LOGICAL THINKING
IN CHILDREN

Research Based on Piaget's Theory

LOGICAL THINKING IN CHILDREN

Research Based on Piaget's Theory

edited by

IRVING E. SIGEL

The Merrill-Palmer Institute

FRANK H. HOOPER

West Virginia University

with Foreword by
Bärbel Inhelder

HOLT, RINEHART AND WINSTON, INC.
New York · Chicago · San Francisco · Atlanta
Dallas · Montreal · Toronto · London

FOREWORD

I was honored to be asked to write the foreword to this important collection of articles on the development of logical thought in children. Under the editorship of Irving Sigel and Frank Hooper, *Logical Thinking in Children* constitutes a tribute to Professor Piaget whose creative work has inspired many of the contributing authors to extend the scope of his original ideas. The book proves conclusively that the Piagetian school of thought is not an end in itself but rather a basis for a great many promising developments.

Studies along Piagetian lines have become so numerous that this publication of a representative sample of papers will be an important tool for research workers. Moreover, the editors' choice and commentaries are such that, even though only one period is treated (that of concrete operations), the different articles all help to bring into focus the essential aspects of the theory of development.

As a Geneva psychologist, I am, of course, particularly interested in such a publication. In the first place, it is clear that child psychology is emerging from relative seclusion to fulfill a double function—to provide a method of dealing with fundamental problems of the acquisition of knowledge and, at the same time, to contribute to the theory of mental development itself. This is a tall order, however, and, as this book makes clear, we have a long way to go before we can resolve all the problems. In fact, we are just beginning to realize that to comprehend the mechanisms of mental development, it is not sufficient to study the competence of children at different ages in certain cognitive fields. This is a first and vital step, but to understand structuring processes inside living organisms we shall have to devise methods which may have more of a biological nature than those employed by most modern psychologists; this approach, to which we attach great importance, seems to be gaining support nowadays, as is shown in some of the work reported in this volume.

Since I had the good fortune to be associated with the discovery of the conservation problem, I am pleased to see that it has opened up a whole new area of research. Conservation problems have always had a particular attraction for American psychologists, and it may be no accident that the first time Piaget referred publicly to this question was during a conference marking the third centenary of Harvard University. Conservation problems have certainly proved to be a great source of new facts regarding both children's thinking and epistemological controversies. In Geneva we have frequently come back to conservation problems, tackling them from different angles; recently we have been studying them in experiments on the regulating mechanisms involved in cognitive development.

Our common aim is to go beyond the first experimental studies which were essentially designed by Piaget from an epistemological and biological point of view and interpreted according to logico-mathematical models. The problem which has to be faced today is whether it is valid to use the original experiments in different ways and from different angles. Is it possible to change the experimental methods and to introduce such concepts as "stimulus change," "stimulus discrimination," and "perceptual cues," without modifying the experiments such that the results are no longer comparable? Is it fruitful to interpret results which are obtained with methods based on those originating from the Geneva point of view within different theoretical frameworks, such as the many varieties of neobehavioristic systems?

Several papers touch upon these problems. It should be remembered that a major concept in Piagetian theory is that knowledge is not a reflection of reality but the result of active interaction between the subject and its environment. The key to the understanding of developmental mechanisms is, in this theory, to be found in the gradual change in modes of interaction. It seems vital for the legitimate use and fruitful interpretation of Piaget-type experiments to take account of this basic tenet. It is reassuring that, at present, this basic concept of the subject's activity seems to be gaining ground in developmental studies. This is seen in *Logical Thinking in Children,* particularly in the contributions of those authors who have been in close contact with the Geneva school—Smedslund, Wohlwill, Elkind, and Smock.

Another fundamental concept of Piaget's theory is that of general structure. No logical discovery analyzed in our experiments can be reduced to an isolated concept, and the search for adequate logical models has thus become necessary. These models are not superimposed upon nor do they precede the experimental results, but they form an integral part of both the experimental design and the theoretical interpretation of the results. Even if the psychological reality of these models has not yet been conclusively proved, they have nevertheless an important heuristic and orientating function. Are models based on the hypothesis of successive additions of separate acquisitions or on the statistical probabilities in strategy-choice really valid for the development and extension of Piaget's original findings? A different theoretical concept and a different line of investigation, although valid and important in themselves, cannot be expected to provide answers to questions emerging directly from Piaget's theory and experiments.

Many articles in this volume concern problems regarding the generalized mental structure underlying specific acquisitions. The general succession of stages seems to be confirmed by all authors, but the relationship between different tasks and substructures, apparently requiring the same mental structure, is still far from adequately explored; what is more, the experimental findings on this point are difficult to interpret. This problem of "décalages horizontaux," or as Wohlwill calls it, "horizontal differential," seems to be one of the most important points which many psychologists are today trying to study in a more direct way. Our current research has led us to believe that the answer to this question will probably not be found by standardizing experiments or by refining statistical methods of treating results. It seems more likely that learning experiments analyzing in great detail the qualitative transformations of the behavior of each subject in the successive phases of training procedures may point the way to furthering our knowledge on the real nature of the "horizontal differential."

We are sure that this collection of recent work, which not only reaffirms a great number of facts at first greeted with scepticism, but also opens up a whole new field of investigation, will prove to be of the utmost benefit to psychologists all over the world. We are very grateful to the editors for making this possible and for their openminded handling of the subject.

MARCH 1968   *Bärbel Inhelder*

Professor of Developmental Psychology

University of Geneva, Geneva, Switzerland

PREFACE

The readings in this volume represent a small but significant body of theoretical and empirical research derived from Piagetian theory. The collection focuses on intellectual development of the young elementary school child, with special reference to acquisition and utilization of conservation concepts. We selected *conservation* as the organizational theme because of its centrality in logical thought within the context of Piagetian theory.

Conservation is of theoretical interest because it reflects cognitive competence of some complexity, while the period of acquisition is the threshold to greater and more complex intellectual growth. Perhaps because of these reasons, considerable research attention has been directed to conservation problems.

The format of this book encompasses reprinted and original articles which are replications of Piaget's reported research, experiments purporting to modify the course of cognitive growth, and some theoretical elaborations and analyses of the Piagetian theory.

The articles selected for each chapter represent diversity of method and motive, and express two crucial issues: (1) replication, in essence, validation studies of the description of cognitive growth, and (2) efforts at modifying the course as charted by Piaget. These articles will enable the reader to acquire an understanding of Piagetian theory and method in the context of a central problem relevant, in theoretical terms, to developmental psychology, and in practical terms, to education of the young elementary school child.

No volume of this nature can come to fruition without the aid of many. First, our thanks to the creator of the system, Jean Piaget, whose creative contributions to the field of developmental psychology are unsurpassed; to his colleague, Bärbel Inhelder, for her gracious acceptance of the task to prepare a foreword to this volume; to the many authors and their publishers for permitting us to reprint their material; and finally, to Hazel McCutcheon without whom our efforts to complete this manuscript would have been to no avail.

The editors of Holt, Rinehart and Winston deserve our thanks for their patience as well as their editorial skills.

No preface is complete, of course, without acknowledging the basic support all husbands engaged in writing receive from their wives—so to Roberta Sigel and Judy Hooper, our many thanks.

MARCH 1968   *I.E.S*
                                                                  F.H.H.

CONTENTS

LOGICAL THINKING
IN CHILDREN

Research Based on Piaget's Theory

INTRODUCTION

* * *

THE RESURGENCE OF interest in cognitive processes and cognitive development during the last fifteen years is reflected in the increased attention developmental psychologists have given to the acquisition of cognitive skills in children. As a result, the output of theoretical and empirical writings identifying various facets of this complex process has markedly increased. There is little doubt that a major source of impetus has been the work of Jean Piaget and his colleagues at the Centre International d'Epistémologie Génétique in Geneva. The significance of Piaget's work in this resurgence stems from the fact that he has provided a comprehensive, stage-dependent, conceptual framework within which cognitive functioning has been intensively studied. No other investigator has produced as encompassing and specific an exposition within a developmental framework of the acquisition of cognitive structures. Piaget, in a prolific output of books and articles, has concerned himself with the developmental stages in the acquisition of concepts in subject matter areas, such as geometry, space, and number, as well as the processes involved in such acquisitions. This combined emphasis on process and product involved in the acquisition of knowledge has resulted in a unique system defining the development of intellective structures.

Piaget's commitment to a developmental orientation has led him to identify stages of growth and their associated ordinal sequence. The transformation of cognitive structure from infancy through adolescence provides the qualitative distinctions and primary focus of Piaget's ontogenetic system. The centrality of the stage construct, as well as the specificity of stage definitions, is a significant contribution of Piagetian theory to developmental psychology. While stages, periods, or level constructs have been integral to descriptive-developmental psychology, their definitions have tended to be general and global. Stages, for example, of psychosexual development have been specified by Freud and extended to a broader dimension in personality development by Erikson (1950, 1959). Some efforts have been made to define stages for intellectual development by Goldstein (1939, 1942), Goldstein and Scheerer (1941), Vygotsky (1962), Werner (1948, 1957), and Werner and Kaplan (1963). However, Piaget has presented the *most* detailed step-by-step description of stages of the course of cognitive development.

As a developmentalist interested in the organism's adaptation to the environment via intelligence, Piaget has studied children from the first year of life to adolescence. The time span is broken up into three major periods: sensorimotor, concrete operations, and formal operations. This

2

volume will concern itself with the period of concrete operations, that is, the time span encompassing the middle-childhood ages of approximately six to eleven years. As Flavell (1963) says, from the point of view of the Piagetian system, "The older child seems to have at his command a coherent and integrated cognitive *system* with which he organizes and manipulates the world about him." It is this system that makes the elementary-school-age child different from his preschool-age counterpart, for now "he gives the decided impression of possessing a solid cognitive bedrock, something flexible and plastic and yet consistent and enduring, with which he can structure the present in terms of the past without undue strain and dislocation, that is, without the ever-present tendency to tumble into the perplexity and contradiction which mark the preschooler" (p. 165).

The rationale for focusing on this period of life is twofold: First, it is the area of concrete operations that has received major attention by investigators outside of Piaget's own laboratory; second, the implications and relevance for education in general, and elementary education in particular, are considerable since Piaget offers a developmental framework within which significant curriculum innovations can be derived.

The interest in the concrete operations period represents a major creative aspect of Piaget's work. As Flavell (1963) has stated:

> It was an act of creative inspiration when Piaget hit upon the idea that a wide variety of cognitive areas—number, quantity, time, and so forth—are in certain crucial respects mastered according to a common procedure: to discover what values do and do not remain invariant (are and are not conserved) in the course of any given kind of change or transformation; . . . There is no question but that the formation of concrete operations is the richest chapter in Piaget's developmental story, in the sense of sheer abundance of highly interesting empirical data. It does not seem likely that all this would or could have come about without the concept of conservation-formation and related unifiers. (p. 415)

This volume is intended to emphasize this significant period of concrete operations with particular attention to the central concept of conservation. Conservation can be defined as the ability of an individual to be aware of the invariant aspects or properties of objects in the face of transformation. For example, the same amount of water exists even when poured from a tall cylinder into a short, flat container. The same value of money exists whether you have one piece in the form of a dollar bill or a hundred pieces in the form of a hundred pennies. Thus, the value is not altered as a function of the transformation of the container or the mode of representing the money. For Piaget, conservation is a central prerequisite for the acquisition and subsequent development of logical thought. Although we primarily associate the conservation concept with various physical and mathematical concepts, its potential application may extend to more general psychological phenomena. The formation of perceptual constancies, stable attitude-value systems, interpersonal perceptions, and self-concepts may all be viewed as special manifestations of a general human need to construct invariants from diverse psychological inputs.

Much of the research undertaken by investigators other than Piaget and his collaborators are replications, or efforts at validating Piaget's findings. A number of studies have been undertaken to replicate Piaget's findings regarding the invariant developmental sequence of quantity conservation, for example, substance, weight, and volume. As we shall see, these studies have tended to be more *supportive* of the sequence of conservation skills but have not confirmed the particular *age-periods* specified by Piaget. Studies representing validation and replication are included in this volume, organized around four core topics; quantity, number, spatial and geometric, and logical operations concepts.

A second body of literature which has become important in recent years deals with the modification of the course of intellectual growth. Certain studies have attempted to determine whether there is a fixed sequence and time for the acquisition of particular concepts. Investigators have attempted to modify the child's knowledge and experience thereby influencing the performance with various types of conservation problems. Many of these studies contribute to an understanding of the basic processes involved in the acquisition of conservation.

Implicit in some of these studies is the question of the invariance of the developmental sequence, a key proposition in the Piagetian system. If children can be taught a particular conservation at any point (at Stage C, for example), and they do not have the prerequisite skills for such acquisition (demonstrated Stage A or B response competencies), then acquiring the conservation skills would cast doubt on the principle of invariance. Piaget has offered relatively little information, at least currently available in English, on the question of stage-sequence modification. Nevertheless, the issue is significant, particularly for those applying Piagetian ideas to the educational scene. There is a great need for research data describing in detail the cognitive capability of elementary school children so that curriculum innovations may be more rationally based, utilizing knowledge about competencies and abilities of children who are, in the final analysis, the consumers of these new curricula. We believe Piaget's work becomes particularly relevant to such thinking. Thus, in addition to the amount of material available, the social consequences of continued study of the concrete operations period further accentuates the need for collections of articles such as these.

This volume will be organized around two topics: one, the replication research, and two, training and modification studies. The reader interested in Piagetian-based results as presented in this volume will notice that a considerable number of the authors have included a concise theoretical exposition of Piaget's general position. Granting that these secondary sources are not the ideal way to grasp the theory, they nevertheless will provide the reader with a basic orientation to the problem at hand. The degree of exposition will vary, but in each case sufficient detail will be supplied to give the reader definition of basic terms, concepts, and problem areas. Our primary goal, however, is not to propound and explicate Piaget's theory as such, but to present some of the current knowledge in a convenient format, and to stimulate additional research endeavors. In addition to the empirical studies, we have included a selection of theoretical articles which deal with some of the more important issues pertaining to the concept of conservation. Finally, the volume includes reflections, speculations, and analyses of the problems of theory and measurement of concrete operations functioning.

The point of view of the editors may be summarized briefly. Piaget has contributed a major system which describes cognitive development. Using a variety of ingenious methodologies to assess specific developmental problems, he has provided insights into the mind of the child. The data arising from such studies lends considerable credence to the ontogenetic principles involved in the development of cognition and strong indications of a unitary, comprehensive system. Much remains, however, to be done to test the validity of the system. Any monolithic attempt to describe or encompass the totality of cognitive growth from birth to maturity is certain to encounter conceptual problems. To believe otherwise is to ignore the immense complexity and inherent spontaneity of man as an intellectual organism or to greatly overestimate our current level of sophistication in the behavioral sciences. Thus, for us, Piaget's theory is not only a description of the child's cognitive world, but also an inspiration for elaboration, extension, and revision. Hopefully we have provided the student and research worker with a broad spectrum of original sources from which an appreciation in depth of the theoretical, methodological, and practical questions relevant to a Piagetian framework can be obtained.

REFERENCES

Erikson, E. H. (1950). *Childhood and society.* New York: Norton.
Erikson, E. H. (1959). Identity and the life cycle. *Psychol. Issues,* 1 (1), Monogr. 1.
Flavell, J. H. (1963). *Developmental psychology of Jean Piaget.* Princeton, N.J.: Van Nostrand.
Goldstein, K. (1939). *The organism.* New York: American Book.
Goldstein, K. (1942). *After-effects of brain injuries in war.* New York: Grune & Stratton.
Goldstein, K., and M. Scheerer (1941). Abstract and concrete behavior: an experimental study with special tests. *Psychol. Monogr.,* 53 (2), Whole No. 239.
Vygotsky, L. S. (1962). *Thought and language.* Trans. by E. Hanfman and G. Vakan. New York: Wiley.

Werner, H. (1948). *Comparative psychology of mental development*, revised ed. Chicago: Follett.

Werner, H. (1957). The concept of development from a comparative and organismic point of view. In D. B. Harris (Ed.), *The concept of development*. Minneapolis, Minn.: University of Minnesota Press.

Werner, J., and B. Kaplan (1963). *Symbol formation: an organismic-developmental approach to language and expression of thought*. New York: Wiley.

CHAPTER

ONE

QUANTITY

CONSERVATION

CONCEPTS

*   *   *

THE DESCRIPTION OF the development of quantity conservation initially reported by Piaget and Inhelder (1962) in *Le Développement des Quantités Chez l'Enfant* has generated a considerable volume of research directed toward replication and validation of the original findings.

Piaget and Inhelder conclude on the basis of their many experiments that initially, children's concepts of quantity are undifferentiated; that is, the child does not have distinct and separate concepts of mass, weight, and volume. The quantitative concept of mass is the first to separate from the undifferentiated whole when the child becomes able to attest to the invariance of mass in the face of transformations. Thus, when presented with two identical clay balls and one of these is altered in shape (rolled into a sausage), the child will attest to identity of quantity in spite of variations in shape. He has made a rational choice not on the basis of appearance, but because he is aware that sheer change of shape does not alter the *amount* of mass. The child has, in effect, conserved mass. Later, quantity concepts of weight and volume separate into two rational concepts.

The developmental invariant sequence described by Piaget is mass, weight, and volume. This sequence is referred to as a *horizontal décalage*, which "refers to a repetition which takes place within a single period in development" (Flavell, 1963, p. 22). The repetition which takes place on the level in question can be described as: A cognitive structure, characteristic of that level, can be successfully applied to task X but not to task Y. A year later, task Y is solved. Cognitive operations used to solve task X are applied to solve task Y. Thus, the child acquiring the concept of conservation of mass, that is, the awareness of the invariance of the quantity of mass, acquires cognitive operations which he will eventually employ in the acquisition of the conservation of weight, and finally of volume.

The studies presented in this chapter are supportive of the horizontal décalage reported by Piaget. In contrast to Piaget's experimental procedures, which have been criticized for failing to employ an objective, experimental approach, the experiments reported here employ standardized procedures, objective modes of scoring and analysis, and reasonably sized samples whose demographic characteristics are defined. Despite divergences in methodology, it is of interest to note the degree of concordance of the work of those authors reported in this chapter with the work of Piaget. These studies include, in addition to replication, extensions in theory and method.

Elkind's findings closely agree with the Piagetian sequence of the discovery of conservation of quantity. This sequence refers to the significant type of quantity-age level interaction which substantiates the horizontal décalage: Mass is conserved earlier than weight, and weight conservation is, in turn, achieved prior to volume conservation. Elkind also discusses the quality of children's responses. These responses provide data on the variation of logical or pseudological explanations for the conservation problems.

The study of substance conservation by Lovell and Ogilvie also essentially agrees with Piaget's original reports.[1] Their results indicate, however, that the three stages postulated for each quantity subtype by Piaget (nonconservation, transitionary, complete conservation) are not sharply defined, nor are they distinct categories. They picture the acquisition of quantity conservation as a very gradual process which generalizes to a wide range of task and material settings only after the child has had sufficient opportunity to explore and manipulate the relevant task dimensions. This emphasis on the role of past experience is supported by the findings of differential conservation performance depending upon which test materials are used. The lack of across-task generalization attests to the fact that conservation is not an all-or-none proposition, but is gradually mastered.

Lovell and Ogilvie also concern themselves with the predicted relationship between conservation performance and the logical operations concepts of compensatory relations, identity, and reversibility. *Compensatory relations* refers to the fact that in a transformation, quantity does not change if the ball of clay is rolled out, for it becomes longer *but* thinner. *Identity* (identical action) is illustrated by the example that the ball that has not been rolled out can be rolled out into a similar sausage as the already altered piece. *Reversibility*, a key concept in Piagetian theory, generally refers to the fact that a transformed object can be returned to its original state; for example, the sausage can be rolled back into a ball. Piaget considers these concepts to be crucial to conservation acquisition. In the case of reversibility, Lovell and Ogilvie find a number of subjects who demonstrate an awareness of the operations concept but who, nonetheless, fail to conserve. This leads them to question the significance of reversibility as a necessary and sufficient condition for conservation performance.

It should be emphasized, in this regard, that reversibility is a rather complex process in Piagetian theory. Two reversibility concepts have been defined by Piaget: *negation*, which applies only to classes, and *reciprocity*, which applies only to relations. Lovell and Ogilvie's criterion for the presence of reversibility is an awareness of the previous state of equality between the stimulus items *within* the conservation task format. Thus, reversibility performance is not measured independently of conservation ability. The identification and subsequent assessment of reversibility as an operation

---

[1] Lovell and Ogilvie (1961) have also replicated Piaget's conservation of weight and substantiated his general findings.

experimentally independent of conservation poses an important methodological challenge which the reader should keep in mind when studying the Lovell and Ogilvie material.

The final Lovell and Ogilvie article deals with the various conceptual subcategories of volume conservation. Volume conservation is a complex behavioral achievement which is not easily assessed in a single experimental presentation. Lovell and Ogilvie administered a series of tasks which tested for the presence of three volume concepts: internal volume, occupied volume, and compensatory-displacement volume conservation. Internal volume refers to the amount of space within a container; occupied volume refers to the amount of space within a container with additional objects in it; and compensatory-displacement volume refers to the effect on the amount of liquid in a container when a solid is placed therein. These concepts were found to differ in terms of relative difficulty. Internal volume was the least difficult to grasp, followed by occupied volume, and displaced volume, respectively. Compensatory-displacement volume conservation was not mastered until approximately eleven to twelve years of age, and this compares favorably with Piaget's initial results from a similar task format.

The degree that the ability to conserve in one situation is generalized and transcended to different situations, which is discussed in subsidiary portions of Lovell and Ogilvie's work, is the focus of Uzgiris' study. Uzgiris finds that the proposed Piagetian sequence of development of the conservation of quantity occurs for each set of material, but that the appearance of conservation with one particular set of material does not necessarily mean we can predict its appearance with other types of stimulus material. In other words, the child solving the conservation problem with the now classical plasticine ball paradigm does not necessarily solve similar problems with other types of material. The horizontal décalage reported by Piaget appears to occur within a class of material but is not evident across a variety of task contents. As in Elkind's study mentioned previously, variance analysis revealed a significant age-type of quantity conservation interaction which is to be expected on the basis of the horizontal décalage. Since a significant age-quantity-material second order interaction is also found (although not discussed), this finding may add further weight to Uzgiris' original premise regarding the interdependence of age, type of conservation, and material.

In their totality, these studies do confirm Piaget's basic findings that conservation of quantity (substance, weight, and volume) appear in an invariant sequence. In addition, the three stages of nonconservation, transitionary, and complete conservation generally have been found within each quantity subclass. Success in conservation, however, is not generalized, nor is there strong evidence supporting Piaget's argument that reversibility is a necessary or sufficient prerequisite for conservation.

These studies, then, raise a number of crucial issues, crucial for Piagetian theory, and crucial for detailing the course of this particular cognitive skill. Some of these issues follow:

(1) What kinds of experiences may be critical in influencing the sequences discovered?

(2) What factors account for the lack of situational generality?

(3) What role do logical operations constructs, such as reversibility and identity, play in relation to conservation acquisition?

(4) How important are the traditional demographic classifications, sex, social class, cultural setting, and scholastic level, to generalizations regarding conservation behavior?

REFERENCES

Flavell, J. H. (1963). *The developmental psychology of Jean Piaget.* Princeton, N.J.: Van Nostrand.

Lovell, K., and E. Ogilvie (1961). A study of the conservation of weight in the junior school child. *Brit. J. educ. Psychol.,* 31, 138–144.

Piaget, J., and Barbel Inhelder (1962). *Le développement des quantités physiques chez l'enfant.* Paris: Delachaux et Niestlé.

CHILDREN'S DISCOVERY OF THE CONSERVATION
OF MASS, WEIGHT, AND VOLUME:
PIAGET REPLICATION STUDY II

David Elkind

INTRODUCTION

This study is the second[1] in a series devoted to the systematic replication of experiments originally performed by the Swiss psychologist, Jean Piaget. For its starting point the present study takes one of Piaget's (1940) investigations dealing with the ages at which children discover the conservation of mass, weight, and volume. Piaget assumes that concepts develop and that the discovery of conservation earmarks the final stage of their development. By studying children's responses to demonstrations of the

[1] For a report of the first study, see Elkind (1961).

Reprinted with the permission of the author and the publisher from *The Journal of Genetic Psychology*, 1961, 98, 219–227. This study was carried out while the writer was a Staff Psychologist at the Beth Israel Hospital in Boston. The writer is indebted to Dr. Greta Bibring, the head of Beth Israel's Department of Psychiatry, and to the members of the research committee for granting him the time to make the study.

conservation of mass, weight, and volume, Piaget sought to uncover the genetic stages in the formation of these concepts. The present study differs from Piaget's investigation in its standardization of his procedures and in its use of statistical design.

In his investigation, Piaget tested for the conservation of mass, weight, and volume by means of the "sausage" experiment. The purpose of this experiment was to determine whether the child could tell that a quantity remained the same (was conserved) after it was changed in appearance. For example, in testing for the conservation of mass Piaget showed the child two clay balls identical in size, shape, and weight. After the child agreed that both balls had equal clay, Piaget made one of the balls into a sausage. Then he asked the child to judge whether the ball and the sausage contained the same amount of clay. Piaget also asked the child to predict— while both pieces of clay were shaped as balls—if they would be the same were one made into a sausage and to explain his judgments and predictions.

Using the sausage experiment to test 5– 12-year-old children, Piaget found that discoveries of conservation followed a regular order that was related to age. The conservation of mass was discovered at ages 7–8; the conservation of weight was discovered at ages 9–10; and the conservation of volume was discovered at ages 11 and 12. These findings, together with his theoretical interpretations, Piaget reported with the aid of a great many illustrative examples but without statistics.

Starting from Piaget's procedures and results the present study was designed to test the hypotheses that, other things being equal, (a) the number of conservation responses does not vary significantly with the Type of Response (prediction, judgment, and explanation) required; (b) the number of conservation responses varies significantly with the Type of Quantity (mass, weight, and volume); (c) the number of conservation responses varies significantly with Age Level; (d) the number of conservation responses varies significantly with the joint effect of Type of Quantity and Age Level (the statistical test of Piaget's age-order of discovery finding). In addition, children's explanations were categorized for comparison with the explanations given by Piaget's subjects.

METHOD

Subjects

One hundred and seventy-five children attending the Claflin School[2] in Newton, Mass., were tested. Twenty-five children were randomly selected from each of the grades from kindergarten to sixth. The mean age and

[2] The writer is grateful to the principal, Dr. Harry Anderson, and teachers of the Claflin School whose friendly cooperation made the study not only possible but enjoyable.

standard deviation for each grade were: Kindergarten, M = 5:8, SD = 3.0; Grade 1, M = 6:8, SD = 3.9; Grade 2, M = 7:7, SD = 3.6; Grade 3, M = 8:6, SD = 3.8; Grade 4, M = 9:7, SD = 3.0; Grade 5, M = 10:7, SD = 2.5; Grade 6, M = 11:9, SD = 5.56 months. Hereafter the grades will be referred to by their age level.

For 125 children at the five oldest age levels, Kuhlmann-Anderson Intelligence Test scores were available. The mean IQ for this group was 109 and the SD was 11.0 points. Most of the children came from middle to upper-middle class homes.

Procedure

Each S was seen individually and questioned three times on each type of quantity. For each quantity S was asked first to predict, next judge, and then explain his conservation or non-conservation responses. The order of the questions and the order of presenting the quantities—mass, weight, volume—was the same for all Ss. A fixed order of presentation was used to provide a more rigorous test of Piaget's findings. Any practice effects resulting from the fixed order should have worked against the differences Piaget found. On the other hand if differences were developmentally determined, as Piaget assumes, then the minimal practice effect over a brief time span should have had little effect.

Tests

In the test for the conservation of mass, two clay balls identical in size, shape, and weight were on the table. E, "Do both balls have the same amount of clay, is there as much clay in this ball as in this one?" S was encouraged to "make them the same," if he doubted the equality of the balls. When S agreed that the two balls were equal E asked, "Suppose I roll one of the balls out into a hot dog, will there be as much clay in the hot dog as in the ball, will they both have the same amount of clay?" (Prediction question.)

After S's prediction E actually made one of the balls into a hot dog while S looked on. E, "Is there as much clay in the ball as in the hot dog, do they both have the same amount of clay?" (Judgment question.) Then E asked "Why is that?" to S's response. (Explanation question.)

Exactly the same procedure was used to test for the conservation of weight and volume. To test for the conservation of weight E asked, "Do they both weigh the same, do they both have the same amount of weight?" etc. And to test for the conservation of volume E asked, "Do they both take up the same amount of space, do they both take up as much room?" etc. On each test the child was initially given the opportunity to handle the balls and to add or subtract clay as he liked to "make them the same."

Scoring

Each conservation response was scored 1 and all non-conservation responses were scored zero. For each S there was a total possible conservation score of 9 and for each Type of Quantity and Type of Response there was a total possible score of three.

Statistical Analyses

To test for the effects of Type of Response, an analysis of variance design described by Lindquist (1953, Chap. 6) was used. In this design chance differences between subjects were controlled by testing all subjects on all types of response.

To test for the separate and combined effects of Age Level and Type of Quantity a different analysis of variance design was used (Lindquist, 1953, pp. 267–273). In this design, chance differences between subjects were controlled for the Type of Quantity variable only, by testing all subjects on all types of quantity.

RESULTS

Type of Response

In his investigations Piaget used children's predictions, judgments, and explanations interchangeably as signs of conservation or non-conservation. In the present study the F for Type of Response was NS and did not approach significance. This finding agreed with Piaget's use of these three types of response as equivalent signs of conservation.

Type of Quantity

Piaget found that, other things being equal, the conservation of mass was easiest to discover, the conservation of weight was of intermediate difficulty, and the conservation of volume was the most difficult discovery of all. The F for Type of Quantity obtained in the present study was 255.55 and was significant beyond the .01 level. Individual t tests for the Type of Quantity means revealed that the mean for each type of quantity was significantly different than every other. For all subjects the average number of conservation responses given for mass was 2.08, the average number given for weight was 1.75, and the average number of conservation responses given for volume was 0.25. The order of difficulty obtained in the present study was the same as the order that Piaget observed.

Age Level

The Swiss children tested by Piaget showed that, other things being equal, their conservation responses increased with age. For the children in the present study the same held true. The F for Age Level was 14.38 and was significant beyond the .01 level. Individual *t* tests of Age Level means showed that the magnitude of the Age Level means increased significantly with age in agreement with Piaget's finding.

Type of Quantity-Age Level Interaction

Piaget's illustrative examples indicated that age group differences varied with the type of quantity in question. For mass there was a marked difference between the 5–6 and the 7–12-year-old groups; for weight there was a marked difference between the 5–8 and the 9–12-year-old groups; and for volume there was a marked difference between the 5–10 and the 11–12-year-old groups in their number of conservation responses.

In the present study the variations in the differences between age groups for each type of quantity appeared as the interaction effect of Type of Quantity and Age Level. This interaction F was 6.93 and was significant beyond the .01 level. Individual *t* tests for age group differences showed that: (*a*) For mass the 5–6 and the 7–11-year-old groups differed significantly; (*b*) for weight the 5–8 and 9–11-year-old groups differed significantly; and (*c*) for volume the 5–10 and the 11-year-old groups differed significantly from each other in number of conservation responses given. These findings agreed with expectations based on Piaget's results.

In Piaget's early studies (1951a) he assigned different tests to the age level at which the percent passing was 75.[3] Although he gave no percentages for the conservation experiments one can assume that he used the same criterion for assigning the conservation of mass to ages 7–8; the conservation of weight to ages 9–10; and the conservation of volume to ages 11–12. The results of the present study were converted into percentages for comparison with Piaget's criterion and these are presented in Table 1.

Table 1 shows that the 70 per cent point for mass was reached at the seven year level but that the 75 per cent point was not reached until age 9. For weight, the 73 per cent was reached at age 9 and the 75 per cent point by age 10. In this study the 75 per cent point for volume was not reached at the 11 year level.

The slight discrepancies between Piaget's results and those in Table 1 for weight and mass could easily be due to the small size of the samples

---

[3] For a test oriented approach to the replication of Piaget's work, see Laurendeau and Pinard (1957).

Table 1

Per Cent[a] *of Conservation Responses
for Mass, Weight, and Volume
at Successive Age Levels (N = 25 at Each Age Level)*

Type of quantity	Age level						
	5	6	7	8	9	10	11
Mass	19	51	70	72	86	94	92
Weight	21	52	51	44	73	89	78
Volume	0	4	0	4	4	19	25

[a] Of 75 possible responses.

used in the present study. The relatively low number of conservation responses at the 11 year level may be due to the fact that Piaget used a somewhat different procedure in his test for the conservation of volume. Piaget had his subjects say whether the ball and the sausage would displace the same amount of water. As a check the same procedure was used with some of the subjects of the present study (after the other testing was completed) and conservation seemed easier to discover by means of the displacement problem.

Children's Explanations

When Piaget interpreted the results of his investigation he made use of children's explanations without categorizing or quantifying them as he did in early studies (Piaget, 1951a). In the present study four types of explanations were distinguished. Two of these were explanations of non-conservation: (*a*) Romancing (Piaget, 1951b, Introd.), it's more because "My uncle said so"; (*b*) Perceptual, it's more because it's, "longer, thinner, thicker, wider, etc." The two types of explanation given for conservation were: (*c*) Specific, "You didn't add any or take any away," "You can roll it back into a ball and it will be the same," and "The hot dog is longer but thinner so the same;" (*d*) General, it's the same because "No matter what shape you make it into it won't change the amount." Table 2 shows the per cent for each type of explanation given at each age level.

Table 2 shows that Romancing and Perceptual explanations decrease with age while Specific explanations first increase and then level off with age. Piaget noted the same types and age trends in the explanations given by his subjects. The explanations are one type of evidence Piaget takes for his theory that as the child's thinking develops, it frees itself from its earlier domination by immediate perception. One step in this liberation is the interpretation of a perceptual effect as the result of a specific action which can be reversed (you can roll it back into a ball). A later step is

Table 2

*Per Cent for Each of Four Types of Explanation
Given at Successive Age Levels
(N = 25 at Each Age Level)*

Type of explanation				Age level			
	5	6	7	8	9	10	11
Romancing[a]	4	3	7	7	0	1	0
Perceptual[a]	85	64	53	57	36	32	33
Specific[b]	11	33	40	36	60	51	49
General[b]	0	0	0	0	4	16	18

[a] Explanation of non-conservation.
[b] Explanation of conservation.

to interpret a perception as but one of a great many possible instances (no matter what shape you make it into it will always be the same). The results in Table 2 agreed with the observations upon which Piaget builds his theory of the developmental changes in the relation between thought and perception.

DISCUSSION

The results of the present study agreed with Piaget's findings regarding the ages at which children discover the conservation of mass, weight, and volume. In both studies: the conservation of mass did not usually appear before the ages 7–8; the conservation of weight did not usually appear before the ages 9–10; and the conservation of volume did not in most cases appear before the age of 11. The discussion will briefly summarize Piaget's interpretation of these results.

Piaget's theory[4] is that concepts of quantity develop in three stages with the final stage earmarked by the discovery of conservation. Children at the first stage have only a general impression of quantity but are capable of judging crude weight, volume, and mass differences. In the sausage experiment they give non-conservation responses because to their general impression the sausage is different than the ball. When they are forced to break down this impression, by the explanation question, then they judge quantity by single dimensions which they are unable to coordinate one with the other.

Those children who are at the second stage have a differentiated impression of quantity and are unable to judge quantity differences two by two

---

[4] For more complete presentations of Piaget's theory, see Piaget (1950, 1957, 1958).

(long-wide, long-narrow, etc.) which Piaget calls *logical multiplication.* Children at this stage give non-conservation responses in the sausage experiment because to their differentiated impression the sausage is both more (in length) and less (in width) than the ball. They are unable to resolve the contradiction, as one child expressed it, "It's more and it's less, I'll take one of each." When these children are forced to explain their non-conservation answers they also judge quantity by single dimensions.

At the third stage children have an abstract quantity concept and judge quantity in unit terms. In the sausage experiment they immediately predict and judge conservation. Their explanations indicate either that the perceived transformation can be cancelled (the sausage can be rolled back into a ball) or that the perceived differences can be equated (what the sausage gained in length it lost in width) and therefore the quantity is the same.

According to Piaget the *equation of differences* results in the formation of ratios and fixed units and underlies abstract quantity and number (Piaget, 1952) concept formation. On the perceptual plane the equation of differences enables the child to discover that an object which changes in appearance can still be the same in quantity. Piaget's theory is that once conservation is discovered it is immediately externalized and the subject has the impression that conservation is a perceptually given property of the object.

The initial appearance of the conservation of mass at ages 7–8 Piaget attributes to the development by that age of logical multiplication and equation of differences which he speaks of as *mental operations.* The time lag before the discovery of the conservation of weight at ages 9–10 and the even greater lag before the conservation of volume at ages 11–12 Piaget attributes to the quantities themselves. He argues that a quantity is difficult to conceptualize, and so to conserve, to the degree that it is associated with the subject's own action. Length, for example was more easily dissociated from the child's action than was weight. In Piaget's theory, therefore, the discovery of conservation is limited both by the maturational level of the subject and by the properties of the object and in this sense it is both a nature *and* a nurture theory.

REFERENCES

Elkind, D. (1961). The development of quantitative thinking: a systematic replication of Piaget's studies. *J. genet. Psychol.*, 98, 37–46.

Inhelder, B., and J. Piaget (1958). *The growth of logical thinking from childhood to adolescence.* New York: Basic Books.

Laurendeau, M., and A. Pinard (1957). Une méthode rationnelle de localization des testes dans échelles d'age. *Canad. J. Psychol.*, 11, 33–47.

Lindquist, E. F. (1953). *Design and analysis of experiments in psychology and education.* Cambridge, Mass.: Riverside.

Piaget, J. (1950). *The psychology of intelligence.* London: Routledge.

Piaget, J. (1951a). *Judgment and reasoning in the child.* London: Routledge.

Piaget, J. (1951b). *The child's conception of the world.* London: Routledge.

Piaget, J. (1952). *The child's conception of number.* London: Routledge.

Piaget, J. (1957). *Logic and psychology.* New York: Basic Books.

Piaget, J., and B. Inhelder (1940). *Le développement des quantités chez l'enfant.* Paris: Delachaux et Niestlé.

A STUDY OF THE CONSERVATION OF SUBSTANCE IN THE JUNIOR SCHOOL CHILD

K. Lovell / E. Ogilvie

INTRODUCTON

The concept of conservation or invariance of substance is an important one. A quantity such as a lump of plasticine, a collection of beads, a length or a volume can be used by the mind only if it remains permanent in amount and independent of the rearrangement of its individual parts. This notion of invariance is indeed essential to any kind of measurement in the physical world. Piaget, using many ingenious experiments, set out to determine if the concept is there in the child's mind from the start or whether it is gradually built up.

It is now becoming generally known that, in Piaget's view, a child's thinking is largely dependent upon perception from 4–7 years of age. During this period thinking tends to be determined by the child "centering" on one aspect, dimension or element of the situation with other aspects ignored. But, from 7–8 years of age he is able to break away from the influence of perception and is increasingly able to apply logical thought to practical problems and concrete situations. Piaget maintains that the concepts that figure in logical thought result from the coordination of actions in which the child combines, dissociates, orders and sets up correspondences. The child gradually appreciates the significance of his actions

Reprinted with the permission of the senior author and the publisher from *The British Journal of Educational Psychology*, 1960, **30**, 109–118.

so that they acquire the form of reversible operations in the mind and thus render his thinking less dependent upon perception.

From his many experiments involving the conservation of continuous and discontinuous quantities, Piaget maintained that children passed through three stages; namely, that of non-conservation, transition and conservation. In a typical experiment, which we have repeated, Piaget or his students would show a child two balls of modeling clay of the same size, one of which is then shaped to look like a sausage. At the first stage the child will deny that the amounts of clay in the "sausage" and ball are now the same. A response such as "It's more because the sausage is longer," might well be found. At the transition stage, he will arrive at the idea of conservation under some conditions, or at one moment, but will lose the idea again under slightly changed conditions; while from 7–8 years onwards it is said that the child feels the logical necessity for conservation and will support it by argument. For example, Piaget (1950, p. 140; 1953, p. 16) maintains that the child will say that the sausage can be returned to the shape of a ball, or what has been lost in one direction has been gained in another, or that nothing has been added and nothing has been taken away.

However, we cannot say how many children were examined by Piaget and his students in this type of experiment, and it was decided to test a group of English children under somewhat more controlled conditions.

EXPERIMENTAL PROCEDURE

This study reports one main and two subsidiary experiments, the latter being of use in clarifying certain points. In the main experiment almost every boy and girl in a junior school in a North of England town was tested individually in an effort to trace the development of the concept of invariance of substance, and to establish the arguments children use to justify their answers. Balls of plasticine were used of diameter about two inches. Providing the child agreed that the amounts of plasticine in the balls were the same to begin with, the subject was considered to be suitable for the experiment. One ball was then rolled out to make a "sausage" and at the same time the child was questioned. All the experiments took place in the Headmaster's room so that no child witnessed the cross examination of another, and the children's replies were recorded verbatim. The procedure which was followed is now given, although it must be stressed that many supplementary questions were asked, and our outline indicates the general form of the procedure and not its exact details. To get the child to give his reasons, we found it necessary to make our approach a flexible one.

APPARATUS   Six balls of plasticine, two equal in size, the others clearly different, and all six of different color.

TECHNIQUE   Ask the child to choose two balls of plasticine which are the same. Say—*Here we have six balls of plasticine. Can you choose the two that are the same?*

If the child replies that they are all different say—*True, in color they are different but I'm thinking of size, of amounts of plasticine. Let us forget the colors; now, which two are equal?*

Child having made the correct choice, say—*Now you have one ball and let me have the other. Will that be fair?*

(1) *Will I have as much plasticine as you?* The reply must be *Yes* before the experiment continues. Equality having been admitted, say—*I am now going to roll your ball into a sausage.*[1] *Watch me.* Action performed. *So now you have a sausage and I still have a ball.*

(2) *Who has the most*[2] *plasticine now?*

(3) *Why do you think so? What makes you so sure?*

(3) (a) *If the sausage is longer why doesn't it have more plasticine in it?* Or, *How can it be longer and still the same?* In the case of "don't know" replies to (3) (a) the child was asked: *What happens as I roll the ball?* Invariably the reply was *It gets longer.* The child was then asked *Anything else?* and, if necessary, *Does it get fatter?*

This was the end of the experiment for those clearly conserving. For non-conservers say—*Watch carefully—I'm rolling your sausage longer still . . . longer still.*

(4) *Now who has most plasticine?*

(5) *Why do you think that?*

(6) *Very well, watch carefully. Let's roll it some more . . . some more. Now who has most plasticine?*

(7) *Why do you think that?* Point out a second aspect of the dimensions—length or breadth—which the child is ignoring by asking the following kind of question. *But my piece of plasticine is fatter. Does this mean that I have more or less plasticine than you?* Pursue this point with similar type questions. The primary aim here is to force the child to consider two dimensions simultaneously and see what changes in thought occur —if any.

(8) *Let's roll your sausage back into a ball.* Action performed. *Who has most plasticine now?*

(9) *Who will have most plasticine if we roll your ball out again into a sausage?*

(10) *Now watch carefully. I am rolling my ball into a sausage.* Action performed at same time. *Who has most plasticine now?*

(11) *Why do you think so? What makes you so sure?*

---

[1] Sometimes the child did the rolling but more frequently it was done by the experimenter.

[2] We have used the word "most" instead of the words "the more." Although grammatically incorrect, we think that the children better understood our question using "most."

The first of the subsidiary experiments was carried out to see if an understanding of addition and subtraction of small pieces of plasticine inevitably produces the concept of conservation. If this is so, then any child who can see that adding/subtracting a piece of plasticine makes a ball more/ less, should maintain his conclusion without regard to subsequent spatial transformation. Thus, a piece of plasticine was removed from a ball and the child was then asked what he thought about the amount of plasticine in the ball. The piece removed was left in the clear view of the child. The experimental ball was then subjected to a spatial transformation and the child questioned again about conservation of plasticine. The following numbers of children were involved: thirty-five at the stage of conservation as found from the main experiment, forty-three at the stage of transition, and thirty-eight at the stage of non-conservation, making one-hundred-and-sixteen pupils in all. Some of the children were subjected to this test at the time of the main experiment.

The second subsidiary experiment was designed to test the hypothesis that a child at the stage of non-conservation in the case of a plasticine ball, is not inevitably a non-conserver in another situation involving quantity; in this case a non-conserver of rubber in a rubber band. Thus, a rubber band was shown to the child; it was then stretched, and he was questioned as to whether or not there was the same amount of rubber in the band as before. Forty-eight children all at the stage of non-conservation in the main experiment undertook this test.

STATEMENT OF THE RESULTS

Main Experiment

The three stages in the development of the concept of conservation of substance have been found. Table 1 shows the number of children at each stage in each of the year groups. It was difficult at times to classify correctly a child at the transition stage.

Table 1

Number of Children in Each Group at Various Stages

	Average Age Yr.	Mo.	Conservation	Transition	Non-conservation	Total
1st year	7	8	30	27	26	83
2nd year	8	10	44	8	13	65
3rd year	9	9	73	15	11	99
4th year	10	8	64	7	4	75
			211	57	54	322

Table 2 shows the percentage number of children at the conservation stage giving various reasons for conserving. Some children gave, spontaneously, more than one reason; and in order to make the meaning of the words used in the table as clear as possible, definitions are first given.

Reversibility. It is difficult to be sure exactly what Piaget means by "reversibilité." Bunt (1950, p. 28) thinks he means that the child must be able to picture to himself the "sausage" returned to the original ball. We were unable to keep to this exact meaning for *reversibility*. Our criterion is that the child gave evidence of his awareness of the equality of the balls at the beginning. The child says in effect, "They were the same before." Of the conservers only five children spoke of rolling the sausage back to a ball which would be identical to the other ball, or pointed out that after rolling back it would be as it was before being rolled out.[3]

Identical action. Child says, in effect, that the ball held by the experimenter can be rolled out into a similar sausage.

Plus/Minus. Child says, in effect, that nothing has been "added to" or "taken from" when the ball was rolled into a sausage.

Coordination of relations. Child says, in effect, that although the sausage is longer it is thinner. Bunt (1950) criticizes Piaget for the use of the term "multiplication of relations," and we have kept to the term "Coordination of relations in compensatory fashion." It appears that, for Piaget, the word "multiplication" means what is sometimes called "logical multiplication," i.e., two factors simultaneously affecting a third. In this case it is height and cross-section jointly affecting volume and he seems to imply something that can be expressed in units. We are not able to keep to Piaget's meaning at this point, if we interpret him correctly.

Weight. Child refers to the fact that the weights of the sausage and ball are the same. The assumption is that the weights of the two balls were the same originally.

Shape. Child says, in effect, that the lump of plasticine has only undergone a change of shape.

We now analyze the replies of the children at the stages of transition and non-conservation. Table 3 shows the number of children in each year group who gave clear evidence of "centering" on one dimension. The criterion was that they replied, "It's more because it's longer" or some essential variation of this at some point. It must be stressed that others might well have "centered" on one aspect but we have no clear evidence of it.

If a child judges by look alone, the aspect of the total situation on which he is "centering" may change. The sausage is bigger one moment and the ball is bigger the next. There is no reason why the child should not switch his "centering," and if he is not conserving then his opinion might change. The criterion was that the child said that a particular object was, say,

---

[3] It will be seen later that some children at the other two stages spoke of rolling the sausage back to a ball which would be bigger/smaller than it was originally.

Table 2

*Percentage of Children in Each Year Group
Giving Various Answers for Conservation*

	Reversi- bility	Identical Action	Plus/ Minus	Coordi- nation of re- lations	Weight	Shape	Don't Know
1st year	57	3	30	30	0	7	13
2nd year	58	12	42	14	5	2	0
3rd year	71	7	29	33	1	0	0
4th year	78	5	19	36	6	6	0

Table 3

*Number of Children in Each Year Group at Transition
and Non-conservation Stages Who Gave Evidence
of "Centering" on One Dimension, and of a Change
of "Centering"*

	Centering		Change of Centering	
	Transition	Non-conserva- tion	Transition	Non-conserva- tion
1st year	21	23	13	14
2nd year	2	3	0	2
3rd year	5	10	3	5
4th year	6	4	3	3
	34	40	19	24

"more" at first and later "less," *without* any prompting or forcing by the experimenter,[4] that is *before* stage 7 in the general procedure. Again, other children might have changed their "centering" from one aspect to another but we have no evidence of their so doing. Table 3 also shows the number of children at the transition and non-conservation stages who changed, without any prompting or forcing, the aspect of the situation on which they "centered."

At stage 7 in the testing procedure the child was forced to observe two dimensions simultaneously. Table 4 shows the number of children in each year group who give clear evidence of being able to consider two dimen-

[4] It must be realized that the fact that the child undergoes the experiment at all, does to some extent force him to think.

sions together. The criterion was that, in essence, the child made reference to two dimensions in compensatory fashion, for example, "It's longer but it's thinner." Table 4 also shows how the children reacted. Those at the transition stage are sub-divided into those who conserved to the end of the experiment and those who conserved for a while but reverted to non-conservation before the end.

Table 4

Number of Children in Each Year Group at Transition and Non-conservation Stages Who Give Evidence of Attending to Two Dimensions

| | Transition | | Non-conservation |
	Can consider two dimensions and conserve at end of experiment	Can consider two dimensions and temporarily conserve	Can consider two dimensions but fail to conserve
1st year	3	3	1
2nd year	0	1	3
3rd year	0	2	1
4th year	1	1	1
	4	7	6

The study of reversibility at the transition and non-conservation stages is of great interest and importance. Table 5 shows the number of children in each age group who gave clear evidence of reversibility as we have defined it. It will be noted that reversibility does not necessarily produce conservation in spite of the fact that it is given as a reason for conservation among conservers.

Table 5

Number of Children in Each Age Group at Transition and Non-conservation Stages Who Gave Evidence of Reversibility

	Transition	Non-conservation
1st year	21	5
2nd year	8	10
3rd year	11	9
4th year	3	3
	43	27

Thus, seventy children can show reversibility as we have defined it, but draw no conclusion from it and remain at the non-conservation or transition stages.

In addition, two children at the transition stage and four at the non-conservation stage showed clear awareness of the possibility of returning the sausage to a ball, but claimed that the ball would be bigger/smaller than the original.

Subsidiary Experiment 1

A small piece of plasticine was taken from the ball. All the children tested, except two, agreed correctly that there was then less plasticine in the ball. The plasticine was then subjected to a spatial change. The thirty-five children who were conservers in the main experiment remain conservers, while Table 6 shows the effect of the experiment on children at the transition and non-conservation stages.

Table 6

*Number of Children Attaining Conservation
After the Subtraction of a Piece of Plasticine*

	Transition		Non-conservation	
	Examined	Conserved or almost so	Examined	Conserved or almost so
1st year	17	10	16	0[a]
2nd year	5	3	10	2
3rd year	14	8	8	4
4th year	7	3	4	3
	43	24	38	9

[a] Two pupils seemed to move some way toward conservation.

Subsidiary Experiment 2

In this experiment we tested to see if non-conservers in the main experiments were also non-conservers in another situation involving invariance of quantity—in this case, of rubber in a stretched rubber band. The results are given in Table 7.

DISCUSSION OF RESULTS

Strong evidence has been produced in support of the three stages proposed by Piaget, and in our view, he was justified in trying to trace the

Table 7

Number of Non-conservers (Main Experiment)
in Each Age Group at Various Stages When Considering
the Quantity of Rubber in a Rubber Band

	Number tested	Conservers	Undecided	Non-conservers
1st year	26	5	2	19
2nd year	11	4	0	7
3rd year	7	5	0	2
4th year	4	3	1	0
	48	17	3	28

development of the concept of invariance of substance. But the stages are not clear cut; the borders between them are zones not lines. Further, we cannot be sure that the group of operations proposed by Piaget of reversibility, combination of compensated relations, and identity, are, in fact, sufficient, although they may well be necessary before the child can attain conservation.

In the case of non-conservers, there is clear evidence that thinking is frequently dominated by perceptual "centering," usually on single dimensions or equalities. Table 3 shows that forty out of fifty-four children at this stage replied to the effect that "it's more because it's longer" or some essential variation of this. The remaining fourteen either could not give a reason or advanced all manner of apparently irrelevant arguments such as, "mine's a sausage"; "you've rolled it." Furthermore, Table 3 shows that twenty-four non-conservers gave clear evidence of a change of "centering" during the experiment and it is possible that this double "centering" may influence the attainment of conservation in some instances.

Piaget (1950, p. 140) has unequivocally stated that the coordination of relations (for example, height makes up for what is lost in length) is necessary before conservation comes about. From Table 4 we see that six non-conservers can consider two dimensions in compensatory fashion when forced to do so, but fail to conserve. Of the children at the transition stage, seven conserve temporarily when forced to consider two dimensions, while a further four conserved at the end of the experiment.

Again, Piaget (1950, p. 141) has stated that the child at the non-conservation and transition stages had, on occasion, admitted a return to the starting point, without this "empirical reversal" constituting a complete reversibility. We do not understand exactly the difference between this "empirical reversibility" and a complete reversibility, but we do know from Table 5 that some children gave evidence of reversibility, as we have defined it, and yet did not conserve.

At the transition stage suggestion is strong in some children. They may give the answer they think is required and not their own opinion, but it was not found difficult to obtain, in answer to later questions, what seemed to us to be their own viewpoint. At this stage the child may begin the experiment by conserving but later resort to non-conservation; or he may begin as a non-conserver, then conserve as the experiment proceeds, and finally revert to non-conservation again. The striking feature about children at this stage is that they are uncertain. The child is stumbling towards the concept of conservation and may revert to non-conservation at any time.

In the final stage the equality of the ball and sausage, from the point of quantity, is always maintained. But one can still note the lingering influence of perception because some children will readily admit that the "sausage" (or ball) *looks* more. In the first year, 13 per cent of the age group were unable to give a reason, but all the other pupils did in all the year groups, and many spontaneously gave more than one reason. Some say, "As they were the same before" (reversibility); some say, "You haven't added any," or "You haven't taken any off," (operation of plus/minus); others say, "Although it's longer it's thinner" (coordination of relations).

A small number of children justify conservation on the grounds that the ball held by the experimenter could be changed into a sausage similar to that held by the testee (identical action). A few children say that their lump of plasticine has only undergone a change of shape, or that the weights of the ball and sausage remain constant. Piaget does not mention these reasons as far as is known to the writers. The last is particularly interesting for Piaget maintains that conservation of weight comes later than conservation of substance. He may well be correct and experiments are being carried out to verify his views. But even now we suggest that substance is conserved more safely when supported by conservation of weight.

In the first subsidiary experiment we have shown that witnessing and agreeing to the operation of subtraction of a small piece of plasticine does not in itself necessarily produce conservation. But it is true that the operation does help the child to fix his attention on quantity rather than on dimension, and it is this that seems to help children to conserve who were previously not doing so. About a quarter of the children tested who were non-conservers in the main experiment, now conserve or almost do so. Among those at the transition stage the move toward conservation is roughly doubled, but this could have been partially anticipated since the lines between the stages are not clear cut. It is the decision in the main experiment, to place all those who change their mind into the transition stage, whether they conserved to the end or not, that enables some children to become conservers after this operation with apparent ease.

In the second subsidiary experiment we have demonstrated that children who are non-conservers in one situation involving quantity, are not inevitably non-conservers in another. Indeed, about one-third of those who were non-conservers in the experiment involving plasticine were conservers in the experiment employing the rubber band. Hyde (1959) also found that some children who were non-conservers in a test using plasticine balls were conservers when a liquid was poured from one vessel into another of different shape. For example, when liquids in similar vessels A and B, which certain children agreed were equal in amount, were poured into glasses C and D, respectively, they agreed that the amounts in the latter vessels were equal in spite of great perceptual differences due to C and D being of entirely different shapes. Yet, when the liquids in A and B were matched again for equality, and the liquid in B was poured into a number of smaller vessels which were all similar to one another, some of those who previously agreed to conservation, now denied it. Beard (1957) also found among sixty children aged 6 and 7 years, that some who were non-conservers when comparing balls of plasticine, could conserve when water was poured from one vessel to a number of smaller ones.

Thus, it seems that children who are conservers of continuous quantities in one situation are not inevitably conservers in another. On this point the more recent findings seem to lead to conclusions at variance with those of Piaget. Our interpretation of his view is that once the concept of the conservation of substance has been attained, it holds in all situations involving conservation of substance. If we have understood him correctly, then our evidence, also that of Hyde and Beard, does not support his viewpoint, which seems to us to hide the particularities of child thinking. It seems rather that the concept is applicable only to highly specific situations at first and that it increases in depth and complexity with experience and maturation. Piaget's view that the child arrives at the concept because he is able to argue logically in concrete situations may or may not be correct. A careful scrutiny of all our evidence does not enable us to prove or disprove his viewpoint. It is equally likely that the concept of conservation of substance—or indeed, any concept—grows out of the interlocking of several organizations of past impressions that normally remain outside consciousness (schemata) which in turn grow out of many and varied experiences. The child may then invoke logical argument to justify the concept which was obtained on other grounds. Or, it may be that experience and the ability to use logical thought aid one another and bring about certainty.

The following points also arise from our study:

(1) Our evidence suggests that in the first two years of junior school there are many children who have not attained much concept of the invariance of substance. It must not be assumed that the children of this school were entirely representative of British junior school children generally, and it is our opinion that in some other junior schools the proportion of conservers might be somewhat higher.

(2) From work reported here and elsewhere, there is, in our view, no doubt that Piaget's type experiments are in themselves learning situations.

(3) Our experiments have shown the grave dangers involved in accepting a child's apparent understanding at face value.

(4) Non-conservation of substance may affect the lives of children and less able adults more than is generally recognised. For example, we have evidence that some children are prepared to pay more money for a piece of toffee when it is in one shape than when it is in another.

(5) Our work has confirmed the considerable verbal confusion known to exist in children in the first two years of the junior school. They confuse such terms as *longer, fatter, shorter, bigger, thicker, smaller.* Here are two examples from first-year children:

"It gets thinner and bigger, it doesn't get fat though." By *bigger* we assume he means *longer.*

"It'll get right long and smaller and smaller." By *smaller* we assume he means *thinner.*

Piaget, too, has read into the child's remarks what he thought the latter meant, although we cannot be sure that either Piaget or ourselves always judged correctly on this issue. To us this confusion supports our view that the idea of quantity grows slowly.

(6) Reversibility, in the sense in which we have defined it, is the most frequently given reason for conservation at all ages.

REFERENCES

Beard, R. M. (1957). An investigation of concept formation among infant school children. Unpublished doctoral dissertation, University of London.

Bunt, L. N. H. (1950). *The development of the ideas of number and quantity according to Piaget.* Gronigen, Djakarta: J. B. Walters.

Hyde, D. M. (1959). An investigation of Piaget's theories of the development of the concept of number. Unpublished doctoral dissertation, University of London.

Piaget, J. (1950). *The psychology of intelligence.* London: Routledge.

Piaget, J. (1953). *Logic and psychology.* Manchester: Manchester University Press.

THE GROWTH OF THE CONCEPT OF VOLUME IN JUNIOR SCHOOL CHILDREN

K. Lovell / E. Ogilvie

INTRODUCTION

Piaget, Inhelder and Szeminska (1960, p. 358) have described an experiment in which a child is shown a set of 1 cm metal cubes which are then put at the bottom of a partly filled bowl of water. The experi-

Reprinted with the permission of the senior author and the publisher from *Journal of Child Psychology and Psychiatry*, 1961, **2**, 118–126.

menter builds a block out of 36 cubes (say, 3 × 3 × 4) while the subject notes how the level of the water rises in the bowl. The child is asked if he thinks the level will change if the arrangement of the cubes is modified (to, say, 2 × 3 × 6). In fact, the subject is questioned about the conservation of volume inside the 36 cubes, i.e. internal volume; about volume as occupied space; and about complementary or displacement volume, i.e. the change in the level of the water in the bowl.

Lunzer (1960), using a procedure very close to that of Piaget, studied the understanding of volume in 24 children ranging in age from 6 to 14 years. Many of the findings of Piaget were completely borne out, but Lunzer did not confirm that the notions of infinity and continuity are necessary before the child can calculate volume in terms of linear dimensions, or before he can grasp the conservation of displacement volume. In the experiment now to be described there were alterations in the procedure that yielded findings that were not brought out either in the work of Piaget or of Lunzer.

The concept of physical volume, embracing the three aspects noted above, is an extremely important one for teacher and child. The latter will make many errors in certain problems in science if this concept is not well developed.

PROCEDURE

Apparatus and General Technique

Apparatus—Twenty-five plastic cubes (dice) of size ⅞ in (2.22 cm); these will be referred to as bricks when questioning the child. A 1 gal (4543 ml) can and a 1 pint can (568 ml), both of these being standard measures found in a primary school.

Technique—A selection of the main questions is given but it must be stressed that supplementary questions were often asked if a point needed elucidating. Each child was questioned individually in the headmaster's room so that no child witnessed the interrogation of another.

PART 1   INTERNAL VOLUME   Twelve cubes were presented as a block arranged as 2 × 2 × 3 (the last figure always represents the height), and another 12 in a block 2 × 3 × 2 (See Fig. 1a).

Question (i): "Here we have two blocks of bricks. If we made two boxes, one for each block of bricks, so that there was just enough room in each box to hold the bricks, would there be as much room in one box as in the other? How do you know? [or] Why?"

One block of cubes was then rearranged as 1 × 2 × 6 (See Fig. 1b).

Question (ii): "If we make another box with just enough room in it to hold this block of bricks [1 × 2 × 6], would that box have the same

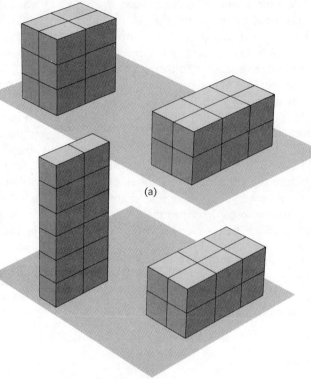

Figure 1   Experimental arrangements of blocks.

amount of room in it as this box [2 × 3 × 2]? How do you know? [or] Why?"

PART 2   OCCUPIED VOLUME   The child was shown the pint can and the gallon can, with the "1 pint" and "1 gallon" marks on the can clearly in view. Moreover, the child was told the amount of water held by each can. The pint can was then filled to the brim with water.

Question (iii): "Before we fill this can [1 gal] with water we are going to put some bricks in like this. [The block 2 × 3 × 2 is placed in the gallon can.] If we now fill this can to the top do we still get the same amount of water in as before, or do the bricks make a difference? How do you know? [or] Why?"

The block 2 × 3 × 2 was then removed from the gallon can.

Question (iv): "Suppose we put this block [1 × 2 × 6] into the 1 gallon can. Are we able to get as much water into the can now as we could with this block [2 × 3 × 2] in the can?"

The questioning was pursued at this point to ascertain if the amounts of water that can be poured into the can are independent of the arrangements of the cubes, provided that the number of cubes remains the same. The subjects were also asked the reasons for their answers.

PART 3 COMPLEMENTARY OR DISPLACEMENT VOLUME   The pint can remained full of water. All the cubes were removed from the gallon can and placed on the table. The experimenter said, "Let's pretend that the gallon can is full of water right to the top just like the pint can, and that I place this block of bricks [2 × 3 × 2] very carefully into the gallon can so that there is no splash." The cubes were lowered very carefully into the gallon can and Question (v) asked.

Question (v): "Is it possible to put the bricks [2 × 3 × 2] into the pint can very carefully without spilling any water? Why do you give that answer? [or] Why?"

Those pupils who answered Question (v) correctly were asked:

Question (vi): "What happens if you place these bricks [1 × 2 × 6] in the pint can instead of these [2 × 3 × 2]? What do you know about the amounts of water spilled over? Why do you give that answer? [or] Why?"

PART 4   Each child was questioned as to whether any water would spill over if just one cube was lowered into (a) the full pint can, and into (b) the full gallon can. If the replies to these two questions were correct, the child was asked if the amounts spilled would be the same. Some children denied that water would be spilled from the full gallon can but thought that it would be spilled from a full pint can.

PART 5   Every child who maintained that the amounts of water spilled were the same, when replying to Question (vi), was asked to compare the amounts of water spilled if (a) a cube used in the experiment, and (b) a cube of exactly the same size and shape but made of lead, and therefore much heavier, were lowered into the full pint can. The question was put in respect of the full pint can rather than the full gallon can since more children thought water would be spilled by one cube being immersed in the former.

Subjects

There were 191 junior school pupils from a North of England town involved in this investigation. Of these 51 were first, 40 second, 45 third and 55 fourth-year children. It is likely that the sample is not entirely representative of English children in general, and it is possible that in other areas of the country a somewhat greater proportion of junior school children with a well-developed concept of physical volume would be found.

RESULTS

PART 1   INTERNAL VOLUME

Table 1

*Number of Children Giving Correct Replies
to Questions (i) and (ii)*

Year	Number of children	Q (i): Box for 2 × 3 × 2 block the same size as box for 2 × 2 × 3 block	Q (ii): Box for 2 × 3 × 2 block the same size as box for 1 × 2 × 6 block
1st	51	44 (86%)	33 (65%)
2nd	40	35 (87%)	27 (67%)
3rd	45	44 (98%)	41 (91%)
4th	55	55 (100%)	51 (93%)
	191	178	152

Table 2

*Number of Children Giving Various Reasons
for Conserving Interior Volume in Question (ii)*

Year	Number of children	Quantity	Identical action	Compensatory relations	Plus/ minus	Reversi- bility	No clear reason given
1st	33	21 (64%)	3	6	1	0	2
2nd	27	19 (70%)	2	5	1	2	1
3rd	41	30 (73%)	5	6	—	1	—
4th	51	33 (65%)	4	3	3	2	2
	152	103	14	20	5	5	5

The headings in Table 2 are defined as follows:

Quantity—Subjects relate the amounts of room in the two boxes to the quantities of cubes which remain unchanged.

Identical action—Subjects say, in effect, that the remaining 2 × 3 × 2 block could be rearranged as 1 × 2 × 6.

Compensatory dimensions—Subjects say, essentially, "This would be a fat box but that would be a big thin one."

Plus/minus—Subjects maintain that cubes have been neither added nor taken away.

Reversibility—Subjects say that the $1 \times 2 \times 6$ block could be changed back to a $2 \times 2 \times 3$ block.

Table 1 clearly shows that when junior school children compared a $2 \times 3 \times 2$ arrangement of cubes with a $2 \times 2 \times 3$ arrangement, almost all recognized that the interior volume was the same in both instances. It cannot be assumed, however, that they necessarily counted the number of cubes in each block; they appeared to observe general likenesses and concluded that the number must be the same. But when the arrangement $2 \times 2 \times 3$ was changed to $1 \times 2 \times 6$ perceptual differences become greater, and then only some two-thirds of the first and second year pupils, and nine-tenths of the fourth year pupils, conserved internal volume. It is possible that these figures would not have been as high if the number of cubes used had been greater.

From Table 2 it is clear that almost three-quarters of the conservers of internal volume in Question (ii), related the amounts of room in the two boxes to the quantity of cubes which remains unchanged. A few children pointed out that a $2 \times 3 \times 2$ block could be rearranged as $1 \times 2 \times 6$, and a few referred to dimensions that compensate for one another.

It is possible that part of the discrepancy in the proportions of correct answers to Questions (i) and (ii) is due to the fact that the answers to Questions (i) were derived from comparing two static situations. For Question (ii), however, one block was seen by the child to be rearranged, and it is feasible that the mere movement of the blocks suggested for some children a change in internal volume.

Of those children who did not conserve interior volume in Question (ii) the most frequently given reason for the inequality of the size of the boxes related to dimensions; e.g. "This box will have more room because it is taller."

PART 2   OCCUPIED VOLUME

Table 3

Number of Children Who Correctly Replied to Questions (iii) and (iv)

Year	Number of children	Q (iii): Could not get as much water in gallon can with $2 \times 3 \times 2$ block in it	Q (iv): Could get the same amount of water in gallon can with $1 \times 2 \times 6$ block as with $2 \times 3 \times 2$ block in it
1st	51	33 (65%)	20 (39%)
2nd	40	29 (72%)	24 (60%)
3rd	45	29 (64%)	25 (56%)
4th	55	49 (89%)	46 (84%)
	191	140	115

Table 4

*Number of Children Giving Various Reasons for Stating
that the Quantity of Water in the Gallon Can
Must be Less if Cubes Are Placed in the Can*

Year	Number of children	Bricks taking up room or essential variation of this	The weight of the bricks will push the water out	Inversion: "If bricks in last, water will spill out"	No clear reason
1st	33	20 (61%)	4	2	7
2nd	29	25 (86%)	1	—	3
3rd	29	23 (79%)	3	1	3
4th	43	43 (100%)	4	2	2
	134	111	12	5	15

It seems likely that the relative sizes of the can and block of cubes are important in relation to Questions (iii) and (iv) and this must be remembered when considering the responses. Using the present apparatus it seems that something like two-thirds of first-year and nine-tenths of fourth-year junior school children realized that after inserting a number of cubes in a gallon can there is less room in the can for water. But not until the fourth year do some 80–90 per cent of junior school children grasp that the presence of the cubes reduced the capacity of the container, *and* that a mere rearrangement of the cubes made no difference to the amount of water that could be put into the can. It must be stressed, however, that had the relative sizes of the object immersed and the container been changed, the number of children giving correct responses at the various ages might have altered somewhat.

Roughly, three-quarters of those who correctly answered Question (iii) said, essentially, that less water could be put into the can because the cubes took up some room. These saw the problem in terms of occupied space. But 12 pupils thought that the weight of the cubes was a determining factor, in the sense that for them water had to be squeezed "out" or "up" so that a heavy block would exclude more water than a light one. Five children anticipated Part 3 by saying that if the bricks were put in last the water would spill out, while 15 gave the correct answer but could not say why.

An examination of the replies of doubtful or incorrect replies to Question (iii) showed that 8 pupils were uncertain of the effect of introducing the cubes into the 1 gal can, and 43 said they would make no difference to the capacity of the container. Of the 43, 27 could give no reason, while 16 said that the water would get "in the cracks" or "under the bricks" or something similar. Thus when children do not understand the relevant factors involved in a physical problem it looks as if they select, as causal agents, plausible elements which happen to strike them.

Table 3 shows the number of correct replies to Question (iv), when the subjects had to compare the amounts of water that could be poured into the 1 gal can with a 2 × 3 × 2 and 1 × 2 × 6 arrangement of cubes. Of the conservers 60 (52 per cent) maintained that the quantities of water were equal, "because there is the same number of bricks" or "the same amount of bricks," and 31 (27 per cent) stated that the two blocks of cubes took up the same space. There were a number of other reasons proposed, but each was given by only very few subjects. An examination of the protocols also revealed that an understanding of interior volume was usually necessary before occupied volume can be understood.

PART 3   COMPLEMENTARY OR DISPLACEMENT VOLUME

Table 5

Number of Children Who Maintained that an Overflow of Water Is Inevitable (Question (v)), and Conserved the Amounts of Water Spilled when the Blocks Were Rearranged (Question (vi))

Year	Number of children	Q (v): Overflow of water inevitable	Q (vi): Conserves the amounts of water overflowing with 2 × 3 × 2 or 1 × 2 × 6 block
1st	51	45 (88%)	28 (55%)
2nd	40	37 (92%)	23 (58%)
3rd	45	43 (95%)	32 (71%)
4th	55	54 (98%)	43 (78%)
	191	179	126

This table indicates that using the present apparatus, almost all junior school children knew that a displacement of water was inevitable when a number of cubes was placed in the full gallon can. When asked about their reasons for their replies to Question (v), 90 (48 per cent) said that "the bricks take up a lot of room" or something similar; and 73 (38 per cent) said that "the heaviness of the bricks makes the water come up," or something essentially similar. Once again it seems that weight of the cubes is a relevant factor for some children. A few pupils each gave a number of other reasons, while 18 knew that water would be spilled but could not say why.

Table 5 also shows that roughly one-half of the first-year and three-quarters of the fourth-year children could conserve the amount of water displaced when a 2 × 3 × 2 block was exchanged for a 1 × 2 × 6 block. Of these conservers 77 (60 per cent) said that the amounts of water displaced were equal "because there's the same number of bricks in each block" or something similar; 36 (29 per cent) thought the amounts displaced were equal because both blocks weighed the same; and 23 (19 per cent) said that the blocks "take up the same room" or made a similar response.

PART 4   The following are the number of children who maintained that water would be spilled if just one cube was lowered very carefully into a full-pint can: 35 (69 per cent) first-year, 28 (70 per cent) second-year, 38 (84 per cent) third-year, and 49 (89 per cent) fourth-year pupils. Table 6 indicates the number of children giving various replies when asked to compare the amounts of water spilled if a single cube was immersed in a full gallon and full pint can.

Table 6

*Number of Children Giving Various Replies when Asked
to Compare the Amounts of Water Displaced if a Single
Cube Is Immersed in a Full Pint and Full Gallon Can*

Year	Number of children	Same amount of water displaced	More water displaced from the pint can	More water displaced from the gallon can	Uncertain
1st	51	11 (22%)	23 (45%)	4	13
2nd	40	11 (28%)	13 (33%)	2	14
3rd	45	20 (44%)	15 (33%)	4	6
4th	55	32 (58%)	21 (38%)	0	2
	191	74	72	10	35

It appears that not until the fourth year of the junior school do 50 per cent of pupils realize that the amount of water displaced by a single cube is independent of the size of the full container within the limits set by the apparatus used.

PART 5   The figures in Table 7 show that the number of children who thought that the weight of an object completely immersed affected the amount of water displaced, decreased with age, but even in the fourth year, only about half understood that the amounts of water displaced were the same.

Table 7

*Number of Children Who Conserved in Their Replies
to Question (vi) Giving Various Answers about
the Amounts of Water Displaced by Two Bricks
of the Same Size and Shape but Different Weight*

Year	Number of children	Same amount of water displaced	More water displaced by heavier cube	Uncertain
1st	28	6 (22%)	20 (71%)	2
2nd	23	9 (39%)	11 (48%)	3
3rd	32	8 (25%)	19 (59%)	5
4th	43	23 (53%)	16 (37%)	4
	126	46	66	14

DISCUSSION

Taking the evidence as a whole it seems as if the concept of physical volume (which embraces interior, occupied and displacement volume) develops slowly during the junior school period, and it is unlikely that any single test will decide if a child fully understands it. If we take success in all the tests that have been described as the criterion of "formal thought" in respect of physical volume, then the number of children who satisfy our criterion are: first-year, 3; second-year, 5; third-year, 5; fourth-year, 21. It is clear that an understanding of physical volume does not, in present circumstances, develop until late in the junior school stage, and even then many children will have gaps in their understanding. Broadly speaking our evidence supports Piaget *et al.* as regards their stages, although we differ concerning developments within stages.

In the development of this concept, as in the growth of other concepts, the child has to learn to eliminate irrelevant factors. This is a slow business.

It is possible, but not certain, that children could learn more quickly about physical volume by being exposed in school to learning situations where the effectiveness of the relevant and non-effectiveness of the irrelevant variables could be made evident in the same experiment. It seems that Piaget *et al.* are optimistic if they think that the single test, in which they employed 36 unit cubes in a bowl, will enable them to distinguish between those who have developed a complete concept of physical volume from those who have not.

Our evidence does not deal with the problem of the calculation of volume as as function of length, breadth and height. Piaget *et al.* (1960) are of the opinion that the ability to understand this calculation depends upon the child having developed the notions of infinity and continuity.

Lunzer (1960) does not agree and thinks that a grasp of these ideas is held to be necessary for the sake of Piaget's theory, which demands the priority of topological concepts over Euclidean ones in child development; he thus casts doubt on a theory that has already been called in question by Lovell (1959).

It may well be possible to measure space inside, or space taken up by, a cube or cuboid before the concept of physical volume becomes well developed. Indeed, teaching a child to calculate volume may well focus his attention on conservation of both interior and occupied volume, providing a good teaching method is employed. It is certain, however, that a child who has not attained a well-developed concept of physical volume cannot employ operational thinking in relation to, say, Archimedes' Principle, or problems of density. In these instances his thinking may lead him into many errors and inconsistencies.

REFERENCES

Lovell, K. (1959). A follow-up study of some aspects of the work of Piaget and Inhelder into the child's conception of space. *Brit. J. educ. Psychol.*, **29**, 104–117.

Lunzer, E. A. (1960). Some points of Piagetian theory in the light of experimental criticism. *J. child Psychol. Psychiat.*, **1**, 191–202.

Piaget, J., B. Inhelder, and A. Szeminska (1960). *The child's conception of geometry*. London: Routledge.

SITUATIONAL GENERALITY OF CONSERVATION

Ina C. Uzgiris

A marked awakening of interest has recently occurred in the work of Jean Piaget on the intellectual development of children, particularly in the studies performed after 1930 (Piaget, 1951, 1952, 1954; Piaget and Inhelder, 1956; Piaget, Inhelder, and Szeminska, 1960; Piaget and Szeminska, 1952; Inhelder and Piaget, 1958). Good summaries of this work are available elsewhere (Anthony, 1957; Berlyne, 1957; Hunt, 1961).

Reprinted with the permission of the author and The Society for Research in Child Development, Inc., from *Child Development*, 1964, 35, 831–841. This paper is based on a dissertation done under the direction of Prof. J. McV. Hunt and submitted to the University of Illinois in partial fulfillment of the requirements for the Ph.D. degree.

At around the age of 7, Piaget finds reasoning becoming operational in that it attains the characteristics of logical and mathematical operations. Although this early operational reasoning is still limited to concrete situations, it nevertheless depends on the availability of invariant concepts or conservations. The most general of these concepts are the ideas of number, space, time, substance, weight, volume, etc. Prior to attaining operational reasoning, children evaluate such quantities by relying almost exclusively on their perceptual appearances. Procedures like measuring, weighing, and enumerating are not used, because children under about 7 years of age are not convinced that length, weight, and number remain invariant through every rearrangement of an object. The study of the development of logical thinking, therefore, must study the attainment of such invariant concepts and the child's coming to recognize them as self-evident.

The attainment of conservation of substance, of weight, and of volume at around the ages of 7, 9, and 12, respectively, was first described in a study by Piaget and Inhelder (1941), and the sequence was verified on a group of mentally retarded children by Inhelder (1944). Furthermore, Piaget and Inhelder (1947) have proposed that this sequence follows the law of logical implication, i.e., that the conservation of weight always implies the conservation of substance, and the conservation of volume always implies the conservation of both weight and substance. Other investigators have generally confirmed Piaget's findings (Carpenter, 1955; Elkind, 1961a, 1961b; Lovell and Ogilvie, 1960, 1961a, 1961b; Smedslund, 1961a).

Piaget used the now classical technique of two plasticine balls to test for the achievement of conservation. Since other investigators were concerned with either replicating the gradual achievement of the invariance of these concepts, the ages at which they are achieved, or with showing the crucial role of particular logical operations, they have also used the two plasticine balls. However, several studies (Beard, 1957; Carpenter, 1955; Hyde, 1959; Lovell and Ogilvie, 1960, 1961a; Lunzer, 1956) have mentioned, mostly parenthetically, that some children who demonstrated conservation of a particular concept with the plasticine balls did not show conservation of the same concept when confronted with a different material, or vice versa.

If each of these levels of conceptual invariance is based on a particular development of logical operations and these operations are organized in a hierarchical sequence, then the type of material used to test for the attainment of the levels of invariance should not affect the sequence of their attainment, although there might be some variation in the time of attainment of a particular concept in the sequence with different types of materials.

The purpose of the present study was to investigate systematically the effect of varying the materials used to test the conservation of substance, weight, and volume on the observed sequential attainment of these concepts.

METHOD

In lieu of a longitudinal study of the sequential attainment of the conservation of substance, weight, and volume with several materials, the technique of scalogram analysis was adopted for cross-sectional data. Although this technique has been most frequently applied in the field of attitude measurement, Wohlwill (1960) has used it to study the development of the concept of number and has discussed at length the assumptions underlying the use of this technique for such a purpose. A somewhat modified version of Guttman's original technique of scalogram analysis, Jackson's Plus Percent Ratio (PPR), discussed by White and Saltz (1957) was chosen in this study.

Subjects

A total of 120 subjects comprised the sample. All the Ss were students at a parochial school in Champaign, Illinois. Since this school is the only one of its kind within the town, it draws students from various socioeconomic groups, and its student body may be considered fairly typical of the town's student population.

The sample of Ss consisted of 20 children from each of the first through sixth grades, 10 boys and 10 girls from each grade. The classroom teachers selected which students would participate in the study, having been asked to pick neither the brightest nor their "problem" cases.

Materials

The following four materials were used in this study:

(1) Plasticine balls, each 2 in. in diameter, of a greenish color.
(2) Metal nuts, ½ in. across and ½ in. high, to serve as metal cubes.
(3) Wire coils, 1¼ in. in diameter, 3 coils high made of multi-stranded, twisted wire.
(4) Straight pieces of red, plastic-insulated wire, each 6 in. long and 1/16 in. in diameter.

Two glass jars and metal-cutting shears were also used in the course of the study.

Procedure

In general, the procedure was very similar to that used by Piaget and Inhelder (1941). Ss were tested individually, in a conference room of the school. They were seated across a table from the experimenter, and all materials to be used in the study were visible on the table. The experiment was introduced by *E* in the following manner:

> When people make a judgment, when they say that two things are alike, or that two things are different, they usually have a reason in mind. It seems that these reasons change as people grow up. I am trying to learn more about this. Therefore, I am going to show you different things and ask you questions about them, and then ask you "why" each time, because I want to know *your* reasons for what you say. OK?

The materials were presented one at a time, in a counterbalanced order, so that each material appeared in the same position an equal number of times in each grade. For any one material, questions regarding the conservation of substance were always asked first, then those regarding the conservation of weight and, finally, those of volume. *S* was always presented with two identical objects made of a given material and was asked if he thought they were alike in terms of the quantity being considered. *S* was urged to make the objects alike or to pick out two others that were alike if he did not think that the ones presented to him were. Once *S* was convinced that the two test objects were identical, one of them was deformed into a different shape and *S* was asked if he thought they were still identical in terms of the quantity considered. To ascertain the conservation of volume, one of the test objects was placed in a glass jar half-filled with water, *S* observed the water level rise, and was then questioned about the amount of water that the other object would displace if immersed in an identical jar equally filled with water, which was also present.

Three deformations were performed on each material, which were repeated for substance, weight, and volume. The deformations were as follows:

Plasticine balls. Of the two identical balls, one was (a) rolled into a sausage; (b) further elongated into a long cylinder; (c) torn into three pieces.

Metal nuts. Of two buildings, each containing 18 nuts arranged 3 by 2 by 3, one was (a) changed into a 3 by 3 by 2 structure; (b) formed into a column with 3 nuts as a base, 6 nuts high; (c) broken up into three separate piles, each with 3 nuts as a base, 2 nuts high.

Wire coils. Of two identical coils of wire, one was (a) slightly stretched; (b) stretched farther into an almost straight piece; (c) about one-third of the strands were separated to form two pieces of wire.

Plastic wire. Of two straight pieces, one was (a) tied with a simple knot; (b) tied with a second knot and twisted to almost a round shape; (c) straightened and cut into three separate pieces.

A standard set of questions was used. *S* was required to give a reason for each response and, sometimes, an additional question was asked to clarify these reasons. The following questions were asked to test for the conservation of substance on the plasticine balls:

(1) Is there as much clay in this ball as in this one?
(2) Is there as much clay in the ball as in the sausage? Why?
(3) Is there as much clay in the ball as in the sausage now? Why?
(4) Is there as much clay in the ball as over here? Why?

The questions were appropriately modified for each type of quantity and each material. *E* did not proceed further until the first question was answered affirmatively. All responses made by *S* were recorded by *E*, verbatim as far as possible.

Method of Analysis

In analyzing the responses and deciding whether a particular *S* was conserving the quantity under consideration, each response following each deformation was evaluated separately, together with the reason for it.

Since the questions were somewhat repetitious, it was conceivable that *S*s could carry over response sets from one quantity to another, so that the quality of the reasons became crucial. Few problems arose in classifying the responses for substance and weight, since whenever *S* stated that the original and the deformed objects were alike in terms of substance or weight, he usually gave an adequate and acceptable reason. However, for volume, quite a number of *S*s maintained that the two objects (the original and the deformed) would make the water rise the same amount, but gave either obviously unacceptable or questionable justifications. Reasons like "because it could be made the same shape as before" or "it just looks like it would" were considered unacceptable, while statements like "there is the same amount in both" or "they both weigh the same" were considered questionable, since they did not deal directly with volume or the three-dimensionality of the two objects. Consequently, those who claimed that the original and the deformed object would raise the water the same amount and gave a questionable explanation were generally asked whether the two objects took up the same amount of space. If they answered this in the affirmative, they were classified as conservers, but if they denied that the two objects took up the same amount of space, their affirmative response to the first question was discounted.

RESULTS

A specific set of criteria was used to rate the response of all *S*s. Responses of a sample of 24 *S*s, four from each grade, were rated independently by two raters. The percentage agreement between the two sets of ratings for the conservation of substance was 99 per cent, for the conservation of weight 97 per cent, and for the conservation of volume 94 per cent.

The differences between the mean scores of boys and those of girls on the four materials at each age level were nonsignificant. Thus, the scores of boys and girls were grouped together in all subsequent analyses.

The effect of the order in which the different materials were administered was also investigated. A compounded score across all three quantities for the two materials administered first and for the two materials administered last was computed for each *S*. The difference between the means of such scores for each grade level and for the sample as a whole was found to be nonsignificant.

Numerical scores were computed by awarding 1 point for each conservation response on each type of quantity for each material. This means that the distribution of scores was quite curtailed, since a *S*'s score could range only from 0 to 3 for any quantity on a given material, from 0 to 9 on any given material, and from 0 to 12 on any given quantity.

Table 1

Scalability of Responses for Substance, Weight, and Volume

Material	Jackson's Plus Per Cent Ratio (PPR)
Plasticine balls	.98
Metal cubes	.98
Wire coils	.98
Plastic wire	.98
Total	.99

Scalogram Analysis

For the scalogram analysis, the ratings on the three separate questions ascertaining the conservation of a quantity on any given material were collapsed into a single judgment of either conservation or nonconservation. Only those who obtained a score of 3 on any one quantity on a given material were classified as conservers.

Insofar as the scalogram analysis is a valid index of the sequential attainment of conservation of the three quantities by individual *S*s, it may be concluded that the conservation of substance, of weight, and of volume is clearly attained in the order postulated by Piaget, since Jackson has suggested a PPR of .70 as the cutoff point of scalability. In fact, out of 120 *S*s, only 8 gave a nonscale pattern on some one of the materials used. It seems that chance factors such as the wandering of a child's attention, fatigue, and the like can easily account for these few exceptions, especially since no single *S* gave a nonscale pattern on more than one material.

Furthermore, the responses scaled for each of the materials separately, so it may be said that conservation of the three quantities develops in the same sequence with various types of materials as well.

Age at Achieving Conservation

Increased conservation with age is an indirect method of assessing the sequential development of conservation. If the various patterns delineated by the scalogram analysis are compared in terms of the mean age of Ss giving each pattern, it can be seen that age increases with the attainment of conservation of the three quantities (see Table 2).

Table 2

Mean Age of Subjects Showing Various Scale Patterns
(+ Indicates Presence of Conservation)

Scale Pattern			
Substance	Weight	Volume	Mean Age
—	—	—	7 years, 9 months
+	—	—	9 years, 3 months
+	+	—	10 years, 0 months
+	+	+	10 years, 7 months

Consistency of Responses across Materials

One way of looking at the consistency of responses across materials is to compare the percentage of Ss conserving substance, weight, and volume at the various grade levels from one material to another. Table 3 shows that there is considerable variation in the percentage of Ss who conserve any given quantity across materials, especially at certain grade levels. Some Ss must change their position in the conservation sequence across materials to give the variation.

A correlational analysis was performed to evaluate further the extent to which individual Ss varied their responses across materials. The scores of Ss at each grade level on one material (summed for all three quantities) were correlated with their scores on all other materials.

Table 4 shows that although none of the correlations are perfect, they indicate considerable consistency. It is also notable that the consistency of responses across materials is greater at some ages than at others. The correlations are high, for instance, at grade 1 when almost no Ss conserve any of the three quantities and at grade 3 when about 90 per cent conserve sub-

Table 3

*Percentage Conserving Substance (S), Weight (W),
and Volume (V) on Different Materials*

		Plasticine Balls			Metal Cubes			Wire Coils			Plastic Wire		
	Mean Age[a]	S	W	V	S	W	V	S	W	V	S	W	V
1st grade	6–11	30	20	0	40	20	0	35	10	5	35	0	0
2nd grade	7–10	70	35	10	70	55	0	55	35	15	45	35	5
3rd grade	8–11	90	65	20	95	80	5	90	60	10	90	60	10
4th grade	10– 0	90	65	15	100	70	20	85	55	5	85	65	10
5th grade	10–11	85	75	15	95	80	30	90	70	25	95	70	10
6th grade	12– 2	90	85	20	100	80	30	95	80	20	95	80	25

Percentage Conserving on (spanning header)

[a] Age in years and months.

Table 4

Correlation of Conservation Responses across Materials

	1st Grade	2nd Grade	3rd Grade	4th Grade	5th Grade	6th Grade	Total
Plasticine balls *with*							
Metal cubes	.80	.56	.76	.47	.31	.51	.72
Wire coils	.81	.84	.84	.58	.48	.33	.75
Plastic wire	.82	.74	.72	.65	.45	.34	.75
Metal cubes *with*							
Wire coils	.78	.60	.74	.58	.46	.82	.75
Plastic wire	.88	.37	.84	.73	.60	.72	.78
Wire coils *with*							
Plastic wire	.82	.77	.73	.62	.77	.91	.83
Average *r*	.82	.67	.77	.61	.53	.66	.76

stance. At grade 6 the correlations tend to be high again when 80 per cent of Ss are conserving weight and practically all are conserving substance. In between these times, when conservation is being achieved, the mean correlation across materials decreases considerably.

Furthermore, a comparison of the percentage of Ss giving only one or two conservation responses for substance, weight, and volume at the various grade levels across different materials indicates a greater preponderance of such responses when the respective conservation schemata are being formed (see Table 5). Thus, such limited conservation responses for substance are most prevalent in grades 1 and 2, for weight in grades 3 and 4, and for volume in grade 6.

Table 5

Percentage Giving One or Two Conservation Responses for Substance (S), Weight (W), and Volume (V) on Different Materials

	Percentage Conserving on											
	Plasticine Balls			Metal Cubes			Wire Coils			Plastic Wire		
	S	W	V	S	W	V	S	W	V	S	W	V
1st grade	5	10	10	20	10	0	10	5	0	10	20	5
2nd grade	5	10	0	5	5	0	20	15	0	30	20	0
3rd grade	5	25	0	10	15	0	5	20	0	0	20	0
4th grade	10	25	5	0	20	5	10	20	0	10	25	0
5th grade	5	15	0	5	10	10	5	5	0	5	25	5
6th grade	5	0	5	0	20	5	5	10	5	5	10	5

Table 6

Analysis of Variance Summary

Source	Sum of Squares	df	Mean Square	Error Term	F
Between subjects	947.383	119			
Age (grade level)	377.279	5	75.456	(b)	5.080[b]
Error (b)	570.104	114	5.001		
Within subjects	2041.750	1320			
Material	12.325	3	4.107	$(w)^1$	6.984[b]
Quantity	1039.406	2	519.703	$(w)^2$	305.889[b]
Material × Quantity	4.394	6	.732	$(w)^3$	1.710ns
Material × Age	5.246	15	.349	$(w)^1$	.593ns
Quantity × Age	78.711	10	7.871	$(w)^2$	4.632[b]
Material × Quantity × Age	20.122	30	.670	$(w)^3$	1.565[a]
Error (w)	881.546	1254			
Error $(w)^1$	201.512	342			
Error $(w)^2$	387.383	228			
Error $(w)^3$	292.651	684			

[a] $p < .05$.
[b] $p < .01$.

Analysis of Variance

The data were cast in a type VI analysis of variance design described by Lindquist (1956, pp. 78–86). The analysis was undertaken with full awareness that the present data do not quite meet all the assumptions. The sample was not selected randomly and the distribution of scores was quite curtailed, but it has been demonstrated that failure to meet the assumptions does not completely invalidate the procedure.

The analysis of variance indicates that the attainment of conservation varies with age, with the type of material used for testing, and with the type of quantity (substance, weight, or volume). It also shows a significant interaction between age and type of quantity conserved, which was expected on the basis of the sequential development of conservation of the three quantities.

DISCUSSION

In general, the results of the present study support Piaget's theory of sequential intellectual development and, particularly, the sequential attainment of conservation of substance, weight, and volume in the above order by each individual.

The ages at which about half the Ss of this sample conserved substance and weight are reasonably consistent with those suggested by Piaget and other investigators. In contrast, only 20 per cent of the sixth-graders (average age, 12-2) were found to conserve volume. This is at variance with Piaget's findings, with those of Lovell and Ogilvie (1961), and of Lunzer (1960); but it corresponds rather nicely with the findings of Elkind (1961), who reported that only 27 per cent of his sample of children between 11 and 12 years of age conserved volume. It may be that this difference in the age at which children come to conserve volume reflects the effect of certain experiential factors, but it also may reflect a difference in testing procedure. Most other studies (Piaget and Inhelder, 1941; Lovell and Ogilvie, 1961b; Lunzer, 1960) asked their Ss to compare how far an object in each of two shapes would cause water to rise in a jar. This may be tapping the conceptualization of volume at a level more concrete (less abstract) than that used here and by Elkind (1961). In the latter cases, the Ss were asked to indicate which shape would occupy the greater space, by verbalizing this either as an explanation for the rise in water level or in reply to a direct question. It is interesting to note that Lovell and Ogilvie (1961) report that only 19 per cent of their Ss who conserved volume, according to their criteria, stated spontaneously, as a reason for equal rise in water level for objects of different shape, the fact that the two objects "take up the same room." Subtle differences in procedure may have appreciable effects on age results and should be carefully investigated.

Furthermore, the conservation of substance, weight, and volume seems to be attained in the same sequence with any material. However, this does not imply a perfect coordination of steps in the conservation sequence across different materials in any one individual. Both the analysis of variance and the correlation analysis lead to the conclusion that an individual's position on the conservation sequence is not constant across materials. The variation does not seem to be systematic, in that there was no single material on which all Ss were either accelerated or lagging behind. It seems more a matter of individual differences, although the discrepancies generally were not large.

Individual past experience may well underlie situational differences and account for the observed inconsistency across the various materials. Although Piaget does not focus on the effects of specific environmental variables on development, he does not deny their importance, as has been sometimes suggested (Wohlwill, 1962), since he describes the schemata as evolving and differentiating in contact with the environment. Encounters with the environment are thought to be desirable and necessary, except that the internal satisfaction of recognition or the confirmation of an expectation is substituted for external reward. It may well be that when a schema is developing, specific contacts with the environment will lead it to accommodate more in certain areas than in others, producing situational specificity in terms of specific past experiences of the individual. But after a certain number or a certain variety of encounters, a schema may develop independence and start to be applied universally. This leads to the expectation that schemata would be in a greater state of flux while developing, showing situational specificity, but once they consolidate, the situational variability would be expected to disappear. The waxing and waning of consistency, to be noted in Table 4, fits such a view.

Another approach to the understanding of the observed situational variability is to look for broader classes of variables that would subsume groups of different materials. Piaget has classified materials into continuous and discontinuous ones. Smedslund (1961b) has observed that the conservation of substance is first achieved with discontinuous materials and only later with the continuous. The present study seems to bear this out. Metal cubes would qualify as the only discontinuous material and it appears that a greater percentage of Ss attained conservation of each of the three quantities on this material. There might well be other salient classifications of materials that would merit investigation and would lead to a better understanding of the observed situational variation.

REFERENCES

Anthony, J. (1957). Symposium on the contribution of current theories to understanding of child development: IV. The system makers: Piaget and Freud. *Brit. J. med. Psychol.*, 30, 255–269.
Beard, R. M. (1957). An investigation of concept formation among infant school children. Unpublished doctoral dissertation, London University.
Berlyne, D. E. (1957). Recent developments in Piaget's work. *Brit. J. educ. Psychol.*, 27, 1–12.

Carpenter, T. E. (1955). A pilot study for a qualitative investigation of Jean Piaget's original work on concept formation. *Educ. Rev.*, 7, 142–149.

Elkind, D. (1961a). Children's discovery of the conservation of mass, weight, and volume: Piaget's replication study II. *J. genet. Psychol.*, 98, 219–227.

Elkind, D. (1961b). Quality conceptions in junior and senior high school students. *Child Develpm.*, 32, 551–560.

Hunt, J. McV. (1961). *Intelligence and experience.* New York: Ronald.

Hyde, D. M. (1959). An investigation of Piaget's theories of the development of the concept of number. Unpublished doctoral dissertation, London University.

Inhelder, B. (1944). *Le diagnostic du raisonnement chez les débiles mentaux.* Neuchâtel: Delachaux et Niestlé.

Inhelder, B., and J. Piaget (1955, orig. French ed.). *The growth of logical thinking from childhood to adolescence.* New York: Basic Books, 1958.

Lindquist, E. F. (1956). *Design and analysis of experiments in psychology and education.* Boston: Houghton Mifflin.

Lovell, K., and E. Ogilvie (1960). A study of the conservation of substance in the junior school child. *Brit. J. educ. Psychol.*, 30, 109–118.

Lovell, K., and E. Ogilvie (1961a). A study of the conservation of weight in the junior school child. *Brit. J. educ. Psychol.*, 31, 138–144.

Lovell, K., and E. Ogilvie (1961b). The growth of the concept of volume in junior school children. *J. child Psychol. Psychiat.*, 2, 118–126.

Lunzer, E. A. (1956). A pilot study for a quantitative investigation of Jean Piaget's original work on concept formation. *Educ. Rev.*, 8, 193–200.

Lunzer, E. A. (1960). Some points of Piagetian theory in the light of experimental criticism. *J. child Psychol. Psychiat.*, 1, 191–202.

Piaget, J. (1936, orig. French ed.). *The origins of intelligence in children.* New York: International Universities, 1952.

Piaget, J. (1937, orig. French ed.). *The construction of reality in the child.* New York: Basic Books, 1954.

Piaget, J. (1945, orig. French ed.). *Play, dreams, and imitation in childhood.* New York: Norton, 1951.

Piaget, J., and B. Inhelder (1941). *Le développement des quantités chez l'enfant.* Paris: Delachaux et Niestlé.

Piaget, J., and B. Inhelder (1947). Diagnosis of mental operations and theory of intelligence. *Amer. J. ment. Defic.*, 51, 401–406.

Piaget, J., and B. Inhelder (1948, orig. French ed.). *The child's conception of space.* London: Routledge, 1956.

Piaget, J., B. Inhelder, and A. Szeminska (1948, orig. French ed.). *The child's conception of geometry.* New York: Basic Books, 1960.

Piaget, J., and A. Szeminska (1941, orig. French ed.). *The child's conception of number.* New York: Humanities Press, 1952.

Smedslund, J. (1961a). The acquisition of conservation of substance and weight in children: II. External reinforcement of conservation of weight and of the operations of addition and subtraction. *Scand. J. Psychol.*, 2, 71–84.

Smedslund, J. (1961b). The acquisition of conservation of substance and weight in children: VI. Practice on continuous versus discontinuous material in problem situations without external reinforcement. *Scand. J. Psychol.*, 2, 203–210.

White, B. W., and E. Saltz (1957). Measurement of reproducibility. *Psychol. Bull.*, 54, 81–99.

Wohlwill, J. F. (1960). A study of the development of the number concept by scalogram analysis. *J. genet. Psychol.*, 97, 345–377.

Wohlwill, J. F. (1962). From perception to inference: a dimension of cognitive development. In W. Kessen and C. Kuhlman (Eds.), Thought in the young child. *Monogr. Soc. Res. Child Develpm.*, 27, (2), Ser. No. 83. Pp. 87–107.

CHAPTER

TWO

NUMBER

CONCEPTS

*   *   *

THE CHILD'S CONCEPTION OF NUMBER by Piaget (1952) is a theoretical treatise with supporting empirical results describing in detail the sequence of the development of the number concept. Piaget distinguishes between the acquisition of number concepts and arithmetic achievement, yet he acknowledges the relationship between the two, since acquisition of appropriate cognitive competencies leads to arithmetic skills:

> Number is organized, stage after stage, in close connection with the gradual elaboration of systems of inclusions (hierarchy of logical classes) and systems of asymmetrical relations (qualitative seriations), the sequence of numbers thus resulting from an operational synthesis of classification and seriation . . . logical and arithmetical operations therefore constitute a single system that is psychologically natural, the second resulting from generalization and fusion of the first. . . . (p. viii)

As can be seen from the above quotation, the evolution of the number concept follows a stage sequence and is intimately related to acquisition of conservation of quantity, since the child can only understand quantification (numbers) when he is capable of preserving wholes (conservation). Numerical conceptions are also linked to the development of the complementary logical operations of classification and seriation.

A number of studies have been reported based on this volume, but only a sample of them are presented in the following chapter. They have been selected because: they replicated Piaget's work with standardized procedures and more clearly described populations (Elkind); they present novel ways to test developmental sequences (Wohlwill); or finally, they permit one to examine the relationships of acquisition of number concepts to related cognitive operations (Dodwell).

Elkind's study is a replication providing documentation of the Piagetian proposition that discrimination, seriation, and numeration follow in that order. In his prologue and conclusion sections, Elkind sets out to clarify Piagetian conceptualizations of the number concept. He provides the reader with a useful elaboration of Piagetian rationale regarding the development of seriation and numeration. The study confirms Piaget's findings concerning the operations relevant to the acquisition of number.

Elkind's methodology involves presentation of various tasks which, while assessing discrimination, seriation, and numeration, were not ordered or scaled a priori by application of a particular scaling methodology.

Employment of scalogram analysis is a method whereby tests are ordered in a logical sequence, thus providing an opportunity for an analogue of longitudinal study. This technique, which we shall have occasion to encounter later in Kofsky's logical classification study, requires the establishment of an hierarchical order, thereby providing a parallel to the description of Piagetian stages. Wohlwill's scalogram analysis is derived from Piaget's description of the developmental sequence of number concept acquisition. Employing a set of ordered tasks, the hierarchy obtained was not as predicted, but the stages in the development of the number concept were found generally in accord with those reported by Piaget. Wohlwill discusses these results at considerable length, both in regard to the implications for general methodology and their relationship to a developmental theory of cognition.

Dodwell set out to test the Piagetian assertion that the number concept develops in an invariant sequence, by assessing the consistency of the child's developmental level across an array of relevant tasks (relation of perceived size to number, seriation, and so forth). Dodwell's research is concerned with the relationships of number concepts to the traditional arithmetic abilities and to logical operations. An initial study (Dodwell, 1960), not represented here, does confirm Piaget's contention that children's ability to count does not necessarily signify comprehension of number. Considerable variability is found within a particular child's performance, as well as between children's performances, in comprehension of the number concept. He finds, moreover, that the sequential stages described by Piaget do not necessarily appear.

The significant aspect of Piagetian theory tested by Dodwell in the study included in this chapter is the relationship of logical classification concepts and the development of cardinal number. Piaget asserts that construction of number is concomitant with the development of logic, and this assertion forms Dodwell's major hypothesis. Although the two abilities were found to emerge over the same general age range, the findings raise questions about the pattern of development because logical classifications may be neither a necessary nor a sufficient condition for number concepts. This type of experiment is central for Piagetian theory since it provides a direct test of the relationship between operations and concepts.

These studies on the acquisition of number tend to confirm Piaget's expectations. Certain questions remain concerning the relation of the concept of number to other cognitive areas:

(1) How interdependent and interlocking are the relations between comprehension of quantification and logical operations?

(2) What are the prerequisites and concomitant cognitive operations necessary and sufficient for the number concept to appear?

(3) Finally, what is the potential value of Piagetian number tasks for classroom diagnostic tools (use in number-readiness assessment, for example)?

REFERENCES

Dodwell, P. C. (1960). Children's understanding of number and related concepts. *Canad. J. Psychol.*, 14, 191–205.

Piaget, J. (1952). *The child's conception of number*. London: Routledge.

DISCRIMINATION, SERIATION, AND NUMERATION OF SIZE AND DIMENSIONAL DIFFERENCES IN YOUNG CHILDREN: PIAGET REPLICATION STUDY VI

David Elkind

INTRODUCTION

The starting point for this sixth replication study is Piaget's book *The Child's Conception of Number* (1952), which represents a variety of experiments dealing with many different facets of the child's number conception. Although some of the experiments reported in the book have been replicated by the writer (1961a, 1961b) and by other investigators, such as Estes, (1956), Wohlwill (1960), and Dodwell (1960), many experiments in the book remain to be explored by means of standarized procedures and statistical techniques. Of the experiments that remain to be explored, those relevant to discrimination, seriation, and numeration[1] of size differences were chosen for the present replication study because they provide a vivid illustration of the complex developments that underlie the child's attainment of an abstract number conception.

Piaget's experiments on discrimination, seriation, and numeration had a dual aim, as did all the experiments reported in his *Number* book. On the one hand, his experiments were designed to demonstrate stages in the development of particular conceptions—namely, that of a series and a seriated class (number). On the other hand, they were designed to demonstrate the development of a conceptualizing ability that transcends the formation of any particular conception and accounts for the similarity in the development of diverse conceptions. In his attempts to achieve his dual aim, Piaget encountered the same difficulties that learning theorists meet when they attempt to study learning apart from performance. Piaget's

---

[1] Piaget speaks of this problem as one of coordinating ordinal and cardinal number. But in fact, as he himself says elsewhere in his discussion (1952, p. 157), the concrete problem is one of seriating classes (constructing numbers). The term *numeration*, though not Piaget's, is a convenient one to designate the application of numerals to a set of elements which are at once classed and ordered.

Reprinted with the permission of the author and the publisher from *The Journal of Genetic Psychology*, 1964, 104, 275–296. This study was supported (in part) by a PHS Small Grant M-3466 from the Department of Health, Education and Welfare, U.S. Public Health Service.

solution was to vary the problems and materials from experiment to experiment so that he could simultaneously demonstrate developmental sequences in the attainment of particular conceptions and, by comparison of these sequences with one another, demonstrate the unfolding of conceptual abilities that can account for the attainment of diverse conceptions. As Piaget does not always make clear the distinction between the dual aims of his investigations, he is frequently misunderstood.[2]

Implicit in Piaget's experiments on number is his assumption that conceptualizing ability derives from the internalization of the child's grouping, ordering, and counting actions—actions that, on the mental plane, give rise to class, relation, and arithmetic operations analogous to those of logic. In each of his experiments, therefore, Piaget presented children with problems of classification, seriation, and numeration that could be solved by the manipulation of concrete materials or by reference to them. By study of the development of the child's grouping, ordering, and counting activities in connection with concrete materials, Piaget hoped to discover the stages in the development of conceptualizing ability, as well as the stages in the attainment of particular conceptions.

Piaget's experiments on discrimination, seriation, and numeration provide a good example of his method. In one of his studies, he used two sets of size-graded sticks. The sticks in the second set were smaller than those in the first set. With his sets of size-graded sticks, Piaget devised three types of tests.

The first test was essentially a control measure and involved simple discrimination problems. For example, the child was asked to select the "largest" and the "smallest" of one set of sticks when the sticks were in disarray upon the table.

A second test involved presenting the child with several seriation problems. First the child was asked to build a "stairway" out of one set of sticks. After the stairway was constructed, the second set of sticks was produced —the child was told that they had been forgotten—and the youngster was asked to insert the new sticks within the stairway.

In the third test, the child was given several numeration problems. On the first problem of the test, the child was confronted with the intact stairway and was asked how many stairs a doll, occupying a particular stair, had had to climb to reach that stair. The second problem of the third test involved asking the child the same question when the stairway was broken apart so that the pieces were unordered as to size. The purpose of these numeration problems was to determine whether a child can coordinate an ordinal position with a cardinal value (the number of stairs climbed).

Piaget found that the discrimination problems were passed at the 4-year level, but that the more complex of the seriation and numeration problems

---

[2] The study of Estes (1956) provides a good example of such misunderstanding.

were not passed until the ages of 6 or 7. Through careful analysis of the typical performance at each age level, Piaget was able to discern three stages in children's ability to seriate and numerate size differences.

At the first stage in the development of seriation (usually at age 4), children generally are unable to seriate sticks above a small number (three or four). At the second stage (usually at age 5), children are able to make a correct seriation after considerable trial and error, but are unable to insert the second set of sticks within the completed stairway. Children at the third stage (usually at the age of 6 or 7) are able to form a stairway and to insert correctly new sticks within it. Piaget observed parallel stages in the development of numeration. Children at the first stage (usually at age 4) are unable to count correctly and cannot determine the number of stairs the doll had climbed. At the second stage (usually at age 5), children are able to tell how many stairs the doll had climbed when the stairway was intact, but not after it was destroyed. Finally, at the third stage (usually at the age of 6 or 7), children are able to say how many stairs the doll had climbed, whether the stairway was together or was in pieces.

Numeration tasks were often performed with fewer elements than seriation problems because Piaget worked with the number of elements that the child could count correctly. With a fixed number of elements, the stages in numeration might well appear at a slightly later age than those reported for seriation. As a fixed number of elements were used in the present study, it was predicted that success on numeration problems would appear later than success on seriation items.

Piaget's presentation of his experiments raises several issues. First, Piaget reported the stages in the development of seriation and numeration by means of illustrative experimental examples of performances at different age levels—but without the aid of statistics. One purpose of the present study was to determine whether similar stages could be found, using standardized procedures and a statistical design.

Second, in discussing the developmental stages, Piaget intimated that the perceptibility of size differences might influence the age at which the stages appeared, but not the order of their appearance. A second purpose of the present study was to determine whether the perceptibility of size differences in one-dimensional, two-dimensional, and three-dimensional materials affects the ages at which the stages appear.

Third, Piaget interpreted the stages as favoring his thesis that the child's growing ability to form class, relation, and number conceptions derives from the conceptualization of his own grouping, ordering, and counting activities. However, as presented in *The Child's Conception of Number*, Piaget's argument is extremely condensed and difficult to follow, especially by those not versed in Piaget's terminology. A third purpose of the present study was to amplify Piaget's discussion on the development of seriation and numeration, with the aid of concepts and examples familiar to American psychologists.

METHOD

Subjects

Ninety children[3] (30 at each age level from 4 to 6) participated in the investigation. The median age for each group was (*a*) 4 years, 6 months; (*b*) 5 years, 7 months; and (*c*) 6 years, 9 months. The 4- and 5-year-old children were from the Wheaton College Nursery and the Country Day Nursery School in Norton, Massachusetts. Six-year-old children were from the Norton Elementary School.

Subjects were heterogeneous with respect to socioeconomic background and intelligence. The 4- and 5-year-old children at the Wheaton College Nursery had fathers who were in business or in the professions. On the other hand, in the majority of cases, the 4- and 5-year-old children at the Country Day Nursery School and the Norton Elementary School came from homes in which fathers were factory, farm, or office workers.

Despite the absence of measurement, it is assumed that the presence of children from a higher socioeconomic class in the 4- and 5-year-old groups raised the general level of intelligence in those groups above that in the 6-year-old group.

Piaget contends that the stages he observed are, at least in part, attributable to maturation and that differences in *IQ* and environmental stimulation should not obliterate differences attributable to growth. If differences between the 4- and 5-year-old children and the 6-year-old children are found, despite the likelihood that the older children have a lower mean *IQ*, the results would strengthen Piaget's argument on the importance of maturation in the attainment of conceptualizing ability.

Materials

BLOCKS   Two sets of size-graded blocks were used for the three-dimensional materials. In each set there were nine blocks. In the first set, the smallest block was a one-inch cube, and the succeeding blocks increased by ½″ increments. In the second set of blocks, the smallest block was a ¾″ cube; the succeeding blocks increased as in the first set. The blocks of both sets were painted a dull orange; the second set was distinguished by red markings.

SLATS   For the two-dimensional materials, sets of size-graded slats were employed. All the slats were 1½″ in width and ¼″ thick. The first

---

[3] The author is indebted to Mrs. Marjorie Ford, Director of the Wheaton Nursery School; to Mrs. Catherine Bauza, Director of the Country Day Nursery School; and to Mr. David Holbert, Principal of the Norton Elementary School, for their friendly cooperation.

set of slats began with a 1½″ slat, and the succeeding slats increased in size by ½″ increments. The second set of slats began with a 1¾″ slat, and the succeeding slats increased by ½″ increments. The slats were painted the same dull orange as the blocks, and the second set were identified by similar red markings.

STICKS   As one-dimensional materials, two sets of sticks, ¼″ in diameter, were used. The lengths of the two sets of sticks were identical to the lengths of the slats. Like the other materials, the sticks were painted dull orange and the second set had red markings.

Tests

DISCRIMINATION   The child was presented with four discrimination problems on the sticks, with four on the slats, and with four on the blocks. A set of nine blocks, slats, or sticks was placed in disarray upon the table and *E* said: "Can you find the smallest? Show me the smallest" (item 1). Then *E* said: "Can you find the largest? Show me the largest" (item 2). Next, *E* asked the child to hide his eyes and when the child did so, *E* disguised the smallest element so that it appeared larger. If it was a block, it was placed in front of other blocks. If it was a slat or stick, it was placed so that its upper edge protruded beyond that of the surrounding elements. The child was then told that he could look, and *E* said: "Find the smallest . . . now, show me the smallest . . ." (item 3). Once the child made his choice, he was asked to hide his eyes again while *E* camouflaged the largest element. If it was a block, it was hidden behind the other blocks; if it was a slat or stick, it was so placed that an element on one side of it protruded above it and an element on the other side protruded below it. Once more the child was asked to look, and *E* said: "Show me the largest . . . now, find the largest . . ." (item 4). Each correct choice was given a score of one. All other choices were scored zero. For any one material there was a possible score of four points. The total possible score was 12 points for the discrimination test as a whole.

SERIATION   For each of the three materials, the seriation items were the same. With a set of nine elements in disarray on the table, *E* said: "Can you make a stairway with the . . . watch me." Then *E* constructed a stairway and made sure that the child watched the procedure. Then *E* mixed the elements and said: "Now, you make one just like mine." If the child failed to seriate nine elements, five were taken away and he was asked to seriate four (item 1). Children who failed to seriate four elements were not tested further. Those who succeeded on four elements were given seven elements to seriate (item 2). If the child failed with seven elements, testing was discontinued. If the child succeeded, he was again given nine elements to seriate (item 3). If the child failed after having seriated four and seven elements, testing was discontinued. Those children who initially, or eventually, were able to seriate nine elements were given five additional elements (picked at random from the second set) and *E* said: "I have some more . . . that also go in the stairway; can you put them where they belong?" (item 4). If the child did not get the idea, *E* demonstrated with one element. Each correct seriation item was given a score of one and, if the child initially succeeded in seriating all nine elements, he was automatically given a point for seriating four (item 1) and seven (item 2). On any one material there was a possible score of four points and a total possible score of 12 for the seriation test as a whole.

NUMERATION   The numeration items, like the seriation items, were the same for all materials. With the elements made into a stairway, *E* asked the child to count the number of stairs (item 1). *E* then said: "Look, a dolly is on this stair." (*E* points to the first stair.) "How many stairs does the dolly have to climb to get on this stair?" Once the child got the idea, *E* pointed to each stair in succession, asking how many stairs the doll had to climb to reach each stair (item 2). Then *E* pointed to the fourth stair and said: "How many stairs must the dolly climb to reach this stair?" After the child's reply, *E* pointed to the seventh stair and repeated the question. For this question (item 3), the child had to tell how many stairs the doll had to climb to reach *both* the fourth stair and the seventh stair to receive credit. Next *E* mixed the elements and said: "If the stairway was together like it was before, how many stairs would the dolly have to climb to reach this stair? (the fourth) . . . and this one?" (the seventh). On this question (item 4), the child had to tell how many stairs the doll had to climb to reach *both* the fourth stair and the seventh stair in order to receive credit. For any one material there was a possible numeration score of four and a total possible score of 12 for the numeration test as a whole.

Procedure

Each child was tested individually three times at intervals of approximately one week. At each test-session a different material was employed. To control for practice effects, the order of presentation of the materials was counterbalanced. At each age level, the 30 children were randomly assigned to one of six subgroups with five children per group. Each subgroup was presented with the materials in one of the six possible orders in which the three materials could be combined.

Experimental Design

As can be seen from the description above, the experiment involved three independent variables: Age, Materials, and Tests. For two of the variables, Materials and Tests, it was possible to administer all the values of each variable to every child. For the third variable, Age, this was impossible; and each value was represented by a different age group. For two within-group variables and one between-group variable, an appropriate design is described by Lindquist (1953). That design, Type VI, was used in this study. Because the scores in the individual cells were small, with consequent small-error terms, the author decided to use the .01 level as the criterion for rejecting or accepting the null hypothesis.

RESULTS

Quantitative Findings

The results of the analysis of variance are shown in Table 1. The various individual tests will be discussed below.

Table 1

Analysis of Variance for Comparing Success on Discrimination, Seriation, and Numeration Tests at Three Age Levels and with Three Materials

Source of variation	df	Sums of squares	Mean squares	F	p
Age	2	213.424	106.712	52.464	.01
Subgroups within Age	87	176.941	2.034		
Materials	2	17.469	8.735	24.815	.01
Tests	2	277.520	138.760	132.278	.01
Age × Materials	4	3.516	.879	2.497	.05
Age × Tests	4	86.220	21.555	20.548	.01
Subgroups within Age × Materials	174	61.236	.352		
Subgroups within Age × Tests	174	182.480	1.049		
Materials × Tests	4	3.620	.905	4.665	.01
Age × Materials × Tests	8	3.284	.410	2.113	.05
Residual	348	67.539	.194		
Total	809	1093.249			

AGE   Piaget's observations imply significant differences between 4-, 5-, and 6-year-old children in the ability to discriminate, seriate, and numerate size differences. In the present study, the F for these three groups was 52.5 and was significant beyond the .01 level of confidence. The means for the three age groups were 21.2 (age 4), 29.7 (age 5), and 32.0 (age 6). Individual t tests for the differences between means indicated that they were significantly different from one another at the .01 level. The increase with age in the size of the mean scores on tests of discrimination, seriation, and numeration is in agreement with Piaget's observations.

TESTS   In his experiments, Piaget found that the discrimination items are the least difficult, that the seriation items are of intermediate difficulty, and that the numeration items (when not made easier by reducing the number of elements used) are the most difficult. Results of the present study gave an F for the three tests of 132.3, significant beyond the .01 level. The means for the three types of tests were 11.6 (discrimination), 8.7 (seriation), and 7.4 (numeration). These means were significantly different from one another as shown by individual t tests. Item analysis revealed that the last item of the seriation test (the insertion problem) was the most difficult of the seriation problems and that the last item of the numeration test (the determination of the number of stairs climbed after the stairway has been destroyed) was the most difficult of the numeration items and, in fact, the most difficult item of all items. The relative difficulty of the three types of test and of the individual item of those tests is consistent with Piaget's results.

MATERIALS   Although Piaget did not to any great degree concern himself with the dimensional characteristics of his test materials, he did suggest that the more perceptible the differences, the more easily they would be mastered. In the present study, this suggestion was tested by varying the dimensionality of the materials. This was done on the assumption that variation in dimensionality might reveal whether successful discrimination, seriation, and numeration of six differences is a function of their discriminability. The F for the three materials was 24.1, significant beyond the .01 level. Individual means were 8.8 (sticks: one-dimensional materials), 9.1 (slats: two-dimensional materials), and 9.8 (blocks: three-dimensional materials). By individual t tests, the differences between means were significantly different at the .01 level. Although the extent of the differences was not great, there was a trend toward more successful discrimination, seriation, and numeration of size differences with an increase in the dimensionality of the materials in which those differences appear. The finding agrees with Piaget's suggestion on the influence of the perceptibility of size differences.

AGE × TEST INTERACTION   According to Piaget, the difference between success on discrimination, seriation, and numeration tests decreases with age because of the increased conceptual ability of the older child. On account of the increased conceptual ability of the older child, one would expect that differences between the three tests would vary between age levels. Statistically, an unequal effect of the tests at each age level would appear as a significant Age × Test interaction. The F for this interaction was 20.5, significant beyond the .01 level. As expected, the table of interactions for these two variables showed that differences between mean scores on tests of discrimination, seriation, and numeration decreased with age, in agreement with Piaget's findings.

AGE × MATERIALS INTERACTION   Although Piaget assumed that the perceptibility of differences might influence the ease with which differences are discriminated, seriated, and numerated, he also assumed that perceptibility of differences does not affect the *order* in which items are passed; rather he held that the order reflects a necessary sequence of development. If Piaget is correct, the differences between age groups should remain relatively the same for each material, although the absolute size of the scores might vary from material to material. In that case, one would not expect a significant Age × Materials interaction, but a significant interaction effect would lead to rejection of the hypothesis that the effects of age are the same for all materials. The F for this interaction was 2.5 and was not significant at the .01 level. In short, it seems reasonable to accept Piaget's view that perceptibility of size-differences affects absolute score-differences, but not relative score-differences between age groups on different materials.

TESTS × MATERIALS INTERACTION   Piaget's position implies that the effects of varying the perceptibility of size differences are more pronounced on difficult tests than on easy tests. If this view is correct, one would expect the effects of materials to be different on different tests and this would appear as a significant Test × Materials interaction. The F for this interaction was 4.7, significant beyond the .01 level. Examination of the table of interactions indicates that the effects of the dimensionality of materials was greatest for the discrimination and the numeration tests and was least for the seriation items. This finding was not expected. It may be that discriminability had the most effect with discrimination and numeration because the children were not as active on these tests as they were on the seriation test; therefore the immediately given differences were of greater significance. Naturally, this hypothesis needs to be checked in another study. It can be said, however, that the effect of the discriminability of differences varies according to the nature of the test.

AGE × TEST × MATERIALS INTERACTION   There was no reason to expect, on the basis of Piaget's findings, that the effects of particular tests and materials would be different at different age levels. In the present study, the test of these particular combinatory effects was tested by the Age × Test × Materials interaction. The F for interaction was 2.1 and was not significant at the .01 level of confidence. Accordingly, the results of this study give no warrant for assuming that the effects of the combination of any one material and any one test varies with age level.

Qualitative Observations

In order to make the foregoing statistical results concrete and to convey some of the behavioral details upon which Piaget builds his interpretations of conceptual development, illustrative examples of performances observed in the present study will be presented. These behavioral observations will also serve as a bridge between the statistics of the preceding section and the theoretical discussion which is to follow.

STAGE 1

Bob (4–7). Bob picked the smallest slat after briefly surveying the elements. For the largest slat, he chose one of the largest elements; when asked whether it was really the largest, he nodded in assent. Bob found the smallest slat when it was disguised but chose the stick that stuck out the farthest in his attempt to find the largest slat.

On the seriation test, Bob arranged the slats in disconnected pairs: GE, HB, EA, etc. In other words, he made several seriations that lacked direction and exactness although the general idea of size differences was grasped. Bob was not able to seriate four slats, and seriation testing was stopped.

When asked to count the steps in the stairway (which E constructed), Bob said: "1, 2, 3, 7, 5, 9, 11." In his attempts to attach these numbers to individual elements, he sometimes counted the same element twice and at other times skipped elements altogether. Bob was not able to grasp the doll-and-stairs problem.

Hal (4–6). Hal picked the smallest slat and the largest slat after carefully comparing them with several others. When the smallest slat was disguised, he found it immediately. On the other hand, he was not sure of the largest stick and said: "I'd better measure," which he proceeded to do. (This is an excellent illustration of Weber's law; i.e., a half-inch differential in length is easier to perceive between short elements than between long ones.)

On the seriation test, Hal put down CABEGFIH but arranged them so that the tops of the elements made a regular stepwise pattern. E then placed a straight-edge along the bottom of the series so that the elements were evenly aligned, but the tops of the elements no longer made a regular stepwise pattern. Immediately, Hal arranged the elements in the stepwise pattern again without regard to the size relations among them. Hal seriated four elements correctly and succeeded with seven elements after some trial and error. But when he had nine slats again, he once more ordered them by arranging the tops in a stepwise pattern.

When Hal was asked to count the stairs in the stairway on the first numeration item, he counted 1, 2, 3, 4, 5, 6, 7, 8, 9, 10, but in his eagerness skipped an element and said there were 10 elements, not nine. *E* asked Hal to count slowly, which he did, and he determined the correct number. When Hal was asked how many stairs the doll had climbed to reach the first step, he tried to count all the steps again. He was not able to get the idea that the number of stairs climbed was determined by the number of the stair.

STAGE 2

Helen (*5–4*). Helen selected the largest and the smallest slats quickly. She did this when they were scattered as well as when they were disguised.

On the seriation test, Helen arranged the elements ABDCEGF and then recognized something was wrong and rearranged the elements several times until she got them right. Then she put H and I together on one side as if the other elements formed a completed series and as if she were starting a new one. When *E* asked: "Can you make these [H and I] into the stairway, too?" Helen added them but reversed the H and I and then got them correctly. When *E* produced five more slats from the second set, Helen attempted to build a second stairway alongside the first. After *E* demonstrated insertion with one element (c), Helen placed c in the stairway but removed C and then she put in f, but removed D. *E* said: "They are all supposed to fit in the stairway. Can you put these [the unseriated pieces] in?" This time Helen put them all in, but in egregiously wrong places, so that the series was AdBCgDcEFaGHIh. When she was asked: "Are they just right?" Helen replied, "Yes."

With the numeration items, Helen had some success. She made no errors in counting the stairs or in grasping that the number of stairs climbed could be determined by the number of the stair occupied by the doll; nevertheless, she did say that when the doll was on the fourth step it had climbed three stairs and that when it was on the seventh step it had climbed six stairs. When *E* (pointing to the fourth step) asked, "But didn't the doll climb this step?" Helen answered, "No, because the doll is on it." (Apparently, at Stage 2, climbing and being on the stair are mutually exclusive concepts. This difficulty in logic is encountered in the formation of many concepts. At a certain stage, youngsters think a boy cannot be a child and a boy at the same time (3). Likewise, at a certain stage in the development of the concept of religious denomination (4), the child thinks that he cannot be an American and a Jew at the same time.) When the stairway was broken, Helen disregarded the order and counted whatever elements were to the right of the designated stair to determine the number of stairs climbed.

STAGE 3

John (*6–4*). John quickly dispensed with the discrimination items.

On the seriation test, John started with the largest slat, I, and each time selected the largest of the remaining elements. He made no errors and the series was constructed in less than a minute.

With the numeration items, John had equal success. He counted the elements correctly; he knew how many stairs the doll had climbed when the stairs were pointed to in succession and when they were pointed to at random. When the stairway was broken, he put it together again to determine how many stairs preceded the designated stair.

Al (7–1). Al performed much like John on the discrimination and seriation items.

On the numeration test, Al was able to tell not only how many stairs the doll had climbed when the stairs were in disarray, but he was able to do so without actually reconstructing the stairway. In addition, when he was asked to say how many stairs the doll would have to climb to reach the top, he did so by subtraction and without reference to the stairway.

The foregoing examples could be multiplied many times to bring out additional nuances and transitional stages in the development of the ability to discriminate, seriate, and numerate size differences; nevertheless, it is hoped that the examples given will make plausible the interpretations to be presented in the concluding section of this paper.

DISCUSSION

In the preceding section, the author presented quantitative and qualitative evidence that is in general agreement with Piaget's observation on the development of the concepts of series and number. Piaget (1952) interpreted his data from the standpoint of his genetic psychology of intelligence. According to Piaget's psychology, conceptualizing ability derives from the internalization of the child's own actions; stages in the development of particular conceptions reveal the sequence of this internalization. In the following pages, an attempt will be made to recapitulate Piaget's interpretation, to extend it, and to make it more concrete than it is in *The Child's Conception of Number*. Obviously, the attempt will involve some bias and distortion, but it is hoped that the presentation will stimulate others to read Piaget and to reach their own conclusions.

Development of Seriation

STAGE 1   At the first stage, the child has only a general impression of a series as a kind of *global* figure in which the whole and the parts are undifferentiated. It is a purely perceptual impression, however, for as soon as the stairway is destroyed the child no longer believes in its existence. Thus, when the child attempts to reconstruct the stairway, he builds disconnected pairs of elements, AC, DG, HB, and makes no attempt to coordinate them. On the other hand, the child's judgment of individual size relations is generally correct, as is shown in his success with the discrimination problems. The two facts—inability to order pairs of relations, and the correct judgment of single relations—show clearly that the child's difficulty is one of coordinating relations as well as of forming a mental representation of the series.

The child's difficulties at the first stage are analogous to those of the infant at the initial stage of the construction of the object (Piaget, 1955). At that stage, the infant ceases to look for the nipple once it has disappeared from sight, even though he is perfectly capable of turning the bottle around so that the nipple is once more accessible. This occurs because the infant is as yet unable to coordinate the visual impression of the back of the bottle with the visual impression of the front of the bottle, just as the older child is unable, at the first stage in seriation, to coordinate individual size relations with the impression of the series as a whole. In the initial stage of construction of object, as well as series, the child mistakes the absence of visual impression for the absence of the real object. He does this because he is unable to make the coordinations that would give the object psychological permanence.

STAGE 2   When the child has reached the second stage (usually age 5), he has attained what Piaget calls an *intuitive representation* of the series as a whole made up of unrelated differentiated parts. It is intuitive representation, a kind of mental picture of the series, that enables the child to construct, after considerable trial and error, a correct seriation in the absence of a model. However, the imaged character of the representation accounts for the child's trial-and-error method and for his inability to insert a second set of elements within a completed series.

The child's trial-and-error behavior involves a beginning coordination of relations, inasmuch as the child eventually reaches a correct seriation, but the coordinations that lead to correct seriation are the *result* of the child's trial-and-error behavior and do not cause it. The reason for the child's trial-and-error behavior is the fact that he tries to construct a figure analogous to his mental representation of the stairway, but the child's mental representation of the series is different from that of an adult.

The adult conceives the series as a set of elements in an order that can be indefinitely extended, whereas the second-stage child imagines the stairway to be a set of elements related only by the fact that they join to form a pattern; consequently, when the child tries to reconstruct the pattern from a set of unordered elements, he regards each element as unique. He can think of no systematic way of selecting them. Put differently, at Stage 2, the child's problem of constructing a series is analogous to that of putting together a jigsaw puzzle; for the adult, the problem is analogous to the construction of a rank order.

It is because the child sees the problem of seriation as a kind of jigsaw puzzle that he selects elements at random and joins them without regard to their size relations. However, when this unsystematic method results in a figure that differs from his imaged representation of the stairway, then, and only then, does the child begin to coordinate the size relations among the elements. For example, if the child places B next to C and A next to C, then the result, BCA, fails to agree with his mental image of the stairway. He then moves A next to B and achieves the seriation, ABC. However, it must be emphasized that the coordination of relations, $A < B < C$, is neither spontaneous nor deduced and is achieved only because of the discrepancy between the imaged and the perceived figures.

The imaged character of the child's representation—or its figural character—at Stage 2 also accounts for the child's strange behavior; i.e., strange from an adult's point of view, when he is confronted with the problems of nesting one set of elements within another. When the second-stage child is given additional elements to insert, he does one of three things: (*a*) he constructs a second series alongside or atop the first, (*b*) he exchanges elements rather than adds them, or (*c*) he inserts elements without regard to their size relations and regards such insertions as correct.

All of these behaviors "make sense" to the adult once it is realized that as soon as the child has completed his stairway, the child regards it as a completed figure or picture to which nothing more can be added. It is for this reason that, when he is given additional elements and is asked to put them within the completed stairway, the child is as baffled as if he had just completed a jigsaw puzzle and were given additional pieces to put within the finished picture. Since he cannot understand how the pieces are to be inserted, he thinks he has not understood *E* and assumes that *E* wants a second stairway, or an exchange of elements, or a longer line of elements. It should be clear, however, that the child's failure to comprehend the directions does not derive from a verbal misunderstanding. He understands what is wanted perfectly well, and *it is because he understands that he is baffled by the problem.*

At Stage 2, the child's performance on the insertion problem complements his trial-and-error attempts at seriation. In trying to form a series, the child does not spontaneously coordinate the relations $A < B$ and $B < C$, etc.; he does so only in connection with discrepancies between perceived and imaged figures. Likewise, when faced with the problem of insertion, the child does not spontaneously attempt to coordinate the relations of the elements to be inserted with those already seriated. Because there is a completed stairway that makes an appropriate match to his mental image of a series, he feels no need to incorporate the second set of elements within the first. So at the second stage in seriation, as at the first, the child's failures are attributable to failures in coordination of relations and the advance of the second-stage child over the first-stage child derives from the fact that, by means of a differentiated image of the stairway, the second-stage child is able to make such coordination and construct a series.

STAGE 3   At the third stage (usually ages 6–7), the child attains what Piaget calls an *operational* concept of a series. Piaget speaks of the concept as operational because the acts of coordination (ordering) begun at the second stage have gradually become internalized and, in the process, take on the characteristics of logical operations. Once the child's ordering activities have become operations, new coordinations—not possible on the intuitive or perceptual planes—make their appearance. For example, at the third stage the child can mentally coordinate the relations A < B and B < C and arrive at the relation A < C without actually comparing A and C as would be necessary on the plane of perception or intuition. Likewise, at Stage 3 the child can mentally order the series in two directions at once, either as A < B < C < D < E < F < G or as F > E > D > C > B > A, whereas on the perceptual plane, as is known from the staircase illusion, he can perceive a stairway as going up or down but not both ways at the same time. In short, the internalization of ordering activities transforms the child's perception (and representation) of the series because he attributes to that perception the results of his own mental activity, whereas previously he merely read the perceptual givens.

In Stage 3, the attribution of the results of mental activity to perception is clearly apparent in the child's seriation. It is marked by rapidity, few errors, and by construction in either direction. To construct a series systematically, as third-stage children do, it is necessary to attribute to each element the relation s > r and s < t because (to form a series) each element must be chosen so that it is smaller than each element that follows it and larger than each element that precedes it. Such attribution cannot be accomplished on the plane of perception or intuition. On these planes the relations s > r and s < t are contradictory and cannot be combined to give a meaningful conclusion. The situation is analogous to the double alternation problem in which the same stimulus points in two different directions at the same time. In the double alternation problem, as well as in the seriation problem, the correct solution can be found only by means of symbolic or operational processes.

With respect to seriation, the coordination of s > r and s < t is accomplished because the child can mentally order the series in two directions at once. When this is done, the child discovers that the relation s > r and s < t are not contradictory but complementary, because they refer to differences in direction—not to differences in substance—and are equivalent to the relations r < s < t. Simultaneously, the child is then able to attribute both relations to (s) and is able to construct a series. However, it must be emphasized that the child would not be able to do this on the perceptual or intuitive plane. He accomplishes it because, at the third stage, he is capable of mentally ordering elements in two directions at once and of attributing this dual relation to particular elements.

Similar reasoning explains the child's rapid and errorless insertions at Stage 3. First of all, at Stage 3, the child attributes relations to the series and is no longer deceived by its whole quality. In other words, he does not assume that the series is complete and that nothing more can be added.

Second, when he picks each element for insertion, say c, he is confronted with the same problem that he encountered in seriation: namely, that of attributing two relations c $>$ C and c $<$ D to c. He resolves the problem by recognizing the equivalence of the relations just mentioned to other relations formed by ordering the elements in a different direction. In short, both seriation and insertion are accomplished rapidly and without error because the third-stage child is able to attribute the results of his mental operations to the perceived elements; in this way he finally overcomes the apparently contradictory relations given in perception.

The Development of Numeration

The development of numeration (the assignment of numerals to elements regarded as classed *and* ordered) parallels the development of seriation and classification (Elkind, 1961b) because the coordinations involved in forming series and classes are also involved in forming seriated classes (numbers). The coordinations involved in forming series and classes are differentiated from those involved in forming seriated classes by the fact that, in attempting to construct a number conception, the child is dealing with elements that, at once, can be ordered *and* classed. Thus, the development of number can be viewed as an attempt to coordinate asymmetric (series) with symmetric (class) relations. This view makes immediately clear the essential unity between the three processes of seriation, classification, and numeration.

STAGE 1   At the first stage (usually age 4), the child has only a global impression of seriated class in which the quantitative differences and the similarities among the elements are undifferentiated. For example, when the child attempts to count the steps of the stairway (disregarding for the moment whether the sequence of numbers he uses is correct), he neglects the differences (and skips elements); he also neglects the similarities (and counts the same element twice). The reason for this behavior is similar to that for global seriation: namely, the child's inability to coordinate relations that, in this case, are the symmetric (class) and asymmetric (difference) relations. Inasmuch as counting for the adult is always the simultaneous ordering and classifying of elements, it is clear that counting for the 4-year-old child is simply an imitation of adult behavior. It is not a true coordination of class *and* order relations. Such a coordination is impossible at the first stage because, at that level, classes, series, and seriated classes do not exist in the adult sense of these terms.

STAGE 2   The child at the second stage (usually age 5) has a differentiated representation of seriated class. Piaget calls such representation intuitive. This intuitive representation amounts to a kind of ambiguous figure that (disregarding differences) can be imaged as a collection of elements similar in appearance or (disregarding similarities) can be imaged as a collection of elements different in size. It cannot be imaged as both at once. This reversible representation of seriated class accounts for the successes and the failures of the second-stage child on the problem of the doll and the stairs.

When the stairway is intact, counting the elements necessarily induces a recognition of their similarities (a sort of reversal of perspective), just as a counting of the unordered elements induces a recognition of their differences. For this reason, when the stairway is intact, it is relatively easy for the child to think of a class in terms of a position. Once the child has counted as far as the stair that the doll occupies, he immediately reverses perspective and sees the stairway as two classes made up of those stairs greater than the number of the stair that the doll is on and of those stairs smaller or equal to the number of the stair that the doll is on. By this method, which amounts to a perceptual rereading of the situation, the child can literally see that the class value of the stairs climbed equals the series value of the stair occupied by the doll.

The proof that this is not a true coordination of series and class values comes from the observation that the child cannot coordinate these values once the stairway is destroyed. When the steps of the stairway are no longer together, the child disregards order and merely counts whatever steps are to the right or to the left of the step occupied by the doll. The reason is that, when the child views the unordered pieces, he recognizes that the unordered pieces can be seriated (since he has already used them to form a series) and that they can be classed (since he has already divided them into two classes to determine the cardinal value of the stairs climbed), but what he cannot do, in the absence of a stairway, is to recognize that the elements can be classed and seriated at the same time. This inability is attributable to the fact that, at Stage 2, the seriated class is a kind of reversible image such that awareness of the one figure automatically destroys awareness of the other.

In the development of numeration, as in the development of seriation, the advances and the limitations of the second stage are determined by the presence of a representational figure. In the seriation problem, the representational figure forces the child to coordinate his construction with the representational image. In numeration the perceptual figure forces the child to reverse the perspective of his representational image. In short, the coordinations that appear at the second stage are due to the matching of mental images and perceived configurations and do not represent a prior understanding that the figure can be constructed by a coordination of relationships.

STAGE 3   At the third stage (usually ages 6–7), the child has attained what Piaget calls an *operational* conception of an ordered class. It is an operational conception because the actions of ordering and classifying, begun at the second stage, have become internalized and have, in the process, taken on the characteristics of logical operations. Once ordering and classifying have become operational, they are potentially capable of being carried out simultaneously. On the intuitive plane they can only be performed sequentially.

Although the coordination of classification and ordering is made possible by their emergence as operations, their coordination into numerical operations cannot actually be achieved without the aid of counting. The reason is as follows: to coordinate the symmetric and the asymmetric operations simultaneously requires that there be actual relations that are at once similar *and* different. No such relations exist on the perceptual or intuitive planes. The perceived relation $A = A'$ (say, in color) cannot be an asymmetric relation, just as the relation $A < A'$ (say, in size) cannot be symmetric. Counting, however, disregards both the perceptual similarities and the perceptual differences and renders elements simultaneously alike, in that they can be counted, and different in the sense that each element has a unique position of enumeration. In other words, counting transforms each element into a *unit*. Once elements are regarded as units, the classificatory operation $A + A' = B$ is transformed into the numerical operation $A + A' = 2A$; the ordering operation $A < A' < B$ is transformed into the numerical operation $A + 2A = 3A$.

It must be remembered, however, that counting achieves the transformation of elements into units only after classification and seriation have become internalized, for only their operational character makes their simultaneous coordination possible. Counting merely provides the concrete materials (units) on which this coordination can operate and, as the preceding discussions of the first and second stages show, does not spontaneously give rise to numerical relations. Put differently, only after seriation and classification become operational is counting regarded as attributing a unit character to each element counted.

At the third stage, the attribution of a unit character to the steps of the stairway is clearly evident in the child's performance on the doll-and-stairs problem. The youngest or least advanced of Stage 3 children reconstruct the entire stairway before counting to the designated stair. More advanced youngsters construct the stairway only as far as the designated stair, but the most advanced children do not even bother to reconstruct the stairway and perform the seriation mentally. Each of these behaviors demonstrates that the child attributes to the stair occupied by the doll both a series value (since he actually or mentally reconstructs the stairway to determine its position) and a class value (since he uses the number of the stair occupied by the doll to say how many the doll climbed). This occurs because counting, at first actual, then mental, transforms each element into a unit.

Once counting renders each element a unit, the operations of seriation and classification applied to these units result in numerical operations. This is not surprising for, as Stevens (1951) has pointed out, numerical operations are appropriate only to elements ordered so that differences between successive elements are equal. Counting thus transforms the stairway into an interval scale that is amenable to arithmetic operations. In their turn, arithmetic operations are nothing other than the operations that are involved in seriating and classifying, as applied to elements, the perceptual similarities and differences of which have been disregarded, and that, as elements, have been rendered simultaneously alike and different by means of the child's actions. The proof that seriating and classifying operations are numerical as applied to units can be observed at the third stage. When the third-stage child has correctly determined how many stairs the doll has climbed by reconstructing the stairway and is asked how many stairs the doll must climb to reach the top, he does not count, but solves the problem by subtraction. That is, once the child has counted the total number of stairs (X) and the number up to and including the stair occupied by the doll (N), he knows immediately that the number remaining to be climbed is $X - N$. In short, classificatory and difference operations become numerical as soon as the members of the class and the series are regarded as units.

Thus, there is an essential unity between conceptual and numerical ability. Both types of ability derive from an internalization of the child's classificatory and ordering actions that become an integrated set of mental operations with logical characteristics. When this system of operations is applied to elements regarded as similar, the result is a classification; when applied to elements regarded as different, the result is a series. When the same system of operations is applied to elements regarded as both alike and different, the result is *number*. However, in contrast to the elements of classes and series, the elements of number are constructed by the child's own actions and are not given in immediate perception or in intuition.

CONCLUSION

This lengthy presentation of Piaget's thesis on the development of seriation and numeration fails to reflect the full depth and scope of his discussion. It is hoped, nevertheless, that the presentation will have made clear at least some of the complexities that underly such an apparently simple task as constructing a stairway or telling how many stairs a doll has climbed to reach a particular position. In attacking any conceptual problem, the child brings to bear a conceptual ability the form of which determines the nature of the particular conception he attempts to attain. Piaget has proposed that this conceptualizing ability derives from an internalization of the child's own actions upon objects and that, depending upon the contents to which they are applied, these internalized actions give rise to classes, relations, and numbers. The present study did not attempt to test Piaget's thesis regarding the development of conceptual ability, but did attempt to repeat those observations that Piaget has reported and on which he builds his thesis.

REFERENCES

Dodwell, P. C. (1960). Children's understanding of number and related concepts. *Canad. J. Psychol.*, 34, 191–203.
Elkind, D. (1961a). The development of quantitative thinking: A systematic replication of Piaget's Studies. *J. genet. Psychol.*, 98, 37–46.
Elkind, D. (1961b). The development of the additive composition of classes in the child: Piaget replication study III. *J. genet. Psychol.*, 99, 51–57.
Estes, B. W. (1956). Some mathematical and logical concepts in children. *J. genet. Psychol.,* 88, 219–222.
Lindquist, E. F. (1953). *Design and analysis of experiments in psychology and education*. Boston: Houghton Mifflin.
Piaget, J. (1952). *The child's conception of number*. London: Routledge.
Piaget, J. (1955). *The child's construction of reality*. London: Routledge.
Stevens, S. S. (1951). Mathematics, measurement, and psychophysics. In S. S. Stevens (Ed.), *Handbook of experimental psychology*. New York: Wiley. Pp. 1–49.
Wohlwill, J. F. (1960). A study of the development of the number concept by scalogram analysis. *J. genet. Psychol.*, 97, 345–377.

A STUDY OF THE DEVELOPMENT OF THE

NUMBER CONCEPT BY SCALOGRAM ANALYSIS

Joachim F. Wohlwill

INTRODUCTION

Although the development of the number concept has been the subject of a considerable amount of experimental research,[1] it seems safe to state

[1] For an annotated bibliography of this research, see Riess (1947).

Reprinted with the permission of the author and the publisher from *The Journal of Genetic Psychology*, 1960, 97, 345–377. This study was carried out under a postdoctoral fellowship from the National Science Foundation at the Institut des Sciences de l'Education in Geneva, Switzerland. The author is indebted to Profs. Jean Piaget and Bärbel Inhelder for their encouragement and support of this work.

that relatively little progress has been made in our understanding of the nature of the developmental processes involved. There appear to be several reasons for this lack. On the one hand, most of the research has been of a normative, cross-sectional nature, and has usually limited itself to the study of one particular task, involving either mainly discriminative functions (e.g., Douglass, 1925; Judd, 1927) or rote counting and enumeration (e.g., Brownell, 1928; McLaughlin, 1935). Even in the more infrequent cases where investigators have compared the course of development for a number of different tasks (Descoeudres, 1946; Giltay, 1936; Long and Welch, 1941), these were selected in fairly unsystematic fashion, without any prior consideration of their possible theoretical significance. The main theoretical accounts, on the other hand, of the development of the number concept, such as that by Piaget (1952), have been lacking in adequate experimental support.

The present investigation represents an attempt to fill this gap. It starts from the theoretical premise that the development of a concept has its origin in an essentially discriminative function of abstraction, proceeding thence by a process of the gradual elaboration of mediating structures to an eventual state in which the concept exists as a purely representational symbolic entity.

This formulation corresponds essentially to the views of conceptual development advanced by Piaget (1950b) and Werner (1957); at the same time, it is consistent with behavioristic interpretations of symbolic functioning (cf. Munn, 1955; Nissen, 1951; Osgood, 1953).

It may be noted that the number concept is ideally suited for the verification of the developmental process postulated here, since it may be dealt with at widely varying levels of abstraction, ranging from the mere discrimination of the quantity of an aggregate of elements to the sophisticated, wholly symbolic conceptualizations of modern algebra. In the present study we shall limit ourselves, however, to but a portion of the total span of development in this area, starting from the point at which verbal mediators are just beginning to be formed, and ending with the first year of primary school. Beyond this point systematic instruction in the manipulation of number symbols presumably determines, to a large extent, the further development of this concept.

METHOD

General Methodological Considerations

The methodological approach adopted for this investigation was dictated by the developmental emphasis to be given to the problem, the basic question concerning the sequence through which an individual passes in the course of the development of the number concept. The normative, cross-sectional type of study, popular though it is in many phases of developmental psychology (including much of the research on the present topic), is of limited usefulness in this respect, since the mere determination of the average age at which a set of problems is solved by a sample of subjects provides us with no real picture of the extent to which the development of the abilities involved in these problems conforms to an orderly sequence. The longitudinal method is clearly more suitable in this respect, but has obvious disadvantages, mainly of a practical nature, in terms of time, expense, loss of subjects, etc.

A different kind of method, which provides essentially the same information about developmental sequences as the longitudinal approach, but which avoids the disadvantages of the latter, consists in an application of the technique of scalogram analysis. Let us consider a set of tasks calling forth behaviors which are thought to be acquired according to a sequential pattern. An analysis of the patterns of successes and failures on these tasks by individuals at varying developmental levels should then reveal whether these tasks constitute a scalable set. If they do, it may be concluded that mastery of a given task presupposes the mastery of all tasks which are below it in the hierarchy of difficulty, which is equivalent to the assertion of a sequential order of development of the functions tapped by these tasks.

Although the technique of scalogram anaylsis has been applied most frequently in the field of attitude measurement (cf. Guttman, 1950), at least one group of investigators (Schuessler and Strauss, 1950; Strauss and Schuessler, 1951) has employed it to study the genetic development of a particular concept—one which is in fact closely related to that of number— the concept of money. In view of the apparently sociogenic nature of this concept it is of considerable interest that these authors were able to construct scales of items involving various aspects of this concept which satisfied the usual criteria of reproducibility.

One defect of the study just cited is the rather arbitrary way in which items were selected for inclusion in the scales, so that the resulting scale types, although in some respects supporting notions of mental development advanced by Piaget and others, are of somewhat limited theoretical import. In the present study, the aim is to provide a sounder theoretical underpinning, by using the concept of levels of abstractness, or degrees of symbolic mediation, as a guiding principle in the selection of the individual tests. By utilizing, as much as possible, tests which on the basis of previous investigations may be assumed to vary on this dimension of abstractness, their relative places in the total sequence may be hypothesized on an a priori basis. Thus the predictive value of this technique is considerably strengthened, in comparison with the approach, current in scalogram-analysis research, of selecting a set of items on a more or less intuitive basis, and rejecting those which turn out not to be scalable.

Experimental Technique

The basic technique employed in this investigation is the matching-from-sample technique. This method has shown itself useful in the study of conceptual responding at infra-human levels, as in the work by Harlow and his associates on monkeys, and at the Yerkes Laboratories on chimpanzees (cf. Harlow, 1951). It has also been applied specifically to the study of number discrimination in various species of birds (cf. Koehler, 1949). Although rarely used with children, the method appears to be promising with nursery-school *S*s, for a variety of reasons: the situation can easily be structured as a game for the child; the method really permits systematic variation of the stimulus material without changing the nature of the tasks; furthermore, verbalization, both on the part of *E* and of *S*, is reduced to a minimum.

Apparatus and General Procedure

The apparatus consisted essentially of a wooden board covered with yellow cardboard and mounted on a base. Three rectangular apertures, 6×10 cm., were cut out of the center of this board, spaced in a horizontal row and separated by intervals of 6 cm. These "windows" were covered by masonite doors opening upwards towards the *S* and covered with white cardboard. Choice cards, 7×7 cm. in size, were hung over these doors. Behind each window a small flat cardboard box was affixed, serving as receptacles for small colored chips used as reinforcers.

The *S* was seated in front of the apparatus, so that his eyes were approximately on a level with the windows. For the initial practice trial, the following *choice cards* were hung over the windows: two blue dots arranged horizontally; three blue dots forming an isosceles triangle, and two purple concentric circles. The *sample card* for this preliminary trial, 10 cm², showed likewise two purple concentric circles (though somewhat larger than those on the third choice card); it was placed horizontally on the table just in front of the apparatus.

E told *S* that he wanted to play a game with him: *E* would hide a chip behind one of the windows and *S* was to try to find it. *E* further informed the *S* that he would be able to find the chip every time if he looked carefully at the (sample) card, for this card told him which was the right window. *E* then waited for *S* to choose and open one of the windows. If the choice was correct, *S* withdrew the chip from the receptacle and placed it in a little box in front of him. In the event of an incorrect choice, *S* was allowed to correct it, until he found the chip; he was urged to look very closely at the card on the table, since there was something on this card which told him which of the windows had the chip behind it. (This correction procedure applied *only* to this single practice trial.)

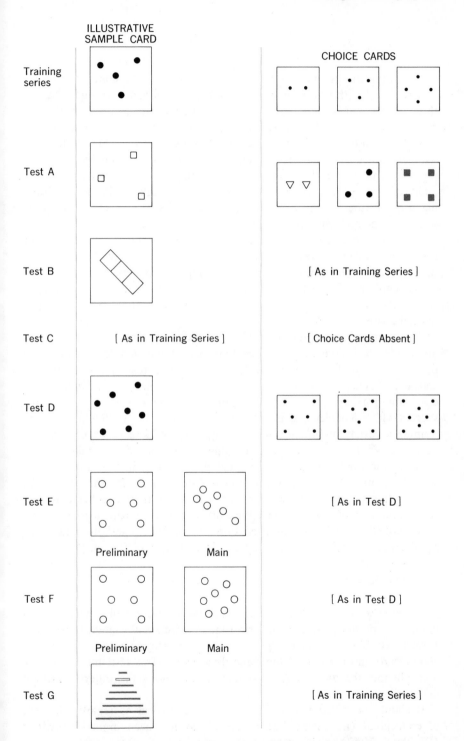

Figure 1   Sample and choice cards used in Training and Test Series.

Training Series

Following the practice trial, the choice card with the concentric circles was replaced with one showing four dots in a diamond arrangement; the three choice cards thus represented the numbers two, three, and four, respectively, arranged from left to right on the windows. These stimuli, as well as those used in the test series, are illustrated in Figure 1, together with examples of the corresponding sample cards. The choice cards remained in place for the length of the training series (they were used in addition in several of the transfer tests that followed; cf. below). The training series further involved the use of a set of 18 sample cards, featuring 2, 3, or 4 dots in varying configurations, none of which were identical to any of the choice cards over the windows. As in the practice trial, the sample cards were placed, one at a time, on the table directly in front of the apparatus. The S was not given the opportunity, however, to correct wrong choices. The criterion of learning was six consecutive correct responses; if this criterion was not met in 48 trials, the S was discarded from the study.

The training series thus elicited from the S a response based on the numerical correspondence between the dots on the sample and those on the correct stimulus card. In itself, however, this response need not be considered evidence for a conceptual response; it may represent rather a discriminative capacity of a fairly primitive order—as suggested by the success which Koehler and his associates (cf. Koehler, 1949) have had in training a variety of birds on number-matching tasks of this type. For our purposes, then, success on this learning phase was merely taken as an index of the lowest level of conceptual development in this area. At the same time this training series constituted a prerequisite for the subsequent transfer tests, in which Ss were required to apply their number-matching set to problems of a more conceptual order. These transfer tests will now be described in their hypothesized order of difficulty, and their assumed significance as an index of conceptual development discussed.

Test Series

ABSTRACTION   This test involved choice and sample cards varying not only in number, but also in form (square, circle and triangle) and color (green, red, blue), in such a way that any given sample card matched each choice card on only one of the three dimensions. This test thus forces the S to abstract the dimension of number from among the other, irrelevant dimensions.

It should be noted that this task is still equivocal as regards the role of conceptual (i.e., symbolic) processes: as has been argued elsewhere (Wohlwill, 1957), abstraction, in the sense of a selective response to one aspect of a stimulus, is best regarded as a basically discriminative process. Nevertheless, particularly in view of the dominance of form and color over number in a multiple-cue matching situation with young children (cf. Descoeudres, 1914), it is clear that *S*s who had recourse to verbal mediators designating the number aspect of the stimuli would be at an advantage here, in the sense of being less likely to abandon their number set.

ELIMINATION OF PERCEPTUAL CUES   The choice cards for this test were those used in the training series (2, 3, and 4 blue dots). The sample cards contained rectangles drawn in outline and divided up into two, three, or four equal, adjacent squares, separated by thin black lines. These rectangles were arranged horizontally, vertically, or obliquely on the various sample cards.

This test differs from the training series in the presumed elimination of any conceivable perceptual cues (such as, total stimulus area, extent of figure-ground segregation) for the discrimination of the numerical correspondence between sample and choice stimuli. A correct response requires, then, the intervention of symbolic processes (specifically counting) mediating this correspondence; accordingly one may hypothesize that this test will be somewhat above the previous one on the difficulty-hierarchy, and that *S*s succeeding on it will likewise solve the previous one.

MEMORY   For this test the sample cards were those of the training series, but the choice cards were removed, i.e., the windows were left blank. The *S* was thus called upon to make his choice by matching a given sample to the window which he had come to associate with the corresponding number.

Lest it be argued that the response here reflects simply a spatial association between the position of the windows and the corresponding number stimuli, it should be pointed out that there was no opportunity in the training series for such specific associations to develop, since the stimuli varied widely among themselves (i.e., in configuration) and generalized number-window associations would thus have required the mediation of schemata representing the individual numbers. Accordingly, a representational basis is assumed for the correct response in this test, leading to its postulated position following Test *B* in the present scale.

EXTENSION   In this test the range of the number continuum was shifted upwards. Six, seven, and eight dots were shown on the choice cards, as well as, in varying configurations, on the sample cards. The test thus constituted an extension of the training series to this higher portion of the number scale.

The justification for placing this test above the previous ones is actually more empirical than rational. It has been shown, both on the infra-human level (Koehler, 1943) and in man (Kaufman, Lord, Reese, and Volkmann,

1949; Taves, 1941), that immediate accurate discrimination of number breaks down above the number six. Thus, once again the intervention of the symbolic process of counting is necessary. It is known, moreover, that enumeration and the functional use of the number scale for numbers above five occurs considerably later than for the smaller numbers (Descoeudres, 1946; Giltay, 1936). Thus the reason for the hypothesized place of this test in the order of difficulty.

CONSERVATION OF NUMBER   For this test the choice cards from the previous one, representing the numbers 6, 7, and 8, were retained. In place of the sample cards, a number of small buttons were employed, which at the start of each trial were arranged in a pattern exactly duplicating the configuration of dots on the corresponding choice card. *S* was told to look at the buttons, for there was one window which looked just like them; he then made his choice. Since the purpose of this preliminary choice was only to inform *S* of the choice card whose dots were in numerical correspondence with the set of buttons, *E* prevented *S* from carrying through an incorrect choice (by stopping him short if he moved to open a wrong window and asking him to try again, urging him to look carefully at the card). For the same reason these preliminary choices were not scored. Following this information portion of the trial, *E* scrambled the buttons by hand, in full view of *S*, calling his attention to *E*'s rearranging of the buttons. *S* then responded anew to one of the windows; for this choice, however, he was kept from counting the buttons (if necessary, by *E*'s covering them with his hand).

This test thus showed whether the *S* could respond in accordance with the principle of the conservation of number, i.e., whether he could maintain the numerical correspondence between the two sets of elements (presumably established for him in the preliminary part of the trial), in the face of a change in the visual arrangement of one set.

The inclusion of this test in the present series was prompted by Piaget's (1952) postulation of the conservation of number as a central step in the conceptualization process. It appeared worthwhile to attempt to verify this assertion in the behavioral terms of our testing procedure. It should be noted that this test differs from the previous ones in demanding a concept, not of an individual number, but of number-in-general, and more particularly of a functional property of this dimension: its independence of configurational aspects of the stimulus aggregate. One would not expect a concept of this superordinate nature to develop prior to the establishment of the subordinate concepts denoting the individual numbers; therefore this test is inserted at a level following Test *D* in the hypothesized developmental sequence.

ADDITION AND SUBTRACTION   This test consisted of a set of trials similar to those of the previous test, with which they were interspersed (cf. below). The only difference between Tests E and F is that in the present test one button was either added to the collection in front of S or subtracted from it, immediately following S's configurational match (i.e., just before E scrambled the set). In either case, E alerted S to the action which he was taking.

It was supposed that these trials would reflect an understanding of the relationship among adjacent numbers. This would again represent a superordinate aspect of the dimension of number. It goes beyond the concept of conservation, however, since the S was required to respond to the change in the numerosity of the buttons, through a symbolic operation of the type $x + 1 = y$. In addition, the S had to recognize the similar relationship among the choice cards. It seemed implausible that the S would be capable of responding to the change in number at this symbolic level, without having first developed an understanding of the characteristic of number as an attribute remaining invariant under configurational changes.

ORDINAL-CARDINAL CORRESPONDENCE   For the purposes of this test, the choice cards of the original training series (denoting 2, 3, and 4) were employed, together with sample cards showing a set of eight solid bars arranged vertically in order of increasing length. The bars were all differently colored, one of them, in red, serving as the cue-bar. This bar was either in second, third, or fourth place in the series. S was told that he should look at the bars, and notice where he found the red bar among all the bars; this would tell him which window was correct.

This test was again suggested by Piaget's work on the number concept (Piaget, 1950a, 1952), in which the integration of the two aspects of number, ordinal and cardinal, is considered to be another focal point in the process of the conceptualization of number. Piaget (1950a, pp. 92–103, 1952, pp. 147–157) appears to regard the conservation of number as developmentally coordinate with the conceptualization of the relationship between ordinal and cardinal number, treating both as essential characteristics of the abstract, "operational" number concept. Nevertheless, it was our hypothesis that the present problem would follow the conservation test in the developmental sequence, on account of the assumed psychological difficulty for the child of bearing in mind simultaneously these quite disparate aspects of number, and the degree of symbolic elaboration of the number concept which appeared to be required for an integration of such abstract order.

The sequence in which these tests were given was the following: C, A, B, G, D, E, F (the last two were given in one joint series of 12 trials, six conservation trials being intermingled with three addition and three subtraction trials). This order was determined in part by practical considerations (such as giving all the tests involving 2, 3, and 4 before those involving 6, 7, and 8), and in part by the requirements of the tasks (thus D preceded E and F, in order to familiarize S with the new stimuli).

All tests normally consisted of six reinforced trials each, with the exception of Test *D*, which was presented for 12 trials, in order to provide adequate familiarization with the choice stimuli for the following conservation test. The criterion for passing was set at five correct responses out of six trials (10 out of 12 for Test *D*).[2]

Supplementary Tests

Two tests were added to the above set at the end of the experimental session. One was essentially a validation of the number-conservation test (*E*), through an adaptation of Piaget's (1952) procedure of direct interrogation. A row of six blocks was laid out in front of the child, and he was asked to place a set of buttons in front of them, so that there would be just as many buttons as blocks. (Mistakes on this part occurred very rarely; when they did, *E* corrected them.) After assuring himself of *S*'s perception of the quality of the two rows, *E* spread out the row of buttons in both directions to approximately twice the length of the row of blocks. *E* then asked *S*: "Now, are there more blocks than buttons, or are there more buttons than blocks, or are there still the same of both?" If *S* denied equality, the two rows were made to coincide again, the *S* reaffirmed their equality, and the above procedure was then repeated, but with the row of blocks now spread out.

In the other test, *S* was simply asked to count forwards to 10 and then, provided he did so correctly, to count backwards from 10. In this latter part, where *S* exhibited difficulty, *E* prodded him by asking: ". . . and what comes before 10? . . . and what's before nine?," etc.

The purpose of this second test was, on the one hand to determine the *S*'s rote-counting ability, and, on the other hand, to explore the relationship between the ability to reverse a series and the higher aspects of the development of the number concepts, as assessed in our Tests *E*, *F*, and *G*. The importance attached by Piaget to the reversibility of operations in the development of conceptual thought generally (Piaget, 1950b), and the number concept in particular (Piaget, 1952), suggested the inclusion of this test, although it is important to bear in mind that the reversal of a verbal chain, such as the number sequence, is not altogether the same kind of phenomenon as the reversibility of mental operations, as it is discussed by Piaget.

[2] On Tests *A*, *B*, *C*, and *G*, *S*s making five correct responses were given an additional three trials with the purpose of setting up a more stringent criterion of eight correct out of nine trials. Since responses on these supplementary trials were, however, almost invariably correct, the uniform criterion of 5 correct was adopted. In addition, in the cases of Tests *C* and *G*, in order to permit later analysis of the results in terms of a more lenient criterion of seven out of nine correct, the three supplementary trials were given also to *S*s making only four correct responses in the first six trials. Due to the length of the experimental session, no supplementary trials were given on Tests *E* and *F*.

Subjects

A total of 77 *S*s were tested in this study. Of these five failed to reach the criterion of learning in the original training series within 48 trials. They were dropped from the study and will not be considered further. The remaining 72 *S*s are divided equally into six age levels, from 4:0 to 7:0, by half-year intervals. With respect to sex, the total group comprises 35 boys and 37 girls.

The *S*s were children enrolled in various kindergartens and primary schools in Geneva, Switzerland.[3] Almost all of them had been and were being exposed to informal and formal instruction in the area of number; for the most part such instruction followed the principles of the Montessori method, which emphasizes the development of the child's powers of observation, through tasks of discrimination or matching among numbers of objects, seriation of a set of objects by magnitude, etc. In addition, most of the children had learned to count; the first-grade children also had some instruction in the rudiments of arithmetic.

EXPERIMENTAL RAPPORT   In general, the motivation of the children seemed quite high—the game aspect of the task apparently maintained their interest throughout the experimental session. In the case of a few of the youngest children, however, attention tended to lag visibly after about 20 minutes (the entire session ordinarily required 30 to 40 minutes). Whenever this became apparent, as was the case for six children, the session was stopped, and resumed on the following day; in these cases, the second session began with the administration of the training series to the original criterion, or with the repetition of the last transfer test passed by the *S*, and continued with the test following the last one completed at the first session.

RESULTS

Order of Difficulty

Considering, first of all, the order of difficulty of the items of the scale, in terms of the number of *S*s (out of the total 72) passing each item, we find the following in Table 1.

[3] The author gratefully acknowledges the generous cooperation of the Geneva Public Schools, and the following private institutions: Ecole Ferrier, Jardin Joyeux and Ecole Champod, in furnishing subjects for this investigation. In addition, the United Nations Nursery School provided valuable assistance in a pilot study from which the present investigation developed.

Table 1

Number of Ss Passing Each Item

B.	Elimination of perceptual cues	49
A.	Abstraction	46
C.	Memory	32
F.	Addition and subtraction	24
D.	Extension	21
E.	Conservation	14
G.	Ordinal-cardinal correspondence	6

The meaningfulness of these figures may be enhanced by referring to Table 2, in which the critical ratios associated with the difference between the proportion of Ss passing each pair of items are listed.

Table 2

Critical Ratios of Differences between Proportions of Ss Passing Each Pair of Tests

Tests	G	E	D	F	C	A	B
G		2.31	3.44	3.84	4.60	6.03	6.41
E			1.94	2.67	3.40	5.49	5.75
D				0.83	2.12	5.00	5.29
F					1.51	4.31	4.64
C						2.99	3.40
A							1.00

An examination of these results discloses two main discrepancies from the hypothesized order: Test *B*, involving numerical correspondence without a perceptual basis was passed by a slightly, but non-significantly greater proportion of Ss than Test *A*, which involved abstraction from irrelevant dimensions. The second discrepancy is rather more pronounced: Test *F* (matching of number after addition or subtraction of an element), instead of occupying a place above Test *E* (conservation), was very significantly easier than the latter, and even came before Test *D* (extension), though the difference between these two items was not significant.

Apart from these reversals, which will be examined more closely below in the discussion of the results for the individual tests, the results conformed to the hypothesized order. Differences between items predicted to be adjacent were significant at the .01 level for *B* vs. *E*, and at the .05 level for *C* vs. *D*, while for *D* vs. *E* the CR of 1.94 just misses the .05 level. In the case of comparisons between non-adjacent pairs, almost all are significant at the .01 level or better, whether we take the predicted or the actually observed order. For the latter, *C* vs. *D* is the only exception, with a CR of 2.12; in terms of the predicted order, the exceptions are *E* vs. *G* (2.31); *C* vs. *F* (1.51), and, as already mentioned, *D* vs. *F* (−0.83). For the test as a whole, furthermore, the rank-order correlation between predicted and observed order is .86.

The mere determination of the order of difficulty of these tests, however, does not in any sense touch on the central question with which we are concerned, viz.: is there a constant, predictable sequence in the order in which mastery of the skills involved in these tasks develops, such that success on any task presupposes success on all prior tasks? The answer to this question will be provided by the results from the scalogram analysis performed on these data, to which we shall now turn.

Scalogram Analysis

Guttman's original technique of scalogram analysis (cf. Guttman, 1950) has been the object of considerable criticism from a variety of sources (e.g., Green, 1954; Torgerson, 1958), due primarily to the lack of objectivity in the ordering of the observed patterns, and the very great dependency of the resultant coefficient of reproducibility on the marginal totals of successes and failures for each item. For the examination of our data, therefore, a more satisfactory analytic technique seemed indicated.

In their recent discussion of measures of reproducibility, White and Saltz (1957) present several alternative mathematical indices for determining the scalability of a set of items. Two of these which appeared to be particularly meaningful were selected for use in the present study. They are Green's index of consistency, based on his method of summary statistics (Green, 1956), and Loevinger's index of homogeneity (Loevinger, 1947).

Both of these indices take into account the marginal totals of passes and fails for each item. Loevinger's technique has the advantage of utilizing all of the information in the data; that is, comparisons are made among all possible pairs of items to determine the relative incidence of error patterns (cases of + responses to the more difficult item coupled with − responses to the easier of the pair). Green's method, while examining only patterns for adjacent pairs of adjacent quadruplets of items, is somewhat less laborious, and allows, in addition, the calculation of an index of reproducibility equivalent to that devised by Guttman. Green's index of consistency, in fact, is simply the ratio of the difference between the observed and the expected (i.e., chance) reproducibility to the maximum value of this difference (i.e., for a perfectly scalable set of items).

Applied to the present data, the two indices actually turn out to be very closely comparable: Green's index of consistency, $I = .616$, and Loevinger's coefficient of homogeneity, $H_t = .620$.

Perhaps the meaning of these figures will become clearer if we consider Green's index of consistency, I. For our data, Rep_A (an estimate of the reproducibility of the responses from the scale types) $= .944$, and Rep_i (the reproducibility to be expected by chance, i.e., on the assumption of independence between responses to individual items) $= .855$, yielding

$$ I = \frac{.944 - .855}{1 - .855} = .616. $$

These figures reflect the fact that with some items showing close to 100 per cent passes or fails (in our case this applies particularly to Test G, with 6 + and 66 —), chance reproducibility will be relatively high. The meaningfulness of even very high observed reproducibilities, such as found here, is accordingly reduced. This problem, which Guttman handles by recourse to a number of somewhat arbitrary and intuitive supplementary criteria for the evaluation of any index of reproducibility, is disposed of by the use of Green's index of consistency, which takes chance reproducibility into account. Following Green's suggestion (Green, 1956) of considering an I above .5 as indicating satisfactory scalability in a test, one may thus conclude that the present set of tests does in fact represent a single scalable dimension. At the same time the deviation of the observed I from its maximal value of 1.00 shows that the responses still fall considerably short of perfect consistency. Pointing to the same conclusion is the fact that only 45 of the 72 Ss exhibited perfect scale-type patterns (i.e., patterns which could be reproduced simply from a knowledge of the number of tests they had passed). This proportion is further reduced to 29 out of 56, or barely over 50 per cent, if the Ss passing or failing all of the tests—who would thus be perfectly fitted under any order of the tests—are left out of consideration.

It should be pointed out, furthermore, that our data fall short of meeting two requirements which are ordinarily considered to be essential in the application of scalogram analysis: our N is below 100, and the number of items is below 10.[4] As far as the number of items is concerned, Green (1956) actually points out that his index of consistency will be largely unaffected by this factor (in contrast to the index of reproducibility which is quite sensitive to changes in number of items). Since little is known concerning the sampling distribution of I, or of other measures of scalability, the effect of reduction in sample size is more uncertain. According to Willis (1954), however, the index of reproducibility is itself invariant for changing values of N, provided N is large in comparison with the number of scale types (the number of items plus one).

N will, of course, affect the SE of an observed reproducibility coefficient; for relatively small samples it is, therefore, important to guard against

---

[4] Practical considerations—particularly the limits imposed upon the length of the experimental session—precluded the addition of further tests to the scale.

differences between observed and expected reproducibilities (Rep_A-Rep_I) which are merely due to sampling error. For this purpose the approximation of the SE of Rep_A proposed by Green (1956) may be used. In the present instance, this difference is found to be highly significant (CR $=$ 8.9). This finding, then, in conjunction with the obtained value for I, suggests that we may with some confidence regard our set as representing a single, cumulative scale. The relevance of this scale to development is indicated, moreover, by its correlation with CA: Eta $=$ .52. (Eta is to be preferred here over r both on logical grounds—the scale cannot be assumed to be an equal-interval one—and on empirical grounds, i.e., significant departure from linearity of regression.)

One further problem which should be discussed in connection with the interpretation of the observed indices of scalability is that of the reliability of the responses to these items. As Green points out (1956), error in the context of scalogram analysis is apt to reflect lack of reliability rather than sampling fluctuation. Since our purpose was not one of test construction, it seems sufficient to note that lack of reliability would only be expected to depress the observed scalability of the items; thus, under more nearly ideal testing conditions a portion of the non-scale patterns might conceivably have been eliminated.

In this connection it is perhaps relevant to cite the results of a replication of the scalogram analysis (utilizing Green's method), employing more lenient criteria for passing on the more difficult tests (Tests C and G: 7 correct out of 9 trials; Tests E and F: 4 correct out of 6 trials; Test D: 9 correct out of 12 trials). Substantially similar indices of scalability are found for this analysis: $\text{Rep}_A = .931$; $I = .595$. (The order of difficulty of the tests remains unchanged.) Although the changed criteria result in a slightly larger number of error patterns—due presumably to decreased reliability—this increase in errors was nearly compensated by a decrease in Rep_I (chance reproducibility). This decrease from .855 to .829 seems to result from the somewhat less lopsided proportion of failures obtained on Test G with the more lenient criterion.

The Individual Tests

In order to provide a somewhat fuller picture of the results obtained on the various tests, we shall now proceed to an examination of each of these in turn, with regard to their theoretical significance in the development of the number concept, as well as to such questions as discrepancies from the predicted order of difficulty and the kinds of errors commonly committed. In addition, the value of Loevinger's coefficient H_{it} (the homogeneity of an item with a scale) is given for each test. This coefficient indicates the extent to which the test scales with the set as a whole, in terms of its power to discriminate Ss with a relatively higher total score from Ss with a relatively lower total score.

ABSTRACTION ($H_{it} = .913$)   This test was predicted to be the easiest in the set, since considerable perceptual support was available for the number-match to be made; in fact this task was the only one which Ss could, in principle, solve on a purely perceptual basis, without the intervention of mediating responses denoting the individual numbers. There were, however, only two Ss who passed this test and no other, suggesting that under the conditions of our transfer situation few if any of the Ss did respond successfully on this direct perceptual basis. The explanation appears to be that for those that were responding at a pre-conceptual level in the training series, the competing dimensions of color and form proved too potent distractors to allow them to maintain their number set. Evidence for this conclusion may be seen in the fact that of the 14 Ss who failed on all items, all but one S made errors on at least five of the six trials of this test, indicating the virtual destruction of their original number-set due to the interference of the color and/or form cues. In contrast, the other 12 Ss who failed this test but passed some other test, and who were thus presumably responding to some extent on a conceptual basis, made an average of 2.75 correct responses on this test. Under the circumstances, then, the emergence of this test as second in order of difficulty, essentially at the level of Test B, is understandable.

It may be noted in passing that of the two competing dimensions, color proved much the more popular as a basis for the children's error responses, accounting for 78 out of a total of 114 errors, or 68 per cent. This finding is in line with the frequently observed dominance of color over form in children of nursery-school age (cf. Brian and Goodenough, 1929; Lindberg, 1938).

This test of abstraction may be considered, then, as an expression of the child's response to number on a conceptual level, albeit in a most elementary sense. Although no direct evidence is available on this point, it presumably reflects the child's ability to verbalize the numbers (implicitly or overtly), thereby making the response more resistant to interference from the irrelevant cues.

ELIMINATION OF PERCEPTUAL CUES ($H_{it} = .891$)   This test, as noted previously, was passed by the largest number of Ss. There is, nevertheless, little reason to doubt the validity of the interpretation originally given this task as involving a symbolically mediated response. Thus it was frequently observed that Ss passing this test counted the squares with their fingers (although the more advanced children did not need to do this overtly). Furthermore, there was again, on this test as there had been in Test A, a fairly sharp differentiation between the performance of Ss who failed all tests and those who passed some other test. The 14 Ss of the former group made an average of only 2.1 correct responses, as against 3.3 for the 9 Ss of the latter group. This difference is significant below the

.05 level ($t = 2.62$, for 21 df). (The fact that the first figure, 2.1 is somewhat higher than the corresponding one in Test *A* need not surprise: in the present test there are no obvious alternative cues on which *S* might consistently base his response; on a random basis one would, therefore, actually expect two correct in six trials on this three-choice problem.)

MEMORY ($H_{it} = .524$)   This test followed Tests *A* and *B* in order of difficulty, as predicted. Indeed, it was rather sharply differentiated from the latter, in the sense that the gap between Tests *C* and *D* was the largest of any gap between adjacent tests (in terms of the number of *S*s passing each). At the same time, there was an appreciable gap (of eight *S*s) between it and Test *F* which ranked immediately above it. This result appears to support the conception of this task as one which involves a conceptual response to the individual numbers, requiring, however, a considerably greater stability or strength on the part of the mediating structures than is the case for Tests *A* and *B*. The absence of the choice cards, and the consequent need to retain them in memory is presumably responsible for this difference, in somewhat similar fashion as in the case of delayed reaction tests (cf. Munn, 1955, pp. 138 ff; also Harlow, 1951, pp. 224 ff).

Nevertheless, in spite of the seemingly well-determined rank of this test, it proved to be one of the least satisfactory, in terms of its homogeneity with the scale as a whole, as seen in the low value for H_{it}. This figure reflects the fact that a considerable number of *S*s passed tests which ranked above Test *C*, but failed on this test. Undoubtedly the memory element of the task contributed to this lack of consistency in the responses on this test: some *S*s evidently had forgotten which window represented which number, as shown in their correct verbalization of the number on the stimulus card preceding their incorrect choices. In this connection, it must be realized that many of the *S*s started with a criterion run on the training series, so that they had only six trials to familiarize themselves with the choice cards; thus their failure to remember their positions is not too surprising. It is possible that this test would have been more meaningful if it had come later in the series, so that the *S*s' associations of the numbers to the windows might have become stabilized.

EXTENSION ($H_{it} = .874$)   This test placed after, rather than before Test *F*, but ahead of Test *E*. Considering the strong dependence of performance on this test on specific learning (i.e., counting), and the associated fact that frequently failures were caused by mistakes in the counting of the dots on the stimulus or choice cards, the homogeneity of this test with the scale is rather high. It seems, then, that differential responding for this part of the number dimension does constitute a conceptual process of a higher order than the previous problems, which involved only the lower numbers. It is plausible to attribute this increased difficulty to the very fact that the number concepts in question no longer benefit from direct perceptual support, thus necessitating the intervention of the symbolic activity of counting.

CONSERVATION ($H_{it} = .842$)   As anticipated, this test was one of the most advanced of the scale; it placed only below Test G in order of difficulty. Its place in the sequence was fairly well determined: the gaps between this and the adjacent tests below and above it, in terms of numbers of Ss passing, were seven and eight respectively (the corresponding CR's are 1.94 and 2.31). Furthermore the frequency-distribution of correct responses on this test was markedly U-shaped, with a mode at 0 (Table 3).

Table 3

Frequency-Distribution for Conservation-Responses on Test E

Number correct	f
0	23
1	17
2	10
3	4
4	4
5	7
6	7

Such a distribution suggests something approaching an all or none character for the comprehension of the concept which this test entails.

These findings lend some support, then, to the importance which Piaget (1952) attaches to the attainment of conservation as a step in the development of the number concept, as well as that of other concepts. In this connection, it may be noted that there was a substantial degree of correspondence between the responses to this test and those made on the verbal form of the conservation problem: of 13 Ss who passed the conservation test, 11 admitted the conservation of number in direct questioning, while there were only 10 such Ss among the 58 who failed the test. (In explanation for these latter cases, it can be argued that our problem involves the *application* of the conservation principle to a concrete situation, as opposed to the verbal form, where it is more a question of the *recognition* of this principle.)

An examination of the relationship between performance on the present test and Test F (addition and subtraction) affords perhaps a somewhat clearer picture of the developmental process involved in the achievement of conservation. It will be remembered that the addition and subtraction trials were postulated to be of greater difficulty than the conservation trials, since they involve a grasp of the relationships among the numbers which did not appear to be essential to the manifestation of conservation. In point of fact, as we have seen, the reverse held true: Test *F* was substantially easier than Test *E*; indeed, there were 12 *S*s who passed *F* and failed *E*, whereas only two *S*s reversed this order (both of these *S*s actually made four correct responses on the six trials of Test *F*, thus barely failing to attain the criterion for passing).

It is nevertheless of interest that there were six *S*s, among the 12 passing *F* and failing *E*, who gave definite evidence of conservation, although "officially" failing the test. There were *S*s who responded incorrectly on the first two or three conservation trials, but showed "learning" in the latter part of the series, as they made correct responses on the last three or four conservation trials. (As the frequency distribution above shows, these six *S*s accounted for all but two of the *S*s with three of four responses on Test *E*; the other two failed Item *F*, but one of these had four correct on this latter test.) The implication of these findings is that the addition and subtraction trials, which were interspersed with the conservation trials, had the effect of suggesting to the *S*s the conservation of the number aggregate in the conservation trials, where no element was either added or subtracted but only the perceptual configuration was changed. If this interpretation is correct, it would be clearly relevant to the understanding of the way in which this concept of conservation emerges, i.e., through a prior conceptualization of the operations of addition and subtraction, at least in their rudimentary forms. This view suggests the possibility of establishing the notion of conservation through repeated exposure to the effects of addition and subtraction.[5]

Finally, an incidental finding which emerges from the errors made on this test is a bias in the direction of a perceived increase in number with a change in configuration. Thus of the 101 errors made on No. 7, 64 were choices of 8, as against 37 choices of 6. A similar effect was seen in the errors made on the addition and subtraction trials of Test *F*: on addition trials involving 6 + 1, 8 was chosen 55 times, whereas on subtraction trials involving 8 − 1, 6 was only chosen 10 times. In view of the fact that the configurational changes effected by *E* in moving the buttons tended to decrease the separation between the buttons, on the average, one admittedly ad hoc explanation for this finding would be that *S*s are more apt to respond in terms of the density of the elements in the configuration than in terms of its area.

[5] Some pilot work along these lines by the author indicates modest success for this approach, depending on the level of development of the *S* at the time the learning takes place. More extensive investigation of this problem is contemplated.

ADDITION AND SUBTRACTION ($H_{it} = .777$)   The results for this test do not require extended discussion. The main finding, that its place in the hierarchy was ahead of Test *D*, instead of following Test *E*, has been discussed already in the previous sections.

We have noted that success on the addition and subtraction trials appeared to be virtually a prerequisite for the manifestation of conservation. Furthermore, there were eight *S*s who passed this test but failed Test *D*; thus it appears that on the lowest level success on this test was based less on a precise realization of the arithmetical relationships involved, (e.g., $6 + 1 = 7$) than on a possibly still rather intuitive perception of the order among the choice cards, and of the effects of addition and subtraction. This interpretation would account also for the somewhat low homogeneity of this item with the total scale.

That passing this test nevertheless reflects something over and above a symbolically mediated response to individual numbers is indicated by the very clear-cut separation between this test and the two lowest (*A* and *B*): there were only two *S*s who passed the present test while failing either of the other two.

ORDINAL-CARDINAL CORRESPONDENCE ($H_{it} = .480$)   As predicted, this test was the most difficult of the set; indeed, only six *S*s achieved the criterion for passing (five correct responses in six trials). There is, however, some doubt whether the conceptualization of the relationship between ordinal and cardinal number is all that is reflected in performance on this test. It could be argued that success here clearly presupposes the selection of an appropriate hypothesis relating the ordinal position of the cue-line to the number to be chosen. It is thus perhaps unrealistic to expect *S*s generally to show an immediate transfer of their previously developed number set to this problem. The fact that six additional *S*s with four correct responses in the first six trials proceeded to respond correctly in the following additional trials which they were given (cf. Footnote 2 above) strengthens this argument.

Under these circumstances the low homogeneity of this item is not too surprising. It should be realized that the value of H_{it} here is partly a function of the lopsided distribution of passes and failures, i.e.: the more the distribution diverges from 50-50, the less tolerance for error is available.

One way of improving the meaningfulness of this test may be suggested: preceding the ordinal-cardinal series, the *S*s' attention could be directed to the ordinal aspect by having choice cards which themselves show the cue-line in differing ordinal positions; this would then be a problem of simple ordinal correspondence. In this way the *S* would presumably be set to respond to the ordinal-cardinal correspondence in the main problem, if he is able to conceptualize this relationship. Exploratory work with this procedure indicates, in effect, that this test is essentially comparable in difficulty to the conservation test.

Finally, one particular mode of responding on this test is worth singling out: There were a number of Ss who, on the basis of their counting of the lines on the sample cards, and in some cases of their verbal explanations at the end of the test, gave evidence of matching the (cardinal) number of lines *up to, but not including* the cue-line to the number of dots on the choice cards. This type of error was already noted by Piaget (1952, pp. 111 ff) as marking a phase antecedent to the integration of the ordinal and the cardinal aspects of number, which requires the identification of the position of an element with the cardinal number of the set of elements which has that position as its boundary.

SUPPLEMENTARY TEST: COUNTING FORWARDS AND BACKWARDS
The results with respect to the Ss rote-counting ability, tested at the end of the experimental session, deserve brief mention. Due to their direct dependence on training experience and practice, they were not included in the main scale of number development, nor expected to show very great consistency in relation to the tests of the scale. This turned out to be the case, particularly for counting forwards (to 10), which all but nine Ss were able to do. Thus this ability by and large preceded the conceptual behaviors demanded by even the lowest-level tests, as shown for instance in the fact that 10 of the 14 Ss who failed all tests counted to 10 without error.

Backward counting, as found previously by McLaughlin (1935), proved to develop substantially later. Even with the help often provided by E (cf. section on methodology above), only 24 Ss gave perfect responses (nine others made one or two mistakes). A general picture of the relationship between this skill and performance on the main tests is given by the following comparison: of the Ss with from four to seven passes on the tests, 16 out of 26 counted backwards without error; of the Ss with from zero to three passes, 8 out of 46 did likewise. This relationship, though clearly significant ($\chi^2 = 12.65$, p. $< .001$), is hardly closer than would be expected for any two functions developing roughly together in time. The relationship with individual tests of the scale is generally consistent with this overall association.

DISCUSSION AND CONCLUSIONS

Three Stages in the Development of the Number Concept

The foregoing discussion of the tests taken individually should not leave the impression that each of these tests represents, in fact, a discrete well-determined point on the scale of conceptual development. The lack of significant separation between various pairs of adjacent tests, as well as the low homogeneity of some of the tests show that such an interpretation is not warranted by the data.

It seems possible, however, to use these results as evidence for the existence of three fairly sharply differentiated stages in the development of the number concept. The dividing points between these stages may be defined by the two most popular response patterns: uniform failures on all tests (14 Ss), and passes on Tests A, B, and C, with failures on the other four tests (8 Ss). If we eliminate, furthermore, Test C from the first group (a procedure which, though ad hoc, is not entirely unjustified, in view of the ambiguity of the meaning of failure on this test pointed out above), the distinction between these stages emerges most clearly: the 29 Ss who failed either Test A or B (or both) accounted for a grand total of only five passes on all of the tests of the second set combined.

The significance of this breakdown of the results is apparent from an examination of the nature of the tests concerned: A through C involves the matching of particular numbers, under conditions of varying amounts of perceptual support for such matching; Tests E through G, on the other hand, invoke higher-order relationships among numbers, representing functional characteristics of the number continuum (as for Test D, which would seem to fit more closely into the first group, it demands, as noted previously, the ability to enumerate which in itself may be suggested as a prerequisite for a mastery of the functional relationships among the numbers).

We may thus describe the process of concept formation in the domain of the number concept in terms of the following three stages: an initial, preconceptual one, in which number is responded to purely in perceptual terms, without any symbolic mediation; an intermediary one, in which the mediating structures representing individual stimuli on this dimension are developed, so that the perceptual support necessary for generalization between two equivalent stimuli on this dimension is steadily reduced; a final one, in which superordinate structures representing the number concept in the abstract, and relating the individual numbers to each other are elaborated, thereby leading to an understanding of such functional principles as the conservation of number and the coordination between ordinal and cardinal number.

This is of course only one among a variety of possible ways in which one may conceptualize the nature of the development of the number concept. Piaget (1950b, pp. 123–155) has described the developmental process in somewhat different, though clearly related terms, proceeding from a stage of pre-conceptual thought through a stage of intuitive thought to the eventual formation of "concrete operations," characterized by conservation and reversibility. This formulation has the advantage of being applicable more generally across several different areas of concept formation; at the same time it covers a rather more restricted range of functions within any given area such as number.

Yet another view of development with respect to the concept of number is presented in the recent work of Gast (1957). This investigator is essentially concerned with the degree of perceptual and functional heterogeneity of the stimulus materials which the child can tolerate in admitting a collection of objects as representing a single cardinal set, for purposes of enumeration, number-matching, etc. He finds an initial stage in which virtually complete homogeneity of the elements is required; a second in which perceptual diversity is possible, within certain limits of qualitative resemblance among the elements, and a final one in which the objects may belong to several disjunctive and altogether disparate classes.

In spite of the differences in emphasis of these various analyses of the developmental process in the formation of the number concept, they doubtless involve, if not the same, at least closely related psychological processes developing in parallel. It should thus be possible to formulate a developmental theory sufficiently general to encompass these various aspects of conceptual development, while still being specific enough to afford predictive power and to relate it directly to the content of particular problem situations.

In any event, the results of our study confirm both the findings of Gast and the theoretical views of Piaget, in demonstrating the existence of a relatively uniform developmental sequence in the area of the number concept. To that extent they contradict the results obtained by Estes (1956), who attempted to differentiate between 4-, 5-, and 6-year-old children on the basis of a series of tests suggested by Piaget's work, notably that concerned with the concept of conservation. Estes found no consistent differences between her age groups on these tests. But in view of the cross-sectional method employed, the relatively small number of *S*s tested (in the face of the well-known individual variation in rate of development) and the apparently inadequate methodology employed, these results can hardly be taken as conflicting evidence with respect to the reality of developmental stages in this area. Certainly our results belie the rather sweeping conclusion which has been made by at least one author on the basis of Estes' study, to the effect that "the 'developmental stage' approach to child behavior continues to suffer critical damage by being subjected to careful empirical test" (Sears, 1958, p. 135).

The Determination of Developmental Sequences through Scalogram Analysis

Since we have in this study employed the technique of scalogram analysis to trace developmental processes, the basic premise of this approach, that scalability of responses to a set of problems is evidence for a single developmental continuum, should be discussed in somewhat more explicit terms.

It is a unique feature of scalogram analysis—as of latent structure analysis, of which the former is but a special case (cf. Torgerson, 1958)— that it scales *both* stimuli (i.e., the items) and subjects simultaneously, on the basis of the same criterion: the response patterns observed. This feature is clearly a double-edged sword: it presents a clear advantage, in so far as it obviates the necessity for an independent measurement device for scaling the items; on the other hand, it places very definite limitations on the logically justifiable interpretations that can be made on the basis of a determination of scalability in a given set of items.

This latter problem does not typically arise in such traditional fields of application of scalogram analysis as that of attitude studies. There the question is usually merely whether a judiciously—and often rather arbitrarily—selected set of items represents a single unidimensional continuum for purposes of measurement, so as to allow one to rank the subjects on this dimension on the basis of their responses to the items.

What we have done in the present investigation, however, goes considerably beyond the determination of an ordinal scale of measurement. In effect, we have inferred, on the basis of the demonstrated scalability of our tests, the operation of a single developmental process, running in the direction of increased symbolic mediation. Such an inference clearly demands two supplementary steps: first, an independent validation, on internal grounds, of the psychological dimension defined by the items, and second, the identification of the ranking of the Ss on this scale with psychological development.

As regards the first point, it may be noted that it would be a matter of ease, for a group of Ss varying in age, to construct a perfectly scalable set of items which would nevertheless fail to represent any specifiable psychological dimension (for instance: ability to walk; achievement of bladder control; ability to define "orange"; ability to drive a car). It is thus apparent that the attribution of a psychologically meaningful developmental process underlying performance on the tests of our scale has to be grounded in the content of the component tests. This consideration argues for the advisability of employing items whose psychological significance is at least to some extent understood, and, more important, to utilize this knowledge in order to formulate an a priori hypothesis concerning the assumed ordering of the items.

In the present study we have attempted to conform to these desiderata by choosing tests for which it was at least possible, on logical and empirical grounds, to advance a hypothetical order of difficulty. The close correspondence found between our hypothesized order and that actually found would seem to confirm the meaning attributed to the developmental sequence which emerged from the patterns of responses.

As for the second point, the interpretation of the scale in terms of a *developmental* sequence is predicated on two assumptions. The first is that with increasing age a change in the direction of a higher scale type would in fact take place. Short of a longitudinal follow-up, this assertion can be verified only by a determination of a substantial correlation between some independent criterion of development (e.g., CA) and the scale type (total score) attained on this set of problems. In our case the correlation between CA and scale type is .52. This correlation is probably as high as should be expected, given the extent of variability in rate of growth in a heterogeneous population; at any rate it appears adequate to justify the equation of our scale with a developmental sequence.[6] The additional assumption which has to be made is that a given subject, if tested at a prior or later point in time, would still respond in conformance with the scale (i.e., only his scale type would be changed, but except for incidental "error" patterns no new response patterns would be found). The validity of this assumption rests on the adequacy of the sampling: it is presumed that a sufficient number of subjects at all stages of development have been tested to disclose the major response patterns that are to be expected at the different levels of the scale.

The Origin of the Developmental Sequence

Of somewhat broader significance is the question of the origin and determinants of a developmental sequence such as the one we have observed. Regularity and consistency in the order of appearance of specific behavior patterns has been used as one criterion for the maturational origin of such behaviors, notably in the area of motor development (cf. Ames, 1937; Shirley, 1931). For a variety of reasons, however, such an inference would not be warranted in the present instance. Not only is the environment of the Ss represented in our sample much too homogeneous, but, more fundamentally, the very nature of this particular developmental sequence precludes the possibility of regarding it as a purely maturational phenomenon, dependent as it is on the formation of mediating symbols which, it would seem, can only be cultural in origin.

Yet, granted that environmental influences can scarcely be ignored as factors in the development of the responses represented in our tests, the actual mechanisms accounting for this sequence still remain to be explained. The main question is whether the changes involved in a child's progression along this sequence represent the product of specific learning due to practice, or whether more generalized experiential effects are at work here.

In the absence of precise knowledge concerning and control over the previous experience of these children, it is obviously not possible to answer this question directly. Let us examine, however, the role of two specific

[6] It might be thought that mental age would provide a better test of validity here. However, apart from the fact that information regarding mental age was not available for these children, none of the intelligence tests presently in use appear to have sufficient "construct validity" (cf. Cronbach and Meehl, 1955) to be of much value in the assessment of the development level attained by a child. As a matter of fact, in the study of the development of concepts of money by Schuessler and Strauss (1950), referred to in the introduction to this article, it was found that partial correlations of scale type with CA were substantially above those with MA.

factors that might be suggested in this connection: those of language and of pedagogical experiences.

With respect to the language factor, one may ask whether progression along our sequence does not merely reflect the mastery of the verbal labels representing the number scale. Several lines of evidence allow us, however, to dismiss this linguistic factor. First of all, the large majority of the children—including 10 of the 14 who failed all tests—could count up to 10 by rote (there were nine Ss who could not, but seven of these children counted at least up to four, without any effect on their ability to solve those problems involving the lower numbers). Secondly, if this factor were chiefly responsible, all tests involving numbers 2, 3, and 4 on the one hand, and numbers 6, 7, and 8 on the other hand, should be mastered simultaneously, but, as our scale shows, this was by no means the case (cf. the significant differences between such pairs of tests as C vs. A, C vs. B, E vs. F, G vs. A, B, and C, Table 2).

In connection with this point regarding the role of language, a different study by the author may also be cited (Wohlwill, 1960). This study showed that the mere availability of verbal labels to designate the number of a visual aggregate is of very little significance in a subject's performance on a learning task which demands a consistent response to a particular absolute number. Even if this result may be attributable in part to the perceptual nature of the task, it illustrates the fallacy of interpreting cognitive performance in terms of verbal habits. The same conclusion appears to be indicated by Martin's (1951) finding that a test of children's spontaneous use of quantitative vocabulary in the description of pictures failed to correlate significantly with a more conceptual test of number ability.

The second factor, that of pedagogical influences, is more difficult to evaluate. It is true that most of these children were in fact exposed to a relatively uniform set of pedagogical experiences, including exercise and instruction in the elementary aspects of number, from the kindergarten period onward. This kind of experience undoubtedly affected the performance of the children on these tasks to some extent. Nevertheless, the tasks had for the most part rather little in common with the practice in rote counting, naming and discrimination of number which constituted the bulk of the scholastic training which the children had received. This is true particularly for our Tests A (abstraction); C (memory); E (conservation), and G (ordinal-cardinal correspondence). Thus it does not seem too plausible to argue that the observed order of mastery of our tests was a direct function of the specific training which the subjects were exposed to in school. The fact that grade in school (i.e., nursery-school level, kindergarten, or first grade) was only very imperfectly related to performance on our tests further weakens this argument.

Having discarded, then, the influence of specific practice due to commonly shared learning experiences on our developmental sequence, one may still attribute it to cumulative learning effects of a relatively non-specific type, such as illustrated in Harlow's (1949) work on learning sets. Alternatively, one might postulate organismic changes of a strictly maturational kind, determining the child's ability to assimilate and make use of his previous experiences and learnings for the solution of the tasks in our test series. But, as for most psychological problems, a sharp differentiation between maturational and experiential factors hardly seems very fruitful here. The real question may be stated perhaps more appropriately in terms of the extent and breadth of the generalization and transfer of particular learned behaviors which are possible at different levels of development. For instance, although the point has not been demonstrated experimentally, it seems most likely that the number of problems necessary for the formation of a discrimination learning set would decrease steadily with increased age (indeed, this does appear to be the case for phylogenetic development; cf. Miles, 1957). In other words, very general experience, assimilated and transformed in the course of development, can to a large extent replace more specific practice as a condition for learning. Applied to our study, this interpretation would attribute the change underlying a child's progress from the first to the second, or from the second to the third phase, not in terms of practice in counting, or experience with the conservation of number, but rather in terms of cumulative experience in the discrimination and identification of number, and in the abstraction of invariant properties from changing stimulus complexes.

The central problem, in any event, appears to be the following: responses to numerical correspondence, above the simplest level, are clearly based on mechanisms of mediated generalization, i.e., on the intervention of internalized symbols representing the numbers. Although such mediating mechanisms have been invoked in the explanation of developmental differences in discrimination learning and transfer (e.g., Alberts and Ehrenfreund, 1951; Shepard and Schaeffer, 1956), and have, in fact, become a central construct in Osgood's (1953) attempt to extend traditional S-R association theory to the area of concept formation, little work has been done thus far on the actual formation of these mediating responses (thus, most of the so-called concept formation literature utilizes concepts which are already in the *S*'s repertoire). Our study can perhaps contribute to this problem by showing the gradual emergence and stabilization of these mediating structures during the course of development; more particularly, it follows this process to the further formation of structures of a superordinate kind, which, in the case of the number concept, form the basis for a truly abstract representation of the dimension of number. Thus this study points the way to the investigation of a problem not heretofore tackled by behavioristic theorists, that of the conceptualization of the relationships among objects, rather than of the objects themselves. Indeed, one might argue that a true concept of an object requires the former, i.e., inevitably involves the formation of superordinate structures relating the object to others which are not instances of the class.

The specification of the developmental sequence is, however, at best a first, descriptive, step in the analysis of the processes involved in concept formation. In future investigation of these problems, an approach appears to be indicated which focuses on the effects of different types of experience, perceptual and linguistic, specific and generalized, on the development of particular aspects of the number concept, and on the differential effects of such experience at different developmental levels. Through such an approach one may hope eventually to gain some insight into the nature of the changes taking place as the child progresses along the developmental scale and achieves an increasingly elaborate and abstract concept of number.

REFERENCES

Alberts, E., and D. Ehrenfreund (1951). Transposition in children as a function of age. *J. exp. Psychol.*, **41**, 30–38.

Ames, L. B. (1937). The sequential patterning of prone progression in the human infant. *Genet. Psychol. Monogr.*, **19**, 409–460.

Brian, C. R., and F. L. Goodenough (1929). The relative potency of color and form perception at various ages. *J. exp. Psychol.*, **12**, 197–213.

Brownell, W. A. (1928). The development of children's number ideas in the primary grades. *Suppl. Educ. Monogr.*, No. 35.

Cronbach, L. J., and P. E. Meehl (1955). Construct validity in psychological tests. *Psychol. Bull.*, **52**, 281–302.

Descoeudres, A. (1914). Couleur, forme ou nombre? *Arch. Psychol.*, *Genève*, **14**, 305–341.

Descoeudres, A. (1946). *Le développement de l'enfant de deux à sept ans*, third ed. Neuchâtel: Delachaux et Niestlé.

Douglass, H. R. (1925). The development of number concept in children of preschool and kindergarten ages. *J. exp. Psychol.*, **8**, 443–470.

Estes, B. W. (1956). Some mathematical and logical concepts in children. *J. genet. Psychol.*, **88**, 219–223.

Gast, H. (1957). Der umgang mit zahlen und zahlgebilden in der frühen kindheit. *Z. Psychol.*, **161**, 1–90.

Giltay, M. (1936). Sur l'apparition et le développement de la notion du nombre chez l'enfant de deux à sept ans. *J. Psychol. norm. path.*, **33**, 673–695.

Green, B. F. (1954). Attitude measurement. In G. Lindzey (Ed.), *Handbook of social psychology*. Reading, Mass.: Addison-Wesley, VI. I, pp. 335–369.

Green, B. F. (1956). A method of scalogram analysis using summary statistics. *Psychometrika*, **21**, 79–88.

Guttman, L. (1950). The basis for scalogram analysis. In S. A. Stouffer *et al., Measurement and prediction.* Princeton, N.J.: Princeton University Press. Pp. 60–90.

Harlow, H. F. (1949). The formation of learning sets. *Psychol. Rev.,* **56,** 51–65.

Harlow, H. F. (1951). Primate learning. In C. P. Stone (Ed.), *Comparative psychology,* third ed. New York: Prentice-Hall. Pp. 183–238.

Judd, C. H. (1927). Psychological analysis of the fundamentals of arithmetic. *Suppl. Educ. Monogr.,* No. 31.

Kaufman, E. K., M. W. Lord, W. T. Reese, and J. Volkmann (1949). The discrimination of visual number. *Amer. J. Psychol.,* **62,** 498–525.

Koehler, O. (1943). "Zähl"-versuche an einem kohlkraben und vergleichende versuche an menschen. *Z. Tierpsychol.,* **5,** 575–712.

Koehler, O. (1949). Vorsprachliches denken und "zählen" der Vögel. In E. Mayr and E. Schüz (Eds.), *Ornithologie als biologische wissenschaft.* Heidelberg: C. Winter. Pp. 125–146.

Lindberg, B. J. (1938). *Experimental studies of color and non-color attitude in school children and adults.* Copenhagen: Levin & Munksgaard.

Loevinger, J. A. (1947). A systematic approach to the construction and evaluation of tests of ability. *Psychol. Monogr.,* **61** (4), Whole No. 285.

Long, L., and L. Welch (1941). The development of the ability to discriminate and match numbers. *J. genet. Psychol.,* **59,** 377–387.

McLaughlin, K. L. (1935). Number ability of preschool children. *Childh. Educ.,* **11,** 348–353.

Martin, W. E. (1951). Quantitative expression in young children. *Genet. Psychol. Monogr.,* **44,** 147–219.

Miles, R. C. (1957). Learning-set formation in the squirrel monkey. *J. comp. physiol. Psychol.,* **50,** 352–358.

Munn, N. L. (1955). *The evolution and growth of human behavior.* Boston: Houghton Mifflin.

Nissen, H. W. (1951). Phylogenetic comparison. In S. S. Stevens (Ed.), *Handbook of experimental psychology.* New York: Wiley. Pp. 347–386.

Osgood, C. E. (1953). *Method and theory in experimental psychology.* New York: Oxford University Press.

Piaget, J. (1950a). Introduction à l'épistémologie génétique. *La pensée mathématique,* Vol. 1. Paris: Presses Universitaires.

Piaget, J. (1950b). *The psychology of intelligence.* New York: Harcourt.

Piaget, J. (1952). *The child's conception of number.* New York: Humanities Press.

Riess, A. (1947). *Number readiness in research.* Glenview, Ill.: Scott, Foresman.

Schuessler, K. F., and A. L. Strauss (1950). A study of concept learning by scale analysis. *Amer. Sociol. Rev.,* **15,** 752–762.

Sears, P. S. (1958). Developmental psychology. *Ann. Rev. Psychol.,* **9,** 119–156.

Shepard, W. O., and M. Schaeffer. The effect of concept knowledge on discrimination learning. *Child Develpm.*, **27**, 173–178.

Shirley, M. M. (1931). The sequential method for the study of maturing behavior patterns. *Psychol. Rev.*, **38**, 507–528.

Strauss, A. L., and K. F. Schuessler (1951). Socialization, logical reasoning and concept development in the child. *Amer. Sociol. Rev.*, **16**, 514–523.

Taves, E. H. (1941). Two mechanisms for the perception of visual numerousness. *Arch. Psychol.*, No. 265.

Torgerson, W. S. (1958). *Theory and methods of scaling*. New York: Wiley.

Werner, H. (1957). *Comparative psychology of mental development*, revised ed. New York: International Universities.

White, B. W., and E. Saltz (1957). Measurement of reproducibility. *Psychol. Bull.*, 1957, **54**, 81–99.

Willis, R. (1954). Estimating the scalability of a series of items—an application of information theory. *Psychol. Bull.*, **51**, 511–516.

Wohlwill, J. F. (1957). The abstraction and conceptualization of form, color and number. *J. exp. Psychol.*, **53**, 304–309.

Wohlwill, J. F. (1960). Absolute versus relational discrimination on the dimension of number. *J. genet. Psychol.*, **96**, 353–363.

RELATION BETWEEN THE UNDERSTANDING OF THE LOGIC OF CLASSES AND OF CARDINAL NUMBER IN CHILDREN

P. C. Dodwell

The problem investigated in this paper concerns the extent to which young children, in developing concepts of number, and of "conservation" of physical quantities, also develop the concept of "class of objects," and the operations and linguistic skills which allow them to deal with the elementary logic of classification and the composition of classes. The problem was investigated at the same time as a general study of children's

Reprinted with the permission of the author and the University of Toronto Press, from *The Canadian Journal of Psychology*, 1962, **16**, 152–160. This investigation was supported by a grant from the Arts Research Committee of Queen's University, whose assistance is gratefully acknowledged. Thanks are due also to Mrs. W. Andriesky who tested the children, and to officials of the Kingston Board of Education and teachers who made it possible.

understanding of numbers was under way (Dodwell, 1960, 1961) and is directly relevant to Piaget's theory of intelligence and the development of the concept of number (Piaget, 1950, 1952).

According to Piaget's theory of number concept development, before a child is able to develop correct operations on numbers, he must develop some basic operations on classes, and some on serial relations. (The operations on numbers are a special subset of these operations, involving relations of both class equivalence and serial order conjointly.) Indeed, it seems plausible on common-sense grounds to expect that a child will have some idea of classes of objects, and subclasses within a more general class, before he can deal with the rather stricter conditions which hold when one deals with the special classes called cardinal numbers. For one thing, the child has frequent occasion to use hierarchical classificatory systems (as: cat and dog are both animals; rose, daisy, and tulip are all flowers) before he learns to use number words to apply to specified— but very general—classes. To quote Piaget's own words: "Our hypothesis is that the construction of number goes hand in hand with the development of logic, and that a pre-numerical period corresponds to the pre-logical level. . . . logical and arithmetical operations therefore constitute a single system . . . the second resulting from generalization and fusion of the first, under the complementary headings of inclusion of classes and seriation of relations, quality being disregarded. . . . the fusion of inclusion and seriation of the elements into a single operational totality takes place, and this totality constitutes the sequence of whole numbers, which are indissociably cardinal and ordinal" (Piaget, 1952, p. viii). This would seem to imply that the development of operations on classes must precede, to a great extent, the ability to reason correctly about numbers. However, Piaget also says: "Hitherto, we have considered number as a seriated class, i.e., as the product of class and asymmetrical relation. But this in no way implies that class and asymmetrical relation come before number. On the contrary, number can be regarded as being necessary for the completion of truly logical structures, as we shall attempt to show. . . . Instead of deriving number from class, or the converse, or considering the two as radically independent, we can regard them as complementary, and as developing side by side, although directed towards different ends" (Piaget, 1952, p. 161). Perhaps it will be thought that these two quotations reflect some inconsistency in Piaget's thinking about the relations of the logical structures for class composition and for number. The natural interpretation of the first quotation would seem to be that the former develops to a considerable degree before the latter. Be that as it may, we should certainly expect, on the basis of the theory, a strong relation to hold between the states of development of the two.

Piaget (1952) reports some experiments on the "logical composition of classes" but, as in most of his other investigations, he fails to specify the number of children studied; nor does he report on the generality of the different types of response at different ages, except to imply rather strongly that there is a high degree of uniformity to the answers given by children of a particular age. The experiments on additive composition of classes purport to investigate the child's understanding of the fact that two groups of things, such as a group of boys and a group of girls, together constitute a single, larger, group of children, and that the group of children is the "additive composition" of the other two. In the normal set notation: B $\cap$ G $=$ C, and B $\cap$ G $=$ O. The actual relation investigated by Piaget is: given these two relations, does the child understand that B $<$ C, or B $=$ C $-$ G. This question was tackled by asking the child questions about groups of beads (white and brown, both wooden), groups of children drawn on paper (boys and girls), and so on. The materials and method of presentation were varied, apparently unsystematically, but the responses of the children appeared to be relatively unaffected, although, for example, questions about the beads were found to be more easily answered if the beads were shown in separate boxes.

It has sometimes been objected that the situations used by Piaget to study understanding of class composition and inclusion are likely to be unfamiliar to the child, and that the questions asked might lead to confusion. The question "Are there more wooden beads, or more brown beads?" seems to suggest that "brown" and "wooden" are mutually exclusive categories, at least to the adult. It is not easy to think of situations and a procedure which will not have these drawbacks in some degree, but an attempt to minimize them was made in the present study, as described below.

EXPERIMENT

The aim of the experiment was to assess the generality of the sorts of response young children, between the ages of five and eight, make when asked about the composition of simple groups of objects. The specific hypothesis investigated concerns the relations between these responses and some of the responses made on the number concept test, that is, that some understanding of class composition is a necessary condition for dealing "operationally" (that is, consistently) with numbers.

Materials

Three different sorts of objects were used: toy plastic dolls, about 4 in. tall, both boys and girls; toy garden tools, rakes and shovels, about 8 in. long; toy cars ("Match box" cars) identical except that some were yellow, some red.

Subjects

The subjects were 60 children, varying in age from five years and two months to eight years and eight months. Twenty of these were in kindergarten. The remainder were in grades I, II, and III, with an average I.Q. of 99.4, range 81–118, as measured on a standard group test of intelligence (I.Q.s were not available for kindergarten children).

Method and Procedure

All the children had previously been tested with the number concept test described elsewhere (Dodwell, 1960, 1961). Each child was tested (not more than four weeks later) individually, to ascertain the extent of its understanding of the additive composition of classes. The use of materials and questioning followed lines rather similar to those described by Piaget, except that the same materials were used with each child, and the questions followed a pre-determined pattern, although the procedure was not completely standardized. Each child was asked questions about six situations, two for each of the three types of material.

First, the child was shown two groups, for instance, one of six rakes and one of five shovels, laid out on a table. The following questions were asked: "Here are some garden tools. Do you know what they are called?" Then "Show me all the rakes" and "show me all the shovels." "Are they all garden tools? Show me all the garden tools." When it had been established that the child understood that the rakes and shovels together constituted the tools, it was asked: "Are there more rakes, or more tools, on the table?" (The question was always asked about the *larger* subgroup). If the answer was wrong, or if the child showed uncertainty, further conversation followed, again emphasizing the relations between the groups, and attempting to elucidate the child's replies. The same procedure was used, but with groups of ten rakes and two shovels; six boys and five girls; twelve boys and two girls; five yellow and six red cars; two yellow and twelve red cars. The order in which the sets of material were presented was varied randomly from child to child.

A word about the choice of materials and numbers of items is in order. The criticism of Piaget's findings mentioned above, that unfamiliarity and verbal confusion may be important determinants of a child's responses, can only be countered either by ensuring that the situation is familiar and the child is not confused by the form of words used, or by trying to assess the importance of the two factors. In the present experiment an attempt was made to ensure that there was no verbal confusion by pointing out the meanings of the words to the child, if it was not quite sure of them, and by allowing and encouraging the manipulation of the objects (for example, "Give me all the tools"). It was thought that, if familiarity were an important factor, some differences in response by boys and girls might show up, since it seems reasonable to suppose that the girls would be rather more familiar with dolls than cars, and conversely for the boys, whereas the tools should be of about equal familiarity for both sexes. The different numbers of items in the subgroups (six and five, as against two and ten or twelve) were included as a measure of the extent to which the relative sizes of the subgroups might affect the answers given.

RESULTS

As in the number concept test and in Piaget's procedure, three types of answer were obtained. The first, characteristic of the youngest children, consisted of replies which showed quite clearly that the child was not able to think simultaneously about the total group and its constituent parts. That is to say, the child did not grasp the relation between the more general category (such as "tool") and the different types of item (rakes and shovels) in that category. The commonest response here was that there were equal numbers of rakes and tools, or (in the two-ten case) that there were more rakes than tools (that is, a comparison of the number of shovels and rakes, rather than the number of tools and rakes). Responses of this type were given a score of 0. At the other extreme were answers which showed quite clearly that the child understood the relation in question and these answers were scored 2. In between were a variety of responses which were indefinite, or in which the child was uncertain whether his answers were correct or not. These answers were scored 1. Thus the maximum possible score, for all six situations together, was 12. (This score will be called the "logic score.") No difficulty was experienced in assigning answers to one of the three categories; sometimes this could be done only after additional questioning, as noted above. The three categories are clearly similar to the stages in number concept development of global comparison, operational judgment, and intuitive judgment respectively, as described by Piaget and confirmed by the writer (Dodwell, 1960).

Treatment of Results

(i) Differences between frequencies of correct answers for the different materials, and different numbers in the subgroups: tests for differences were non-significant in both cases, using a χ^2 test.

(ii) Sex differences. There were no significant differences, again on a χ^2 test, either between sexes or between sexes with the different materials.

(iii) Effects of age and I.Q. Older children, and the more intelligent children, tended to do better than others, as one might expect, although the correlations were not high (see Table 1).

Table 1

Relation between "Composition of Classes" and Other Measures

Correlation	r	N	P
(1) Age; comp.	.238	60	< .05
(2) I.Q.; comp.	.338	40	< .01
(3) Point score; comp.	.273	60	< .025
(4) "A score"; comp.	− .282	60	< .025

(iv) There was similarly a low, but significant, correlation with over-all score (point score) on the number concept test, and a negative correlation with the "A score" on that test, the "A score" measuring the child's tendency to give answers in the "global" (perceptual) category (see Table 1).

More detailed comparisons of ability to answer correctly in the two situations (number test, composition of classes) were made in the following way: in the number concept test the two items which seem to show most clearly the child's understanding of cardinal numbers are the ones labelled "provoked correspondence" and "unprovoked correspondence," in which questions are asked about sets of equal numbers of eggs and eggcups and red and blue poker chips respectively, in different positions and configurations (see Dodwell, 1960, for a detailed description of the items).[1] Answers to the two items were scored 2, 1, or 0, according to their adequacy. Tetrachoric correlations were computed between correct and incorrect answers (that is, 2 against 1, or 0) on both these tests and the six situations used in the present study.

(v) Correlations between answers about composition of classes and about number concepts. Table 2 shows the correlations, all but one of them low, and all but four insignificant. This indicates that there is very little tendency, in general, for ability to answer correctly in one situation to be associated with ability to answer correctly in the other, although all the correlations are in the expected direction.

(vi) On the other hand, there is a very significant tendency for correct answering of the 6/5 problems to be associated with correct answering

---

[1] Basically, these two items measure the extent to which a child can understand and use the concept "cardinal number" in a situation wherein any perceptual correspondence between the two sets is disrupted. In one case (provoked correspondence) there is an obvious perceptual and utilitarian correspondence between individual members of the two sets (an egg can fit into each cup) but this is not true of the two sets of poker chips. In both cases the child had to set up a perceptual correspondence between the two sets, which was then disrupted by the experimenter, by bunching one of the sets together. The child was then asked whether this perceptual disruption had any bearing on the equivalence of the numbers in the two sets.

110   *Number Concepts*

Table 2

Tetrachoric Correlations between
"Logic" Scores and "Number" Scores

	Provoked	Unprovoked
6/5 tools	.18	.15
6/5 dolls	.16	.04
6/5 cars	.30[a]	.25[a]
10/2 tools	.23	.67[b]
12/2 dolls	.26[a]	.23
12/2 cars	.19	.15

[a] $p < .05$.
[b] $p < .01$.

of the 10 or 12/2 problems. A contingency table yielded a χ^2 of 22.4 ($p < .01$).

Expressing the over-all relation between the composition of classes scores and the two number test scores presents something of a problem, since neither score is really dichotomous or continuous. Since the total score on the former varies between 0 and 12, it was taken as a continuous variable, and the other two as dichotomous (again 2, as against 0 or 1).

(vii) The biserial correlation between "logic" scores and provoked correspondence is .19; between "logic" scores and unprovoked correspondence, .20. Neither is significant. It could be argued that the correlations do not tell us precisely *how* the two types of concept are related. We might find that a strict relation held in one direction, but not in the other. For example, it might be the case that understanding of the logical compositions is a necessary condition for understanding numbers (as seems to be implied by Piaget) but not conversely. To examine this possibility, the numbers of children answering the number questions correctly for different "logic" scores were tabulated. These numbers are expressed as proportions in Table 3 for frequencies of four or more.

(viii) No regular pattern is discernible in the proportions answering correctly as a function of score on the "logic" test.

(ix) Similarly no marked pattern is discernible in the logic answers, as a function of answers on the number concept test. Although there is some tendency for the two to be associated, we find for instance that four children do very poorly on logical composition, although they have perfect scores for number concepts (Table 4). Other anomalies will be obvious from an inspection of the table. With such low frequencies in most of the cells, the table is not appropriate for applying a χ^2 contingency test.

(x) Finally, the extent to which the "logic" questions and the "number

Table 3

Proportions Answering Questions about
Number Correctly, as a Function of Score
on Logical Composition Test

Comp. score	N	Provoked correspondence	Unprovoked correspondence
12	6	.67	.50
11	8	.63	.63
10	7	.57	.43
8	5	1.00	.40
7	4	.50	.50
6	7	.71	.26
4	13	.38	.31
3	4	.75	.50

Table 4

Answers to Questions about Logical Classes
as a Function of Answers to Number Concept Questions

Number score (provoked & unprovoked correspondence)	N	Logical composition score									
		12	11	10	9	8	7	6	5	4	3–0
4	24	3	4	3	2	2	2	1	1	4	0
3	11	0	2	1	0	3	0	3	0	1	1
2	7	1	1	1	0	1	1	0	1	0	0
1	9	2	1	2	0	0	0	2	0	2	0
0	9	0	0	0	0	0	1	0	0	5	3

concept" questions form a single scale was examined by Goodenough's modification of the Cornell scalogram technique (Edwards, 1957). The coefficient of reproducibility turned out to be .6, so that they form, at best, a "quasi-scale."

DISCUSSION

The results of this investigation show a fairly consistent, although negative, pattern. Understanding of the nature of hierarchical classification, to the extent that this is shown by ability to answer correctly questions which involve simultaneous consideration of the whole class and its (two) component subclasses, appears to develop to a large extent independently of understanding of the concept of cardinal number (as measured in the tests for provoked and unprovoked correspondence). Of course it could be argued that neither of these is a reliable or valid test. As to the first of these, reliability, the high degree of association between answers in the 6/5 and in the 10 or 12/2 situations (Results, vi) suggests that this test measures fairly consistently. As to the reliability of the two items from the number concept test, the first twelve pairs of papers from the short retest group (Dodwell, 1961) were examined (these being the only ones readily available) and, of the 24 pairs of answers to the questions on provoked and unprovoked correspondence, only one changed from the first to the second test. This is not a random sample from the original 60 pairs of papers, since most of the children in it were relatively high scorers. However, it does suggest that there is considerable stability in the answers to these questions. It is not known how valid the tests used may be. However, the total number concept test has good validity, and the questions used in the present investigation certainly appear to be relevant to the subject matter purportedly under investigation.

Although there is no clear relation between the development of the two types of concept, either in terms of priority of appearance or concomitance, they both develop within the same age range. It can be argued, as was done in the case of the number concept test (Dodwell, 1960), that variability is largely due to learning of specific responses for particular types of situation and material, and generalization of such responses to novel situations is imperfect. No doubt in some cases children answer "by chance," that is, they say something without realizing that it *is* the right (or wrong) answer because they do not understand the question, but in other cases it may well be that the child fails to answer correctly simply because it fails to see the relevance of an already learned sequence of operations, or concepts, to the situation at hand. In this connection it is worthwhile pointing out that, whereas a considerable amount of instruction in the use of the number words is given in school, there is little, if any, teaching of the concepts of hierarchical classification which the child has to pick up for himself. This may be a considerable factor in determining the ways in which the two groups of concepts develop.

These considerations lead the author to believe that an adequate picture of the development of logical, numerical, and other concepts will only be attained by intensive longitudinal study of individual children. What can be said, on the basis of the results here reported, is that the pattern of development is neither as regular, nor as simple, as Piaget has suggested. Whether more consistent relations would be found in longitudinal studies remains to be seen.

REFERENCES

Dodwell, P. C. (1960). Children's understanding of number and related concepts. *Canad. J. Psychol.*, 14, 191–205.
Dodwell, P. C. (1961). Children's understanding of number concepts: characteristics of an individual and of a group test. *Canad. J. Psychol.*, 15, 29–36.
Edwards, A. L. (1957). *Techniques of attitude scale construction.* New York: Appleton-Century-Crofts.
Piaget, J. (1950). *The psychology of intelligence.* London: Routledge.
Piaget, J. (1952). *The child's conception of number.* London: Routledge.

CHAPTER

THREE

SPATIAL

AND

GEOMETRIC

CONCEPTS

*   *   *

THE CHILD'S CONCEPTION OF SPACE (Piaget and Inhelder, 1956) and *The Child's Conception of Geometry* (Piaget, Inhelder, and Szeminska, 1960) are the two seminal volumes upon which the studies presented in this chapter are based. Since the geometric concepts are viewed as a direct outgrowth of spatial concepts, these two areas are presented together.

The major thesis of Piaget and his colleagues expressed in these volumes is that the child's *conception* of space and its *measurement* (geometry) proceed in an invariant stage sequence generally occurring as follows: from (1) topological concepts (the spatial relationships involved in a single object, for example, boundedness), to (2) projective concepts, where objects are not viewed in isolation but are seen as a coordination of objects in space, to (3) Euclidean concepts, such as angularity, parallelism, and distance. Historically, within the development of Western thought, the emergence of these concepts was Euclidean, projective, and topological, respectively, the sequence that is recapitulated in our educational curriculum. In contrast to the historical sequence, the results of Piaget's studies show that the ontogenetic pattern of acquisition is indeed the same as the *logical* sequence cited above. Extension of Euclidean concepts of space to measurement of that space is discussed in the studies on the concepts of geometry. Thus, the two areas are related since the child first has to develop a concept of space before he acquires concepts of measurement of that space. Acquisition of these concepts is coordinated with the growth of logical reason, so that the child's ultimate knowledge of spatial and geometric ideas cannot be divorced from the development of logical thought. The course of this development is complex, involving the emancipation from an egocentric view of the physical world and acquisitions such as representational thought and coordination of multiple dimensions. Accomplishments in these aspects of growth lead to capabilities in managing spatial and geometric concepts developed in an orderly, logical, and objective fashion.

The main propositions of Piagetian theory are found in the articles which follow. Dodwell's introductory statements not only capture the flavor of Piaget's theory, but also provide enough of its substance to allow one to follow the subsequent studies with considerable accuracy. Piaget's ideas on the development of geometric concepts are detailed in the Lovell, Healy, and Rowland article, which also reports broad confirmation of Piaget's stages of growth for such geometric concepts as length, distance, and angularity. A summary of the essentials of Euclidean space conceptions

116

is found in the Shantz and Smock article, chiefly in relation to distance conservation. A more discursive statement of general Piagetian theory as well as detailed discussions of the specific Piagetian concepts relevant to development of length (metric), order (seriation), and transitivity are found in the article by Braine. Although this author offers a critique directed at issues of length, conservation, measurement, serial order, and logical transitivity, a number of his comments are germane to such issues as stage concepts, with methodology in particular, and Piagetian concepts in general. The reader may find it worthwhile to reexamine some of the previous readings in the light of Braine's comments.

As in the development of number, so in the study of space and geometry, one of the major issues is the degree to which the child's spatial concepts become generalized. One of the major theses propounded by Piaget is that the child acquires a number of ideas which coalesce, enabling him to deal with other concepts. Piaget uncovers the child's conception of space by employing a variety of tasks. These tasks, unfortunately, are seldom administered to the same child. Dodwell provides just such data in the first article of this chapter. By administering a wide array of tasks to the same child and working with children of different age levels, Dodwell is able to assess not only interrelationships among various spatial problems, but also performance differences among diverse age groups. Leaving the problems of the developmental sequence within the same child (longitudinal research), Dodwell's study raises two important issues regarding the Piagetian research: (1) the problem of assigning the child to a particular stage, since considerable intra-individual variability is found; and (2) the confirming of the development sequence in broad outline only, which raises questions on such issues as the invariance of the predicted logical pattern.

The Shantz and Smock study is another variation of the idea of two operations presumed by Piaget to occur sequentially. Using first-grade children, these authors set out to assess whether the child's conservation of distance occurs developmentally prior to his comprehension of horizontality and verticality. They confirmed Piaget's contention that distance conservation does develop prior to the understanding of the Euclidean coordinate system; that is, horizontality and verticality can be judged independently of the immediate context. The article also makes a methodological contribution by showing the relationship between pictorial representations and three-dimensional representations of the same problem.

The equivocality of Piaget's results concerning acquisition of spatial concepts is further attested by Braine. Focusing on logical operations in general, expressed particularly in the study of length and its transitivity (for example, $A > B$, $B > C$, therefore $A > C$), Braine attempts to deal with substantive as well as methodological issues. He provides evidence supporting the relationship between acquisition of seriation and transitivity. This study was one of the first to raise the question, in empirical terms, of the role of instructions in Piagetian tasks. Criticizing the use of verbal methods, Braine employs nonverbal techniques in his tasks. Braine's discussion of this matter has given rise to a controversy with Smedslund (see "Reflections," Chap. 7).

Such methodological modifications, along with criticism of various elements of Piagetian theory, contribute points of clarification. Despite procedural changes, Braine offers vivid support for Piaget's proposition that certain operations and concepts are interdependent. He offers substantial support for developmental stages, but for him the chronological ages of appearance are earlier than those reported by Piaget.

These studies of geometric and spatial concepts are critical examples of Piaget's contention concerning the interlocking nature of cognitive processes in development. In reviewing these studies the reader should reflect on the similarities and differences between tasks presumably assessing similar phenomena, and should attempt logical integrations where possible. Braine's reservations should be held in mind while reviewing the other studies.

REFERENCES

Piaget, J., and Barbel Inhelder (1956). *The child's conception of space.* London: Routledge.

Piaget, J., Barbel Inhelder, and Alina Szeminska (1960). *The child's conception of geometry.* New York: Basic Books.

CHILDREN'S UNDERSTANDING
OF SPATIAL CONCEPTS

P. C. Dodwell

In *The Child's Conception of Space* (Piaget and Inhelder, 1956) rather extensive investigations of children's understanding of spatial concepts and relations are described, investigations based on experimental procedures which are typical of the practice of Piaget and his co-workers in their recent studies. As in many of his investigations, Piaget claims to

Reprinted with the permission of the author and the University of Toronto Press, from *The Canadian Journal of Psychology*, 1963, 17, 141–161. This investigation was supported by a grant from the Arts Research Committee of Queen's University, whose assistance is gratefully acknowledged. Thanks are due also to the various school authorities for their cooperation, and to students in the Department of Psychology at Queen's who took part in the study.

demonstrate a fairly clear progression in spatial concept development with age, and, as in many previous instances, he can be criticized for basing his generalizations on inadequate evidence. He gives no indication of the number of children tested, of the consistency of trends from one stage to another with age, or—more important—the consistency of the steps in the progression within individual children. The investigation here reported is an attempt to verify some of Piaget's conclusions concerning spatial concepts on a fairly large sample of children, and is thus parallel to an earlier investigation of the development of number concepts (Dodwell, 1960, 1961).

PIAGET'S THEORY

Piaget's theory of the development of spatial concepts, like his theory of number concept development, is a particular application of his general theory of intelligence (Piaget, 1950), which was briefly outlined in the introduction to the study on number concepts (Dodwell, 1960) and will not be repeated here. However, some important new concepts are introduced, the most important being the concept of *sub*-logical (spatio-temporal) operations, which are distinguished from logico-arithmetical operations mainly on the grounds that they involve notions of proximity and continuity. These notions are not strictly necessary for the first steps in logico-arithmetical operations (that is, the logic of classes) but are clearly required in the development of spatial concepts.

The theory of the development of spatial operations and concepts is, roughly, that the first spatial operations the child comes to understand involve primitive notions of proximity, enclosure, and boundary which are entirely non-metric in character. Piaget makes a perfectly reasonable distinction between *perceived* space and *conceived* space: whereas a quite young child may be able to distinguish perceptually between, say, a square and a circle, this does not mean that the child can conceptualize this difference, or marshal the operations which are necessary for making anything more than a perceptual distinction. *Understanding* spatial properties and relations, as opposed to perception of similarities and differences between spatially extended objects, involves operations which are thought of as "virtual" or "internalized" actions. It is interesting to note that the "psychologically primitive" operations of order, proximity, enclosure, etc. correspond quite closely to the "mathematically primitive" concepts used in that branch of geometry known as topology, which also deals with the most general, and usually non-metric, properties of space. In this there is quite a close parallel to the relations between the logical primitives on which mathematics is based, and the primitive notions the child develops before coming to understand numbers (cf. Dodwell, 1960).

One tends to think of Euclidean geometry as *the* "natural" geometry, and hence that children should easily come to understand space in terms of Euclidean concepts. According to Piaget, however, the use and understanding of such concepts is preceded first by the development of topological operations and concepts, as described above, and then by operations and concepts of a projective character, for example those required for an understanding of perspective.

The stages in the development of spatial concepts in Piaget's theory are a good deal more complex than in the case of number concepts. However, the same sorts of stages are envisaged, starting with "global" comparisons, proceeding through an "intuitive" stage, at which the child starts to grasp the correct operations and the relations between them, to a stage of "concrete operations" at which the correct operations are used in a consistent fashion. This is complicated, however, by the simultaneous development from topological to projective to Euclidean concepts, so that the *sorts* of operation the child uses change at the same time as he is learning *what* operations and groupings of operations are.

PIAGET'S EVIDENCE

Piaget's study of spatial concepts is divided into three parts, corresponding to the three types of geometrical concepts outlined above. In investigating the topological stage he made use primarily of drawings, "haptic" perception (perception by touch, without vision), linear and circular order (as with beads on a string), the study of knots, and situations involving the concept of continuity—for example, the number of points on a line, the end result of indefinitely repeated bisection of a line, and continual reduction in size of a geometric figure.

Understanding of projective properties was investigated by such techniques as: observing children's ability to *construct* straight lines using numbers of discrete objects, getting them to draw various perspective figures, asking questions about the projection of the shadows of objects, the relations between objects perceived from different points of view, sections through solid geometric figures such as a cylinder or cone, etc.

The transition from projective to Euclidean concepts was investigated in terms of "affine" transformations (transformations preserving parallels) with "Lazy Tongs," in terms of understanding of similarity and proportion in figures such as the rectangle and triangle, and in terms of the understanding of systems of horizontal and vertical reference axes. None of Piaget's procedures have been described here in detail, since many of them are followed fairly closely in the tests to be described below: in general he avoids basing his conclusions on a single demonstration situation, but tends to use two or more situations both of which require use of the same sorts of operation. However, as noted above, he does not give any idea of the generality of his findings, either between children at the same age or between different tests allegedly chosen to demonstrate similar or identical operations in action within the same child.

PROCEDURE

Aim

To assess the generality of the sorts of spatial concepts and their development, as reported by Piaget and his co-workers (Piaget and Inhelder, 1956); to examine age trends, the consistency of the reported activities at different ages and stages, and to assess these factors as evidence for a theory of cognitive development based, first, on the notion of the formation of operational groupings, and secondly, on the progression from topological to Euclidean spatial concepts.

Method

Three persons took part in the investigation, two of them as testers, and all three as scorers. *S*s were 194 children in Kingston public schools, ranging in age from five years and one month to eleven years and three months, and in I.Q. (measured on a group test) from 80 to 136 (no I.Q.s were available for kindergarten children). The average range of I.Q. was somewhat over-represented at the expense of the extremes, and all children were in either kindergarten or Grades I, II, or III. Age distributions within grades were similar to those reported previously (Dodwell, 1960); the children were in three different schools and were drawn from all socio-economic levels. The test was administered individually and took in most cases about 20–30 min. per child. Thirty-four different situations or items were used in the test, which was divided into seven main subsections. The order in which the items were administered was standardized, as was the scoring procedure and, to a large extent, the use of subsidiary questioning. However, some latitude was allowed in the latter respect, since the point of such questioning is to follow up ambiguous answers and clarify the processes of thought which led to them.

The seven subgroups of the test, which follow quite closely some of the situations used by Piaget, are listed in Table 1.

Subgroup I Construction of Straight Line (Items 1–5)

In the first subsection, understanding of the *construct* "straight line" was investigated (as opposed to the *discrimination* between straight and curved lines). (1) The child was confronted with a heavy cardboard disk, about 14 in. in diameter, placed on a fairly large table, and about 12 in. from its edge. Ten colored plastic toothpicks on plasticine bases were also

Table 1

Subgroups of the Spatial Concept Test

Sub-group	Name	Materials and/or method
I	Construction of straight line	"Telegraph poles"
II	Drawing shapes	Pencil and paper, shapes to be copied.
III	Plane figures, lines, points, and continuity	Pencil and paper, demonstration by tester.
IV	Horizontal and vertical coordinates	Bottles, "boat," plumbline, pictures.
V	Geometrical sections	Plasticine solid geometrical models, sections to be drawn.
VI	Similarity and proportion	Shapes, similar shapes to be drawn around them, by parallel lines.
VII	Coordination of perspective	Table model with mountains, pictures of "points of view."

placed on the table, and the tester said: "These are telephone poles [indicating the toothpicks] and I would like you to set them up so that they will be in a straight line beside a straight road. I will put in the one that will be at the beginning of the line and the one that will be at the end and I would like you to put in the ones in between that go to make the straight line." The end-posts were placed some distance apart from each other on the circumference of the disk, at the ends of a cord parallel to the diameter of the disk sagittal to the child. The child's performance was noted down on a standard test blank, which listed the common types of response as indicated by Piaget (in this case: posts arranged in a straight line; posts follow curve of circle; posts form zigzag line; posts at random over surface; evenly spaced; bunched). Checking one or more of the items served to characterize the response in most cases, but if some substantially different response occurred, it was noted separately. The procedure was repeated using (2) a cardboard square, with end posts at the corners of the side closest to the child, (3) with the circle, placing the end points so that the cord joining them ran obliquely to the sagittal axis, (4) with the square, so that the end points were on the base and on the left side of the square. Lastly in this subsection, the posts were placed on the square in a non-straight line, and the child asked to straighten them (5). If the child did not spontaneously sight along the line, it was moved to various positions around the table and asked which positions would help to show if the line were straight or not.

Subgroup II Drawing Shapes (Item 6)

The child was asked to draw a picture of a man (to make sure that it had *some* drawing ability: however, this was not scored) and then was asked to copy a series of 20 shapes, ranging from the "topological" shapes shown in Figure 1 through various simple geometrical shapes (circle, square, triangle, ellipse, rectangle) to more complex shapes, such as a pair of circles intersecting, touching, and separated, an equilateral triangle enclosed in a circle, etc. The purpose here was to try to discover the extent to which children can draw the shapes with (*a*) topological, (*b*) projective, and (*c*) Euclidean properties correctly reproduced.

Figure 1 The topological shapes used as models in subgroup II.

Subgroup III Points and Continuity (Items 7–12)

Items in this subgroup deal with understanding of the concept of point, and the ideas of continuity and limit in a very elementary sense. (7) The tester first said: "I am going to draw a box [square] on this sheet of paper. Here right beside it I would like you to draw the smallest box that can possibly be drawn, one so small that no one could make one smaller." (The common alternatives here were: draws a smaller square; draws immediately the smallest square; draws a series of squares decreasing in size; does not draw a smaller square. Distinguishing between the first two of these alternatives was almost always quite easy.) The same procedure was repeated for a *bigger* square (8): here the "biggest" square was taken as one which followed fairly closely the edges of the paper. For item 9: "Here is a straight line drawn on a sheet of paper. Under it I want you to draw a straight line just half as long as this one. . . . I want you to draw one just half as long as the one you just drew. . . ." etc. When the child had drawn his "smallest" line, the tester said (10): "You can do a lot of things in your mind, can't you? Well then, try to imagine that you are going to go on cutting up this little bit [line] without stopping. How long could you go on cutting it up like this? . . . What is going to be left in the end?"

Next (11), the tester took a fresh sheet of paper, drew a line about an inch long on it, and asked: "How many lines do you need to get a big one like this?" and then (12), drawing two points about an inch apart: "How many points are there between these two points? Draw in the points. . . . Could you get any more points in? What would you have if you drew in as many points as you could possibly draw?" Following this was an item (13) concerning the limit for the "smallest" square; in this case the child was allowed to "cut up" the square (by drawing dividing lines through it); the child was asked what the final product of this process would be. If it said "nothing at all," it was asked: "What would you get just before nothing at all?" As before, all responses were recorded, either as one of the standard responses, or as a separate response where necessary.

Subgroup IV Horizontal and Vertical (Items 14–20)

This group concerns the understanding and use of systems of horizontal and vertical reference axes. The materials used consisted of two narrow-necked bottles, one with straight parallel sides and a flat base, the other spherical, each about one-quarter full of a colored liquid; two other empty jars, one each of the types described; a cork with a matchstick fixed to it, and perpendicular to one of the flat faces; a plumbline with a bob shaped like a fish; a plasticine model of three mountains; and various pictures of the jars.

Item 14: "We are going to tip the straight jar over like this. . . . Will the water stay where it is, or will it move? Show with your finger on the jar where the water will be. . . . Draw on your picture of the jar (tilted) where the water will be when it is tipped. . . . Now we will see whether it is right. . . . Were you right? Now draw what you see." This was repeated with the *round* jar (15) and in both cases the tilt was about 45°.

Item 16: "Here are some pictures of jars with water in them." [Three jars, one vertical, one horizontal, one tilted at 45°.] "Take them one at a time and tip them so that the water looks right," followed by item 17: "Here are some [6] pictures of jars with water in them. Some of them are tipped so that the water looks right [4] and some are not [2]. Put all the ones that are right in one pile and all the others in another pile." So far the items in this subgroup have been concerned with a horizontal reference axis (the surface of the water). The remaining items deal with a vertical reference axis.

Item 18: With the parallel-sided jar: "Here is a cork with a matchstick in it. Let's pretend that it is a little boat. We will let the boat float on the water in the jar. Which way does the mast of the boat point now? [Jar vertical.] We are going to tip the jar, and I want you to draw the way the mast will look with the jar tipped: I will tip the *empty* jar the way this jar is going to be tipped [45°]. Now draw the little boat. . . . Now we will tip the jar with the water in it and see if you were right. Were you right?

Draw it again the way it should look." This procedure was repeated with the jar tipped through 90° (Item 19).

Item 20, again with the parallel-sided jar: "Here is a line with a fish on it. We will hang it inside the empty jar. Now we will tip the jar like this [45° tip demonstrated with similar jar] and I would like you to draw the way the string would look with the jar tipped. Now let's see if you were right [tip jar with line in it]. Were vou right? Now please make your drawing look right."

Item 21: "Here is a mountain, and here are some posts [9]. I would like you to plant three posts nice and straight on the top of the mountain. . . . Plant three posts on the ground nearby. . . . Plant three posts on the slopes of the mountain. . . . Now *draw* the mountain with four trees nice and straight on the sides."

Subgroup V Geometrical Sections (Items 22–27)

The problems in this group concern understanding of the sections of a three-dimensional geometrical figure. The materials used were a plasticine cylinder, a rectangular parallelepiped, a cone, and a hollow rubber ball.

For item 22 the child was shown the cylinder, and a knife. The tester said: "I am going to cut this roller in the middle like this [perpendicular to the main axis, indicated by a gesture]. I would like you to draw the side you'll see where it has been cut. . . ." Then, showing a cut section: "Did you think it would look like that?" The same procedure was repeated with the cone (23), the parallelepiped (24), the hollow ball (25), a longitudinal section of the cylinder (26), and an oblique (elliptical) section of the cone (27).

Subgroup VI Similarity and Proportion (Items 28–33)

Drawings of isosceles and scalene triangles and of a rectangle were used, and a ruler provided. The items were designed to elucidate understanding of similarities and proportions.

Item 28, showing the isosceles triangle: "Do you know what we call this drawing? [Yes, it looks like a tent and is called a triangle.] I am going to draw a line just below the bottom of this triangle [actually, parallel to its base]. I would like you to start with this line and make a bigger triangle just the same shape as this other one, around the outside of it. You may use this ruler to help you draw it, and you may turn the paper any way you like." The same procedure was repeated with the scalene triangle (29) and rectangle (30), and with the rectangle having one diagonal drawn in and produced, to see if the child would use this to help obtain a similar figure (31).

Item 32: "Here are some pictures [eight pairs of similar figures and three pairs of dissimilar ones]. Each picture has two triangles on it. The triangles may be exactly the same shape, or they may be of different shapes. Put all the pictures with triangles that are the same in this pile, and all the others over here." This was repeated, with cards showing pairs of rectangles (33).

Subgroup VII coordination of Perspectives (Items 34–35)

Materials. A papier mâché model of three mountains on a square base, with various identifying details, such as a truck parked on one mountain, a sheep on another, a tree on the third; in addition each mountain was a different color (green, brown, grey); a doll; and 10 pictures representing different views of the scene.

Item 34: "These pointed things are mountains, and from different sides you can see different things. I will put this little doll at different places, and then I would like you to pick out the picture that shows what the doll would see from those places." Four positions were used, one the child's own position, and opposite the three other sides of the model.

Item 35: "Here is a picture that shows what the doll would see from one side of the scene. Look at it carefully and then show me where the doll would be standing to see this picture." The same procedure was repeated for four different positions of the doll, and the child was not allowed to move around the model at any time. As with previous items in the test, boxes were provided on the test blank for common types of answers, and unusual or ambiguous responses were noted down in full.[1]

RESULTS

Description and analysis of the results of this test are not by any means as straightforward as in the case of the number concept test: first of all, because the range and variability of responses is greater in the present test, and the categorization of responses not so objective in all cases, and secondly because several different processes appear to be developing concurrently. As was mentioned above, according to Piaget the child develops through different stages characterized by changing concepts of space (topological, projective, Euclidean), but at the same time it is elaborating the "mental structure" of operations, and groupings of operations. Also a number of the items in the present test depend for their solution on drawing ability, and this is something which is developing rapidly during the age range under investigation (of course this development is probably dependent to some extent on the changes in spatial concepts, but it seems doubtful whether this is the only factor involved).

---

[1] Copies of the test blank are available on request to the author.

On the whole Piaget's assertions about the development of spatial concepts, as measured by the present types of test situation, were corroborated, although not in all respects, as will become evident in the descriptions below. It was not found possible to assign any child to a particular stage of development, either in terms of the type of spatial (geometrical) concepts the child entertained, or the correctness of its answers within a particular conceptual framework. Thus a child might get all solutions to one set of problems correct in terms of projective characteristics, yet in another set it might not grasp even the topological relations involved. Furthermore, the division of responses into "global" (perceptual), "intuitive," and "operational" categories, according to the adequacy of a response, was not in all cases as readily or reliably attainable as in the number concept study (Dodwell, 1960). However, responses were classified in this way, the labels A, B, and C stages being used, as before. So far as possible Piaget and Inhelder's classification into stages was followed, at least approximately. The relations of the A, B, and C stages to the sometimes more complex subdivisions of Piaget and Inhelder are noted in the appropriate places below.

QUALITATIVE OBSERVATIONS

These qualitative observations can best be followed by referring back to Table 1 which lists the methods and materials for the various subgroups.

Subgroup I Construction of Straight Line

This set of items is concerned with ability to construct a straight line, and Piaget's findings are borne out, to the extent that many of the younger children could place their posts between the end-posts, but did not attempt to space them evenly or in a straight line. Rather, they seemed to be satisfied with an arrangement of "linear proximity." (This Piaget calls "stage I.") Another common response among younger children was to follow the edge of the platform on which the line was to be constructed, thus forming a curved, or even two-sided "straight line" between the end-posts. (Piaget's "stage II.") Characteristically, such children did not see the advantages of viewing the line of sticks from a particular point of view to "get them straight," whereas older children, even if they did not spontaneously sight along the line, were easily convinced of the advantage of doing so, and of course were not influenced in their constructions by the contour of the platform. Division into stages A, B, and C on any one item was not difficult in this subgroup and corresponded to Piaget's stages I, II, and III: however, so many children displayed different types of behavior between the different items in the subgroup (despite their apparent similarity—see description in previous

Table 2

Characteristics of Responses to Items
in Subgroup I (5 items) in Terms of Age

	Typical behavior	*N*	*Mode*	*Range*
Stage A	"Linear proximity," with no attempt to form straight line.	11	7.3	5.3– 8.3
Stage B	Follows model edge, often in two separate lines.	36	7.0	5.3–10.3
Stage C	Forms straight line, posts usually evenly spaced between end points.	66	8.8	5.8–11.3
Mixed		81	5.8	5.3– 9.8

section) that a special "mixed" category was included, and proved to be the largest single category.[2] Table 2 demonstrates the main characteristics of the responses in this subgroup, on the basis of age. It is evident that the age overlap of the different stages is very great, and the size of the "mixed" category strongly suggests that clear verification of the Piagetian stage of development for a particular child, even within such a homogeneous group of items, often cannot be made even approximately.

Subgroup II Drawings of Shapes

From the point of view of classification, this set of items was, perhaps, the most troublesome. It may seem, a priori, that it should be fairly easy to decide whether or not a shape has been drawn so that Euclidean, projective, topological, or no characteristics of the model are more or less faithfully reproduced. However, in many cases the decision is not so simple, especially as the level of drawing competence is obviously relevant. Thus, a child that has to draw an equilateral triangle inscribed in a circle may, in the attempt to get the sides of the triangle of equal length, fail to have them join on the circle, so that the result is not even topologically correct. How does one score such a drawing? After several attempts at classification, and discussion of the results, the three scorers managed to agree on just over 80 per cent of the drawings, classified independently, and no further improvement seemed likely.

As one might expect, the level of drawing competence increased with age. The youngest children frequently did not draw their shapes even

---

[2] The criterion for classifying a child as in the "mixed" category for a subgroup was that at least two of the responses within the subgroup should be rated differently from the remainder. Thus a child given four As and one B in subgroup I would be rated as in category A, but a child with three As and two Bs would be rated "mixed."

topologically correctly, but were more often correct in a topological than in a projective or Euclidean sense. Older children, on the other hand, tended to make progressively more of their drawings correct in the latter two senses, but in view of the uncertainties of the scoring procedures, it seems hardly worthwhile to elaborate on these changes, except to state that even among the oldest children some non-Euclidean drawings were made.

Subgroup III Points and Continuity

Piaget interprets a crude notion of continuity as the end-product of elaborating operations of ordering, seriating, and enclosing, and distinguishes three stages in its development. Evidence was found for his first two stages (the third being a stage of "formal understanding" occuring only at about 11–12 years of age): in the first stage children are held to be unable to draw "largest" and "smallest" figures since, as Piaget puts it, "they lack an operational schema of seriation (Piaget and Inhelder, 1956, p. 128), are unable to subdivide a line or figure more than a very few times, and consider the ultimate elements of indefinitely repeated division to have the same shapes as the original figures. Also, a line cannot be understoood as a collection of points.

Table 3 shows some characteristics of age levels in this subgroup: there was only one child that could be characterized as "pure A," that is, that had no concept of continuity at all, and the most striking feature of the table is the enormous preponderance of the "mixed" category. This very large "mixed" category suggests that the development of the operations concerned may proceed in a rather haphazard fashion. The question of whether or not there is a discernible pattern in the "mixed" response group is taken up below. In the second stage subdivision leads to a "point," but the point is still thought of as having extension, its shape depending on the mode of subdivision and the process as having a finite number of steps. The "building up" of a line or surface is understood, in an elementary sense, as the reverse of the process of subdivision. A third stage was identified (stage C, which is not the same as Piaget's final, formal, stage) in which a "point" is understood as being without spatial extension, and the number of points in a line or surface as being unlimited. Naturally these notions are only entertained by children in a very elementary and crude way.

Here is a typical "mixed" set of responses, made by a boy aged eight years and ten months, of average intelligence: (7) To the "smallest box" instruction, the boy responded by drawing a *series* of squares of decreasing size, one beside the other (rated B). (8) To the "largest box" instruction he responded also by drawing a series, one outside the other (B). (9) Asked to draw a series of lines of decreasing size, he did so, ending up with a point (C). (10) Asked how much further his point could be cut up, he said "about three more times" (rated B, since the response was not

Table 3

*Characteristics of Responses to Items
in Subgroup III (6 items) in Terms of Age*

	Typical behavior	*N*	*Mode*	*Range*
Stage A	Inability to draw "largest" and "smallest," inability to subdivide line, or "construct" line out of points.	1	6.8	—
Stage B	Draws series, to find smallest, or largest figure. Subdivision of line not completed.	23	7.3	5.3– 9.8
Stage C	"Largest" and "smallest" found immediately. Subdivision of line, and composition of line from points understood.	6	8.3	5.8– 9.8
Mixed		164	8.3	5.3–11.3

entirely determined by perceptual properties—the line had already been reduced to a point). Asked what would be left, after a final division, he said "a little bit" (B). (11) Asked how many lines go to make a longer line, he said "about seven" (A), and (12) that a given line would be made up of about 12 points (some of which he drew—spaced apart (A)). Asked what one would have when all the dots had been drawn in, he said "a jumble of little dots" (A). (13) The final product of dividing up a square was said to be "a tiny bit of the square" (not "a square") (B). Evidently this boy has the beginnings of an understanding of "continuity," in an elementary way, but is not able to apply his ideas too consistently.

Subgroup IV Horizontal and Vertical Axes

Again, all the substages and stages described by Piaget were observed, and the results were divided into three stages corresponding to Piaget's stages I, II, and III. At stage A, the child has no conception of horizontal and vertical, cannot draw the water levels or plumblines, nor relate movements of the jars to different pictures of the water levels, etc. At stage B, the rudimentary concepts of horizontal and vertical appear, but cannot be maintained with respect to an external reference point, or line: that is, when the jar is tilted, the water level or plumbline tends to tilt with it. At the third stage, C, the levels are correctly predicted and drawn, as are the directions of plumblines. Table 4 shows distributions of these stages over age: Piaget mentions ages four to five as typical for stage A, and "after seven to eight" for stage C. The present findings suggest that the age limits cannot be so precisely identified, and the enor-

Table 4

*Characteristics of Responses to Items
in Subgroup IV (8 items) in Terms of Age*

	Typical behavior	N	Mode	Range
Stage A	No idea of horizontal and vertical axes, either in prediction, drawing or recognition of pictures.	15	6.3	5.8–10.3
Stage B	Some recognition of axes, but not maintained when jar tipped.	9	8.8	5.3–10.3
Stage C	Correct prediction, drawing and recognition of axes.	12	8.3 and 9.3	7.3– 9.8
Mixed		158	8.3	5.3–11.3

mously preponderant "mixed" category again suggests very little regularity in the developmental pattern.

As an example from the "mixed" category, the boy whose responses were described under subgroup III above was able to predict the direction of the mast and water level perfectly well when the cork was tilted in the bottle (stage C) but placed sticks on the mountain, and drew them, perpendicular to the mountain sides (stage B). He was also unable to predict the water levels for the initial items in the subgroup. There is possibly a learning effect here, since responses to the bottle problems improved: however, a number of other children gave more adequate answers to the early items in the subgroup than to the later ones, so it is certain that not all children in the "mixed" category are there because they learned how to answer this type of question while the test was in progress.

Subgroup V Geometric Sections

Three main stages in developing the ability to predict the results of sectioning a geometrical solid are described by Piaget, and all three were observed in the present study. First stage responses are characterized by inability to reproduce even an approximation to the section, and are frequently characterized by a "medley of viewpoints"; that is, the child may draw part of the solid object, with perhaps one or more smaller figures inside it to represent the section. Evidently it cannot "abstract" the section from the object and the operation of cutting. The second stage is characterized by progressively greater ability to imagine the section and to draw it, although imperfectly. In the third stage the problem is solved at once and the section drawn correctly. Piaget mentions ages four to six years as characteristic of the first stage, about five and a half to seven years for the second. The age ranges found in this study are shown in Table 5. Again, the "mixed" category is very large, indicating that the "mental construction" of a section is not an "all-or-nothing" affair; that is, consistency from one situation or object to another is comparatively exceptional. Moreover, only one child was consistently in stage B, and very few consistently in stage C. The age overlap for the stages is again enormous.

Table 5

Characteristics of Responses to Items
in Subgroup V (6 items) in Terms of Age

	Typical behavior	*N*	*Mode*	*Range*
Stage A	No reproduction of cross-sections; often a "medley of viewpoints."	82	7.3	5.3–11.3
Stage B	Partially correct drawings of sections.	1	9.8	—
Stage C	Fully correct drawings, and correct predictions of cross-sections.	12	9.3	5.8–11.3
Mixed		99	—[a]	5.3–10.3

[a] No clear mode.

Subgroup VI Similarities and Proportions

The results are quite straightforward in this group. In the first stage, "drawing a similar figure" means simply "drawing another figure around the given model"—usually with more or less straight sides, and usually the right number of sides, but with no attempt to make corresponding sides in model and drawing parallel. The second stage is characterized by fairly careful drawing, but inconsistency in achieving parallels. In the third stage, a similar enlarged figure is correctly produced, with all sides parallel to the corresponding sides of the model. Piaget distinguishes a number of substages in this development, but since the evidence in Table 6 indicates that it is not possible to assign most children to a category, even when just three categories are employed, further refinements were not attempted.

Subgroup VII Coordination of Perspectives

Only two of Piaget's stages are relevant here, each one divided into two substages. In practice it seems impossible to distinguish between the

Table 6

Characteristics of Responses to Items
in Subgroup VI (6 items) in Terms of Age

	Typical behavior	N	Mode	Range
Stage A	No idea of drawing parallels to produce similar figures.	8	6.3	5.6– 9.3
Stage B	Inconsistency in drawing sides parallel to model to produce similar figures.	14	7.3	5.3– 9.3
Stage C	All sides drawn parallel to those of model.	10	—[a]	7.3–10.3
Mixed		162	—[a]	5.3–11.3

[a] No clear mode.

Table 7

Characteristics of Responses to Items
in Subgroup VII (2 items) in Terms of Age

	Typical behavior	N	Mode	Range
Stage A	No coordination of position and "point of view" of doll. Chooses view from *own* position, or at random.	44	5.8	5.3– 9.3[a]
Stage B	Partially correct, transitional responses.	30	8.3	5.3–10.3[a]
Stage C	Complete coordination of position and perspective view of model.	11	9.8	8.3–10.3
Mixed		109	7.3	5.3–11.3

[a] Plus a "straggler" at 11.3.

middle pair of these substages (IIB and IIIA), both of which are "transitional," and have been labeled B in the present classification.[3]

The behavior characteristic of stage A (Piaget's stage IIA) is a lack of ability to coordinate position of the doll ("point of view") with a particular view of the model, the child either always choosing the picture of the model as seen from his own position, or choosing a picture at random. Stage C again is the stage characterized by ability to coordinate position and perspective view of model perfectly, and stage B includes various partly correct transitional types of response. Again, responses were observed in all three stages, A, B, and C, but there was a preponderance of "mixed" responses. Table 7 gives the relevant data. Rather

[3] The division into stages does not always correspond very closely with the division used by Piaget, who tends to distinguish a number of substages. In general the system used here is to distinguish the (usually easily recognizable) stages A and C, and to lump together all "transitional" responses as stage B.

exceptionally, Piaget mentions the number of children observed in this case (Piaget and Inhelder, 1956, p. 212), namely, one hundred, between the ages of four and twelve years. However, he fails to give any indication of age ranges, except to mention that stage C is usually found after about seven to eight years of age. As a matter of fact, the separation into stages is here rather clearer than in most of the other subgroups, despite the large mixed category, and the age ranges and modes are approximately what one might expect from Piaget's theory, except that the upper limits for stages A and B are rather high.

QUANTITATIVE TREATMENT OF RESULTS

A point score was devised, points being awarded for correct answers and solutions to problems. Also, an A score was computed, which consisted simply of a count of the number of responses classified as in group A. It should be noted that A responses are those which show no evidence of grasping spatial concepts of widely different types; for instance, in subgroup I an A response indicates inability to arrange a set of posts in a straight line, except in the topological sense of making the posts neighbors, whereas in subgroup VII it indicates inability to understand the coordination of position and perspective. However, the A score can be considered a rather general measure of primitiveness in grasping spatial concepts, and it is not surprising that it has a fairly high negative correlation with the point score, as shown in Table 8. This table also shows a number of other test characteristics: as one would expect, there is a considerable correlation with age, and an even more marked correlation with mental age. The partial correlations indicate that mental age is a source of variation at least as important as chronological age alone. This result is in conformity with other findings on the relation of Piagetian stages to

Table 8

Test Characteristics[a]

Items correlated	r	N
Total score, A score	−.69	194
Total score, M.A.	.69	152
Total score, C.A.	.56	194
Total score, M.A. (C.A. constant)	.52	152
Total score, C.A. (M.A. constant)	.22	152
Total score, I.Q.	.31	152
Total score (test-retest)	.95	20

[a] Test mean = 91.6; standard deviation = 20.45; error of measurement = 4.8.

mental and chronological age (Dodwell, 1961; Harker, 1960; Carpenter, 1955). A group of 20 children was re-tested with the test approximately one week after the first administration, and the test-retest correlation demonstrates that the test is satisfactorily reliable. This may be an over-estimate of reliability, since the children were drawn from a fairly wide age range. However, calculation of r from the actual differences between scores on first and second administrations of the test, according to Gulliksen's formula (Gulliksen, 1950, formula (5), chap. 4, p. 40) yielded a value of .92 indicating a genuinely high reliability.

Table 9 shows the intercorrelations between the scores on items in the various subgroups. The "battery" is too small to make a factor analysis worthwhile, but a cluster analysis (Harman, 1960) was performed to determine which, if any, of the tests could be considered as forming well-defined clusters. The analysis was entirely inconclusive: there is no evidence to suggest clustering. Inspection of the intercorrelations does not suggest any striking hypotheses or obvious points of confirmation for Piaget's theory; the fact that all the correlations are positive is not surprising, and probably is due simply to the fact that all the types of geometrical conceptualization tested tend to improve with age. On the basis of Piagetian theory, one might expect high correlations between groups of items apparently requiring use of similar or identical operations, but in the absence of any evidence for clustering, there is no point in pursuing speculations on this point.

Table 9

Intercorrelations of Subgroup Scores

| | Subgroup | | | | | | |
Subgroup	I	II	III	IV	V	VI	VII
I		.37	.40	.38	.20	.07	.40
II			.46	.50	.25	.43	.38
III				.64	.34	.05	.30
IV					.24	.49	.52
V						.10	.35
VI							.37
VII							

It has been noted already that, within subgroups of the test, a mixed category of responses is generally far more common than any one of the pure categories, and usually the mixed category is larger than all the others put together. It is possible that, within the mixed category of a subgroup, meaningful patterns of response can be discerned. On the other hand, it may be that the "mixed" answers are fairly irregular in their patterns of occurrence. To attempt to resolve this question, all responses to items in subgroup III were analyzed in the following way:[4]

There are seven items in the subgroup, and the response to each one could be classified as an A, B, or C response, in terms of its adequacy, as defined above.

The record of every child that had at least one fully correct (type C) response in the subgroup was examined.[5] In order to discover what pattern, if any, there might be among the various responses given by these children, the frequency of occurrence of correct responses to *both* of all possible pairs of items in the subgroup was computed, as was frequency of occurrence of all the various possible combinations of pairs of correct and incorrect answers. These are shown in Table 10. It is immediately evident from this table that consistent type-C responses are the exception rather than the rule: in only one case (items 9–12) does the number of consistent type-C responses exceed every other type. This is hardly surprising, since it has already been noted that a mixed category (for children rather than test items) is the single largest category. Of more interest is the question of the relations which hold among the various sorts of mixed-type responses. The important ones appear to be the following:

(i) Starting with the last line in the table, one observes that a child that answers items 7, 8, or 9 with an A response has almost no likelihood of giving any C responses. On the other hand, type A responses to items 10, 11, and 12 are quite frequently associated with C responses to other (later) items. This is quite consistent with what one would expect on the basis of Piaget's theory: items 7 and 8 are concerned with the operations of seriation (according to Piaget) and an A response indicates no understanding of this operation. Without this understanding, one could hardly expect correct solutions to other problems about points, limits, and so on to be given. Similarly, item 9 is concerned with subdivision of a line, and some understanding of this operation would seem to be a prerequisite of correct solutions to the later items.

(ii) On the other hand, it is quite clear, from inspection of the fourth line in the table, that B responses to the first two items (7 and 8) are readily compatible with correct solutions to later items, but this is again consistent with Piaget's theory, since the B response in this case (described earlier) involves drawing a *series* of squares, rather than the smallest or largest square immediately, that is, an understanding of seriation, but not one that is applied immediately to the problem of "largest" and "smallest."

(iii) It is clear that the marked difference between lines four and five has disappeared, and even possibly been reversed, in the last few columns of the table, although it is difficult to see why such a reversal should occur.

[4] Subgroup III was chosen for this analysis partly because it seemed to be one of the most interesting subgroups, partly because the sorts of operation required to answer questions correctly seemed to be fairly easily recognizable.

[5] This choice of response type is arbitrary, but serves to keep the figures down to a reasonable size. Also, it emphasizes the distinction between correct and incorrect responses, which is probably the most reliable of the possible partitions of the responses.

Table 10

Relations between Stages in Subgroup III

Stages[b]	Items[a]										
	7–8	7–9	7–10	7–11	7–12	7–13	8–9	8–10	8–11	8–12	8–13
C–C	14	10	1	4	13	4	28	2	14	25	8
C–B	5	8	14	5	0	12	17	33	14	1	23
C–A	0	1	5	11	6	1	4	14	20	24	19
B–C	25	60	4	29	65	18	47	3	19	48	15
A–C	0	0	0	0	0	0	2	0	0	2	1
	9–10	9–11	9–12	9–13	10–11	10–12	10–13	11–12	11–13	12–13	
C–C	4	23	55	15	4	4	0	21	11	13	
C–B	51	15	3	34	1	1	2	3	14	33	
C–A	23	37	17	28	2	0	3	5	8	29	
B–C	2	11	11	8	22	41	15	13	2	2	
A–C	0	0	9	2	8	29	8	42	10	7	

[a] The items are: 7, draw smallest box; 8, draw largest box; 9, subdivide line; 10, imaginary end product of subdivision; 11, number of lines in longer line; 12, number of points in a line; 13, subdivide box.

[b] The stages (rows) are interpreted as follows: C–C means that, for the pair of items at the column head (items 7 and 8 in the first column), type C responses were made to both—in this case by 14 children. C–B means that the first of the pair (item 7, in the first column) was answered with a C response, but the record of the pair (item 8, in the first column) with a B response. There were five children in this category, for the first column. The remaining row symbols are interpreted in a similar way.

(iv) The interpretation of the difference between lines four and five for the lefthand columns of the table given is supported to some extent by the frequencies in lines two and three. There are no consistent differences between these two rows, and of course neither one represents any possible "learning" effect. Rather they give an estimate of what might be termed "random" moves between stages.

(v) A rather striking fact emerges when one compares, within a column, the sum of the frequencies of rows two and three with the sum of the frequencies for rows four and five. There is an inverse relationship; a rank order correlation yields a highly significant negative value of $\rho = -.75$. This might be interpreted in the following way: if an item is one which can be solved on the basis of learning within the test situation, there is a low probability that it will be answered wrongly when earlier items have been answered correctly. On the other hand, if the solution is not so learnable, there is a greater chance of the items being answered incorrectly following earlier correct solutions. This is only an interpretation, and it is clear that the evidence is far from conclusive on this point.

(vi) By inspection, the most "learnable" responses are to questions 9, 11, and 12, and the least "learnable" are correct responses to items 10 and 13. It may be noted that these last two are questions to which the child had to answer in terms of what he could *imagine* rather than what he could *do*.

The sorts of relation found among the answers to questions in subgroup III were not common to all subgroups. Similar analyses were undertaken for subgroups I and IV which showed, in the first place, that subgroup I is much more homogeneous than the others, in the sense that the frequency of "both correct" was always higher than for any other response pair. Secondly, for subgroup I the lines corresponding to lines 2–5 of Table 9 showed none of the patterns described above for subgroup III. Subgroup IV, on the other hand, showed the same pattern of negative correlation between lines 2 and 3 on the one hand, and lines 4 and 5 on the other. Inspection of these four lines in Table 11 seems to indicate that while "learnability" is higher in this group than in subgroup III, items 16 and 17 are especially high in this characteristic. Interestingly enough, these two items involve sorting and identifying pictures, whereas the remaining items in the subgroup concern actual manipulation of the jars and their contents.

Thus, some of the points that emerge in the detailed breakdown of the mixed responses appear to be compatible with Piaget's theory, and even

Table 11

Relations between Stages in Subgroup IV

	Items[a]								
Stages	14–15	14–16	14–17	14–18	14–19	14–20	14–21	15–16	15–17
C–C	26	38	43	19	31	25	10	38	37
C–B	18	4	1	16	9	9	33	5	6
C–A	1	1	0	8	4	12	3	1	0
B–C	18	26	31	14	18	18	7	27	38
A–C	0	44	87	9	18	37	20	43	86
	15–18	15–19	15–20	15–21	16–17	16–18	16–19	16–20	16–21
C–C	18	28	25	11	102	41	59	59	29
C–B	15	13	6	32	5	60	44	12	79
C–A	8	1	9	1	1	14	12	38	4
B–C	15	18	20	7	44	7	9	19	10
A–C	8	17	34	27	11	1	4	2	1

	17–18	17–19	17–20	17–21	18–19	18–20	18–21	19–20	19–21	20–21
C–C	36	62	73	35	28	31	10	39	16	19
C–B	89	70	25	120	9	6	30	9	48	58
C–A	33	27	64	6	3	6	3	16	2	2
B–C	6	5	8	2	30	36	16	33	17	6
A–C	0	0	1	0	6	14	11	7	5	12

[a] The items are: 14, predict water level in tilted straight jar; 15, predict water level in tilted round jar; 16, tilt pictures to show correct levels; 17, sort pictures showing levels; 18, draw boat and mast 45°; 19, draw boat and mast 90°; 20, draw plumbline 45°; 21, put posts on mountain.

to some degree tend to confirm it (for example, points (i), (ii), and (iii) above). Others are neutral with respect to the theory.

DISCUSSION

No doubt more elaborate analyses of the relations between single items both in the same and in different subgroups might be attempted, but it appears to me that a sufficiently detailed exposition has been given to show, as has been shown before (for example, Dodwell, 1960, 1962), that the patterns which emerge in this sort of study of cognitive development are complex, and certainly not completely compatible with Piaget's statements about the topic. However, it should also be noted that further examination within mixed categories (as in the latter part of the results section) might reveal further factors which are consonant with the theory.

Since the sorts of behavior which Piaget describes as characteristic for certain ages and stages of development have been observed, and since his theoretical account is a satisfying, coherent one (see, for instance, Hunt, 1961), it seems sensible to look for possible reasons why the pattern of development should be blurred rather than clear, rather than to reject the theory out of hand, especially if one has no better substitute to offer. I have suggested elsewhere (Dodwell, 1960, 1962) that the obvious factors which might tend to disrupt the clear pattern of stages Piaget describes, are things such as special interests and training, amount of formal instruction, and the difficulties of learning to apply a set of rules or operations learned in one context to a new situation. Part of Piaget's theory is that, once an operation or grouping of operations has been acquired, its deployment in novel situations should present few, if any, difficulties: however, this is not a logical requirement of the theory, and it seems entirely reasonable to assume that such response generalization is halting and inadequate at first, but improves with practice. Any school boy who has learned (and understood) Newton's laws, for example, and has subsequently had to apply them to problems in mechanics, would no doubt agree that this can happen. It would certainly be interesting to study more intensively the possibilities of teaching children to apply operations already used correctly in one situation to a second situation in which the operations are not applied spontaneously, and to compare such ability to learn with that of children who do not apply the operations correctly in any situation. If Piaget is close to being correct, rapid learning would be expected in the first instance, virtually no learning in the second.

No attempt was made to validate the test described. No obvious external criterion is available, since geometry is not taught in school to children of the age range under consideration. The content validity of the test seems to be high; however, probably the best way to validate a test of this sort would be through a factorial study, using established measures of spatial aptitude and understanding. Such a study was beyond the scope of the present investigation.

It has been pointed out before, and is worth emphasizing again, that an adequate understanding of the development and attainment of concepts in children will not be reached through the type of rather general investigation here reported. Such investigations should be supplemented by more intensive longitudinal studies which attempt to unravel some of the threads out of which the fabric of intellectual growth is woven.

REFERENCES

Carpenter, T. E. (1955). A pilot study for a quantitative investigation of Jean Piaget's original work on concept formation. *Educ. Rev.*, **7**, 142–149.

Dodwell, P. C. (1960). Children's understanding of number and related concepts. *Canad. J. Psychol.*, **14**, 191–205.

Dodwell, P. C. (1961). Children's understanding of number concepts: characteristics of an individual and of a group test. *Canad. J. Psychol.*, **15**, 29–36.

Dodwell, P. C. (1962). Relations between the understanding of the logic of classes and of cardinal number in children. *Canad. J. Psychol.*, **16**, 152–60.

Gulliksen, Harold (1950). *Theory of mental tests.* New York: Wiley.

Harker, Wilda H. (1960). Children's number concepts: ordination and cardination. Unpublished Master's thesis, Queen's University.

Harman, H. H. (1960). *Modern factor analysis.* Chicago: University of Chicago Press.

Hunt, J. McV. (1961). *Intelligence and experience.* New York: Ronald.

Piaget, J. (1950). *The psychology of intelligence.* London: Routledge.

Piaget, J., and B. Inhelder (1956). *The child's conception of space.* London: Routledge.

GROWTH OF SOME GEOMETRICAL CONCEPTS

K. Lovell ╱ D. Healey ╱ A. D. Rowland

In their book *The Child's Conception of Geometry*, Piaget, Inhelder, and Szeminska (1960) give details of many ingenious experiments which they used to study the growth of the child's understanding of measurement

Reprinted with the permission of the senior author and The Society for Research in Child Development, Inc., from *Child Development*, 1962, **33**, 751–767.

and other concepts of metrical (Euclidean) geometry. This paper describes our findings when 12 of these experiments, sometimes slightly adapted, were given to both Primary and Educationally Subnormal (E.S.N.) Special School Children.[1] All the experiments were undertaken individually by the children in their own schools, and their replies were recorded verbatim. As the length of the paper must be restricted, only the essentials of the study can be given. Details of the exact apparatus used, instructions, precise questions asked, and other data obtained may be obtained from the authors. Furthermore, it must be assumed that access can be made to the book, for the length of the paper would be prohibitive if the experiments were described in any detail. The discussion will comment on some educational implications of the study.

METHOD

Experiments

The experiments carried out are listed below; page numbers indicate where relevant details may be found in *The Child's Conception of Geometry*. In the next section details of each experiment are given.

(1) Reconstructing Relations of Distances.
(2) Conservation of Length. The length of lines and the coincidence of their extremities.
(3) Conservation of Length. Comparison of length and change of position.
(4) Measurement of Length.
(5) Subdividing a Straight Line.
(6) Locating a Point in Two-Dimensional Space.
(7) Angular Measurement. Measuring angles.
(8) Angular Measurement. Measuring triangles.
(9) A Problem of Geometrical Loci. The straight line.
(10) Subtracting Smaller Congruent Areas from Larger Congruent Areas.
(11) The Measurement of Areas. Unit iteration.
(12) Subdivision of Areas and The Concept of Fractions.

A study of the Conservation of Volume has also been made but is published elsewhere (Lovell and Ogilvie, 1961).

Subjects

Experiments 1, 4, 5, 8, 9, and 11 were undertaken by the following: (a) Ten pupils in the 5-year-old age group, and 15 in each of the age groups 6, 7, 8, and 9, making 70 primary school pupils in all. The children within each age group were chosen to represent all levels of ability

---

[1] In England, children between 5 and 11 years of age attend Primary School. Educationally Subnormal Special Schools contain the least able of the school educable English pupils. There are about .8 per cent of the school population in such schools, and their ages range from about 8 to 15 or 16 years.

as far as possible. (b) Ten pupils in each of the age groups 9, 10, 11, 13, and 14 in E.S.N. Special Schools.

Experiments 2, 3, 6, 7, 10, 12 were undertaken by: (c) Seventy primary school children selected exactly as in (a) above but from another school. (d) Ten pupils in each of the age groups 9, 10, 11, 14, and 15 in E.S.N. Special Schools.

General Technique

After the subject had been introduced to the materials, he was asked to perform certain standard tasks and asked certain questions, the general procedure being kept as close to that of the Geneva school as possible. It must be stressed, however, that the experimenter was quite free to vary the procedure by asking supplementary questions if it was thought that these would be helpful in eliciting further information.

Usually Piaget *et al.* give details of three stages of thinking, stages II and III being frequently divided in "A" and "B" levels. They also combine stages I and IIA in the case of some experiments. We kept as close as possible to the criteria for the various stages laid down by the Geneva school in assessing our protocols, but occasionally it was necessary to introduce intermediate stages such as IIA-IIB, IIB-III, etc.

As already stated, the children's replies were recorded verbatim. The protocols were first examined by the two experimenters (D.H. and A.D.R.) and the child's thinking, as reflected in the protocol, assessed as at one or other of the stages. Each protocol was then examined independently by the senior author (K.L.) and the level of thinking again assessed. Our assessments were usually in complete agreement; in the very few cases where there was a difference of opinion a compromise had to be reached. It is not thought that the experimenters' knowledge of the children biased the assessments which they made, since the independent assessor (K.L.) did not have the same detailed knowledge of the pupils.

EXPERIMENTS AND RESULTS

The individual experiments are first briefly described, and the results immediately follow each description. The correlation between chronological age and stage was calculated separately for the Primary and E.S.N. groups using Kendall's tau coefficient. These coefficients are included in the tables of results.

Experiment 1   Reconstructing Relations of Distance

Two plastic "Red Indians," each 3 in. in height, were placed on a table about 20 in. apart. The child was asked if he thought the Indians were "near together" or "far apart." When he had given his reply, the E placed a hardboard screen between the figures and asked the S whether they were still as "near" or as "far apart" depending on his first reply. If the child was of the opinion that the screen altered the distance between the Indians, he was asked to give a reason. The screen was removed and replaced by a piece of wood 2 in. wide and 1 in. high (i.e., lower than the Red Indians). The same question was repeated in this new situation.

Table 1

Experiment 1. Relations of Distance

			Stage			
				IIB		
Age (years)	I	IIA	Type A	Type B	III	Total
Primary Group						
5	9	0	1	0	0	10
6	5	6	4	0	0	15
7	8	2	2	0	3	15
8	4	0	6	1	4	15
9	1	2	7	1	4	15
	tau = .47, significant at the .01 level.					
E.S.N. Group						
9	6	0	1	3	0	10
10	4	0	1	3	2	10
11	7	0	0	2	1	10
13	4	1	3	0	2	10
14	3	0	2	2	3	10
	tau = .31, significant at the .01 level.					

In order to test the symmetrical character of the clear interval between the Red Indians, the child was asked: "Is it as far from there to there (AB), as it is from there to there (BA)?" The E indicated these distances by running his finger along AB and BA. Finally the questions were repeated with the Red Indian at different levels.

Criteria for Stages:
    Stage I. Introduction of screen puts an end to the distance relationship between A and B, since the two parts and the whole distance cannot be coordinated.
    Stage IIA. The width of the screen is not regarded as part of the distance between A and B, and the over-all distance is thought to be less.
    Stage IIB, Type A. Distance and lengths still regarded as heterogeneous, but the symmetrical character of the interval is recognized, i.e., AB = BA.
    Stage IIB, Type B. The over-all distance is conserved but the distance relationships are asymmetrical.

Stage III.   Distance is conserved regardless of intervening objects and the symmetry of the interval is recognized.

Experiment 2   Conservation of Length. The Length of Lines and the Coincidence of Their Extremities

The subject was presented with a straight wooden rod of length 5 cm. and a longer undulating thread of plasticine shaped like a snake. The objects were placed side by side a few millimeters apart, with their endpoints in exact alignment, and the child was asked to compare the lengths of the two objects. If he said that they were equal, he was made to run

Table 2

Experiment 2.   Length of Lines and Coincidence of Their Extremities

	Stage				
Age (years)	*I*	*IIA*	*IIA-IIB*	*IIB*	*Total*
Primary Group					
5	3	3	0	4	10
6	2	4	1	8	15
7	1	4	0	10	15
8	0	4	0	11	15
9	1	4	0	10	15
	tau = .26, significant at the .01 level.				
E.S.N. Group					
9	4	5	0	1	10
10	0	4	0	6	10
11	0	3	2	5	10
14	1	4	1	4	10
15	0	1	3	6	10
	tau = .47, significant at the .01 level.				

his finger along the two lines and the question was repeated. Next, he was shown what happened when the plasticine was straightened, and the question was repeated. Finally, the plasticine was twisted back to its original shape and the original question put again.

Criteria for Stages:
   Stage I.   The length of the line is estimated by its endpoints.
   Stage IIA.   Judgment is modified by movement of fingers. Child reverts to original judgment on static inspection again.
   Stage IIB.   Aware of the intervals which lie between the endpoints.

Experiment 3   Conservation of Length. Comparison of Length and Change of Position

Subjects were given two 5-cm. rods. The latter were placed with their extremities coinciding, and almost all the children agreed that the rods were of the same length. The following procedures then took place: (a) one rod was pushed about half a centimeter ahead of the other, (b) the rods were placed to form the letter T, (c) the rods were placed at an acute angle to one another but touching. On each occasion the subjects were asked if the two rods were still of the same length. The experiment was then repeated using two 10-cm. rods.

Table 3

Experiment 3.   Comparison of Length and Change of Position

	Stage			
Age (years)	*I and IIA*	*IIB*	*III*	*Total*
Primary Group				
5	9	1	0	10
6	11	2	2	15
7	10	1	4	15
8	6	1	8	15
9	3	2	10	15
	tau $= .42$, significant at the .01 level.			
E.S.N. Group				
9	10	0	0	10
10	8	1	1	10
11	8	1	1	10
14	8	1	1	10
15	6	1	3	10
	tau $= .38$, significant at the .01 level.			

Criteria for Stages:
   Stages I and IIA.   The stick that is moved is judged to be longer. The child thinks in terms of the further extremities.
   Stage IIB.   Uncertainty is characteristic of this stage. The child may reply correctly with a pair of sticks in one position but not in another, or with one length of stick.
   Stage III.   The child recognizes that the sticks are, and must be, the same length.

Experiment 4   Measurement of Length

The child was presented with strips of card arranged in various shapes and pasted on to hardboard, the strips being presented in pairs. The pupil was asked to compare these "lines" and say whether they were equal or whether one was longer. When he had made a response, he was provided with short strips of card 3 cm. and 6 cm. long and asked to measure the lines to verify his initial estimate. If he was unable to make use of the cards, the experimenter showed him how to apply the unit card by marking off two or three intervals on the test lines. These intervals were regarded as "steps" which a little man made as he walked along the road. The subject was asked to find out how many steps the man would take if he walked from one end to the other of each of the two lines in the three pairs presented for comparison.

The first pair of lines consisted of an L-shaped line with limbs of 9 cm. and 3 cm. and a line bent at right angles and having limbs each 6 cm. in

Table 4

Experiment 4.   Measurement of Length

| | Stage | | | |
Age (years)	I and IIA	IIB	IIIA	Total
Primary Group				
5	10	0	0	10
6	9	4	2	15
7	4	5	6	15
8	0	6	9	15
9	0	3	12	15
	tau = .55, significant at the .01 level.			
E.S.N. Group				
9	8	2	0	10
10	5	4	1	10
11	5	4	1	10
13	4	3	3	10
14	8	2	0	10
	tau = .29, significant at the .01 level.			

length. The second pair consisted of a line bent to form an obtuse angle and one bent to form an acute angle. The arms of the former were 15 cm. and 9 cm., and of the second 21 cm. and 3 cm. For the third pair there was a V-shaped line with the two limbs each 18 cm. long and a line bent to form an obtuse angle, the arms being 24 cm. and 12 cm. long.

Criteria for Stages:
Stages I and IIA. The construction of a unit of measurement is impossible. Subdivision is sometimes used without change of position, or change of position at the expense of subdivision.
Stage IIB. The transitivity of relations beginning to be understood.
Stage III. Subdivision is generalized. Subjects can measure the lines with the 3 cm. and 6 cm. cards and express the latter length in terms of the former.

Experiment 5   Subdividing a Straight Line

Two wires, A_1C_1 and A_2C_2, which are equal in length were placed parallel to one another with their ends in alignment. The child was told that a bead on the wire was a train traveling along a railway line. The experimenter moved his bead from A_1 to B_1, and the child was asked to move his bead to do a journey of the same length. Subjects were provided with a ruler, string, strips of card of varying length which they were invited, but not shown how, to use.

Table 5

Experiment 5.   Subdividing a Straight Line

	Stage				
Age (years)	*I and IIA*	*IIB*	*IIIA*	*IIIB*	*Total*
Primary Group					
5	7	3	0	0	10
6	6	9	0	0	15
7	5	8	0	2	15
8	1	11	2	1	15
9	3	8	0	4	15
	tau $= .39$, significant at the .01 level.				
E.S.N. Group					
9	8	2	0	0	10
10	6	4	0	0	10
11	2	7	1	0	10
13	4	4	0	2	10
14	8	2	0	0	10
	tau $= .21$, significant at the .01 level.				

The experimenter commenced by moving his bead from A_1, the child being invited to move his bead from A_2 so that the segment A_1B_1 equaled the segment A_2B_2. This procedure was repeated with the subject having to move his bead from the other end C_2 so that $A_1B_1 = C_2B_2$.

A_2 was next moved 4 in. to the left of A_1, so that C_2 was 4 in. to the left of C_1. The subject was again asked to move his bead to B_2 on A_2C_2, starting from C_2, and making $C_2B_2 = A_1B_1$. Keeping A_2C_2 in the same position relative to A_1B_1, the experimenter then moved his bead 15 in. from A_1—a distance longer than any of the measuring instruments provided. The child was again asked to locate B_2 so that $A_1B_1 = C_2B_2$.

Finally the wire A_2B_2 was replaced by a wire A_3C_3 which was shorter than A_1B_1. The wires were still parallel but A_3B_3 was displaced 4 in. to the right of A_1C_1. The experimenter moved his bead 6 in. from A_1 and the subject was asked to move his bead 6 in. from C_3.

Criteria for Stages:

Stages I and IIA. Length of travel determined solely by point of arrival so the problem is solved only when the points of departure are in alignment.

Stage IIB. A given length can be reproduced with reasonable accuracy by visual estimate.

Stage IIIA. Measurement is possible if the measuring rod provided is equal to, or longer, than the distance to be measured. If the distance is longer, two or more measuring rods are placed in prolongation.

Stage IIIB. Subjects apply a short ruler by iterate stepwise movements, thus reducing the total distance to multiples of the unit length.

Table 6

Experiment 6.   Locating a Point

Age (years)	Stage						Total
	I	*I-IIA*	*IIA*	*IIB*	*IIIA*	*IIIB*	
Primary Group							
5	7	2	1	0	0	0	10
6	6	4	3	1	1	0	15
7	3	4	6	2	0	0	15
8	2	0	3	2	3	5	15
9	1	0	1	4	8	1	15
tau = .57, significant at the .01 level.							
E.S.N. Group							
9	5	2	3	0	0	0	10
10	5	1	2	0	1	1	10
11	2	0	3	3	1	1	10
14	1	0	6	2	1	0	10
15	1	0	5	1	3	0	10
tau = .64, significant at the .01 level.							

Experiment 6   Locating a Point in Two-Dimensional Space

Children were each given two rectangular sheets of plain white paper, identical in size. The first (S_1) was placed on the top right-hand corner of a piece of hardboard, the second (S_2) at the bottom left-hand corner.

Sheet S_1 contained a red dot (P_1) about half way between the center of the sheet and its upper right-hand corner. The E asked the subject to draw in a dot (P_2) on the other sheet (S_2) in exactly the same position as the dot (P_1) on the first sheet (S_1), so that if the two sheets were superimposed P_2 would fall over P_1. As the paper was semitransparent, the coincidence of the dots could be confirmed by putting one sheet over the other. A ruler, strips of cardboard, and lengths of thread were provided. It was suggested to the child, if necessary, that he use these, but he was not shown how to do so.

Criteria for Stages:
   Stages I and IIA.   Visual estimation only.
   Stage IIB.   Subject begins to use tools to measure. But measurement in one direction only.
   Stage IIIA.   Two dimensions are considered; the subject tries to coordinate them by trial and error.
   Stage IIIB.   Two measurements are made and coordinated at once.

Experiment 7   Angular Measurement. Measurement of Angles

The procedure consisted of placing a drawing of two supplementary angles, ADC and CDB, on a table behind the subject and asking him to reproduce the drawing on a sheet of white paper. It was made clear to the child that his drawing must be an exact copy of the one supplied as a model. He was provided with a ruler, compass, string, and strips of card

Table 7

Experiment 7.   Measuring Angles

Age (years)	Stage					Total
	I and IIA	IIB	IIB-IIIA	IIIA	IIIB	
Primary Group						
5	10	0	0	0	0	10
6	9	1	1	4	0	15
7	5	2	1	7	0	15
8	0	5	0	7	3	15
9	1	2	2	5	5	15
tau = .55, significant at the .01 level.						
E.S.N. Group						
9	8	2	0	0	0	10
10	2	8	0	0	0	10
11	1	5	1	3	0	10
14	3	5	0	2	0	10
15	2	2	0	5	1	10
tau = .58, significant at the .01 level.						

which he was invited, but not shown how, to use. Although he was not allowed to move the model or to draw while looking at it, he was permitted to study and measure it as often as he wished and to make construction lines on the model if he desired.

Criteria for Stages:
   Stages I and IIA. Visual judgment only, no attempt at measurement whatever.
   Stage IIB. AB or DC or both measured. Slope of line estimated visually.
   Stage IIIA. AD, DB measured separately; AB measured, DC measured. Subject tries to maintain the correct slope of the the line DC using ruler, finger, pencil, etc.
   Stage IIIB. AD measured. AC and CB measured to fix point C thereby ensuring the correct slope of CD. A number of subjects at this stage and nearly all at the beginning of stage IV measure the perpendicular distance from C on to AB.

Experiment 8 Angular Measurement. Measuring Triangles

The procedure of experiment 7 was repeated using the drawing of an obtuse angled triangle instead of the drawing of the angles.

Table 8

Experiment 8. Measurement of Triangles

	Stage				
Age (years)	*I and IIA*	*IIB*	*IIIA*	*IIIB*	*Total*
Primary Group					
5	9	1	0	0	10
6	13	2	0	0	15
7	8	7	0	0	15
8	4	6	4	1	15
9	0	14	0	1	15
	tau $= .51$, significant at the .01 level.				
E.S.N. Group					
9	9	1	0	0	10
10	6	4	0	0	10
11	4	6	0	0	10
13	5	5	0	0	10
14	7	3	0	0	10
	tau $= .26$, significant at the .01 level.				

Criteria for Stages:
   Stage I. Subject fails to draw a three-sided figure of any description.
   Stage IIA. Three-sided figure produced but subject relies exclusively on perception.

Stage IIB. The three sides of the model measured. These reproduced without taking into account the angular separation.

Stage IIIA. An attempt is made to take slope into consideration, either by maintaining a ruler at a constant slope while transferring it from ruler to copy or coordinating the three sides by trial and error.

Stage IIIB. The height of the triangle is measured as well as the three sides; at stage IV lines are constructed outside the figure.

Experiment 9 A Problem of Geometrical Loci. The Straight Line

The *E* and *S* sat opposite one another at a rectangular shaped table. The child was given a number of beads, and he was requested to place them so that each bead was equidistant from himself and the *E*. In the second part of the enquiry he is asked to find points equidistant from two pennies.

Table 9

Experiment 9. Geometrical Loci—The Straight Line

	Stage					
Age (years)	*I*	*IIA*	*IIB*	*IIB-III*	*III*	*Total*
Primary Group						
5	4	5	1	0	0	10
6	4	4	6	0	1	15
7	1	5	4	1	4	15
8	1	5	3	0	6	15
9	2	2	3	2	6	15
tau = .42, significant at the .01 level.						
E.S.N. Group						
9	3	4	3	0	0	10
10	3	7	0	0	0	10
11	1	5	3	1	0	10
13	1	8	1	0	0	10
14	5	5	0	0	0	10
tau = .02, not significant.						

Criteria for Stages:

Stage I. Subjects lack an intellectual notion of distance and make a random placement.

Stage IIA. The point of equidistance situated at the midpoint is found, but it is not possible for other points to be established which satisfy the condition of equidistance.

Stage IIB. Beginnings of generalization in relation to symmetry (beads on both sides of midpoint); continuity (interpolation of beads in the interval between equidistant beads); infinity (progressive iterations).

Stage III. Locus is seen to be continuous in both directions and extending to infinity.

Experiment 10   Subtracting Smaller Congruent Areas from Larger Congruent Areas

The child was shown two identical sheets of cardboard painted green, each 20 cm. by 30 cm. These represented fields. He was asked to compare the fields and agree that there was the same amount of grass on each. Following this, he was shown a toy cow and asked if it had the same amount of grass to eat in each of the fields. Small cube (counting) beads were then placed on the fields to represent houses. In one field the beads were placed end on like houses in a road, while in the other field the beads were spread about in disarray. To begin with, one bead was placed in each field, then two, three, etc. After each increase in the number of beads the child was asked to compare the amounts of grass left in each field for the cow to eat.

Table 10

Experiment 10.   Subtracting Smaller Congruent Areas from Larger Congruent Areas

| | Stage | | | | | |
Age (years)	*I*	*I-IIA*	*IIA*	*IIB*	*III*	*Total*
Primary Group						
5	2	1	2	0	5	10
6	1	1	0	3	10	15
7	2	0	3	0	10	15
8	1	0	2	2	10	15
9	0	0	0	1	14	15
tau = .29, significant at the .01 level.						
E.S.N. Group						
9	3	4	3	0	0	10
10	0	3	4	0	3	10
11	2	3	4	0	1	10
14	2	1	3	2	2	10
15	1	1	6	1	1	10
tau = .38, significant at the .01 level.						

Criteria for Stages:
   Stage I.   Difficult to pursue enquiry.
   Stage IIA.   Equality recognized only when one house in each field.
   Stage IIB.   Equality of remaining areas recognized up to a certain number of houses (varying with the child).
   Stage IIIA.   Conservation of area. Responses show operational thinking.

Experiment 11   The Measurement of Areas. Unit Iteration

Subjects were given (a) shapes made up of a number of squares and a separate unit square; (b) shapes made up of squares and adjoining triangles, and both a separate unit square and a separate unit triangle such that the latter was formed by cutting a unit square along a diagonal. In (b) there was also the problem of converting the number of unit squares into unit triangles, as the areas of the complete shapes could only be expressed as whole numbers in terms of the unit triangles.

Table 11

Experiment 11.   Measurement of Areas—Unit Iteration

	Stage					
Age (years)	*I*	*IIA*	*IIB*	*IIIA*	*IIIB*	*Total*
Primary Group						
5	4	5	1	0	0	10
6	4	7	4	0	0	15
7	3	6	3	1	2	15
8	0	4	8	0	3	15
9	0	4	7	2	2	15
	tau = .47, significant at the .01 level.					
E.S.N. Group						
9	2	6	2	0	0	10
10	1	7	2	0	0	10
11	2	6	2	0	0	10
13	1	5	4	0	0	10
14	1	4	5	0	0	10
	tau = .36, significant at the .01 level.					

Criteria for Stages:

Stage IIA.   Subjects make judgments of size by reference to the perceptual appearance of the figure even when they have counted the number of squares in each and satisfied themselves as to their numerical identity.

Stage IIB.   The figures in (a) are correctly equated, but there is no decomposition of the figures in (b) in terms of homogeneous units (squares and triangles regarded as equivalent units).

Stage IIIA.   Figures in (b) compared by making compensatory transformations, i.e., parts of the figures can be transferred to vacant sites so that a comparison can be expected.

Stage IIIB.   The figures of (b) are measured by unit iteration. The area of the unit square can be expressed in terms of the area of the unit triangle and vice versa.

Experiment 12   Subdivision of Areas and the Concept of Fractions

Each subject was shown a circular slab of plasticine about 2 in. in diameter and told that it represented a cake. His first task was to cut the "cake" into two pieces so that he and the experimenter each had the same amount to eat. Next he was asked to cut a similar circular slab of plasticine into three equal parts. On both occasions he was questioned as to whether the sum of the pieces equaled the whole.

In the second part of the enquiry the child was given a circle, square, and rectangle cut in paper. He was asked to divide each into three equal parts first by drawing lines with a pencil and then by cutting with scissors.

Table 12

Experiment 12.   Subdivision of Areas and the Concept of Fractions

Age (years)	Stage						Total
	I	*I-IIA*	*IIA*	*IIB*	*IIB-IIIA*	*IIIA*	
Primary Group							
5	1	1	8	0	0	0	10
6	2	0	12	1	0	0	15
7	0	0	6	5	2	2	15
8	0	0	2	9	2	2	15
9	0	0	2	4	1	8	15
	tau = .59, significant at the .01 level.						
E.S.N. Group							
9	2	3	5	0	0	0	10
10	3	1	6	0	0	0	10
11	1	1	6	2	0	0	10
14	1	0	8	1	0	0	10
15	0	1	8	1	0	0	10
	tau = .44, significant at the .01 level.						

Criteria for Stages:
    Stage I.   Plasticine divided into little pieces without using up the whole, or the whole divided into unequal pieces.
    Stage IIA.   Divides into halves, usally divides into four by a double dichotomy. Frequently conserves amounts but no proper reasoning. Trisection not possible.
    Stage IIB.   May trisect square and rectangle; trisection of circle not solved without trial and error. The whole conserved intuitively.
    Stage IIIA.   Trisection at once. The whole conserved operationally.

DISCUSSION

The main stages in the growth of certain geometrical concepts proposed by Piaget, Inhelder, and Szeminska have been broadly confirmed among English school children. The protocols could be classified into the stages enumerated by the Geneva school providing a few intermediate stages were occasionally introduced. However, the number of children at the various stages were not always what one would expect from the book. In the present study it seems likely that there were more primary school children in each age group than in the Geneva work and that they were more representative of children generally. It is not known how many Geneva children undertook the various experiments; rarely is it stated, as on page 106, that 59 children aged 4 to 9 years were used in the experiments involving the Conservation and Measurement of Length. In the present work an attempt was made to get representative samples of English primary school children so as to obtain some idea of the likely performance of these or of representative samples of American elementary school children. Moreover, the present work has been extended to include E.S.N. Special School pupils.

The tau values yield a mean correlation coefficient between CA and stage of .46 in the primary school children and .36 in the E.S.N. school pupils. Experiments 2 and 10 are relatively easy for the former, and experiment 9 is hard for the latter group. In retrospect it appears that the 14-year-olds in the E.S.N. group which undertook experiments 1, 4, 5, 8, 9, and 11 were less able than the 13-year-old group. This fact almost certainly accounts for the tendency displayed in the results of experiments 4, 5, and 9 for there to be a curvilinear relation between age and stage. A third point of interest is the small number of 8-year-old children at stage IIB in experiment 3. It is now a well recognized feature of the Piaget-type experiments that some children do not appear to pass through intermediate stages but proceed from stage I to stage III direct. Thus, Mannix (1960) found that, in tests involving number concepts, not all children showed second stage responses very similar to those reported by Piaget.

While E.S.N. children tend to go through the same earlier stages as ordinary primary school pupils, the over-all performance of the 14- to 15-year-olds is about the same as that of an average 7- or 7- to 8-year-old primary school child. This parallels the findings of Lovell and Slater (1960) in the growth of the concept of time in Primary and E.S.N. Special School children. The results of a number of experiments from Piaget and Inhelder's book *La genèse des structures logiques élémentaires* carried out at Leeds University (Lovell, Mitchell, and Everett, 1962) also confirm the low level of operational mobility (to use a Piagetian term) attained at 15 by the least able school educable children. In other words, few of the least able school educable children reach Piaget's stage of concrete operational thinking.

The Child's Conception of Geometry has very important implications for the teacher. It shows how in the field of geometrical concepts, as in many other fields, children may acquire a certain verbal facade, or they may perform some action by rote since they have been "taught," without having the operational mobility to understand what they are doing. It is impossible in this paper to develop this in relation to each experiment; just two experiments will be considered which bear directly on the measurement of straight lines.

In experiment 4 one finds, at stages I and IIA, the child either changes the position of the unit-measure without adequate subdivision of the line, or the line to be measured is subdivided but the unit-measure is not applied correctly. Stage IIB is marked by the beginnings of an operational synthesis (i.e., a synthesis carried out in the mind) of subdivision and relations of order and change of position. The child can now break up the line into successive segments and move the card in a definite order, using reference marks that are fairly accurate. The initial demonstration by the E seems to help the S to achieve a measure of coordination and to understand how to use the common measure. But this "learned" understanding does not immediately lead to subdivision in terms of homogeneous units. Ss count the segments without caring if they are all of the same size. At stage III, however, pupils compare unit lengths and discover that the small card (3 cm. long) is half the 6 cm. unit-card, so that the length of the line can be correctly expressed as multiples of the 3 cm. or 6 cm. lengths. The present evidence suggests that one third of 7-year-olds, one half of 8-year-olds, and about three quarters of 9-year-olds are at stage III.

In experiment 4 subdivision is suggested to the S by the initial demonstration of the E, so that the choice of a unit is imposed. To complete the investigation of the growth of metric operations, experiment 5 reverses the technique. Children are asked to locate a particular segment on a straight line and a variety of measuring instruments are available to them, this approach standing midway between spontaneous measurement and deliberate suggestion as in experiment 4.

Given two straight lines, A_1C_1 and A_2C_2, the ends of which may or may not be in alignment, the subject is asked to find a point B_2 on A_2C_2 to correspond with a point B_1 on A_1C_1, such that the segment A_2B_2 equals segment A_1B_1. The subject is free to use a ruler, a stick, strips of manila cardboard, pieces of string of varying lengths, and a pencil.

The key feature of the responses at stages I and IIA is that children fail to conceive of the length of a "journey" as an interval between the point of arrival and point of departure, but think of it only in terms of the former. Thus B_2 is placed opposite B_1 regardless of whether A_2 is opposite A_1. During substage IIB Ss solve the problem intuitively and fail in accurate measurement, except when this is achieved by trial and error. Ss rely on a visual estimate to place B_2 and see no need to measure unless they are instructed to do so. Measurement for them is merely a check. At stage III, however, children make a visual estimate only if the problem is too easy; otherwise they always measure A_1B_1 before measuring A_2B_2. But two substages are observed. At substage IIIA pupils achieve only a qualitative transitivity in their use of a common measure. When the stick or ruler is equal to the distance required or longer, the child can perform the measurement; when the stick or ruler is shorter, he simply prolongs it by using supplementary lengths. At stage IIIB, however, the newly acquired concept of a unit enables him to apply an iterative stepwise movement to a short ruler. Thus true measurement of length begins when the child recognizes that any length may be decomposed into a series of intervals which are known to be equal because one of them may be applied to the others in turn.

The figures given in Tables 4 and 5 suggest that many children in primary schools are successfully measuring length without fully understanding the nature of the actions they are engaging in. It is not, of course, suggested that measurement be postponed until it can be fully understood. Rather, the experiences the child undergoes help to build up *schemas* out of which arises later understanding. The important thing for the teacher is to know to what extent a child is performing a given operation with understanding and to what extent he is performing in rote fashion. These tables also show the very poor operational mobility of the older E.S.N. children many of whom can use a ruler successfully for measurement since they have been "taught" how to do so. We are in no sense objecting to this; indeed, it is necessary for the teacher to get these children to acquire whatever skills he can, for the latter greatly help the personal and social competence of such pupils.

REFERENCES

Lovell, K., B. Mitchell, and I. R. Everett (1962). An experimental study of the growth of some logical structures. *Brit. J. Psychol.*, **53**, 175–188.

Lovell, K., and E. Ogilvie (1961). The growth of the concept of volume in junior school children. *J. child Psychol. Psychiat.*, **2**, 118–226.

Lovell, K., and A. Slater (1960). The growth of the concept of time: a comparative study. *J. child Psychol. Psychiat.*, **1**, 179–190.

Mannix, J. B. (1960). The number concepts of a group of E.S.N. children. *Brit. J. educ. Psychol.*, **30**, 180–181.

Piaget, J., B. Inhelder, and A. Szeminska (1960). *The child's conception of geometry*. London: Routledge.

DEVELOPMENT OF DISTANCE CONSERVATION AND THE SPATIAL COORDINATE SYSTEM

Carolyn Uhlinger Shantz/Charles D. Smock

Piaget and Inhelder (1956) and Piaget, Inhelder, and Szeminska (1960) postulated a sequential development of the child's representation of space, culminating in the acquisition of a Euclidean structuring of space. The coordinates of Euclidean space may be described as a grid of lines crossing each other perpendicularly in three dimensions. The presence of such a conceptual coordinate system is attested to when horizontality and verticality become independent of the perceptual properties of objects and immediate surround. Thus, the presence of the horizontal concept is demonstrated when the child is able to refer the water level in a tilted bottle to the table level, rather than to any particular property of the bottle. Likewise, if the child has acquired the concept of verticality, figures on a mountain, for example, are related to ground level rather than to the mountainside.

It is Piaget and Inhelder's (1956) contention that the conservation of distance is a prerequisite for the development of the coordinate system. There are two cognitive operations involved in distance conservation: (*a*) distance must remain constant whether the space between two points is filled or empty, and (*b*) distance must remain identical between two points regardless of the direction of travel ($AB = BA$). The developmental priority of distance conservation to the coordinate system has received empirical support, according to Piaget, in terms of the general age of emergence of distance conservation at approximately 7 years of age compared to emergence of the coordinate system at 9 years of age. However, Piaget notes that the use of a coordinate system appeared in his subjects from 6½ to 12 years of age, and equally large age ranges have been found by independent studies (Dodwell, 1963; Smedslund, 1963). The overlap in ages of emergence of distance conservation and the coordinate system does not provide a clear test for determining whether these two concepts emerge simultaneously or sequentially, particularly in the sequence hypothesized by Piaget. A more direct test of the hypothesis would be provided by testing both concepts in the same children. The purpose of the present study is to test Piaget's hypothesis that every child using the coordinate system also conserves distance, and every child who is unable to conserve distance is unable to demonstrate the coordinate system concept.

Reprinted with the permission of the authors and The Society for Research in Child Development, Inc., from *Child Development*, 1966, 37, (4), 943–948. The authors wish to express their appreciation to Dr. Walter Emmerich for his assistance in the formulation of this study.

Studies by Dodwell (1963) and Rivoire (1961) suggest that the variability in age of emergence of the coordinate system may be due in part to the way in which the task is presented. Specifically, there appeared to be a differential performance associated with the use of objects or pictures as stimuli. Since the number of spatial dimensions of stimuli appears to be particularly germane to the study of space concepts, and there are indications of its effects, the second purpose of this study is to determine the comparability of data relevant to two spatial concepts derived from two-dimensional (drawings) and three-dimensional stimuli (objects).

METHOD

Subjects

Ten boys and ten girls from one first-grade class in a rural elementary school were subjects (*Ss*). Their ages ranged from 6 years, 4 months to 7 years, 10 months with a mean of 6 years, 9 months.

Experimental Measures

DISTANCE CONSERVATION   Five items were designed to determine whether *S* conserved distance (*a*) if the distance were filled or empty (*FE*), and, with five additional items, (*b*) if the direction of movement were changed (*DM*). To assess *FE* distance conservation with objects, for example, two 2½-inch trees were placed before *S* 8 inches apart, and *S* was asked whether the trees were "far apart" or "near together." A board higher than the trees was placed halfway between them and *S* was asked, "And now, are they far apart (or near together)?" A child who conserves distance will assert that distance remains the same whether the space is filled or empty; nonconservers make a variety of responses, the most common being that the distance is less because the board "uses up" some of the space between the trees. Four additional *FE* tests varied the type of figures (pigs or trees) and height of the interposed object (higher or lower than figures). Table 2 presents the exact combinations used in this and all other tests. The variations were designed to provide a more stringent test of conservation. For example, Piaget et al. (1960) found that some children conserve only if the barrier is lower than the figures.

The same basic *FE* task was presented in five drawings, but with a matching-to-standard method. A standard picture showed two trees 6 inches apart with no object between them. The *S* designated his preference for calling that distance "far apart" or "near together." The *E* presented three comparison pictures of the same figures at varying distances and said, "Now here are some trees—some have fences between them and some don't. Now find two trees that are just as far apart (or near together) as these [referring to the standard]." In the remaining four items, the same variations in figures and screen height were used as with objects; in some cases, the standard had a fence between the figures and the correct match did not, or vice versa.

Distance conservation with *DM* was determined with objects by asking *S* to indicate whether or not it is "just as far from here to here [left tree to right tree] as from here to here [right tree to left tree]." As this was said, *E* moved her finger at equal rates in each direction. A child who has the concept of conservation will assert the symmetrical character of distance regardless of travel direction; the child who does not will assert it is "further" in one direction. The four remaining tests varied the figures, height of figures, or one figure was raised 3 inches off the table.

The five *DM* tests with drawings were the same as with objects except for slight variations in the size of the drawn figures, and the method of inquiry was the same.

COORDINATE SYSTEM   Five tests were constructed to assess each of the concepts of horizontality (*H*) and verticality (*V*). The former concept task with objects consisted of presenting an upright bottle one-quarter filled with dark liquid. The *S* indicated with his finger on an identical, but empty bottle, what would happen to the water level when the empty bottle was upside down. (At no time did *S* have an opportunity to observe the filled bottle change in orientation.) If *S* has acquired the horizontal concept, the water level is related to an external level, such as the table; if not, *S* may respond in many ways, such as relating the water level to a particular side of the bottle. Four additional items varied the orientation and shape of container.

With drawings, *E* presented a drawing of a quarter-filled bottle the same size as the actual bottle; *S* drew on "empty" drawings the water level he expected at orientations similar to those used with objects.

Verticality was tested by presenting a clay-covered styrofoam pyramid ("mountain") with a 60° slope on which figures with pins in their base were to be placed "nice and straight" by *S* at five sites verbally designated by *E*. If *S* has acquired the vertical concept, objects are placed on the mountain in reference to external axes, such as vertical to the table or parallel to the walls; if not, he relates objects to the most proximal perceptual configuration, that is, perpendicular to the slope of the mountain.

A drawing of the mountain with a 60° slope was presented for each *S* to draw freehand figures at similar sites under the same directions as with objects. The *H* and *V* responses with drawings and objects which deviated 10° or less from the correct axis were considered correct.

Procedure

Half the *S*s were administered the tasks with objects and then drawings, and half had the reverse order. Within either sequence, half of those

*S*s had distance conservation tests first and coordinate tests second, or the reverse order. The *S*s were randomly assigned to each of the four orders of testing. In all cases, the five tests of each concept (*FE, DM, H, V*) were administered sequentially in the order listed in Table 2. At no time was the adequacy of *S*'s response indicated by *E*.

RESULTS AND DISCUSSION

The first hypothesis concerned the developmental priority of distance conservation, that is, every child using the coordinate system would also achieve conservation of distance, but failure to conserve would preclude success on the coordinate tasks. The criterion of successful performance was passing four or five of the five items of each concept. Contingency table distributions of *S*s are presented in Table 1. Since such a distribution provides a direct test of the hypothesis, χ^2 analyses were not done.

Table 1

Distribution of Subjects on Two Spatial Concepts Assessed with Drawings and Objects

Distance Conservation Concept	Drawings (Coordinate Concept)		Objects (Coordinate Concept)	
	Pass	Fail	Pass	Fail
Pass	5	8	4	7
Fail	0	7	1	8

The task using drawings yielded five *S*s who used both concepts and seven who used neither. No child used the coordinate concept who did not show distance conservation. The eight *S*s who evidenced conservation but not the coordinate concept constitute the most relevant supporting evidence for the hypothesis of priority of distance conservation. The same trends were found using objects with the exception of one *S* whose performance may be interpreted as a refutation of the hypothesis or a case of measurement error. The assessment of both concepts in a larger number of *S*s would be required to clarify which of the interpretations is more tenable.[1]

An item analysis of the percentage of correct responses is given in Table 2. There is evidence that *S*s found distance conservation easier with

[1] An analysis of variance indicated significantly more correct answers on conservation items than on coordinate items ($p < .01$), which is also consistent with the hypothesis. There was no significant difference between sexes on the total number of correct responses.

Table 2

Percentage of Subjects Passing Each Item

Concepts and Items	Drawings	Objects
Distance conservation		
Filled vs. empty space:		
Trees with high screen	95	75
Trees with two low cubes	100	75
Trees with low screen	95	80
Pigs with high screen	100	70
Pigs with one low cube	95	80
Direction of movement change:		
Equal height trees	90	85
Unequal height trees	80	80
One raised tree	65	65
Pigs on level	80	90
One raised pig	85	75
Coordinate system		
Horizontal:		
Bottle upside down	100	95
Bottle tilted 45° left	35	60
Bottle on side	75	80
Box tilted 45° right	30	35
Box on side	80	85
Vertical:		
Tree on right side	45	40
Doll on left side	35	25
Flag at summit	100	95
Doll on level ground	100	100
Tree on left side	45	50

drawings than objects. The major difficulty in applying the coordinate concept appears when the child is confronted with the *tilted* line both in drawings and objects.

The second aspect of the study concerned a comparison of drawings and objects as stimuli. The difference between stimuli in an analysis of variance of correct responses was not highly significant ($p < .12$). This trend toward a greater number of correct responses with drawings than objects was sufficiently strong, however, to warrant further analysis. Of 20 *S*s, 19 passed the *FE* conservation task with drawings, while only 14 passed with the same items administered with objects. There are three factors which may have facilitated *FE* conservation with drawings. The drawings may have provided more cues for correct response, for example, the additional structure provided by the borders of the card. Several children were observed comparing the distance of trees from the edge of the card rather than distance between the trees. Second, the potential "movability" of tree-objects versus tree-drawings may have hindered identity of distance with or without barriers. And third, the matching-to-standard method with drawings may have assisted in recognition of identity. There is no theoretical or empirical reason (Piaget et al., 1960) to suspect that filled versus empty space conservation is an easier concept to acquire than conservation with change in direction of movement. Indeed, with objects, *FE* and *DM* conservation were passed by exactly the same number of Ss. A significant stimuli x concept interaction ($p < .05$) appeared to be primarily a function of the frequency of success with *FE* tasks with drawings.

The impact of the type of stimuli was further evident as an order effect: Ss who had objects first and drawings second performed better than those under the reverse order of stimuli ($p < .10$). This finding not only indicates the importance of evaluating such order effects in repeated measurement designs but suggests that training of spatial concepts may be most effective with manipulation of objects preceding two-dimensional presentation of tasks.

In summary, the data are consistent in general with the hypothesis of the developmental priority of distance conservation to the coordinate system. A longitudinal analysis of the development of these concepts is a necessary next step in the investigation of the ontogeny of spatial representation.

REFERENCES

Dodwell, P. C. (1963). Children's understanding of spatial concepts. *Canad. J. Psychol.*, 17, 141–161.

Piaget, J., and B. Inhelder (1956). *The child's conception of space.* London: Routledge.

Piaget, J., B. Inhelder, and A. Szeminska (1960). *The child's conception of geometry.* New York: Basic Books.

Rivoire, J. L. (1961). The development of reference systems in children. Unpublished doctoral dissertation, University of Arizona.

Smedslund, J. (1963). The effect of observation on children's representation of the spatial orientation of a water surface. *J. genet. Psychol.*, 102, 195–201.

THE ONTOGENY OF CERTAIN
LOGICAL OPERATIONS: PIAGET'S FORMULATION
EXAMINED BY NONVERBAL METHODS
Martin D. S. Braine

The experiments reported are concerned with the work of Piaget on the development of intelligence in children. Piaget's theory has two aspects. First, it is a theory of intelligence: Piaget believes that the development of intelligence consists in the development of an ability to perform logical operations. Second, Piaget makes specific statements about the ages at which certain types of reasoning develop. He claims that as children grow older certain specified groups of logical operations develop in the average child at given ages. In his studies the principal ages of transition are reported to be at 7 and 11 yr., approximately. At around age 7, the operations of the spatial and class interpretations of the Boolean calculus make their appearance in children's thinking; at around age 11, the operations of the propositional interpretation appear.[1] The appearance of the opera-

[1] For the calculus and its various interpretations, see, for example, Langer (1953). Piaget's logical system differs from the Boolean calculus, but the differences can be neglected for the purposes of this study. The interested reader may refer to his treatise on logic (Piaget, 1949).

The operations of the Boolean calculus are called *conjunction* and *disjunction*. A conjunction of classes is denoted in the English language by the qualification of a noun by an adjective, as, for instance, "white sheep" (i.e., objects that are *both* white, *and also* sheep). A disjunction of classes is often expressed by the words *and* and *or*, as, for instance, "men *and* women," "barren mountains, *or* fertile valleys."

A spatial conjunction is expressed in the two following examples: "The United Nations building is located at 42nd Street *and* the East River Drive," "a straight line is the region *common to* two intersecting planes." Spatial disjunction indicates partition or composition, e.g., "Canada *and* the United States make up North America."

Abridged from Braine, M. D. S. "The Ontogeny of Certain Logical Operations: Piaget's Formulation Examined by Nonverbal Methods"; *Psychological Monographs; General and Applied*; 1959, Whole No. 475. Copyright 1959 by the American Psychological Association and reproduced by permission of the publisher and the author. This study is based upon a doctoral dissertation submitted to the Department of Psychology, New York University Graduate School of Arts and Science. The writer wishes to express his thanks to Elsa Robinson who sponsored the research, and to H. L. Teuber for his invaluable suggestions and criticisms. The writer is also indebted to Marjorie Cornell and Elsie Stange for making available the subjects and the facilities of their nursery schools. The work was partially supported by the Commonwealth Fund of New York through their grant to H. L. Teuber and the Psychophysiological Laboratory, New York University-Bellevue Medical Center.

tions of the spatial interpretation are revealed in Piaget's studies by changes at around age 7 yr. in the child's manner of using measuring instruments and in his performance on a number of tasks supposedly demanding conception of, or reasoning about, spatial relations (Piaget and Inhelder, 1956; Piaget, Inhelder, and Szeminska, 1948). The operations of the class interpretation are revealed by the development of number concepts and by the disappearance of certain anomalies in the child's class concepts (Piaget and Szeminska, 1952). The appearance of propositional operations at age 11 is attested, according to Piaget, by the child's performance on a variety of reasoning tasks (Piaget, 1955; Piaget and Inhelder, 1953).

The notion that the nature of intelligence lies in the performance of logical operations is not new in psychology. It is clearly implicit in Spearman's (1923) identification of intelligence with "eduction of relations" and "eduction of correlates."[2] Moore (1929) seems to have had a similar view. Attempts to find logical models for schizophrenic thinking (Arieti, 1948; Von Domarus, 1944) also implicitly make the assumption that the only proper model for "normal" reasoning was described by Aristotle.

Piaget's theory differs from those of previous investigators, first, in that it aims to give a description of the *development* of intelligence, and second, in that his logical model for reasoning is worked out in great detail and is derived from modern symbolic logic (Piaget, 1949). Piaget attempts to support his theory with a good deal of evidence, although the validity of some of it has been questioned (Fraisse and Vautrey: 1952a, 1952b).

Testing Piaget's theory in detail will obviously prove a monumental task, not only because of its tremendous scope, but also because some of his concepts do not have a sufficiently firm basis in experimental operations. The investigation reported here is intended as an attempt to examine the validity of Piaget's theory within a limited context. His views on the development of length measurement and of concepts of order in children have been singled out for study. The development of length measurement is discussed in the next section and order concepts in the section following. In both these sections special attention is paid to Piaget's views on the specific ages at which particular types of responses develop.

The ontogenesis of measurement provides a particularly convenient point of departure since the logic of measurement has been well analyzed by workers interested in the bases of science (Bergmann and Spence, 1944; Campbell, 1920; Nagel, 1930). In the next section an experiment is reported in which the development of a particular inferential response in children is traced. This response is the inference that a stick, A, is longer than another stick, C, when it has been demonstrated that A is longer than

---

A conjunction of propositions asserts the joint truth of two propositions, often by the use of the word *and,* for example, "Fabius was born at the rising of the dog-star, *and* Fabius will perish in the sea." A disjunction of propositions carries the meaning "either . . . or . . . (or both)."

[2] Piaget (1953b) presents a derivation of these concepts from his own theory.

a measuring rod, B, and that B is in turn longer than C. In logical symbolism this may be written A > B.B > C. ⊃ .A > C.[3] According to Nagel and other logicians this inference is one of those fundamental in length measurement (i.e., all length measurement tacitly assumes the validity of this inference). . . .

[In the original article, the relationship between the development of the inferential response A > B.B > C. ⊃ .A > C and of the discrimination of position order is investigated.] Piaget believes that the development of inferences such as A > B.B > C. ⊃ .A > C is one aspect of the development of a more general ability to perform logical operations. The task Piaget has set himself is to give a detailed description of these logical operations and of their formal interrelations. He believes that this will enable us "to construct by means of the algebra of logic a deductive theory to explain some of the experimental findings of psychology" (Piaget, 1953b, p. 26). Although Piaget does not make this explicit, a basic postulate of his theory of intelligence certainly appears to be that operations, inferences, or concepts which are logically interdependent (i.e., the definition of the one involves reference to the other, or both derive from the same interpretation of a logical calculus), will be found to develop in association with each other in children's thinking. It may be noted that experimental refutation of Piaget's views about the specific ages at which particular groups of operations develop does not refute this postulate. With this postulate it may be predicted that order concepts and the inference A > B.B > C. ⊃ .A > C develop in association in children's thinking.

If the postulate that logically interdependent operations develop in association is generally valid, it follows that there should be periods of transition in the development of intelligence, during which particular groups of operations develop. If such ages of transition exist—and they may not be at 7 and 11 yr. as Piaget claims—then changes in the nature of intelligence during childhood should be observable and reflected in a changing factorial composition of intelligence tests. Failure to find such changes would cast serious doubt on any theory which seeks to relate intellectual development to the performance of logical operations. In the section on ages of transition, this study concludes with an examination of the evidence for such changes reported in the literature.

THE DEVELOPMENT OF LENGTH MEASUREMENT IN
    CHILDREN

The part played by the logic of measurement in Piaget's description of lengthmeasuring behavior in children is considered. Piaget's experiments are discussed and certain criticisms of his techniques are suggested. A study

[3] To be read: "*If* (A is longer than B) *and* (B is longer than C) *then* (A is longer than C).

which uses different techniques to study the development of certain of the inferential processes involved in measurement is then reported. The results are compared with Piaget's.

Theoretical Considerations

According to many logicians, measurement is possible in a dimension only when relations between objects in the dimension fulfill certain axioms, the so-called axioms of measurement (Bergmann and Spence, 1944; Nagel, 1930). From these, certain laws may be derived. For example, the truth of the following seven laws is always tacitly assumed whenever length is measured.[4]

$$A = B.B = C. \supset .A = C$$
$$A = B.B > C. \supset .A > C$$
$$A = B.B < C. \supset .A < C$$
$$A > B.B = C. \supset .A > C$$
$$A > B.B > C. \supset .A > C$$
$$A < B.B = C. \supset .A < C$$
$$A < B.B < C. \supset .A < C$$

When length is measured, it is also assumed that lengths are additive, i.e., any length is composed of shorter lengths added together. Consequently, some arbitrary unit (e.g., in., cm.) may be defined and the length of a measured object is the number of units which have to be added together to compose another object equal in length to the first. It is the existence of this additive operation that, among other things, enables one to talk meaningfully of the length of a path which is not straight, e.g., the perimeter of a triangle whose length is the sum of the lengths of the sides.

Piaget's description of the development of measurement in children consists of an account of the development of children's understanding and use of these laws.

Piaget treats these laws not only as empirical statements which are demonstrably valid, but as behavioral processes initiated by the child S. For example, the expression $(A + B)$ can be regarded either as a length, or as a record of the behavior of some S: "S picks up B and places one end of B next to one end of A." If S does not displace B physically, but does so only implicitly or "in his imagination," then the expression $(A + B)$ can be regarded as representing an implicit displacement or operation performed by S on A and B.

In most studies of length judgment in children, the Ss have been asked to compare two lengths. The method used by S to arrive at a judgment is likely to depend both on the stimulus conditions and on the manner in which S is obliged to communicate his judgment to E.

[4] A, B, and C represent any three lengths and ">," "<," and "=" designate the relations "longer than," "shorter than," and "equal in length to," respectively.

The importance of the stimulus conditions in length judgment may be illustrated by two prototype examples. In the first example, a length A in one room is to be compared with another somewhat shorter length C in another room by the following procedure: in the first room a convenient third object, B, is juxtaposed with A and it is found that A is longer than B; B is then carried into the other room and juxtaposed with C and it is found that B is longer than C; it is concluded that A is longer than C. For the second example, suppose that the stimulus conditions are altered so that A and C are in the same room standing upright next to each other on the top of a table; it is then immediately clear that A extends upwards beyond the highest point of C, i.e., that A is longer than C.

Let us say that in the first case A is "inferred" to be longer than C, and in the second case that A is "perceived" to be longer than C. This appears to be not inconsistent with conventional usage of these words in the English language. In the remainder of this section the word *inference* is used to refer to the kind of method by which the length judgment is arrived at in the first example, and the judgment itself is called an *inferential response*. The terms *perception* and *discrimination* will often be used to designate the length judgment in the second example.

Critique of Piaget's Techniques

In Piaget's work the stimulus conditions are rarely identical with those of the two prototypic examples above; distinguishing between an inferential and a discriminatory response therefore becomes a diagnostic problem. In his experiments the stimuli to be compared have sometimes been solid objects and sometimes the paths traced by moving objects. The stimuli have been straight or bent to form a "zig-zag," and the spatial relations between the stimuli have been varied. The response has sometimes been a judgment expressed verbally, and sometimes S has been asked to construct a length equal to a given length, with or without uncalibrated measuring rods available. In all experiments either E or S has used words such as *big, little, short, long, same length, measure*, etc., so that a certain vocabulary development is presupposed.

The standardization of the Binet test (see Terman and Merrill, 1937) indicates that average children between the ages of 3–0 and 3–6 are able to obey a verbal instruction to pick out the longer of two sticks 2 in. and 2½ in. in length at least 82% of the time, when the sticks are placed parallel so that the longer overlaps the shorter at both ends. It is an open question whether the word *longer* is understood at this age to apply to other spatial relations between the sticks.

In two experiments by Piaget (Piaget, 1946, Ch. 3; Piaget et al., 1948, Ch. 6), the Ss were aged 4–8 yr. The E moved a bead a certain distance along a wire and S was required to move another bead the same distance along a second wire.[5] The shape and relative positions of the wires together with the typical errors of the youngest *S*s are shown in Fig. 1. The errors made by most of the *S*s aged 4–6 yr. were always of the same nature: they moved their bead to a position, P′, directly opposite the position, P, of *E*'s bead, thus failing to take account of the differing points of departure of the two beads. The responses of these *S*s were thus correct only in arrangement "(b)" in Fig. 1. The *S*s of intermediate age were correct in arrangements "(a)" and "(c)," but not in "(d)" or "(e)." The *S*s aged 7 and 8 yr. were correct in all arrangements. Following their response all *S*s were given an unmarked ruler to measure the distances. The youngest *S*s just laid the ruler across the two beads perpendicular to the wires. Not until after age 7 yr. were the *S*s able to measure adequately. Piaget interpreted his findings to indicate that his youngest *S*s identified "length" with "final position occupied"; the typical errors indicated the "finalism" which is characteristic of children of this age, and which reflects the fact that the logical operations basic to measurement are not yet available to them.

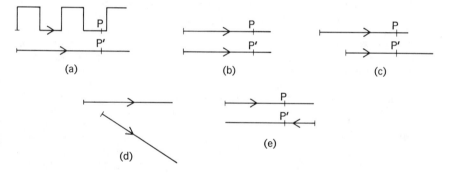

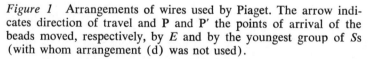

Figure 1   Arrangements of wires used by Piaget. The arrow indicates direction of travel and P and P′ the points of arrival of the beads moved, respectively, by *E* and by the youngest group of *S*s (with whom arrangement (d) was not used).

Fraisse and Vautrey (1952a) criticize Piaget's procedure and, in a study which also employed the paths traced by moving objects as stimuli, they found no evidence for "finalism" in young children's perception of length. Their *S*s were aged 4–6 to 5–6, the age of Piaget's youngest *S*s. Fraisse and Vautrey found that *S*s who were told to indicate the starting positions of the objects responded correctly more often than *S*s whose response was not prefaced by this instruction. Moreover, *S*s who made errors had usually indicated the starting position incorrectly, their response being appropriate to the starting position indicated. The authors suggest that the errors typical

[5] "Veux-tu faire marcher l'autre tram pour qu'il fasse juste le même long chemin?" (Piaget, 1946, p. 56).

of Piaget's youngest Ss reflect not a peculiarity of their conception of length, but their failure to notice or to recall the starting positions of the objects.

If the errors made by Piaget's Ss do not constitute evidence to support his diagnosis of their length judgments as "pre-logical," then the only support for this diagnosis lies in the inappropriateness of the measuring behavior of his Ss.

The inception of measurement is examined in greater detail in another of Piaget's studies (Piaget, 1953a; Piaget et al., 1948, Ch. 2). Piaget invited children to build with blocks a tower equal in height to a tower already built by E. However, the table on which E's tower stood was higher than the table on which S was to build his tower and was some distance from it. Sticks longer, shorter, and equal to the height of the model were available to Ss. Piaget (1953a) summarizes his results as follows:

> The youngest children build up the second tower to the same visual level as the first, without worrying about the difference in height of the tables. They compare the towers by stepping back and sighting them. At a slightly more advanced stage a child lays a long rod across the tops of the two towers to make sure that they are level. Somewhat later he notices that the base of his tower is not at the same level as the model's. He then wants to place his tower next to the model on the same table to compare them. Reminded that the rules of the game forbid him to move his tower, he begins to look around for a measuring standard. Interestingly enough, the first that comes to his mind is his own body. He puts one hand on top of his tower and the other at its base, and then, trying to keep his hands the same distance apart, he moves over to the other tower to compare it. Children of about the age of six often carry out this work in a most assured manner, as if their hands could not change position on the way! Soon they discover that the method is not reliable, and then they resort to reference points on the body. The child will line up his shoulder with the top of his tower, mark the spot opposite the base on his thigh with his hand and walk over to the model to see whether the distance is the same.
>
> Eventually the idea of an independent measuring tool occurs to the child. His first attempt in this direction is likely to be the building of a third tower next to and the same height as the one he has already erected. Having built it, he moves it over to the first table and matches it against the model; this is allowed by the rules. The child's arrival at this stage presupposes a process of logical reasoning. If we call the model tower A, the second tower C, and the movable tower B, the child has reasoned that B = C and B = A, therefore A = C.
>
> Later the child replaces the third tower with a rod, but at first the rod must be just the same length as the height of the tower to be measured. He then conceives the idea of using a longer rod and marking the tower height on it with his finger. Finally, and this is the beginning of true measurement, he realizes that he can use a shorter rod and measure the height of the tower by applying the rod a certain number of times up the side.
>
> The last discovery involves two new operations of logic. The first is the process of division which permits the child to conceive that the whole is composed of a number of parts added together. The second . . . enables him to apply one part upon others and thus to build a system of units. (pp. 77–78)

It can be seen that Piaget's diagnosis of a child's ability to perform the inferences basic to measurement is based entirely on his measuring behavior. However, it seems to the writer that a child's measuring behavior may reflect his knowledge of measuring technique as much as it does his ability to reason logically about length. Piaget's 5- and 6-yr.-old *S*s tended to use their own bodies as measuring rods. The human body is, of course, a clumsy and inadequate measuring instrument, yet the fact that a young child does not immediately perceive its imperfections and select a better tool may not necessarily indicate a deficiency in his logic. One may recall that in the cultural history of measurement it required a considerable period of time before adult human beings came to adopt more objective units of measurement than parts of the human body. Consider the behavior of the child who "measures" the height of a tower by placing one hand at its base and the other at its summit. Piaget claims that such behavior indicates deficient understanding of the logic of measurement, because the child fails to realize that it is impossible to keep the distance between the hands constant as he walks from one tower to the other: the child's measuring rod is elastic. However, the opposite point of view can be argued. To the writer such behavior suggests that the child has a rather sound knowledge of the logic of measurement, but is woefully inexpert in its practice! Such behavior appears to show a good knowledge of the seven paradigmatic rules of inference involved in measurement enumerated earlier.

Another factor which may be important in Piaget's studies of measurement is the child's motivation. Piaget relies on the inherent interest of the tasks for the child. However, it is possible that the older children are more interested than the younger *S*s in measurement and the additional accuracy it makes possible.

In another experiment (Piaget et al., 1948, Ch. 5) designed to study children's understanding of the additive operation involved in length measurement, the stimuli were two "roads" composed of match sticks of unequal length placed end to end. Two sets of sticks were initially lined up parallel to each other, and without overlap, to form two equally long lines. The *S* was asked whether the "roads" were the same length or not. Even the youngest *S*s were able to respond "Yes" to this question.

One line of sticks was then altered so that the "road" was no longer straight, but formed a "zig-zag." The *S* observed the alteration. He was then asked again whether the "roads" were the same length or not. This question was sometimes rephrased, the child being asked, if an ant were to walk along each road, whether one ant would walk farther than the other.

It was found that the youngest children (aged 4–6 yr.) did not consider the lines the same length after the rearrangement had taken place; they considered either the straight line to be longer because it extended beyond the other one, or else they thought the "zig-zag" line to be longer because of the turns. There was an intermediate stage where some rearrangements were considered to alter the length and some were not. Around ages 7 and 8 yr. (Stage III), the line was known to be the same length irrespective of the rearrangement of its parts.

This experiment is one of the rare ones in which Piaget reports some results numerically. Fifty-nine children between the ages of 4 and 9 were examined. Responses classified in Stage III were shown by only 10% of those aged 6–0 to 7–0, by 50% of those between 7–0 and 7–6, and by 75% of those between 7–6 and 8–6.

No manipulation of measuring instruments is required of the child in this experiment, but Piaget's questions are very complex for young children. Indeed, the use of words such as *long* or *length* (which appear in the questions) to refer to lines which are not straight presupposes comprehension of the additive operation involved in measurement, since the length of a line which is not straight is defined as the sum of the lengths of its straight parts. Comprehension of Piaget's questions by the child would therefore of itself indicate understanding of the additive character of lengths. Piaget's results can thus only be regarded as equivocal, since it is unclear precisely what he is studying. The development of this additive operation could perhaps be examined more adequately if the experiment were redesigned as a length-discrimination task in which selection of the longer of two sticks (at least one of which is bent to form a zig-zag) led to, say, a candy reward. At whatever age the additive operation develops (if there is such an age) one would expect an increase in skill in visualizing a line as composed of displaceable parts, and therefore a sudden improvement in the accuracy of discrimination at this age.

Vocabulary development may well be a factor in many of Piaget's experiments. Its confounding effects cannot be eliminated unless nonverbal methods of presenting the tasks to the Ss are used. The notion of employing nonverbal techniques has methodological importance. Historically, one of the important contributions of comparative psychology has been the consistency with which processes of reasoning or concept formation, which at one time were considered by some to be peculiar to the human species, have been elicited in lower animals, once the appropriate nonverbal tasks have been designed. Fields' (1932) study of concept formation in the rat provides an example of this. The success of Harlow (1951), and Evarts and Nissen (1953) in teaching subhuman primates to solve conditional matching problems employing the Weigl principle is a more recent instance, which suggests that the kind of thinking called "abstract" by Goldstein and Scheerer (1941) can occur in primates other than man.[6]

No theory which postulates levels of conceptual development can be regarded as definitely established when the supporting data are obtained through extensive verbal communication with Ss who differ in their ability to verbalize. This principle applies not only when the human species is

[6] Moreover, deficits in "abstraction" following brain injury may not be the peculiar privilege of man! Cf. Riopelle, Alper, Strong, and Ades (1953).

compared with phylogenetically lower animals, but also, within the human species, when aphasics—and perhaps also schizophrenics—are compared with "normals," and in ontogenetic studies of young children. The main purpose of using nonverbal techniques is therefore not to discredit the notion of "levels" or "stages" of development, but to provide more convincing evidence for them.[7]

Conservatively interpreted, the evidence suggests the following conclusions:

(1) In the absence of measurement, the accuracy of length judgment in young children varies with the nature and the spatial arrangement of the stimuli judged. Where the lengths are the paths traced by moving objects, failure to notice or to recall the relative starting positions is an important source of error.

(2) Selection and manipulation of instruments for measuring length becomes increasingly adequate between the ages of 4 and 8 yr. in the average child who has had no special tuition.

(3) There is reason to question Piaget's belief that performance of the inferences and logical operations basic to measurement emerges at the approximate age of 7 yr. in the average child. Piaget's findings may reflect his methods of investigation.

To evaluate this criticism of Piaget, a length-discrimination task was designed in which the difference in length between the stimuli could not readily be perceived but had to be inferred, using the rule $A > B.B > C. \supset .A > C$. This rule has the status of an axiom in the logic of measurement. The S did not manipulate any measuring instruments during the task so that skill in the use of measuring rods was not a controlling factor. Every time the child made a correct response he obtained a small piece of candy, so that he was not motivated only by the inherent interest of the task.

Tracing the development of this inferential response in children makes it possible to subject to empirical test Piaget's view that the inferences fundamental to length-measurement develop in children at around age 7 yr.

Method

SUBJECTS   The Ss were children from two day nurseries in New York City, partially supported by the Division of Day Care of the New York City Department of Welfare. There were 41 Ss, 18 boys and 23 girls, who ranged in age from 3–6 to 7–0. The distribution by age is shown in Table 1. The children in these nurseries are almost all children of working

---

[7] The writer is indebted to H. L. Teuber for suggesting the use of nonverbal techniques. In numerous conversations he has persistently reiterated that, if a theory postulates an alteration of thought (rather than language) processes either during development or as a result of brain injury or disease, then the possibility of demonstrating this alteration on nonverbal tests is clearly implied.

mothers who live in low-income housing projects in New York's lower East Side. Although the socioeconomic status and education of the parents are below average for New York City, in the opinion of the nursery authorities and of the writer, it is doubtful that the children are below the country-wide average in general intelligence. IQs are available for very few of the children, but those that are range from 89 to 118 and thus are in harmony with this general impression.

Of the 41 *S*s, 37 also received the order-discrimination task described in the next section. To 16 of these, the order-discrimination task was administered before the task now described.

APPARATUS   The apparatus consisted of 15 upright pieces of wood painted a turquoise color, screwed to a flat base painted black. Each of these could be placed to rest on a low orange pedestal, constructed so that a piece of candy could be concealed in the pedestal beneath the base of the upright. The apparatus also contained two orange measuring sticks. The 15 uprights are shown in Fig. 2. Two of these 15 are shown in Fig. 3 being measured in turn with a measuring stick. The longer of the two measuring sticks, which measured 11⅜ in. and 11¾ in., is shown in Fig. 3. Each of the measuring sticks was designed with a spigot on top which passed over the shorter of the two uprights, thus clearly revealing the relative lengths of the uprights and measuring stick. This spigot can be seen best in the left part of Fig. 3.

The purpose of constructing the uprights with arms at their upper and lower extremities was to increase the difficulty of making accurate discriminations of their relative lengths by direct visual comparison. It was expected that the arms would induce a slight degree of illusion (Müller-Lyer effect) in the apparent length of the uprights.

PROCEDURE   The task consisted of a series of discrimination problems with the stimuli (the uprights) presented in pairs. There were three phases. In the first phase the uprights used were always clearly different in height. Half the children learned to obtain a reward by selecting the longer upright, the remainder by selecting the shorter upright. In the second phase *S* was required to find the rewarded upright when the two uprights in each trial were objectively, but not discriminably, different in length, and where each was compared in turn, by *E*, with a measuring stick of intermediate size. The *S* had to *infer* which was the longer (or shorter) upright, by the rule A > B.B > C. ⊃ .A > C. In the third phase the question, "Which is the taller [or shorter]?" was posed verbally as *E* measured the uprights with the measuring stick. Thus, in Phase 1 each child was taught the relation "longer than (or "shorter than"). Phases 2 and 3 tested whether this relation was transitive or intransitive for the child: in Phase 2 a nonverbal method was used, and in Phase 3 the nonverbal method was

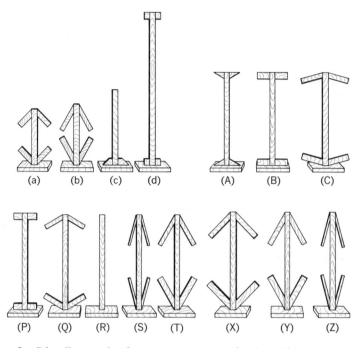

Figure 2 Stimuli used in the measurement task. (a), (b), (c), and (d) were used only in training and retention trials. (A), (B), and (C) were 11¾₁₆ inches tall, (P), (Q), (R), (S), and (T) 11⁹₁₆ inches, and (X), (Y), and (Z) 11¹⁵₁₆ inches.

supplemented by verbal instructions. The precise details of procedure in the three phases were as follows.

Phase 1: Training. The *S* and *E* sat opposite each other, with the long edges of a low rectangular table between them. The *S* was first shown how to lift one of the uprights and find candy under it. The uprights were then presented in pairs. Half the children in each age group always found candy under the taller upright, the remainder under the shorter upright. The uprights in each pair were clearly different in height: during Phase 1 no two of the uprights designated in Fig. 2 by capital letters were ever paired together. The uprights designated d and P in Fig. 2 constituted the first pair of training stimuli. This pair was presented in successive trials until *S* had achieved eight successive correct comparisons. The pair d-P was then removed and a-X substituted for it. When *S* had performed six successive correct comparisons of a and X, these were removed and d-P reinstated. If *S* did not remember whether the candy was under d or P, he was retrained. Pairs d-P and a-X were then presented on successive trials until both discriminations were retained simultaneously. The pairs a-P, P-d, d-X, and X-a were then presented in successive trials until all four discriminations had been learned and retained simultaneously. If *S* proved unusually slow in learning to transpose the concept taught, these pairs were presented individually in successive trials until learned. Then c-R was introduced and *S* was trained on this if necessary. Then the pairs b-c, c-R, R-d, d-Y, Y-c, c-a were presented successively until all the discriminations involved were retained simultaneously. When this point was reached, uprights designated by lower-case letters in Fig. 2 were paired at random in successive trials with uprights designated by capital letters until eight successive correct comparisons of different pairs of uprights were made. The *S* was then considered to have learned whichever of the concepts "longer than" or "shorter than" he had been taught and Phase 2 was initiated. When the training phase required more than one session with an *S*, pairs of stimuli were presented in subsequent sessions in the same sequence as they had been presented in the first sesions: that is, the child was always trained from the beginning again, although the success criteria for the discriminations learned in prior sessions were somewhat relaxed.[8]

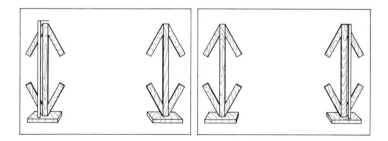

Figure 3   Example of a measurement trial: The measuring stick is juxtaposed with each upright in turn.

During Phase 1, the position of the correct upright was varied, but it was not always varied randomly. It was found that random variation of the correct position was an ineffective training technique since it generally provided accidental partial reinforcement of an *S*'s wrong hypotheses or habits. Many *S*s tended to reach for the upright nearest their preferred hand. It was found that the only effective way of countering this was to put the correct upright consistently on *S*'s nonpreferred side until the position habit was abandoned. In general, during Phase 1 a random position sequence was employed from which *E* departed periodically in order to avoid reinforcing incorrect hypotheses that *S* appeared to be developing.

---

[8] The success criteria were selected following Hilgard (1951, Table 5, p. 535) which gives the number of successive correct responses required for statistical significance as a function of the total number of trials.

At the beginning of the training in Phase 1 the uprights were placed on the table a few inches apart in front of *S*. They were gradually moved away from each other until one was on *S*'s extreme left and the other on his extreme right: these were the positions the upright occupied in Phase 2, in order to render direct visual comparison of their heights more difficult.

Phase 2: Measurement and retention. This phase consisted of a minimum of 40 trials. Eighteen of them were "measurement" trials. Ten were "trials without yardstick" and there were at least 12 retention trials.

The uprights were always presented in pairs as in Phase 1, and the candy was always under the same upright (the "longer" or the "shorter") as it had been in Phase 1. In the retention trials the same combinations of stimuli were used as had been used in the training trials of Phase 1. However, in the measurement trials and trials without yardstick only uprights designated in Fig. 2 by capital letters were used. The objective differences in height between the stimuli were therefore always quite small. It will be noted that among the 11 uprights designated by capital letters in Fig. 2, there are 39[9] possible pairings in which there is a small true difference in height. In a few pretesting sessions the 28 pairs which seemed most difficult to discriminate by direct visual comparison were selected and 18 of these were randomly assigned to the measurement trials. The remaining 10 pairs were used in the trials without yardstick.

During measurement trials *E* juxtaposed one of the measuring sticks with each upright in turn, the left-hand one first, as shown in Fig. 3. The measuring stick was always shorter than one of the uprights and longer than the other. It was placed vertically on the base of each upright and rotated so that the spigot passed over the top of the shorter upright or rested against the side of the longer upright (see Fig. 3). If *S* did not seem to be watching during this procedure, the stick was knocked against the top of the upright to attract his attention and he was told, "Look at the tops of them." The *S* was not permitted to touch either of the stimuli until the measurement had been performed. The measuring operation was often prefaced by the words, "Wait, we are going to try and help you find the candy." If the child failed to lift one of the uprights immediately after the measuring operation had been performed, this operation was repeated and then he was instructed, "Find the candy." The criterion for successful "measurement" was 13 correct trials out of 18.

The trials without yardstick were the same as the measurement trials except that the entire measuring procedure was omitted. The *S* was instructed, "See if you can find the candy without help this time." The purpose of the trials without yardstick was to test the accuracy of *S*'s discrimination of the lengths of the uprights without measurement in order to show that in the measurement trials *S* had "inferred" rather than directly perceived the longer (or shorter) upright.

[9] Fifteen pairings of A, B, C with P, Q, R, S, T + 9 pairings of A, B, C with X, Y, Z + 15 pairings of P, Q, R, S, T with X, Y, Z.

In the retention trials pairs of uprights clearly different in height, as in Phase 1, were used. The retention trials were included in order to ensure that *S*s who were unable to find the correct upright in the measurement trials still retained the concept "longer" (or "shorter"), i.e., to ensure that failure on measurement trials did not occur simply because *S* had forgotten the problem "instructions," taught in Phase 1. When failure occurred on any of the retention trials the original length discrimination was retaught as in Phase 1 to the same criterion of eight successive correct comparisons of eight different pairs of stimuli, before the measurement trials and trials without yardstick were continued. No *S* was retrained more than three times.

The measurement trials were given in pairs, and between every pair of measurement trials a trial without yardstick was inserted. The retention trials were distributed among the 28 measurement trials and trials without yardstick: between every fourth and fifth of these trials, two retention trials were inserted.

Throughout Phase 2 the position of the correct upright was varied randomly.

Phase 3: The procedure in this phase depended on whether *S* had reached the criterion of success in the measurement trials of Phase 2. If *S* had failed to reach this criterion, the following procedure was adopted. Two uprights similar in appearance (e.g., S and Z or T and Y in Fig. 2) were first placed next to each other and inclined together until the tops touched. The *S* was told to put his finger on the top of the one that was "taller or bigger" (or, "shorter or smaller"). The *S* then watched a piece of candy being put under the taller upright (or the shorter, whichever concept had originally been learned). The positions of the uprights on the table were then rapidly interchanged several times so that *S* lost track of the one with the candy. The uprights were then measured as in the Phase 2 measurement trials. As each upright was being measured, (*S* was instructed to point to the "one that is longer or taller" (or, the "one that is smaller or shorter"). Thus, an *S*, for whom the longer upright had previously been rewarded, now pointed to the measuring rod as the shorter upright was being measured, and to the longer upright as this was measured. When both had been measured, he was told, "Find the candy under the one that is longer or taller." The main purpose of the supplementary verbal instructions in Phase 3 was to ensure that *S* had noticed the relative lengths of the uprights and measuring rod. Not more than six trials were given. To be credited with success, *S* had to respond correctly in five successive trials.

If *S* had reached the criterion on the Phase 2 measurement trials, it was desirable to make doubly sure that he had succeeded by a genuine process of inference. A book was placed under one of the pedestals so that the bases of the pedestals were no longer at the same level. Two uprights similar in appearance (e.g., S and Z or T and Y) were again selected and placed one on each pedestal. The child was asked which was the taller (or shorter, if he had originally learned this discrimination). Following his answer the uprights were measured in the usual manner, and he was then asked whether his original judgment had been correct or not. The uprights were reshuffled several times and this procedure repeated until *S* had demonstrated without error in 5 trials that he was able both to maintain and to change his original judgment, depending on the facts as indicated by measurement.

Results and Discussion

LEVEL OF PERFORMANCE ATTAINED   One *S* failed to reach the learning criterion in Phase 1 and was therefore excluded from the subsequent phases.[10] The remaining 40 *S*s all learned the original length discrimination in Phase 1, and to all of these *S*s Phases 2 and 3 were therefore administered.

Fifteen *S*s failed to reach the criterion of 13 correct measurement trials in Phase 2, and also failed in Phase 3. These *S*s therefore failed to find the longer or shorter upright by inference in both phases. An additional 5 *S*s failed to reach the criterion in the measurement trials of Phase 2, but made an inferential response in Phase 3, when the nonverbal method was supplemented by verbal instructions. The remaining 20 *S*s were successful under both conditions; there were no *S*s who reached the criterion in Phase 2 but failed to do so in Phase 3.

The percentage of *S*s within each 8-mo. age interval between 3–6 and 6–10 who successfully found the correct upright following the measuring procedure is shown in Fig. 4. This graph shows separately the increase with age of the percentage of *S*s reaching the criterion in the measurement trials of Phase 2, and those who made an inferential response in either Phase 2 or Phase 3. It can be seen that a regular development appears to occur, and that in this sample the threshold age at which 50% of children made the inference studied is somewhat between 4–2 and 5–5. In Table 1 the development with age is shown in terms of the mean number of correct responses in the 18 measurement trials.

The improvement in performance with age in the trials without yardstick is also shown in Fig. 4 and Table 1. A criterion of eight correct choices in the 10 trials without yardstick was used in Fig. 4.[11] It can be seen that

[10] This child was aged 5–0. In three training sessions she failed to learn even the first discrimination (between P and d). The writer has no explanation for this failure.

[11] This criterion errs on the lenient side: $p = .054$ of obtaining by chance eight or more correct responses in 10 trials. This criterion was selected because it is comparable to the criterion used in the measurement trials ($p = .048$ of finding 13 or more correct in 18 trials).

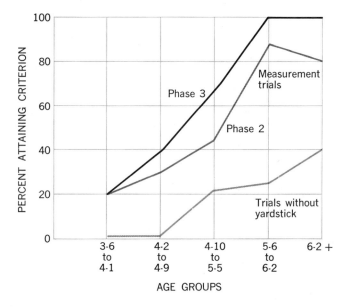

Figure 4   Percentage of Ss finding the correct upright by inference (measurement trials) and by direct comparison (trials without yardstick).

in all except the oldest age group the average number of correct responses in the trials without yardstick is close to the chance level. Even in the oldest age group accuracy is considerably less than in the measurement trials.

Since the use of the measuring stick is the only factor that distinguishes the measurement trials from the trials without yardstick, the greater accuracy in the measurement trials is attributable to the Ss' use of the cues provided by the measuring procedure. Further evidence that the children successful in the measurement trials found the longer or shorter upright by inference is provided by the fact that all these children were able to find the correct upright in Phase 3, when the bases of the uprights were at different levels.

The evidence that the children successful in the measurement trials were using an inferential procedure is thus convincing. The results suggest also that the lack of success of the children who did not reach the criterion in either the measurement trials of Phase 2 or in Phase 3 cannot be explained simply as a failure to retain the original concept "longer" or "shorter," taught in Phase 1. Evidence for this is found in the retention trials of Phase 2. Of the 15 children who failed in both the measurement trials of Phase 2 and in Phase 3, six responded correctly in all 12 retention trials, five failed in one retention trial and had to be retrained once, and three had to be retrained twice. One S was discontinued on Phase 2 because of consistent failure to retain the discrimination. Of the 20 chil-

Table 1

*Number of Correct Responses as a Function of Age
in the Measurement Trials and Trials
without Yardstick of Phase 2*

| Age Group | N | Mean Number Correct Responses | |
		18 Measurement Trials	10 Trials Without Yardstick
3– 6 to 4–1	5	9.5	5.0
4– 2 to 4–9	13	10.2[b]	4.6
4–10 to 5–5	9[a]	12.4[d]	6.0
5– 6 to 6–1	8	14.8[d]	5.7
6– 2 to 7–0	5	15.6[d]	7.2[c]

Note. The statistical tests were based on the null hypothesis that Ss' scores are distributed as predicted by the binomial expansion, with $N =$ no. of trials and $P = q = .5$. Thus, where $n =$ no. of Ss in an age group, $z = $ (Mean Score of age group $- Np$) / $\sqrt{Npq/n}$.
[a] One S excluded who failed to learn the initial length discrimination in Phase 1.
[b] Significant at the .05 level.
[c] Significant at the .01 level.
[d] Significant at the .0001 level.

dren who reached the criterion on the measurement trials, three had to be retrained once and one twice. Thus, Ss who failed to make an inferential response also tended to forget the discrimination taught in Phase 1 somewhat more often than Ss who made an inferential response. This is not surprising since the former Ss were in general younger and more distractible. But it is extremely unlikely that failure to reach the criterion in the measurement trials is due to a simple failure to retain the original discrimination. It may be recalled that the retention trials were spaced among the measurement trials and trials without yardstick in such a way that any failure to retain the discrimination would be very quickly discovered. If this happened, Ss were then retrained before any further measurement trials or trials without yardstick were administered. Thus one or two failures of retention would not vitiate the results in the measurement trials of Phase 2. Moreover, an S is not considered to have failed to have made an inferential response unless he also failed in Phase 3 with the supplementary verbal instructions.

Three variables probably unrelated to successful "measurement." Whether or not an inferential procedure was used seemed unrelated to the location of the candy under the longer or shorter upright. For 20 Ss the reward was consistently under the shorter upright, and of these, eight failed to make an inferential response. Of the remaining 20 Ss, seven failed to find the longer upright by inference.

Sex of S also seemed to be unrelated to success or failure in finding the correct upright by inference. Of 18 boys, eight failed to make an inferential response, and of 22 girls, seven failed. The difference is statistically insignificant.

Some of the Ss received the order-discrimination task described in the next section before receiving this task. Of the total group of 40 Ss, 16 received the order task first. Of these only four failed to make an inferential response, whereas 11 of the remaining 24 Ss failed. However, the Ss who received the order-discrimination task first were generally older. This was because a few young Ss inopportunely went on vacation after receiving the order task. Unlimited time was not available and it was therefore desirable to begin the measurement task early, since, owing to the lengthy Phase 1 training, it required several sessions to administer to the younger children. Of the 21 children under 5–0, 14 took the measurement task first and 10 failed to make an inferential response. Of the seven who took the order task first, four failed to make an inferential response. Chi square, even without Yates correction, is very small; even for the whole group of 40 Ss chi square is not significant. Thus there is no evidence that prior experience with the order task affected the Ss' success in making an inferential response in the measurement task.

Temporal course of performance in Phase 2. In Fig. 5 the temporal course of performance in the 18 measurement trials is shown separately for the group of 20 Ss who reached criterion and for the remainder who did not. It can be observed that there was no tendency to learn on the part of Ss who failed; their performance never deviated far from the chance level. The 20 Ss who reached criterion performed significantly better than chance even on the first three trials, and the improvement that followed took place very quickly. Moreover, even on the first measurement trial, 16 of these Ss found the correct upright.[12] The evidence therefore indicates that Ss who reached criterion on the measurement trials tended to use the inferential procedure from the beginning of Phase 2.

In Fig. 6 the course of performance on the 10 trials without yardstick is shown. It is noteworthy that the Ss who reached the criterion on the measurement trials performed consistently better than the remainder. That is, the Ss who made an inferential response also tended to discriminate the relative lengths of the uprights better when no inferential procedure was involved. In the last four trials without yardstick their performance even rose to a level significantly better than chance.

This correlation raises some very interesting questions. In particular, it might lead one to suggest that the dichotomy originally made between "inferred" and "perceived" length differences may not be as absolute

---

[12] $p < .05$ that this is a chance occurrence.

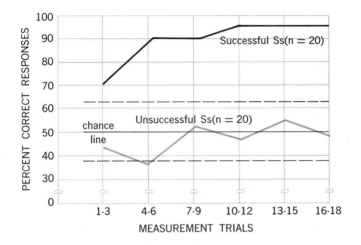

Figure 5 Temporal course of performance on the measurement trials. The "successful" *S*s are those who reached the criterion. The parallel broken lines enclose the region between the minimum score significantly greater than chance and the maximum score significantly less than chance ($p = .05$).

psychologically as it is logically. This question is complicated and a discussion of it is deferred until it can be treated within the context of the totality of the results.[13] At this point one may note only that the *S*s who made an inferential response were older. Also, in the specific stimulus conditions used in this experiment, discrimination of the lengths of the uprights without the aid of the measuring stick is quite complex, because of the slight degree of illusion presumably induced by the arms at the upper and lower extremities of the uprights.[14]

Qualitative results. For the purposes of description, the *S*s' behavior may be grossly categorized into three types. However, there were many *S*s who did not fall clearly into any type. Also, at the beginning of the experiment it was not known how they would behave. On looking back at the protocols, it was found that for some of the *S*s run first there was no adequate record of the presence or absence of many of the behaviors later observed carefully.

The *S*s who failed to make an inferential response appeared to have no

[13] See section entitled Changes in "Set" Associated With the Emergence of Measurement.

[14] It will be recalled that the uprights were deliberately constructed in this manner in order to increase the difficulty of discriminating their relative lengths without the aid of the measuring sticks. If the *S*s had shown a moderate or high degree of success in the trials without yardstick, it would have been difficult to prove statistically that *S*s who were successful in the measurement trials had used an inferential procedure.

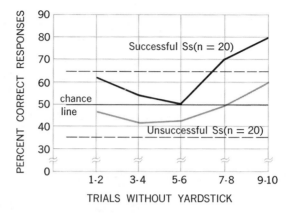

Figure 6 Temporal course of performance on the trials without yardstick. The "successful" *S*s are those who reached the criterion in the measurement trials. The parallel broken lines enclose the region between the minimum score significantly greater than chance and the maximum score significantly less than chance ($p = .05$).

comprehension of the measuring operation in Phase 2. They did not spontaneously watch the measuring procedure except on the first few trials. Their attention had to be constantly attracted to the measuring sticks by various means, with the result that administering Phase 2 so that the measurement was at least observed, if not understood, proved to be quite exhausting to *E* and probably to *S* also, and often required several sessions. On the trials without yardstick these *S*s did not seem to compare the uprights visually. They gave no more than a quick glance at each and then reached for one of them. It was as if the possibility of an imperceptible difference in length was beyond their comprehension.

To others, who were generally the older *S*s, the nature of the task was quite clear. For example, one *S* verbalized, "I know one's bigger but they look the same." These *S*s would watch the measurement intently. During the trials without yardstick they attempted to assess the uprights carefully and often leaned back as far as they could in their chair to bring them closer together in their field of vision; they often glanced from one upright to the other several times. In general, these *S*s found the measurement trials rather easy and one even urged *E* not to use the measuring sticks because that "gave it away."

There was a very interesting third group, into which fell many of the younger *S*s who made an inferential response. Like the first group, they did not spontaneously watch the measuring procedure in Phase 2, but when their attention was drawn to it, they proved able to find the candy with the aid of the measuring stick. Some of these *S*s might find the candy two or three trials in a row, while paying attention, and still fail to watch spontaneously the measuring procedure in subsequent trials. Their behavior recalls the observations of Goldstein and Scheerer (1941) in which they argue that abstract thinking is an "attitude" rather than an "ability"; these *S*s were able to make an inferential response, but did not spontaneously attempt to do so. Some of the *S*s in this group reached the criterion in the measurement trials of Phase 2, whereas others only demonstrated their inferential ability in Phase 3, where the verbal instructions permitted *E* to take a more active role in fixing the *S*s' attention. Like the *S*s of the first group, these *S*s showed no comparison behavior in the trials without yardstick of Phase 2. This group was small: only eight *S*s fell unequivocally within it.

Role of verbalization. The spontaneous verbalizations of the children did not throw much light on the processes involved in solving the task. Of the task-related verbalizations, most occurred during Phase 1 or during the retention trials of Phase 2 (i.e., when the difference in length between the uprights was large). Examples of these are: "It's under the big one," "The little one," "The baby one," "Which one's up," "The teeny one." Interestingly, it appeared that when an *S* says, "It's under the big one," this should not necessarily be construed by *E* to mean "It's always under the big one." An *S*'s verbalization often seemed to refer only to a particular trial, and he might select the incorrect stimulus on the very next trial.

There was no evidence that verbal cues were of much help in solving the measurement trials. Spontaneous verbalization during Phase 1 of the location of the candy under the longer or shorter upright was not related to the performance of an inferential response. No child spontaneously verbalized the measuring procedure. At the end of the task several *S*s were asked how the use of the measuring stick helped them find the candy. All except two said they did not know. Of these two, one answer was, "Because it [the stick] makes it [the upright] smaller." The other answer was, "If the thing [measuring stick] is bigger than there [upright] and the other one the stick's smaller, it's there." Both these *S*s were girls aged 5–6. The latter child was the one, cited earlier, who verbalized, "I know one's bigger but they look the same." The performance of this *S* was interesting. During the measurement trials she pointed occasionally to one or the other of the two uprights, as if she were trying to verbalize the solution of the problem to herself subvocally. These efforts seemed to be more confusing than helpful to her: in the 18 measurement trials, she failed the first trial, solved the next six, then made four successive errors, followed by seven successive correct responses. She did not become similarly confused in the trials without yardstick, finding the objectively taller upright after careful visual comparison in 9 of the 10 trials. Even when the question "Which one is taller or bigger?" was posed verbally by *E* in Phase 3, she almost became confused again but managed to correct herself. She gave the impression that she was trying to form the series long-upright—measuring stick—short-upright, but, having formed the series, she forgot which end was which!

In general, although the location of the candy under the longer or shorter object was often verbalized, there was no evidence that any verbal cues were used which related specifically to the inferential procedure: no audible words were used in the measurement trials which were not also used in the initial learning and in the trials without yardstick. In the one S who appeared to be seeking to use verbal cues during the measuring procedure, these cues seem to have been more confusing than helpful.

SIGNIFICANCE OF RESULTS FOR PIAGET'S THEORY   The most important single result of this study is the finding that the inferential response $A > B.B > C. \supset .A > C$ can be elicited in children substantially earlier than Piaget leads one to believe. If Piaget's finding that children do not manipulate measuring instruments effectively until around age 7 or 8 yr. is valid, then children can perform this inferential response long before they are able to measure adequately. While the availability of this response may be a necessary condition for adequate measurement, it is therefore not a sufficient condition. One plausible reason for the apparent time lag between the development of the inference studied in this experiment and the development of adequate measuring behavior in Piaget's research is that manipulation of measuring instruments requires considerable learning of specific measuring techniques. Adequate measuring behavior may also demand interest in measurement and in achieving the additional accuracy that it makes possible. It is likely, therefore, that many of Piaget's studies, which he believes investigate the development of children's performance of the logical operations implicit in measurement, should be reinterpreted as studies of the development of skill and interest in the techniques of measurement. Inferential responses of the kind investigated here may be available to many of his Ss, particularly those of intermediate age.

The experimental technique used also differed from Piaget's in the manner in which the stimuli were presented. Piaget used instructions which contained the words "same length," and "measure," or synonyms of these. Until Phase 3 at least, the task was presented nonverbally, except for the instruction, "Find the candy"; moreover, the words "longer" or "shorter," introduced in Phase 3, were preceded by the considerable training in length-discrimination involved in the previous phases. Probably this difference in technique is a factor contributing to the difference between the present results and Piaget's. It is particularly likely that the nonverbal method facilitated the success of the youngest children making an inferential response.

The fact that the findings of this experiment indicate that Piaget is mistaken about the specific age at which the inferences basic to measurement develop raises the question: Is it possible—and if possible, is it desirable—to attempt to decide at what age these inferences develop in children? In this sample of children, presumably of average intelligence, and under the particular stimulus and response conditions employed here, this age was found to be somewhere between 4–2 and 5–5. However, it would be incautious to assert that this is the earliest age at which these inferences can be elicited in average children. Although a considerable effort was made to use experimental operations simpler than Piaget's, it is quite possible that further study would lead to the discovery of procedures in which the inferential response studied could be elicited in still younger children, thus demonstrating that some relevant factor was overlooked in the present experimental design.

The crucial theoretical issue concerns the usefulness of postulating the existence of an "emergent" formal reasoning factor in the development of children's length judgment.

It could be argued that if the apparent "age of emergence" is a function of the particular manipulanda and discriminanda involved and of their mode of presentation to *S*, then the concept of an emergent level is unsatisfactory in that it lacks parsimony and could even obstruct psychological analysis. One might be forced to postulate as many "levels" as there are different experimental operations for eliciting the same alleged psychological process.

One weakness of this argument against the "levels" concept is that it could clearly be transposed and used to attack, not only Piaget's, but any concept of emergent levels. Moreover, one can argue that there must be some point between birth and maturity at which the kind of inferential process studied in this section develops in the average child. The reason why Piaget's results differ from those reported here is not simply that there is a difference in experimental procedures, but is, the writer believes, because in designing his experiments Piaget fails to eliminate important variables which are not involved in the definition of the processes he sets out to investigate. That is to say, in his studies of measurement, Piaget claims to be studying the development of the formal reasoning inherent in measurement; he is probably actually studying primarily the development of skill or interest in the use of measuring rods, or perhaps the development of children's understanding of certain words. The results obtained here therefore lend support to the notion of an "emergent" reasoning process in the development of children's length judgments, although the establishment of "emergent levels" is a more complex experimental problem than Piaget apparently seems to believe.

It is clear that if one seeks to state an age at which a particular type of response develops, the only age which is not completely arbitrary is the earliest age at which this type of response can be elicited using the simplest experimental procedures. To establish these "simplest" procedures requires the discovery and systematic exploration of all relevant factors. The experiment reported can be interpreted as a step in this direction. Such a program of research would presumably result either in a clear operational definition of the alleged "emergent" process, or in convincing evidence that the notion of an "emergent" reasoning process in children's conception of length is unsatisfactory because no clear distinction between the "higher" and "lower" processes can be found. There is nothing in this study to suggest that the formal reasoning inherent in measurement cannot be defined experimentally.

CHANGES IN "SET" ASSOCIATED WITH THE EMERGENCE OF MEASURE-MENT   In presenting the qualitative results, differences in behavior were described, which seemed broadly related to age. The oldest *S*s showed the most comparison behavior, especially in the trials without yardstick: they tended to lean back in their chairs to facilitate visual comparison of the uprights; they paused before responding and looked intently at each upright, often giving each several glances. Such behavior indicates that they readily transferred the set to discriminate length, learned in Phase 1 with the large and obvious length differences, to Phase 2 where the length differences were small. In contrast to this, comparison behavior was conspicuous by its absence in many of the youngest *S*s. This fact suggests that perhaps differences in length too small to be readily perceptible did not have much significance for the younger children. It was as if they were not "trying" to find the longer upright when the differences were small, not because they were unmotivated, but because they failed to recognize the possibility of a difference in length too small to be noticed. They seemed to lack the attitude of the older *S*s expressed in the words, "I know one's bigger, but they look the same."[15]

Thus, there is evidence that two kinds of behavior develop. First, there is the development of the inferential response, which is revealed quantitatively in the increasing success with age in the measurement trials of Phase 2. Second, there is a change with age in the "attitude" or "set" adopted toward small differences in length, which seems to consist in a greater tendency with increasing age to transfer the set to discriminate length from large obvious differences to small barely perceptible ones. This change in "attitude" is revealed quantitatively in the better-than-chance success of the oldest *S*s in the trials without yardstick.

The question must be raised whether there is any connection between these two phenomena. Is the development of the inferential response related to the phenomenon referred to as a change in attitude? On this issue there are three possible hypotheses which are worth exploring, although the present data do not clearly indicate which hypothesis is valid.

The first hypothesis is that the change in "attitude" or "set" and the inferential response develop quite independently and are unrelated in the

---

[15] If this interpretation is correct, it raises the more general problem of how and when children learn to make the conceptual distinction between a "real" and a "phenomenal" world. This problem has been largely ignored by experimental genetic psychology outside Geneva. No general discussion of it is attempted here.

individual child. If this is so then there should have been no tendency for the *S*s who made an inferential response to have done better in the trials without yardstick than those who failed to make an inferential response. In the total sample this was certainly not true. The relationship can be clearly seen in Fig. 6. However, when age was taken into account the correlation was equivocal. Matching the seven youngest *S*s who made an inferential response with *S*s of the same age who failed to do so, it was found that those who made an inferential response obtained a mean score on the trials without yardstick significantly higher than the others ($t = 2.47$, $df = 6$, $p < .05$); however, both means (5.7 and 4.4) can themselves be readily explained on the hypothesis that the *S*s were responding at random. Consequently the evidence against the first hypothesis is ambiguous. The remaining hypotheses both assume a relationship.

The second hypothesis is that the change in attitude is the determining variable and that the development of an inferential response is dependent on it. That is, the adoption by *S* of the more "mature" set is a precondition for the occurrence of an inferential response: unless *S* realizes the uprights differ in length and consequently seeks the longer, he will not infer the longer upright in the measurement trials. Plausible though this hypothesis may be, the evidence is against it. The best evidence is qualitative. Although all *S*s who showed comparison behavior also made an inferential response, there were at least eight *S*s who made an inferential response but who showed no comparison behavior in the trials without yardstick: there was no change in posture to bring the uprights closer together in the field of view, the response was not preceded by several ocular shifts from one stimulus to the other, and there was no verbalization which suggested that these *S*s realized the stimuli differed in length. Thus, an inferential response could occur in the context of behavior associated with the more "primitive" set. The quantitative evidence of Fig. 4 points in the same direction: inferential responses occurred in much younger *S*s than did any success in the trials without yardstick. Unfortunately, however, the quantitative evidence is inconclusive because of the illusion presumably induced by the arms placed at the upper and lower extremities of the uprights: the possibility cannot be dismissed that the younger *S*s failed to discriminate to a degree better than chance because they were deceived by the illusion, and not because their "set" was inappropriate.

The evidence, although primarily qualitative, is more consistent with the third hypothesis, which is that the change in attitude toward barely perceptible length differences is dependent upon the prior development of inferential processes of the type studied. Should this hypothesis prove valid, it could be explained on the theory that the development of the inferences basic to measurement leads to the establishment of a concept of length as a dimension in which continuous small increments are possible. A frame of reference might then be created within which barely perceptible length differences could acquire meaning.

To decide definitely between these hypotheses a detailed exploration would be necessary of the minimum length difference discriminated as a function of age, both with and without measurement, and with stimuli which do not give rise to an illusion. It would be interesting to know whether the smallest length difference noticed by children decreases steadily as a function of age, or whether there is a sharp decrease at any period which might correspond to the change in "attitude" toward small differences which is suggested by the present data.[16] If there is such a sharp decrease, it would be interesting to know whether or not it is associated with the development of inferential responses of the kind studied here, and whether these inferential responses usher in the sharp decrease in DL, or follow it. Some of the issues raised by this study might then be resolved.

Recapitulation

Some aspects of the logic of length measurement were discussed and a series of studies of length judgment were reviewed. These included a group of studies by Piaget in which he attempted to diagnose children's grasp of the logic of measurement through their manner of using measuring rods. He found children under 7 yr. deficient in this respect. A number of criticisms of Piaget's work and general methodology were discussed. It was suggested that adequate use of measuring rods by children may involve factors other than the performance of the logical operations basic to measurement. In particular, learning of effective measuring techniques may be an important factor.

To investigate this possibility a task was constructed in which no manipulation of measuring rods was demanded of the Ss. They were required to make deductions about the relative lengths of two nearly equal upright sticks, using the rule, $A > B.B > C. \supset .A > C$. This inference has the status of an axiom in the logic of measurement. The experimental procedures were adapted from work with animals, so that it was possible to present the task with a minimum of verbal communication between E and S. Vocabulary development, an uncontrolled factor in Piaget's studies, is therefore unlikely to be a factor influencing the results. The methodological importance of this innovation was stressed.

It was found that with these procedures, the inferential response $A > B.B > C. \supset .A > C$ was elicited approximately two or three years before the age at which Piaget claims it first becomes available to children.

Unless Piaget incorrectly reports the age at which children begin to manipulate measuring rods properly, it is clear that factors other than

---

[16] It is assumed, of course, that the DL is explored using an experimental technique in which S is first trained to discriminate large length differences, and then the smallest length difference to which he will generalize this discrimination is studied.

correct reasoning according to the axiomatic standards of the logic of measurement are involved in his studies. These factors are probably vocabulary development (particularly, comprehension of the meanings of words such as "measure," "same length," etc.) and the development of skill and interest in the technique of length measurement. The effect of these factors is probably to conceal the reasoning ability of many of Piaget's Ss.

The results indicate that the definition of "emergent levels" of development is a complicated problem. The objection that the apparent "age of emergence" is dependent on the specific experimental procedures utilized does not pose insuperable difficulties for the concept of "levels." This objection does, however, suffice to demonstrate that any stated "age of emergence" must be arbitrary until the effects of all relevant variables have been systematically explored, so that extraneous factors (e.g., vocabulary development, skill in the use of measuring rods, etc.) which may hinder the younger Ss from responding to the relevant cues (the relative lengths of uprights and measuring stick) are identified and eliminated. With this qualification, the experiment reported lends support to Piaget's notion that the formal reasoning inherent in length measurement constitutes an "emergent" process in child development.

The experimental task also contained some trials in which the two nearly equal uprights were compared by direct visual comparison. Qualitative aspects of the behavior of some of the older Ss in these trials suggested that they adopted an "attitude" or "set" which was different from that of many of the younger Ss, and which assisted them to achieve some measure of success in these discrimination trials. The possible genetic relationship of this change with age in "attitude" or "set" to the development of the inferential response was discussed. The evidence, although not conclusive, suggests that once a child is capable of the inferences basic to measurement, he may develop a concept of length as a dimension, as a result of which he more readily adopts a "set" to discriminate small differences in length. A method of examining this hypothesis experimentally was suggested.

{ The section "The Development of a Concept of Position }
{ Order" is omitted. }

THE RELATION OF ORDER DISCRIMINATION TO THE INFERENTIAL RESPONSE $A > B.B > C. \supset .A > C$

In the previous sections it was shown that, although Piaget may be mistaken about the specific ages at which order discrimination and the inferential response $A > B.B > C. \supset .A > C$ develop, there is nothing to indicate that his concept of levels of development should be rejected.

In this section and the following one, Piaget's theory of intelligence, which contains his definition of general levels of intellectual functioning, is discussed. This theory suggests specific predictions about the relationship between discrimination of order and the inferential response studied.

Piaget's Theory of Intelligence

According to Piaget, logical reasoning consists of a group of "emergent" intellectual functions. He refers to these as "operational thinking," with which he identifies "intelligence." His theory of intelligence, therefore, attempts to give a detailed definition of logical reasoning in the following manner.

Piaget's basic postulate is that mature intellectual processes are isomorphic with the "operations" of bivalent logic.[17] An example may clarify this use of the term "isomorphic." "Addition" of numbers is an intellectual process occurring in children when they do arithmetic; it is presumed to be isomorphic with the "additive operation" discussed by mathematicians. Similarly, deduction is an intellectual process (or processes) which can be placed in correspondence with one or more logical definitions. Piaget's definitions of the logical operations with which intellectual processes are assumed to be isomorphic are similar, but not identical, to the operations of the spatial, class, and propositional interpretations of the Boolean calculus, as described in texts on logic. Thus, the principal processes for which he finds isomorphic logical definitions are conjunction and disjunction of classes, of regions of space and of propositions,[18] and the corresponding relations of class inclusion, geographical or spatial inclusion, and implication. These processes are assumed to be, so to speak, the "atoms" of which intelligence is made. This part of Piaget's theory is essentially an essay in formal logic rather than psychology. According to Piaget, the relation between the logical definitions and the corresponding intellectual processes is analogous to the relation between pure geometry and physical geometry,

---

[17] It is difficult to phrase this postulate so as to avoid becoming embroiled in epistemological argument. The epistemology of the connection between reasoning process and logical operation is still disputed among logicians. To identify logical operation and reasoning process is Boole's fallacy and Piaget is well aware of this. The term "isomorphic" has been selected to express the postulated relation between logical operation and intellectual process in order—hopefully—to circumvent the epistemological issues. The use of this term does not do violence to Piaget's generally expressed views (Piaget, 1949, pp. 1–31; 1950, pp. 18–37; 1953b).

[18] The logical definitions of these operations may be found in most introductory texts in symbolic logic (e.g., Langer, 1953). Piaget's own definitions are expressed somewhat differently, but a review of these differences would complicate this discussion unnecessarily. See Piaget (1949; or 1950, pp. 43–47) for a brief summary of Piaget's system. For examples of these operations in ordinary speech, see Footnote 1.

or to the isomorphism between complex algebra and certain properties of alternating current electric circuits.[19]

Psychologically, the terms *conjunction* and *disjunction* are ambiguous. To illustrate the meaning intended here, class conjunction will be discussed in some detail. A conjunction of classes is that class whose members share the attributes of two other classes: thus, the class of white sheep is the conjunction of the class of white objects and the class of sheep, the class of balls (with exceptions) is the conjunction of the class of spheres and the class of playthings.

It might be argued that whenever we identify an object we perceive (e.g., a white sheep) we are performing a conjunction of classes, since any perceptual identification requires the simultaneous recognition of a number of different cues. If class conjunction is interpreted psychologically as the recognition of combinations of cues, it is obvious that it is an extremely primitive process which occurs early in phylogenetic development: many nonverbalizing organisms certainly discriminate classes of objects on the basis of combinations of cues. The apparent ubiquity of logical operations, viewed from this standpoint, appears to have led Lashley (1956) to assert that the operations of bivalent logic are coincident with the existence of nervous tissue, and this has led him to insist upon the need for a "neurology of logic."

Whether or not one selects a logical model for perception appears to be a matter of taste; many workers prefer a statistical model or one taken from information theory (e.g., Attneave, 1954; Binder, 1955). It is clear that whatever the reasoning processes are to which Piaget refers in his studies, they are *not* the processes involved in perceptual identification as discussed in the preceding paragraph. Unfortunately, the writer has not been able to find an adequate discussion by Piaget of this ambiguity in his concept of logical operation; consequently, the interpretation of his conception that follows is the writer's.

In the English language, a conjunction of classes is denoted by a syntactical device: the qualification of a noun by an adjective as, for example, in the phrases "white sheep," "navigable rivers," etc. To render the following discussion more concrete, suppose that the English language be modified so that a conjunction of classes is expressed by the nonsense syllable "ZIK." In this modified English, white sheep would be denoted by the phrase "ZIK-whitethings-sheep"; navigable rivers would become "ZIK-navigable-waters-rivers"; balls would be denoted by the same word, "balls," but might also be represented by the phrase "ZIK-spheres-playthings." It is clear that the words "balls" and "ZIK" have quite different meanings. Knowledge of the meaning of the words "ball" and "white sheep," reflected in correct identification of these objects, is not the same as knowledge of the meaning of the word "ZIK," reflected in the proper usage of this term.

---

[19] In a book review, Isaacs (1951) discusses this point in relation to Piaget's theory.

The latter, let us say, reflects a general concept of class conjunction, which is not indicated by perceptual discrimination of either balls or white sheep. I believe it is to this, the discrimination of the meaning of the word "ZIK," that Piaget's theory refers when he uses the term *multiplication* or *conjunction of classes.*

There are many words and phrases in the English language which have a meaning as abstract as that of "ZIK" in the modified English discussed above. "Like," "similar to," "same as," "analogous to," "type of," "kind of," "species," "genus," "both . . . and," "either . . . or," "is a," "common to," are a few examples. These words express general characteristics of classes and have no reference to any specific class. The intellectual processes which Piaget's theory, as it is construed here, treats as isomorphic to the logical definitions of conjunction and disjunction of classes and of the relation of class inclusion are the kinds of processes which are reflected in the understanding and proper usage of such words and phrases.

The distinction made between the learning of names of objects and the learning of words such as "ZIK" is not new to psychology. It seems closely related to the distinction Lashley (1938) has made between "first-order generalizations" and "second-order generalizations." Examples in the literature of first-order generalizations are learning to discriminate "triangularity per se" (Andrew and Harlow, 1942; Fields, 1932, 1936; Gellerman, 1933; Lashley, 1938),[20] and to distinguish the identical elements in Hull's (1920) Chinese ideographs. Lashley's example of a problem whose solution requires second-order generalization is the "oddity" problem (Harlow, 1951; Lashley, 1938). The writer would suggest that other examples among nonverbal tests are the "sameness-difference" problem administered to chimpanzees (Robinson, 1955), and the experiments reported in the present paper. Examples of verbally communicated problems involving second-order generalization are provided in studies of the learning of logical relations by children (Kreezer and Dallenbach, 1929; Schooley and Hartmann, 1937).

It may be noted that the distinction between "abstract" and "concrete" thinking made by Goldstein and Scheerer (1941) appears to have much in common with Piaget's distinction between "operational" and "preoperational" thinking and with Lashley's between first- and second-order generalizations.[21] All these distinctions appear to follow that made by logicians between "class" and "class of classes."[22]

Assuming the validity of the postulate that mature intellectual processes

---

[20] That is, learning to choose triangular stimuli, as against other shapes, irrespective of the size, color, or orientation of the stimuli.

[21] However, as in his discussion of amnesic aphasia, Goldstein (1948) sometimes appears to suggest that it is the nominal aspects of speech which are most clearly related to "abstract" thinking, whereas in Piaget's theory, it would be, of course, the syntactical aspects.

[22] Cf. Russell's (1920, Ch. 2) definition of number.

are isomorphic with the operations of bivalent logic,[23] Piaget adopts the following research method. He sets children problems whose solution requires a certain line of logical reasoning. He then observes how children at various ages solve these problems, and he tries to observe the method of solution. Consideration of the ages of the children who solve the problem leads Piaget to specify the age at which the reasoning process involved in the problem develops.

He finds that certain types of problems are solved at the same age. Although he never explores the intercorrelations between success and failure on different problems, he concludes that reasoning processes develop in groups at particular ages. Specifically, he claims that the processes of class conjunction, class disjunction, and the concept of the relation of class inclusion develop in children at approximately 7 yr. of age. He also claims that the analogous operations of the spatial interpretation of Boole's system[24] develop at the same age. At around 11 yr., the child becomes capable of reasoning with propositions. That is, the processes of conjunction and disjunction of propositions develop at this age along with the concept of the relation of implication.

It can be seen, therefore, that Piaget's notion that reasoning processes develop in groups clearly implies the postulate that where operations, inferences, etc., are mutually interdependent (i.e., the logical definition of the one involves reference to the other, or that both derive from the same interpretation of a logical calculus), then the corresponding reasoning processes develop in association in children's thinking.[25] Thus, the operations of class conjunction, class disjunction, and the concept of the relation of class inclusion all derive from the class interpretation of the Boolean calculus and would therefore be expected to develop in children as a group. Later it will be shown that position order and the proposition $A > B.B > C. \supset .A > C$ (where ">" is interpreted "longer") are logically interdependent and, as an illustration of how Piaget's theory might operate, this postulate will be used to predict a high correlation between success in the tasks described in the two previous sections.

Summarizing Piaget's theory schematically, it consists, first, of a set of logical definitions with which the intellectual processes subsumed under the title "intelligence" are postulated to be isomorphic. Second, it postulates

---

[23] One may note that there is no a priori reason why bivalent logic, rather than any of the polyvalent logics, should be selected as the model for reasoning.

[24] As noted in Footnote 1, Piaget's system differs somewhat from Boole's but the differences can be neglected for the purpose of this study.

[25] The proposition that logical and ontogenetic priority correspond would seem to be a corollary. That is, where one logical definition is dependent on another, the intellectual process corresponding to the latter develops earlier. That there is at least some truth in this proposition is suggested by many educational practices based on common sense: for example, children are customarily taught to add numbers before they are taught to multiply, presumably because multiplication logically presupposes addition.

implicitly that where the logical definitions are interdependent or derive from the same interpretation of a logical system, the corresponding intellectual processes will be found to develop in association in children's thinking. Third, the theory contains a group of empirical laws stating the ages at which certain groups of processes develop. One may note that the ages indicated in these empirical laws could readily be altered where necessary without changing the main structure of Piaget's theory.

A CRITICISM OF PIAGET'S CONCEPT OF INTELLECTUAL PROCESS   In theory construction in psychology, intellectual processes have the theoretical status of hypothetical constructs. A hypothetical construct requires two kinds of specification. First, it is specified in terms of its relations to other constructs of a theoretical system. In Piaget's theory this kind of definition is contained in the two postulates that intellectual processes are isomorphic to definitions of logical operations, and that when the logical definitions are interdependent the corresponding intellectual processes develop in association. However, in modern behavioral theory a hypothetical construct of this kind requires specification of the experimental operations through which it may be elicited, and of the characteristics of the response which testifies to its presence; without this it lacks empirical reference. Unfortunately, there is little in Piaget's theory which fulfills this function. The goal of his experiments is not to provide adequate specifying procedures, but only to provide situations in which he can diagnose the character of intellectual processes through a series of acute observations of the Ss' behavior and language. The tasks he uses are therefore not intended to serve as specifying experimental procedures, and the results from the experiments reported in the previous sections demonstrate that the tasks used by him in his studies of length measurement and of concepts of position order are inadequate for this purpose. It may be that Piaget's view that psychological processes do not need to be specified in terms of experimental procedures leads him to neglect the need for careful experimental design, with the result that he sometimes overlooks important variables.

This criticism exposes an important weakness of Piaget's theory—namely, that its roots in empirical fact are not entirely adequate. The power of his theory lies in the fact that it is potentially capable of giving a detailed and precise account of the development of intellectual functioning, and that numerous predictions may be derived from a few simple postulates.

Derivation of the Genetic Association
of Order Discrimination with the Inferential
Response $A > B.B. > C. \supset .A > C$

As an example of how Piaget's theory might operate, this relationship will be derived using the postulate that when definition of logical operations are interdependent, the intellectual processes isomorphic to these operations develop in association. It follows from this postulate that, if there is a clear relation between the definition in logic of serial order and the proposition A > B.B. > C. ⊃ .A > C, then discrimination of position order and the inferential response A > B.B > C. ⊃ .A > C develop together in children.

The relation in logic between "order" and rules of the form A > B.B > C. ⊃ .A > C is clearly stated by Russell in a discussion of the definition of order. Russell (1920) states, "We must not look for the definition of order in the nature of the set of terms to be ordered. . . . The order lies, not in the *class* of terms, but in a relation among the members of the class, in respect of which some appear as earlier and some as later" (pp. 30–31).

According to Russell, ordering relations are asymmetric, transitive, and connected.[26] That is, the property of transitivity of a relation is part of the definition of order, or, as Nagel (1930) states, it is an "axiom" of order. The rule, A > B.B. > C. ⊃ .A > C merely states the transitive nature of the relation "longer than."

Given that a relation is asymmetric,[27] and disregarding the property of connectedness,[28] one may therefore predict that as the relation becomes transitive for a child, he should begin to distinguish different sequential arrangements of objects ordered with respect to it.

A particular kind of series is specified by its generating relation. Thus, the relation "heavier than" gives rise to a series of weights. The relations "after" or "before" give rise to temporal series. The relation of class inclusion gives rise to a class hierarchy (e.g., Greeks: men: mortal beings: etc.). Similarly, in a position sequence, such as that involved in the order-discrimination task, the relevant relation is spatial: "left of," or "right of." The asymmetric transitive relation involved in the length-measurement task

[26] A relation is asymmetric if, holding between x and y, it does not also hold between y and x (e.g., longer than, left of, father of). A relation is transitive if, holding between x and y, and also between y and z, it holds between x and z (e.g., longer than, left of, same as). A relation is connected if it has the property that, "given any two terms of the class to be ordered, there [is] one which precedes and another which follows. For example, of any two integers, . . . one is smaller and the other greater; but of any two complex numbers this is not true" (Russell, 1920, p. 32).

[27] I have been unable to think of any experimental operations for investigating an S's understanding of the asymmetry of a relation, which differ from operations used to train him to discriminate the relation.

[28] Connectedness is a property of the number series in which Russell was principally interested. It is not, however, a property of all series: for example, it is a property of positions on a scale (no two positions being identical), but it is not necessarily a property of objects measured against a scale (since two of these may be the same). In the experiment reported, the Ss were presumably comparing lengths of objects, not positions on the length scale.

is also a spatial relation, but a different one, namely, "longer than" (or "shorter than"). In order, therefore, to predict that the development of a grasp of the transitivity of the relation "longer than" will be associated with the genesis of discrimination of position sequences ordered with respect to the relation "left of" or "right of," it is first necessary to show that the relation "longer than" can be defined in terms of the relations "left of" and "right of." However, the relation "longer than" can indeed be so defined: the statement "OA is longer than OB" is a verbal shorthand for some more awkward statement such as, "When OA and OB are juxtaposed so that their left hand extremities, O, are coincident, then the relative positions of their other extremities will be such that OA overlaps OB, i.e., such that A is to the right of B." Thus, relative length is defined in terms of overlapping positions, and it is therefore possible to treat the relation "longer than" as a special case of the left-right relation.

It can therefore be predicted that discrimination of position order and the inferential response $A > B.B > C. \supset .A > C$ will be found to develop in association in children, or—to say the same thing in different words—the age at which the relation "longer than" becomes transitive for children should be closely related to the age at which different serial arrangements of a set of objects are distinguished.

A MACHINE MODEL   The derivation of this prediction might be represented more concretely in the following manner. Suppose we construct a machine which will perform the inference $A > B.B > C. \supset .A > C.$ Into one end of this machine we feed the relations between A and B, and between B and C; the machine performs the inference and we read off its deductions concerning the relations between A and C. Now let us construct a second machine which will perform the order discriminations of the order task. Russell's logical analysis of order informs us that there is no operation performed by the first machine which the second machine cannot also perform. Moreover, the first machine can perform certain operations of the second machine: it can discriminate the sequence of three objects.

In the two previous sections, some similarities between the behavior of children and of these hypothetical machines were investigated as a function of age. Logical analysis demonstrates that these two machines are in important respects two versions of the same machine. Consequently, when an *S* behaves like one of these machines, he should also behave like the other. One may therefore make the two following predictions: First, the ages of first appearance of order discrimination and of the inferential response $A > B.B > C. \supset .A > C$ will be found to be closely related. Since the age of first appearance is difficult to establish more than approximately, the second prediction is more significant: there should be an extremely high correlation between the two tasks.

Empirical Evidence

Figure 7 portrays the increase with age of the percentage of Ss who made an inferential response either in Phase 2 or Phase 3 (i.e., without or with the supplementary verbal instructions) of the measurement task. Juxtaposed with this is the graph showing the increase with age of the percentage of Ss who reached the criterion in any of the series of the order task. The latter curve is identical to that for Series C with three colors per card, since all Ss who reached the criterion in any series were successful in Series "C."

It can be seen that the course of development is almost exactly the same on the two tasks. The youngest age group is the only one at which there is a difference of more than a few percentage points between the two curves and this difference is caused entirely by one S who made an inferential response in the measurement task but failed to show any concept of order.[29]

The fact that the two developmental curves shown in Fig. 7 are almost superimposable confirms the prediction, but it would be dangerous to attach too much significance to it. Future investigation may well demonstrate that with other experimental procedures, either or both of the responses studied can be elicited in children of average intellectual capacity younger than these Ss. If such should be the case, the close correspondence between the two curves would be revealed as fortuitous.

More significant is the fact that there was a strong tendency for Ss either to fail both tasks or to pass both. This tendency occurred in all age groups. Altogether 37 Ss took both tasks. Of these, 12 failed both, 22 showed some measure of success in both, 2 made an inferential response in the measurement task but completely failed to discriminate order, and one failed to make an inferential response but reached the criterion in some of the series of the order task. Even when one eliminates the two oldest age groups, in which 100% of Ss passed both tasks, and the youngest age group, in which almost all Ss failed both tasks, the correlation remains high. Considering, then, only the children aged 4–2 to 5–5, it was found

---

[29] The age of this child was 3–8 and her adjustment to the order task was so unusual that the task cannot be regarded as a fair test of order discrimination for her. After the measurement task she discovered that other Ss, who had not eaten the candy they had won, had had their earnings wrapped up for them in a piece of paper. Every piece of candy she won she then wanted wrapped up at once in a similar piece of paper and placed some distance away from her so that she would not be tempted to eat it immediately. Her attention was focused much more on what was going to happen to the candy than on the task. Once she had won three or four pieces responding randomly she was content and wanted to leave the conflictful experimental situation. Little significance can be attributed to her failure to reveal any concept of order.

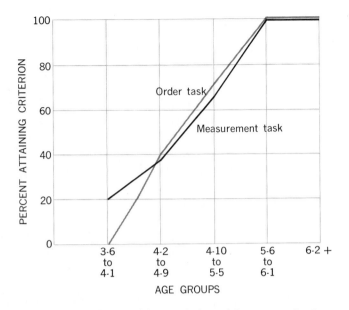

Figure 7   Percentage of *S*s making an inferential response in the measurement task and discriminating order. The number of *S*s in each age group was 5, 13, 9, 8, and 5, respectively, for the measurement task, and 5, 12, 11, 11, and 5, respectively, for the order-discrimination task.

that of the 20 children who took both tasks, 9 failed both, 9 were successful in both, 1 made an inferential response but showed no concept of order, and 1 showed some concept of order but failed to make an inferential response. Chi square = 12.8 ($p < .0001$), and the correlation (tetrachoric) is .96 ($\phi = .80$). In fact, in view of the impossibility of constructing tests of perfect reliability, the correlation appears to be as high as can be expected in careful psychological research.

Thus both predictions are substantially fulfilled. Discrimination of position order and the inferential response A > B.B >C. ⊃ .A > C were found to have the same course of development with age, at least in this sample of children and under the experimental conditions employed. Also, children who made an inferential response in the measurement task were also found to discriminate order, and vice versa.

Discussion

Colleagues with whom these results have been discussed have sometimes made the point that some degree of correlation between the tasks would be expected, since success on both tasks is probably correlated with intelligence test scores. In purely statistical terms, this point is no doubt valid. However, these tasks were designed in order to test a prediction derived from Piaget's theory of the development of intelligence and, in terms of Piaget's theory, success on them, by definition, reflects intelligence. It therefore begs the question to invoke intelligence to explain the correlation found, since the nature of intelligence is itself the subject of the investigation.

For this reason, intelligence tests were not administered to the Ss. One would, of course, expect that success on both tasks would correlate with mental age. The kind of inference demanded in the measurement task has been regarded since Aristotle as a manifestation of intelligence; stringing a chain of beads in a given order is a recurrent test item on the Binet.

It is known that correlations between individual test items at the preschool level are typically low relative to correlations between items at higher age levels (Goodenough, 1954, p. 466). Considering the age of the Ss, the correlation found is thus higher than one would expect on the general grounds that all tests of intellectual functioning correlate. However, the size of the correlation obtained is difficult to evaluate statistically because the sample is small and because it is not possible to establish confidence limits for a tetrachoric correlation or phi-coefficient.

One may note that Piaget's theory does not predict that all tests of intellectual functioning, paired indiscriminately, would correlate with each other. Between success in two carefully designed tasks such as the ones used here, one of which demands a grasp of the transitivity of the spatial relation "longer than," and the other of which demands the discrimination of sequences ordered with respect to an associated spatial relation, it predicts a very high correlation. But there appears to be nothing in Piaget's theory which would predict a particularly high correlation between success in these two spatial tasks and, for example, success in any task used to explore the development of operations of classification.[30, 31]

Conclusion

In the correlation found between order discrimination and the inferential response A > B.B > C. ⊃ .A > C, a prediction derived from a postulate implicit in Piaget's theory has been empirically verified. Within the

---

[30] It is interesting to speculate that the distinction between the operations of the class and spatial interpretations of the logical calculus in Piaget's theory might provide a theoretical basis for the verbal and spatial factors usually found by factor analyses. It still appears to be a matter of interpretation in factor analysis whether the so-called verbal factor is truly a linguistic factor, or whether it relates to reasoning about class membership, relations between classes, etc., which provide the content of so many verbal tests.

[31] An unpublished study of the development of the class-inclusion relation, employed many of the Ss used in the experiments reported here. There was no obvious correlation between solution of the "class-inclusion" problem and success in the length-measurement and order-discrimination tasks. Unfortunately, the small number of Ss and the variety of factors found to be related to solution of the class-inclusion problem greatly limit the significance of this finding.

restricted context of this study, the data confirm the validity of the postulate that when the definitions of logical operations are interdependent, the isomorphic intellectual processes develop in association. Whether this postulate can be verified over a much wider range of children's intellectual responses and thus provide a solid empirical basis for Piaget's theory of the development of intelligence is a matter for further research. . . .

SUMMARY AND CONCLUSIONS

Piaget's theory of the development of intellect has been examined in a number of ways. The first and primary purpose was to select two areas of intellectual functioning discussed by Piaget and to subject to detailed investigation his description of the development that takes place during childhood within these areas. This purpose was accomplished in the second and third sections. In the second section, the development in children of certain logical inferences, whose validity is tacitly assumed when length is measured, was studied. In the third section, the development of children's concepts of position order was investigated. In each case Piaget's theory, his research methods, and the nature of his evidence were reviewed and discussed, and an experiment was conducted to evaluate certain weaknesses in his approach, suggested by the discussion.

The second purpose was to discuss Piaget's theory of the development of intelligence, to derive an hypothesis from it and to test this hypothesis. The hypothesis concerned the expected correlation between a child's performance of one of the inferences basic in the logic of measurement, and his possession of a concept of position order, reflected in the discrimination of sequences of objects arranged in different orders.

The third purpose was to assess in a general manner the concordance of Piaget's concept of levels of development with the available data on the development of intelligence as measured by intelligence tests.

The evidence suggests the following conclusions.

(1) The inference $A > B.B > C. \supset .A > C$ (where ">" is interpreted "longer than"), which has the status of an axiom in the logic of length measurement, is generally available to children at least two years before the age at which Piaget locates its development. Factors other than correct reasoning according to the axiomatic standards of the logic of measurement therefore appear to be involved in his studies. The difference between Piaget's experimental procedures and those used here suggests that these factors are the development of skill and interest in the techniques of length measurement, and perhaps vocabulary development (especially, comprehension of the meanings of words and phrases such as "measure," "same length," etc.). The effect of these factors is probably to conceal the reasoning ability of many of Piaget's Ss.

(2) Children show some concept of position order, in general, at least two years before the age at which Piaget places the development of order discrimination. It was found that the number of items in the sequences to be dis-

criminated is an important variable disregarded by Piaget. It is likely, though not proven, that discrimination of order is facilitated for the younger Ss and the shorter sequences (i.e., less than seven items) when the task is presented using relatively nonverbal methods.

(3) There is nothing in the data which suggests that Piaget's concept of "emergent levels" of development should be rejected. The objection that the apparent "age of emergence" is a function of the particular task manipulanda and discriminanda was considered in some detail. This objection is not fatal for a concept of levels although it suffices to show that the problem of establishing levels is somewhat more complicated than Piaget appears to have envisaged. The reason why Piaget's results differ from those obtained here is not, in the writer's opinion, because his notion of levels is inapplicable, but because in his research design he fails to eliminate important variables which are not involved in the definition of the processes he sets out to investigate, and which hinder many of his Ss from responding to the appropriate cues.

(4) Piaget's theory of the development of intelligence predicts accurately the high correlation in the individual child between the availability of the inference $A > B.B > C. \supset .A > C$ and the possession of a concept of position order.

(5) The available data on the development of intelligence as measured by intelligence tests suggest that there are periods of transition during the preschool years during which the nature of intellectual functions changes. These data support the notion of phases or levels in the development of intellect and seem rather difficult to account for on any other basis. However, the period of transition most relevant to this examination of Piaget's theory appears to occur during the middle and late preschool years, rather than at approximately age 7 yr., as Piaget reports. The evidence thus suggests, once again, that Piaget probably places too late the development of the intellectual processes upon which his theory bears.

While discussing Piaget's theory of intelligence, it was noted that, although his theory is in some ways admirably precise and clear, his conception of psychological process is at variance with that of modern behavioral theory. For Piaget, intellectual processes are not hypothetical constructs, which require specification in terms of the experimental procedures by which they may be elicited, but realities which need only to be diagnosed through intuitive analysis of an S's behavior and language. In his research his major effort is therefore expended on analysis of his Ss' methods of solution of problems, rather than on experimental design. This method of approach perhaps leads him to overlook relevant variables, with the result that he is misled as to the age of development of the processes he is investigating. In this respect, one contribution of the present study is that it begins to provide more carefully designed experimental procedures for eliciting a few of the processes upon which his theory bears.

In view of the many criticisms that have been made of Piaget, it should be emphasized that the data reported provide considerable support for his notion of emergent levels and also, within the limited scope of these experiments, for his conception of the emergent processes as "operational" thinking.

REFERENCES

Andrew, G., and H. F. Harlow (1942). Performance of Macaque monkeys on a test of generalized triangularity. *Comp. Psychol. Monogr.*, **19** (3).

Arieti, S. (1948). Special logic of schizophrenic and other types of autistic thought. *Psychiatry*, **11**, 325–338.

Attneave, F. (1954). Some informational aspects of visual perception. *Psychol. Rev.*, **61**, 183–193.

Bergmann, G., and K. W. Spence (1944). The logic of psychophysical measurement. *Psychol. Rev.*, **51**, 1–24.

Binder, A. (1955). A statistical model for the process of visual recognition. *Psychol. Rev.*, **62**, 119–129.

Campbell, N. R. (1920). *Physics: the elements*. London: Cambridge.

Evarts, E. V., and H. W. Nissen (1953). Test of "the abstract attitude" in chimpanzees following ablation of prefrontal cortex. *AMA Arch. Neurol. Psychiat.*, **69**, 323–331.

Fields, P. E. (1932). Studies in concept formation: I. Development of the concept of triangularity by the rat. *Comp. Psychol. Monogr.*, **9** (2).

Fields, P. E. (1936). Studies in concept formation: IV. A comparison of white rats and raccoons with respect to their visual discrimination of certain geometric figures. *J. comp. Psychol.*, **21**, 341–355.

Fraisse, P., and P. Vautrey (1952a). La perception de l'espace, de la vitesse, et du temps chez l'enfant de cinq ans: I. L'espace et la vitesse. *Enfance*, **5**, 1–20.

Fraisse, P., and P. Vautrey (1952b). La perception de l'espace, de la vitesse, et du temps chez l'enfant de cinq ans. II. Le temps. *Enfance*, **5**, 102–119.

Gellerman, L. W. (1933). Form discrimination in chimpanzees and two-year-old children: I. Form (triangularity) per se. *J. genet. Psychol.*, **42**, 3–27.

Goldstein, K. (1948). *Language and language disturbances*. New York: Grune & Stratton.

Goldstein, K., and M. Scheerer. (1941). Abstract and concrete behavior: an experimental study with special tests. *Psychol. Monogr.*, **53**, (2), Whole No. 239.

Goodenough, Florence L. (1954). The measurement of mental growth in childhood. In L. Carmichael (Ed.), *Manual of child psychology*, second ed. New York: Wiley.

Harlow, H. F. (1951). Primate learning. In C. P. Stone (Ed.), *Comparative psychology*, third ed. New York: Prentice-Hall.

Hilgard, E. R. (1951). Methods and procedures in the study of learning. In S. S. Stevens (Ed.), *Handbook of experimental psychology*. New York: Wiley.

Hull, C. L. (1920). Quantitative aspects of the evolution of concepts. *Psychol. Monogr.*, **28** (1), Whole No. 123.

Isaacs, N. (1951). Review of J. Piaget, "Traité de logique." *Brit. J. Psychol.*, **42**, 185–188.

Kreezer, G., and K. M. Dallenbach (1929). Learning the relation of opposition. *Amer. J. Psychol.*, **41**, 432–441.

Langer, Susanne K. (1953). *An introduction to symbolic logic*, second ed. New York: Dover.

Lashley, K. S. (1938). The mechanism of vision: XV. Preliminary studies of the rat's capacity for detail vision. *J. genet. Psychol.*, **18**, 123–193.

Lashley, K. S. (1956). Cerebral organization and behavior. Address to the Association for Research in Nervous and Mental Diseases, New York.

Moore, T. V. (1929). The reasoning ability of children in the first years of school life. *Stud. Psychol. Psychiat., Catholic Univer. of Amer.*, **2** (2).

Nagel, E. (1930). Measurement. *Erkenntnis*, **2**, 313–333.

Piaget, J. (1946). *Les notions de mouvement et de vitesse chez l'enfant.* Paris: Presses Universitaires.

Piaget, J. (1949). *Traité de logique.* Paris: Colin.

Piaget, J. (1950). *The psychology of intelligence.* London: Routledge.

Piaget, J. (1953a). How children form mathematical concepts. *Scientific Amer.*, **189** (5), 74–79.

Piaget, J. (1953b). *Logic and psychology.* Manchester: Manchester University Press.

Piaget, J. (1955). *De la logique concrète de l'enfant à la logique propositionelle de l'adolescent.* Paris: Presses Universitaires.

Piaget, J., and Barbel Inhelder (1953). *La génèse de l'idée de hasard chez l'enfant.* Paris: Presses Universitaires.

Piaget, J., and Barbel Inhelder (1956). *The child's conception of space.* London: Routledge.

Piaget, J., Barbel Inhelder, and Alina Szeminska (1948). *La géométrie spontanée de l'enfant.* Paris: Presses Universitaires.

Piaget, J., and Alina Szeminska (1952). *The child's conception of number.* London: Routledge.

Riopelle, A. J., R. G. Alper, P. M. Strong, and H. W. Ades (1953). Multiple discrimination and patterned string performance of normal and temporal-lobectomized monkeys. *J. comp. physiol. Psychol.*, **46**, 145–149.

Robinson, J. S. (1955). The sameness-difference discrimination problem in chimpanzee. *J. comp. physiol. Psychol.*, **48**, 195–197.

Russell, B. (1920). *Introduction to mathematical philosophy*, second ed. London: G. Allen.

Schooley, M., and G. W. Hartmann (1937). The role of insight in the learning of logical relations. *Amer. J. Psychol.*, **49**, 287–292.

Spearman, C. (1923). *The nature of intelligence.* London: Macmillan.

Terman, L. M., and Maud A. Merrill (1937). *Measuring intelligence.* Boston: Houghton Mifflin.
Von Domarus, E. (1944). The specific laws of logic in schizophrenia. In J. S. Kasinin (Ed.), *Language and thought in schizophrenia.* Berkeley, Calif.: University of California Press.

CHAPTER

FOUR

LOGICAL

OPERATIONS

* * *

ESTS OF TWO basic Piagetian notions, themes which have been
reiterated throughout the volume,[1] appear in this chapter: the
invariance of the development of logical operations and the linkage
between operations. These themes have been reflected in the content of
specific tasks (for example, quantity and number), whereas in this chapter
the operations themselves are more clearly examined.

One basic Piagetian contention is that parallel invariant stage sequences
exist for classification and for seriation. Kofsky examines the stage sequence
of classification behavior, while Lovell, Mitchell, and Everett set out to
explore linkages between classification and seriation.

According to Kofsky (1966), the invariant sequence of the development
of classification skills has "not been tested by observing the chronological
development of a large number of Ss, cataloguing the steps leading up to
learning" (Kofsky, 1966, p. 1). She constructed eleven experimental tests,
based upon the report of Inhelder and Piaget, to determine, first, whether
the order of difficulty corresponds to that described by Piaget, and second,
whether mastery of a particular classification rule reflects mastery of previous rules. To test this latter contention, Kofsky employed a scalogram
analysis.

The observed order of task difficulty was in accord with theoretical expectations. A significant correlation between age of the children and number
of successful completions was also found. The scalogram analysis indicated that the invariance of the task mastery sequence was only partially
substantiated. Some of the more advanced tasks were passed while subjects
failed earlier, theoretically prerequisite, tasks. Kofsky interprets her results
in the context of methodological issues which need to be considered before
final determination of the validity of these Piagetian propositions is made.

Lovell, Mitchell, and Everett attempt to identify the relationships among
a number of classification and seriation tasks. In doing so, they replicated
many of the experiments originally reported by Inhelder and Piaget (1964).
The study utilized cross-sectional samples of primary pupils and a group
of educable retarded children.

In contrast to Inhelder and Piaget, Lovell *et al.* presented the entire task
array to each subject in the sample. This procedure permitted them to assess

---

[1] For a detailed discussion of the original ideas, see Inhelder and Piaget (1964),
Piaget (1952), Piaget and Inhelder (1956), and Piaget, Inhelder, and Szeminska
(1960).

the degree of intra-individual consistency for the classification-seriation behaviors in question. They present results, in terms of the number of children at each of the stages of development, for four tasks: addition of classes, multiplication of classes, visual seriation, and multiplication of asymmetrical transitive relations. Although the data are not reported in terms of individual performance patterns (see Lovell, Mitchell, and Everett, Table 2), the children consistently demonstrated a given stage-type behavior across the four task settings. The authors conclude that operational mobility (Stage II) for the four logical tasks appear in primary school children at about the same time. This conclusion supports the view that seriation and classification are parallel achievements. In addition to these main considerations, the study also reports a number of task instructions and stimulus material manipulations which have significant effects on the children's performances in a particular operations setting.

The holistic nature of Piagetian theory is further exemplified in the Shantz study, which is aimed at testing the degree of association between logical operations. She offers direct evidence concerning the co-relationship of three logical operations: multiple classification, asymmetric logical relationality, and asymmetric spatial relationality. Tasks representing these multiplicative abilities were given to seven-and-one-half-, nine-and-one-half-, and eleven-and-one-half-year-old children. The results offer only moderate support for Piaget's claim of close interdependence of logical structures and related abilities. Also, there was considerable variation in the task intercorrelations across the age range tested.

In this chapter, the studies have focused upon related aspects of the same complex processes involved in the development of logical operations. Varying degrees of confirmation of Piaget's original proposition were found. Additional research directed toward the unresolved issues should be of value. To this end, the reader may wish to consider the following questions:

(1) What prevents the appearance of maximum levels of concordance in the evolution of specific structures?

(2) Is it reasonable to expect concordance of logical operations at *each* stage of growth, or are there separate courses in the development of logical thought which become integrated at particular points in time and under certain conditions?

(3) What generalizations can be made from cross-sectional data as to the intra-individual course of development?

(4) What is the role of language, perceptual factors, and intellectual ability in influencing the role and degree of linkage among the logical operations?

(5) Are the best possible tasks used as measures of the operations?

(6) What methodological revisions are necessary to provide more specific and definitive tests of sequence and convergence of operations?

(7) How much learning is there within each task so that the application of multiple tasks to the same child does not, in fact, create artifactual correlations?

REFERENCES

Inhelder, Barbel, and J. Piaget (1964). *The early growth of logic in the child: classification and seriation.* New York: Harper & Row.

Kofsky, E. (1966). A scalogram study of classificatory development. *Child Develpm.,* 37 (1), 191–204.

Piaget, J. (1952). *The child's conception of number.* New York: Humanities Press.

Piaget, J., and Barbel Inhelder (1956). *The child's conception of space.* London: Routledge.

Piaget, J., Barbel Inhelder, and Alina Szeminska (1960). *The child's conception of geometry.* New York: Basic Books.

A SCALOGRAM STUDY
OF CLASSIFICATORY DEVELOPMENT

Ellin Kofsky

One of the fundamental assumptions of Piaget's theory of cognitive growth (Inhelder, 1962; Inhelder and Piaget, 1958) is that there is a fixed order in which concepts are acquired which is determined by the child's increasing ability to use complex logical operations. The theory has not been tested by observing the chronological development of a large number of *S*s and cataloguing the steps leading up to learning. Instead, the Genevans have used a cross-sectional approach in which groups of *S*s of different ages are given tasks which vary in complexity. Although it has been demonstrated (Piaget and Inhelder, 1956; Piaget, Inhelder, and Szeminska, 1960) that as the logical complexity of the task increases, the average age at which the task is mastered rises, the Genevans also have not reported enough data on the performance of individual *S*s on a wide variety of tasks to prove that the order of development is the same for all learners. More recent studies (Dodwell, 1961; Laurendeau and Pinard, 1962; Peel, 1959; Uzgiris, 1962; Wohlwill, 1960) have combined scaling techniques with the

Reprinted with the permission of the author and The Society for Research in Child Development, Inc., from *Child Development*, 1966, 37 (1), 191–204. This report is based on a doctoral dissertation submitted to the Department of Psychology, University of Rochester, in 1963. The author would like to thank John H. Flavell for his continuous guidance in executing and reporting the study and Donald Gardner and Bette Watson of the Rush-Henrietta, New York, school system and Elizabeth Staub and Marion Fulbright of Rochester, New York, for their assistance in making arrangements and securing pupils for this study.

cross-sectional approach to explore individual patterns of mastery of conceptual tasks. If one assumes that the most mature logical operations are also the most difficult, one can test whether the order of difficulty is the same for all learners. In other words, each *S* who has learned a skill of a given level of difficulty should also have acquired all the easier skills. It was decided to use the same research strategy in the exploration of the development of classificatory skills.

Past research in classification tasks has focused on how children learn (*a*) to form one class (Bruner and Olver, 1963; Inhelder and Piaget, 1959; Lovell, Mitchell, and Everett, 1962; Morf, 1959; Vigotsky, 1962), (*b*) to change their criteria for categorization (Heald and Marzolf, 1953; Lovell, Mitchell, and Everett, 1962), and (*c*) to compare the size and contents of different classes (Dodwell, 1962; Hyde, 1959; Inhelder and Piaget, 1959; Piaget, 1952).

A more detailed explanation of the steps by which children learn inclusion is offered by Inhelder and Piaget (1959). On the basis of their hypotheses, development appears to proceed in 11 partially ordered steps. They contend that classification begins when the child groups together two objects that are equivalent because they look alike in some way (resemblance sorting). As the child grows he learns to extend the scope of his grouping from two, to more than two (consistent sorting), to all the objects that could be considered equivalent in some respect (exhaustive sorting). The child also learns which are acceptable categories for grouping. Physical proximity becomes a less favored means of categorizing since the resulting groupings are transitory (conservation). Experiences in constructing one class at a time prepare the child for forming successive and simultaneous classifications and for understanding class inclusion. Slowly the child begins to recognize that objects do not belong exclusively in different categories (multiple class membership), and he actively tries out different groupings of objects, choosing first one and then another single attribute as a focus for grouping (horizontal classification). As his logical abilities develop, his method of choosing criteria becomes more complex. He chooses single attributes and then combinations of attributes to construct successive classes (hierarchical classification). His use of combinatorial structure (Inhelder and Piaget, 1958) enables him to form classes that stand in an inclusion relationship to each other.

Class inclusion is thus the product of experiences in which the child finds diverse attributes to guide his groupings (Morf, 1959) and diverse schemes of attribute combination. There is a second group of experiences that enable children to understand class inclusion. When children start to recognize that objects belong to more than one class, they also begin to describe the way in which classes overlap by using terms like "some" or "all." Once the children have the verbal tools for comparison, they can begin to construct classes that stand in an inclusion relationship and can experiment with the complementary processes of joining subclasses to form a superordinate class (A+A′) and dividing superordinate classes into constituent parts (B—A′). Piaget has argued that class addition is a simpler logical feat than class subdivision and therefore is found among younger children. Constructing superordinate classes from subordinate classes involves finding some common feature shared by the groups that allows them to be grouped together. The focus on the communalities between subclasses and the superordinate group helps the classifier to keep in mind the logical relationship between the subclass and the whole superordinate class. But when *S* is separating the superordinate class into more specific subclasses, the focus is on the attributes that distinguish the subclasses from each other and from the superordinate class so that it is harder for *S* to realize that the parts he has just produced out of the whole superordinate class are related to each other. It is obvious that as the child becomes more flexible in grouping (horizontal classification), he is also able to subdivide classes or join them more easily. Morf (1959) has demonstrated that reclassification skills and logical subdivision and addition develop at the same time and are prerequisites for learning class inclusion. One more insight is necessary, reversibility, before inclusion can be understood. When the child knows that combination and division are opposite processes, inclusion is within his grasp, and quantitative comparisons of subclasses and larger groups become possible.

Figure 1 summarizes the theory of development of classificatory rules. These rules were translated into 11 experimental tasks which were used to test two aspects of Piaget's theory: (*a*) that the order of difficulty of these tasks corresponds to the developmental sequence described by Piaget, and (*b*) *S*s who have acquired a particular rule have also mastered all the simpler prerequisite rules.

METHOD

Subjects

The experimental sample consisted of 122 children who were attending nursery or elementary school in Rochester, New York. There were 10 girls and 10 boys at each age level between 4 and 9 years, except in the 7- and 4-year-old groups which contained an additional child. The children selected were above average in intelligence. Their level of intellectual functioning was determined by a composite of three measures: father's occupation, teacher's rankings of class standing, and scores on a group intelligence test. The *S*s were also screened for defects in color vision, form discrimination, and vocabulary by means of an adaptation of the Stanford-Binet discrimination-of-forms test (Terman and Merrill, 1960) and a vocabulary test.

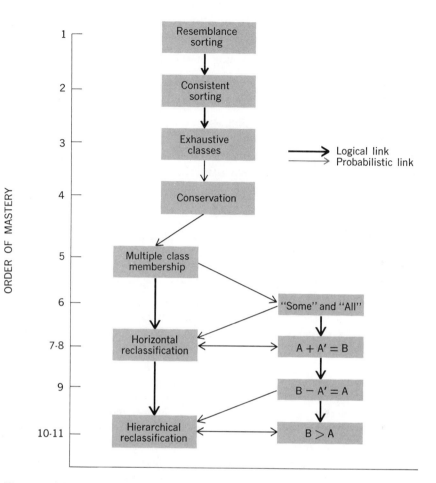

Figure 1 Predicted sequence of development of classificatory skills.

Procedure

Tasks were developed that required Ss to demonstrate their understanding of each of the 11 classificatory operations by correctly manipulating a set of geometric blocks. The blocks were 1 inch thick and had a plane surface of approximately 4 square inches in area. The plane surfaces were either square, circular, or triangular, and the colors of the blocks were usually blue, red, green, or yellow. The labels employed by Ss in describing the colors and shapes during the initial screening device were subsequently used by E to describe the blocks throughout the regular testing session. During the testing procedure each of the 11 tasks was administered in a random order to individual Ss to control for the effects of learning.

The testing sessions lasted approximately one-half to three-fourths of an hour. In order to avoid fatigue, the youngest children were seen individually for two 20-minute sessions. The rest of the subjects were questioned individually in one session. Responses were written down verbatim and later scored by *E*. A description of the tasks and the scoring criteria follows.

RESEMBLANCE SORTING (RS)   Four patterns of 8–10 blocks were constructed in front of the child. After each pattern was assembled, *E* pointed to one of the blocks that was part of the design and said, "Find me another block like this. Choose from these two." The choice consisted of a second block, which was taken from the pattern but did not resemble the first in color or shape, and a third block, which was either the same color or shape as the first. The third block was not one of those used to construct the pattern. Each *S* was to point to his choice and to explain his reason for making it. One design consisted of a row of houses with yellow triangular roofs and red square bases. The block to be matched was a red square. The subject could choose its mate from a yellow triangle in the pattern or a yellow square. The other designs are presented in Kofsky (1963).

A successful sorter made three correct matches on the basis of form, color, or some perceptual property, for example a triangle and a square could be considered alike because "they both have corners."

CONSISTENT SORTING (CS)   A mixed array of blocks consisting of two red, one green, one blue, and one brown triangle; a red, a yellow, a blue, and a green square; and a red, a yellow, and a blue circle was presented to *S*, who was to place together some things that "were alike" and to explain the reason for his grouping. Subjects who grouped just two objects were encouraged to find more things that were alike.

Consistent classifiers selected three or more objects which were alike in some perceptual feature.

EXHAUSTIVE SORTING (EC)   A collection of blocks, including a red and a blue circle, one green and two blue squares, two red and two green triangles, was shown to *S*. He was to choose a block and put it in a box along with all the others that were "like it." After the first box was filled, the procedure was repeated with the remaining blocks until all the blocks had been chosen.

In an exhaustive sort, *S*s consistently used an attribute to select the contents of each box and filled the box with all the blocks that possessed the criterial attribute.

CONSERVATION (CON)   A group of nine triangles, each a different color, was placed on a paper plate and labeled with a nonsense syllable name, MEF, selected from the Glaze list (Hilgard, 1951, p. 544) of three-letter combinations eliciting minimal associations. The subject was asked if all the blocks were still called MEF's under three conditions: (*a*) after the blocks were removed from the plate and scattered on the table; (*b*) after *S* constructed a pattern with the triangles and one block was removed from the pattern; (*c*) if *E* should take a block home. The last two questions were also asked about the specific block that was removed. The procedure was then repeated with a group of nonsense shapes called WUB's.

A successful *S* asserted consistently that MEF's and WUB's retained their identity despite all the changes because each block possessed some attribute that made it a WUB or a MEF. For example, "It's still a MEF because it's a triangle, too." An acceptable alternative explanation mentioned a condition under which class membership is invariant, such as "A MEF is a MEF wherever it is."

MULTIPLE CLASS MEMBERSHIP (MM)   A set of triangles varying in size (large or small) and color (red or green) was placed in front of *S*. The plane surface of the small triangles measured 4 square inches in area, and the large ones were approximately 9 square inches in area. The large triangles were either red or green, but all the small ones were red. The object of the task was to determine whether any of the blocks could be placed in more than one category.

The experimenter asked:

(*a*) This is a bag full of red things. Do all of the small things belong in the bag with the reds? Why? (Yes, all of the small blocks are red.)
(*b*) This is a bag for triangles. Do the greens belong in the bag? Why? (Yes, the greens are triangles.)
(*c*) Do the reds go in the bag for triangles? Why? (Yes, all the reds are triangles.)
(*d*) This is a bag for small blocks. Do the greens belong in it? Why? (No, the greens are all large.)

The order of questions was varied for each *S*. Successful performance entailed three correct responses. Acceptable answers for this and other tasks appear in parentheses.

HORIZONTAL RECLASSIFICATION (HR)   The eight wooden blocks to be sorted included pairs of reds, yellows, greens, and blues. One of each color was a triangle and the other a square. Each S was (*a*) to sort all the objects that were alike into classes, (*b*) to sort a different way, and (*c*) to explain each complete grouping.

To pass the test, *S* was required to sort the blocks into groups in which (*a*) all the blocks were alike in some respect, and (*b*) all the objects possessing the criterial attribute were included in the group. Subsequently *S* changed his criteria for sorting to produce a new arrangement which conformed to the above requirements. In other words, one time he sorted completely by color and another time by shape.

HIERARCHICAL CLASSIFICATION (VC)   In this task there were seven triangles, four of which were red and the rest blue, which were arranged in two parallel rows. Each row contained both reds and blues. The *E* said, "All of these are called MEF's [points to each], but only some are TOV's. What are MEF's? Which are the TOV's?" The child was to point to the MEF's and TOV's and explain his actions. TOV, like MEF, was selected from the Glaze list of nonsense syllables eliciting few associations.

To classify correctly, *S* had to define MEF's in terms of some attribute shared by all the members of the group (such as "triangle"). TOV's were defined by an attribute shared by one part of the group but not the entire group (such as "blue").

"SOME" AND "ALL" (SA)   There were nine blocks differing in color and shape. Among the six blue figures were two triangles and four squares. The three red figures were all triangles. In Inhelder and Piaget's (1959) notation, a superordinate class is called B, its subclasses A and A', with A the larger of the two subclasses. The class of blue figures (B) contained four squares (A) and two triangles (A'). The class of triangles (B) contained three reds (A) and two blues (A'). Each *S* had to determine whether the members of the superordinate class (B) were all members of one subordinate class (A), and the converse, if all the A's belong to B. The order of questions varied randomly among the *S*s. As in other tasks, the categories of blocks were mixed so that the subdivisions were not readily apparent to *S*. First *S*s were asked to find the reds, blues, triangles, and squares. Then *E* asked:

(a) Are all of the reds (A) triangles (B)? Why? (Yes, every red is a triangle.)
(b) Are all the triangles (B) red (A)? Why? (No, some triangles are blue.)
(c) Are all of the squares (A) blue (B)? Why? (Yes, every square is blue.)
(d) Are all of the blues (B) squares (A)? Why? (No, there are some blue triangles.)

Three correct responses were necessary for passing.

WHOLE IS THE SUM OF ITS PARTS (A + A')   Two blue wooden squares were mixed in among a half-dozen red ones. The experimenter asked:

Are all of these squares? Are the red ones square? Are the blues square? I am going to tell you a story. Mary and Joan wanted to build a very high tower using all these [*E* demonstrates]. Mary said they could make the highest tower if they took all the red and all the blue blocks and put them together. Joan said they could get the tallest house if they put all the squares together. Who was right? Mary? Joan? Both? (Both, since the reds and blues are all squares.)

If you put the reds and blues together would there be more of them, or more squares, or as many reds and blues as squares? (There are as many reds and blues as squares since the reds and blue are squares.)

Two correct answers were required for passing.

CONSERVATION OF HIERARCHY (B — A') The same arrangement of blocks as in the preceding task was used. The opening question was also the same. Then *E* asked:

If I took away all the reds, are there just blues left, just squares left, or both blues and squares? Why? (Both blues and squares since the remaining blocks are all blue and square.) If I took away all the reds, would there be more blues or more squares left or as many blues as squares? (Since all the remaining blocks are blue and square, there are as many blues as squares left.)

Again, two correct answers were needed for success.

INCLUSION (B > A) The arrangement and kind of blocks were the same as in the SA task. However, in this task the children had to compare the number of objects in different classes by answering the following questions:

(*a*) Are there more blues (B) or squares (A)? Count them. (More blues, since there are six blues and four squares.)
(*b*) Are there more reds (A) or triangles (B)? Count them. (More triangles, since there are five triangles and three reds.)
(*c*) Are there more triangles or blues? Count them. (More blues, since there are five triangles and six blues.)

The order of the questions varied, and sometimes the subclass name was stated first, sometimes the superordinate. Two correct responses were required for passing.

RESULTS

The data were analyzed to elicit information about age differences in classificatory skills and the validity of Piaget's theories of classificatory development and of the invariant nature of development.

Each *S* received a score based on the number of tasks he had passed. The means and SD's for the successive age groups are presented in Table 1. An analysis of variance of age effects ($F = 17.27$, $df = 5/116$, $p < .01$) and correlation of age with score ($r = .86$, $p < .01$) were both significant. Tukey's test indicated that the age continuum was divisible into three segments. The 9-year-olds performed better than the 7- and 8-year-olds, who, in turn, were superior to the younger *S*s. When *S*s were grouped into

Table 1

Classification Scores as a Function of Age

Age Group (years)	N	Mean	SD
4	21	4.00	1.11
5	20	5.00	1.58
6	20	5.85	1.68
7	21	7.66	1.61
8	20	7.95	1.56
9	20	9.35	1.11

Table 2

Percentage of Subjects in Each Age Group Passing Each Task

	Age Group (Years)						
Task	4	5	6	7	8	9	Total
CS	90	90	95	100	100	100	96
RS	81	95	85	100	95	100	94
EC	43	75	80	90	90	90	77
SA	52	50	90	90	85	95	77
MM	10	35	60	90	95	100	65
A + A'	29	40	65	81	75	90	62
B − A'	14	20	45	66	80	95	55
CON	29	35	60	43	45	75	45
HR	10	25	20	66	70	90	45
B > A	29	20	10	19	45	60	31
VC	10	25	0	14	20	40	17

two age categories, 4–6 years and 7–9 years, a significantly greater number in the older group passed all tests except CS, CON, and VC.

Table 2 analyzes in greater detail the proportion of Ss passing each task. There appear to be six different levels of difficulty in these tests of classificatory logic, with the tasks at each step differing significantly from the tasks at the preceding level in the proportion of passes ($p < .05$). The steps are: (a) the ability to match objects (RS) and collect small groups of objects (CS) which share common features, both of which appeared well within the grasp of all the children tested; (b) understanding "some and all" relationships and proficiency in forming exhaustive classes (EC), which occurred in a majority of the 5-year-olds; (c) a grasp of the elementary relations among objects and classes in a hierarchy including the knowledge that an object can belong to more than one class (MM) and that the total number of objects in the subclasses is equal to the extension of the superordinate class (A + A'), which was demonstrated by most of the 6-year-olds; (*d*) conservation of hierarchy (B — A'), conservation (CON), and reclassification (HR), which were performed successfully by most of the 7-year-olds; (*e*) knowledge of inclusion, which was apparent in most of the 9-year-olds; and (*f*) hierarchal classification, which was mastered by less than half of the oldest group.

The rank-order correlation of the predicted logical sequence with the obtained sequence of difficulty of the tasks was .87 ($p < .01$).

In order to determine whether *S*s who solved a given task had also mastered all of the tasks thought to be logical prerequisites, a scaling technique was employed. The tasks were ranked in order of difficulty on the basis of the proportion of *S*s passing each task, and *S*s were ranked in order of proficiency as determined by the number of tasks they had passed. Each *S* occupied one row in the matrix and each task a column. The resulting table, presenting individual patterns of passes and failures, was the source of several analyses.

Table 3

Homogeneity of Items with Test Score

Item	H_{it}	Item	H_{it}
CS	0.500	B — A'	0.958
RS	0.351	CON	0.894
SA	0.757	HR	0.906
EC	0.738	B > A	0.948
MM	0.931	VC	0.945
A + A'	0.951		

The item-test homogeneity, or H_{it} (Loevinger, 1947), was computed for each task in order to determine the extent to which each *S*'s total score predicts whether he will pass a particular item. If there is an invariant order of difficulty, *S*s who pass a particular item should have passed at least as many tests as the rank order of the item, and *S*s who fail should have passed fewer items. The only *S*s to pass the most difficult task should be those who have passed all others. Table 3 presents the H_{it}'s for each of the tasks. The discriminative efficiency of seven of the tasks was 0.9; only two tasks, the easiest, yielded H_{it}'s below 0.7. We may, therefore, conclude that most items were sufficiently discriminative to suggest regular stages in the development of categorizing skills.

High H_{it}'s are not sufficient evidence for an invariant order, however, since all the people who pass item 4 may have passed three other items, which were either easier or harder than item 4. If there were a set order of mastery, every S passing a difficult task would also pass all the easier. Interitem homogeneity, or H_{it} (Loevinger, 1947) is a statistic that measures for pairs of items the extent to which passage of a difficult item implies passage of an easier one as compared to what might be expected by chance. As Table 4 indicates, only 19 of the 55 interitem comparisons exceeded 0.500. If the items with average H_{it}'s exceeding this level are listed, CS appears to be the easiest followed by EC, MM, A + A' and B — A'. The rest of the tasks are not as well ordered as the differences in proportion of people passing each task, presented in Table 2, would lead one to believe. At best there is a partial order.

Table 4

Interitem Homogeneities

	B > A	HR	CON	B − A'	A + A'	MM	SA	EC	RS	CS
VC	0.239	0.285	0.106	0.366	0.621	0.595	0.355	−0.721	0.659	1.000
B > A		0.220	0.012	0.358	0.501	0.228	0.167	0.059	−0.375	1.000
HR			0.243	0.377	0.442	0.652	0.376	0.683	0.694	1.000
CON				0.261	0.302	0.652	0.366	−0.030	0.083	−0.070
B − A'					0.644	0.577	0.258	0.528	0.480	1.000
A + A'						0.552	0.406	0.228	0.539	1.000
MM							0.371	0.371	0.779	0.228
SA								0.381	0.358	0.351
EC									0.073	1.000
RS										.096

The heterogeneity of the tasks and of sequences of mastery was further illustrated by an examination of the number of response patterns. Ideally, 12 patterns should occur, failure of every item or every one except the easiest, or two easiest, etc. Yet 63 appeared. Only 27 per cent of the Ss passed all the items up to a certain point and failed the rest.

Finally, the number of times Ss passed easier and failed more difficult items was counted for the total response matrix. Although irregularities occurred in 10 per cent of the cases, by chance 16 per cent of the items would be expected to show reversals. The Reproducibility (Green, 1956) of 0.90 is, therefore, not significant. An acceptable scale with a Reproducibility of 0.93 and an Index of Consistency of 0.50 was obtained by eliminating data from the CON, EC, and B > A tasks. Much of the improvement was due to the omission of items that were tied in difficulty with other items and produced a disproportionate number of errors in scaling. On the new scale, 51 per cent of the Ss showed a perfect sequence of passes and failures, and the variety of response patterns was reduced to 40. The reliability of the eight-item sequence must be tested on a new population.

Piaget has contended not only that there is a fixed order in which skills emerge but also that a particular skill is mastered through a fixed sequence of stages. If so, it might be expected that Ss would be fairly consistent in the method of solution on tasks so that they can be reliably characterized as belonging to one stage or another. Yet on any one task, a third of the Ss showed wide variations in approach. Most consistency occurred on the A + A′ task, on which 84 per cent were consistent, and least on B > A, on which 17 per cent used the same kind of reasoning for all questions.

It is also possible to categorize the errors on tasks on which a sufficient number and variety of mistakes were made. The incidence of specific types of errors among the older and younger halves of the Ss can then be compared. It might be expected that the two groups would fail tasks for different reasons. The following are some examples of these analyses. Many Ss failed the two sorting tasks, EC and HR, because they were unable to form consistent classes; others failed because they were unable to execute the rule specific to the task, exhaustive sorting or reclassification. Although it might be predicted that the younger failures would be most likely to be inconsistent sorters, such was not the case. (EC: $\chi^2 = 0.05$, $df = 1$, $p <$ .90; HR: $\chi^2 = 1.73$, $df = 2$, $p < .50$). On VC failures either formed one class or two mutually exclusive classes, rather than inclusion classes. Inability to form more than one class at a time should be more prevalent among younger Ss, but it was not ($\chi^2 = 0.47$, $df = 1$, $p < .50$).

On the SA tasks, Piaget (1952) described two common fallacies: (a) all the members of the superordinate class B are also members of one subclass A; (b) none of the members of the superordinate class B are members of the subclass A. These errors represent two separate stages of development with young children falling prey to the first type of error and older Ss to the second type. The data do not support this contention ($\chi^2 = 0.68$, $df = 2$, $p < .50$).

Admittedly, the number of failures on each question was small. Parceling the errors into age and error combinations resulted in even smaller frequencies. Yet the data seem to confirm the findings of many other replications of Piaget's work (Dodwell, 1960; Hyde, 1959; Lovell, Mitchell, and Everett, 1962; Lunzer, 1960), that individuals vary in the sequence of mastery of cognitive tasks and the steps by which they master a particular cognitive task.

DISCUSSION

One might well ask then whether logical development does possess any regularities. Perhaps scaling the difficulty of tasks is not the most adequate way of exploring the question, because the scaling technique confounds experimental errors with population variations in the course of development. A few examples may suffice to substantiate this argument. The fundamental operations tested may indeed be mastered in a fixed sequence, yet the variations in instructions and material from task to task may have had such a strong effect on performance that the regularities were masked. It is well known (Hyde, 1959; Lovell, Mitchell, and Everett, 1962) that performance on comparable tasks is susceptible to variation due to subtle differences in experimental procedure. Lovell reports that one-third of the nonconservers in an experiment involving a plasticine ball were perfectly sure that the content of a rubber band remained the same no matter how far it was stretched. It may also be argued that a task that requires verbalization from the child is inherently different from a task that requires manipulation of material no matter how similar the content of the two. Unfortunately, changes in experimental tasks tend to affect Ss differentially, since Ss who are in the process of acquiring an operation may be the most susceptible to experimental manipulations (Dodwell, 1960; Lovell, Mitchell, and Everett, 1962).

This difficulty is compounded by the relative unreliability of children's performance. Young Ss are often less aware of the need to be consistent and are more likely to perform in a random fashion on tasks than adults. Therefore, the use of a brief sample of Ss' behavior may not constitute the most appropriate data for scaling development.

It is also possible that the scalogram model may not be the most accurate picture of development, since it is based on the assumption that an individual can be placed on a continuum at a point that discriminates the exact skills he has mastered from those he has never been able to perform. It is debatable whether development is so abrupt. Perhaps each child is capable of a broad range of behavior. He can perform one operation under a wide variety of circumstances, another harder one under more limited conditions, and a third still more difficult one on rare occasions. A better way of describing individual growth sequences might employ probability statements about the likelihood of mastering one task once another skill has been or is in the process of being mastered.

Finally, the use of cross-sectional data to describe a course of longitudinal development may be fallacious. The rank order of difficulty of items for a given group may not correspond to the sequence by which items are mastered. Similarly, in a younger group the existence of gaps in performance which are filled in in an older group may not be suitable evidence on the course of development, since there is no guarantee that the younger group when older will perform as the older group did.

Elaborate longitudinal studies may not be the only way of exploring regularities in development, however. One fairly productive line of research has been the delineation of the experiences that promote the acquisition of particular operations (Ervin, 1960; Feigenbaum and Sulkin, 1964; Morf, 1959; Wohlwill, 1959). If all children of a given level of ability need a certain type of experience to learn a new skill, one type of developmental regularity may have been unearthed. Perhaps learning situations mirror the pattern of cognitive growth.

REFERENCES

Bruner, J. S., and R. R. Olver (1963). Development of equivalence transformations in children. *Monogr. Soc. Res. Child Develpm.*, 28 (2), Ser. No. 86, 125–140.

Dodwell, P. C. (1960). Children's understanding of number and related concepts. *Canad. J. Psychol.*, 14, 191–205.

Dodwell, P. C. (1961). Children's understanding of number concepts: characteristics of an individual and of a group test. *Canad. J. Psychol.*, 15, 29–36.

Dodwell, P. C. (1962). Relations between the understanding of the logic of classes and of cardinal number in children. *Canad. J. Psychol.*, 16, 152–160.

Ervin, S. M. (1960). Training and a logical operation by children. *Child Develpm.*, 31, 555–563.

Feigenbaum, K. D., and H. Sulkin (1964). Piaget's problem of conservation of discontinuous quantities: a teaching experience. *J. genet. Psychol.*, 105, 91–97.

Green, B. F. (1956). A method of scalogram analysis using summary statistics. *Psychometrika*, 21, 79–88.

Heald, J. E., and S. S. Marzolf (1953). Abstract behavior in elementary school children as measured by the Goldstein Scheerer Stick Test and the Weigl Goldstein Scheerer Color Form Sorting Test. *J. clin. Psychol.*, 10, 59–62.

Hilgard, E. R. (1951). Methods and procedures in the study of learning. In S. S. Stevens (Ed.), *Handbook of experimental psychology*. New York: Wiley.

Hyde, D. M. (1959). An investigation of Piaget's theories of the development of the concept of number. Unpublished doctoral dissertation, University of London.

Inhelder, B. (1962). Some aspects of Piaget's genetic approach to cognition. *Monogr. Soc. Res. Child Develpm.*, 27 (2), Ser. No. 83, 19–34.

Inhelder, B., and J. Piaget (1958). *The growth of logical thinking from childhood to adolescence*. New York: Basic Books.

Inhelder, B., and J. Piaget (1959). *La genèse des structures logiques élémentaires*. Neuchâtel: Delachaux et Niestlé.

Kofsky, E. (1963). Developmental scalogram analysis of classificatory behavior. Unpublished doctoral dissertation, University of Rochester.

Laurendeau, M., and A. Pinard (1962). *Causal thinking in the child*. New York: International Universities.

Loevinger, J. (1947. A systematic approach to the construction and evaluation of tests of ability. *Psychol. Monogr.*, 61 (4), Whole No. 285.

Lovell, K., B. Mitchell, and I. R. Everett (1962). An experimental study of the growth of some logical structures. *Brit. J. Psychol.*, **53**, 175–188.

Lunzer, E. A. (1960). Some points of Piagetian theory in the light of experimental criticism. *J. child Psychol. Psychiat.*, **1**, 191–202.

Morf, A. (1959). Apprentissage d'une structure logique concrète. In J. Piaget (Ed.), *Etudes d'épistémologie génétique*, Vol. 9. Paris: Presses Universitaires. Pp. 15–83.

Peel, E. A. (1959). Experimental examination of some of Piaget's schemata concerning children's perception and thinking and a discussion of their educational significance. *Brit. J. educ. Psychol.*, **29**, 89–103.

Piaget, J. (1952). *The child's conception of number.* New York: Humanities Press.

Piaget, J., and B. Inhelder (1956). *The child's conception of space.* New York: Humanities Press.

Piaget, J., B. Inhelder, and A. Szeminska (1960). *The child's conception of geometry.* New York: Basic Books.

Terman, L. M., and M. A. Merrill (1960). *Stanford-Binet Intelligence Scale.* Boston: Houghton Mifflin.

Uzgiris, I. C. (1962). On the situational generality of conservation. Unpublished doctoral dissertation, University of Illinois.

Vigotsky, L. S. (1962). *Thought and language.* Cambridge, Mass.: M.I.T. Press.

Wohlwill, J. F. (1959). Un essai d'apprentissage dans le domaine de la conservation du nombre. In J. Piaget (Ed.), *Etudes d'épistémologie génétique*, Vol. 9. Paris: Presses Universitaires. Pp. 125–135.

Wohlwill, J. F. (1960). A study of the development of number by scalogram analysis. *J. genet. Psychol.*, **97**, 345–377.

AN EXPERIMENTAL STUDY OF THE GROWTH

OF SOME LOGICAL STRUCTURES

K. Lovell╱B. Mitchell╱I. R. Everett

INTRODUCTION

The ability to classify has long been recognized as an important aspect of the cognitive processes. From the time of Binet, questions involving classification have been found in intelligence tests; Goldstein and Scheerer (1945) used tests of classification to study the lack of flexibility of thinking said to occur amongst certain clinical cases; more recently Semeonoff and

Reprinted with the permission of the senior author and the publisher from *The British Journal of Psychology*, 1962, 53, 175–188.

Trist (1958) have given details of a number of tests involving classification together with the mode of administration and assessment. Lovell (1955) using group versions of the Wisconsin, Trist–Hargreaves and Vinacke Sorting Tests with a non-clinical population of adolescents and young adults, showed that there is an ability involved in classifying the above-named and other materials, over and above the well recognized g, $v:ed$ and k abilities. In the work of Piaget and Inhelder (1959), however, there is a major attempt to analyze the successive forms and stages through which children pass in classifying material, and to relate the development of classification to the growth of logical structures.

Piaget himself in his earlier work studied the problem of the logical subset in a verbal context, but in his later research he became more convinced that classifications and seriations were the result of mental operations (i.e., actions which have become internalized, which are carried out in the mind and are reversible). He considered that the formation of concepts and the underlying systems of classification was due to something more fundamental than socio-linguistic communication, language being a necessary but not a sufficient condition for the formation of classes and the structure of relationships. The work of Oléron (1956) supports this view to some extent, for he found that deaf mute children completed elementary operations of classification, but were retarded in more complex conceptual systems. Luria and Yudovich (1959) also report that an improvement in language and verbal formulation assisted the classifying process in Twin A ('Yura').

This paper describes an experimental study involving the individual testing of children, using experiments of the type described in Piaget and Inhelder's book *La genèse des structures logiques élémentaires*, together with three experiments which bear a close resemblance to certain of those given in Piaget's book *The Child's Conception of Number*. Only the essentials of the study can be given here, details of the presentation of materials, instructions, further questions asked, and other data obtained, may be obtained from the authors. It is assumed that access can be had to Piaget and Inhelder's book.

PROCEDURE, RESULTS AND DISCUSSION

First Series of Experiments

In this part of the study five experimental techniques were used. The population consisted of 10 children, representative of all levels of ability, in each of the age groups 5 to 10 in a primary school, and 10 children in each of the age groups, 9, 11, 13, 15 in E.S.N. (Educationally Subnormal) special schools. It is not possible to say how many tests were given to any one group of children in the Geneva studies.

EXPERIMENT 1 SPONTANEOUS CLASSIFICATIONS OF GEOMETRICAL SHAPES AND LETTERS: ADDITIVE CLASSIFICATION   The material consisted of five groups of shapes, each containing six elements. The groups were composed of squares, triangles, circles, rings and half rings. All six elements in any one group were identical in shape and size. Two elements were made of blue and one of pink plastic foam; three elements were made of manila of which two were covered with red, and one with blue plastic tape. The material also included six letters of the alphabet. The letters L, T, P were cut in plastic foam, the first in pink, the last two in blue; while the letters L, X, T were cut in manila covered with plastic tape, the first two in red and the last in blue. All the elements were presented in disorder in front of the subject and the general instructions were: "Put together things that go together" or an essential variation of this. Later, subjects might be told to put the elements in "a better order" or to arrange the elements in "a better way."

Stage 1 classifications gave the elements arranged in short or long lines, or in small incomplete groups. The latter were extremely unstable and the subjects often placed elements together, took them away, or rearranged the spatial arrangement of the elements after they had declared "I've finished." Two squares might be placed together in a short line, then a circle and a square. A long line might alternate between shape and shape, color and color, material and material. Collections were determined more by spatial shape than by inclusive elements; Piaget termed this type of classification "figural." At Stage 2 (non-figural collections) classifications showed a breaking away from spatial arrangement and there was more emphasis on similarities and differences among the elements. It is in effect a stage between figural collections and classes representing inclusion. Classification proper was found at Stage 3.

Each of the three stages can be divided into sub-stages although it is our intention here only to state the subdivisions for Stage 3. At Stage 3*a* all the elements are classed together according to one criterion, namely, shape, material, color, form. They are then subdivided according to a further criterion. Stage 3*b* indicates that all the elements are classified and subdivided according to two criteria, and at Stage 3*c* all the elements are classified and subdivided according to three criteria. The number of children at Stage 3*c* should be comparable with the numbers of children making three classifications in Experiment 6; this point will be referred to again when that experiment is discussed.

The results for Experiments 1, 2, 3 and 4 are combined in Table 2.

EXPERIMENT 2 MULTIPLICATIVE CLASSIFICATION   The material consisted of sixteen cards, 2 by 2 in., on which pictures of rabbits were painted; eight cards showed similar rabbits running, four being painted black and four being painted white; eight cards showed similar rabbits sitting, four being painted black and four painted white. There was also a box 10 by 6½ in. painted black inside, and a similar-sized one painted white inside, and a further box 9 by 12 in. subdivided into four equal sections by movable partitions.

The sixteen cards were presented in disorder and the following kinds of instructions were given, and questions asked:

(1) "Put together those that are alike, those that go together."

(2) Present the black and white boxes. "Put some in this box and some in that box."

(3) Present the box with the four partitions. "Put together those that are alike and put them in different parts of this box."

(4) One partition of the box used in (3) was taken out, subdividing the rabbits into black running and sitting in one half, and white running and sitting in the other half. "Can you put these (indicating the black running rabbits), with these (indicating the black sitting rabbits)?" "Why?" "Can you put these with these (indicating the white running and white sitting)?" "Why?"

(5) The first partition was replaced and second partition removed, subdividing the rabbits into black running and white running in one half, and black sitting and white sitting in the other half. "Can you put these (indicating the black running rabbits) with these (indicating the white running rabbits)?" "Why?" "Can you put these with these (indicating the black sitting and white sitting)?" "Why?"

In (4) and (5) the rabbits are classified in dichotomies: by color, i.e. white and black; then by shape, i.e. running and sitting. The questions determine whether the subject understands that once the four subclasses have been separated they can be reunited; in (4) by additive classes black running, black sitting, also white running, white sitting; in (5) by additive classes black running, white running, also black sitting, white sitting. If the subject is able to place a subclass in both dichotomies, he has shown the ability to understand multiplicative classification.

Using the above approach we observed the subjects' spontaneous arrangements and by questioning we could determine how the latter had been made.

At Stage 1 we find obvious figural arrangements, i.e. mixed groups of black and white, sitting and running rabbits. We also found arrangements in four subclasses in accordance with perceptual similarities but without any evidence of the extension of a unified class. Thus although the subject may relate black running and white running rabbits in perceptual relationships, when asked "Can we put these with these?" he might respond "No." At Stage 2 there is some extension of a class, but there is no evidence of a multiplicative system either in spontaneous arrangement in boxes, or in response to questions. Finally at Stage 3, subjects consistently show relationships of a multiplicative nature. Thus we find arrangements in the box such as

White running	Black running
White sitting	Black sitting

and questions are answered with adequate proof.

EXPERIMENT 3 ANTICIPATION AND VISUAL SERIATION   The subjects were first presented with four cardboard squares all of different sizes, and they were asked to "put the squares in order." Any child who was unsuccessful was helped, and when the series was constructed he was questioned further to ascertain if he understood what "putting in order" meant.

When it was clear that the child had understood his instructions, he was presented with ten rods in a certain disordered arrangement, the same for each child. The rods were of 1 sq. cm. cross section, their lengths ranged from 1 to 10 cm., and they were of ten different colors (they were in fact, the Cuisenaire materials). A base line was provided on a piece of cardboard.

The experimenter said to the child, "Look at these sticks carefully. You are going to put them in order. Show me which one will go here, which will go next and so on." The child had first to anticipate the series (without moving the sticks) that he later had to construct, and the task of the experimenter was to trace the development of the coordination of anticipation and past actions.

At Stage 1 figural type solutions were found. Both the anticipations and actions indicated a lack of coordination of intension and extension in relation to the rods. For example, a child G.H. age 5 years 2 months anticipated the rods in the sequence (of length) 6, 1, 4, 2, 9, 10, 3, 5, 8, 7. He then made the following series: 8, 2, 9, 10, 5, 4, 16, 7, 3. At Stage 2 we find anticipations and constructions partly correct, while at Stage 3, pupils both anticipated and constructed the series correctly.

EXPERIMENT 4 MULTIPLICATION OF ASYMMETRICAL TRANSITIVE RELATIONS   The material consisted of sixteen cardboard squares each 2½ by 2½ in. Each square contained a painting of a tree leaf. The leaves were in four different sizes and four different shades of green so that they could be arranged simultaneously according to size and shade. If I, II, III, IV, indicate order of size, and 1, 2, 3, 4 indicate order of color, the elements were arranged as in Table 1. In addition there were duplicate cards for II2, III2, I1, II4.

The sixteen cards were presented to the subject in disorder and he was asked to arrange them as he thought best. A series of standard instructions and questions was used according to the nature of his spontaneous reactions. The instructions and questions included:

"Please put them in order." "Can you put them in a better way?" "Can you make more groups?" "Can you put the dark ones together and the light ones together?" "Can you put them so that you can find the big leaves right away?" "Can you put them so that you can find the same color right away?"

If the subject was unable to construct the table, the elements of one dimension were arranged for him and he was asked to put the others in

Table 1

Arrangements of Elements in the Table
Illustrating Multiplication of Asymmetric Transitive Relations

	*1*ᵇ	*2*ᵇ	*3*ᵇ	*4*ᵇ
Iᵃ	I 1	I 2	I 3	I 4
IIᵃ	II 1	II 2	II 3	II 4
IIIᵃ	III 1	III 2	III 3	III 4
IVᵃ	IV 1	IV 2	IV 3	IV 4

ᵃ Indicates order of size.
ᵇ Indicates order of color.

order. If he was unable to do this a second dimension was constructed for him and the child was again asked to complete the table.

When the subject had completed the table, element II2 was withdrawn and the four duplicate elements were presented with the instruction, "Put in the one which will go here."

At Stage 1 there was an absence of seriation, and the intension and extension of classes were not coordinated. During Stage 2 there was evidence of differentiation and partial coordination of intension and extension. At Stage 3 the operation of multiplicative asymmetrical transitive relations was complete.

EXPERIMENT 5 THE HIERARCHICAL CLASSIFICATION OF ANIMALS
The materials consisted of three toy ducks, three toy birds that were non-ducks (robin, turkey, hen), and five toy animals that were non-birds (pig, dog, sheep, goat, horse). There were also box *A* (3 by 3 in.), box *B* (6 by 6 in.), and box *C* (9 by 9 in.); each of these had 1 in. high transparent sides. The boxes were placed one inside the other so that when the animals were placed in the respective boxes, inclusive relationships could be observed. Thus animals (non-birds) go in box *C*, birds (non-ducks) in box *B*, and ducks in box *A*.

Only a selection of the questions asked is given below. These relate to general questions of inclusion, (*a*) to (*f*), quantification of inclusion, (*g*) to (*j*), further quantification of inclusion, (*k*) to (*n*):

(*a*) "Can you put the ducks in this box (*B*)?" "What is this box (*B*) for?"
(*b*) "Can you put the ducks in this box (*C*)?" "What is this box (*C*) for?"
(*c*) "Can you put these birds (indicating birds non-ducks) into this box (*C*)?"
(*d*) "Is it right to put these (indicating non-birds) into this box (*B*)?"
(*e*) "Is it right to put these (indicating birds non-ducks) into this box (*A*)?"
(*f*) "Is it right to put these (indicating non-birds) into this box (*A*)?"
(*g*) "All these (indicating all the animals) belong to a farmer. Has he more ducks than birds, or less?"

(*h*) "Has he more birds than animals, or less?"
(*i*) "Are there more birds or more animals?"
(*j*) "Are there more ducks or more birds?"
(*k*) "If you killed all the birds will there be any animals left?" "Which?"
(*l*) "If you killed all the ducks will there be any birds left?" "Which?"
(*m*) "If you killed all the animals will there be any birds left?" "Which?"
(*n*) "If you killed all the birds will there be any ducks left?" "Which?"

The results of the first series of experiments are now discussed under two heads.

(1) Table 2 shows that, with the apparatus used in these experiments, the ability to achieve Stage 3—that of operational mobility—is achieved in addition of classes, multiplication of classes, visual seriation and multiplicative asymmetrical transitive relationships at about the same time in primary school children. This is the first time that this has been shown through giving the four tests to the same children. Although Piaget and Inhelder say that the ability to perform addition and multiplication of classes appears *pari passu*, they do not present data from the same children to support their claim. The increase in operational mobility between 7 and 8 years of age also confirms the view of the Geneva school.

Table 2

Number of Children at Stages 1, 2, 3 in Experiments:
Addition of Classes, Multiplication of Classes,
Visual Seriation, Multiplication of
Asymmetrical Transitive Relations

Age in years	No. of children	Stage 1				Stage 2				Stage 3			
		A[a]	M[b]	VS[c]	MTR[d]	A	M	VS	MTR	A	M	VS	MTR
					Primary school								
5	10	3	5	1	3	7	5	6	5	0	0	3	2
6	10	1	0	1	0	6	8	5	7	3	2	4	3
7	10	0	0	0	0	6	5	3	7	4	5	7	3
8	10	0	0	0	0	0	0	1	1	10	10	9	9
9	10	0	0	0	0	2	2	0	1	8	8	10	9
10	10	0	0	0	0	1	1	2	1	9	9	8	9
					E.S.N. school								
9	10	3	3	7	6	7	7	2	4	0	0	1	0
11	10	0	0	2	0	7	6	6	8	3	4	2	2
13	10	0	0	0	0	4	5	2	4	6	5	8	6
15	10	0	0	0	0	1	3	0	6	9	7	10	4

[a] Addition of classes.
[b] Multiplication of classes.
[c] Visual seriation.
[d] Multiplication of asymmetrical transitive relations.

In all four tests, children at Stage 1 showed no consistency in their actions. Indeed, there seemed to be a complete lack of ability to see and plan the next step. At Stage 2, however, the beginning of a construction seemed to be remembered, for there was some coherence between one move and the next. But there was no sudden jump to Stage 3 as one might expect if visual perception was relied upon exclusively. Rather, it seemed that the move from Stage 1 to Stage 3 was closely related to the improvement in the coordination of retroactions and anticipations, attention being increasingly directed to and from the partial solutions. Because of the nature of the materials and procedures it was not possible to estimate the influence of language. From our observations it would appear that language plays only a small part in the formation of these types of logical structures, but we cannot be sure since language might have been used covertly. However, we are inclined to agree with the Geneva school that language is not in itself a sufficient condition for the formation of these structures; for if classification depended greatly on language, logical additions should be easier than logical multiplication since sentence structure, e.g. "The black and the white rabbits ran" should tend to aid logical addition.

The performance of 15-year-old E.S.N. special school pupils is about equal to that of 7- to 8-year-old children in primary schools. This is frequently found in the other experiments reported here and clearly parallels the findings of Lovell and Slater (1960) in respect of the development of the concept of time in E.S.N. special school children. It is noticeable that visual seriation was rather easier, and multiplicative asymmetrical transitive relations rather more difficult for the 15-year-old E.S.N. children than the other experiments. The former finding is probably due to the fact that these children have had some years of this type of activity both within and without school.

(2) Table 3 shows the number of children giving correct responses to questions of inclusion of the type, "Are all the ducks birds?" and "Are all the animals birds?" Many subjects answered correctly with a "yes" or "no" but were unable to provide a satisfactory reason; these were not assessed as passing the item. The hard questions are those of the kind "Are all the ducks animals?" and "Are all the birds animals?" when these questions are related to the action of putting ducks or birds in the class of animals containing non-birds as well. It seems as if birds, including ducks, are not included within the class of animals for many primary school children. Piaget and Inhelder (1959) certainly asked "Are all the birds animals?" ("Les oiseaux sont des animaux?") and we kept close to the form of questioning laid down by the Geneva school. It was only afterwards that we became wise to the difficulty the children experienced. At the beginning of the experiments when all the animals were together each child was asked "What are all these?" or similar. The usual reply was "animals" or "farm animals." But when the groups were separated, many subjects no longer looked upon birds as animals. Perhaps the Geneva children were

Table 3

Number of Children Responding Correctly
to Questions of Class Inclusion
and Hierarchical Classification Involving Animals

		Question number and type of question					
Age in *years*	*No. of* *children*	(*a*) All ducks birds?	(*e*) All birds ducks?	(*b*) All ducks animals?	(*c*) All birds animals?	(*f*) All animals ducks?	(*d*) All animals birds?
		Primary school					
7	10	9	8	2	2	9	9
8	10	10	8	3	2	10	10
9	10	10	9	1	1	10	10
10	10	10	10	5	5	10	10
		E.S.N. school					
9	10	3	6	3	3	6	6
11	10	6	7	3	4	10	9
13	10	6	6	1	4	10	9
15	10	7	7	5	7	10	10

abler, or language or slight culture patterns differences affect the issue. The E.S.N. children at 15 are again equal to the 7- to 8-year-old primary school children in performance except that they do much better in questions (*b*) and (*c*). Perhaps sheer experience of life has helped these older E.S.N. pupils to appreciate that ducks are animals.

In Table 4 one can see how difficult questions of quantification of inclusion are when cast in certain forms. As soon as these questions were posed the children seemed to ignore the concrete materials in front of them and instead to deal with the problem at an abstract verbal level. This is confirmed in our view by the figures in Table 5 where the concreteness of the situation was maintained to some extent by asking what the results would be if certain classes of animals were killed. In these instances the number of correct responses rose.

Once again there is an increase in the number of correct responses between 7 and 8. Questions (*b*) and (*c*) in Table 3 and question (*m*) in Table 5 again reveal the difficulty children have in looking upon birds as animals. It is very doubtful if the small number of correct responses to these questions is due to lack of operational mobility *per se*.

This experiment involving animals is not a satisfactory one although at first sight it would appear to provide great interest. It is believed that the class of animals is more abstract than most of the other classes involved in this study. Perceptual relationships are not evident, and these do have some relevance since concrete logical operations cannot be dissociated from the

Table 4

Number of Children Responding Correctly
to Questions Involving Quantification in Relation to Inclusion

Age in years	No. of children	(g) More ducks than birds?	(h) More birds than animals?	(g)+(h) correct	(i) More birds or more animals?	(j) More ducks or more birds?	(i)+(j) correct	All questions correct
				Primary school				
7	10	0	0	0	0	0	0	0
8	10	3	3	3	1	2	1	0
9	10	3	4	3	0	0	0	0
10	10	6	6	6	2	3	2	1
				E.S.N. school				
9	10	0	0	0	1	1	1	0
11	10	0	0	0	0	0	0	0
13	10	1	0	0	0	0	0	0
15	10	2	2	2	1	2	1	0

intuitive content of the elements to which the operations apply. The early unstable and indefinite verbal concept does not help the children to appreciate the significance of their actions in relation to animals (pig, dog, robin, duck, etc.) which they do not usually think of as being associated in real life. They are familiar with squares and circles being associated, and with different kinds of flowers found in a bunch of cut flowers or growing in a garden, but not at first with a rather odd collection of animals. Thus retroactive and anticipatory processes have no significance in relation to the class of animals as a whole in this experiment.

Second Series of Experiments

In this part of the study five experimental techniques were used. The population consisted of 10 children, representative of all levels of ability, in each of the age groups 5, 6, 7, 8, 9–11 years in a primary school, and 25 children in each of the age groups 10–13 and 14–15 years in E.S.N. special schools. The primary school was situated in a somewhat lower socio-cultural area than was the primary school used in the first series of experiments. In retrospect we have reason to believe that the 8-year-old primary group was rather less able than the other year groups.

EXPERIMENT 6 VISUAL CLASSIFICATION   The material consisted of four large blue squares of side 5 cm., four small blue squares of side 2½ cm., three large blue circles of diameter 5 cm., three small blue squares of diameter 2½ cm., and a large red circle of 5 cm. diameter. Later, the

Table 5

Number of Children Responding Correctly
to Questions of Quantification in Relation to Inclusion

		Question number and type of question						
Age in years	*No. of children*	(n) Kill all birds any ducks left?	(l) Kill all ducks any birds left?	(n)+(l) correct	(m) Kill all animals any birds left?	(k) Kill all birds any animals left?	(m)+(k) correct	All questions correct
				Primary school				
7	10	4	9	4	2	8	2	1
8	10	8	10	8	2	8	2	2
9	10	10	10	10	1	10	1	1
10	10	9	10	9	5	10	5	5
				E.S.N. school				
9	10	4	8	3	4	4	1	0
11	10	1	8	1	2	5	0	0
13	10	5	10	5	5	8	4	4
15	10	5	10	5	4	9	3	3

following material was added if necessary; one large red square of side 5 cm., one small red circle of 2½ cm. diameter, one small red square of side 2½ cm.

The procedure followed these general lines:

(*a*) The first group of elements was placed in front of the child and he was asked to put them into groups as he liked. This was to give him preliminary practice in sorting the elements.

(*b*) The child was asked to put the elements into two groups, e.g. "Can you put these in two lots that are different from each other." The child was further questioned to find out his criterion. The subjects usually grouped by shape.

(*c*) He was then asked to find another way of sorting the elements into two groups. The subjects often grouped by size on this occasion.

(*d*) The child was asked to find a third way of arranging the elements in two groups. This was often the unique class, which consisted of all the blue pieces in one group, and the one red piece forming the other group. The subject had, of course, to attribute to the one red square the properties of a class. If he was unable to make the unique class, the second group of elements was added and he was again asked to make the third classification. No child tried to make the unique class for his first classification; four made it for their second classification but none of these was able to make a third classification.

The results for Experiments 6 and 7 are displayed in Table 6, the figures in brackets indicating the number of children who could sort the material into two groups in three different ways without the addition of the three red pieces; i.e. these figures give the number of children who could form the unique class as one of three ways of classifying the material. These numbers, when added to the corresponding numbers under the other columns headed V, give a total of 10 for each primary school age group.

EXPERIMENT 7 TACTILE-KINESTHETIC CLASSIFICATION   The material consisted of sixteen elements all made of wood. These comprised two balls of 4 cm. diameter, two balls of 2 cm. diameter, two cubes of side 4 cm., two cubes of side 2 cm., two circles of 4 cm. diameter, two circles of 2 cm. diameter, two squares of side 4 cm., two squares of side 2 cm. All the squares and the circular discs were 0.2 cm. in thickness. A frame was made so that a cloth could be draped over it in such a way that the child could not see objects placed behind the cloth, but the experimenter could observe the actions made by the child in handling the objects. Furthermore, the top of the frame was low enough for the child and interviewer to see one another; conversation was thus helped.

Table 6

*Number of Children Who Were Able to Make 0, 1, 2 or 3
Classifications, by Visual and Tactile-kinesthetic
Perception*

Age in years	No. of children	No classifications		One classification		Two classifications		Three classifications	
		V[a]	TK[b]	V	TK	V	TK	V	TK
				Primary school					
5	10	2	2	6	3	1	4	1(1)	1
6	10	0	0	4	5	6	4	2(0)	1
7	10	0	0	4	1	4	6	4(2)	3
8	10	1	0	4	5	3	2	4(2)	3
9–11	10	0	0	0	0	6	4	6(4)	6
				E.S.N. school					
10–13	25	1	1	14	16	9	4	1(1)	3
14–15	25	1	1	15	10	7	8	2(2)	6

[a] Visual perception.
[b] Tactile-kinesthetic perception.

The objects were placed in a tray behind the cloth and the child told to feel the objects, to remember their "feel," and to place them in one or other of two boxes (also behind the cloth) that he had seen earlier. Thus:

(*a*) The child was asked to place the objects in the two boxes so that there would be the same sort in each box.

(*b*) The objects were placed in the tray again, well mixed, and the child told to find another way of sorting the objects into the two boxes.

(*c*) The objects were placed in the tray a third time, well mixed, and the child was asked to find a third way of sorting the objects into the boxes.

The three classifications made were shape ("rounds" *v.* "squares"), size ("big" *v.* "little"), volume or third dimension ("thick" *v.* "thin").

EXPERIMENT 8(*a*) ADDITIVE COMPOSITION OF CLASSES INVOLVING MARKED PERCEPTUAL DIFFERENCES   The materials consisted of twenty plastic "poppet" beads, of which eighteen were brown and two white. The beads were laid out in disorder on a piece of blue paper. The child was instructed to pick up some of the beads and examine them; it was pointed out at the same time that the beads were of the same material throughout and not just painted on the surface. A series of questions were put to the subject and a selection of these is given:

"Are there more brown ones or white ones?"

"Are there more plastic beads or are there more brown ones?"

"If I made a necklace of white beads, and I made another necklace of brown beads, which necklace would be the longer?"

"If I made a necklace of the plastic beads, or if I made a necklace of brown beads, which necklace would be the longer?"

In the case of some children who did not answer the last question correctly, they were asked to make the actual necklaces and the question was repeated. In no case did the child change his answer.

Table 7

Number of Children Giving Correct Responses
to Questions Involving Additive Compositions
of Classes and Relations of Inclusion
Using Colored Beads and Flowers

Age in years	No. of children	Stage 1		Stage 2		Stage 3	
		Beads	Flowers	Beads	Flowers	Beads	Flowers
		Primary school					
5	10	10	10	0	0	0	0
6	10	5	6	2	2	3	2
7	10	4	7	2	1	4	2
8	10	4	4	3	3	3	3
9–11	10	0	1	0	0	10	9
		E.S.N. school					
10–13	24	14	17	6	4	5	4
14–15	25	9	14	7	7	9	4

EXPERIMENT 8(*b*)   Experiment 8(*a*) was repeated with materials which were well known and which had specific names. The children were presented with twenty red roses and three daffodils, all the flowers being artificial. The names of the flowers were clearly stated. If a particular child called the daffodils, say, daisies, this was accepted and the name kept throughout. Great care was taken to establish that the terms "red" and "yellow" were understood. A series of questions were put to the child, a selection of which is given:

"If they were growing in a garden like this (flowers standing upright) and you wanted a very big bunch, must you pick the flowers or the roses?"

"If I pick the daffodils what will be left?"

"Are there more flowers or are there more roses?"

At Stage 1 subjects were unable to grasp the relationship between the part and the whole as well as between the parts themselves. Stage 2 was a transitional stage in that they sometimes answered correctly and sometimes did not; while at Stage 3 they were able to relate the parts to one another and to the whole in each question.

EXPERIMENT 9 THE USE OF THE WORDS "ALL" AND "SOME" IN SITU-ATIONS INVOLVING COLOR AND WEIGHT   A box totally enclosed a lever balance, the latter controlling the positions of an apple concealed within the box. The apple appeared only when the "heavy" boxes weighing 5 oz. each were placed on the platform, the remaining "light" boxes weighed 4½ oz. each. There were three light red boxes, three light blue boxes and three heavy red boxes, all the boxes being of the same size. The following procedure was followed:

(*a*) The experimenter said, "Some of the boxes placed here (platform) make the apple appear, some boxes do not" (demonstrated).

(*b*) "Place each of the boxes here (indicating platform) one at a time."

(*c*) "Place the boxes here (indicated) that make the apple appear, and place the boxes there (indicated) that do not make the apple appear." The subjects had to place the boxes side by side on their respective parts of the table and not on top of one another.

Four preliminary questions were then asked to focus the pupils' attention on to certain relevant variables:

(i) "Why did you place the boxes here?" (indicating those that made the apple appear).

(ii) "Why did the apple appear?" (Here the child has to abstract the concept of weight.)

(iii) "Did the red boxes make the apple appear?"

(iv) "Did the blue boxes make the apple appear?"

The main questions followed: These included:

"Are all the heavy boxes red?" (*Hr*) "Why?"

"Are all the blue boxes light?" (*bl*) "Why?"

"Are all the red boxes heavy?" (*rH*) "Why?"
"Are all the light boxes blue?" (*lb*) "Why?"
Each question was asked twice and the second of the two answers was recorded. By this means children were able to "correct" their first answer if they could in much the same way as the children in Geneva did. The results are displayed in Table 8.

Table 8

Number of Children Responding Correctly
to Questions Involving the Use of the Words "All" and "Some"
in Situations Involving Color and Weight

Age in years	No. of children	Hr All heavy ones red?	bl All blue ones light?	rH All red ones heavy?	lb All light ones blue?	Hr + bl	rH + lb	All correct	Hr + lb (W)
				Primary school					
5	10	4	9	8	5	4	4	2	2
6	10	7	10	10	7	7	7	6	6
7	10	9	8	10	7	7	7	5	7
8	10	9	6	8	8	5	6	4	7
9–11	10	8	10	10	10	9	10	8	8
				E.S.N. school					
10–13	25	18	17	20	13	11	10	3	7
14–15	25	15	17	18	17	8	17	7	12

The results are now very briefly discussed under a number of heads.

(1) Table 6 shows that among the primary school population, the number of children making three classifications is about the same whether visual or tactile-kinesthetic perception is used. When the unique class is one of the three classifications, made visually, tactile-kinesthetic perception gives rather better results. This is generally in keeping with Piaget's prediction although we have demonstrated the fact by giving both tests to the same group of children. Among E.S.N. special school children three classifications were made rather more easily using tactile-kinesthetic perception compared with visual perception. We have clear evidence that all children tend to "search" less among the variables using visual perception.

Some children could make classifications but were unable to define the criterion verbally. The E.S.N. children especially had difficulty in naming the common quality of the elements. This again suggests that simple classificatory processes do not greatly depend on language, although later a verbal term to describe a class may well allow the child to extend his operations.

The number of children making three classifications in these two experiments is comparable, as one would expect, with the number of children at Stage 3c in Experiment 1 where the elements were classed and subdivided according to three criteria. The number of primary school children in each age group who were at Stage 3c of Experiment 1 is given below:

Age in years	5	6	7	8	9	10
Number of children	0	0	0	4	3	6

The corresponding figures for E.S.N. special school children:

Age in years	9	11	13	15
Number of children	0	0	0	3

These experiments involving classification make it clear that the degree of operational mobility available to the child is reflected in his ability to coordinate the increasing number of variables when criteria are changed.

(2) It appears from Table 7 that the attainment of Stage 3 in the additive composition of classes and relations of inclusions is rather more difficult when using the flowers than when using the beads. As the flowers were brightly colored there was greater perceptual contrast than with the beads, and this might be responsible. The number of 8-year-olds reaching Stage 3 is small; this might be due to the fact that 8-year-olds in our population were rather a poor group. On the other hand, Hyde (1959) reports only 7 out of 48 European children at Stage 3 in an identical experiment using beads. Judged against her figures, our 8-year-olds did well.

(3) Table 8 reveals that it is rather easier to deal with the questions of the type "Are all the blue (color) ones light?" than "Are all the light (weight) ones blue?" When reference to abstract weight comes first in the question there is a tendency to reverse the question. As was explained earlier, the subjects were asked each question twice and so were allowed to "correct" their first answers just as Piaget and Inhelder permitted their subjects to do. The infant and the E.S.N. children frequently changed a right answer to a wrong one, whereas the older junior children corrected wrong answers to right ones. Even so, answers to individual questions tend to be unstable and a better indication of the understanding of the pupils is obtained from columns 5 to 8 reading from left to right.

CONCLUSION

Over-all the results reported here agree fairly well with those of Piaget and Inhelder. It has been possible to confirm many of their predictions by giving a number of tests to the same pupils, these pupils being drawn from a known population of school children. In addition the work has been extended to cover E.S.N. special school pupils and it has shown the limited ability of the pupils to develop logical structures.

We acknowledge the great co-operation that we received from the head teachers of the schools that were involved in the study. Our thanks are also due to the children who patiently tried to answer the many questions that they were asked.

REFERENCES

Goldstein, K., and M. Scheerer (1945). *Tests of abstract and concrete thinking.* New York: Psychological Corporation.

Hyde, D. M. (1959). An investigation of Piaget's theories of the development of the concept of number. Unpublished thesis, University of London Library.

Lovell, K. (1955). A study of the problem of intellectual deterioration in adolescents and young adults. *Brit. J. Psychol.* 46, 199–210.

Lovell, K., and A. Slater (1960). The growth of the concept of time: a comparative study. *J. child Psychol. Psychiat.*, 1, 179–190.

Luria, A. R. and F. Ia. Yudovich (1959). *Speech and the development of mental processes in the child.* London: Staples.

Oléron, P. (1956). *Recherches sur le développement mental des sourds-muets.* Paris: C.N.R.S.

Piaget, J., and B. Inhelder (1959). *La genèse des structures logiques élémentaires.* Neuchâtel: Delachaux et Niestlé.

Semeonoff, B., and E. Trist (1958). *Diagnostic performance tests: a manual for use with adults.* London: Tavistock.

A DEVELOPMENTAL STUDY OF PIAGET'S THEORY OF LOGICAL MULTIPLICATION

Carolyn Uhlinger Shantz

Intensive investigation of children's thinking has led Piaget to propose that there is a substantial correspondence between certain logico-mathematical structures and the organization of children's practical and cognitive actions. In order to model most accurately the structure and limitations of thought processes during the age span of 7 to 11, approximately, Piaget

Reprinted with the permission of the author and the publisher from *The Merrill-Palmer Quarterly*, 1967, 13, 121–137. A modified version of this paper was read at the American Psychological Association meeting in New York City, September, 1966. This paper is based on research reported in a dissertation submitted in partial fulfillment of requirements for the Ph.D. degree at Purdue University. The author is greatly indebted to Dr. Charles D. Smock for his direction and assistance as major professor. The author's appreciation is also extended to Sisters Frieda and Therese Eileen, principals of St. Lawrence and St. Mary's Schools, respectively, in Lafayette, Indiana, for their generous cooperation.

invented a structure called the grouping, which combines properties of structures in modern mathematics. The grouping is composed of one operation (addition or multiplication) applied to certain elements (classes, logical relations, or space) and the relations between elements (symmetrical or asymmetrical). The child's actions of combining, ordering, disassociating, etc., represent the type of thought operations which Piaget holds to be identical to logical operations within a given logical system. Following Bourbaki, Piaget believes it is necessary to analyze separately structures dealing with classes, logical relations, and space.

The correspondence between logical and psychological structures may be supported by two phenomena: contemporaneous emergence of formally similar structures and the close relationship of these structures throughout development in middle childhood. Piaget has asserted in several works (Piaget, 1952, p. 240–243; 1960, p. 145; Inhelder and Piaget, 1964, p. 282, 290) that the multiplication of classes, logical relations, and spatial relations evidence these two phenomena as a reflection of their formal similarity.

The data which Piaget marshals in support of his hypothesis are the similarity in ages of emergence and improvement with age of each ability. In all cases each ability was assessed in different groups of children. Lunzer (1960), in particular, has noted the hazard of Piaget's position: the only methodologically defensible procedure for testing the hypothesis that logical interrelatedness of two or more structures reflects their psychological relatedness is the assessment of relevant abilities in the same group of children.

It is the purpose of this study to investigate the degree of relationship among the three multiplicative groupings within the same individuals at a given age level and to determine the extent to which this relationship and level of performance vary among age groups. The particular groupings under study were selected for their importance within Piaget's theory, as well as providing a test of the general hypothesis. In contrast to the more familiar and specific numerical connotation of "multiplication," the term is defined as the simultaneous combination of two or more elements such as two class attributes ("red and square"), two asymmetric logical relations ("longer and darker"), or two asymmetric spatial relations ("above and to the left of . . ."). Such concepts are identical to the more well-known "conjunctive concepts."

The importance of these multiplicative structures resides in the position they hold as precursors to adolescent systems of combination, in the case of class multiplication; and, as processes underlying some of the most complex concepts attained in the concrete-operational stage—conservation, in the case of asymmetric logical relations, and, Euclidean space concepts in the case of asymmetric spatial relations.

Concrete class multiplication is exemplified by the combination of all class attributes of one series with all attributes of another series, such that red and blue are combined with circle and square to produce four subclasses of red squares, red circles, blue squares, and blue circles. Each subclass is defined by the simultaneous presence of two attributes. Piaget views such combinatorial ability as the forerunner of adolescents' ability to systematically find all combinations and permutations of variables, as in the scientific method.

The second ability under study, multiplication of asymmetric logical relations, is thought by Piaget to be involved in conservation concepts (Flavell, 1963). The experimental paradigm for conservation is the following: given two tall, thin glasses A and B filled with equal amounts of water, and the contents of B poured into a short, wide glass C, the question is posed as to the equality of water in A and C. Piaget contends that as the child is able to consider the relation of C to A ("wider than" *and* "shorter than" A), i.e., as he sees the relations as compensatory, he asserts equality (conserves amount). Multiplication of asymmetric relations, like class multiplication, is the joint consideration of elements within two or more series. In this case, the series are continuous dimensions (e.g., length, shade of color, size) and elements within the dimensions are values.

The third ability, spatial multiplication, also involves continuous dimensions, in this case the spatial dimensions of the horizontal and vertical axes rather than logical dimensions. The joint consideration of sites along two dimensions, when combined, defines a point on a surface. Euclidean space is thought to be based upon the child's ability to locate objects and sites in space in terms of the intersects of three dimensions (right-left; before-behind; up-down).

There have been no correlational data presented by Piaget in support of his hypothesis of a close relationship among the three multiplicative abilities. To date the major supporting evidence is Smedslund's study (1964) of several Piagetian processes, among which were the multiplication of classes and logical relations. He found that children tended either to pass both class and relational multiplication tasks (43%) or fail both (41%).

In view of the significance of the hypothesis of close relationship among groupings for Piaget's operational theory, the present study was undertaken. If the abilities to multiply classes, logical relations, and spatial relations develop in close association, it would be expected that within each age group a high correlation in performance would hold among the three multiplication tasks. It would also be expected that the three abilities would improve with increasing age.

METHOD

Subjects

Ss were 24 children, 12 boys and 12 girls, at each of three age levels, 7½, 9½, and 11½ ($N=72$). At each age level, Ss were within three months of the half year (e.g., 7 years, 3 months to 7 years, 9 months). This age criterion resulted in *S*s within one age level coming from two grades: the 7½-year-olds were about equally divided between first- and second-grades; about one-third of the 9½-year-olds were in the third grade, and the remaining in the fourth-grade; all of the 11½-year-olds were in combined fifth- and sixth-grade classes. *S*s were drawn from a total of 13 classes.

Each teacher selected children from her class who evidenced "average achievement" *for their age*. The mean intelligence scores for each age group, based on 58 *S*s for whom tests were available, are presented in Table 1. All *S*s were drawn from two parochial schools representing primarily lower middle-class families in a small midwestern town.

Experimental Measures

Multiplication of classes was assessed by the revised children's form of the Raven's Progressive Matrices Test (1956). A typical matrix problem requires the selection of one design from six alternatives which combines two class attributes, such as circle versus square and stripes versus solid interior, in order to complete the matrix. The index of multiplicative ability was the total number of correctly solved matrices out of 36.

Table 1

Intelligence Test Data on a Portion of
the Study Sample (N=58)

Age Level	N	Intelligence Test	Mean I.Q.	SD
7½ years	11	Kuhlmann-Anderson	113.2	5.3
9½ years	24	Kuhlmann-Anderson	108.3	5.8
11½ years	11	Kuhlmann-Anderson	106.2	7.0
11½ years	12	Otis Quick-Scoring Mental Ability Test	107.5	6.2

A multiple relations test (MRT) was specially constructed to assess the multiplication of asymmetric logical relations. As in the Raven's test, *S*'s task was to fill in one intersect of a matrix. However, the entire matrix was not presented, as it is in the Raven's test. Instead, only the diagonal of a "conceptual" matrix was used, i.e., that part of a matrix presenting the one-to-one changes along both dimensions. For clarity, the term "matrices" will be used to refer to the tasks rather than the more exact "diagonals of matrices."

The matrices were constructed from various combinations of five continuous dimensions: orientation (A), amount of border (B), shade of

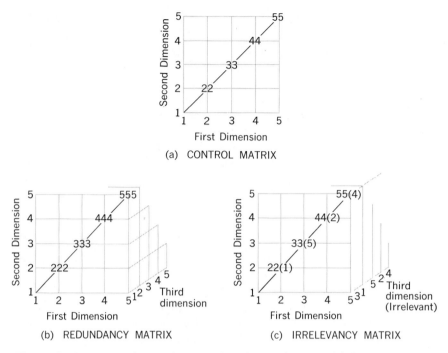

Figure 1 Structure of complete matrices for each type of information upon which MRT is based. Numbers represent ordered values within each dimension.

color (C), size (D), and degree of emptiness (E). Each of these continuous dimensions was divided into five ordered values, e.g., C ordered from black, to dark gray, medium gray, medium light gray, and light gray.

A total of 15 matrices were constructed, five of which were labeled "control" matrices, five "redundant" matrices, and five "irrelevant" matrices. Each of the control matrices was made from two dimensions (specifically, AB, CD, EA, BC, DE). The values of both dimensions were systematically ordered, e.g., in the CD matrix, values becoming progressively lighter (C) and larger (D). Each of the redundant matrices was constructed from three systematically ordered dimensions (ABC, CDE, EAB, BCD, DEA), the third dimension being considered as redundant information. Each of the irrelevant matrices had two systematically ordered dimensions with the third dimension presented in randomly ordered values, labeled irrelevant information (see Fig. 1).[1] The combinations of dimensions for these five matrices were ABD, CDA, EAC, BCE, and DEB.

The task was presented in the form of a strip of five cells, the first cell

---

[1] An analysis of the effects of these information parameters on the ability to multiply logical relations indicated, briefly, that redundant information did not have significant facilitative effects, but irrelevant information did have the predicted detrimental effects (Shantz, 1967).

combining the first values of both dimensions in a design, the second cell combining the second values, etc. The fourth cell was blank for *S* to insert the correct choice from 12 alternatives presented on a choice board. The geometric designs used as vehicles for value combinations differed among all matrices.

Table 2

*Combinations of Values for Matrices and Choice Boards
for Each Type of Information*[a]

Type of Matrix Information	Value Combinations of Each Matrix	Value Combinations on Each Choice Board		
Control	1–1	1–4	3–4	4–4
	2–2	2–3	4–1	4–5
	3–3	3–2	4–3	5–4
	5–5	3–3	4–4	5–5
Redundancy[b]	1–1–1	1–4–2	3–4–3	4–5–5
	2–2–2	2–3–5	4–3–3	5–1–4
	3–3–3	3–2–1	4–3–4	5–5–4
	5–5–5	3–3–3	4–4–4	5–5–5
Irrelevancy[c]	1–1–3 (1)	1–4–2	3–4–3	4–4–4
	2–2–1 (2)	2–3–5	4–1–4	4–5–5
	3–3–5 (3)	3–2–1	4–3–3	5–4–5
	5–5–4 (5)	3–3–3	4–4–3	5–5–5

[a] The first number or each pair of triplet represents the value of the first dimension, the second number is the value of the second dimension, etc. For example, 3–2 represents the third value of the first dimension combined with the second value of the second dimension.

[b] Correct choices are 4–4–4 and 4–3–4; other correct combinations, 3–4–4 and 4–4–3, were not included among the choices.

[c] The third number in each *matrix* triplet is the value of the irrelevant dimension which appeared in the cells ranked 1, 2, 3, 5 (in parentheses); the third number in each *choice* triplet is the cell rank.

The 12 choices offered represented only a small portion of the total possible combinations and were selected to clarify the frequency of different types of errors children make in such a task. Types of errors were defined, generally, by the amount of distance from the correct intersect (4–4). Table 2 presents the specific combination of values in the matrices and choice boards. The frequencies of each type of choice among the 12, illustrated with the control matrices, were as follows: two choices were correct (4–4); two choices combined the correct value on one dimension with a very deviant value on the second dimension (1–4, 4–1); two choices combined one correct value and a third value (3–4, 4–3); two choices combined one correct value and fifth value (5–4, 4–5); two choices were incorrect on both dimensions, one of which was fairly deviant (2–3, 3–2); and two choices, also incorrect on both dimensions, were adjacent to the correct intersect (3–3, 5–5). The 12 choices were presented in four staggered rows on each board, and the positions of choices randomized across all boards.

The total 15 matrices were presented in three standard orders, the primary limitation upon random ordering being the condition that no two matrices were presented sequentially which would allow *S* to use similar dimensions for correct response, e.g., *BC* and *BCE*.

After initial administration of the 15 matrices, "limits testing" was done on those redundant and irrelevant matrices which *S* had failed: *E* pointed to particular choices and asked whether the combination was acceptable or not to complete the matrix. Those combinations which *S* accepted were "pitted" against one another to the point where *S* designated the "best" choice, or in some cases, best choices to complete the matrix.

The two major indices of ability to multiply logical relations were (1) the total number of correctly solved matrices on initial testing, and (2) the number of correctly solved matrices in limits testing added to the initially correct number.

The multiplication of spatial relations was assessed by a modified version of Piaget's landscape task (1956). Two identical landscapes of open country were employed (see Fig. 2). Four rather wedge-shaped quadrants were formed by the intersection of a road and stream; two houses, a group of trees, a hill, and bridge were located on identical points on each land-

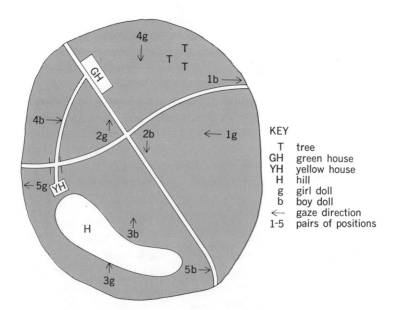

Figure 2   Schematic drawing of unrotated landscape.

scape. Two dolls, a boy and girl, were placed by *E* at five standard pairs of positions facing various directions as shown in Fig. 2. *S*'s task was to place two identical dolls in the same positions and facing the same direction as *E*'s dolls, but with *S*'s landscape rotated 180°. *S*'s landscape was made on a styrofoam base to allow for puncturing a paper beneath the landscape for each doll placement; both landscapes were covered with non-drying clay to allow each puncture to be rubbed out. *E* visually estimated gaze direction after each pair of placements.

S's ability to combine simultaneously the reversed horizontal and vertical dimensions was measured by both doll placement and direction of gaze. The latter was measured in 5° units such that a gaze of 17°, for example, was scored 15°. Exact measurement appeared unwarranted in view of the manner in which responses were initially obtained. The scoring systems used for the two measures are presented in Table 3. In both cases scores could range from a perfect performance of 10, to 50. The total spatial performance index was the sum of placement and gaze scores. Since doll placement presumably required simultaneous use of two reversed dimensions and gaze only one, analyses were done on gaze and placement scores separately as well as together.

Table 3

Scoring Systems for Responses to Landscape Task

	Position Responses	Gaze Responses
Score	Placement within circle of:	Deviation from correct direction
1	1-inch diameter around correct location	0°–5°
2	¾-inch diameter beyond the first circle	10°–15°
3	¾-inch diameter beyond the second circle	20°–25°
4	¾-inch diameter beyond the third circle	30°–35°
5	Placement beyond 3¼-inch diameter circle	40° and beyond

Procedure

*S*s were tested individually on the MRT and landscape tasks in one session which averaged approximately 50 minutes. The Raven's test (RPM) was administered with standard instructions (1956) to groups of eight *S*s; the time elapsing between individual testing and RPM testing varied from one week to one month. Individual testing for 60 *S*s was done in a mobile laboratory, and the remaining *S*s were tested under similar conditions in one of the schools.

Each *S* was randomly assigned to two order conditions: the sequence of MRT and landscape tasks, and one of the three standard MRT orders.

Prior to administration of MRT, five seriation pre-tests were presented in random order to each *S* in which each of the five dimensions was presented singly so as to familiarize *S* with the dimensions, the values within dimensions, and the basic task of ordering values. *S* described the dimension presented and the value he thought would complete the order of four cells, the third being blank. When the description was incorrect, *E* briefly described the dimension in a standard manner with emphasis upon the transformation of values from one cell to the next. The choice board of six alternatives was presented, *S* made his selection, and was told whether it was correct or not. If *S* erred, the correct choice was designated by *E* and the standard description reiterated.

Then the 15 matrices were introduced with the following instructions:

> Now I'll show you some puzzles that are a little harder. There is more than one thing changing in these new puzzles, so you must look carefully at everything that is changing. This time I won't ask you any questions first. You look at the puzzle (*E* points to stack of matrices faced down) to figure out the things that are changing. Then look at the big board (*E* points to stack of choice boards faced down) and find the picture that goes in the puzzle as quickly as you can. Point to it as soon as you find it. I am going to time you, but take enough time to be sure you've found the best one to fit in the puzzle. All right? Do you understand?

Each matrix with its choice board was presented on vertical stands in front of *S* while *S*'s eyes were closed, and timing began from the moment *S* opened his eyes until he indicated his choice.[2] The reason for each choice was asked. At no time was the adequacy of the choice or reason indicated by *E*. Upon completion of the MRT, *E* tested limits without timing as previously described.

The two landscapes were presented initially in the same orientation, the similarity of objects on both pointed out, and *S* was given two practice trials. A screen was inserted between the landscapes and *S*'s landscape slowly rotated 180° while *S* watched. After *E* placed two dolls, *S* was told to "figure out" where to place his dolls on his landscape so they would be standing near the same landscape objects and right at the same spot as *E*'s dolls, and looking at the same things. As *E* placed each doll, she referred to position as "standing here" and gaze as "looking this way" regardless of position and gaze direction so as not to verbally differentiate for *S* changes in gaze and position. The references to position and gaze were alternated sequentially in an effort to direct *S*'s attention equally to both aspects of the task. *S* was free to view *E*'s landscape as often as he wished. The order of pairs of positions was randomized for all *S*s. After each pair of placements, *S*'s responses were recorded.

[2] The latency measure was employed as an index of "information-processing time." An analysis indicated that several combinations of independent variables were significant sources of variation of the latency data (Shantz, 1967).

RESULTS

It was hypothesized that there would be a high correlation among the three multiplicative tasks within each age level. Since the landscape data did not meet the requirements of parametric correlational statistics, the degree of correlation was evaluated by the coefficient of concordance, W. The following measures were intercorrelated: RPM total score (multiplication of classes); TS, total space score on the landscape task (multiplication of spatial relations); and, two measures of MRT performance (multiplication of logical relations)—the number of correctly solved matrices on initial testing (IT) and that number plus additional correctly solved matrices on limits testing (LT).[3] There was a significant association among all three tasks for each set of data for the 7½-year-olds: RPM, TS, IT ($W = .54$, $X^2 = 37.23$); and, RPM, TS, LT ($W = .56$, $X^2 = 38.71$), $p < .05$ in each case. Likewise, the 9½-year-olds' performance correlated significantly for both sets of data: RPM, TS, IT ($W = .62$, $X^2 = 42.44$); and, RPM, TS, LT ($W = .69$, $X^2 = 47.33$), $p < .01$ in both cases. For the oldest group, however, correlations among tasks only approached the lower level

Table 4

Rank-Order Correlations Among Tasks
for Each Age Level (N=24)

	Age Levels		
Tasks	7½ years	9½ years	11½ years
Total space, IT	.42[a]	.38[a]	.25
Total space, LT	.58[b]	.50[b]	.24
Total space, RPM	.30	.43[a]	.18
Position, IT	.36[a]	.29	.13
Position, LT	.50[b]	.43[a]	.19
Position, RPM	.38[a]	.50[b]	.15
Gaze, IT	.34[a]	.37[a]	.29
Gaze, LT	.52[b]	.46[a]	.17
Gaze, RPM	.07	.31	.22
RPM, IT	.24	.48[a]	.37[a]
RPM, LT	.20	.69[b]	.42[a]

[a] $p < .05$ (rho = .343).
[b] $p < .01$ (rho = .485).

[3] The IT data were obtained under timed conditions, whereas the LT data were not. The latter measure represents maximal performance and is confounded, to a greater degree than IT data, with sequence effects.

of significance: RPM, TS, IT ($W = .51$, $X^2 = 35.05$); and RPM, TS, LT ($W = .50$, $X^2 = 34.71$), $p < .10$ in both cases.

The rank-order correlations between pairs of tasks for each age group are presented in Table 4. For the youngest group, correlations between MRT and the space task, as each was variously measured, were significant beyond the .05 level. All correlations which were not significant involved the relationship of the multiple classification test (RPM) to other tasks. The data for the 9½-year-olds indicate fairly uniform correlations among all tasks, the primary difference with the youngest group being the significant correlations of RPM to other tasks. The oldest group evidenced consistently low correlations between the space task and other tasks, the only significant correlations involving the RPM and MRT.

It was also expected that all multiplicative abilities would improve with increasing age. The mean (or median) performance of each group on all tasks is presented in Fig. 3, and reveals an almost linear trend in performance as a function of age. For clarity, the total space score is not presented but falls between the position and gaze scores for each group. All

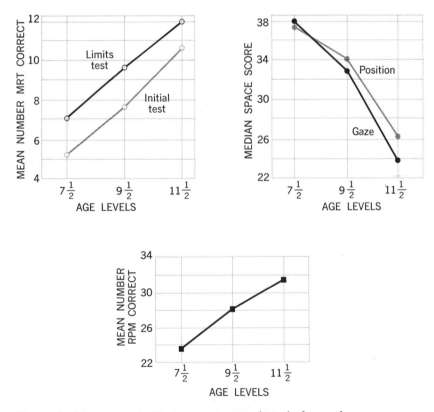

Figure 3 Mean (or median) scores on each task for each age level. (Higher scores indicate poorer performance on space task.)

differences between age groups were significant ($p < .05$ and $< .01$) with one exception: landscape placement scores for the 7½- vs. 9½-year-olds did not reach the lower level of significance.

The effects of two independent variables, order of tasks and sex, for each of the three multiplication tasks were analyzed and neither was found significantly ($p < .05$) to influence performance.

Since Piaget's theory is a theory of intelligence, measures of "products" of reasoning would be expected to show a moderate association with tests of operations. Although this was not an explicit hypothesis of the study, one-tailed tests were employed on the correlations between intelligence measures and the three experimental tasks (see Table 5). The MRT

Table 5

Correlations of Intelligence Scores with Each Task

			RPM	MRT IT	Total Space
Age	*N*	*Intelligence Test*	*r*	*r*	rho
7½ years	11	Kuhlmann-Anderson	−.23	+.38	−.32
9½ years	24	Kuhlmann-Anderson	+.40[a]	+.20	+.52[b]
11½ years	11	Kuhlmann-Anderson	+.42	+.42	−.04
11½ years	12	Otis Quick-Scoring Mental Ability Test	+.06	+.13	+.19

One-tailed tests:
$N=11$, [a] $p < .05$ ($r=.521$; rho$=.519$); [b] $p < .01$ ($r=.685$; rho$=.735$)
$N=12$, [a] $p < .05$ ($r=.497$; rho$=.506$); [b] $p < .01$ ($r=.658$; rho$=.712$)
$N=24$, [a] $p < .05$ ($r=.344$; rho$=.343$); [b] $p < .01$ ($r=.472$; rho$=.485$)

measures are the total number of matrices solved in initial testing, and, for the landscape task, the total space scores. The latter scores required the use of the non-parametric correlation statistic, rho. The correlations were not significant for the youngest and oldest groups; however, RPM and space scores correlated significantly ($p < .05$ and $p < .01$, respectively) with intelligence scores for the 9½-year-olds.

The response alternatives offered in each of the three multiplicative tasks allowed for an analysis of types of errors, particularly in terms of errors on two dimensions as compared to one dimension in the RPM and MRT. On the RPM, the percent of choices which were errors on *both* dimensions was 4%, 8% and 1% for 7½-, 9½- and 11½-year-olds, respectively. In contrast, errors on one dimension only accounted for 20%, 13%, and 7% of the choices for each age group. Similar trends were found for the MRT: of all choices, 22%, 13%, and 6% were errors on both dimensions of the two-dimensional matrices for 7½-, 9½-, and 11½-year-olds, respectively. Errors on one dimension only were 36%, 27%, and

17% of total choices for each age group. The percentages of various choices on RPM and MRT cannot be compared directly since the RPM offers other types of choices, such as incorrect orientations, irrelevancies, and incomplete patterns. In summary, for each test, two-dimensional errors were less frequent than one-dimensional errors for each age group, and, with one minor exception, both types of errors decreased with increasing age.

Landscape performance, for which there is a scarcity of data in the published literature, was evaluated first by Piaget's criteria of successful performance. That is, incorrect placements are those in the wrong quadrant or on the wrong side of a nearby object; all other placements are considered correct, regardless of the amount of distance error within the correct quadrant. The median number of correct placements for 7½-, 9½-, and 11½-year-olds was 6.8, 8.6, and 9.7, respectively, of a possible 10. The amount of distance error in placements and gaze deviations were incorporated in the scoring system developed for this study, and provide a second measure of landscape performance. The median scores for each age group, presented in Fig. 3, indicate that placement and gaze responses were quite similar within age levels although no attempt was made to "equate" the two scoring systems. Prior to applying the scoring system, gaze deviations were plotted and revealed an interesting phenomenon in the youngest group: a tendency to make more errors in the 90°–100° range. That is, Ss tended to make quarter-rotations, possibly through confusion of horizontal and vertical axes or mere incomplete rotations.

The final analysis of landscape performance dealt with the relative difficulty of particular positions and gaze directions as shown in Fig. 2. First, all age groups found certain positions and gaze directions difficult, reflected in significant correlations among the three age groups of frequency of position errors ($W = .89$) and frequency of gaze errors ($W = .94$), $p < .01$ in both cases. There was substantial variation in the relative difficulty of particular positions across ages, poorest performance generally being on 3g and 4g (see Fig. 2). The former error appeared to be a constant error induced by the curvature of the hill, and the second error due to placement of the doll on the incorrect horizontal side of the trees. The easiest positions were 4b and 5b. The least accurate gaze orientations, as assessed by summed scores, were on 3g and 3b. Again, the curvature of the hill and edge of the landscape seemed responsible; Ss made the dolls' gaze perpendicular to the hill rather than themselves. The easiest gaze reversal was on 4b.

DISCUSSION

The results of this study appear to have some important theoretical implications and raise some complex methodological problems. The general hypothesis stated that the three multiplicative abilities would be closely associated within each age level. First, there were significant correlations (W) among the three tasks in the younger two groups, but in the oldest group the obtained correlations were significant only at the .10 level. The correlations for pairs of tasks within each age level indicated that correlations among tasks (W) were a function of different task relationships. In the youngest group, correlations between the space task and MRT were consistently greater than correlations of RPM to other tasks. In the 9½-year-old group, all three tasks appeared to have fairly similar degrees of relationship. In contrast to the youngest group, the 9½-year-olds had some of the highest correlations with cross-classification and spatial tasks, relationships which continued in the 11½-year-old group. Most pairs of tasks in the oldest group, however, did not correlate more than would be expected by chance. These correlations between pairs of tasks, as well as among tasks, in the oldest group raise a question: Does the association among multiplicative abilities decrease with increasing age or are the lower correlations in the oldest group dependent upon other factors? The higher correlations among all tasks for the 9½-year-olds compared to the youngest group are suggestive of greater, not lesser, association with age. Likewise, the relative lack of variability of performance on most tasks for the 11½-year-olds, i.e., near-perfect performance, has the statistical effect of limiting the size of correlations (Guilford, 1956). Relevant data would tend to support this conclusion. In the oldest group, the mean number of correct matrices on initial testing was nearly 11 of a possible 15 with a standard deviation (SD) of 2.4; mean number of correct gaze and position responses (scores 1–4) was 16.4 of a possible 20, SD of 3.7; and RPM mean score was 32 of a possible 36, SD of 3.4. Such low variability essentially disallowed a clear test of the general hypothesis for the oldest group.

Two questions arise in relation to Piaget's hypothesis. First, to what degree are the correlations among the three tasks greater than those which might occur among other unrelated abilities of the same individuals? This is a question of discriminative validity, primarily, and research designed to define "multiplication" in terms of what it is not would be an important extension of study on the hypothesis. In this regard, the intelligence test data which were available do not provide a clear means of establishing discriminative validity. As noted previously, a moderate correlation might be expected between intellectual operations and concepts measured on intelligence tests. This is particularly true in the case of the Kuhlmann-Anderson Test which includes subtests requiring spatial concepts and ordering, both of which would tend to increase the correlations with the experimental tasks. Nevertheless, it is noteworthy that several of the correlations between intelligence test scores and the experimental tasks were as great, or greater, than correlations between experimental tasks. These correlations suggest that a "general intelligence" factor can account for some of the variability in performance on the experimental tasks.

Second, to what degree do the results of this study support Piaget's hypothesis that a *close* relationship exists among multiplicative abilities? The magnitude of the correlations appear to provide only moderate support for the hypothesis. Although the correlations between tasks differed significantly from zero, for the most part in the younger groups, a more meaningful comparison would be the difference in degree of association between these tasks and some minimal correlation which might be expected between dissimilar tasks given to the same individuals. Moreover, the correlations between tasks seldom account for more than 25% of the variance.

There are also several methodological issues raised in the present study. As noted previously, the landscape task and MRT, as each was variously measured, correlated significantly in the youngest group. The degree to which these correlations indicate association of abilities or shared method variance is an important consideration. The methods used to assess multiplication of logical relations and spatial relations are quite different. The MRT presented stimuli in a fairly structured manner, whereas the landscape task did not; in fact, the degree to which children actually construct a cognitive matrix to solve the landscape problem is moot. The location of a doll on a rotated surface and consideration of the relative values of color and size have some "face validity" as quite independent methods. The extent to which these differences constitute "independence" of methods would determine in part the degree to which correlations could be viewed as relations of abilities.

On the other hand, the differentiation between logical relations and spatial relations as elements is relatively unclear in the experimental tasks of this study, which is also the case with Piaget's tasks (Inhelder and Piaget, 1964). Specifically, the MRT appears to be a quasi-logical relations task in that the majority of dimensions used may be conceived of as primarily spatial: orientation, length of border, spatial area (size), and ratio of filled to unfilled area ("emptiness"). These are similar to the types of relations Piaget refers to as logical, e.g., height and width of containers (1952). This lack of clarity may be due in part to the difficulty of representing logical relations in concrete stimuli. For example, Piaget typically uses kinship relations when discussing the theoretical nature of groupings with logical relations; yet, in his most direct assessment of multiplying logical relations, he employed shades of color and size (Inhelder and Piaget, 1964). In summary, then, the higher relationships between MRT and space tasks found in the younger two groups are limited somewhat by the fact that spatial elements appeared in both tasks.

It is important to note that several major hypotheses in Piaget's theory are similar to the one studied here. For example, Piaget hypothesizes that *addition* of classes, logical relations and spatial relations emerge simultaneously and develop in close association throughout middle childhood, and further, that addition and multiplication of classes, for example, evidence the same phenomenon (Inhelder and Piaget, 1964, pp. 282–290). It appears that testing these hypotheses may well entail some of the same methodological problems raised in the present study.

In conclusion, there is a growing body of research relevant to multiplicative skills which bears mentioning. As outlined previously, Piaget has hypothesized that the multiplication of relations, in particular, underlies conservation concepts. It would be his contention that if one wished to teach a particular concept, such as conservation, the most likely method to use would be one which induced or "activated" the requisite operations (in terms of his theory). Yet a review of the conservation training literature suggests that training in the past has been quite specific to the type of conservation studied and by such methods as direct reinforced practice, verbalized rules, or confrontation with the "empirical facts," for the most part resulting in "remarkably little success" in inducing conservation (Flavell, 1963, p. 377). Recently, however, a pilot study by Sigel, Roeper, and Hooper (1966) indicated that training on multiplication of classes, multiplication of relations, and reversibility was effective in producing quantity conservation in four or five children in a training group compared to a control group. This finding was replicated in a slightly larger group by the same authors. Sonstroem (1966) also found training on multiplication of relations with manipulation of materials, compared to reversibility training, an effective procedure for eliciting quantity conservation. Although the hypothesis concerning the relationship among multiplicative abilities bears further study, particularly longitudinal study, it may be that determining whether these abilities are necessary and/or sufficient for conservation concepts will provide a more fruitful means of understanding their role as intellectual processes.

REFERENCES

Flavell, J. H. (1963). *The developmental psychology of Jean Piaget.* Princeton, N.J.: Van Nostrand.

Guilford, J. P. (1956). *Fundamental statistics in psychology and education.* New York: McGraw-Hill.

Inhelder, Barbel, and J. Piaget (1964). *The early growth of logic in the child: classification and seriation.* New York: Harper & Row.

Lunzer, E. A. (1960). Some points of Piagetian theory in the light of experimental criticism. *J. child Psychol. Psychiat.,* 1, 191–202.

Piaget, J. (1952). *The child's conception of number.* London: Routledge.

Piaget, J. (1960). *The psychology of intelligence.* Paterson, N.J.: Littlefield, Adams.

Piaget, J., and Barbel Inhelder (1956). *The child's conception of space.* London: Routledge.

Raven, J. C. (1956). *Guide to using the colored progressive matrices.* London: Lewis.

Shantz, Carolyn U. (1967). Effects of redundant and irrelevant information on children's seriation ability. *J. exp. child Psychol.,* **5**, 208–222.

Sigel, I. E., Annemarie Roeper, and F. H. Hooper. (1966). A training procedure for acquisition of Piaget's conservation of quantity: a pilot study and its replication. *Brit. J. educ. Psychol.,* **36**, 301–311.

Smedslund, J. (1964). Concrete reasoning: a study of intellectual development. *Monogr. Soc. Res. Child Develpm.,* **29** (2), Ser. No. 93.

Sonstroem, Anne M. (1966). On the conservation of solids. In J. S. Bruner, Rose R. Olver, and Patricia M. Greenfield (Eds.), *Studies in cognitive growth.* New York: Wiley. Pp. 208–224.

CHAPTER

FIVE

TRAINING

RESEARCH

*   *   *

IN THIS CHAPTER attention is directed toward the role of specific training programs in cognitive development. The identification of the type and amount of experience germane to the growth of logical thought is an important issue for Piagetian theory. Despite Piaget's claim of the significance of the environment, his reports do not specify, but appear to minimize the significant experiential forces which may influence the organism's developmental transitions from one stage to another. In contrast, American psychology has long stressed the significance of learning, perhaps a reflection of its strong environmentalistic persuasion. Experience is usually viewed in learning terms as the external reinforcements which become the determinants of intellectual growth. This position implies that the organism is plastic, virtually *tabula rasa*, and, hence, modifiable, given its basic neurophysiological integrity.

For Piaget, the environment plays a facilitating role by providing the necessary stimulation. There is a heavy emphasis on "inner organization and mutual coordination of the subject's schemata" (Smedslund, 1961a, p. 85). As described so ably by Flavell (1963), Piaget's theory employs an adaptation model where the individual, himself, plays a very active role which is expressed in his actions on the environment. The organism comes in contact with reality, takes in the information (assimilation), and makes the appropriate adjustments to this newly acquired knowledge (accommodation). These assimilation-accommodation processes are central for intellectual growth. Thus, for Piaget, "the organization of space, objects, and other fundaments of human experience are not given at the outset but are constructed in the course of complex and interesting evolutions . . ." (Flavell, 1963, p. 263).

The acquisition of knowledge evolves in an orderly way. First, the organism acts on reality. This is followed by a period when actions no longer need to be acted out in the environment but become internalized, covert, and representational in nature. There is a consistent and constant integration and reintegration of knowledge—new pieces of information are acquired and made parts of larger wholes. This process is called *equilibration*. Development is a long-term, continuous, dynamic interaction between the organism and the environment, expressed in identifiable stages or periods which, according to Piaget, follow an invariant sequence. We have already identified the stages in particular intellectual areas such as quantity, number, and spatial concepts.

Learning and maturation, however, are not *the* identifiable processes by which these cognitive gains are accumulated. Piaget does not deny that learning processes are involved, but he does not believe that learning, as described by American learning theory, is a fruitful way to explain the development of logical reasoning. Rather, consideration has to be given to the organism's covert *organization* of reality.

It is in the context of considerations such as these that the following training studies are presented. Their value resides in their contribution to theoretical and practical questions. On the theoretical side, these studies concern themselves with the learning conditions necessary for knowledge acquisition, the generalizability of these knowledges, and the basic modifiability of the organism at various developmental levels. The resultant changes in cognitive structures, as a function of only certain training conditions, highlight the fact that modification appears to be the consequence of the interaction of the method of training, the content area involved, and the developmental level of the particular child. Thus, these studies are of inestimable value in providing critical tests of Piaget's theory.

The practical contribution of these studies can be assessed from the perspective of general educational practice, curriculum building, and specific teaching strategies. They represent the use of teaching procedures derived from Piagetian theory (for example, conflict situation), and from traditional learning theory (for example, direct reinforced practice). These training techniques are applied to acquisition of various conservation concepts.

The initial Smedslund paper presented in this chapter deals with a number of possible interpretations of conservation acquisition. Brief descriptions of nativism, maturation, learning, and equilibration as theoretical approaches to conservation phenomena are included. Smedslund compares the relative merits of reinforcement-based learning as opposed to equilibration models in providing an adequate explanation of cognitive growth. Although he favors the equilibration position, Smedslund definitely acknowledges the role of experiential factors on thought processes, provided that the developmental level, the active explorations, and the internal sources of reinforcement for the child are taken into consideration.

Most of Smedslund's research is based on the proposition that conservation is acquired through repeated exposures to conflict situations. This point of view is consistent with Piaget's equilibration theory. Smedslund's experiments use an array of procedures to assess the relative significance of conflict. Not only is Smedslund concerned with conservation acquisition, but also with the extinction of conservation, once it is acquired. Thus, children who have demonstrated weight conservation responses following guided experiences with a balance have returned to nonconservation behavior when confronted with a contradictory setting rigged by the experimenter (Smedslund, 1961a).

Smedslund devised training procedures which coupled a stimulus deformation with either the addition or subtraction of the material in question.

Ideally, this procedure creates an ambiguous situation (for example, if the subject contends that compressing the stimulus array reduces its amount, a piece would be added simultaneously) which induces cognitive conflict and demands some type of resolution. The results of two studies dealing with quantity concepts (Smedslund, 1961b, 1961c) indicate that exposure to the conflict situations, without explicit reinforcement, may be an effective means of inducing conservation performance in some subjects. This is especially true of experiences dealing with discontinuous quantity materials. Similar results are found by Smedslund (1963) in his application of various conflict-situation strategies to length conservation.

Sigel, Roeper, and Hooper also question the efficacy of direct, reinforced training on the conservation tasks. They feel that such direct training often fails to take into account the logical prerequisites for conservation acquisition as defined by Piaget (*multiple classification, multiple relationality,* and *reversibility,* for example). These investigators, training children in these operations, succeeded in eliciting conservation of substance and weight.

Some questions remain: Are all these processes equally relevant? What role does each of them play? Answers are not yet available in terms of conservation of quantity, but some answers are forthcoming for the concept of number. The Wallach, Wall, and Anderson study provides some evidence for the role of reversibility. Basing the investigation on a previous training study which assessed the role of reversibility (Wallach and Sprott, 1964), the investigators undertook to determine whether reversibility training facilitated number conservation. Since comprehension of addition and subtraction are said to be involved in number conservation, Wallach, Wall, and Anderson also set out to determine this relationship. Finally, they were interested in discovering whether children generalize to conservation of liquid. The finding that reversibility training, and not addition and subtraction, induces conservation leads these investigators to stress the role of reversibility. Reversibility alone is not considered as the necessary and sufficient condition for conservation. Rather, reversibility *and* the avoidance of misleading cues combine to induce conservation. Although these results appear to cast some doubt on Piaget's emphasis on the role or reversibility, the reader should carefully assess Wallach, Wall, and Anderson's concept of reversibility as well as their training procedure.

It will be noted that reversibility training is similar to number correspondence training within variations of spatial relationships. "In Piaget's view, reversibility is a necessary by-product of the equilibration-of-structures process; a psychological system which is strongly equilibrated must entail the balancing and compensating functions supplied by negation and reciprocal operations . . ." (Flavell, 1963, p. 243). The two types of reversibility are *negation* and *reciprocity,* "the first of which applies only to classes and the second only to relations. With classes as elements, reversibility expresses the notion that every direct operation has an inverse (element or operation) which cancels it, that is, negates it. When complementary classes are added together, a null or empty class is produced; for example, 'cats + noncats = 0' " (Langer, 1953, pp. 128, 147). Likewise, addition is cancelled by subtraction and multiplication by division. In a relational structure, reversibility takes the form of reciprocity as follows: if "A is darker than B," the reciprocal is "B is lighter than A," and the combination of these two terms yields an "equivalence statement" (A = A). Reciprocity expresses one relation between two elements in its complementary way; there is no direct action upon the elements themselves for this would alter the relation (such as making B darker than A)" (Shantz, 1966).

The concept of reversibility employed in the Wallach, Wall, and Anderson study does not clearly encompass these processes as defined by Piaget. It may be for that reason that task transfer occurs to a similar content area but not to the conservation of liquid in their study.

Many of the studies included in this chapter contain comparisons of the relative effectiveness of a number of distinct training methods derived from different theoretical premises. Wohlwill and Lowe's investigation of number conservation employs training procedures based upon reinforcement, differentiation, and Piagetian inference. These three training methods differed minimally. Nonverbal, performance training effects were not found to generalize to the conventional, verbal conservation task formats.

Gruen evaluated the effects of two training procedures: direct, reinforced practice versus cognitive-conflict experience. He also pretrained half his sample on such relational terms as *more* and *same*, which are considered essential for adequate task understanding and performance in the classical conservation setting. The combination of verbal pretraining and cognitive-conflict experience were found to be the superior training approach. The transfer of training from number conservation to length and substance conservation performance is also evaluated by Gruen.

Zimiles' commentary is primarily directed toward the Wohwill and Lowe study, although his discussion is relevant to all the present attempts to induce number conservation. He stresses the initial functional utility of perceptual cues in the child's judgment of size and quantity dimensions. These cues gradually lose their value as the child masters certain quantification abilities (for example, counting and measuring) which are intrinsically more accurate in mediating quantity estimates. Which one of these approaches the child relies upon in conservation situations may depend upon the specific instructional set or the child's interpretation of the experimenter's expectations, as well as the subject's position in the developmental sequence.

Beilin finds verbal instruction techniques to be effective in facilitating conservation of number and length. A number of the theoretical and empirical questions raised in the studies already mentioned are combined in Beilin's experiment. According to Beilin, what is frequently ignored is the relationship between learning and the unitary nature of logical growth, an assertion often attributed to Piaget. Beilin sets up a comprehensive study examining a number of critical issues: (1) the unity of conservations of area, length, number; (2) the effects of specific methods of training on conservation of number and length; and (3) the generalization of these experiences to conservation of area. He incorporates the conflict technique described by Smedslund by using the verbal and nonverbal techniques which involve reinforcement and nonreinforcement. The results indicate training effects, particularly for the test (for example, number and length conservation) in which the child was trained. Of all the training techniques used, didactic-rule training was the most effective in producing significant posttest differences. It is of interest that generalization did not occur for the area tasks. Beilin discusses the implication of this major result. The fact that increased generalization was not found indicates that convergence is not a direct function of training experiences, but seems dependent on the developmental level of the child.

The study by Beilin, Kagan, and Rabinowitz attempts to determine whether language and perceptual training experiences can play a significant role in the production of symbolic imagery represented by a water levels task. The majority of the neobehavioristic approaches to cognition stress the salience of verbal mediation mechanisms in the development of conceptual thought. This may be contrasted with the contention of the Genevan researchers who view language not as a determinant, but as a symbolic medium for logical thought processes. For the latter position, spatial-geometric conceptions such as the representation of horizontality-verticality are particularly well served by perceptually-oriented symbolic imagery.

In contrast to the Beilin research dealing with conservation acquisition through verbal rules, the perceptual training methods were found to be superior to verbal techniques in generating significant pretest-posttest differences. Spatial concepts of horizontality are more dependent upon nonverbal imagery than upon conventional language processes. None of the training approaches resulted in significant generalization to a related transfer task. In addition to the general theoretical and methodological implications of the present findings, the authors discuss the possible differential requirements of conservation and spatial representation tasks, and the role of socioeconomic variables.

Although most of the training studies that have utilized direct reinforcement or empirical demonstrations have not been successful, Kohnstamm feels that conventional learning approaches can be effectively applied to Piagetian concept tasks. Elaborating and extending the initial work of Morf (1959) on class inclusion relations, Kohnstamm set up three training conditions based upon verbal instruction, pictorial demonstrations, and guided practice with neutral geometric material, respectively. The latter training condition proved significantly effective on immediate posttesting, and later assessment indicated that the induced learning was stable and generalizable to new task materials. These results were obtained with five-year-old children. Piaget's norms have shown that problems of the present type (that is, conservation of the superordinate class when composed of two subordinate classes, such as flowers = tulips + roses) are not generally mastered until seven to eight years of age. Kohnstamm's efforts may be of major importance in delineating the potential role of guided experiences on Piagetian logical concept development.

These training or modification studies represent a range of methods (direct reinforcement, cognitive-conflict or self discovery, didactic lessons with demonstrations and perceptual reorientation) employed with a number of substantive areas. In addition to content-specific task analysis and developmental level considerations, there remains a need to identify exactly what accounts for the successful modifications, and what kinds of learning environments need to be created for maximal effectiveness.

The significance of the present studies rests upon their contribution to cognitive-development theory as well as to educational practice. They reveal that experiential variables must be considered in any comprehensive evaluation of Piagetian theory. It is evident that no single type of training is equally effective for all kinds of problems. Verbal and nonverbal procedures have differential effects depending upon the class of problem or the subject area in question. A major problem in assessing the effectiveness of the training techniques in these studies may be to ascertain whether the induced changes are truly indicative of cognitive reorganization, rather than a product of an intuitive awareness or pseudoconservation. Not to be overlooked is the relationship of timing and type of training to the developmental level of the child. Undoubtedly, the effectiveness of training is mutually dependent upon the developmental level of the child, the class of problem, and the kind of training technique used.

These results provide two valuable guidelines for the educator: First, they provide criteria by which curriculum units can be analyzed for sequence and relevance to the development of cognitive behaviors; and second, they assess teaching strategies relative to these curriculum considerations.

The discussion by Hooper concluding this chapter emphasizes the potential value of utilizing cognitive development information in problems of educational application. Three points of contact between Piagetian research and the educational field are suggested, and these correspond to the related aspects of curriculum content and timing, and optimal teaching strategies. A number of interesting parallels between cognitive acquisitions and social science concepts are presented.

A number of important questions remain which should be kept in mind when reading the following articles:

(1) Which of the various training procedures are most effective? Why?
(2) Would similar modification procedures be successful for different content areas?
(3) To what extent is the interaction of content area, developmental level, and specific training approach present in each training attempt?
(4) Can training procedures be constructed to test the stage invariance of a particular concept?
(5) Given the results of these training studies, what implications do they have for modification of Piagetian theory and for behavioristic learning theory?
(6) Piaget (1964, pp. 17–18) provides the following criteria for cognitive reorganization: (a) stability over time, (b) degree of transfer across tasks, and (c) acquisition of new, more complex cognitive operations. To what degree do the present studies meet these conditions?

REFERENCES

Flavell, J. H. (1963). *The developmental psychology of Jean Piaget.* Princeton, N.J.: Van Nostrand.
Langer, S. (1953). *An introduction to symbolic logic.* New York: Dover.
Morf, A. (1959). Apprentissage d'une structure logique concrète (inclusion): effets et limites. In A. Morf, J. Smedslund, Vinh-Bang, and J. F. Wohlwill, L'apprentissage des structures logiques. *Etudes d'épistémologie génétique,* Vol. 9. Paris: Presses Universitaires. Pp. 15–83.
Piaget, J. (1964). Three lectures. In R. E. Ripple and V. N. Rockcastle (Eds.), *Piaget rediscovered.* Ithaca, N.Y.: Cornell University Press.
Shantz, C. U. (1966). A developmental study of Piaget's theory of logical multiplication. Unpublished doctoral dissertation, Purdue University.
Smedslund, J. (1961a). The acquisition of conservation of substance and weight in children: III. Extinction of conservation of weight acquired "normally" and by means of empirical controls on a balance. *Scand. J. Psychol.,* 2, 85–87.
Smedslund, J. (1961b). The acquisition of conservation of substance and weight in children: V. Practice in conflict situations without external reinforcement. *Scand. J. Psychol.,* 2, 156–160.
Smedslund, J. (1961c). The acquisition of conservation of substance and weight in children: VI. Practice on continuous versus discontinuous material in conflict situations without external reinforcement. *Scand. J. Psychol.* 2, 203–210.
Smedslund, J. (1963). Patterns of experience and the acquisition of conservation of length. *Scand. J. Psychol.* 4, 257–264.
Wallach, L., and R. L. Sprott (1964). Inducing number conservation in children. *Child Develpm.,* 35, 1057–1071.

THE ACQUISITION OF CONSERVATION
OF SUBSTANCE AND WEIGHT
IN CHILDREN: I. INTRODUCTION

Jan Smedslund

This series of articles will be concerned with the following specific problem: What processes are involved in children's acquisition of conservation of substance and weight? These phenomena are defined as follows. A subject has conservation of substance when he thinks the amount of substance in an object must necessarily remain unchanged during changes in its form, as long as nothing is added or taken away. Similarly, a subject has conservation of weight when he thinks the weight of an object must necessarily remain unchanged during changes in its form, as long as nothing is added or taken away.

The classical test for the study of conservation of substance and weight employs pieces of plasticine. The child is presented with two equal balls of plasticine and is told that they are equally heavy. Then one of the balls is changed into a sausage or something else, and in the test of conservation of substance the following standard question is asked: "Do you think there is more plasticine in the ball, or the same amount in both, or more in the sausage?" The corresponding question in the test of conservation of weight is: "Which is heavier, the ball or the sausage, or do they weigh the same?" After the child has answered the question he is asked: "Why do you think so?"

Children with conservation of substance answer that the objects contain the same amount of plasticine because they contained the same amount in the beginning; because only the shape is changed; or because nothing has been added or taken away. Children with conservation of weight answer that the objects weigh the same, and use the same arguments as in the case of conservation of substance. Children who do not have a principle of conservation usually rely on perceptual features of the objects: The sausage contains more because it is longer; the ball weighs more because it is thicker and rounder, because it looks a little bigger, etc.

TRANSITION AGES

Several earlier studies have established the generality of the developmental transition from non-conservation to conservation in the domains of substance and weight. The classical study of Piaget and Inhelder (1941)

Reprinted with the permission of the author and the publisher from *Scandinavian Journal of Psychology*, 1961, **2**, 11–20.

first drew attention to these phenomena. These writers did not report the exact number and ages of their subjects, but stated that conservation of substance is reached on the average around 7–8 years, and conservation of weight around 9–10 years. Furthermore, their data seemed to indicate that conservation of substance and weight are invariably acquired in this order, i.e. subjects with conservation of weight always have conservation of substance but not vice versa.

The generality of this sequence seemed to be confirmed in parallel studies of children's interpretations of the melting of sugar in water and of the swelling of popcorn on a hot plate. In each situation they observed some children who asserted conservation of substance and denied conservation of weight, but they observed no children who asserted conservation of weight but denied conservation of substance. This early study was conducted by means of Piaget's *méthode clinique*, which consists of flexible and intuitively directed conversation and play. This method has proved very fruitful in the initial steps of research, but has the drawback that it cannot be exactly replicated, and it allows for unknown degrees of subjectivity in the procedure and interpretations.

A study by Inhelder (1944) verified the substance–weight sequence and indicated that these tests, together with those of conservation of volume and transitivity of weight, may have considerable diagnostic utility in practical application. The general developmental level of feeble-minded children and adults was reported as being clearly reflected in the test responses.

A large scale standardization by Vinh-Bang (in preparation) has provided reliable and exact information on the transition ages in the population of Geneva. Nearly 1500 children between 4 and 12 years of age were given a battery of some thirty objective tests, including conservation of substance and conservation of weight. The 50 per cent level for the acquisition of conservation of substance is at 7½ years, and the corresponding level for conservation of weight is at 8 years. (See also Vinh-Bang, 1959). The study of Lovell (1960) in England gave approximately the same results. On the other hand, Smedslund (1959) found somewhat earlier transition ages in a group of children (sons and daughters of delegates to the international committees and organizations) from a socio-economically superior milieu in Geneva.

The studies of conservation of number by Slater (1958) in England and by Hyde (1959) with European and non-European subjects in Aden further support the hypothesis that the rate of development of concepts of conservation is influenced by environment.

POSSIBLE INTERPRETATIONS

Historically, the diverging interpretations of the phenomena of cognitive development may be traced to the conflict between the classical philosophical schools of *empiricism* and *rationalism*. Briefly stated, the former assumes that everything that is in the mind comes from experience. The latter asserts that there are certain structures and categories which impose themselves by necessity upon the human mind and which exist independently of any experience. In contemporary psychology one may discern at least four major interpretations of the type of developmental phenomena to be studied here (and combinations of them).

Nativism

According to this point of view, the human nervous system is organized in such a way that the intrinsic validity of the inference of conservation is immediately recognized at the moment when the child has acquired a knowledge of the empirical elements involved. This line of thought assumes that even very small children are always logical *within those limited areas where they have sufficient knowledge*. Development is seen as a process where appropriate inferential behavior is immediately applied to every new domain of experience.

Learning Theory

This continues the old empiricist tradition and assumes that the child acquires the concepts of conservation as a function of repeated external reinforcements. According to this point of view, the subjective validity and necessity of the inference of conservation derives from an *empirical law*. The children discover empirically that as long as nothing is added or taken away, objects maintain the same amount of substance and the same weight, irrespective of changes of shape.

Alternatively, learning theorists may interpret the development transition as resulting from *social* reinforcements. The sanctions from adults and older children may gradually lead to the "correct" behavior relative to physical substance and weight. The training in the rules of language may contribute in various ways to the same outcome.

Maturation Theory

This theory asserts that logical structure may not be present from the beginning in children's behavior, but that it develops as a function of nervous maturation and independently of experience. No amount of experience can bring about a given type of inferential behavior in a child who is not mature enough, and once he has reached a sufficient degree of nervous maturation his experiences are immediately integrated into a logical framework. Small children may be "illogical," but there is nothing one can do about it, just wait for nature to take its course.

Equilibration Theory

This is the position of Piaget (1950, 1957) and his co-workers, who assert that logical structure is not originally present in the child's thinking, but that it develops as a function of an internal process, equilibration, which is heavily dependent on *activity* and *experience*. This point of view differs radically from that of learning theory, since practice is not assumed to act through external reinforcements, but by a process of mutual influence of the child's activities on each other. Logical inferences are not derived from any properties of the external world, but from the placing into relationship (*mise-en-relation*) of the subject's own activities. The process of equilibration is not identical with maturation, since it is highly influenced by practice which brings out latent contradictions and gaps in mental structure, and thereby initiates a process of inner reorganization. The theory is somewhat similar to Festinger's (1957) theory of cognitive dissonance and Heider's (1958) theory of balance, but is more general.

These are, briefly, the four main theories of the mechanisms of cognitive development. Needless to say, many psychologists may choose intermediate positions, e.g. by postulating some kind of *interaction* of learning and maturation.

Nativism and learning theory represent opposite positions with respect to the role of experience, but they share the idea that children's thinking is essentially similar to that of adults. Both theories assume that in situations with insufficient knowledge adults will behave like children, and that in situations with sufficient knowledge children will behave like adults.

CRITICAL DISCUSSION

The well-established findings of Piaget and his collaborators in a variety of fields seem to have excluded *nativism* as a serious possibility. (For a summary of many of these findings see Piaget, 1950, pp. 129–147.) Children below a certain age do not, for example, have notions of conservation, and they seem to acquire these notions at a relatively late stage of their development. Young children show amazingly "illogical" behavior even in situations where they seem to be in possession of all the relevant knowledge necessary for a correct conclusion. A child may know that nothing has been added to or taken away from a piece of clay, and still assert that the amount of clay and the weight has increased or diminished when the form is changed from ball to sausage. Even when every possible precaution is taken to ensure that the child has grasped the essential elements of the situation, one may observe the same type of perception-bound, "irrational" behavior.

We must conclude that the available evidence is clearly against the theory that logical structure follows automatically when the elements of a situation have been understood.

It is most tempting to apply some variant of *learning theory* to the developmental process. However, this application encounters a number of obstacles, some of which stem from the fact that it is so difficult to imagine how conservation can be established by external reinforcements in the normal life of children.

Let us begin with conservation of substance. According to Piaget and Inhelder (1941) this notion is established before conservation of weight and volume, i.e. before there exists any unequivocal empirical criterion of conservation. The subject cannot *observe* the conservation of substance during changes in form. On the contrary, his perceptual schemata lead him to suppose that the amount changes, and he has to fight to overcome the impact of how things "look." "It *looks* as if there were more in the ball, but I *know* it can't be." Thus, the child acquires conservation of substance by learning to *ignore* the appearance of things and his own direct experience.

In the experiment of melting sugar in water (Piaget and Inhelder, 1941), some children with conservation of substance asserted that the melted sugar was still there, even though they thought that the glass with the sugar would weigh exactly the same as the other glass with pure water, and that the water level would be the same in the two glasses. In this case, the child ignores the visual disappearance of substance, and asserts conservation without relying on a single empirical support. Even the taste is supposed to disappear after some time. It is difficult to imagine by what means children in normal conditions could be led by their observations to assume exact conservation of substance.

There are at least three possible auxiliary hypotheses, which depart more or less from a strict learning theory interpretation, but which nevertheless attribute a crucial role to external reinforcement.

(1) The subject may have learned empirically that objects become larger when something is added to them and smaller when something is taken away. This may be generalized in some complex way to the class of situations where nothing is added or taken away and where consequently no change is assumed.

The difficulty with this explanation is that even very young children understand that nothing has been taken away or added in the conservation test, and still think that the amount of substance has increased or decreased. They do not appear to regard the absence of adding and taking away as a relevant argument for conservation, and this is really the crucial problem.

Why does this argument suddenly become relevant and lead to the idea that conservation is logically necessary?

(2) It may be thought that the discovery of *empirical reversibility*, i.e. the fact that one may return to the point of departure after a deformation, would be sufficient to induce conservation. More generally, the set of expectancies associated with other possible deformations remains unchanged by any given deformation, and by some complex mechanism this might lead to the notion of conservation.

A large amount of evidence shows that empirical reversibility cannot explain the acquisition of conservation. Even very young children know practically always that one may return to the starting point; the sausage can be remade into a ball that contains exactly as much plasticine as the unchanged standard. Even so, the sausage is seen as containing *more* or *less* plasticine than the standard! Finally, it should be noted that in the experiment with the melting of sugar, children assert conservation of substance even though the melting process is not empirically reversible in their field of experience.

(3) One may assume that the lack of conservation of substance stems from a *difficulty of recall*, and that this can be improved upon by a process of "learning to learn." Perhaps the small child is unable to recall the initial state of equality, after just one presentation? This hypothesis is clearly contradicted by the available evidence, since the children, with few exceptions, do remember the initial state. However, they do not feel that the initial state of equality is relevant for the judgment of the state after the deformation, and learning theory probably cannot easily provide an explanation of how this is changed.

The preceding considerations are equally valid for conservation of weight. In this case, however, learning theory might seem to be in a somewhat better position, since weight is a directly observable factor. Perhaps children learn directly that weight does not change with changes in form? Again the answer seems to be negative. It is well known that the direct kinesthetic–tactile impression of weight is highly unreliable and extremely sensitive to irrelevant visual stimuli. We have repeatedly observed how children *confirm* their idea of non-conservation by weighing the objects in their hands. "Yes, I can feel that the sausage is heavier than the ball"; "the ball is much heavier now," etc. Again, we must conclude that the children acquire conservation *against* the perceptual appearance of things.

It has been suggested that children learn conservation of weight by means of scales. The answer to this is that children relatively seldom play with scales. Furthermore, the scales designed for children and available in the nurseries are technically rather primitive and do not easily lend themselves to any test of the principle of conservation.

A direct learning interpretation of the acquisition of conservation of weight also fails to explain why conservation of substance seems regularly to precede it genetically, although conservation of substance has no unambiguous observable referent.

Learning theorists may also try to explain the transition from non-conservation to conservation as a result of accumulated direct and indirect *social reinforcements.* We are aware of no evidence pointing to any direct training in these matters in the homes, and the sequential development· of the various notions does not have any obvious connection with the teaching program in nurseries and schools. On the other hand, as mentioned above, several recent studies have shown an effect of children's socio-economic and cultural background on the speed of acquisition of the various concepts of conservation. This is in accordance both with a learning theory interpretation and an equilibration theory interpretation. The former would attribute the acceleration to a higher frequency of direct and/or indirect reinforcements, whereas the latter would assume that certain environments more frequently than others confront the child with complex intellectual problems, thus forcing him to organize his thinking.

Altogether, we may conclude that, despite apparent difficulties, one cannot discard the possibility of a learning theory interpretation of the acquisition of notions of conservation. Among recent authors on this subject, Apostel (1959) apparently believes in this possibility, whereas Berlyne (1960) introduces so many new assumptions into the Hullian framework that it becomes almost indistinguishable from the equilibration theory.

The *maturation theory* is in some ways a relatively plausible one. It takes account of the general observations of pre-logical behavior and of the absence of evidence for direct learning. The great difficulty from this point of view is (*a*) to explain the *time lag* between the occurrence of the various notions of conservation (Piaget, 1950; Vinh-Bang, 1959), and (*b*) to explain the accelerating versus the retarding effects of the various environments. These two types of observations show that the maturation hypothesis is invalid as a general explanation, and that maturation can at most be a necessary condition for certain other processes to occur. The main problem is to discover the nature of these other processes.

Most of the arguments so far presented are not only *against* the three other interpretations, but also *for* the equilibration theory. The following tentative conclusions may be drawn from the preceding discussion: that the existing evidence seems to exclude nativism as a possible interpretation, and that maturation can at most be a contributing factor in providing the necessary neurological conditions for the acquisition of the successively more complex cognitive levels. The respective validities of learning theory and equilibration theory remain undetermined, although many findings seem to point against the former. In what follows, we will focus on the problem of how experience influences cognitive development, and on the question of learning versus equilibration. A brief review of some relevant earlier studies will conclude this introductory paper.

RELEVANT PREVIOUS STUDIES

The direct predecessor of the present investigations was a study by Smedslund (1959). It was designed to show the effects of direct external reinforcement on the acquisition of conservation and transitivity of weight.

The experiment on conservation learning included three groups of subjects between 5;10 and 7;1, who consistently asserted nonconservation. Group A ($N = 8$) went through a series of 30 empirical controls on a pair of scales, permitting direct observation that objects do not change weight during deformation. Group B ($N = 8$) likewise had 30 controls on the scales, but 11 of the items of deformation were exchanged for items of addition and subtraction.

It was thought that if the learning theory interpretation were true, group A should learn more and faster than group B, since A had only direct reinforcements of the response category to be learned. On the other hand, equilibration theory would lead one to expect more improvement in group B, since this involved practice on the operations of addition and subtraction, whose combination is assumed to lie beneath the concept of conservation. ("Nothing is added and nothing is taken away.") Finally, there was a group C ($N = 5$) which did not take part in any practice sessions, and which functioned as a control.

There was a considerable amount of learning in both the experimental groups and no significant difference between them, although group A had slightly better results. Taken at their face value these results seemed to indicate that a concept of conservation of weight may be acquired as a function of external reinforcements. Furthermore, the slight advantage of group A over group B was in the direction of confirming the learning theory interpretation and went against the equilibration theory.

However, there are at least two alternative interpretations of the findings which, if true, would radically change the conclusions.

(1) It is quite possible that what occurred was a simple response learning leading to a *pseudoconcept* without the quality of insight and necessity that accompanies the genuine concept. The genuine concept of conservation is inaccessible to experimental extinction, whereas the outcome of simple response learning would presumably be easy to extinguish. In article III of this series the outcome of an experimental test of this possibility will be reported.

(2) The possibility of an easy response learning in group B (the majority of the items involved simple deformations which were identical to those in group A), may have inhibited any tendency to active cognitive reorganization induced by the small number of addition/subtraction items; cf. the discussion of Gréco's experiments below. A more crucial test would be to compare a condition with only addition/subtraction items with a

condition with only deformation items. The outcome of such an experiment is described in article II of this series.

The experiment of Wohlwill (1959) on the acquisition of conservation of number is highly relevant for our purpose. A subject has conservation of number when he thinks that the number of objects in a collection must necessarily remain unchanged during changes in the spatial arrangement of the collection, as long as nothing is added or taken away.

Wohlwill posed the problem of whether conservation of number develops from the operations of adding and subtracting by means of some inferential process, or whether it results from direct reinforcement. He decided to check this by comparing the outcome of direct external reinforcement of conservation with the outcome of reinforcement of the operations of adding and subtracting.

The results show a not quite significant but highly suggestive superiority of the group trained on additions and subtractions as compared with the group trained directly on conservation over deformations. Since ordinary S-R learning principles would lead one to expect more learning in the latter group, this experiment represents a very suggestive strengthening of the equilibration theory. Wohlwill's data are at variance with our own, reported above, and this provided further encouragement to repeat our experiment with a more clearcut design involving only addition/subtraction items versus only deformation items.

The study of Gréco (1959a) concerns the learning to understand successive spatial rotations. The materials were a cardboard tube and a wooden rod to which were fastened a black, a white, and a red bead, in that order. The rod with the beads is moved into the tube until it is completely hidden and the child is asked: "Which color comes out first at the other end?" This simple question is answered correctly by most children at the age of 5–6 years. The tube with the rod inside is then rotated slowly and horizontally 180 degrees, once or twice, and the question of which color comes out is again asked. Gréco was interested in whether young children could learn to understand the meaning of the successive rotations of the tube. To the adult the rotations form a kind of logical grouping. The rotations may be combined with each other to deduce the effect, and the outcome is considered as *logically necessary*. If red is expected to come out in the direct order, then black must come out after one rotation and red again after two rotations.

Gréco's design involved two main experimental groups, D and S. The subjects in group D learned one rotation and two rotations separately to perfection, before they were presented with a mixed set of items containing both one and two rotations. The subjects in group S were mainly trained on the mixed set of items. The subjects in both groups learned to anticipate correctly the outcome of both one and two rotations. After a period of between one and three months a post-test was given to test the stability of the achievements. Furthermore, the *generalization* to *n* rotations was studied and the *transfer* to an analogous situation (a rotating disk with red and black placed in diametrically opposite positions). The data show a striking difference between the two groups. The children in group D had forgotten practically everything they had learned, whereas the children in group S had retained almost everything. The children in S also showed a considerable, but not complete generalization to *n* rotations and some transfer to an analogous situation.

Gréco's conclusion is as follows: In this situation it is possible for most pre-school children to learn behavior that is seemingly equivalent to the performance of older children. However, this learning seems to proceed in two ways which lead to quite different results. The subjects in group D seemed to have learned the outcome of one and two rotations separately as empirical laws and with no understanding of their "necessary" character. The subjects in group S never had a possibility to learn in this way; directly confronted with the more complex mixed set of items, they were probably forced into an intense "structuring activity." Apparently this led them to understand that two rotations represent the outcome of one rotation and another rotation.

These findings seem to strengthen the hypothesis that situations which permit simple response learning are detrimental to the occurrence of more profound cognitive reorganizations. Unfortunately, the two experimental conditions differed in several other respects, such as standardized versus clinical procedure, and massed versus distributed practice. This makes the interpretation very uncertain.

The experiment of Morf (1959) concerned the acquisition of certain operations of class-inclusion. In a typical test the subject is presented with a collection of wooden beads, most of which are brown and a few are white. The subject is led to acknowledge explicitly that all the beads are made of wood and that most of them are brown and only a few are white. Finally, the following question is asked: "Can you tell me whether there are more brown beads or more beads made of wood?" The typical answer of the 5–6 year old is: "There are more brown beads because there are only two or three white ones."

No amount of reformulation or rearrangement of the materials seems to bring these children to understand the correct answer. Morf wanted to find out whether it was possible for children to acquire the operations of class-inclusion as a function of some kind of training or practice.

Very briefly, the findings were as follows: With a method of various empirical controls and with several concrete materials the outcome was completely negative as far as the correct answer was concerned. The outcome of a method of free play was likewise negative. A third technique tried to make the relations between the total class and the subclasses directly visible, but again there was no real learning. Finally, some success was obtained with a technique involving exercise of the operations of *logical multiplication.*

The children were trained in seeing objects as being simultaneously members of two or more classes, and this induced learning in 7 of 30 subjects. These results, as far they go, are more in accordance with equilibration theory than with ordinary learning theories.

Churchill (1958) in a study of the acquisition of conservation of number, apparently succeeded in inducing conservation to a considerable extent, but the exact procedure is not given in the summary that has been available.

TENTATIVE GENERALIZATIONS

The preceding experiments are mostly very complex and exploratory and have served to raise questions rather than answer them. Nevertheless, they permit us to formulate certain tentative generalizations, which may act as a frame of reference for further research.

(1) The possibility of inducing a cognitive reorganization depends on the subject's already available schemata. If he has a structure which already approaches the given notion, the probability of the desired reorganization is high, whereas if he is still far from the notion, the chances are small that he will change sufficiently during a limited series of experimental sessions. Gréco (1959b) was able to show that children of the same age as those in the experiment with the rotating tube were unable to learn an exactly analogous but purely empirical and arbitrary problem. The probable reason was that the subjects in the former experiment already had a beginning "intuition" about the rotations, whereas the subjects in the latter experiment had to start from scratch. The studies of children's learning at different age levels by Gréco (1959b), Goustard (1959), and Matalon (1959) all demonstrate directly how the ability to profit from experience depends on the initial developmental level.

(2) Situations which permit immediate and simple response learning with empirical control are unlikely to lead to any profound cognitive reorganization. This is exemplified by Gréco's group D and by our own groups A and B. For evidence supporting this interpretation see article III of this series.

(3) Situations stressing empirical control, which do not permit simple response learning, may or may not induce a cognitive reorganization, which probably depends on the conditions mentioned under (1). Morf's groups with empirical control and our own experiment on learning of transitivity of weight (Smedslund, 1959) gave completely negative results. Correct inferences of transitivity and class-inclusion involve different stimuli and different responses in each new situation, and thus would be expected to

yield little learning on the basis of current learning theories. These situations would also be expected to yield little improvement on the basis of equilibration theory, since they emphasize the empirical outcomes instead of the activities of the subject. Positive results were found in Gréco's group S.

(4) Direct exercise of the relevant operations is likely to induce cognitive change to the extent that the conditions mentioned under (1) are favorable. This is exemplified by Morf's group, trained on the multiplication of classes, and by Wohlwill's addition/subtraction group.

These are only vague statements with little predictive value. In the subsequent articles attempts will be made to determine the exact conditions for the acquisition of conservation of substance and weight and to construct a more specific theory.

REFERENCES

Apostel, L. (1959). Logique et apprentissage. In J. Piaget (Ed.), *Etudes d'épistémologie génétique,* Vol. 8. Paris: Presses Universitaires. Pp. 1–138.

Berlyne, D. E. (1960). Les équivalences psychologiques et les notions quantitatives. In J. Piaget (Ed.), *Etudes d'épistémologie génétique,* Vol. 12. Paris: Presses Universitaires. Pp. 1–76.

Churchill, E. M. (1958). The number concepts of the young child. Leeds: *Leeds Univer. Res. Stud.,* 17, 34–49; 18, 28–46.

Festinger, L. (1957). *A theory of cognitive dissonance.* New York: Harper & Row.

Goustard, M. (1959). Etude psychogénétique de la résolution d'un problème (Labyrinthe en T). In J. Piaget (Ed.), *Etudes d'épistémologie génétique,* Vol. 10. Paris: Presses Universitaires. Pp. 83–112.

Gréco, P. (1959a). L'apprentissage dans une situation à structure opératoire concrète: les inversions successives de l'ordre linéaire par des rotations de 180°. In J. Piaget (Ed.), *Etudes d'épistémologie génétique,* Vol. 7. Paris: Presses Universitaires. Pp. 68–182.

Gréco, P. (1959b). Induction, déduction et apprentissage. In J. Piaget (Ed.), *Etudes d'épistémologie génétique,* Vol 10. Paris: Presses Universitaires. Pp. 3–59.

Heider, F. (1958). *The psychology of interpersonal relations.* New York: Wiley.

Hyde, D. M. (1959). An investigation of Piaget's theories of the development of the concept of number. Unpublished doctoral thesis, University of London.

Inhelder, Barbel (1944). *Le diagnostic du raisonnement chez les débiles mentaux.* Neuchâtel: Delachaux et Niestlé.

Lovell, K., and E. A. Ogilvie (1960). A study of the conservation of substance in the junior school child. *Brit. J. educ. Psychol.,* 30, 109–118.

Matalon, B. (1959). Apprentissages en situations aléatoires et systematiques. In J. Piaget (Ed.), *Etudes d'épistémologie génétique*, Vol. 10. Paris: Presses Universitaires. Pp. 61–91.

Morf, A. (1959). Apprentissage d'une structure logique concrète (inclusion): effets et limites. In J. Piaget (Ed.), *Etudes d'épistémologie génétique*, Vol. 9. Paris: Presses Universitaires. Pp. 15–83.

Piaget, J. (1950). *The psychology of intelligence.* London: Routledge.

Piaget, J. (1957). Logique et équilibre dans les comportements du sujet. In J. Piaget (Ed.), *Etudes d'épistémologie génétique*, Vol. 2. Paris: Presses Universitaires. Pp. 27–117.

Piaget, J., and Barbel Inhelder (1941). *Le développement des quantités chez l'enfant.* Paris: Delachaux et Niestlé.

Slater, G. W. (1958). A study of the influence which environment plays in determining the rate at which a child attains Piaget's "operational" level in his early number concepts. Unpublished dissertation, Birmingham University.

Smedslund, J. (1959). Apprentissage des notions de la conservation et de la transitivité du poids. In J. Piaget (Ed.), *Etudes d'épistémologie génétique*, Vol. 9. Paris: Presses Universitaires. Pp. 85–124.

Vinh-Bang. (1959). Evolution des conduites et apprentissage. In J. Piaget (Ed.), *Etudes d'épistémologie génétique,* Vol. 9. Paris: Presses Universitaires. Pp. 3–13.

Vinh-Bang. (in preparation). Elaboration d'une échelle de développement du raisonnement. Genève: Institut des Sciences de l'Education.

Wohlwill, J. (1959). Un essai d'apprentissage dans le domaine de la conservation du nombre. In J. Piaget (Ed.), *Etudes d'épistémologie génétique,* Vol. 9. Paris: Presses Universitaires. Pp. 125–135.

THE ACQUISITION OF CONSERVATION OF SUBSTANCE AND WEIGHT IN CHILDREN: III. EXTINCTION OF CONSERVATION OF WEIGHT ACQUIRED "NORMALLY" AND BY MEANS OF EMPIRICAL CONTROLS ON A BALANCE

Jan Smedslund

In the first article in this series (Smedslund, 1961a) two main theories of the origin of principles of conservation were described. The first main-

Reprinted with the permission of the author and the publisher from *Scandinavian Journal of Psychology*, 1961, **2**, 85–87.

tains that such principles ultimately derive from some kind of reinforcement mediated by external stimuli ("Learning theory"). The second assumes that the principles of conservation derive primarily from the inner organization and mutual coordination of the subject's schemata. Before children acquire conservation of substance and weight, they already have the conception that adding means increment in amount and that subtracting means decrement. By coordinating these two operations into an organized whole, the absence of adding and subtracting is eventually seen as meaning no change in amount, i.e. conservation ("Equilibration theory").

In two earlier studies (Smedslund, 1959, 1961b) it was shown that 5- to 7-year-old children may acquire a notion of conservation of weight by means of controls on a balance. When the invariance of the weight of an object over deformations was empirically demonstrated a number of children began to assert conservation of weight even in situations where the balance was not present. This fact would seem to support the learning theory interpretation. On the other hand, it may be that such acquisition involves a pseudoconcept of conservation only, without the functional properties of a "normally" acquired concept.

This paper reports an experiment testing two predictions about the extinction of conservation. On the basis of learning theory one may expect that a notion of conservation can always be extinguished, regardless of whether it has been established in the laboratory or in normal life. This follows from the assumption that notions of conservation are dependent on external reinforcement. On the other hand, it follows from equilibration theory that a genuine principle of conservation should be practically impossible to extinguish, since it reflects an inner "logical" necessity. The experiment is not decisive since the interpretation of the outcome will have to rest on many uncertain assumptions. However, it will serve to reveal some of the functional properties of artificially and normally acquired notions.

PROCEDURE

A number of 5- to 7-year-old children were given the pretest of conservation of weight described by Smedslund (1961b). The subjects who showed no traces of conservation were given two training sessions with empirical controls of conservation of weight on a balance. The training sessions were identical to those described in the earlier paper.

In the posttest, 11 subjects gave only correct answers and explanations referring to the initial state (they weigh the same because they weighed the same in the beginning). These 11 subjects and 13 subjects of the same age who already showed complete conservation of weight in the pretest, participated in the extinction trials. The extinction of the principle of conservation of weight was attempted by cheating the subjects. Three items were prepared for the extinction procedure, but sometimes only the first or the first two were employed (notably when extinction occurred after the first or second item). All the objects were made of plasticine. In presenting each item the subject was told that the two objects weighed the same.

(1) *Two brown balls.* One of them is changed into a *sausage* and a piece is taken away from it, inconspicuously. The child is asked to predict whether the two objects will now weigh the same or whether one of them will weigh more, and if so, which one. The objects are placed on the balance and lack of conservation is observed. Finally, the subject is asked to explain why the ball is heavier than the sausage.

(2) *Two red bricks.* One is changed to a *cake* and a piece is taken away, inconspicuously. Prediction, control and explanation.

(3) *Two green sausages.* One is changed into a *ball* and a piece is taken away, inconspicuously. Prediction, control and explanation.

RESULTS

The main outcome of the experiment is shown in Table 1.

None of the subjects who had acquired the principle during the experiment showed any resistance to extinction, whereas about half of the subjects who had acquired the concept in a "normal" way maintained it in the face of apparent non-conservation. The typical behavior of those who did not resist was to show little surprise and to switch rapidly back to non-conservation with explanations referring to the perceptual appearance of the objects: "The ball weighs more, because it is rounder and fatter," "The brick will weigh more, because it is bigger," etc. The subjects who resisted said: "We must have taken a little away from that one (the lighter object)," "I think you have taken away some of the clay!" "We must have lost some clay on the floor," etc.

Table 1

Number of Subjects Who Showed Resistance versus Non-resistance to Extinction in Groups Having Acquired Conservation of Weight by Means of Controls on a Balance Scale (E) and in Normal Life (N)

	Group E	Group N
Resistance	0	6
Non-resistance	11	7

DISCUSSION

The results seem to show that the subjects who acquired a notion of conservation by means of controls on the balance had learned only a relatively arbitrary empirical law. They were not very shocked or surprised when the law was falsified, and rapidly modified their predictions and explanations. On the other hand, several subjects in the group who had acquired the notion of conservation in a "normal" way, did not give up their conception, and thought that some material had been taken away.

The occurrence of resistance to extinction in group N is consistent with the equilibration theory. From the learning theory point of view it may be argued that the significance of the resistance is unclear; after all, there were only three extinction trials, and the concepts may have been overlearned by the subjects in group N. With more extinction trials all the subjects might have given up the idea of conservation. This argument is not very cogent in view of the explanations given by the subjects who resisted. They seemed to regard the change in relative weight as a sign that something had been taken away (or added to the other object), and this mechanism should make them fairly independent of the empirical outcomes.

It should be noted that it was impossible to predict extinction from the subject's initial explanations. The subjects in the two groups generally gave the same types of explanations before the extinction trials. The most frequent was: "They will weigh the same because they weighed the same in the beginning." Obviously, this explanation may be given by subjects with highly different concepts of conservation; and, consequently, one should not rely too much on the verbal behavior in making inferences about the functional properties of a concept of conservation.

REFERENCES

Smedslund, J. (1959). Apprentissage des notions de la conservation et de la transitivité du poids. In J. Piaget (Ed.), *Etudes d'épistémologie génétique,* Vol. 9. Paris: Presses Universitaires. Pp. 85–124.

Smedslund, J. (1961a). The acquisition of conservation of substance and weight in children: I. Introduction. *Scand. J. Psychol.,* 2, 11–20.

Smedslund, J. (1961b). The acquisition of conservation of substance and weight in children: II. External reinforcement of conservation of weight and of the operations of addition and subtraction. *Scand. J. Psychol.,* 2, 71–84.

THE ACQUISITION OF CONSERVATION
OF SUBSTANCE AND WEIGHT
IN CHILDREN: V.
PRACTICE IN CONFLICT SITUATIONS
WITHOUT EXTERNAL REINFORCEMENT

Jan Smedslund

According to learning theory, concepts of conservation are established as a function of external reinforcement; according to the equilibration theory they are acquired by a process of internal reorganization, independently of external reinforcement (Smedslund, 1961a). Consequently, if one could produce acquisition of conservation in a situation *without* external reinforcement, it would be a strong argument in favor of the equilibration theory.

Certain observations in an earlier experiment (Smedslund, 1959) are of interest in this connection. The first three items in a test of conservation of weight were simple deformation items (the child was questioned about the relative weight of two equally heavy objects after one of them had been deformed). For the fourth item a small piece of plasticine was taken away from one of two equally heavy balls and placed clearly visible on the table. Then the other ball was changed into a sausage and the child was asked: "Do you think the ball weighs more, do you think they weigh the same, or do you think the sausage weighs more?"

Twenty-one subjects responded correctly to all four items in the test, and 24 subjects did not respond correctly to any of the items. Eleven subjects responded incorrectly to the first three items (pure deformation) but correctly to the fourth item, and one subject responded correctly to the first three items but not to the fourth. (It should be mentioned that in a pure addition/subtraction situation, which did not belong to the test, all the subjects responded correctly; they all knew that an object becomes heavier when something is added to it and lighter when something is subtracted from it.)

The fourth item is a situation in which the two schemata of deformation and addition/subtraction come into *contact* and perhaps *conflict*, and where sometimes one and sometimes the other dominates. More concretely, the subjects who think that weight is changed when the ball is changed into a sausage, have to combine their impression of this change in weight with

Reprinted with the permission of the author and the publisher from *Scandinavian Journal of Psychology*, 1961, **2**, 153–155.

Table 1

List of Items in the Practice Sessions

Item no.	Objects	First transformation	Second transformation
		Session I	
1	Yellow sausages	Much thicker sausage $+V$	$-V$
2	Red cylinders	$+V$ a little thinner cylinder	Equal cylinders
3	Orange snakes	Much thinner snakes $-V$	Equal snakes
4	Green cakes	$-K$ ball	$+K$
5	Blue blocks	Ball $+K$	Equal blocks
6	Brown balls	$+K$ slightly squeezed ball	$-K$
7	Green snakes	A little thicker snake $-V$	Equal snakes
8	Red sausages	$-V$ snake	$+V$
9	Orange cylinders	A little thinner cylinder $+V$	$-V$
10	Brown blocks	$+K$ a little higher block	Equal blocks
11	Yellow cakes	Much thicker cake $-K$	Equal cakes
12	Blue balls	$-K$ slightly squeezed ball	$+K$
		Session II	
13	Red snakes	Ball $+V$	Equal snakes
14	Green blocks	$+V$ cake	$-V$
15	Yellow balls	Egg $-V$	$+V$
16	Blue cylinders	$-K$ much thinner cylinders	Equal cylinders
17	Orange sausages	A little thicker sausage $+K$	Equal sausages
18	Brown cakes	$+K$ a little thinner cake	$-K$
19	Red blocks	A little flatter block $-V$	$+V$
20	Brown snakes	$-V$ ball	Equal snakes
21	Yellow cylinders	A little thinner cylinder $+V$	Equal cylinders
22	Blue cakes	$+K$ much thicker cake	$-K$
23	Green sausages	A little thicker sausage $-K$	$+K$
24	Orange balls	$-K$ a little squeezed ball	Equal balls
		Session III	
25	Blue snakes	Ball $+V$	Equal snakes
26	Brown sausages	$+V$ much thinner sausage	$-V$
27	Orange cakes	A little thicker cake $-V$	$+V$
28	Green cylinders	$-K$ a little thinner cylinder	Equal cylinders
29	Red balls	Snake $+K$	Equal balls
30	Yellow blocks	$+K$ a little higher block	$-K$
31	Orange blocks	Much flatter block $-V$	$+V$
32	Blue sausages	$-V$ ball	Equal sausages
33	Yellow snakes	Much thicker snake $+V$	Equal snakes
34	Brown cylinders	$+K$ a little thinner cylinder	$-K$
35	Green balls	A little squeezed ball $-K$	$+K$
36	Red cakes	$-K$ a little thinner cake	Equal cakes

A plus sign means the adding of a small piece and a minus the taking away of a small piece. The adding and subtracting in the same item always refer to the *same* piece. V = deformed object, K = not deformed object.

the observation that a piece is taken away from the other ball. If they think that the deformation into a sausage has made object A heavier, this is in agreement with the knowledge that object B has become lighter (since a piece has been taken away) and there is really no conflict; object A is judged as heavier. On the other hand, if the deformation of object A into a sausage is seen as making object A lighter, there will be real conflict, since object B has also become lighter. The child has to reach a decision as to the relative size of the two changes, and the state of inner conflict and uncertainty preceding this decision may well have the effect of inducing pronounced cognitive changes, especially if the same type of situation is repeated.

These observations led to a tentative hypothesis about the normal origin of the concept of conservation of substance. It is assumed that a person is confronted repeatedly with situations where the addition/subtraction and the deformation schemata come into contact. In some situations one of these schemata is activated much more strongly than the other, and the weaker schema is simply inhibited. But in many situations both the schemata are activated with approximately the same strength and a *cognitive conflict* will occur, sometimes evidenced by hesitation, looking back-and-forth, and signs of uneasiness and tension. Since the addition/subtraction schema presumably has greater clarity, simplicity and consistency, it will gradually or suddenly begin to dominate, whereas the deformation schema with its high degree of ambiguity, complexity and internal contradiction will be weakened and will eventually disappear completely, even in pure deformation situations without addition/subtraction.

To test this hypothesis a number of situations were designed in which the conflict between the two schemata would be maximal, and the subjects consequently be forced toward some kind of cognitive reorganization.

PROCEDURE

Thirteen children between 5;6 and 6;6 participated in the experiment. First, the pretests of conservation of substance and weight and of transitivity of weight were administered (see Smedslund, 1961b). The children were selected according to the strict criterion of no correct answers in the pretests of conservation of substance and weight. The three practice sessions were on three successive days.

Throughout the pre- and posttests and the practice sessions the experimenter took great care to maintain a completely neutral and indifferent attitude toward all responses of the subject. Thus, as far as could be ascertained, the subjects received no systematic and unambiguous external reinforcement.

Objects of colored plasticine were used. The two objects in each item were always identical in color, form and volume and the children were informed that they contained the same amount. Every item consisted of one deformation and one addition or subtraction, followed by the standard question, and then of the reverse transformation of either the addition/subtraction or the deformation, also followed by the standard question: "Do you think there is *more*, or the *same amount* or *less* plasticine in this one than in that one?" The deformations were either very small and barely perceptible, medium sized (e.g. change of a thick sausage to a thin sausage), or large (e.g. change of ball to snake). The pieces that were added or taken away were always small relative to the size of the objects. A piece that was taken away was always placed nearby on the table, and a piece that was added was always stuck lightly on top of the object. If a piece was added prior to a transformation of form, it was taken off during the transformation and then immediately replaced. In Table 1 the transformations in each item are listed in the order in which they occurred in the experiment.

RESULTS

Certain trends could be clearly observed during the practice sessions. Five of the subjects consistently, and nearly from the beginning, adhered to the addition/subtraction schema and ignored the deformations. The remaining eight subjects seemed to be consistently dominated by their perceptual schema of change of weight over deformations, and remained in this state. The data as a whole show very little change from session I to session III. The initial signs of conflict (if there were any) very soon disappeared, and each subject consistently followed one of the available schemata without bothering about the other.

Four of the five subjects who followed the addition/subtraction schema in the practice sessions changed from no traces of conservation in the pretest to several correct answers with S_L-explanations (symbolic–logical) in the posttest. S_L-explanations contain explicit references to the absence of addition/subtraction or to logical necessity (see Smedslund, 1961b). None of the subjects who followed the perceptual schema of deformations showed any change from pre- to posttest.

Some of the observed changes may be described briefly:

Subject No. 123 (5;6). Item I in the pretest on conservation of substance (ball changed to a ring): "There is more in the ball." "Why do you think so?" "Because it is round." Same item in posttest: "The same amount, because you haven't taken any plasticine away."

Subject No. 125 (5;6). Item I, pretest: "There is more in the ball." "Why do you think so?" "Well . . ." Posttest: "They are the same." "Why do you think so?" "Because if you take two equal (objects) they have to be equal all the time." (In the next item she adds to this explanation: "They will be equal whatever you do to them.")

Subject No. 133 (6;6). Item 4 (ball changed to cross), pretest: "There is more in the ball." "Why do you think so?" "Because it is not so much spread out." (Indicates with his hand how the cross is extended in all directions.) Same item, posttest: "There is the same amount in both." "Why do you think so?" "Because you have not added anything."
  Subject No. 134 (6;6). Item 1 (ball changed to ring), pretest: "There is more in the ball." "Why do you think so?" "Because it is bigger." Same item, posttest: "The same in both." "Why do you think so?" "Because you did not take anything off that one." (Points to the ring.)

DISCUSSION

The theoretical importance of the observed individual changes stems from the fact that they apparently occurred in a complete absence of external reinforcement. The belief in conservation of substance did not seem to be acquired by observations of an empirical law, or by reinforcement from the experimenter, but as a solution of a conflict between the incompatible schemata of addition/subtraction and deformation, or some other kind of conflict.
  The transition from no trace of conservation to conservation accompanied by S_L-explanation is not very frequent. In our earlier studies only five such cases out of more than a hundred possible ones were observed. Three of them occurred in a group trained by external reinforcement on a balance scale (Smedslund, 1959), one in a control group given only pre- and posttests (Smedslund, 1961b), and one in a group practising on transitivity of weight (Smedslund, in press). Thus, there are some grounds for believing that the present method may be more effective in inducing conservation than most of the previous ones.

REFERENCES

Smedslund, J. (1959). Apprentissage des notions de la conservation et de la transitivité du poids. In J. Piaget (Ed.), *Etudes d'épistémologie génétique,* Vol. 9. Paris: Presses Universitaires. Pp. 85–124.
Smedslund, J. (1961a). The acquisition of conservation of substance and weight in children: I. Introduction. *Scand. J. Psychol.,* **2,** 11–20.
Smedslund, J. (1961b). The acquisition of conservation of substance and weight in children: II. External reinforcement of conservation of weight and of the operations of addition and subtraction. *Scand. J. Psychol.,* **2,** 71–84.
Smedslund, J. (in press). The acquisition of transitivity of weight in children. *J. genet. Psychol.*

THE ACQUISITION OF CONSERVATION
OF SUBSTANCE AND WEIGHT
IN CHILDREN: VI. PRACTICE IN
PROBLEM SITUATIONS
WITHOUT EXTERNAL REINFORCEMENT

Jan Smedslund

The promising outcome of the experimental technique described in the preceding article (Smedslund, 1961b) encouraged us to continue the study of the effects of practice in conflict situations without external reinforcement. Conclusive positive results would mean support of the hypothesis that concepts of conservation are acquired as a function of internal equilibration rather than by external reinforcement.

Since the schema of addition/subtraction seems to be of fundamental importance in the acquisition of conservation of substance, it was decided to introduce some items of addition and subtraction in the pretests. This would yield some information both about the relationship between addition/subtraction and conservation at the pretest level, and about the possibility of predicting acquisition on the basis of the pretest results on addition/subtraction. A factor of continuity/discontinuity of material was also introduced in order to study its effects at the pretest level and in the process of acquisition.

The practice sessions were designed as complex conflict situations without external reinforcement. Two groups of subjects were trained on continuous and discontinuous material respectively (plasticine and small pieces of linoleum), and a third group served as control. The subjects for the three groups were selected on the basis of the strict criterion of no correct responses in the four items of conservation in the pretests. Because of this strict criterion, and because the pretests with their items on conservation and addition/subtraction frequently induced immediate acquisition of conservation (see below), it was necessary to test a total of 154 children in order to get 45 suitable subjects for the experimental groups.

PRETESTS

Four pretests with a total of twelve items were administered individually to a total of 154 children in nurseries distributed fairly evenly over the districts of Oslo. The ages ranged from 4;9 to 7;3 with an average of 6;2.

Reprinted with the permission of the author and publisher from *Scandinavian Journal of Psychology*, 1961, 2, 203–210.

After the usual standard question in tests of conservation (Smedslund, 1961a), the subject was asked: "Why do you think so?"

The continuous material consisted of plasticine and the discontinuous of small squares (0.5×0.5 cm) of thin linoleum in various colors, in piles of 48 pieces.

Conservation of substance with continuous material:
  (1) Two equal balls of red plasticine. One of the balls changed into a ring.
  (2) Two equal balls of green plasticine. One of the balls changed into a cross.

Addition/subtraction with continuous material:
  (3) Two equal balls of brown plasticine. A small piece is taken away from one of them and placed on the table in plain view of the child.
  (4) The small piece is placed back on the ball, but on top of it and plainly visible.
  (5) A small piece (of the same size as the first one) is placed on top of the other ball.
  (6) The small piece is removed again.

Conservation of substance with discontinuous material:
  (7) Two equal piles of blue pieces. One of the piles is changed into a ring.
  (8) Two equal piles of yellow pieces. One of the piles is changed into a cross.

Addition/subtraction with discontinuous material:
  (9) Two equal piles of black pieces. One piece is taken away from one of them and placed on the table plainly visible to the child.
  (10) The piece is placed back on the pile.
  (11) A piece is added to the other pile.
  (12) The piece is removed again.

It should be noted that items 4–6 engender several conflicts between the correct response and perception. In No. 4 the correct response is that both balls contain the same amount, although one has a small piece on top and the other has not. In No. 5 both balls have a piece on top, but the correct answer is that one of them contains more clay than the other. Finally, item 6 repeats the situation of item 4.

Items 10–12 do not involve the same type of perceptual distortion as items 4–6. A piece of linoleum does not stand out from the entire pile in the same way as a piece of plasticine on top of a ball stands out from the ball.

The children's responses were scored as correct or incorrect, and the explanations were scored as perceptual (P), symbolic (S), with the sub-class symbolic-logical (S_L), or ambiguous (A) (cf. Smedslund, 1961a). In the case of additions and subtractions it was impossible to distinguish between S- and S_L-explanations. Practically all these S-explanations were of the type: "You added that piece," "You took a piece away," "You placed it back again," etc.

Results of Pretests

It may be gathered from Table 1 that conservation and addition/subtraction seem to form an approximate developmental sequence for both

Table 1

The Relationship between Conservation of Substance
and the Operations of Addition/Subtraction
with Continuous and Discontinuous Material[a]

	Continuous material		Discontinuous material	
	Non-conservation	Conservation	Non-conservation	Conservation
Addition/subtraction	29	39	45	58
Not addition/subtraction	77	9	46	5

[a] Criterion: only correct answers and S-explanations. $N = 154$.

Table 2

The Relationship between Conservation of Substance
with Continuous and with Discontinuous Material[a]

	Continuous material	
	Non-conservation	Conservation
Discontinuous material		
Conservation	20	43
Non-conservation	86	5

[a] Criterion: only correct answers and S-explanations. $N = 154$.

types of material, as revealed by the small number of subjects who appear to have conservation but not addition/subtraction. In view of the high susceptibility of children to all kinds of momentary distractions, it seems unreasonable to expect any better regularities.

Table 2 also gives an approximation to a developmental sequence, this time suggesting that subjects rarely acquire conservation of continuous quantities before they have acquired conservation of discontinuous quantities.

In Table 3 the relationship between the operations of addition/subtraction with continuous and with discontinuous material is presented. The data strongly suggest that, for the type of concrete material studied, addition/subtraction on discontinuous material regularly precedes addition/subtraction on continuous material.

Table 4 shows that addition/subtraction with continuous material and conservation with discontinuous material are of about the same difficulty and moderately intercorrelated.

Finally, conservation with continuous material and addition/subtraction

Table 3

The Relationship between the Operations of Addition/Subtraction with Continuous and with Discontinuous Material[a]

	Continuous material	
	Not addition/ subtraction	Addition/ subtraction
Discontinuous material		
Addition/subtraction	37	66
Not addition/subtraction	49	2

[a] Criterion: only correct answers and S-explanations. $N = 154$.

Table 4

The Relationship between the Operations of Addition/Subtraction with Continuous Material and Conservation of Substance with Discontinuous Material[a]

	Continuous material	
	Not addition/ subtraction	Addition/ subtraction
Discontinuous material		
Conservation	18	45
Non-conservation	68	23

[a] Criterion: only correct answers and S-explanations. $N = 154$.

with discontinuous material are compared in Table 5. As might be expected on the basis of the preceding tables, these two tests form a very clear developmental sequence. Subjects very seldom acquire conservation of continuous quantities before the addition/subtraction of discontinuous quantities.

The relationships between the individual test items will not be presented in detail since they do not seem to reveal much of theoretical interest. The intercorrelation between the two items on conservation of substance in each subtest is very high, confirming the findings previously reported (Smedslund, 1961a). In the subtests on addition/subtraction most errors occur in items 6 and 12.

Several times during the pretests, subjects were encountered who responded negatively to the test of conservation of continuous quantities, but positively in the case of discontinuous quantities. Since these subjects were

Table 5

The Relationship between Conservation of Substance with Continuous Material and the Operations of Addition/Subtraction with Discontinuous Material[a]

	Continuous material	
	Non-conservation	Conservation
Discontinuous material		
Addition/subtraction	59	44
Not addition/subtraction	47	4

[a]Criterion: only correct answers and S-explanations. $N = 154$.

excluded from the learning experiment proper (only subjects with consistently negative responses in both pretests of conservation were admitted), the test on continuous quantities was repeated with 17 of them in order to see if the success on discontinuous quantities would spread to continuous quantities. Furthermore, the hypothesis was tested that transitions should not occur in those subjects who did not yet have addition/subtraction of continuous quantities. With the criterion of only correct responses and S-explanations, 11 subjects of the 17 acquired conservation with continuous material as a function of the presentation of the pretest. The acquisitions did not seem to be clearly related to initial presence/absence of addition/subtraction of continuous quantities.

The pretest findings may be summarized in the following diagram, where the numbers in parentheses refer to the number of subjects observed at the given stages.

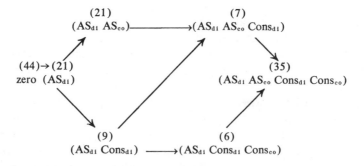

Less than six per cent of the subjects fall outside this schema. The spontaneous changes observed during the pretests and the changes observed in the practice sessions are generally, but not invariably, in agreement with the diagram. For the time being it can only be seen as a rough picture of certain general tendencies in the data.

Discussion of Pretest Results

Two complementary interpretations are suggested by the pretest findings. One is that the processes involved in the earlier stages may somehow be constitutive of those involved in the later stages. This refers particularly to the idea that conservation is the result of a completely reversible grouping of the operations of addition and subtraction. The test of addition/subtraction of discontinuous material would seem to be a relatively pure test of the capacity to keep in mind and to combine mentally the operations of addition and subtraction (undisturbed by conflicting perceptions), and the data seem to show quite conclusively that mastery of this test is a necessary condition for passing the two tests of conservation. In the domain of number this is confirmed by the recent findings of Wohlwill (1960).

The other interpretation is that development is a function of the amount of disturbance of perception in each situation. It is obvious that the disturbing influence of perception is at a minimum in the test of addition/subtraction of discontinuous material and is much higher in the other three tests. Furthermore, it is also quite plausible that the presence of perceptually separate and invariant parts in the discontinuous material should facilitate an additive composition of these parts, and thereby conservation. By an additive composition we mean that the whole object is seen as a sum of its parts, which also means that as long as all parts are retained, the whole will be conserved. This atomistic composition and its relation to conservation has been discussed in detail by Piaget and Inhelder (1941).

Our interpretation of the pretest data may be summarized as follows. The concepts of conservation are symptoms of an additive composition of the objects. Development in this area consists in a progressively more structured and balanced organization of the operations of addition and subtraction (equilibration). This equilibration is accompanied by an increasing resistance to perceptual disturbance.

The next step in the study of these phenomena should be to design a test containing a variety of operations of addition/subtraction in order to determine more exactly the properties of the AS-system which are linked with conservation. Without such data further theorizing seems futile.

THE EXPERIMENTAL PROCEDURE

One control group and two groups practising on continuous and discontinuous material, respectively, took part in the experiments. In order to maximize the comparability of the groups, only children with no correct answers in the two pretests of conservation were included. These children were matched in groups of three with respect to the pattern of responses on the two pretests on addition/subtraction, and the children in each trio were randomly assigned to groups, one child to each group. There were 15 subjects in the Co-group (practice on continuous material), 15 in the Di-group (practice on discontinuous material), and 14 in the K-group (control).

Following the pretests, the members of groups Co and Di were given a maximum of three training sessions on three successive days. The sessions were interrupted as soon as the transition to conservation occurred, and consequently only those subjects who did not acquire conservation during the practice period had three full sessions. A complete trial session comprised five items, each with differently colored material.

The items were composed according to the schema shown below. A and B are the two identical balls or piles with which each item started. The child was always informed at the beginning of an item that the two balls (piles) contained exactly the same amount. I–IV and *a–e* are the various steps and substeps in the item. Def. A means deformation of object A, +A means that a piece is added to A, and —A means that a piece is taken away from A. The standard question is asked after each deformation, addition or subtraction. A > B means that there is more in A than in B, A = B that there is the same amount in both, and ≠ means > or <. The sequence +A —A always refers to the addition and subtraction of the *same* piece.

I	II	III	IV
(*a*) Def. A If child says A > B, then:	(*a*) Def. B and —B	(*a*) Def. A and —A	(*a*) Def. B and —B —A
(*b*) —A	(*b*) —A	(*b*) —A (another piece)	(*b*) +A +B Proceed to next item.
(*c*) +A If child says B > A, then:	(*c*) +B Proceed to III.	(*c*) +A (*d*) +A Proceed to IV.	
(*b*) —B			
(*c*) +B In both cases proceed to II. If child says A = B, then:			
(*b*) Def. B In what fol- lows: If child says ≠, return to I*a*, if =, continue:			
(*c*) Def. A Two new ob- jects C and D.			
(*d*) Def. C			
(*e*) Def. D Posttest.			

Sequence of deformations

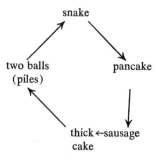

The circle with the arrows indicates the sequence of deformations. A session may start at any point in the circle. If the first deformation was to a snake, then the next should be to a pancake, then to a sausage, etc.

This schema is the result of a compromise between the need for a variable and flexible procedure (which maximizes the chances of inducing a cognitive change) and the need for comparability and clear communication. The procedure may seem highly complex when communicated verbally, but with a little practice it is carried out nearly automatically by the experimenter. The assistant recorded the responses in a simple code on specially prepared sheets.

The posttests were identical to the pretests. They were given immediately after the child had manifested conservation throughout the items Ia–Ie (see the schema), or at the end of the third practice session. The control group was posttested three days after the pretest.

Throughout the pre- and posttests and practice sessions, the experimenter took care to maintain a completely neutral attitude to all the responses of the children, and never to inform them of the correctness of the responses.

RESULTS

Table 6 shows the changes from pre- to posttests in the three groups. The Di-group had the most frequent acquisitions of conservation, then the Co-group, whereas only two subjects in the control group improved, one of them only on continuous and the other only on discontinuous material. The next step in the analysis was to study the individual transitions in order to see whether they conform with the hypothetical sequence that was inferred from the pretest material. This sequence may briefly be expressed as follows: all tests negative→addition/subtraction of discontinuous material→addition/subtraction of continuous material, and roughly at the same time conservation of discontinuous material→conservation of continuous material. Of 30 subjects who changed in some way during the

Table 6

The Changes in Number of Correct Responses in the Various Subtests for the Three Matched groups[a]

	Scores improving	Scores unchanged	Scores getting worse
Co-group			
$Cons_{co}$	4	11	—
AS_{co}	8	3	4
$Cons_{di}$	5	10	—
AS_{di}	5	6	4
Di-group			
$Cons_{co}$	8	7	—
As_{co}	8	3	4
$Cons_{di}$	6	9	—
AS_{di}	5	8	2
Control Group			
$Cons_{co}$	1	13	—
AS_{co}	7	7	0
$Cons_{di}$	1	13	—
AS_{di}	3	11	0

[a] "Cons" and "AS" refer to the subtests of conservation and addition/subtraction, "co" and "di" to the continuous and the discontinuous material.

experiment, only two seemingly developed in a way that does not fit the hypothetical sequence. These two subjects both changed from completely negative pretests to conservation of continuous quantities, one of them with all the other tests negative, and the other with addition/subtraction of discontinuous quantities only.

DISCUSSION

The main trends in the data are quite clear. They permit us to conclude with some confidence that frequent transitions from non-conservation to conservation may be induced in situations without any known external reinforcement. Furthermore, practice of the given type on discontinuous quantities apparently leads to more frequent transitions than practice on continuous quantities, which in turn leads to more frequent transitions than the mere presentation of the pretests.

The procedure is too complex to permit an exact delimitation of the effective factors in the practice sessions. At the moment one may only presume that the variable and complex problems presented to the child start some kind of active internal reorganization, resulting in sudden "insights," and that practice on discontinuous material is more stimulating in this respect than practice on continuous material. The next step is to attempt to make a gradually more refined diagnosis of the cognitive processes involved. A recent book by Berlyne (1960) contains much relevant material on conflict and cognitive change.

Finally, it may be appropriate to emphasize that a type of cognitive change has been produced that seems to lie outside the field of application of ordinary theories of reinforcement. It is hoped that data of this type will help to give wider perspectives on the difficult problems of developmental learning.

REFERENCES

Berlyne, D. (1960). *Conflict arousal and curiosity*. New York: McGraw-Hill.
Piaget, J., and B. Inhelder (1941). *Le développement des quantités chez l'enfant*. Paris: Delachaux et Niestlé.
Smedslund, J. (1961a). The acquisition of conservation of substance and weight in children: II. External reinforcement of conservation of weight and of the operations of addition and subtraction. *Scand. J. Psychol.*, 2, 71–84.
Smedslund, J. (1961b). The acquisition of conservation of substance and weight in children: V. Practice in conflict situations without external reinforcement. *Scand. J. Psychol.*, 2, 156–160.
Wohlwill, J. (1960). A study of the development of the number concept by scalogram analysis. *J. genet. Psychol.*, 97, 345–377.

A TRAINING PROCEDURE FOR ACQUISITION
OF PIAGET'S CONSERVATION OF QUANTITY:
A PILOT STUDY AND ITS REPLICATION

Irving E. Sigel/Annemarie Roeper/Frank H. Hooper

INTRODUCTION

Conservation is defined by Flavell (1963, p. 245) as "the cognition that certain properties (quantity, number, length, etc.) remain invariant (are conserved) in the face of certain transformations (displacing objects or object parts in space, sectioning an object into pieces, changing shape,

Reprinted with the permission of the senior author and publisher from *The British Journal of Educational Psychology*, 1966, 36, 301–311.

etc.).". This process is considered by Piaget (1952, p. 3) as "a necessary condition for all rational activity." On the basis of extensive studies, Piaget identifies three stages of development for each type of conservation: stage 1, in which no conservation is found, and the child focuses in this instance on irrelevancies; stage 2, a transitional period, in which the child is dominated by the perceptual appearances and in which conservation may or may not appear; stage 3, the stage of natural conservation, in which the child readily and logically demonstrates understanding of invariant properties in the face of transformations. The stages are presumed to be fixed and invariant, irrespective of the properties under study. There is an additional developmental sequence which exists across the different quantity subclasses. Conservation of substance appears at about 8 to 10 years of age, preceding conservation of weight which is apparent between the ages of 10 to 12. Functional acquisition of volume occurs after the age of 12. The invariant sequence of the development of substance, weight and volume conservation has generally been verified, with certain qualifications, in a number of studies by Elkind (1961a, 1961b, 1961c), Kooistra (1963), Lovell (1961) and Smedlund (1961a, 1961b, 1961c, 1961d, 1961e, 1961f).

Can conservation be induced in the child? Piaget (1952) holds that for conservation to appear the child must be able to perform the following operations: multiple classification, multiple relationality, atomism, reversibility, and seriation. We contend that conservation can be induced if the training procedures embody these prerequisite operations.

PREVIOUS TRAINING RESEARCH

The majority of previous attempts at conservation modification or acceleration have dealt with areas other than quantity concepts. These include number conservation, Wohlwill (1960), Wohlwill and Lowe (1962) and area conservation, Beilin and Franklin (1962). Training results in these studies have essentially been negative. Piagetian concept acquisition has not proved amenable to laboratory training techniques based upon traditional learning approaches, e.g., see Flavell (1963, pp. 370–379). The studies which have attempted to induce conservation generally, provide no information as to the child's ability to employ any or all of the prerequisite operations. They merely indicate the extent to which the child can conserve (Bruner, 1964, and Smedslund, 1961a). Further, these investigators shed no light on the relationship between the mental operations, e.g., multiple classification, and conservation.

Piaget assigns a clearly subordinate role to language as a necessary condition in the development of conservation, holding that changes in cognitive structure are not accomplished via verbal enrichment or sophistication. Bruner, however, contends that acquisition of conservation is related to linguistic experiences. He reported a study by Frank who tested the Bruner (1964, p. 5) hypothesis that "improvement in language should aid this type (conservation) of problem solving." Activation of language would enable the child to be less dominated by perceptual forces in the setting, less inhibited in utilizing symbolic processes, and consequently, be able to deal with the conservation problem. Frank, using subjects aged 4 to 7, tested the children on the classic paradigm of conservation of continuous quantity (liquid), in one case with the materials in full view, and for several conditions in which the beakers were screened. In the latter condition the child is asked to verbalize. Increases in conservation responses occurred under the screened conditions and the older subjects maintained correct responses in posttest and transfer task situation. These results are offered by Bruner (1964, pp. 6–7) as support for the significance of verbalization in conservation acquisition.

Unfortunately, the report of this experiment is condensed and open to alternative interpretations. Selective attention toward the salient cues of constant water quantities, especially in the screened situation, may be the operative factor, irrespective of any verbalization that occurs. Practice effects via the recall of the treatment condition would not necessarily demand a language activation rationale. In particular, we would have to know how the experimenter examined the influence of problem-specific queries across a number of conservation settings. Although Bruner reports no significant improvements for pretest–posttest controls, Smedslund has found changes following task administration, irrespective of training methods employed. The possibility of learning within the task situation still remains.

Another set of studies involving the acquisition of the conservation of weight has been reported by Smedslund (1961a, 1961b, 1961c, 1961d, 1961e, 1961f). Working with children from 5 to 7, Smedslund attempted to train children to conserve weight by employing two training procedures. In one situation he reinforced trials in the conservation of matter. He altered the form of one of the balls of clay and asked the child to predict which one would weigh more. The child's prediction was tested directly by placing the object on a scale in the child's presence. A second procedure was to add or subtract pieces of plasticine and show the child the relative effect of these actions. The assumption in this latter approach was that if the addition-subtraction schema were exercised, the child would more easily acquire conservation of weight. The results for this study were essentially negative.

One experiment in this series by Smedslund is of considerable interest in that it provides exciting possibilities for inducing conservation by the creation of cognitive conflict, i.e., competing cognitive systems. Smedslund reasoned that creation of such conflict would induce cognitive reorganization. Two kinds of transformations were employed, i.e., deformation by changing the shape, and addition and subtraction of quantity. Thus, if the child was inclined to think that flattening out a piece of clay increased its size, and that subtracting a piece of it would decrease its size, the experimenter would employ both actions at the same time and ask the child whether the transformed and subtracted item was the same or less than the standard. Presentation of two conflicting approaches is presumed to give the subject a situation in which he has to pause and decide between the conflicting possibilities. Of all the conditions Smedslund employed to induce conservation, the conflict paradigm was the most successful.

A recent study by Gruen (1964) compared verbal pre-training on number conservation, in combination with direct reinforced practice, against a verbal cognitive conflict paradigm drawn from Smedslund's approach. Although training effects were generally small, a significant difference between verbal conflict training and control groups was demonstrated. In addition, Beilin (1965) found a verbal-rule instruction method to be effective in the inducement of length and number conservation. Tests on an area generalization task revealed a notable absence of any transfer effects.

It may be that facilitating as cognitive conflict is, it may have to be more intensive as well as extensive. In Smedslund's studies only five of thirteen subjects manifested changes in conservation ability. Why not all, in view of their common exposure to the training? Our contention is that conservation can be induced only by training the child in the prerequisites to such mental operations. Such training may, in fact, induce conflict since it exposes the child to experiences which force him to reorganize cognitively.

The potential role of operational reversibility in mediating conservation development is indicated by Eifermann and Etzion (1964) for adult subjects, and by Wallach and Sprott (1964) for young children. The latter study utilized a reversibility training approach very similar to that found in the final sessions of the present enrichment program. Experimental training groups of 6–7-year-old children were found to differ significantly from controls on discontinuous quantity conservation and numerical correspondence responses.

RATIONALE FOR PROPOSED TRAINING PROGRAM

To conserve, the child must be able to emancipate himself from the perceptual demands of the situation, to know that the size or shape of the items can be changed, i.e., be transformed, and still not lose every one of the initial attributes, and to acknowledge that objects are multidimensional. Given that the child learns that objects can be classified and reclassified on the basis of any one of the single attributes, he is now in a position to learn that objects can be classified and reclassified on the basis of two or more attributes. Combining two or more dimensions of objects signifies the beginning of multiplicative relations, an operation that leads to the creation of a large array of classes. Since objects have a large number of possible class memberships, classifications are, to a degree, relative. The creation of classes becomes dependent on the criteria selected as bases for classification. An interesting by-product of this is the awareness that class membership of an item may be defined by the individual, since it is he who decides what attributes to use.

The above operations are presumed to be critical for the acquisition of conservation. What about the schemas? Piaget proposes the schema of atomism, the awareness that objects are made up of minute particles. The transformations are said to relocate these particles in space without changing their number. It is our contention that such knowledge is unnecessary for the level of comprehension of conservation under discussion here.

In summary, then, we conclude that conservation is possible only when the mental operations of *multiple classification, multiple relationality,* and *reversibility* are present as the cognitive structure basic to adequate conservation performance. The goal of our program was to train children in these operations.

PLAN OF THE INVESTIGATION

Subjects

Ten children, ranging in age from 4·9 to 5, were divided in two groups of five and comprise the Pilot sample. One group was designated Training Group and the other Control. No significant age differences were found between the two groups. The mean Stanford-Binet I.Qs. were 149 for the T group and 152 for the C group. Unfortunately, school withdrawals prevented posttesting of one training and two control subjects. All children were in regular attendance at a nursery school at which the second author was Director. This school provides a rich and stimulating curriculum.

Conservation Tasks

Each of the ten children was given conservation tasks of continuous quantity (plasticine) for substance, weight, and volume, and one conservation of liquid substance. The tests were administered in the classical way. A child passed a conservation task when he could indicate that at least in two of the three transformations the two items were still identical in terms of the property under discussion. Posttests were administered two weeks after the training period.

Teaching Procedures

Of particular significance in this report is the teaching procedure used. The Training Group gathered in Mrs. Roeper's office for their sessions, each of which was tape recorded. The children were told that they were going to do some work, and nothing was said about the relationship between the work in Mrs. Roeper's room and the testing experiences.

On the basis of the theoretical position presented earlier, the training focused on multiple labeling which was followed by multiple classification and multiplicative relations. Finally, reversibility was introduced. In Table 1 we have a verbatim account of the teacher introducing an object, in this case a banana, and the encouragement toward labeling. This is followed by another object, an orange. This same procedure is followed. Having focused on the characteristics of each, the teacher presents two similar objects and asks the children to label differences between the tangerine and the orange. Having identified the difference, she now proceeds to discuss similarities.

We assume that directing the children's attention to the similarities, as well as the differences of objects, facilitates perception of comparison and distinction. The children begin to enumerate the comparisons and each one is accepted by the teacher as legitimate. This is contrary to some of their experiences on intelligence tests, for example, where such acceptance is not possible or responses are not given the same reward. Having ascertained and verbalized apparent similarities such as shape and color, the teacher introduces another basis of classification, in this particular case, functional attributes. Having worked with the two different objects, yet of the same general class, she now introduces the original banana, which is different, and focuses on similarities again. The process of naming the additional attributes, searching for class labels, and defining criteria of class membership goes on until the group, under the teacher's guidance and stimulation, has exhausted the possibilities. Following this, the children were introduced to the idea of multiplicative relations in which two criteria are coordinated as a basis of classification, e.g., "Can you think of two things that you are at the same time?" Starting with the personal, that is the egocentric, the teacher moved to non-personal objects.

Reversibility was the final operation to be introduced. The children were given a constant number of pennies, which were divided among them. The goal here is to demonstrate that irrespective of how the pennies are divided or arranged on the table, the total remains the same and can be recombined to form a pile equal to the original one.

The opportunity to use language and language formulas, and to provide schemas in the context of learning particular information was deliberate. We also believe that opportunities for cognitive reorganization were provided, in that the children learn two or more attributes of an object which can be combined to define another class. Thus, through structural teaching involving verbalization and demonstrations, we sought to bring to the children's attention the fact that objects have multiple characteristics (multiple classification), that these can be combined in various ways to produce new categories (multiple relations), and that categories of objects can be reorganized and brought back to the original (reversibility).

Table 1

Portion of Verbatim Transcript of a Training Session
Dealing with Multiple Attributes of Objects

TEACHER: Can you tell me what this is, Mary?
MARY: A banana.
TEACHER: What else can you tell me about it?
MARY: It's straight.
TEACHER: It's straight. What else?
MARY: It has a peel.
TEACHER: It has a peel. . . . Tom, what can you tell me about it?
TOM: Ummm . . . It has some dark lines on it.
TEACHER: Uh-huh.
TOM: It has some green on it.
TEACHER: What can you do with it?
TOM: You can eat it!
TEACHER: That's right! . . . Now let's see . . .
CHILDREN: . . . I love bananas!
TEACHER: What is this?
CHILDREN: An orange.
TEACHER: Is it really an orange?
CHILDREN: Uh-huh. . . . Yes.
TEACHER: Look at it closely.
CHILD: It's an artificial one.
TEACHER: Oh, that's right, it's an artificial one . . . But, what else can you tell me about it?
CHILDREN: You can eat it . . . It is round . . .
TEACHER: Uh-huh.
CHILDREN: . . . Orange.
TEACHER: That's right!
CHILD: It has a stem.
TEACHER: Now, look at this one . . . What's this?
CHILDREN: An orange . . . orange.
TEACHER: And what can you do with it?
CHILDREN: You can eat it . . . and it's round . . .
TEACHER: It is round . . .
CHILD: It has a peel . . .
TEACHER: It has a peel . . . Now, look at these two things. Are they the same?
CHILDREN: No.
TEACHER: What's different?
CHILDREN: This one . . . this one here is pressed in on the side a little . . . this one is lighter.
TEACHER: Do you know what this really is? This is a tangerine . . . and this is an orange. Now tell me in what ways they are alike.
CHILDREN: This is smaller and that's bigger.
TEACHER: I said, "In what way are they alike?"
CHILDREN: They are both round . . . they both have a stem . . . both orange.
TEACHER: They both have a stem, both round, both orange: Anything else alike about them?
CHILD: They're both fat.
TEACHER: Uh-huh. What can you do with them?
CHILDREN: We can eat them . . .
TEACHER: We can eat them . . . Now, tell me, what's the same about all these things?

CHILD: These are round, but this isn't.

TEACHER: I said, what is the same about them, not what's different about them.

CHILDREN: They're both round . . . they're round . . . they're round . . . and they are both artificial.

TEACHER: They're all artificial, and, . . . are they all round?

CHILD: No.

TEACHER: What about the banana?

CHILD: It's straight.

TEACHER: But, . . . tell me something else that's the same about all of these things.

CHILD: . . . They have . . . all have a peel.

TEACHER: That's right, too, but what can you do with all of them?

CHILDREN: You can eat them!

TEACHER: That's right! That's the same about every one of them. Do you have a name for all of them?

CHILDREN: Yes!

TEACHER: What?

CHILD: A banana.

TEACHER: A banana? No, . . . is there something that you can call all of them?

CHILDREN: Fruit . . . fruit.

TEACHER: And what's the same about all fruit?

CHILDREN: They are all round except bananas.

TEACHER: No, . . . why do you call all of these things fruit?

CHILDREN: Because you can eat them.

TEACHER: You can eat them.

CHILDREN: And they are food.

TEACHER: And they are food. If I had a piece of bread here, would that be fruit too?

CHILDREN: No.

TEACHER: Why not?

CHILDREN: Because it is not sweet . . . not round . . .

TEACHER: Because it is not sweet. I think that's a good reason . . . and, you eat bread too?

CHILDREN: Yes.

TEACHER: But is still not a fruit . . . right?

CHILDREN: Yes.

TEACHER: Now, can you tell me again what this is? We talked about it yesterday.

CHILD: A pencil.

TEACHER: What else can you tell me about it?

CHILDREN: It's round. . . . You said you were going to put it in . . .

TEACHER: That's right . . . Ah . . . Tom, what is this?

TOM: Chalk.

TEACHER: What else can you tell me about it?

TOM: It's white.

TEACHER: Gail, tell me, what's the same about these two things?

GAIL: They're both round.

TEACHER: What else?

GAIL: . . . . . . Ummm . . .

TEACHER: John, tell me, what's the same about these two things?

JOHN: . . . both write.

TEACHER: That's right! There are two things that are the same about it. Tell me what they are?

JOHN: Well. . . . I don't know . . .

TEACHER: What are they, Mary?

MARY: They're round and they write.

TEACHER: Very good!

Although each of these sessions was planned in advance, a rigid schedule could not be followed. The children did not always conform to the teacher's expectation, at times they gained insight so quickly that the teacher had to vary her procedure. The sessions lasted only twenty to thirty minutes and were discontinued as soon as the teacher noticed that the children seemed to lose interest. The Control Group would also come into Mrs. Roeper's office, but were engaged in discussions of social studies problems. They would discuss such matters as community helpers and their social roles. In this way, both groups were given special treatment, differing in specific content. It will be noticed that the training procedure did not focus directly on the tasks that were used in the posttesting, nor was any reference made to that situation. We believe, as far as the children were concerned, they were unaware of the relationship between the two.

INITIAL RESULTS

The results of the pilot sample are shown in Table 2. Each child in the Training Group was able to solve correctly at least one more conservation task in the posttesting than in the pretesting session. The most dramatic change is that of Gail who responded correctly to the posttest problems involving substance, weight, and volume. Tom and Mary showed smaller gains, but nevertheless, did do better on the posttraining testing than on their pretraining tests.

For the Control Group children, two out of the three were unable to solve any of the conservation tasks on the pretraining tests and were also unable to solve any of the tasks on the posttraining testing. One child in the Control Group, Em, who was able to solve two of the conservation tasks, was able to solve all of them in the posttraining.

In discussing the findings, we must keep in mind that the children are of comparable I.Q. chronological age, social status and educational level. The answers to the differences in the abilities to resolve the conservation tasks cannot be attributed to any of these variables.

RESULTS OF REPLICATION STUDY

The results of the first training session were sufficiently encouraging to warrant a replication. In the selection of the second sample, we made certain that none of the ten children could conserve. The children were assigned randomly to the training and control groups, the average ages were 4·3 and 4·5, respectively, and mean Stanford-Binet I.Q. scores were identical, 143·8. Identical testing and training procedures, as described in the first situation, were used.

The results of the pre- and post-conservation testing are presented in Table 2.

Table 2

*Responses of Training and Control Groups in
Two Conservation Experiments*

Study I

Training Group

	Pretesting				Posttesting			
Subjects	*Sub.*	*Liq. Sub.*	*Wt.*	*Vol.*	*Sub.*	*Liq. Sub.*	*Wt.*	*Vol.*
Gail	0	0	0	0	+	0	+	+
Tom	0	0	0	0	0	+	+	0
Martha	+	0	0	0	+	0	+	0
Mary	0	0	0	0	+	0	0	0

Control Group

Ma	0	0	0	0	0	0	0	0
Je	0	0	0	0	0	0	0	0
Em	+	†	0	0	†	†	+	+

Study II
Training Group

Ruth	0	0	0	0	+	+	†	0
Joby	0	0	0	0	0	0	0	0
Nelson	0	0	0	0	+	0	0	0
Jody	0	0	0	0	+	+	+	0
Tracy	0	0	0	0	0	0	+	0

Control Group

Al	0	0	0	0	0	0	0	0
Su	0	0	0	0	0	0	0	0
Car	0	0	0	0	0	0	0	0
Ja	0	0	0	0	0	0	0	0
Ji	0	0	0	0	0	0	0	0

In the pretest, not one child was capable of conserving. In the posttest, we find that four of the five children were able at least to conserve one or more properties. It is particularly interesting to note that Child 5 was able to conserve weight but not substance or liquid substance. Beyond the objective pass-fail considerations, the training subjects revealed a heightened awareness and verbal sophistication within the posttest setting. Thus, the children not only increased in their ability to conserve correctly, but also showed an increase in their ability to verbalize the underlying operations and the salient dimensions of the criterion test situation. The Control Group showed no change in conservation ability or verbalization skills.

DISCUSSION AND CONCLUSION

How can we explain these particular findings? The only significant difference in the educational experience of the Training and Control Groups was the training session during the five-week period. These findings indicate that given training in such operations as multiple classification and reversibility, conservation, at some level, has a greater probability of appearing.

We do have the single case of the child in the first Control Group who showed a change over the course of the five-week period. This may be due to the child's already exhibited ability to conserve which was highlighted by the experimental situation. Yet, we find no such phenomenon in the second Control Group, e.g., no conservation in the pretest, none in the posttest. This strongly supports the contention that the child who can conserve is in the process of demonstrating it in more situations. If we discount, then, the child Martha in the Training Group, and Em in the Control Group, who had shown pretest conservation, we find that the children in the first Training Group who had no conservation did acquire conservation ability, whereas this was not the case in the Control Group. The children who show no such ability are able to solve conservation problems *only* after the training experiences. This suggests that the testing situation may not be an influence unless some ability to profit from the experience is present. Combining the two samples, eight training and seven control subjects indicated pretest non-conservation. There were no posttest successes for any of the seven control subjects. In contrast, of the eight training subjects, five conserved substance, three conserved liquid substance, five conserved weight, and one subject succeeded on the volume task. Pass-fail contingency comparisons show differences between training and control performances on the substance and weight cases, e.g., Fisher Probability Test significance level of .025.

The sequence of development, described by Piaget and confirmed by Elkind, Kooistra, Lovell, and Smedslund, appears in this study with the exception of one subject, Tracy, in our replication sample. The degree to which the enrichment experiences were assimilated by the Training Group is reflected in the type of response given to the inquiry questions in the post-training session. The children verbalized their explanations in an articulate way, employing statements of reversibility, for example, as explanations. During the posttesting session, in response to the question, "Do I have more or less, or the same amount of clay?" the answer was much more complex than in the pretraining session. The child answered, "This piece is the same as this piece (points to the shape-transformed stimuli), it looks the same, it is the same. It is the same clay, it is turned into a ball just like that (points to the comparison stimuli), then you changed it into something else. It looks the same, the same amount of clay." What is of interest in this case is that the explanations are at levels expected as a consequence of training experience. The children who did not have any training showed little change in verbalization patterns from initial to post-training test situations. Even when giving the wrong answer, the Training Group was more articulate and fluent than the Control Group.

The results demonstrated in the ability to articulate as well as in the ability to answer the questions correctly are to be explained primarily as a function of the training experience. Such a conclusion is warranted on theoretical as well as empirical grounds. Reading the transcripts, it becomes readily apparent that the children become sensitized to the multiplicity of attributes of objects and to the possibility of coordinating combinations of attributes. They seem to be encouraged by such an experience to make inferences, that is, to view objects in terms of their classificatory relationships to other objects. The encouragement to verbalize their ideas about objects and to direct attention to the multidimensionality of objects may have played an important part in the child's assimilation of this new knowledge. Such encouragement to verbalize, in conjunction with the prerequisite operations, may combine to provide the appropriate experiences necessary for the child to acquire conservation. In this sense, Bruner's emphasis upon the verbal aspect of the situation may well be correct.

The quantitative and qualitative analyses of the results of this study provide support for the basic hypothesis that training programs focusing on prerequisites for relevant cognitive operations influence the resultant cognitive structures. This modification of cognitive structure, directed by such a training procedure, provides for the emergence of new sets of abilities and demonstrates the interdependence of cognitive stages and precursors. On the basis of this position, conservation *per se* need not be taught directly. Possessing the necessary prerequisite, children may "discover" conservation as a principle and apply it to substance, weight and volume. Increased affirmation of their competence in a specific area could be obtained through extended practice. They already have the necessary logical structure, in this instance, to master conservation of continuous quantity. Children having experience with conservation of continuous quantity could then be exposed to discontinuous quantities, number, etc. In this way, progress toward comprehensive logical thought can be developed. Insofar as stage placement within a given quantity conservation type is concerned, the present training subjects were probably at a transitionary or intuitive level. It appears reasonable that transitionary stage individuals would derive the greatest benefit from the training experiences. Unfortunately, no attempt was made to determine stage location in this study.

REFERENCES

Beilin, H. (1965). Learning and operational convergence in logical thought development. *J. Exp. child Psychol.*, **2**, 317–339.
Beilin, H., and I. C. Franklin (1962). Logical operations in area and length measurement, age, and training effects. *Child Develpm.*, **33**, 607–618.
Bruner, J. S. (1964). The course of cognitive growth. *Amer. Psychologist*, **19**, 1–15.
Eifermann, R. R., and D. Etzion (1964). Awareness of reversibility: its effect on performance of converse arithmetical operations. *Brit. J. educ. Psychol.*, **34**, Pt. 2, 151–157.
Elkind, D. (1961a). The development of quantitative thinking: a systematic replication of Piaget's studies. *J. genet. Psychol.*, **98**, 37–46.
Elkind, D. (1961b). Children's discovery of the conservation of mass, weight, and volume: Piaget's replication study II. *J. genet. Psychol.*, **98**, 219–227.
Elkind, D. (1961c). Quantity conceptions in junior and senior high school students. *Child Develpm.*, **32**, 551–560.
Flavell, J. H. (1963). *Developmental psychology of Jean Piaget*. Princeton, N.J.: Van Nostrand.
Gruen, G. E. (1964). Experience affecting the development of number conservation in children. Unpublished doctoral dissertation, University of Illinois.
Hunt, J. McV. (1961). *Intelligence and experience*. New York: Ronald.
Kooistra, W. (1963). Developmental trends in the attainment of conservation, transitivity, and relativism in the thinking of children: a replication and extension of Piaget's ontogenetic formulations. Unpublished doctoral dissertation, Wayne State University.
Lovell, K. (1961). *The growth of basic mathematical and scientific concepts in children*. New York: Philosophical Library.
Piaget, J. (1952, 3rd impression, 1964). *The child's conception of number*. London: Routledge.
Smedslund, J. (1961a). The acquisition of conservation of substance and weight in children: I. Introduction. *Scand. J. Psychol.*, **2**, 11–20.
Smedslund, J. (1961b). The acquisition of conservation of substance and weight in children: II. External reinforcement of conservation of weight and of the operations of addition and subtraction. *Scand. J. Psychol.*, **2**, 71–84.
Smedslund, J. (1961c). The acquisition of conservation of substance and weight in children: III. Extinction of conservation of weight acquired "normally" and by means of empirical controls on a balance. *Scand. J. Psychol.*, **2**, 85–87.
Smedslund, J. (1961d). The acquisition of conservation of substance and

weight in children: IV. Attempt at extinction of the visual components of weight concept. *Scand. J. Psychol.*, **2**, 153–155.

Smedslund, J. (1961e). The acquisition of conservation of substance and weight in children: V. Practice in conflict situations without external reinforcement. *Scand. J. Psychol.*, **2**, 156–160.

Smedslund, J. (1961f). The acquisition of conservation of substance and weight in children: VI. Practice on continuous versus discontinuous material in conflict situations without external reinforcement. *Scand. J. Psychol.*, **2**, 203–210.

Wallach, Lise, and R. L. Sprott (1964). Inducing number conservation in children. *Child Develpm.*, **35**, 1057–1071.

Wohlwill, J. F. (1960). A study of the development of the number concept by scalogram analysis. *J. genet. Psychol.*, **97**, 345–377.

Wohlwill, J. F., and R. C. Lowe (1962). Experimental analysis of the development of the conservation of numbers. *Child Develpm.*, **33**, 153–157.

NUMBER CONSERVATION: THE ROLES
OF REVERSIBILITY, ADDITION-SUBTRACTION,
AND MISLEADING PERCEPTUAL CUES

Lise Wallach╱A. Jack Wall╱Lorna Anderson

The present experiment was designed to answer several questions arising from a previous study (Wallach and Sprott, 1964) in which number conservation was induced in children. The Ss in that experiment had been 6- and 7-year-olds who recognized that the number of a set of dolls and the number of a set of beds were equal when there was one doll in each bed, but who said the number was different when subsequently, before their eyes, the dolls were taken out of the beds and placed closer together. The procedure which led them to recognize that the number remained equal was to show them repeatedly that the dolls could be fitted back into the beds again when they had been placed closer together or further apart, though not when a doll or a bed was added or taken away.

The results of this previous experiment were interpreted as indicating that conservation under operations that remove defining attributes could be induced through experience with reversibility of these operations. However, it has been proposed (Wohlwill and Lowe, 1962; Smedslund, 1962) that experience with addition and subtraction may be critical for conservation,

Reprinted with the permission of the senior author and The Society for Research in Child Development, Inc., from *Child Development*, 1967, 38, 425–442.

and such experience, as well as experience with reversibility, was involved in the training procedure. Our first question, therefore, was whether conservation could be induced by training in reversibility alone—that is, whether the procedure would still be effective if it showed only that the dolls could be fitted back into the beds again when they had been put closer together or further apart and did not show what happened when a doll or bed was added or removed.

Secondly, we wished to see whether conservation could be induced by training in addition and subtraction alone without training in reversibility. We thought that the answer might throw some light not only on the question of the effectiveness of experience in addition and subtraction itself, but also on the suggestion made by Zimiles (1963) that a brief experimental procedure which appeared to induce number conservation might do so only because a number set was aroused by the procedure. Addition and subtraction should certainly be at least as capable of arousing such a set as reversibility.

The earlier study had found that the induced number conservation transferred readily to new sets of objects. We now wished to see whether a wider kind of transfer might also occur; specifically, whether number conservation induced by experience with the dolls and beds would transfer to conservation of the amount of a liquid. Much direct transfer of this kind seemed unlikely, so we included a transitional series of tasks less and less like the dolls and beds and more and more like the liquids, for use when the children did not transfer directly.

A final question that we hoped to answer, if possible, was whether conservation of the quantity of a liquid could itself be induced by training in reversibility. The procedures were thus arranged so that children who did not acquire conservation of the quantity of a liquid through transfer were given an opportunity to acquire it through reversibility training.

METHOD

Subjects

The Ss were 56 children whose ages ranged from 6 years and 1 month to 7 years and 8 months with a mean of 6 years and 11 months. They were all in the first grade of a predominantly middle-class public school in a small university town.

Pretests

The child was seated at a table with E, and another adult sat nearby recording.

DOLL PRETEST   Six dolls and six beds were on the table, the beds lined up and the dolls in a pile in front of them. The S was asked to put one doll in each bed. The E then asked, "Are there more dolls than beds?" If S said there were not, E went on, "Are there more beds than dolls?" If S again said there were not, E continued, "Are there the same number of dolls as beds?"

If all three questions were answered appropriately, E said, "Now watch what I do." One by one, he took each doll out of its bed and placed it in a row in front of the beds but closer together, so that the last bed had no doll in front of it. Then E asked, "Now are there the same number of dolls as beds?" If S said there were, E asked, "How do you tell?" If S said there were not, E asked, "Which are more?"

LIQUID PRETEST   The E filled two identical, narrow glasses to the very top from a pitcher of green-colored water. The child was asked whether both glasses were filled exactly to the top, and adjustments were made if necessary. The E then asked, "Is there the same amount to drink in each glass?"

If S said there was, E again said, "Now watch what I do." Explaining what he was doing as he did it, he poured the water from one of the two identical, narrow glasses into a low wide glass. Then, indicating the two glasses with water in them, E asked, "Now is there the same amount to drink in this glass and in this glass?" If S said there was, E asked, "How do you tell?" If S said there was not, E asked, "Which has more?"

Classification of Subjects

On the basis of their performance on the pretest, the Ss were classified into five categories, as follows:

(1) Not meeting criteria: The Ss who did not assert equality between the dolls and beds when the dolls were in the beds, or between the amount of water in the two identical, filled glasses (three Ss), or who failed to follow instructions (one S). Placement in this category precluded placement in any other.

(2) Conservation: The Ss who asserted both that the number of dolls was the same as the number of beds when the dolls were closer together, and that the amount of liquid in the wide glass was the same as that in the narrow one.

(3) Nonconservation: The Ss who asserted neither that the number of dolls was the same as the number of beds when the dolls were closer together, nor that the amount of liquid in the wide glass was the same as that in the narrow one.

(4) Partial conservation—dolls: The Ss who asserted that the number of dolls was the same as the number of beds when the dolls were closer together, but who did not assert that the amount of liquid in the wide glass was the same as that in the narrow one.

(5) Partial conservation—liquid: The Ss who did not assert that the number of dolls was the same as the number of beds when the dolls were closer together, but who did assert that the amount of liquid in the wide glass was the same as that in the narrow one.

Participation in the experiment ended with the pretest for *S*s in the not meeting criteria and conservation categories. The *S*s in the other categories received additional training and testing as follows (details of the procedures will be described below): The nonconservation *S*s and the partial conservation—liquid *S*s were divided within each category by alternate assignment (the order of *S*s was at the convenience of the teacher) into groups receiving doll reversibility training and doll addition-subtraction training. Immediately following the training, both groups were given a doll posttest which, except for the delayed posttest, was the end of the experiment for the partial conservation—liquid *S*s. Nonconservation *S*s who did not show conservation in the doll posttest were then given liquid reversibility training and subsequently a liquid posttest. Nonconservation *S*s who did show conservation in the doll posttest were immediately given the liquid posttest to test for direct transfer. If direct transfer did not occur, they were then given training on the transfer series, and, if this also did not lead to liquid conservation, they were given liquid reversibility training, and the liquid posttest was repeated. The *S*s in the partial conservation— dolls category were given liquid reversibility training and then the liquid posttest immediately following the pretest. Nonconservation and both partial conservation groups of *S*s were given both doll and liquid delayed posttests 2–6 weeks after the training. See Figure 1.

Doll Training Procedures

DOLL REVERSIBILITY TRAINING   As in the pretest, *S* was again asked to put one of the six dolls in each of the six beds. Then *E* took the dolls out of the beds and put them closer together. This time, however, *E* asked, "Do you think a doll can be put back in every bed now? Or will there be a bed without a doll? Or a doll without a bed?" Regardless of *S*'s answer, he was then asked to try to put a doll back in each bed.

When the dolls were back in the beds, *E* once more took them out and now placed them further apart, so that the last doll had no bed behind it. The *S* was asked the same questions concerning the possibility of putting the dolls back in the beds and then again asked to try to put them back.

This procedure was repeated, with the dolls being placed closer than the beds one time and further the next, until *S* had correctly predicted four times in succession that the dolls could be put back in the beds.

DOLL ADDITION-SUBTRACTION TRAINING   The *S* was again asked to put one of the six dolls in each of the six beds. Then, however, a low screen was placed between *S* and the beds in such a way that the beds were effectively hidden. (The screen was used so that *S* could not simply rely on perception to tell whether there was a doll in each bed, but he would have to make use of his knowledge of dolls or beds being taken away or added.)

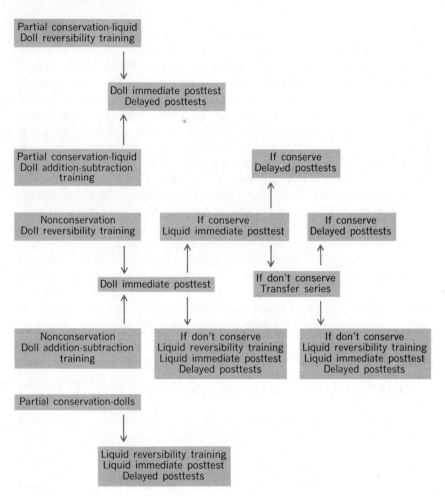

Figure 1 Sequence of procedures for different groups.

The E said, "I'm going to take one doll away," and he reached behind the screen and took a doll out of its bed. Indicating a box with one doll in it at S's side, E gave the doll to S, saying, "Would you put it in this box?" When S had complied, E asked, "Do you think there is a doll in every bed now? Or is there a bed without a doll? Or a doll without a bed?" Regardless of S's answer, the screen was then removed, and he was allowed to see that there was one bed without a doll.

The screen was replaced, and E said, "Now would you give me one doll from the box and I'll see if I can put it in a bed." The E took the doll which S gave him and placed it, behind the screen, into the empty bed. Then E asked, "Do you think every doll is in a bed now? Or is there a doll without a bed? Or a bed without a doll?" After S answered, the screen was again removed, and he was allowed to see that every doll was in a bed, with no beds left over.

After this, the screen was again put back, and *E* said, "Would you please give me one doll from the box again, and I'll see if I can put it in a bed again." The doll which *S* handed *E* was laid down, behind the screen, next to the row of beds. Then *E* asked again, "Do you think every doll is in a bed now? Or is there a doll without a bed? Or a bed without a doll?" After *S* answered, the screen was again taken away.

The screen was replaced, and *E* said, "Now I'm going to take one doll away again." He took the doll that was lying on the table without a bed from behind the screen and gave it to *S*, saying, "Would you put it in the box?" Then *E* asked, "Do you think there is a doll for every bed now? Or is there a bed without a doll? Or a doll without a bed?" After *S* answered, the screen was taken away again.

This sequence was repeated until *S* had correctly described the situation behind the screen four times in succession.

Immediate Posttests

DOLL IMMEDIATE POSTTEST   The six dolls were again in the six beds standing in a row. (This was automatically the case at the end of the reversibility training; *E* added or took away where necessary to make it the case at the end of addition-subtraction training.) As in the pretest, *E* took the dolls out of the beds and put them closer together so that the last bed had no doll in front of it. Then *E* said, "Now I'll ask you something else again. Are there the same number of dolls as beds?" If *S* said there were, *E* asked, "How do you tell?"

LIQUID IMMEDIATE POSTTEST   The first part of the liquid posttest was the same as the liquid pretest, with the same glasses being used. Now, however, if *S* said there was not the same amount to drink in the one narrow glass and in the wide glass into which the water from the other narrow glass had been poured, *E* stopped without asking which had more. If, on the other hand, *S* said there was the same amount to drink in these two glasses, *E* asked how he knew this and then repeated the procedure with several variations.

The first variation was to have the two identical, narrow glasses filled only part way, with *S* serving to judge when the second had "just the same amount" as the first. If *S* showed conservation again when the water from one of the narrow glasses was poured into the wide one, this procedure was repeated with two identical vases and a square pitcher in place of the original glasses. Finally, regardless of whether the new containers were used and of whether conservation occurred with them, the original glasses were filled to the top once more. The original procedure was followed again except that now, instead of all the water, only about two-thirds was poured from the narrow glass into the wide one.

Liquid Training Procedures

TRANSFER-SERIES TRAINING   The transfer series consisted of a series of successive tasks, all of which were presented only if S answered each question correctly. If at any point an incorrect answer occurred, transfer-series training was discontinued, and liquid reversibility training was instituted. The tasks were as follows:

(1) Again, the six dolls were put in the six beds. Then E took them out and put them closer together so that the last bed had no doll in front of it. The E asked, "Are there the same number of dolls as beds?"

(2) Five 3 × 5-inch cards were laid out in a row, and S was given five checkers and asked to put one on each card. The E asked, "Are there the same number of checkers as cards?" Then E took the checkers off and put them closer together in a row in front of the cards so that there was one card without a checker in front of it, and asked, "Now are there the same number of checkers as cards?"

(3) Five black checkers were placed in a row parallel to and aligned with five red ones. The E asked, "Are there the same number of red and black checkers?" Then E put the black checkers much closer together and asked, "Now are there the same number of red and black checkers?" After S answered, E spread the red checkers far apart and out of line and repeated the question.

(4) The S was given one large bead at a time and asked to put them in a row. The E took one bead for himself every time he gave S a bead and made a row parallel to and aligned with S's. When each row had six beads, E asked, "Are there the same number of beads in your row as in my row?" Then E put his beads much closer together and asked, "Do we still have the same number of beads?" After S answered, E spread S's beads further apart and out of line and asked the same question again.

(5) The E again gave S one large bead at a time and gave himself a bead each time he gave one to S, but this time S was asked to put the beads in a pile, and E did likewise. When there were seven beads in each pile, E asked, "Do we have the same number of beads?" Then E spread his beads out and asked, "Do we still have the same number of beads?" When S had answered, E put his beads into a glass and repeated the question.

(6) The E gave S and himself each eight small beads, one at a time, and each of them put his beads into a little glass. (The two glasses were identical and different from those used previously.) The E asked, "Do we have the same number of little beads?" Then E took his beads out of the glass and spread them out on the table, asking, "Now do we have the same number of beads?" Then he said, "Now let me put them back in the glass," and he did so. When they were back in, E said, "Now I'll pour them into another glass," and he poured them into a larger, wider one (different from that used previously). Then E asked, "Do we still have the same number of beads?"

(7) The little glasses, first empty, were dipped into a basket containing small beads so that they were filled with beads. The E asked, "Are both glasses filled to the top?" and he made adjustments when necessary. Then E asked, "Are there about the same number of beads in each glass?" After S answered,

E poured the beads from one of the little glasses into the larger, wider glass and, indicating the two glasses with beads in them, asked, "Now are there about the same number of beads in this glass and in this glass?"

(8) Little stones (of the kind used for mosaics) were poured from a pitcher into the two little glasses, filling them, and *E* asked, "Are they both filled to the top?" and made adjustments if necessary. Then *E* asked, "Are there about the same amount of little stones in each glass?" Then *E* poured the little stones from one of the little glasses into the larger, wider one and, indicating the two glasses with stones in them, asked, "Now are there about the same amount of little stones in this glass and in this glass?"

(9) The green water was poured into the two little glasses, filling them, and *E* asked, "Are they both filled exactly to the top?" and made adjustments when necessary. Then *E* asked, "Is there the same amount to drink in each glass?" After *S* answered, *E* poured the water from one glass into the larger, wider one and, indicating the two glasses with water in them, asked, "Now is there the same amount to drink in this glass and in this glass?"

(10) The liquid posttest was repeated.

LIQUID REVERSIBILITY TRAINING   Depending on whether water had just been used or not, *E* said, "Now we're going to do something more with water," or "Now we're going to do something with water again." He placed two identical glasses different from any used previously next to each other and filled each glass, saying, "I'm going to pour it into this glass to the very top just like we did before, and now I'm going to pour it into the other glass to the very top." Then *E* asked, "Are they both filled exactly to the top?" and made adjustments if necessary.

Then *E* said, "Watch me," and poured the water from one of the two identical glasses into a new, wide glass, which stood next to the glass which still had water in it. The *E* said, "Now I'm going to ask you something different. If I pour this water back in the empty glass, will it be filled just like this one?" After *S* had made a prediction, *E* poured the water back and asked, "Is it . . . ?" (full, or like the other, etc., whatever *S* has predicted) or "Did it . . . ?" (run over, etc.).

With the appropriate modifications in wording, this procedure was repeated until *S* had made three correct predictions in succession. Three different sets of glasses were used in order.

Delayed Posttests

DOLL DELAYED POSTTEST   Three tasks were given in succession:

(1) The *E* gave *S* six toy soldiers and asked him to line them up. The *E* then aligned another row of six to *S*'s row and asked, "Are there the same number of soldiers in your row and in my row?" Then *E* put his soldiers closer together so that one of *S*'s stood alone and asked, "Now are there the same number of soldiers in your row and in my row?"

(2) The *E* asked *S* to put one of five spoons in each of a row of five bowls, and asked, "Are there the same number of spoons as bowls?" Then *E* took

the spoons out and put them in a row closer together so that there was one bowl without a spoon in front of it and asked, "Now are there the same number of spoons as bowls?"

(3) The *E* asked *S* to put the six dolls in the six beds, asked if they were the same number, and then took out the dolls and put them closer together so there was a bed without a doll in front of it, as previously. The *E* asked, "Now are there the same number of dolls as beds?" If *S* said there were, *E* pointed to the bed without a doll in front of it and said, "But look, here is a bed without a doll in front of it. Aren't there more beds?"

LIQUID DELAYED POSTTEST   Four tasks were given in succession:

(1) The *E* filled one of two identical opaque cups (not used previously) part way, then said he wanted to put "just the same amount" into the other cup and adjusted until *S* said he had done so. The *E* then asked, "Is there the same amount to drink in each cup?" Then, saying, "Now watch what I do" and explaining as he went along, *E* poured the water from one of the cups into a transparent jar. Indicating the two containers with water in them, *E* asked, "Now is there the same amount to drink in the jar and this cup?"

(2) The second task was the same as the first except that both cups were filled exactly to the top (as judged by *S*) instead of only part way.

(3) The third task was again like the first except that now the previous test glasses were used instead of the two cups and the jar.

(4) The fourth task was like the second, but still using the previous test glasses. At the end, if *S* said there was the same amount in the two different glasses, *E* said, "But look, in this glass the water goes all the way up to the top, but in this glass it doesn't go nearly so high. Isn't there more water in this glass?"

RESULTS

Pretests

NUMBER AND AGE OF CHILDREN IN EACH CATEGORY   As may be seen in Table 1, approximately the same number of children fell into the conservation and the nonconservation categories. Liquid conservation was present without doll conservation for a sizable number of children, while doll conservation was present without liquid conservation for fewer. The ages of the children were quite comparable in all the categories.

NONCONSERVATION ANSWERS   As was found previously, most children who did not show number conservation said there was a greater number of the items which were more spread out. Of the 28 giving nonconservation answers in the doll pretest, 26 said there were more beds than dolls, while only 2 said there were more dolls.

Most, if not all, of the children giving nonconservation answers in the liquid pretest said there was more liquid in the narrow glass, in which it reached a greater height. This was true for 19 subjects; the data are not clear for the other 2.

Table 1

Number and Age of Children in Each Category

Category	N	Mean Age[a]	Age Range[a]
Nonconservation	16	6–10	6–1 to 7–4
Doll reversibility training	8	6–10	6–7 to 7–4
Doll addition-subtraction training	8	6–10	6–1 to 7–4
Partial conservation—liquid	12	6–11	6–6 to 7–5
Doll reversibility training	6	6–11	6–8 to 7–5
Doll addition-subtraction training	6	6–11	6–6 to 7–3
Partial conservation—dolls	5	7–1	6–5 to 7–8
Conservation	19	7–0	6–7 to 7–5
Not meeting criteria	4	6–11	6–7 to 7–4
Grand total	56	6–11	6–1 to 7–8

[a] In years and months.

Doll Reversibility versus Addition-Subtraction Training

CONVERSATION ON DOLL IMMEDIATE POSTTEST   Doll reversibility training had a strong effect on conservation, while addition-subtraction training did not. When the dolls were closer together than the beds in the first posttest, only 2 of the 14 Ss given doll reversibility training still said the number of dolls and the number of beds were not the same; the other 12 all changed to conservation answers. On the other hand, 12 of the 14 Ss given doll addition-subtraction training continued with nonconservation, while only 2 changed to conservation. (χ^2 for the difference is 11.57, $p < .001$ with 1 df.)

DOLL DELAYED POSTTEST   All Ss who after training changed to conservation in the doll immediate posttest also gave conservation answers throughout the entire doll delayed posttest, except that 2 of the 12 Ss who had received reversibility training succumbed at the end to E's suggestion against conservation.

NUMBER OF TRAINING TRIALS TO CRITERION   Doll reversibility training, with a median of 4, took somewhat fewer trials to criterion than doll addition-subtraction training, with a median of 6, but the difference is not significant. (χ^2 for the median test is 2.30, $.10 < p < .20$ with 1 df.)

Transfer to Liquid

DIRECT TRANSFER   Only nonconservation Ss, who had shown neither doll nor liquid conservation in the pretest, could be used to test for direct transfer to liquid when they had acquired doll conservation through training. This meant that there were only eight *S*s available, as doll conservation was developed by only one of the eight nonconservation *S*s given addition-subtraction training, and seven of the eight given reversibility training. Of these eight, only one *S* showed conservation on the liquid posttest after training with the dolls, thus providing essentially no indication of direct transfer at all.

TRANSFER SERIES   With this one *S* removed, only seven *S*s remained for the transfer series. Four of these seven gave liquid conservation answers in the liquid posttest at the end of the series, although one of the four answered incorrectly on the last question. All four continued to maintain liquid conservation in the delayed posttest. The other three *S*s gave incorrect answers in the third task of the transfer series.

Liquid Reversibility Training

Sixteen *S*s were available for liquid reversibility training. These included the three *S*s above who failed to transfer either on the direct test or on the transfer series, the seven addition-subtraction-trained *S*s and the one reversibility trained nonconservation *S* who did not acquire doll conservation with training, and the five partial conservation—dolls *S*s.

CONSERVATION ON LIQUID POSTTEST   Only 4 of these 16 *S*s gave clear conservation answers in the liquid posttest following liquid reversibility training; 1 more gave a nonconservation answer first but immediately corrected himself; and 11 gave clear nonconservation answers. The 5 *S*s who did give conservation answers at this point, immediately or not, continued to give them throughout the delayed posttest, except that one succumbed to the nonconservation suggestion at the end. These data do not, however, provide much support for the effectiveness of reversibility training for liquid conservation, a point to be further discussed below.

ABILITY TO PREDICT   The predictions called for in liquid reversibility training were clearly very easy. Of the 16 Ss, 14 made correct predictions on every trial—that is, predicted from the start that the initial glass would be full again when the water was poured back. The remaining 2 *S*s predicted incorrectly only on the first trial.

How Ss Said They Could Tell Number or Amount Were the Same

It will be recalled that *S*s who said number or amount were the same in the pretest or in the immediate posttest were thereupon asked, "How do you tell?" The answers to this question were independently coded by two of the investigators into the following nine categories:

(1) Equality Before. Referred to the fact that every bed had a doll in it before the dolls were taken out, or that the two identical glasses had been equally full before the water from one was poured into the different glass.

(2) Reversibility. Referred to the fact that a doll could be put back in every bed, or that the water could be poured back into the original glass and the two identical glasses would both be full again.

(3) Addition-Subtraction. Referred to the fact that nothing had been added or taken away.

(4) Closer or Wider. Noted that the dolls were closer together than the beds, or that the glass into which the water had been poured was wider than the original one.

(5) Number. Referred to specific numbers (possible only with dolls, not with liquid).

(6) Matching. Showed how the dolls could be matched with the beds, pointing to successive doll-bed pairs saying something like, "this goes with this, this goes with this," etc. (again possible only with dolls).

(7) Extra Doll. Showed that there was one doll between two beds, or without a bed, or that two dolls were "sharing" a bed (again possible only with dolls).

(8) Don't Know. Indicated lack of knowledge by saying, "Don't know," by not answering, or by restating the equality without a reason (e.g., "because this has as much as this").

(9) Miscellaneous. Any other answers.

If a child gave two different reasons for saying the number or amount were the same, his answer was scored as half in one category and half in the other. The investigators agreed on the coding of all but five of the 79 answers; these five were coded again by one of the investigators. The frequency with which answers in the different categories were given by Ss who first said the number or amount were the same after various experiences may be seen in Table 2. (It should be noted that these answers are not all independent; a given S may appear both under dolls and under liquid.)

Table 2 supports the effectiveness of training in that the reasons which Ss gave after training for saying the number or amount were the same were not appreciably different from the reasons which Ss gave who did not require training to say they were the same. The main difference seems to be that the latter Ss somewhat more often gave answers in the "Don't know" or "Miscellaneous" categories. This would suggest that the trained Ss were, if anything, clearer about the reasons for conservation than the untrained ones.

However, contrary to expectation, neither reversibility nor the lack of anything having been added or removed was very often given as the reason for number or amount being the same. The most frequent reason, by far, with the dolls was that there was an extra doll in the line. With the liquid, two reasons were much more frequent than any others: that the amount had been the same before, and that the glass into which the water had been poured was wider than the glass from which it came. These points will be further considered in the Discussion.

Table 2

Frequency of Different Reasons for Saying Number or Amount Were the Same

Point at Which S Said Number and Amount Were the Same	Equality Before	Reversibility	Addition-Subtraction	Closer or Wider	Number	Matching	Extra Doll	Don't Know	Miscellaneous
Dolls									
Pretest (conservers)	2	0	1	0	2½	1	9½	5	3
After reversibility training	3	2	0	1	1	1	4	0	0
After addition-subtraction training	0	0	0	0	0	0	2	0	0
Total for dolls	5	2	1	1	3½	2	15½	5	3
Liquid									
Pretest (conservers)	17	0	0	12	—	—	—	2	0
After doll training (direct transfer)	0	0	0	0	—	—	—	0	1
After transfer series	2	½	0	1½	—	—	—	0	0
After liquid reversibility training	2	0	0	1	—	—	—	2	0
Total for liquid	21	½	0	14½	—	—	—	4	1

DISCUSSION

Several of the questions which gave rise to this experiment are clearly answered by the results. Our first question was whether, in order to induce number conservation, it was necessary for the reversibility-training procedure which had been found effective in a prior experiment to include, as it had, experience with addition and subtraction. The answer is no; the procedure was as effective here without addition-subtraction experience as it was previously with such experience.

This suggests—but does not necessarily imply—that number conservation is not affected by training in addition and subtraction. In the absence of reversibility training, training with addition and subtraction might still lead to conservation. Our second question was whether this was the case. The answer again is no, at least for the particular addition-subtraction training procedure that we used.

Further, the lack of effectiveness of this procedure indicates that the basis for the success of the reversibility training is not that it arouses a number set, as implied by Zimiles' (1963) suggestion. Such training in addition and subtraction ought to be at least as likely, if not much more likely, to arouse a number set as the training in reversibility.

Another question which seems clearly answered is whether the number conservation induced by our reversibility-training procedure transfers directly to such different conservations as that of the amount of a liquid: it does not. Such transfer is not expected from the point of view that what is critical for conservation of a property is recognition of the reversibility of operations that remove the defining attributes of this property, as suggested by Wallach and Sprott (1964). Our number-conservation training procedure was designed to lead to the realization that when objects had been paired together—a defining attribute of equality—they could be paired again despite intervening changes in arrangement. The procedure would not be expected to indicate that when a liquid which had originally filled one of two identical containers had been poured into a different container, it would exactly fill the first again if it was poured back.

On the other hand, it was found that conservation of the amount of liquid did follow upon the number-conservation training procedure for some children, when the differences between conserving amount of liquid and number were minimized by a series of intervening steps. What this was due to cannot be clearly answered at present. It is possible that the series led the children to realize that the pouring of a liquid is reversible as well as the rearrangement of the dolls, but it is also possible that other processes, particularly that of direct suggestion, were responsible.

The results so far discussed were all essentially in line with expectation and as such appear to support the view that conservation was induced as the result of recognition of reversibility. However, some doubt is thrown upon this interpretation by two other results: (*a*) the reasons which *S*s gave for conservation answers, and (*b*) the failure of liquid reversibility training to have a strong effect.

It will be recalled that one reason was given more frequently than reversibility or any other for saying the number of dolls was the same as the number of beds when the dolls were closer together, whether or not training had been necessary for number conservation to be shown. This reason was that there was an extra doll in the line not aligned with a bed—that is, that there was a doll between two beds, or that two dolls were "sharing" a bed, etc. This suggests that the effectiveness of the doll reversibility-training procedure may have been due, not to the experience with reversibility per se, but to the opportunity which this experience gave for the removal of a distorted perception. That is, initial nonconservation answers may have resulted from seeing the dolls and beds as paired with one bed left over; the training procedure may then have led to the realization that this was not correct—that the dolls and beds were not paired with one another, and that therefore the bed apparently left over at the end did not imply inequality in the number of dolls and beds.

The main effect of the reversibility-training procedure with the dolls, then, may have been to lead the *S*s to stop using a misleading perceptual cue. Conservation probably never occurs when a situation provides what the subject takes to be a clear perceptual cue for nonconservation. Removing such cues has been shown to be effective in an experiment by Frank (Bruner, Olver, and Greenfield, et al., 1966), and making the *S*s stop using such a cue although it is still present may have been—with or without the experience of reversibility per se as well—a crucial factor in the success of our doll reversibility-training procedure.

If this was the case, it would not be hard to understand why reversibility training was relatively ineffective with the liquid although it was so effective with the dolls. While reversibility training in the doll situation may have indicated that the bed left over at the end of the line was misleading by showing that the other dolls and beds were not paired, there was nothing in the reversibility training in the liquid situation to discourage the use of misleading cues (such as the height of the liquid).

The doll reversibility-training procedure, then, may well have been successful, not because it led the *S*s to recognize reversibility, but because it led them to stop relying on a misleading cue. It is, in fact, not clear to what extent the recognition of reversibility—which did, of course, exist—resulted from the experience with reversibility provided by this training procedure and to what extent it was due to prior experience. Both in the present study and in our earlier one (Wallach and Sprott, 1964), sizable proportions of the *S*s predicted correctly the first time they were asked that the dolls could be put back into the beds; others did not. It is clear that the *S*s who did predict correctly the first time already knew about reversibility from prior experience, though they may not have thought about it until the question was asked. The Ss who did not predict correctly the first time may also already have known about reversibility and been misled by misperceiving the dolls and beds as paired with a bed left over—that is, they might have been able to predict correctly in a situation which was less misleading perceptually. It is possible, then, that the experience with reversibility provided by the training procedure actually contributed very little to the recognition of reversibility.

In view of the new interpretations suggested by this study, the success of the doll reversibility-training procedure can no longer be regarded as providing evidence for the role of the recognition of reversibility in conservation. This procedure, which previously appeared to induce conservation by leading the Ss to recognize reversibility, probably did so, at least in large part, by leading them to stop using misleading cues.

We still believe, nonetheless, that the recognition of reversibility is necessary for conservation. The Ss would not have conserved, we submit, if they had not realized (whether on the basis of the training procedure or prior experience) that the dolls could be fitted back into the beds again. The lack of use of misleading cues is not in itself sufficient to account for their believing at the end of the experiment that the number of dolls was equal to the number of beds despite the rearrangement. If a S stopped seeing the dolls and beds as paired with a bed left over, this would just mean that a previous reason for believing in inequality no longer obtained; it would not yet provide a basis for believing in equality. Why should the number of dolls and beds be regarded as remaining the same? It seems clear that the use of appropriate perceptual cues does not provide the answer either; seeing the dolls first in the beds and then being taken out is a crucial part of the procedure. When Ss who had attained conservation were shown the dolls and beds as arranged in the conservation test situation without first seeing the dolls in the beds, they typically took a much longer time to say whether the number of dolls and beds was the same and often answered incorrectly.

An explanation is still needed, then, given that the Ss stopped using misleading cues, of the fact that—at the end of the experiment—number was thought to remain the same after the dolls had been taken out of the beds and placed closer together. We believe that recognition of the fact that the dolls could be fitted back into the beds again—that the rearrangement was reversible—can explain this; no factor suggested by other interpretations of conservation seems capable of doing so (cf. Wallach and Sprott, 1964). In order for conservation answers to be given, a S must, we think, realize that the dolls and beds could be exactly paired again, as well as not use misleading perceptual cues.

Quite generally, recognizing reversibility as well as not using misleading perceptual cues would seem to be necessary for conservation. Conservation cannot be attained when a cue for nonconservation is relied on. But that misleading cues are not used is insufficient per se to account for a property being regarded as the same after certain transformations. The only factor that does seem able to account for this is recognition of the reversibility of the transformations. We believe, therefore, that in order for a child to conserve, he must both recognize reversibility and not rely on inappropriate cues.

REFERENCES

Bruner, J. S., Rose R. Olver, and Patricia M. Greenfield (Eds.), (1966). *Studies in cognitive growth.* New York: Wiley.
Smedslund, J. (1962). The acquisition of conservation of substance and weight in children: VII. Conservation of discontinuous quantity and the operations of adding and taking away. *Scand. J. Psychol.,* 3, 69–77.
Wallach, Lise, and R. L. Sprott (1964). Inducing number conservation in children. *Child Develpm.,* 35, 1057–1071.
Wohlwill, J. F., and R. C. Lowe (1962). Experimental analysis of the development of the conservation of number. *Child Develpm.,* 33, 153–167.
Zimiles, H. (1963). A note on Piaget's concept of conservation. *Child Develpm.,* 34, 691–695.

EXPERIMENTAL ANALYSIS
OF THE DEVELOPMENT
OF THE CONSERVATION OF NUMBER

Joachim F. Wohlwill / Roland C. Lowe

In Piaget's (1950) theory of intellectual development, a central role is assigned to the child's conceptualization of the principle of "conservation," i.e., his realization of the principle that a particular dimension of an object may remain invariant under changes in other, irrelevant aspects of the situation. For instance, children who lack conservation will assert that the relative weight of two objects has changed when the shape of one of them is altered or that numerical equality between two collections of objects no longer holds following a change in the length over which they extend. This

Reprinted with the permission of the senior author and The Society for Research in Child Development, Inc., from *Child Development*, 1962, 33 (1), 153–167. This investigation was supported by a research grant to the senior author from the National Science Foundation (G-8608). Nelson Butters assisted in the collection of data.

phenomenon, which has been demonstrated for a variety of other dimensions, including those of volume, area and length, represents, according to Piaget, a manifestation of the immature level of functioning of the child's mental processes and of their failure to conform to the operational structures of logical thought.

Although Piaget has described some of the precursors of this notion of conservation in children who have not yet attained this level, little is known thus far about the specific ways in which the transition from lack of conservation to the presence of conservation takes place. It is apparent, however, that an adequate explanation of this problem ultimately requires a clearer understanding of the psychological processes at work in this transition phase.

One approach to this goal is to expose children presumed to be slightly below the age of onset of conservation to selected, systematically manipulated learning experiences, designed to call into play different factors believed to be important in the development of conservation. Any differential changes in the children's tendency to give conservation responses should then reflect the role played by the particular factors manipulated. At the same time, a more detailed examination of the interrelationship among different tasks involving conservation and closely related concepts should likewise extend our understanding of the nature of this problem.

The domain of number lends itself particularly well to the investigation of the development of conservation, for several reasons. First of all, recent empirical work (Dodwell, 1960; Elkind, 1961; Wohlwill, 1960) has given strong support to the notion that the attainment of the level of conservation marks a clearly defined stage in the formation of the number concept. Secondly, in this domain the problem of conservation can be readily related to development in other aspects of the number concept (e.g., counting, arithmetical skills, etc.), rather than constituting the somewhat isolated, *sui generis* problem which conservation appears to represent for such dimensions as weight or volume. Thirdly, and most importantly, the number dimension occupies a unique position in regard to the question of conservation, insofar as the number of elements contained in a particular collection is exactly identifiable by the corresponding integer; by the same token, the *fact* of conservation—i.e., that the number of a collection remains invariant under changes in the spatial arrangement of its elements—is readily verifiable, through the operation of counting. This feature creates an opportunity for assessing the role of symbolic, mediational processes, as well as of reinforcement, in the development of conservation.

This very uniqueness of the number dimension represents of course a potential limitation, as regards the applicability of the results to the problem of conservation in general. It is of considerable interest, therefore, that a rather similar investigation of the acquisition of the conservation of weight has simultaneously been carried out by Smedslund (1961); its results will thus provide us with a valuable basis for comparison, as we will note in the discussion section.

THREE ALTERNATIVE THEORETICAL VIEWS

OF NUMBER CONSERVATION

If one looks closely at the problem confronting the child in the conservation situation, several different interpretations of the acquisition of this principle suggest themselves. We may label these alternatives the reinforcement hypothesis, the differentiation hypothesis, and the inference hypothesis.

The *reinforcement* hypothesis would propose that, as a child obtains increasing experience in counting numerical collections of different types and in different arrangements, he gradually learns that alterations in the perceptual dimensions of a set do not change its number, i.e., that the same number is obtained from counting the set after as before such a change. Accordingly, systematic reinforced practice in counting rows of elements prior and subsequent to changes in the length of the rows should promote conservation.

The *differentiation* hypothesis would interpret lack of conservation in the young child as a response to an irrelevant but highly visible cue (length) which typically shows substantial correlation with that of number. The child thus has to learn to differentiate the dimension of number from this irrelevant cue. Repeated experience designed to neutralize the cue of length, and thus to weaken the association between it and the dimension of number in the child's thinking, should be expected, then, to facilitate conservation responses.

The *inference* hypothesis, finally, is based in part on Piaget's (1959) own analysis of the role of learning in the development of logical operations. Piaget maintains that experiential factors can only become effective, in this realm of development, to the extent that it builds on the child's previously developed structures of thought, as through the activation of a reasoning process prior to, but logically related to the one to be developed. In the case of conservation, one possible implication might be that by dint of cumulative exposure to the effects of adding an element to a collection, or subtracting one from it, the child may be led to *infer* conservation as the result of a change involving neither addition nor subtraction. This implication is supported, incidentally, by the explanations frequently voiced by children who admit conservation, e.g., "it's still the same, because you haven't taken any away."

Prior work by the senior author also bears on this last alternative. First, in the course of a sequential analysis of the development of the number concept (Wohlwill, 1960), it was found that success on tasks involving simple addition and subtraction not only regularly preceded success on a task embodying the principle of conservation, but appeared, in a certain number of subjects, to lead to the emergence of conservation responses. In a previous pilot study (Wohlwill, 1959), it was found, furthermore, that subjects given a limited set of trials involving addition and subtraction subsequently made more conservation responses than subjects given equivalent training on conservation, though the difference did not reach significance.

The results of this pilot study suggested the possibility of a more extended investigation of the development of the conservation of number, by bringing to bear each of the above-mentioned theoretical interpretations in the context of a small-scale learning experiment and determining the effectiveness of the various conditions of learning in bringing about conservation, both in a limited and a generalized sense. This is the main aim of the study to be reported, a subsidiary purpose being to provide information regarding the cross-situational generality of number conservation and its relationship to other types of number skills.

METHOD

The experiment was conducted in two sessions over two successive days (except for two *S*s, for whom the interval between sessions was two and six days, respectively). The general design called for (a) a predominantly verbal pretest, partly of a diagnostic character, to reveal *S*'s ability to deal with number concepts, and partly dealing specifically with conservation; (b) a "nonverbal" test of conservation given in the form of a series of multiple-choice trials; (c) a training series on tasks presumed to be related to number conservation; and finally (d) a repetition of both the nonverbal and verbal tests of conservation to provide a measure of learning or change with respect to the understanding of this notion. This design is summarized in Table 1.

Table 1

Design of the Study

Order	First Day	Order	Second Day
(1)	Diagnostic questions	(1)	Training series (trials 10 to 18)
(2)	Verbal conservation pretest	(2)	Nonverbal conservation posttest
(3)	Pretraining in number matching	(3)	Verbal conservation posttest
(4)	Nonverbal conservation pretest		
(5)	Training series (trials 1 to 9)		

Procedure

DIAGNOSTIC QUESTIONS

(1) *Number Production.*   S was shown a pile of red poker chips and was told, "Give me six of them."

(2) *Number Equivalence.*   E laid out a row of seven red chips. S was told, "Put down just as many of your chips over here (indicating an imaginary row paralleling E's row), as I have here."

(3) *Number vs. Length.*   E laid out a row of six blue chips extending beyond the limits of his own row of seven red chips (S's row being longer than E's). S was asked, "Who has more chips, you or I?" If he answered that he had more, but without having counted the chips, he was asked, "How do you know?"

These three questions concerned, respectively, the child's ability to (a) reproduce a particular cardinal number, (b) establish a relationship of numerical equivalence between two collections, and (c) respond to the dimension of number independent of irrelevant perceptual cues (e.g., length).

VERBAL CONSERVATION PRETEST

(4) Two rows of seven chips each, one blue and the other red, were placed parallel to each other so that both rows were of the same length, and the chips in one row were directly opposite those in the other. S was asked, "Who has more chips, you or I?" This question, hereafter referred to as Q, was repeated for all the items in this part.

(5a) E then extended the red row in both directions to a length about twice that of the blue row. (Q)

(5b) The red row was subdivided into two rows of four and three chips placed parallel to S's blue row. (Q)

(5c) The red chips were placed in a vertical pile in front of the blue row. (Q)

(5d) The red chips were inserted into an opaque tube. (Q)

Question 4 served chiefly a preparatory function, i.e., to set up the following questions of conservation. Question 5a represented the main criterion of number conservation, while 5b to 5d indicate the generalizability of conservation. Accordingly, questions 5a to 5d were cumulative: if a S did not assert equality at any point, the remaining questions were omitted.

(6) Questions 4 and 5a were repeated with 12 chips in each row instead of seven.

The suggestive nature of the questions (Q) used above ("Who has more chips, you or I?") requires comment. It should be noted that its initial use (in question 4) is in a situation where perceptual cues mitigate against

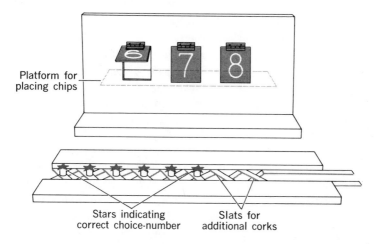

Platform for placing chips

Stars indicating correct choice-number

Slats for additional corks

Figure 1 Apparatus for nonverbal conservation and training trials, showing device for presenting variable-length rows of sample numbers and display-board for choice numbers.

the child's following the suggestion of inequality implicit in the question: the matched rows of chips afford a strong cue for direct perception of equivalence.[1] Second, the suggestion applied both in the pre- and the posttests and thus may be presumed to have played a constant role on both occasions.

PRETRAINING IN NUMBER MATCHING   The apparatus used here, shown in Figure 1, consisted of an upright panel containing three windows which had the numerals 6, 7, 8 inscribed on them from left to right. The *S*s were told they were going to play a game, in which they would find a chip hidden behind one of the windows, and that the object of the game was to get as many chips as they could. For the pretraining phase, the procedure consisted in presenting singly a series of six 5 by 5 in. cards showing six, seven, or eight colored stars arranged in simple configurations. On each trial a colored chip was hidden behind the corresponding window. *S* was informed that the number of stars on the card would tell him behind which window the chip was hidden and urged to count the stars. When *S* opened the correct window, he was instructed to remove the chip and

---

[1] All but 14 of the *S*s did in fact resist *E*'s suggestion, usually through some such answer as "we both do" or "you and me." The 14 *S*s who failed to do so were made to count the two rows, whereupon the question was again put to them. If *S*s persisted in following the suggestion of inequality, *E* confronted them with the results of their counting and, if necessary, told them outright "So we both have the same, don't we?" This procedure was necessary in order to proceed to the following part, where *S*s' prior knowledge of the equivalence of the two rows had to be presupposed.

place it onto a board at his side. He was told to fill up the board with chips; if he found "a lot" of them, he would on the following day receive a toy. The purpose of this series was to create a set in the child to respond to number, as well as to familiarize Ss with the specific numbers shown. A correction procedure was used which involved having Ss correct any mistakes made in counting the stars and guiding S to the correct window when, as occasionally happened, a S counted correctly but made an incorrect choice.

NONVERBAL CONSERVATION PRETEST   This series consisted of three two-phase trials. Ss were presented with a row of colored stars, either six, seven, or eight in number, mounted on a set of corks which rested on a series of connected scissors-like slats. This apparatus, depicted in Figure 1, permitted lengthening or shortening the row while preserving the straight-line arrangement. E told S that he was to count the stars in order to find the chip behind the correct window. Following S's initial response, he was made to return the chip to E, who replaced it behind the same window, and then, depending on the trial, either extended or shortened the row of stars. S was allowed to count only on the first phase; he thus had to find the correct window on the second phase on the basis of the knowledge gained in the first and in the face of the perceptual changes in the row of stars.

TRAINING   There were four conditions of training: Reinforced Practice, Addition and Subtraction, Dissociation, and Control. The three experimental conditions were designed to relate, respectively, to the reinforcement, inference, and differentiation hypotheses presented in the introduction. Each training series consisted of 18 trials, broken up into two sets of nine which were administered on successive days. The apparatus used was the same as in the conservation pretest trials.

(1) *Reinforced Practice* (RP).   The procedure here was the same as for the preceding conservation trials, with this modification: if S made an incorrect response on the second phase of the trial, he was told to count the stars, so as to find out which window he should have chosen. E then exposed the chip behind that window but did not allow S to remove the chip.

(2) *Addition and Subtraction* (A&S).   These trials were similar to the conservation trials, except that on two-thirds of the trials, following the S's initial response after counting, E either added or subtracted a star at the end of the row before changing its length. The remaining third of the series consisted of straight conservation trials which were interspersed with the A&S trials.

(3) *Dissociation* (Diss.).   Unlike the above, these were single-phase trials, with the length of the row varying from one trial to the next over a range of four times the smallest length. S was urged to count the stars and open the corresponding window; if correct, he received the chip. Over

the series of trials each number of stars appeared equally often at each of the different settings of length.

(4) *Control.* This series of trials consisted likewise of single-phase trials as in the Dissociation condition, but the length of the row remained fixed throughout at its minimum spread.

POSTTESTS   The *nonverbal* conservation posttest, consisting of three conservation trials as in the pretest, followed immediately upon the completion of the training trials. (For *S*s in groups Diss. and Control, *E* prefaced these trials with a remark to the effect that they would again have to find the chips twice in a row, the second time without counting.) Any *S* responding correctly on the last trial of this posttest was asked: "How did you know where to look for the chip that time?"

The *verbal* conservation posttest, consisting of a repetition of questions 4 through 6 as given in the pretest, concluded the experimental session.

At the end of the second session, each child was shown a variety of dimestore toys from which he picked one to take back with him as his "prize." Altogether, each of the sessions lasted about 20 to 25 minutes per child. The children's level of attention and motivation appeared to have remained high throughout these sessions, the "game" aspect of the situation apparently having proved effective in capturing their interest. This was reflected in their universal eagerness to return to it when called for the second session.

Subjects

Subjects for this study were 72 kindergarten children, 35 boys and 37 girls, with a mean CA of 5 years, 10 months. (This age level was selected as one at which most children would still show lack of number conservation, while yet being old enough to be able potentially to profit from the learning experience; in other words, an interaction between learning and developmental level is presumed.) There were 18 *S*s in each condition of training, *S*s being assigned to their group according to a predetermined order. The four subgroups were closely matched as to their mean CA. (The range of the means was one month.)

The children were enrolled in the kindergarten classes of three public schools in Worcester, Massachusetts, located in predominantly lower-middle-class neighborhoods. They thus had been and were being exposed to a variety of activities in the area of number skills, consisting mainly of counting, number-matching, and identifying simple numerals.[2]

[2] The authors are greatly indebted to the principals and teachers of the Freeland, Columbus Park and Woodland Elementary Schools in Worcester, Massachusetts, for their splendid cooperation in providing subjects and facilities for this investigation. We also wish to acknowledge the assistance of the Worcester Country Day School in connection with a pilot study from which this investigation evolved.

RESULTS

The presentation of the results of the experiment is divided into three sections: the verbal pretest, including the diagnostic and verbal conservation questions; the learning of nonverbal conservation; and the transfer of training to the verbal posttest.

Verbal Pretest

Considering first the diagnostic questions, only one of the 72 Ss failed question 1, while four failed question 2. On question 3, however, only 20 Ss gave a correct response (i.e., based on counting the chips either before or in justification of their judgments). These results show that the Ss had adequate facility in counting and dealing with numbers symbolically in simple situations, such as producing a required number of elements and in matching two groups for number. Their success on these two tasks, however, contrasted sharply with their performance on question 3 where the task required the abstraction of number as independent from certain irrelevant perceptual cues. It should be noted that, since this question followed question 2 without a break, some Ss may have seen E take a chip from his row in setting up question 3. Thus, some of the correct responses may have been facilitated by this circumstance. In fact, nine Ss explicitly based their answers on this cue. (Control over this factor in a subsequent study did indeed result in lowering still further the number of Ss succeeding on this question, so as to equate it in difficulty with the conservation question, 5a.)

On the verbal conservation items, only nine of the 72 Ss answered correctly on question 5a. A breakdown of the incorrect responses shows that 41 Ss responded to the length of the rows, while 22 responded to the density of the elements. This tendency to regard the longer row as more numerous was also found on question 3 of the diagnostic questions.

As for the generality of the Ss' concept of number conservation, of the nine Ss who succeeded on question 5a, six extended their conservation to 5b, five to 5c, and four to 5d. On question 6, on the other hand, involving conservation for 12 elements, seven of these Ss showed conservation, in addition to one who had not responded correctly on question 5a. Thus, when conditions were qualitatively different, generalization was somewhat lower than it was when the new situation differed only in a quantitaive way.

Nonverbal Conservation Learning

Table 2 summarizes the performance of each group on the verbal and nonverbal tests of conservation, before and after the learning series.

Table 2

*Performance on Conservation
Before and After Training*

Condition of Training	Verbal Conservation[a]			Nonverbal Conservation[b]		
	Pretest	Posttest	Net Change	Pretest	Posttest	Net Change
A&S	1	3	+2	1.05	1.77	+.72
RP	2	3	+1	1.22	1.50	+.28
Diss.	4	2	−2	1.05	1.16	+.11
Control	2	4	+2	1.44	1.96	+.52

[a] Number of Ss giving correct responses on question 5a.
[b] Mean correct responses out of three trials.

An anlysis of variance revealed no significant differences among training groups with respect to learning of nonverbal conservation ($F = 1.73$; $p > .05$ for 3 and 68 df). However, the mean over-all difference scores differed significantly from 0 ($t = 3.95$; $p < .01$), showing that for the total group as a whole conservation did increase from pre- to posttest.

A comparison between the responses of the A&S and RP groups on the conservation trials of their respective training series shows that the former Ss were correct on 48 per cent of their trials, while the latter were correct on 47 per cent. It will be recalled that only six conservation trials were given in the A&S series, while the RP series consisted wholly of 18 conservation trials for which, in addition, a correction procedure was used. Hence, direct training on conservation was no more effective than the more intermittent practice afforded on the A&S trials.

It was also found that the A&S group had greater success on the A&S trials than on the straight conservation trials: for the former, 59 per cent of the responses were correct, as compared to the 48 per cent for the conservation trials. This finding, which is consistent with the results of previous research (Wohlwill, 1960), represents of course a prerequisite for the use of the A&S trials as a training experience.

The training trials under the control and dissociation condition, which involved only rote counting, were quite easy for these Ss: a near perfect performance was the norm.

Transfer of Training to Verbal Posttest

With respect to verbal conservation, there were very few changes in any group. The number of Ss showing conservation of number on the pretest was nine, while 12 Ss showed it on the posttest. Two Ss changed to conservation from the A&S group, two from the Control group, and one from the

RP group. Two *S*s, in the Diss. group, who had shown conservation on the pretest, failed to do so on the posttest (cf. Table 2).

It is interesting to note that, whereas on the pretest of verbal conservation only four of the nine *S*s having conservation showed perfect extension of this concept on items 5b through 5d, on the posttest nine of the 12 *S*s showing conservation did show this extension, the remaining three *S*s belonging to the group of five who had not shown conservation on the pretest. This seems to indicate the unstable nature of the *S*s' conservation, as acquired in this situation.

Of the 12 *S*s showing conservation on question 5a of the posttest, 11 again showed conservation for 12 elements (question 6).

DISCUSSION

In this section we will consider some of the more specific implications of the results for the nonverbal conservation learning and for the transfer to the verbal test, leaving until a later section certain more general conclusions suggested by this investigation.

Nonverbal Conservation Learning

As regards the "learning" of conservation within the limited context of the training trials, a significant amount of improvement from pre- to post-test did take place for the group as a whole, but the lack of significant differential effects due to the conditions of training and the fact that the Control group gained more than either the Reinforced Practice or the Dissociation groups clearly prevents us from attributing beneficial effects to any specific learning condition.

The failure of the RP group to outperform the others nevertheless deserves comment. It had actually been anticipated that this group, which received essentially one continuous series of conservation trials, would as a result of this extended practice show the greatest amount of learning from pre- to posttest, although such learning might not necessarily transfer to the verbal posttest. The contrary results bear out the ineffectiveness of continued reinforced practice in bringing about conservation responses, even of a purely empirical sort (i.e., "pick the window where the chip was before"), which the above-mentioned pilot study (Wohlwill, 1959) had already hinted at in a much shorter training series. Whether a still more extended series than that used in the present study might have yielded a greater amount of learning remains an open question, of course.

The greatest amount of improvement from the pre- to the posttest trials, on the other hand, took place in the A&S group, exposed to 12 addition and subtraction trials, set off against six conservation trials; these results are thus at least consistent with the possible role of a process of inference (i.e., conservation as the end-product of changes involving neither addition nor subtraction) to which the previous studies (Wohlwill, 1959, 1960) had pointed.[3]

Finally, as regards the virtual absence of learning in the Dissociation group, it might be suggested, in retrospect, that the very act of counting the stars interfered with directing the child's attention to the cue of length, which the condition was designed to neutralize. If so, no improvement on the conservation trials, based on explicit disregard of the biasing cue of length, would result.

Transfer to Verbal Conservation Questions

Perhaps the major finding of the study is that none of the above procedures proved in any way effective in leading to an understanding of the principle of number conservation, such as the verbal posttest demanded. For instance, over the four training groups combined, a total of 10 *S*s shifted from zero or one conservation responses on the nonverbal pretest to three on the posttest, yet these shifts did not bring with them a single change to conservation on the verbal posttest.

In explanation for this failure of the noverbal conservation learning to transfer to the verbal posttest, one might suggest that the nonverbal learning situation favored the development of an essentially empirical rule, i.e., "the correct number remains the same as before after *E* shortens or lengthens the row," or simply "look for the chip behind the window where the chip was just previously." If this were the case, little if any transfer to the very different situation confronting the child in the verbal conservation questions would be expected. The verbalizations elicited from those *S*s who made a correct response on the last posttest conservation trial lend some support to this argument: many of the *S*s actually gave no meaningful explanation for their choice at all (e.g., "I just knew," or "I thought hard about the stars"), while most of the rest responded in such terms as "It was there before."

Interestingly enough, Smedslund (1961), on the basis of his work on the learning of the conservation of weight, similarly argues for the very limited, nonconceptual nature of such learning. In his study, *S*s were exposed to an extended series of judgments of the relative weight of two masses of plasticine, before and after one of these was deformed in shape; each judgment was reinforced by weighing the two objects on a balance.

---

[3] It is worth noting that in a subsequent study, modeled closely after the present one, training with addition and subtraction again resulted in the greatest amount of improvement in (nonverbal) conservation, though the superiority over the control group still failed to be significant. In other respects, too, this study, in which the learning series was increased to 24 trials and the pre- and posttests of conservation to six trials each, yielded results which were closely comparable to those reported here.

While *S*s did learn to anticipate correctly the conservation of weight of the deformed object, the author feels that this learning was mainly that of an empirical fact, rather than of a logical principle, as shown both in the kind of explanations offered by the children, and in the lack of transfer of the learning to problems embodying logically equivalent principles (e.g., transitivity relationships).[4] Parenthetically, it is worth noting that in Smedslund's study a training procedure embodying addition and subtraction of matter, in a manner somewhat analogous to that of our A&S condition, yielded nearly as much learning as continued practice on conservation problems.

There remains, however, an alternative interpretation of our results. It is based on a major difference between the nonverbal and verbal tests of conservation, which might itself have accounted for the lack of transfer observed: while the nonverbal test involved a match between a given collection of elements and the corresponding, symbolically indicated number, the verbal test entailed rather the equivalence of the numerosity of two collections of elements. Thus, it is conceivable that the children did in fact learn, in their nonverbal training, that the *absolute* number of elements remained unchanged, without transfering this principle to the *relative* number of elements in two collections, in the verbal test. Implausible as this possibility may seem to a sophisticated adult, it is borne out by the total inefficacy of asking the children to count the two collections after a nonconservation response on the verbal posttest: of 23 *S*s who were asked to do so, 19 persevered in their nonconservation responses when the question was repeated, immediately after ascertaining that there were seven chips in each row. Most recently, furthermore, Gréco (1962) has obtained clear evidence that children may show conservation in the first or absolute sense, without showing it in the second or relative sense.

Finally, the use of nonverbal methods in the investigation of children's thinking deserves brief comment. While the ineffectiveness of the nonverbal training procedures in our study may seem to cast doubt on the fruitfulness of such methods, they have been used to good advantage in several other recent studies (Braine, 1959; Wohlwill, 1960); moreover, the pitfalls of the verbal interrogation approach, at least as used by Piaget, have been

---

[4] Perhaps more convincing evidence on this point comes from an ingenious "extinction" procedure which Smedslund (personal communication) has most recently utilized. This consisted in confronting *S*s with apparent nonconservation, the weight of the deformed object being altered by surreptitiously adding or removing a small amount of plasticine. Under these circumstances *S*s who had acquired conservation through their learning experience readily acceded to the lack of conservation which they seemed to be witnessing, i.e., abandoned their recently "learned" conservation. In contrast, *S*s who had developed conservation spontaneously tended to invent explanations in order to reconcile this apparent contradiction, such as "we must have lost something on the floor."

Since the preparation of this paper portions of Smedslund's work (including the material of the personal communication referred to in the previous paragraph) have appeared in print (1961).

persuasively analyzed (Berko and Brown, 1960, pp. 536f; Braine, 1959).[5] Perhaps the central point is that it is incumbent on those applying nonverbal methods to determine, by varied and appropriate transfer tests, the breadth and depth of the child's understanding of the principles or concepts in question—a point which appears of special relevance to the application of automatic teaching methods to instruction in this and similar areas.

CONCLUSIONS

Although the predominantly negative outcome of this investigation does not allow us to give any definitive answer to the question posed at the outset, concerning the mechanisms involved in the child's acquisition of the concept of the conservation of number, a few general conclusions regarding this problem may be permissible.

First, the strong tendency of the children in this investigation to respond on the basis of differences in length in making numerical comparisons between two collections, even without the element of perceptual *change* introduced in the conservation situation (cf. question 3), lend some weight to the interpretation of lack of conservation as a failure to differentiate number from irrelevant perceptual cues, pointing to an aspect of the problem which appears to have received insufficient attention in Piaget's theoretical account of conservation.

Second, the consistent tendency across several studies for the A&S conditions to yield the most improvement in nonverbal conservation suggests that a process of inference may be operative in the development of number-conservation, even if this inference may be too limited in scope to lead to a generalized understanding of the principle. In view of the fact that children typically receive considerable experience in simple addition and subtraction in the very time period in which conservation generally appears (i.e., in late kindergarten and early first grade), this factor merits further attention.

Third, our investigation highlights the considerable gap separating the ability to *enumerate* collections by counting from a true understanding of the number concept, as it is reflected in the principle of conservation. In this respect the present results are entirely in agreement with those obtained in previous work on the development of the number concept (Dodwell, 1960; Wohlwill, 1960). Furthermore, even repeated identification of a

---

[5] Relevant in this connection is a study most recently reported by Yost, Siegel, and McMichael (1961), demonstrating considerable positive transfer from a non-verbal presentation of a probability-relationship problem to the corresponding verbal version of this problem as used by Piaget. These authors likewise found that by their nonverbal procedures the problem could be dealt with successfully at a much earlier age than Piaget had found, thus confirming the similar findings of Braine (1959).

collection with a particular number symbol, independent of length, appears to be relatively ineffective in bringing about conservation, thus raising the question of the adequacy of a mediation-theory approach to this particular aspect of concept formation.

In a more positive vein, two suggestions for future attacks on this problem might be offered. The first is to construct a set of learning experiences which would not only be more extended but, more important, cover a wider variety of situations (i.e., stimulus materials, configurations, specific numbers involved, etc.). This would be in line with Harlow's (1951) emphasis on *generalized* experience as a prerequisite for the learning of broad concepts and principles in primates as well as in man. It is plausible to suppose, in fact, that it is precisely such generalized experience—in the classroom, at play, and in other everyday activities of children of this age level—which represents the basis for the seemingly spontaneous appearance of conservation in the child.

The second suggestion is to undertake a thorough, intensive analysis of the ontogenesis of conservation in a selected number of children followed longitudinally. Special attention might be paid to the types of explanations given by the child at various stages, as well as to the stability and generalizability of conservation responses once they appear. Inhelder and Noelting (1957), at the University of Geneva, have in fact already launched such a longitudinal project, with preliminary results that appear promising.

REFERENCES

Berko, J., and R. Brown (1960). Psycholinguistic research methods. In P. H. Mussen (Ed.), *Handbook of research methods in child development*. New York: Wiley. Pp. 517–557.

Braine, M. D. S. (1959). The ontogeny of certain logical operations: Piaget's formulation examined by nonverbal methods. *Psychol. Monogr.*, 73 (4), Whole No. 475.

Dodwell, P. C. (1960). Children's understanding of number and related concepts. *Canad. J. Psychol.*, 14, 191–203.

Elkind, D. (1961). The development of quantitative thinking: a systematic replication of Piaget's studies. *J. genet. Psychol.*, 98, 37–46.

Gréco, P. (1962). Quotité et quantité. In J. Piaget (Ed.), Structures numériques élémentaires. *Etudes d'épistémologie génétique*, Vol. 13. Paris: Presses Universitaires.

Harlow, H. F. (1951). Thinking. In H. Helson (Ed.), *Theoretical foundations of psychology*. Princeton, N.J.: Van Nostrand. Pp. 452–505.

Inhelder, B., and G. Noelting (1957). Le passage d'un stade au suivant dans le développement des fonctions cognitives. *Proc. 15th Int. Congr. Psychol.*, Brussels. 435–438.

Piaget, J. (1950). *The psychology of intelligence*. London: Routledge.

Piaget, J. (1959). Apprentissage et connaissance. In J. Piaget (Ed.), La logique des apprentissages. *Etudes d'épistémologie génétique*, Vol. 10. Paris: Presses Universitaires. Pp. 159–188.

Smedslund, J. (1961). The acquisition of conservation of substance and weight in children. *J. Scand. Psychol.*, **2**, 71–87.

Wohlwill, J. F. (1959). Un essai d'apprentissage dans le domaine de la conservation du nombre. In J. Piaget (Ed.), L'apprentissage des structures logiques. *Etudes d'épistémologie génétique*, Vol. 9. Paris: Presses Universitaires. Pp. 125–135.

Wohlwill, J. F. (1960). A study of the development of the number concept by scalogram analysis. *J. genet. Psychol.*, **97**, 345–377.

Yost, P. A., A. E. Siegel, and J. E. McMichael (1961). Nonverbal probability judgments by young children. Paper read at Society for Research in Child Development, University Park, Pa.

EXPERIENCES AFFECTING THE DEVELOPMENT
OF NUMBER CONSERVATION IN CHILDREN

Gerald E. Gruen

A considerable amount of interest in cognitive development has been generated by Piaget's (1950) theory of intellectual development. Much of the resulting research has been concerned with the transition in cognitive processes that occurs as the child advances from preoperational reasoning to reasoning at the concrete-operational level. One of the most important components of this transition is the acquisition of various "conservations." The term "conservation" refers to the realization that a particular dimension of an object may remain invariant under changes in other, irrelevant dimensions. For example, a child is said to conserve number when he realizes that the numerical equality between two collections of objects remains unchanged following a change in the spatial arrangement of the objects, provided no objects are added or taken away.

Piaget (1957) theorizes that the transition from nonconservation to conservation occurs through the "equilibration process," an internal process

Reprinted with the permission of the author and The Society for Research in Child Development, Inc., from *Child Development*, 1965, 36 (4), 963–979. This experiment is adapted from a paper submitted in partial fulfillment of the requirements for the Ph.D. degree at the University of Illinois. The author wishes to thank the directors and teachers of the following kindergarten and nursery schools for their cooperation in making Ss available: The Playtime Nursery School, the Busy Bee Nursery School, the ABC Nursery School, and Westview Kindergarten in Champaign, Illinois; and the Maryville kindergarten in Granite City, Illinois.

heavily dependent upon activity and experience. According to Smedslund (1961a), equilibration theory "differs radically from that of learning theory, since practice is not assumed to act through external reinforcements, but by a process of mutual influence of the child's activities on each other. Logical inferences are not derived from any properties of the external world, but from the placing into relationship (mise-en-relation) of the subjects' 'own activities.'" For a fuller discussion of equilibration theory see Flavell (1963).

Several investigators have attempted to test Piaget's equilibration theory by determining the kinds of experiences that facilitate conservation (Greco, 1963; Morf, 1963; Smedslund 1961b, 1961c, 1961d, 1961e; Wohlwill and Lowe, 1962). Smedslund (1961b), investigating conservation of weight, and Wohlwill and Lowe (1962), investigating conservation of number, have compared the relative effectiveness of training procedures derived from Piaget's equilibration model and a more conventional learning-through-reinforced-practice model. Neither of these experimenters found either kind of procedure to be significantly superior to the other in inducing conservation. Nor did they find that the children subjected to these special training techniques outperformed their respective control groups. In a later experiment, however, Smedslund (1961e) found that it was possible to induce conservation of substance in children by means of a training procedure designed to induce "cognitive conflict," which is, according to Smedslund, an essential condition for the development of conservation in the child. Cognitive conflict supposedly induces a reorganization of the child's intellectual actions, which proceeds along the lines postulated by Piaget's equilibration theory. This reorganization then leads to the conservation strategy. Children exposed to this type of training were found to outperform their no-training control group on a posttest of substance conservation, but their performance was not directly compared to a group of children receiving reinforced practice on conservation.

In the present investigation of number conservation, an attempt is made to compare directly the relative effectiveness of training procedures derived from Smedslund's (1961d, 1961e) cognitive-conflict hypothesis and a conventional learning-through-reinforced-practice hypothesis. The training procedures derived from the former hypothesis are designed to induce internal cognitive conflict that will bring about conservation of number. However, they do not permit the kind of external feedback that the training procedures derived from the learning-through-reinforced-practice hypothesis do. The latter provide external feedback, through the process of counting, of the relative number of elements in two collections of elements. The "reinforcement" involved in this procedure is strictly a "knowledge-of-results" kind of reinforcement, no external rewards being given until the end of the experiment. In this respect, the procedure is more comparable to Smedslund's (1961b) procedure with conservation of weight than it is to Wohlwill and Lowe's (1962) procedure with conservation of number. The purpose of this study is not to discover a procedure that will permit early conservation training but, rather, to isolate some of the variables that may play a role in the acquisition of conservation.

The present investigation has one further purpose. The majority of the investigators interested in the acquisition of various Piagetian thought forms have used verbal techniques. Typically, the experiments of these investigators have shown agreement with the findings of Piaget (1950) and Piaget and Inhelder (1948) that conservation and other concrete-operational thought forms do not appear in children until they reach the age of 7 or 8 years. Braine and Shanks (1965a, 1965b), however, using nonverbal assessment techniques, have found several kinds of conservation in children 4.5–5.5 years old. Their findings suggest that a child may have the ability to perform a given operation, such as conservation, without having the verbal skill necessary to adequately comprehend and respond to verbal techniques of assessing conservation.

In the present experiment, a verbal-assessment technique is used, but an attempt is made to insure that all Ss understand the key words that E uses in this verbal assessment. The key words involved are "more" and "same." Half of the Ss in each of the experimental and control groups are pre-set to interpret these words to mean more or same in number, and only in number, and not to associate these words with length, a variable that typically shows substantial correlation with number. The other Ss receive no pretraining on these terms. It is expected that those Ss receiving the verbal pretraining will outperform the other Ss on a posttest of number conservation.

METHOD

The experiment was conducted in two sessions over two successive days. Table 1 shows the order of procedure on each day.

The general design of the experiment was the classical transfer of training paradigm consisting of (*a*) pretests of conservation of number, length, and substance; (*b*) verbal pretraining; (*c*) the major training for conserva-

Table 1

Order of Procedure

Order	First Day	Second Day
1	Pretest	Refresher pretraining trials (10–13)
2	Pretraining trials (1–9)	Training trials (17–32)
3	Training trials (1–16)	Posttests

tion (involving two experimental groups trained on conservation of number and one no-training control group); and (*d*) posttests of conservation of number, length, and substance. There were three training conditions and two pretraining conditions (verbal pretraining vs. no verbal pretraining). Thus, the experiment was a 3 × 2 factorial design.

Subjects

Subjects for this study were 90 nursery-school and kindergarten children, 50 girls and 40 boys, between the ages of 4–6 and 6–4. The mean age of the *S*s in each of the six experimental conditions varied between 5–0 and 5–2, the over-all mean age being 5–1. These *S*s were selected from a total of 210 children who were given pretests of addition/subtraction and conservation of number (see below). Any child who demonstrated his ability to count from 1 to 9 and who also had a rudimentary understanding of addition/subtraction, but lacked the ability to conserve number, was selected for participation in the experiment. Of the 120 *S*s who were excluded from further participation in the study, 17 were excluded because they were unable to count from 1 to 9, 73 were excluded because they failed the addition/subtraction prestest, and 30 were excluded because they passed the number-conservation pretest. Selected *S*s were assigned at random to the six experimental conditions.

Apparatus

The materials necessary for the pre- and posttest were six plasticine balls of approximately equal weight and volume; nine white and nine blue poker chips; two yellow sticks, both 12 in. long; and four V-shaped figures of black cardboard pasted on a 28 × 22 in. sheet of white cardboard. The arms of the V-shaped figures formed an angle of approximately 50°. The arms were 4½ in. long and ⅜ in. wide. Two of the four V-shaped figures were placed with their apexes 12 in. apart and their arms pointing outward, and the other two were placed with their apexes 12 in. apart and their arms pointing inward. This was intended to produce the Müller-Lyer (M-L) illusion.

Blocks of wood of various sizes were the only materials necessary for verbal pretraining. There were 12 1×1×¾-in. blocks, 10 2×1×¾-in. blocks, 4 3×1×¾-in. blocks, and 2 5×1×¾-in. blocks. Half of the blocks of each size were painted black, and half were painted white.

The apparatus used in the training of each of the experimental groups consisted of two crisscrossing, scissors-like devices which were parallel to each other. These devices were attached to metal handles that could be pushed and pulled to lengthen and shorten them. Corks were mounted on pegs located at the junctions of the crisscrossing devices. The corks could be easily removed from, and replaced on, these pegs. This apparatus permitted lengthening or shortening of each row of corks independently, while maintaining an approximately equal distance between the corks within a particular row. Trinkets for charm bracelets and M&M chocolate candies were used as rewards.

Procedure

S was seated at a table directly opposite *E* and told that he was going to play a number of games.

ADDITION/SUBTRACTION PRETEST   Two piles of nine poker chips each, one pile made up of white chips and the other of blue chips, were placed on the table before *S*. *E* announced to *S* that both piles contained the same number of chips. Then *E* took a chip away from one of the piles and placed it on the table where it was plainly visible to *S*. The standard conservation question (Q)[1] was then asked: "Do you think there are more blue chips in this pile, the same number of blue chips and white chips, or more white chips in this pile?" After *S* answered Q, *E* always asked: "Why do you think so?" Following this, the chip was placed back on the pile from which it had been removed, and these questions were repeated. *E* then added a chip to the other pile, and finally, removed it again, asking these same two questions after both the addition and the subtraction.

S had to answer all four of these items correctly and explain his answers in terms of the operations that *E* had performed on the piles of chips (e.g., "you took one chip away from this pile," or "you put a chip back on that pile," etc.) before he was permitted to continue in the experiment.

CONSERVATION PRE- AND POSTTESTS   Immediately following the addition/subtraction pretest, *S* was tested for conservation of number, length, and substance, in that order.

(1) *Number*.[2] Two rows of seven chips each, one blue and the other white, were placed parallel to each other so that both rows were of the same length, and the chips in one row were directly opposite those in the other. *E* then directed *S* to count the number of chips in each row. Following this, *E* deformed one of the rows of chips and asked Q plus the question, "Why do you think so?"

The following three deformations were repeated two times each, making a total of six items which were administered in a random order; the row

---

[1] This same general question is also used to get at conservation of number, length, and substance. It is modified to make it appropriate for each kind of conservation. Hereafter, it will be referred to as Q.

[2] The procedures used in the number conservation pre- and posttests were adapted from procedures used by Wohlwill and Lowe (1962), with slight modifications.

of blue chips was deformed on one-half of the trials and the row of white chips on the other half: (*a*) *E* extended one row of the chips in both directions to a length about twice that of the other row; (*b*) *E* subdivided one row of chips into two rows of four and three chips placed parallel to the other row of seven chips; (*c*) *E* placed one row of chips in a vertical pile in front of the other row.

(2) *Length.* Two 12-in. yellow sticks were held upright and close together with their lower ends on the table directly before *S*. After *S* had seen that the two sticks were equal in length, *E* slowly laid the sticks down on the M-L figures previously described, creating a perceptual illusion in which one stick appeared longer than the other. *E* then asked Q plus the question, "Why do you think so?"

This same procedure was repeated three times. For one-half the *S*s the M-L illusion was varied so that first the stick on *E*'s right looked longer, then the one on *E*'s left, and then the one on *E*'s right again. For the other half of the *S*s the order was left-right-left.

(3) *Substance.* *E* presented *S* with two balls of plasticine, equal in weight and volume, and told *S* that they contained the same amount of clay. If *S* did not think that the two balls looked as though they contained the same amount of clay, he was instructed to make them equal by subtracting from one ball and/or adding to the other. After *S* was satisfied that the two balls were equal, *E* rolled one of the balls into another form saying: "Now I change this one into a——[sausage, ring, or cross]." After each of the three deformations, Q plus the question, "Why do you think so?" were asked.

VERBAL PRETRAINING   On the first experimental day, one-half the *S*s were given nine verbal pretraining items, each item beginning with two rows of wooden blocks placed parallel to each other. For six of these nine items, one row contained a greater number of blocks than the other row but was shorter in length. This was accomplished by using longer blocks in the row with the least number of blocks. The items having an unequal number of blocks in each row were the following: eight 1-in. blocks versus two 5-in. blocks; seven 1-in. blocks versus three 3-in. blocks; and six 1-in. blocks versus four 2-in. blocks. These three items were given, in random order, twice. On half the trials the front row had the greater number of blocks, and on half the back row had the greater number. For the remaining items, the two rows contained the same number of blocks and were equal in length. These three items had either five 1-in. blocks, six 1-in. blocks, or four 2-in. blocks in each row. On the second experimental day, *S* was again given the three items having an unequal number of blocks in each row and an item having five 1-in. blocks in each row.

On each item *S* was directed to count out loud the number of blocks in each row. Then Q was asked. If *S* responded incorrectly, *E* directed him to count out loud the number of blocks in each row again and then said, for example, "Yes, there are seven blocks in this row and three blocks in that row, so this row has more blocks than that row." Following this, *E* asked, "Now, which row is longer, this one or that one?" If *S* responded incorrectly, *E* said, "No, you see this row sticks out further this way and that way, so it is longer."

Those *S*s who did not receive verbal pretraining were given another task that involved about the same amount of interaction between *S* and *E* as the verbal-pretraining task. In this task, *S* was asked to take from a number of blocks placed before him a certain number that were to be placed on an 8-in. × 11-in. sheet of white paper that *E* had before him. The number of blocks that *S* was asked to place on the white paper varied from 2 to 10. On each trial, after *S* had placed what he thought to be the correct number of blocks on the paper, *E* asked him to count the blocks to see if he was correct. As in the verbal-pretraining conditions, nine trials were given on the first day and four on the second.

TRAINING FOR CONSERVATION   The two experimental groups and the control group all received training on the apparatus, previously described, that permitted the lengthening or shortening of parallel rows of corks.

(1) *Direct-training group.* The apparatus was placed on the table before *S* with the two horizontal rows running parallel to the front of the table. *E* held up a bag of prizes (trinkets) and told *S* that if he did really well in this game he would receive some prizes at the end of the game. He was instructed to do his very best.

While the rows were in the starting position, *E* directed *S* to count the number of corks in each row. The *E* then lengthened or shortened one of the rows of corks by manipulating the metal bar attached to one end of the apparatus. After each deformation Q was asked. *E* neither confirmed nor corrected *S*'s response to Q. After he responded *S* was directed to count the number of corks in each row a second time. The only external feedback *S* got as to whether his response to Q was correct or incorrect was the knowledge he obtained through counting. If *S* counted correctly the number of corks in each row, *E* confirmed that he had done so by saying, "That's right." If *S* counted incorrectly the number of corks in each row, *E* corrected him.

On half the trials there was an equal number of corks in each row, while there was an unequal number (one row having one more cork than the other) on the remaining trials, thus requiring the conservation of inequality. This was necessary in order that these trials would not be too easy and to prevent response stereotypy.

The items used are shown in Table 2. Starting position A refers to the row nearest *S*, B to the row farthest from *S*. Each of these eight items were used four times, and the order of their occurrence was randomized. These are not the only transformations possible, but in each there is an inconsist-

Table 2

Direct-Training Items

Items	Starting Position	Transformation
1	A = B	A elongated
2	A = B	B elongated
3	A > B	B elongated
4	B > A	A elongated
5	A = B	A shortened
6	A = B	B shortened
7	A > B	A shortened
8	B > A	B shortened

ency between length of row and number of corks in a row. Thus, it is necessary for S to make a conserving response in order to answer Q correctly.

(2) *Conflict group*. The procedure in this group was identical to that in the direct-training group except that every item consisted of one deformation, followed by Q, and then, rather than a recount of the number of corks in each row, a number of subtractions from the row which S believed to have more corks. Each time E subtracted a cork he asked, "Now which row has more corks, this row or that row?" In order to insure that a conflict between the operation of the deformation and the operation of subtraction had actually occurred, E continued to subtract corks until S changed his answer to this question.

When subtracting a cork, E always removed the third cork from the end of the row first (the corks are numbered from 1–9, beginning at the end of the row on E's left). If more subtractions were necessary E then removed the seventh cork; next, the fifth, fourth, sixth, second, and eighth, in that order. This left only one cork at each end of the row. No S required this many subtractions before he changed his answer as to which row had more corks. When a cork was taken away it was always placed nearby on the table where it was plainly visible to S. Between the trials, E was careful to shield the apparatus from the view of S with a 10-in. × 22-in. sheet of cardboard while the corks were placed back on the pegs from which they had been removed and the lengths of the rows were adjusted to make them even. This procedure was necessary to insure that S did not receive any external feedback as to the correctness of his response to Q.

The number of corks (nine) in each row and the length of the rows on the apparatus were made identical at the beginning of each item. This made possible only 4 transformations: lengthening or shortening either the front or back row. These 4 items were repeated 8 times in random order, making 32 items altogether.

(3) *Control group*. The rows of corks remained at their minimal

spread on all trials for Ss in this group. The corks were removed from both rows, and nine corks were placed directly in front of S and nine in front of E. On each trial E placed a number of corks on the pegs sticking up in row B, the row nearest E. E always placed the first cork on the peg at the end of row B and continued placing the other corks on adjacent pegs. After E had finished placing the appropriate number of corks on row B, he said, "See if you can place as many of these corks on that row as I have placed on this row." This procedure was repeated for 32 trials, with the number of corks used on each trial varying between two and nine. As in the other training groups, Ss in this group were told that they could win prizes if they did well in the game.

RESULTS

Classification of the Children's Explanations

The pre- and posttests of conservation called for an explanation in addition to a response to the conservation question. These explanations were divided into three categories: (a) conserving explanations—those clearly indicating conservation; (b) nonconserving explanations—those clearly indicating nonconservation; and (c) ambiguous explanations—those not clearly indicating either conservation or nonconservation. E attempted to get Ss to elaborate and give further explanation of ambiguous explanations by interjecting some neutral statement, such as, "Tell me more," following each such response.

The explanations actually given by the Ss were recorded on tape and transcribed. Two scorers then scored the explanations given as either conserving, nonconserving, or ambiguous responses. An estimate of the reliability with which these responses could be categorized was then obtained. A total of 1,080 responses were involved, 540 for number conservation and 270 each for length and substance conservation. The two judges agreed on 1,063, or 98 per cent, of their classifications. A ϕ correlation coefficient of .96 was obtained as an estimate of the overall interjudge reliability. The separate interjudge-reliability coefficients or the number, length, and substance data, respectively, were: .97, .96, and .88.

Addition/Subtraction

A total of 193 Ss were given the addition/subtraction pretest. Of these, 120 Ss answered all four of the items correctly, while 33 Ss failed all four items. Of the remaining 40 Ss, 31 passed the first two items but failed the last two. The first two items consisted of subtracting one chip from one of two piles of chips, followed by replacing that chip back on the pile from which it had been removed ($- +$). Conversely, the last two items consisted of adding one chip to one of two piles of chips, followed by subtracting that same chip from the pile to which it had been added (+ —). Only 3 Ss passed the last two items (+ —) after they had failed the first two (— +). Five Ss passed one of the first two items (— +) but failed both of the last two (+ —), and one S failed one of the first two items (— +) and one of the last two items. None of the 30 Ss who were excluded from the study because they had passed the number-conservation pretest failed any of the four addition/subtraction items.

Verbal Pretraining

The 45 Ss in the verbal-pretraining condition were given 13 verbal-pretraining trials, 9 on the first day and 4 on the second day. The mean number of trials on which no errors were made for each S was 10.42. Only one S made errors on as many as 7 trials, and only 4 Ss made errors on the second experimental day.

Number Conservation

The scores on the number posttest ranged from 0 to 6, with 49 of the 90 Ss making scores of 0 and 12 Ss making scores of 6. Forty-one of the 90 Ss made at least one conserving response, and 31 made three or more conserving responses. Table 3 shows the mean number of conserving responses per S for each of the six experimental conditions.

Table 3

Mean Number of Number-Conservation Responses per S for the Experimental Groups

	Training Groups		
	Control	Direct Training	Conflict
Pretraining groups:			
Verbal pretraining	2.00	1.40	3.33
No verbal pretraining	0.67	1.80	1.60

A plot of the deviations of the scores within each group from their group means revealed that the data were positively skewed and bimodal. Therefore, only nonparametric analyses of the data were considered appropriate.

A Kruskal-Wallis one-way analysis of variance (Siegel, 1956) of the posttest data revealed a significant difference among the six experimental groups (H = 12.09; 5 df; p < .05). Using the Mann-Whitney U test (Siegel, 1956), it was found that this difference was due to the greater number of conserving responses made by Ss in the conflict-plus-verbal-pretraining group than by Ss in the control group with no verbal pretraining (U = 49; p < .02). None of the other differences among the six experimental groups was significant.

In order that an estimate of the effect of the verbal-pretraining variable could be obtained, the three groups that had received verbal-pretraining were combined and compared with the three groups that had not received verbal-pretraining. A Mann-Whitney U test revealed that this variable was not significant (Z = 1.39; p = .16). However, when all Ss who received conflict training were combined and compared with all Ss who received direct training and all Ss in the control condition, a Kruskal-Wallis one-way analysis of variance did reveal a significant difference among the training groups (H = 7.20; 2 df; p < .05). This difference was due to the greater number of conserving responses made by Ss in the conflict group than by Ss in the control group, as was shown by the Mann-Whitney U test (Z = 1.92; p = .05).

One other analysis was performed on the number posttest data. This was a χ^2 analysis of the frequency with which Ss in each of the six groups reached a criterion of three or more (50 per cent) conserving responses. This analysis did not yield a statistically significant difference between the groups although significance was approached (χ^2 = 10.28, 5 df; .05 < p < .10). The frequencies are presented in Table 4.

Table 4

Number of Ss Who Made Three or More Conserving Responses on the Number Conservation Posttest

	Training Groups		
	Control	Direct Training	Conflict
Verbal pretraining	5	4	10
No verbal pretraining	2	5	5

Length Conservation

Table 5 shows the number of Ss who conserved length on the pretest and posttest. Although there was no significant over-all improvement in length conservation from pretest to posttest, a Kruskal-Wallis one-way analysis of variance did reveal significant differences among the groups in

Table 5

*Number of Ss Who Conserved Length
on Pretest and Posttest*

	Posttest	
	Nonconservers	Conservers
Pretest:		
Conservers	8	21
Nonconservers	50	11

their change scores from pretest to posttest ($H = 11.56$; 5 df; $p < .05$). The Mann-Whitney U test showed that the only group to improve significantly more than the control group without verbal-pretraining from pretest to posttest was the conflict-plus-verbal-pretraining group ($U = 26$; $p < .02$). The mean improvement score for Ss in the conflict-plus-verbal-pretraining group was 0.6, while that for Ss in the control group without verbal-pretraining was 0.2.

Substance Conservation

Table 6 shows the number of Ss who conserved substance on the pretest and posttest. As with the length-conservation data, there was no significant overall improvement in substance conservation from pretest to posttest. However, a Kruskal-Wallis one-way analysis of variance did reveal significant differences among the groups in their change scores from pretest to posttest ($H = 23.18$; 5 df; $p < .001$). The Mann-Whitney U test revealed that the only group to improve significantly more than the control group without verbal-pretraining from pretest to posttest was the conflict group without verbal-pretraining ($U = 63$; $p < .05$). The mean improvement score for Ss in the conflict group was 0.47, while that for Ss in the

Table 6

*Number of Ss Who Conserved Substance
on Pretest and Posttest*

	Posttest	
	Nonconservers	Conservers
Pretest:		
Conservers	4	5
Nonconservers	71	10

control group was —0.07. The negative improvement score of the control group indicates that they did slightly poorer on the posttest of substance conservation than they did on the pretest.

Transfer of Training

The primary reason the tests of conservation of length and substance were included in this study was to provide a means of assessing the generalizability of laboratory-induced conservation. Specifically, in this study it is of interest to know the extent to which those Ss who acquired the ability to conserve number also acquired the ability to conserve length and/or substance. Table 7 provides this information. Columns (1) and (2) include only those Ss who made no conserving responses on the pretest of conservation of length. The 29 Ss who conserved on the pretest of conservation of length are not included because they were already able to conserve length when the experiment began and did not acquire this ability during the experiment. Similarly, columns (3) and (4) include those Ss who made no conserving responses on the pretest of conservation of substance. Of course, none of the Ss made conserving responses on the pretest of number conservation.

Table 7

Number of Ss Acquiring Number Conservation
Who Incidentally Acquire Other Conservations

	Length[a]		Substance[b]	
	Nonconservers (1)	Conservers (2)	Nonconservers (3)	Conservers (4)
Number:				
Conservers	17	10	26	9
Nonconservers	33	1	45	1

[a] The 29 Ss who made conserving responses on the pretest of length conservation are not included.

[b] The nine Ss who made conserving responses on the pretest of substance conservation are not included.

Columns (1) and (2) show that 10, or 37 per cent, of these 27 Ss who acquired conservation of number also acquired conservation of length, while only 1, or 3 per cent, of the 34 Ss who did not acquire conservation of number during the experiment acquired conservation of length. Fisher's exact-probability test (Siegel, 1956) reveals that the difference in these two proportions is highly significant ($p = .0007$). Columns (3) and (4) show that 9, or 26 per cent, of those 35 *S*s who acquired conservation of number also acquired conservation of substance, while only 1, or 2 per cent, of the remaining 46 *S*s who did not acquire conservation of number during the experiment acquired conservation of substance. Applying Fisher's exact-probability test to these data reveals that the difference in these two proportions is also highly significant ($p = .002$). Thus, there appears to be some tendency for those *S*s who acquire conservation of number during the experiment to also acquire conservation of length and/or substance.

DISCUSSION

In one sense, the most obvious conclusion one might draw from the data of this experiment is that neither confronting the child repeatedly with the invariance of numerical values in the face of irrelevant perceptual changes nor devising situations to induce internal cognitive conflict is particularly effective in inducing number conservation. Over one-half of the *S*s who received one of these two kinds of training did not make even one conserving response on the posttest of number conservation.

Nevertheless, there were a substantial number of *S*s who acquired conservation of number during this experiment. The overall improvement becomes more impressive when it is compared with the improvement in conservation that occurred in previous studies that have attempted to induce conservation in children experimentally (Smedslund, 1961b, 1961c, 1961d, 1961e; Wohlwill and Lowe, 1962).

If we compare those *S*s who received only direct training with those *S*s who received only training designed to produce internal cognitive conflict, there is little to choose between them. There was approximately the same amount of improvement in both groups. However, if all the *S*s (both those who received verbal-pretraining and those who did not) who received direct training are compared with all the *S*s in the cognitive-conflict condition, it can be seen that the *S*s exposed to cognitive conflict outperformed those given direct training, although the difference between these two groups did not reach statistical significance. Thus, although it may not be definitely concluded from these data that either direct external feedback or internal cognitive conflict was more effective in inducing number conservation in these children, the direction of the results tends to support Smedslund's (1961d) equilibration-through-internal-cognitive-conflict hypothesis.

It should be remembered, however, that the direct training procedure used in this study involved reinforcement of the "knowledge-of-results" kind. Thus, it differed from a similar procedure used by Wohlwill and Lowe (1962), who, in an attempt to induce number conservation by reinforced practice, rewarded correct responses to the conservation question with chips that could be exchanged at the end of the experiment for toys.

It also differed from their procedure in that theirs involved a match between a given collection of elements and the corresponding symbolically indicated number, whereas the direct training procedure of the present study involvd a comparison of the *relative* number of elements in two collections. Since the posttest of number conservation in both studies involved the comparison of the relative number of elements in two collections, it would be interesting to see what effect direct confirmation of responses to the conservation question by external rewards would have on a training procedure such as the one used in this study.

Since there was a significant difference between the two conflict groups combined versus the two control groups combined, it seems clear that number conservation can be acquired without any kind of direct external feedback if one can induce appropriate cognitive conflict in a child.

However, the verbal-pretraining alone was about as effective as either direct training or cognitive conflict in the inducement of number conservation. Table 3 shows that the mean number of conserving responses for Ss in the control-plus-verbal-pretraining group was 2.00, while that for Ss in the direct training (without verbal-pretraining) group was 1.80, and that for Ss in the conflict (without verbal-pretraining) group was 1.60. This indicates that an experimenter who uses a verbal test of conservation must be certain that Ss understand the language he is using. Otherwise, a child capable of conserving may be deemed a "nonconserver" erroneously.

The most interesting characteristic of the verbal-pretraining, however, was the facilitative effect it had in inducing conservation when it was combined with the cognitive-conflict training. One possible reason for this effect of verbal-pretraining follows from the fact that the child in the conflict situation hears the word "more" quite often. Having been given the verbal-pretraining, the child supposedly understands that the word "more" refers to the relative number of elements in two collections of elements. He is not likely to lose this understanding if his verbal-pretraining is followed by training in the conflict situation, because in that situation he is exposed to, and must respond to, the word "more" repeatedly. Using the word "more" a great number of times places a great emphasis on the *relation* between the two rows of elements involved. It is interesting to note that the children in the training groups other than the conflict group do not have so much emphasis placed on this relation. Thus, they are not as likely to make direct comparisons of the number of elements in the two rows. Focusing one's attention on the relation between two sets of elements may very well be an important aspect of the acquisition of conservation of number.

Generally speaking, training the children on conservation of number did little to increase their ability to conserve length and substance. This seems to indicate either that the process of conserving is acquired for each concept separately and independently and is not a general ability which, once acquired, can operate for all concepts and materials, or, alternatively, that the ability to conserve number, when it is acquired in the laboratory over a few days, may not have as much depth or generality as conservation acquired "naturally" over a long period of time. Both these statements are probably true. Previous studies indicate that the acquisition of conservations of various sorts will appear at different ages in the same child (Elkind, 1961), and Smedslund (1961c) has shown that the ability to conserve weight, when acquired through laboratory training, will extinguish faster than will "naturally" acquired conservation of weight.

Finally, the findings of this study seem to support Smedslund's (1964) finding that the − + operation is easier and appears developmentally earlier than the + − operation. Further, the fact that none of the 30 *S*s who had number conservation on the pretest failed any of the four addition/subtraction items, while 90 *S*s had addition/subtraction but not conservation, is empirical evidence to support the hypothesis that the addition/subtraction operation logically and developmentally precedes conservation.

REFERENCES

Braine, M. D. S., and B. L. Shanks (1965a). The conservation of a shape property and a proposal about the origin of the conservations. *Canad. J. Psychol.*, **19**, (3), 197–207.

Braine, M. D. S., and B. L. Shanks (1965b). The development of conservation of size. *J. verb. Learn. verb. Behav.*, **4**, 227–242.

Elkind, D. (1961). Children's discovery of the conservation of mass, weight and volume: Piaget replication study II. *J. genet. Psychol.*, **98**, 219–227.

Flavell, J. H. (1963). *The developmental psychology of Jean Piaget.* Princeton, N.J.: Van Nostrand.

Gréco, P. (1963). L'apprentissage dans une situation à structure opératoire concrète: les inversions successives de l'ordre lineaire par les rotations de 180°. Cited by J. H. Flavell, *The developmental psychology of Jean Piaget.* Princeton, N.J.: Van Nostrand. Pp. 375–376.

Morf, A. (1963). Les relations entre la logique et le language lors du passage du raisonnement concret au raisonnement formel. Cited by J. H. Flavell, *The developmental psychology of Jean Piaget.* Princeton, N.J.: Van Nostrand. P. 375.

Piaget, J. (1950). *The psychology of intelligence.* Trans. by M. Piercy, and D. E. Berlyne. London: Routledge.

Piaget, J. (1957). Logique et équilibre dans les comportements du sujet. In L. Apostel, B. Mandelbrot, and J. Piaget, Logique et équilibre. *Etudes d'épistémologie génétique*, Vol. 2. Paris: Presses Universitaires. Pp. 27–117.

Piaget, J., and B. Inhelder (1948). Le role des opérations dans le développement de l'intelligence. *Proc. 12th Int. Congr. Psychol.*, 102–103.

Siegel, S. (1956). *Nonparametric statistics for the behavioral sciences.* New York: McGraw-Hill.

Smedslund, J. (1961a). The acquisition of conservation of substance and weight in children: I. Introduction. *Scand. J. Psychol.,* 2, 11–20.

Smedslund, J. (1961b). The acquisition of conservation of substance and weight in children: II. External reinforcement of conservation of weight and of the operations of addition and subtraction. *Scand. J. Psychol.,* 2, 71–84.

Smedslund, J. (1961c). The acquisition of conservation of substance and weight in children: III. Extinction of conservation of weight acquired "normally" and by means of empirical controls on a balance scale. *Scand. J. Psychol.,* 2, 85–87.

Smedslund. J. (1961d). The acquisition of conservation of substance and weight in children: V. Practice in conflict situations without external reinforcement. *Scand. J. Psychol.,* 2, 156–160.

Smedslund, J. (1961e). The acquisition of conservation of substance and weight in children: VI. Practice on continuous versus discontinuous material in conflict-situations without external reinforcement. *Scand. J. Psychol.,* 2, 203–210.

Smedslund, J. (1964). Concrete reasoning: a study of intellectual development. *Monogr. Soc. Res. Child Develpm.,* 29 (2).

Wohlwill, J. F., and R. C. Lowe (1962). An experimental analysis of the development of the conservation of number. *Child Develpm.,* 33, 153–167.

A NOTE ON PIAGET'S CONCEPT
OF CONSERVATION

Herbert Zimiles

In his discourse on the development of the number concept Piaget (1952) gives central emphasis to the concept of conservation as an essential principle that forms the basis for a framework of numerical reasoning. He describes conservation as developing in three stages: an initial stage in which perceptual factors exclusively determine the judgment of quantity, an intermediate stage of transition when perceptual as well as conserva-

Reprinted with the permission of the author and The Society for Research in Child Development, Inc., from *Child Development,* 1963, 34, 691–695. The author is grateful to Barbara Biber and Martin Kohn for their critical reading of the manuscript.

tion considerations influence the judgment, and finally a last stage of complete conservation. These stages are, according to Piaget, one manifestation of a general trend from a perceptual-intuitive to an operational orientation, which characterizes the development of conceptual thinking.

Some of the most thoughtful experimental analyses of Piaget's theoretical speculations regarding the development of number concept have been recently conducted by Wohlwill (1960, 1962). In an attempt to gain some further understanding of the factors that contribute to the development of the principle of conservation, Wohlwill and Lowe (1962) report a study in which they evaluated the relative contribution of three forms of specific training on the development of conservational thinking. The three experimental conditions of training were: (a) Reinforced Practice—*S* determined the number of objects immediately before and immediately after their spatial arrangement (in terms of their spread in a horizontal line) had been changed; (b) Addition and Subtraction—*S* was trained in observing the effects of addition or subtraction of one object from a larger aggregate on the determination of the number of such objects after their spatial arrangement had been changed; and (c) Dissociation—*S* received practice in counting an aggregate of objects under varying spatial arrangements. All the experimental conditions as well as the Control Condition, wherein *S* was given practice in counting the row of a varying number of objects always presented in the same spatial arrangement, were found to have significant effects on a nonverbal measure of conservation, but virtually no demonstrable effect on verbal tests of the same characteristic. Moreover, although no reliable differences in effectiveness were found among the four training procedures employed, the greatest changes were observed in the Control and Addition and Subtraction conditions, those least concerned with providing explicit training in conservational thinking. It is the primary purpose of this note to help account for such perplexing results and, in so doing, to emphasize an aspect of number concept development which tends to be neglected.

Although Wohlwill suggests that the role of lack of differentiation between numerical and perceptual estimates of quantity may have been insufficiently considered, he himself helps to obscure this issue by repeatedly describing the tendency to judge quantity on the basis of greater length or density as a response to 'irrelevant perceptual cues." It must not be overlooked that the concept of quantity exists for the child prior to the concept of conservation. The earliest ideas about quantity are nonconservational and are based exclusively on perceptual cues of length, density, height, weight, and so forth. These dimensions constitute the definition, insofar as there is a definition, of quantity for the preschool child. Such perceptual cues may be misleading in the experiments by Piaget and Wohlwill in the same sense that the trapezoidal rooms were misleading in the Ames experiments, but in both instances such perceptual cues have great relevance.

Accordingly, it would seem more accurate to describe the development of the concept of quantity as something that gradually changes in the direction of greater clarity and precision. The preschool child possesses not one, but a great many definitions of quantity. His concept of quantity is somewhat amorphous and ambiguous. He does not demand the level of clarity, internal consistency, and logical rigor that the analytic adult mind does.

With the advent of counting, cardination, and ordination, the child adds to his concept of quantity. He now employs counting as well as perceptual estimates of magnitude to make quantitative evaluations. Just as before when quantitative evaluations based on length and density tended to correlate with each other, so now evaluations based on perceptual cues and on counting also tend to agree with each other, but also, as before, not perfectly. As he gains facility with the counting schema, he begins to rely more and more on such methods for quantitative evaluations since they provide more precision, differentiation, and information and because they are universally employed and easily communicated. His need for precision and accuracy has increased as he has begun to master complexity, and his exposure to numbers has in turn introduced him to levels of precision never before encountered. The new criteria of precision introduced by the use of number systems facilitate the evaluation of the efficiency of alternate methods of quantitative estimation and consequently lead to their abandonment insofar as they contradict quantitative numerical evaluations.

But these prior methods of quantification do not totally disappear, rather their influence wanes. Restaurants still use thick glasses with high bases so that the capacity of their glasses will be overestimated; packagers of food and other produce are continually exploring methods of creating the impression of great quantity; many people still feel that two dollars in change is either more, or less, money than two bills. Such factors continue to operate in the adult and may be regarded as a manifestation of the wish-fulfilling function of perception. It may be appropriate to consider them as irrelevant in the case of the adult, but it is important to remember that they constitute the definition of quantity for the child.

Let us return to Piaget's developmental stages. Children who respond at the nonconservational level have a less stable, less differentiated, prenumerical concept of quantity. It is a multidimensional concept; it encompasses whatever perceptual magnitudes are involved in a particular situation. It is therefore most probable that these children will respond to the word "more" in terms of whatever dimension is suggested by the E. Since children do not possess a fixed, specific concept of quantity, they will interpret E's manipulation of specific perceptual dimensions as an indication of the particular concept of quantity required by the task.

The child in the intermediate stage is one who employs a rudimentary command of numbers together with various perceptual criteria in his evaluation of quantity. He has not yet had sufficient experience with number systems to reduce the role of perceptual factors in quantity estimation. The third and final stage, that of complete conservation, appears when there has been sufficient opportunity to master cardination and to compare counting with alternative perceptual methods of quantification.

These considerations help to explain some of Wohlwill's findings, for example, the difference between the verbal and nonverbal test results. The verbal test presents a situation in which one of two rows of objects, previously indicated as equal, undergoes a spatial, but not a numerical re-arrangement. For the child who possesses many concepts of "more," the tendency of the E to manipulate a specific aspect of quantity (i.e., length) is likely to be decisive in determining the dimension of quantity to which the child will respond. At no time in the verbal test is a specific request made for a numerical rather than a spatial response. This is in sharp contrast with the nonverbal test procedure where S's response to the altered spatial arrangement must be made in terms of numerical symbols rather than ambiguous language. According to the interpretation presented here, the necessity to respond in terms of number serves as a set to use numerical rather than spatial criteria, hence the superiority of nonverbal as opposed to verbal test performance in both the pre- and postsessions.

In this regard, Wohlwill reports that, when 23 Ss were asked to count the two collections after having given nonconservational responses in the verbal posttest, 19 repeated their nonconservational response when the question was asked of them again. These results demonstrate that at least four Ss could adopt the numerical set when it was suggested to them. With respect to the remaining 19, it remains possible that the suggestion implied by the counting was not explicit enough for them to abandon their spatial set. If this is true, it is dramatic evidence of how disconnected these two different concepts of quantity are in the minds of some of these children.

The same explanation may account for the substantial differences found between the pre- and post-nonverbal tests. All four training periods entailed counting activity involving the objects appearing on the nonverbal test of conservation. This interpolated experience facilitated the adoption of a number set during the posttest sessions and thereby improved performance.

The reasons for the differential effect of certain training conditions, i.e., the slightly greater gains achieved by the Control and Addition and Subtraction conditions, may be attributed to the same factor. The Control condition was the only one of the four training periods in which no spatial rearrangement of the test objects took place. The numerical, rather than the perceptual, cue was manipulated. In the Addition and Subtraction condition the length of the row was varied, but this was probably obscured by the novelty of adding or subtracting an object on two thirds of the trials, once again supporting a numerical rather than a spatial orientation. On the other hand, the Dissociation condition generated the most conflict between the spatial and numerical attitudes. S was required to count rows of varying length, thereby observing that the length and number of a row were completely unrelated, but was never given any indication as to which dimension of quantity was favored by *E*. Since on the test trials it was the length variable that was manipulated, it is to be expected that *S* would be more inclined to turn to the spatial orientation. In a similar manner, but to a lesser degree, the Reinforced Practice training period also gave prominence to the variation of length, this time under a circumstance when the number was unchanged. Consequently, both the Dissociation and Reinforced Practice conditions tended to inhibit the adoption of a number set.

These speculations are reinforced by the findings of an earlier study by Wohlwill (1960). As part of a scalogram analysis of number concept development, Wohlwill investigated the level of conservational thinking by having *S* count a group of buttons and then estimate their number after the aggregate had been scrambled so that the buttons were closer together. The preponderance of nonconservational responses regarded the more dense group as being more numerous. These results are in contrast with Wohlwill and Lowe's findings in which the longer of two rows rather than the shorter or more dense array was usually considered to be greater. These trends of response would appear to be contradictory. They have in common, however, the fact that in both cases *S* considered the aggregate manipulated by *E* as larger. The decisive cue in both instances appears to be the change introduced by *E*.

According to the present analysis of the development of conservation of quantity, it is not to be expected that short training periods of the type employed by Wohlwill and Lowe will be effective in changing the child's approach to conservation. The move from the first to the second stage of conservational thinking requires the assimilation of counting and other number skills, abilities which cannot be cultivated in a short training period. The transition from the second to the third stage where there is a more exclusive reliance on numerical reasoning in the attitude toward conservation is also not likely to develop within a short period of time. For it requires a gradual familiarization and incorporation of the mechanics and implications of numerical reasoning. Whatever changes do occur during an experimental procedure most probably will result from *S*'s changing interpretation of those criteria of "more" that *E* would like him to employ. Although the growth of concepts of quantity may undergo dramatic spurts, quantitative reasoning is seen as unfolding in the manner suggested by Werner (1957) for all forms of cognition, from the diffuse to the articulated, from the indefinite to the definite, from the labile to the stabile. The introduction and mastery of specific symbol systems represent landmarks in this transition, and from the viewpoint of the logical structure of mathematics the acquisition of complete conservation marks an important point in development, but it is the essential continuity of the developmental process which must not be overlooked.

REFERENCES

Piaget, J. (1952). *The child's conception of number.* New York: Humanities Press.
Werner, H. (1957). *Comparative psychology of mental development,* revised ed. New York: International Universities.
Wohlwill, J. F. (1960). A study of the development of the number concept by scalogram analysis. *J. genet. Psychol.,* 97, 345–377.
Wohlwill, J. F., and R. C. Lowe (1962). Experimental analysis of the development of the conservation of number. *Child Develpm.,* 33, 153–167.

LEARNING AND OPERATIONAL CONVERGENCE IN LOGICAL THOUGHT DEVELOPMENT

Harry Beilin

The description of cognitive development as either unitary or non-unitary eludes consensus. Among the prominent developmental theories, Piaget's has often been characterized as a unitary conception, but Piaget and his colleagues discount this interpretation.[1] It is possible to see how

[1] Inhelder, in an introduction to a Lovell work (1961) says, "Even where Dr. Lovell suggests some differences between his findings and ours we see convergence. For example, Dr. Lovell has rediscovered a point on which Piaget has always insisted, that a concrete operation is not generalizable into all contexts, but remains specific to a particular context." The difficulty that a number of researchers have had on this score with the Piaget system is evident also in the report of the Feinberg and Laycock (1964) findings that three tasks involving the same principle but differing in their physical parameters were differentially difficult for a group of subjects. Feinberg and Laycock politely suggest that a "structural" theory of the type that Piaget proposes cannot ignore data that contradict unity. Either these investigators (who conducted their experiment in Geneva at the 'Institut des Sciences, de l'Education') were not aware of the Geneva position on the issue, knew it but did not accept it, or else believed a logical contradiction exists between the Piaget position and the demonstrated lack of unity in performance.

Reprinted with the permission of the author and the publisher from *Journal of Experimental Child Psychology,* 1965, 2, 317–339. This study was supported in part by Public Health Service Research grants M-5681-01 and M-5681-02 from the National Institute of Mental Health. The author would like to thank Dolores Hughes, Rheba Horn, Harriet Gans and Carl Zlatchin for their assistance in the research, as well as Dr. Morris Pincus and the teachers of the New York City school system whose cooperation made the collection of data possible. The author is greatly indebted to Mrs. Irene Gillman for a careful and constructive reading of the manuscript.

such a view could be attributed to the Geneva group in light of their detailed elaboration of a cognitive architecture and the central place within it given to stage theory. In an effort to clarify their position, Piaget and his colleagues distinguish between the sequential order of stages and achievements within a stage. In the former instance, development (by stages) is viewed as progressing in fairly fixed order; in the latter, the existence of a general stage with simultaneous development of a variety of cognitive systems is denied. Although there is no structural coordination among various developmental systems within a stage, there is functional "convergence." Inhelder suggests, for example, that conservation abilities are not achieved simultaneously (as in the conservation of volume, weight, and mass), because of greater difficulty in dealing with some physical parameters than others. On the other hand, she says it was from the observation of the "surprising concordance of structural order in the mechanisms of thought" that the stepwise character of cognitive functions was theorized. This may account for the insistence upon a fixed order of stages (Tanner and Inhelder, 1956, p. 125). Inferring both structural invariance and response variability from the same body of data, however, places the Geneva group in the position of offering either a paradox or a contradiction. It undoubtedly accounts for the ambiguity of an important aspect of their theory.

Various studies have attempted empirical clarification of the issue. They provide a variety of data, which in the main, support a non-unitary view, particularly of within-stage development, but the data are not unequivocal (Dodwell, 1960, 1962, 1963; Lovell, 1961; Beilin and Franklin, 1962; Smedslund, 1964; Almy and Chittenden, 1963; Feinberg and Laycock, 1964; Uzgiris, 1964).

Another issue, not usually associated with discussions of operational unity, concerns the effect of experience (through training) on logical thought development. The role of such experience is not clear. Although the Geneva group considers experience to have a significant place in cognitive development, Piaget seems lukewarm to the idea that experience alone may significantly alter developmental patterns.

Some investigators have recently tried to test the Piaget assertions concerning experience and learning. Among these learning studies two issues seem to bear the burden of investigation. The first reflects an attempt to evaluate the effects of reinforcement and nonreinforcement procedures in the achievement of logical thought (Wohlwill and Lowe, 1962; Smedslund, 1961a, 1961b, 1961c, 1961d, 1961e). These studies, in the main, support the Piaget nonreinforcement view of cognitive change, but again not without qualification.

The second issue involves the differential efficacy of verbal and nonverbal training procedures. This problem is of particular importance since the Geneva group is committed to the view that verbal processes become articulated with logical thought only after the development of (nonverbal) infralogical and logical schema. Some of these studies (Wohlwill, 1960a, 1960b; Ervin, 1960b) demonstrate the limitations of verbal training and reflect some skepticism of the role of verbal mediation in logical thought, although the opposite view is also given expression (Braine and Shanks, 1965).

What gets little attention in these studies is the possible relation between learning and the unitary character of logical development. The present study was designed to investigate this relation and to pursue a number of objectives relative to the other issues already highlighted. Specifically, we have studied the unity of conservation performance independently and in relation to the effects of training. In addition, we have experimentally tested the possible differential effects of reinforcement and nonreinforcement, as well as verbal and nonverbal training procedures.

METHOD

There were three phases to the study: (1) pretraining tests of number, length, and area conservation; (2) training with four experimental procedures on number and length conservation; and (3) posttraining transfer tests of number, length, and area conservation. The pretraining tests provided data for a determination of the unity or convergence of conservation performance, as well as a baseline for the comparison of posttest data. The posttest data indicated the effects of training, and the convergence of posttraining conservation performance.

A test of "numerosity" was given prior to the pretests for an assessment of "number language" comprehension.

Apparatus and Materials

The number and length conservation "tests" were concept attainment tests based upon a nonverbal reinforcement procedure. In both number and length tests reinforcement for correct response was given by buzzer and red tokens. An incorrect response yielded neither buzzer nor token. A red light served as a signal for *S* to make his choice between response alternatives.

NUMBER CONSERVATION APPARATUS   For the test of number conservation a modification was made of the Wohlwill-Lowe number censervation device (Wohlwill and Lowe, 1962). The W-L equipment consists of two parts, a number rack for displaying three numbers, and a part which consists of an expanding and contracting apparatus on which is placed a row of corks. The corks can be moved together or apart by pushing a handle at the end of the device. Wohlwill and Lowe measured number conservation by requiring *S* to choose the number (of three in the display rack) corresponding to the number of corks on the apparatus. After *E* expanded or contracted the array of corks, *S*'s second choice of a number served as the measure of number conservation. (Nonconserving children chose a different number when the row was stretched or contracted.) Since response in this procedure relies on the use of number symbols, a modification was made for the present experiment. The apparatus was widened to form a platform (covered with cork sheet) on each side of the expanding-contracting apparatus. This permitted a row of corks to be arranged on each side of the moving corks. (The center row corks were held in place by pins molded to the apparatus. The side row corks were secured to the base by pins in the corks.)

In the pretest and training series the cork tops were painted with red enamel. For posttesting the tops were painted blue and paper gold stars affixed to them.

LENGTH CONSERVATION APPARATUS   The number conservation test provided the model for length conservation measurement. This task was also nonverbal (i.e., the concept sought was not verbalized to the child) and the reinforcement procedure was the same. The lengths used were discontinuous and made of 1-inch sticks ¼ inch in diameter. Three columns of straight lengths were laid out in parallel (approximately 8 inches apart) on a square cork board (2 × 2 feet). The top ends of all lengths were aligned.

In the pretest and training series the sticks were red and round (1 × ¼ inch) (slightly flattened on one side to keep from rolling); in the posttest series they were green and square (1 × ¼ × ¼ inch).

AREA CONSERVATION APPARATUS   The area conservation task differed from the others in that a transformation of the stimulus materials (particularly with regard to the irrelevant physical property) was not made before the subject's eyes. Judgment of area equality was made of areas already altered in configuration. The subject was provided, in essence, with an analogue to the second half of the number and length trials. Because of this difference the task has been referred to as measuring "quasiconservation." For the test a Visual Pattern Board (VPB) was used. The apparatus and stimulus materials are more fully described elsewhere (Beilin, 1964). The VPB consists of a display panel and a control box. By the insertion of a prepatterned template into the control box, it is possible to present on the display panel any pattern of lighted areas within a 12 × 12 matrix of squares. Three kinds of patterned *pairs* were presented. In one series, the areas were equal and spatially congruent. In the second series, the areas were unequal and spatially noncongruent (e.g., 4 squares vs. 5), and the third (quasiconservation) series consisted of pattern pairs, equal in area, with transformed configurations which made them spatially non-congruent.[2]

PROCEDURE

Preliminary Test of Numerosity

The purpose of this test was to determine whether a child had or lacked receptive language capacities that might affect his success in the conservation tests, although it was recognized that more than language ability was being tapped.

The test assessed his knowledge of equality ("same"), inequality ("more," "less"), "number production" and "number equivalence" terms. It consisted of four items:

(1) Number production: *S* was shown a pile of thirteen red chips and told, "Give me six of these. Now, give me eight. Now, give me twelve."
(2) Number equivalence: *E* laid out a pile of seven red chips. *S* was told, "Make a pile with as many of your chips over here as these here."
(3) Inequality: *E* laid out a pile of seven red chips before himself and five before *S*. "Who has more chips, you or I?" Then, "Who has less chips, you or I?"
(4) Equality: *E* laid out six chips before himself and six chips before *S* and asked, "Do you have more, less or the same chips as I?"

Pretests

Following the preliminary test, all *S*s were tested for conservation of length (Pre L), conservation of number (Pre N) and conservation of area (Pre A). Half of the *S*s were given Pre L first; half Pre N first. Pre A was given last to all subjects. An interval of at least one day separated the administration of each test. *S*s were tested individually.

In the number conservation test (Pre N) there were 2 practice and 12 test trials. Each trial consisted of two parts. In the first part, *S* was shown the number apparatus with its three parallel columns of corks. One column was equal in number as well as length to the middle (stimulus) column (i.e., the corks were in one-to-one correspondence). The other column was unequal in number and also in length to the middle one (i.e., in length covered from first to last cork). The *S* was instructed to choose the row which was "like" the middle one and to respond by pressing a button at the base of either of the response columns. If correct, he heard

---

[2] Equality and inequality series performance data are reported elsewhere (Beilin, 1964). Correct responses were not reinforced, although they were in the other conservation tasks. The *S*s were not trained for this test, which was used as a transfer measure in the posttest.

a buzzer and was given a token. After S responded, E expanded or con-tracted the stimulus column so that the first and last corks were aligned with the first and last corks of either the shorter or longer (irrelevant cue) response column (Fig. 1(a)). No corks were removed or added. All con-tractions and expansions were made in sight of S. After each change, S was again asked to choose the column that was "like" the middle one, and his correct responses were reinforced in the same manner. It was presumed that the reinforcement would serve to provide S with information as to which of the concepts (length covered vs. number) represented in the array was the one sought in the test. On half the trials the incorrect (i.e., irrelevant cue) column was shorter than the middle one, and on half it was longer. The number combinations changed in each trial.

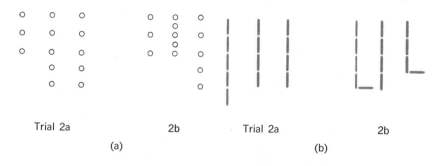

Trial 2a   2b   Trial 2a   2b

(a)   (b)

Figure 1   Sample conservation test trials: (a), number; (b), length.

At the end of the 12th test trial, S was asked why he chose the column he did. The interrogation and answers were recorded on a tape recorder.

The length conservation test (Pre L) also consisted of 2 practice and 12 test trials, and each trial was in two parts. First, S was shown three parallel columns of sticks. Sticks within a column were placed end to end with no space between them. The left column was approximately in line with the left reinforcement buzzer button; the right column in line with the right button. The third, or stimulus column, was placed midway between. One column was equal in length to the middle column, and the other was either longer or shorter than the middle one. S was asked to choose the left or right column "like" the middle one and to press the button near it. Reinforcement was given as in the number test. On the second half of each trial, E changed, in sight of S, the *two outer columns* by aligning the beginning and terminal points of the *incorrect* column with the middle column (i.e., the "incorrect" column was put into a non-straight form so that its "end" was aligned with the middle column). The "correct" column was made perceptually different from the stimulus column by having its terminal point *not* coincide with the stimulus length (i.e., by also making it a non-straight figure) (Fig. 1(b)). After the change, S was again asked to choose the row "like" the middle one. Length combinations were changed in each trial.

At the end of the 12th trial, S was asked why he chose the column he did. The interrogation and answers were tape recorded.

In the area conservation test (Pre A), there were a total of 36 trials. In each trial a *pair* of light patterns was presented on the display panel of the Visual Pattern Board. S was asked if the two figures covered the "same" or "different" amounts of space. For 14 trials 2 $\times$ 2 stimulus patterns were used; on 22 trials 3 $\times$ 3 patterns were used. There were 16 (2 $\times$ 2 and 3 $\times$ 3) quasiconservation trials which constituted the area test of the study. The basis for making conservation judgments was determined in the interrogation.

Scoring Procedures

There were three criteria used in scoring. One, the performance criterion, was based upon S's correct responses in the tests. The second criterion was a qualitative verbal report criterion based upon E's judgment of S's response rationale. A third criterion represented a combination of the performance and verbal report criteria.

PERFORMANCE CRITERIA   For length and number tests an S's response was counted correct if he chose, on *both* parts of a trial, the column of sticks (corks) which was the same length (number) as the stimulus column. If an S responded correctly on any five of the last six trials, he met the "pass/fail" *performance* criterion for conservation. The Ss were classified as *conservers* if they met the pass/fail criterion on both number and length tests; as *transitional conservers* if they passed only one, and as *nonconservers* if they passed neither test. Another performance measure used in the study was simply the correct number of responses in a test.

In the area quasiconservation trials, a response was correct if S said the two figures covered the *same* amount of space. Correct response on any eight of the ten 3 $\times$ 3 quasiconservation trials met the performance criterion for conservation.

VERBAL REPORT CRITERIA   An S was judged on the basis of his verbal response in the number and length test interrogation, as a *conserver*, a *nonconserver*, or a *transitional conserver*. The criteria for judgment were as follows:

If an S had no idea, that is, if he could not verbalize in any manner the principle of conservation of length (or number) (i.e., that the length (or number) remained invariant even when visually altered), he was classified as a *nonconserver*. If an S had a partial, ambiguous or unclear idea of the conservation principle, he was judged as a *transitional con-*

server. If *S* verbalized clearly the principle of length and number conservation, he was considered a *conserver.*

The reliability of judges' classifications of verbal reports according to these criteria was subjected to study. Four reliability checks were made between independent categorizations of the same reports. The per cents of agreement were 82%, 90%, 81%, and 61%. The last low reliability estimate was interpreted as due to one judge's lack of understanding of the classification criteria.

The verbal report criterion for the area test was met if a child gave an "iterative" or "translocational" explanation for his responses. That is, if he recognized area equality by counting the units in each pattern or by making the configurations equal through an ideational relocation of one unit.

"COMBINED" CRITERIA   The *S*s were classified by a combination of the performance and verbal criteria in the following manner:

The *S*s who met *both* qualitative and (pass/fail) performance criteria for *both* length and number tests were classified as *conservers.* The *S*s who met this criterion in the pretest were not assigned to a training or control group ($N = 6$). Although not assigned to a treatment group, these *S*s were tested on the posttests.

The *S*s who had various combinations of passing and failing according to the aforementioned criteria were classified as *transitional conservers.* For example, an *S* who met the performance criterion on Pre N and not on Pre L or passed on the verbal and failed on the performance criterion qualified for this category ($N = 51$).

The *S*s who failed to meet any of the conservation criteria on length and number were classified as *nonconservers* (Pretest $N = 113$).

Assignment of Ss to Treatment Groups

Upon completion of testing, *S*s were assigned to a training or control group with an attempt to balance for age (above- or below-median) and performance on the pretests (Pre L and Pre N). Nonconservers and transitional conservers (classified according to the *combined* criterion) were distributed as evenly as possible among training and control groups (Table 1).

Training

Four training procedures were employed in the experiment: (1) *Nonverbal Reinforcement* (NVR), $N = 31$; (2) *Verbal Orientation Reinforcement* (VOR), $N = 33$; (3) *Verbal Rule Instruction* (VRI), $N = 33$; and (4) *Equilibration* (EQ), $N = 34$. All training was given in two sessions.

Table 1

Assignment of Subjects to Treatment Groups

Treatment	*Age*[a] Below median	Above median	*Pretest Classification* Transitional	Nonconserver
Training Group				
NVR	15	16	8	23
VOR	17	16	11	22
VRI	16	17	10	23
EQ	17	17	10	24
Control	17	16	12	21
Total	82	82	51	113

[a] Median age: 5 years, 4 months.

There was a control group (C), $N = 33$, which received no training but participated in normal class activities for the equivalent period.

Presentation order of training was counterbalanced (i.e., half of the Ss were trained first on length and half first on number). Each S was trained in both number and length, but received only one kind of training (e.g., NVR).[3] No S was trained on the area conservation test. The control group was given no training, but was pre- and posttested.

Three of the training procedures (NVR, VOR, and VRI) were extensions of the pretraining test procedure (i.e., each utilized the pretest nonverbal reinforcement procedure as a base). The NVR training procedure was a repeat of the nonverbal pretest with an increased number of trials (viz., 36). The VOR procedure included verbalization of the concept in the instructions and on each trial so that S would be *verbally oriented* to the relevant attribute (i.e., "You have to figure out which is the same length (or number) as this one.")

VERBAL RULE INSTRUCTION   provided S with a statement of the rule to be applied to the problem in each instance of an unsuccessful trial re-

---

[3] Presentation order of pretests was counterbalanced (i.e., half of the Ss were given Pre L first, half Pre N first). The data indicate that there were no significant differences between the group receiving a given test first and the group receiving the same test second, either on pretests or on posttests. One difference (number) approaches significance ($p < .10$), however, which suggests that the presentation of Pre L first has a slight transfer effect on Pre N—but not vice versa. If success on Pre L (where lengths are discontinuous) were dependent on Ss' counting, then Pre N given first should have facilitated performance when Pre L followed. The fact that it did not, indicates that Pre L performance success is dependent upon some other variable. The same data indicate further that the Pre L test is generally easier than the Pre N test.

sponse. The VRI group was given the same starting instructions as the VOR group. After each trial S was asked why he chose the column or line he did. E judged whether S gave an adequate conservation explanation. On any length trial where S responded incorrectly and/or gave an inadequate conservation explanation, the principle of conservation of length was explained as follows: "Whenever we start with a length like this one [pointing] and we don't add any sticks to it or take away any sticks, but only move it, it stays the same length even though it looks different. See, I can put them back the way they were, so they haven't really changed." For number trials, the conservation rule was explained as follows: "Now I am moving them. See, they are standing in a different place, but there are just as many dots as before. They only look different. See, I can put them back just the way they were, so you see, there are still the same number as before because I did not add any dots or take away any dots. I only moved them." In this training series there were also 36 trials.

The EQ procedure was an adaptation of the deformation method used by Smedslund (1961a) in which the spatial arrangement of objects undergoes transformation, without the addition or subtraction of objects or parts, for the ostensive purpose of creating "cognitive uncertainty." It was hypothesized (by Smedslund) that this procedure generates cognitive disequilibrium. The uncertainty (or disequilibrium) provokes an internal organization of available schemata that facilitates problem solution and terminates in cognitive certainty (equilibrium). This procedure is consistent with the general Piaget model of cognitive change and is offered as an alternate to the associative, S-R reinforcement model. For EQ training, the stimulus pattern underwent a series of "deformations" in sight of S. There were twelve different trials repeated three times (i.e., 36 trials).

The first six length trials employed two sets of six red 1-inch sticks. The last six trials used two sets of eight red 1-inch sticks. At the start of the first trial S was shown two parallel columns of sticks (A and B) (Fig. 2(a)). The S was asked if the two rows of sticks were the same length. In the trials that followed, Column B underwent a series of deformations, ultimately returning to its original configuration. Column A was kept intact as a continuing reference for the child, but was not referred to by E. After each deformation S was asked if the new form was the same length as before it had been moved.

Specific instructions were: "In this game you have to figure out if these two lines of sticks are the same length." If a child appeared not to understand what the word "length" meant, E added: "You have to figure out if an ant walking along these two sets of sticks would have the same distance to walk."

After each deformation E asked: "Is it the same length or a different length from before? Would an ant still have the same distance to walk?"

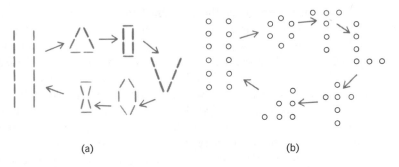

Figure 2   Equilibration method trials 1–6: (a), length; (b), number.

No reinforcement was given on any of the trials in this training procedure.

In equilibration training for number conservation, a parallel procedure was used, except for the use of corks instead of sticks (Fig. 2(b)). Specific instructions were: "In this game you have to figure out if these two rows are the same or different. If these were candies and this side was mine, and this side was yours, would you have more, less or the same as I?" After each deformation, *E* asked: "Are there the same number of candies now or are there a different number from before?"

Posttests

All *S*s were retested for number (Post N), length (Post L) and area (Post A) conservation when training was completed for the entire group. Subject order in posttesting across all groups was on a random basis (except where children were not available because of illness). The *S*s were not retested any sooner than one day after training and the average time gap between the last training session and the first posttest session was three weeks. Approximately one-third were tested within two weeks and two-thirds within three weeks. Some children who were ill were not retested till about eight weeks later.

The period from pretest to posttest ranged from about 8 to 16 weeks.

The procedures for retesting were identical with those used in pretraining except that the test materials and combinations of numbers and lengths of the test trials were changed. Green 1 × ¼ × ¼-inch sticks were substituted for red ones in the length test and gold stars against a blue background for red cork tops in the number test. The VPB apparatus and test stimuli, however, were identical to those used in the area pretest.

Posttests on number and length were considered a "near" transfer (i.e., the tests were based upon the same concepts as those the *S*s were trained on and closely related materials were employed), whereas the area posttest was intended as a "far" transfer (i.e., the task was unlike the training tasks except for the presumed commonality in conservation operations).

Subjects

Subjects were obtained from six kindergarten classes in one New York City elementary public school. The classes were in a school annex located in a middle-income housing project. A majority of *S*s was drawn from this project. All but ten of the *S*s were white. There was an attrition of 20 *S*s during the course of the testing due to persistent illness, moving, etc. The median age of the sample was five years and four months. Each child was tested and trained individually. There were ten sessions with each child (except the control children): three pretesting, four training (two number and two length) and three posttesting sessions. The sessions averaged about 40 minutes. A total of 170 *S*s were in the final sample. Five *E*s participated and were rotated in testing and training sessions.

RESULTS

There are two general analyses: the first concerns the efficacy of training method. The measure of such effectiveness is obtained from the change in performance from pretest to posttest, as a function of training procedure.

The second general analysis concerns the convergence of conservation performance before and after training. The measures of convergence are applied to pretest and posttest performance.

Training Effects

The consequences of training for above- and below-median age groups are represented first according to the "combined criterion" (performance and verbal report) (Table 2). There are fair to substantial increases from pretest to posttest in the number of *S*s meeting number and length conservation and transitional conservation criteria. While there is no significant difference among the treatment groups in pretest performance, posttest differences (in an overall chi-square analysis) are significant for the total group ($p < .01$) and the below-median age group ($p < .01$). This suggests that significant performance differences among groups after training are due principally to differential training effects upon younger subjects. There is an increase in the control group from pretest to posttest of nine per cent (of total *N*) who are conservers and a 22% increase in the number of transitional conserving subjects. A McNemar test of the relation of pretest to posttest proportions of nonconserving and conserving (pooled with transitional) subjects on length and number tests is significant

Table 2

Conservation Level on Combined Number and Length
Pre- and Posttests by Age and Training Procedure[a]

	Age—above median									
	NVR		VOR		VRI		EQ		C	
	Pre	Post	Pre	Post	Pre	Post	Pre	Post	Pre	Post
No conservation	75	19	56	38	59	6	65	24	62	19
Transitional	25	56	44	44	41	53	35	41	38	62
Conservation[b]	0	25	0	19	0	41	0	35	0	19

Chi squares for conservation level vs. treatment: pretest: $p =$ n.s. posttest: $p =$ n.s.

	Age—below median									
	NVR		VOR		VRI		EQ		C	
	Pre	Post	Pre	Post	Pre	Post	Pre	Post	Pre	Post
No conservation	73	27	76	41	81	6	76	53	65	47
Transitional	27	67	24	35	19	50	24	41	35	53
Conservation	0	7	0	24	0	44	0	6	0	0

Pretest: $p =$ n.s. Posttest: $p < .01$.
[a] Per cent of Ss meeting criterion.
[b] Conservation classification based upon combined (performance and verbal report) criterion ($N = 164$).

($p < .01$), indicating that the proportion of Ss who improve is statistically significant. These increases may be attributed to the fact that the pretests and posttests are in themselves training sources, a fact which has been observed in similar studies (Beilin and Franklin, 1962). It could also be attributed, however, to other phenomena associated with the time span between pre- and posttesting. The greatest increase in number of conservers and transitionals from pretest to posttest is in the VRI group.

Similar results are evident when improvement from pre- to posttest is assessed according to the (absolute) number of correct response measure and the pass/fail performance measure (Table 3). With the former criterion, any improvement in an S's responses (e.g., five correct to six correct) is considered an improvement. Table 3 shows the per cent of Ss who improve, as well as the per cent of Ss who change from fail to pass according to the more demanding pass/fail criterion. The percentage of Ss who improve in the VRI group is significantly greater than the percentage of Ss in the control group who improve, with both measures on number and length tests. For the area test there is no significant difference between the percentage of subjects improving in any training group

Table 3

Percent of Ss Showing Improvement
from Pre- to Posttests within Treatment Groups
according to Performance Criteria
(Pass/Fail and Correct Number of Responses Measures)[a]

Treatments	Correct number of responses			Pass/fail criterion		
	Number	Length	Area	Number	Length	Area
Training Group						
NVR[b]	60	61	35	31	37	13
VOR	67	76	24	32	39	6
VRI	87[c]	94[d]	30	67[d]	77[d]	3
EQ	59	71	26	27	39	12
Control	58	51	15	19	17	6

[a] Ss passing on both pre- and posttests are excluded.

[b] Ns change as different numbers of "pass-pass" (pre to post) Ss are excluded in each group.

Chi squares for comparison of *single* training group vs. control, Ss improving vs. Ss not improving:

[c] $p < .05$.

[d] $p < .001$.

Chi squares for comparisons of *combined* training groups vs. control, Ss improving vs. Ss not improving (correct no. of responses measure): length $p < .05$; (pass/fail measure): length $p < .01$, Number $p < .10$.

and the percentage improving in the control group. For area test performance there is no significant difference for either measure between the *combined* training group increase and the increase for the control group, although for length tests the difference between the four training groups combined and the control (for each measure) is significant. With the "correct number of responses" measure, the chi square for length is significant ($p < .05$); with the "pass/fail" measure, length is again significant while number only approaches significance ($p < .01$ and $p < .10$), respectively. The principal contributor to the overall differences is, again, the VRI group.

The increases in the above-median age group seem, in the main, to be greater than those in the below-median age group (Table 2). Further indication of age difference is to be found in Table 4. Age differences in conservation level for above- and below-median age groups are significant only with the "verbal report criterion" (pretest chi square $p < .01$; posttest $p < .05$). Differences are also evident with the "performance" and "combined criterion," but they only approach an acceptable level of significance ($p < .10$). The relatively small difference between the age

Table 4

*Percent of Ss Classified by Conservation Level and Age
on Length and Number Pre- and Posttests
according to Performance, Verbal Report
and Combined Criteria*

	Pretest (N = 170)[a]					
	Performance criterion[b]		Verbal report criterion[d]		Combined criteria[b]	
Level	Above median age	Below median age	Above median age	Below median age	Above median age	Below median age
Nonconserver	80	90	62	76	60	73
Transitional	12	9	26	23	35	26
Conserver	8	1	12	1	5	1

	Posttest (N = 164)					
	Performance criterion[b]		Verbal report criterion[c]		Combined criteria[b]	
Level	Above median age	Below median age	Above median age	Below median age	Above median age	Below median age
Nonconserver	38	55	24	39	21	35
Transitional	24	22	38	40	51	49
Conserver	38	23	38	21	28	16

[a] Includes 6 conservers classified according to combined criteria; these *S*s are not included in posttest table. Control *S*s are included in both pretest and posttest tabulations.

Chi Squares for conservation level vs. age as a function of criterion used:

[b] $p < .10$.

[c] $p < .05$.

[d] $p < .01$.

medians of the older and younger groups (about six months) may in large measure account for the limited difference between age groups on the performance measure.

CONSERVATION AND NUMEROSITY TEST PERFORMANCE   For the number production part of the numerosity test, 78.8, 67.6, and 48.2 per cent of *S*s ($N = 170$) counted out correctly 6, 8, and 12 objects respectively. In judging who had "more" objects, 94.1% of *S*s were correct and 85.3% were correct in judging who had "less." In judging "same" 47.6%

were correct, although a greater percentage of Ss (56.4) could make an equivalent pile (to E's) of seven objects.

Of 81 Ss who responded correctly to "same" in the numerosity tests, 15 per cent passed on Pre L, 15 on Pre N and 12 on Pre A (with "pass/fail performance" criterion). Of the 89 who failed, 6 per cent passed on Pre L, 6 on Pre N and 2 on Pre A. Although passing "same" is a better predictor of success on pretest, failing "same" does not preclude success. Posttest performance indicates that of the "pass same" group, 51 per cent passed Post L, 47 Post N and 21 Post A. Of the "fail same" group, 44 per cent passed Post L, 35 Post N and 4 Post A. Differences in posttest performance, then, are almost completely eliminated except in the Area test, for which no training was given. Performance in the numerosity test is not predictive of ability to profit from training, although the difference between pass and fail groups on Post A suggests there may be some relation to transfer in the posttest.

Table 5

Performance on Numerosity Test ("same number")
Related to Pretest and Posttest Conservation Performance[a]

Numerosity Test		Pretest			Posttest		
"Same"	N	Length	Number	Area	Length	Number	Area
Pass	81	15	15	12	51	47	21
Fail	89	6	6	2	44	35	4

[a] Percentage of Ss passing according to pass/fail performance criterion.

In general, then, training results in improved conservation performance. This improvement is not uniform (either for age group or method) and the only training method that results in significant number of Ss improving, compared with the number improving within the control group, is VRI. Training, however, is not sufficient to insure transfer to a conservation test for which there was no training. Training appears, among kindergartners, to be somewhat more effective with older than younger children. Although understanding of "same" (number) is a better predictor of success in pretests, not understanding "same" does not preclude success, and training appears to remove all pretest differences in such comprehension.

Convergence

PRETEST CONVERGENCE   Performance between pretests (i.e., according to "correct number of responses" measure) was correlated. The correlation is greatest between length and number performance ($r = .44$, $p < .01$). There is less correlation between each of these tests and the area test (length-area $r = .23$, $p < .01$; number-area $r = .05$, $p = $ n.s.).

Another measure of pretest convergence is the number of *S*s who passed single tests relative to those who passed two or more tests. Excluding the control group and the six "full" conservers, there are 15 *S*s who passed only one test (according to the "pass/fail performance" criterion) and 4 who passed two or more.

POSTTEST CONVERGENCE   The correlation between number and length tests after training ($r = .72$, $p < .01$) is greater when compared with pretest correlation ($r = .44$). There is little or no difference in length-area and number-area correlations. In correlating pretest with posttest performance the correlation is greatest for the area test ($r = .50$, $p < .01$) and less for the others (number $r = .37$, $p < .01$; length $r = .29$, $p < .01$). These data support the conclusion that training has the least effect upon altering area test status (i.e., the test for which there is no training).

The number of *S*s who passed only one test on posttest (whether number, length, or area) is 32 (39% of *S*s who passed at least one test) and 48 (61%) of *S*s passed two or more. These proportions are *inverse* to what appears on pretest when 15 (79%) passed only one test and 4 (21%) passed two or more. Training, then, has the effect of facilitating convergence although this is limited mostly to the length and number tests.

In examining convergence prior to training, it is possible to apply two measures. First, there is the measure which indicates the number of *S*s who passed one test in relation to those who passed at least two. This measure has already been indicated (i.e., on pretest 21% passed two tests whereas 79% passed only one). Second, there is the measure indicated by the proportion of *S*s who passed number, length and area of those who passed at least number and length. Relative to this measure, there are six *S*s who passed number and length on pretest. Of these, four also passed area (66%). After training, however, the per cent of those who passed at least length and number (according to the combined criterion), who also passed area is only 24% (i.e., 8 of 34 *S*s).

If we look for the pretest group which contains the highest proportion of *S*s who passed two posttests (considering only number and length independent of area performance), we find that of *S*s who passed one pretest, 67% (8 of 12) passed both posttests. Of those who passed neither pretest, 31% (36 of 117) passed both posttests. Of those *S*s who failed both number and length on pretest, 24% (28 of 117) passed one posttest and failed the other. Those who passed at least one pretest, therefore, had the greatest likelihood of passing "maximally" on posttests. Similar results are found when an analysis is made of performance with three pretests rather than two. The group most likely to profit from training is

Table 6

Consistency of Verbal and Performance Responses on Pre- and Posttests Verbal Report Responses

		Pretest			Posttest		
		Fail	Pass[a]	Total	Fail	Pass	Total
Performance	Pass	4	15	19	7	81	88
Responses	Fail	113	32	145	46	30	76
	Total	117	47	164	53	111	164

Pass verbal and performance criteria[b] (15/51)	29%	Pass verbal and performance criteria[b] (81/118)	69%
Pass performance criterion[b] (19/51)	37%	Pass performance criterion[b] (88/118)	74%
Pass verbal criterion[b] (47/51)	92%	Pass verbal criterion[b] (111/118)	94%
Pass verbal (and performance)[c] (15/19)	79%	Pass verbal (and performance)[c] (81/88)	92%
Pass performance (and verbal)[d] (15/47)	32%	Pass performance (and verbal)[d] (81/111)	73%

[a] Pass refers to *S*s who perform as transitional conservers or better.
[b] As a proportion of total *S*s who pass at least one criterion (pretest $N = 51$; posttest $N = 118$).
[c] As a proportion of the total *S*s who pass performance criterion.
[d] As a proportion of the total *S*s who pass verbal criterion.

that group whose members have at least some (but not the fullest) conservation ability, i.e., the group who passed one pretest as compared to the groups that passed no or two pretests.

VERBAL REPORT AND PERFORMANCE MEASURE CONVERGENCE   In addition to verbal and nonverbal training technique differences, we were interested in the convergence of verbal and performance responses.

A measure of such convergence is obtained from the number of *S*s who passed[4] both verbal response and performance response measures relative to the number of *S*s who passed at least one of these criterion measures (verbal or performance). On pretest the proportion (15/51) is 29%. On posttest this value is 69% (81/118).

We determined also the proportion of *S*s who passed the verbal report criterion of those who passed at least one criterion. This proportion for pretests is 47/51 or 92%. For posttests the proportion is 111/118 or 94%. On the other hand, the proportion who met the performance response criterion of those who met at least one criterion is, on the pretests, 19/51 or 37%, and on posttests is 88/118 or 74%. It is evident (on both pretest

[4] "Passing" for this analysis includes both transitional conservers and conservers.

and posttest) that the likelihood of a person who met the performance criterion giving the correct verbal report is substantially greater than the likelihood of a person who met the verbal report criterion also meeting the peformance criterion. This is true in spite of the fact that substantially more *S*s met both criteria on posttest than on pretest.

In general, then, the convergence data may be ordered into different levels of performance. On pretest, there are those who passed no tests, those who passed one of the two training tests, those who passed two (but not the third test) and those who passed all three. Training has the effect of increasing the number of *S*s who could pass two or more of the tests. Training is most likely to be effective for the pretest group who passed one pretest. The proportion of those who passed at least length and number on the posttests, who also passed the area posttest, ostensibly as a result of the training procedures (24%), is not as great as the proportion of *S*s who passed at least length and number on pretest, who also passed the area pretest, without formal training (66%). The likelihood of *S*s who passed the performance tests (at least at the transitional conserving level) similarly passing according to the verbal report criterion, is much greater than the likelihood of *S*s who passed the verbal report criterion also passing the performance criterion.

DISCUSSION

The effect of training in improving performance from pretest to posttest is evident for the tests in which *S*s were trained (i.e., number and length conservation), although not for the test in which *S*s were not trained (i.e., the area test). Each treatment group in the study, including the control group, has a significant number of *S*s who improved in performance from pretest to posttest. There is only one training group, however, which has significantly more *S*s improving than the control group, namely, the VRI group. The procedure used in training this group involved: (1) the presentation of a problem-solving task which led to either success or failure, and (2) with failure, the provision of a verbal statement of the conservation (i.e., problem-solving) principle. The principle, if properly applied, could lead to correct performance in the task. The essential features of the VRI procedure were: (a) the method was verbal, (b) an affective response was generated to failure which, hypothetically, could have led to greater subject attention and/or to cognitive uncertainty, (c) reinforcement was given, and (d) the procedure offered a model which was applicable to a variety of instances of the principle.

It is often argued that "didactic" methods are relatively ineffective in facilitating learning. The didactic method of the present study, however, emerged as the only one which led to a significant number of *S*s showing improvement (over the control group). On the other hand, it did not transfer to an analogous conservation task, but then neither did the NVR, VOR, and EQ methods. The significant feature of the VRI method which facilitated learning requires identification since some of its attributes were shared with other methods. The VRI method was verbal, but so were the VOR and EQ procedures—at least in the sense that the concept sought was verbally identified and these other methods did not facilitate conservation learning. The VRI method could have acted to orient S to the relevant features of the stimulus array, but then again, this was the distinctive feature of the VOR method. The VRI employed a reinforcement procedure, but so did NVR and VOR. Another possibility is that the VRI procedure created cognitive uncertainty which was altered by some kind of cognitive integration or reorganization. Again, the EQ method was employed specifically for this purpose and its effects were not significantly different from the control's. In relation to the EQ method, one may argue that either Ss were not provided with the schemata that had to be integrated during training or else Smedslund's assertions about the efficacy of the method were not borne out. Smedslund has emphasized that two schemata are needed for conservation, the deformation schema and the addition/subtraction schema. In a later paper Smedslund (1961d) stresses the greater importance of the addition/subtraction than the deformation schema in conservation learning. In our analogue to the equilibrium procedure, object arrangements were deformed without the addition or subtraction of elements so that the addition/subtraction schema was only dealt with indirectly. If Smedslund's assertions are confirmed, then the fairest test of the EQ method was not made in the present experiment. It is nevertheless instructive that the method, even as used, was no better than the control procedure. The emphasis upon the addition/subtraction schema may be methodologically necessary, since the VRI procedure alluded to both deformation and addition/subtraction in the statement of the rule. It is therefore not possible to conclude that the EQ method cannot influence performance. In spite of this latter limitation, it would appear that the most salient feature of the VRI procedure is its 'model' or algorithm feature (i.e., it provides S with a model or rule for processing relevant input data).

A question remains, however, as to why the verbal model or rule was not used effectively to transfer to the area task. The limitation of verbal model training is highlighted by the fact that of the Ss who conserved before training on the number and length tests, a large proportion (66%) were also able to perform on the area test. This condition did not prevail after training. Training (of the type reported here) is therefore not sufficient to foster generalization to the extent to which it exists among children who have acquired the capacities in a nonformal fashion. At the same time, training does make a transition from nonconservation to "full" conservation possible for at least some children. It suggests also that some element beyond verbal model training is necessary for "full" conservation, which no other training procedure is able to provide either, but which is achieved in less formal learning settings. In addition, the data relating verbal to performance success suggest that the ability to give correct verbal conservation responses is not sufficient in itself to insure performance success. The evidence of *S*s being able to give correct verbal responses relative to the conservation tasks (both before and after training) and not being capable of meeting the performance criterion represents confirmation of the "mediation deficiency hypothesis" (Reese, 1962). It suggests, too, that processes other than verbal learning are involved, in that verbal training does not result in extensive use of verbal responses as mediators. Confirming the mediation deficiency hypothesis does not identify the nature of mediation in later development. Two possibilities exist: (1) in later development verbal responses will account for logical thought (as some verbal mediationists would hold), or (2) in later development conservation ability will result from the acquisition of nonverbal logical structures independent of verbal elements (as some holding to the Piaget view would assert).

The convergence data support the view of most investigators that, prior to training, there is relatively little convergence of conservation performance across tasks. The training data reveal that training leads to a greater number of *S*s who show improved performance, but mostly in the tasks for which they were trained. Conservation training is most likely to affect *S*s who are at a transitional conservation level; those who are nonconservers or closest to "full" conservation are less likely to profit from such training. Training is not sufficient to make for extensive conservation across all tasks. The acquisition of conservation abilities appears to involve, then, a transaction in which experience, in itself, although contributing considerably to improved performance, does not lead to a generalized conservation capacity. There is a difference between how much is achievable through formal training and how much is achievable without such formal training. Even in nonformal conservation acquisition, however, where convergence is most extensive, only 66% (albeit with a small number of cases) performed successfully on the three conservation tasks. Learning may facilitate convergence but not extensive convergence without, apparently, interaction with maturational processes.

REFERENCES

Almy, M., and E. Chittenden (1963). Young children's thinking: understanding of the principle of conservation. Paper presented at meetings of The Society for Research in Child Development, Berkeley, Calif.

Beilin, H., and I. C. Franklin (1962). Logical operations in area and length measurement: age and training effects. *Child Develpm.*, 33, 607–618.

Beilin, H. (1964). Perceptual-cognitive conflict in the development of an invariant area concept. *J. exp. child Psychol.*, 1, 208–226.

Braine, M. D., and B. L. Shanks (1965). The development of conservation of size. *J. verb. Learn. verb. Behav.*, 4, 227–242.

Dodwell, P. C. (1960). Children's understanding of number and related concepts. *Canad. J. Psychol.*, 14, 191–205.

Dodwell, P. C. (1962). Relations between the understanding of the logic of classes and of cardinal number in children. *Canad. J. Psychol.*, 16, 152–160.

Dodwell, P. C. (1963). Children's understanding of spatial concepts. *Canad. J. Psychol.*, 17, 141–161.

Ervin, S. M. (1960a). Transfer effects of learning a verbal generalization. *Child Develpm.*, 31, 537–554.

Ervin, S. M. (1960b). Training and a logical operation by children. *Child Develpm.*, 31, 555–563.

Feinberg, I., and F. Laycock (1964). Ability of blindfolded children to use landmarks to locate a target. *Child Develpm.*, 35, 547–558.

Lovell, K. (1961). *The growth of basic mathematical and scientific concepts in children.* New York: Philosophical Library.

Reese, H. W. (1962). Verbal mediation as a function of age level. *Psychol. Bull.*, 59, 502–509.

Smedslund, J. (1961a). The acquisition of conservation of substance and weight in children: II. External reinforcement of conservation of weight and of the operations of addition and subtraction. *Scand. J. Psychol.*, 2, 71–84.

Smedslund, J. (1961b). The acquisition of conservation of substance and weight in children: III. Extinction of conservation of weight acquired "normally" and by means of empirical controls on a balance. *Scand. J. Psychol.*, 2, 85–87.

Smedslund, J. (1961c). The acquisition of conservation of substance and weight in children: IV. Attempt at extinction of the visual components of the weight concept. *Scand. J. Psychol.*, 2, 153–155.

Smedslund, J. (1961d). The acquisition of conservation of substance and weight in children: V. Practice in conflict situations without external reinforcement. *Scand. J. Psychol.*, 2, 156–160.

Smedslund, J. (1961e). The acquisition of conservation of substance and weight in children: VI. Practice on continuous versus discontinuous material in problem situations without external reinforcement. *Scand. J. Psychol.*, 2, 203–210.

Smedslund, J. (1964). Concrete reasoning: a study of intellectual development. *Monogr. Soc. Res. Child Develpm.*, 29 (2).

Tanner, J. M., and B. Inhelder (Eds.), (1956). *Discussions on child development*, Vol. 4. New York: International Universities.

Uzgiris, I. E. (1964). Situational generality of conservation. *Child Develpm.*, 35, 831–841.

Wohlwill, J. F. (1960a). Absolute versus relational discrimination on the dimension of number. *J. genet. Psychol.*, 96, 353–363.

Wohlwill, J. F. (1960b). A study of the development of the number concept by scalogram analysis. *J. genet. Psychol.*, 97, 345–377.

Wohlwill, J. F., and R. C. Lowe (1962). Experimental analysis of the development of the conservation of number. *Child Develpm.*, 33, 153–167.

EFFECTS OF VERBAL AND PERCEPTUAL
TRAINING ON WATER LEVEL REPRESENTATION

Harry Beilin∕Jacob Kagan∕Rhea Rabinowitz

In the view of Piaget and Inhelder, human language serves essentially as a symbolic "vehicle" for thought. Although it functions well in the communication of conceptual data, it is less adequate for the communication of perceptual events. For the perceptual domain, symbolic imagery serves the principal communication function. Although symbolic imagery is inadequate for symbolizing logical and arithmetic operations, it is quite relevant to the symbolic representation of "geometric intuitions" where a partial isomorphism exists between spatial representations and spatial relations on which geometric "operations" are performed (Inhelder, 1965).

In the development of this position, the Geneva group has conducted a series of studies involving "reproductive, evocative, and anticipation imagery" with a variety of materials which could be visually and figurally

Reprinted with the permission of the senior author and The Society for Research in Child Development, Inc., from *Child Development*, 1966, 37 (2), 317–328. This study was supported in part by a USPHS research grant from the National Institute of Child Health and Human Development (HD-925). The authors are indebted to Dr. S. Waxman and the personnel of the Greenburgh District No. 8 schools, Hartsdale, New York, who made possible the collection of the data. The training programs cited in this paper were modeled after an experimental programed instructional series for "Mathematics Vocabulary Improvement," developed by L. G. Gotkin, J. Chaikin, and J. Graham for the Center for Programed Instruction, Teachers College, Columbia University. The authors are indebted to Dr. Gotkin for making the programs available to them.

represented. The Geneva position is of particular theoretical interest in light of the more significant role given to language in both perceptual and cognitive functioning by neobehaviorists and others. These latter theorists are also less likely to accept the view that the ability to manipulate imaginal representations is dependent upon the development of relevant operative thought mechanisms.

The present experiment was an attempt to determine whether language and perceptual experience can play a significant role in symbolic imagery. It was conducted in relation to the representation of water levels or water surfaces, a phenomenon described in some detail by Piaget and Inhelder (1956).

The ability to represent water levels was studied by Piaget and Inhelder with a variety of tasks involving the rotation of straight- and round-sided jars partially filled with water. Children copied water levels and, with line drawing responses on outline figures, anticipated the water levels in covered jars tilted at various angles. Their formulation of water level representation reflects a stagewise progression which is consistent with their characterization of other developments in the period of concrete operations.

In an attempt to demonstrate that "experience" with reality is itself insufficient for the development of adequate symbolic imagery, Smedslund (1963) provided children with such experience by drawing their attention to the surface of the water as a jar was rotated through 360°. His results show almost no improvement in performance from pre- to posttest among Ss who had no correct pretest drawings. There was greater improvement among those who had at least one correct response. No S responded correctly or even nearly correctly on all test drawings as a result of the experience.

Two studies have dealt with the results of cultural experience upon water level representation. R. Feurstein,[1] in a training study of 14–16-year-old Moroccan immigrants in Israel, using the anticipation method, found striking performance deficits when compared with the Piaget "norms." With a training procedure in which S copied the observed water level after making an anticipation response, he found reductions in errors in all orientations of the jars. He also found differences favoring response to straight-sided jars compared to round-bottomed flasks, a result contrary to both Piaget's findings and theory. Vernon (1965), in a study of West Indian and English children which employed a large battery of tests, including the "tilted jar" procedure, found water level performance differences between the two samples to be "quite small," whereas differences between the groups in Piaget conservation tasks were substantially greater.

The present experiment, again, was undertaken to study more fully the influence of language and perceptual experience upon anticipation imagery

---

[1] Research Unit, Child Guidance Clinic, Youth Aliyah, Jerusalem, Israel. Personal communication.

in water level representation. In light of the evidence that water level representation might be sensitive to the effects of social and cultural experience, it was thought desirable to test performance and training effects with children differing in cultural and social experience.

METHOD

A pretest-training-posttest-transfer design was used. The pretest, posttest, and transfer test were based upon an anticipation method, with choice of one water level representation, from a series of drawings of jars in the same orientation, serving as the dependent variable. The transfer test utilized round-bottomed Florence flasks, whereas straight-sided jars were used in pretests, posttests, and training.

There were two types of training procedure. Perceptual training involved visual confirmation of water level following an anticipation response made to the water level in a covered jar oriented at a particular angle with the horizontal. There were two variations of this procedure.

Verbal program training involved verbal instruction in the concept of horizontality, the water level principle, or both. Instruction was provided through a programed instructional procedure presented in booklet form. Four groups were given various combinations of verbal training.

There were three control groups that received no training. One group was administered only the pretest and transfer test. A second group received the pretest, posttest, and transfer test with the demonstration jar covered prior to pretest. The third group was given the same tests as the second, but the demonstration jar was uncovered prior to the pretest. There was an additional group that was administered only the transfer test. The data for that group were not used in the main analysis.

Procedure

The Ss were seated at their desks in a classroom. The E stood behind a desk in the front of the room. Pencils and booklets were distributed, and E told the children they were to play a game.

PRETEST   The E placed a straight-sided gallon jar, half filled with red-colored water, on the desk. He covered the jar with a green opaque stretch stocking which made the water no longer visible but kept the visual outline of the jar intact. The Ss were instructed to select in their answer booklets, from among eight pictures of jars, the picture that represented the water level correctly. Each pictured jar was about 1 inch high and outlined in black. The water surface was indicated by a red line, and the water itself (either above or below the water line) was shown by red stippling. All jars on a page were tilted in the same direction as the jar used by *E*.

The choice alternatives reflected the combination of two variables. The first involved the relation of the water line to a reference system either internal or external to the jar. There were four such reference choices: with the water line (*a*) horizontal, (*b*) parallel to the base of the jar, (*c*) parallel to the side, and (*d*) diagonal. The second variation was of the body of water in the jar relative to the effect of gravity, that is, either the water was above the water line, defying gravity, or below, in accord with it. For each internal or external reference choice there were two gravity options for a total of eight alternatives. The correct choice in each series, of course, was the "water level horizontal—water below line" representation.

There were eight trials with the jar tilted and held in a preset bracket at angles of 45°, 90°, 135°, 180°, 225°, 270°, 315°, and 360° (top-up position). When the jar was presented at angles of 180° and 360° (vertical positions), the alternatives having the correct water level, regardless of the gravity position of the water, became identical with the alternatives in which the water level was parallel to the base. When the jar was presented at angles of 90° or 270° (horizontal positions), these alternatives became identical with those in which the water surface line was parallel to the sides. In order to eliminate this duplication, one set of alternatives was replaced by another having the water lines drawn diagonally from one side to the other. These differed from the other set of oblique alternatives in that the direction of the slant of the water lines was reversed. The *S* responded by circling one of the eight alternatives on the answer sheet. The placement of alternatives was randomized (using a table of random digits) for each trial. The posttest procedure was the same as that of the pretest.

PERCEPTUAL TRAINING   Two of the six training groups received perceptual training. There were eight training trials paralleling the eight jar positions used in the pretest.

PM group. Ss were shown the demonstration jar. After being covered, the jar was rotated in the aforementioned orientations. After each anticipation response (in which *S* indicated, by marking one picture out of a series, what he imagined the water level to be), the jar was uncovered, and *S* could compare his predicted water level with the "real" water level. The series was repeated twice for a total of 16 trials.

PNM group. Ss followed the same procedure except for two changes. First, the Ss made no written response to the representation of the water level. Second, for the anticipation response they were instructed to "think of what the water would look like." When the jar cover was removed, they were told to "see if it's like what you thought it would be."

The PNM method differed from the PM method, then, in that in the

PNM method there was no forced motor response or forced choice of a pictorial representation of the imaginal response.

VERBAL PROGRAM TRAINING   Verbal instruction was given through two programs. One was devoted to the water level principle, the other to the concept of horizontality. A sample frame from the water level program contained the following: "When water is in a glass, the top of the water makes a *water line* across the glass. It starts at A and ends across at B" (an outline drawing illustrated this). "Does this glass have a water line?" (the outline drawing showed the same glass as above but with no A-B notation). "Yes-No."

The horizontal program contained this in a sample frame: "Here are three lines" (illustrated: one vertical, one horizontal, one oblique line). "The middle one is horizontal. Is this line horizontal?" (the line was oblique). "Yes-No."

There were 15 frames in each program. The *E* read the text of each frame aloud while *S* followed silently. A "yes" or "no" response to each frame was made by circling the printed word. After all *S*s had answered, *E* told them the correct answer. There was a second *E* in each room to assure that directions were properly followed.

The two verbal programs were given in the following combinations to different groups to test their individual and combined effects:

Water level concept (V-WL). The water level program was given twice to each child.

Horizontal concept (V-H). The horizontal program was given twice to each child.

Horizontal and water level concepts (V-H-WL). The *S*s in this group were given both programs, with horizontal prior to water level training (once each).

Water level and horizontal concepts (V-WL-H). This group also received both programs but in reverse order from the prior group.

Each *S* given a verbal program made 30 training responses.

TRANSFER TEST   The transfer test procedure was identical to the pretest and posttest procedure except that the rectangular gallon jar was replaced by a 1,000-millimeter Florence flask with a large round bowl and long cylindrical neck. The response alternatives were patterned after those of the pre- and posttests.

CONTROLS   There were three control groups, none of which received training. The first control group (CU), which received pretest, posttest, and transfer test, was shown the water level in the pretest jar before it was covered by the opaque stocking. The second group (C) did not see the demonstration jar uncovered prior to pretest. The third (CNP) received no posttest, that is, they were administered only the pretest (uncovered) and transfer test.

Subjects

The experiment was initially conducted with third-grade children aged 8–9 years. Pretest data showed that a substantial number of Ss had reached the operational level of performance. Since our primary interest was in training Ss who did not meet the operational level criterion, it became necessary to obtain data from younger children. The experiment was then conducted with second-grade children.

The second-grade Ss were 180 white and Negro pupils enrolled in a school in Westchester County, New York. Their ages ranged from 6 years, 2 months to 8 years, 2 months with a mean of 7 years, 6 months. The school system operates under the so-called Princeton Plan. All second-grade children in the school district attend the same school. There is no sorting within grade, by ability or other criteria, for the purpose of instruction. There were nine heterogeneously grouped classes used for the principal part of the study. Experimental treatments were randomly assigned to available class groups. After all data had been collected, Ss were classified for socioeconomic status (SES) according to father's occupation with the Warner scale (Warner, Meeker, and Eells, 1949). For the present analysis, the occupational categories were collapsed into two SES groups with occupational classes one through three designated as "middle class" and occupational classes four through seven designated as "lower class." Age and IQ data (Kuhlmann-Anderson Test) for all Ss were available from school records.

The nine groups ($N = 180$) did not differ significantly on age, IQ, race, and SES. For the training study, those Ss who had maximum scores in the pretest were withdrawn from the analysis. There were 28 such Ss. A re-analysis of the nine groups, with these Ss removed, indicated that the nine groups still did not differ significantly on age: $F (8, 143) = 1.35, p =$ n.s.; IQ: $F (8, 143) = .90, p =$ n.s.; race: $\chi^2 = 13.97, df = 8, p =$ n.s.; or SES: $\chi^2 = 14.35, df = 8, p =$ n.s.

RESULTS

Training Effects

SCORE CRITERION   The final sample of nine treatment groups included 152 children after the 28 Ss with perfect scores were removed. The remaining Ss had scores which varied discretely from 0 to 7 of a possible total of 8 (Table 1).

Table 1

*Treatment Group Means and Standard Deviations
for Pretest, Posttest, and Transfer Test Scores*[a]

			Pretest		Posttest		Transfer	
Group	N	Treatment	Mean	SD	Mean	SD	Mean	SD
PM	17	Perceptual-motor response	4.94	1.95	7.06	1.39	5.59	1.87
PNM	20	Perceptual-no motor response	4.45	2.33	6.50	1.85	4.90	2.02
V-WL	12	Verbal program-water level	5.75	1.48	6.33	1.87	5.25	2.38
V-H	20	Verbal program-horizontal	3.85	2.32	4.80	2.67	4.10	2.53
V-H-WL	14	Verbal program-horizontal-water level	5.07	.99	5.86	1.75	5.44	1.74
V-WL-H	13	Verbal program-water level-horizontal	3.77	1.96	5.38	2.18	4.85	1.62
C	18	Control (jar covered)	4.39	2.09	4.72	2.67	5.05	1.62
CU	19	Control (jar exposed)	4.95	2.09	4.95	2.44	4.47	2.19
CNP	19	Control (no posttest)	4.42	2.29	—	—	4.53	2.29
Total	152		4.59	2.90	5.66	2.22	4.86	2.07

[a] Pretest operational Ss not included.

A one-way analysis of variance of pretest scores showed no significant differences among the nine group means: F (8, 143) = 1.34, p > .10. The analysis of posttest scores, excluding the CNP group, showed significant differences among the eight groups: F (7, 125) = 3.01, p < .01. Kramer's (1956) extension of Duncan's multiple range test for group means with unequal Ns was used to test for the significance of differences between means. The mean scores of both Perceptual Training groups (PM and PNM) were the largest and differed significantly from all other group mean scores except from that of the Water Level group (V-WL). The mean score of the V-WL group differed significantly from the mean scores of the CU and the V-H groups. No other mean differences were significant. A one-way analysis of variance of transfer test scores showed no significant differences among the nine means: F (8, 143) = .98, p > .25. On the basis of the posttest and transfer test analyses, it appears that perceptual training and the verbal water level program did improve choice of correct water level representations, but this improvement did not generalize to a task utilizing the same concept in jars of different outline.

Of the pretest operational Ss, 28 per cent were also operational on the transfer test. Of 133 trained Ss, 27 per cent became operational on posttest. Of this latter group, 25 per cent were also operational on the transfer test. These data indicate two things. First, the Piaget contention that round-sided flasks are easier for water level representation than straight-sided jars is not borne out. A comparison of the percentage of errors made per trial on posttests and transfer tests (Table 3) supports this conclusion, as do the data from Table 1, which show transfer means to be lower than posttest means for every treatment group but one. Second, training contributes as much to transfer among those who were nonoperational on pretest yet operational on posttest, as to those who were operational on pretest. This finding differs from what has been observed with conservation performance (Beilin, 1965).

STAGE CLASSIFICATION CRITERION   A second set of analyses was based upon stage classification of *Ss*' pre- and posttest performance. These classifications derive from the Piaget and Inhelder (1956) developmental sequence (Table 2).

Table 2

Criteria for Stage Classification Based upon Response Pattern; Pre- and Posttest Subject Distribution

	Position of Jar			Pre-test[b] (N)	Post-test[b] (N)
	Horizontal	Vertical	Diagonal		
Stage III—*External reference:*					
IIIB—Operational	passed 2 of 2	passed 2 of 2	passed 4 of 4	24	55
IIIA—Partial-					
operational	passed 2 of 2	passed 2 of 2	passed 1–3 of 4	61	57
Transitional	passed 2 of 2	passed 2 of 2	failed 4 of 4	6	8
Stage II—*Internal reference:*					
IIB—Inconsistent		any other combination		45	20
IIA—Base					
Response[a]	failed 2 of 2	passed 2 of 2	failed 4 of 4	16	12
Stage I—*No reference:*					
I—Nonoperational	—	passed 0 or 1	—	5	5

[a] A child was placed in the Base Response category if he chose an alternative having the water parallel to the base eight out of eight times.
[b] CNP group not included.

Ss were classified for pretest and again for posttest performance. Tallies were made of *Ss* with higher posttest than pretest classifications against those with lower posttest classifications. A Wilcoxon matched-pairs signed-ranks test showed that if an *S* changed classification from pre- to post-test, he was more likely to change to a higher than to a lower classification

($Z = 4.8$, $p = .00006$). The groups that had the largest and significant percentage of Ss moving to a higher classification were the PM (67%), PNM (64%), V-WL-H (54%), and V-H (48%) groups. Whereas the perceptual training groups improved according to both criteria, the V-WL-H group improved by the classification analysis alone, and the V-WL group improved more than the controls by the score analysis.

With errorless performance as the criterion, the overall percentage of Ss who went from nonerrorless pretest performance to errorless posttest performance was 27 per cent. Of the 36 posttest concept attainers, a large proportion (83%) were classified as *partial-operational* (IIIA) on pretest. Viewed another way, 49 per cent of the pretest *partial-operationals* became *operational* on posttest compared to 30 per cent of the *transitionals*, 11 per cent of the *inconsistents*, and 0 per cent of the *base-response* and *non-operational* groups. Thus the procedures employed here produced errorless performance in only about one out of four children, and those children who did reach an *operational* level were most likely to have had some prior ability.

Form and Orientation

Piaget and Inhelder suggested that jars placed in a horizontal or vertical orientation should yield occasional success because of the coincidence of jar orientation with horizontal or vertical axes. The present data show (Table 3) that the vertical jars (top-up and top-down) yielded the fewest pretest errors (7%, 12%). The jars placed horizontally (facing left and right) were next in difficulty (35%, 27%). The most difficult were those placed on the oblique, with the upside-down orientations (both facing left and right) among them more difficult (69%, 63%) than those facing up (41%, 56%).

The difficulty with jars oriented upside-down may be related to the greater number of gravity choice errors made in that orientation. The largest number of gravity errors, based upon a classification of gravity responses, was made to the jars in the oblique upside-down orientation (facing left and right: 13%, 19%) compared with the right-side-up jars in the same oblique orientations (facing left and right: 6%, 5%).

DISCUSSION

The evidence shows that anticipation imagery indicated in water level representation was improved through training. Perceptual training, on the whole, was more effective than verbal training. Both perceptual training procedures yielded significantly larger posttest scores than the controls, according to both score improvement and stage level improvement criteria. One of the verbal methods, the water level program, led to significant

Table 3

Percentage of Ss Making Water Level Errors per Item (N = 133)

	(bottle)	(bottle)	(bottle)	(bottle)	(bottle)	(bottle)	(bottle)	(bottle)
Pretest	7	41 (89)[a]	35	69 (85)[a]	12	63	27	56
Posttest	5	37	17	50	5	44	17	42
Feurstein Study (N = 30)[c]								
Pretest	0	31	10	62	6	—	—	48
Posttest	0	24	3	48	6	—	—	34

	(flask)	(flask)	(flask)	(flask)	(flask)	(flask)	(flask)	(flask)
Transfer Test	2	44	27	69	10	55	29	62
Control[b]	0	57	29	52	9	62	33	67
Feurstein Study (N = 30)[c]								
Pretest	17.5	70	35.5	85	21	—	—	90
Posttest	7	60	14	78	7	—	—	67

[a] Percentages in parentheses are estimated from Smedslund's (1963) data (*N* = 27).
[b] *N* = 21. This group received only the transfer test—it is not elsewhere used in the analysis.
[c] We are grateful to Dr. Feurstein for making these preliminary data available.

gains over the control by the score criterion, and the water level–horizontal program combination led to more *S*s improving according to the classification criterion, as did the horizontal program itself.

Of the two perceptual training procedures, the one embodying anticipation imagery, motor response to figural representation, and visual confirmation (PM) was more successful than the method employing only anticipation imagery and visual confirmation (PNM), although the latter led to significant improvement as well. Success of these procedures indicates that when a child can develop an image of a complex object with at least a minimum of success, this image can be modified effectively by a confrontation with reality which leads to a more accurate representational schema. In general, the greater effectiveness of perceptual training suggests that water level representation is more dependent upon nonverbal than verbal mediational processes.

Among the verbal training procedures, the water level program was effective according to both criteria employed. The horizontal program led to stage level change that was significant alone and also when it followed water level principle instruction. It appears that both specific concept training (water level) and general concept training (horizontally) lead to improvement, although the evidence for the latter is weaker. Although verbal training led to significant improvement, the verbally transmitted information was not translated by most *S*s into a mediational system as effectively as the perceptual experience translated into nonverbal mediators (or schemata). In addition, there is confirmation of the Piaget and Inhelder assertion of a relationship between symbolic imagery and operativity, from the evidence that full operational performance was achieved with training only by *S*s with some measure of pretest success.

In the case of both perceptual and verbal training, there was no significant transfer to the round-bottomed flasks. This would be more of a paradox if Piaget and Inhelder's contention that round flasks should be easier to deal with than straight-sided vessels were true. Our data show that water level representation for round flasks is equal to or more difficult than for straight-sided flasks, and Feurstein's preliminary data indicate it to be more difficult (Table 3). We are in agreement with Piaget and Inhelder that round flasks do not provide the child with a ready reference system of spatial coordinates, but this offers no assurance that the child is thus forced to external references more than if he were dealing with straight-sided jars. Straight-sided jars provide a reference system with the attributes of verticality and horizontality fairly evident. In fact, *S* may be oriented, by their vertical and horizontal characteristics, to other plane surfaces, such as the tabletop. The round jars, which lack straight-line reference, may keep the *S*'s attention within the jar rather than lead him to the external axes.

The lack of transfer to a task that utilized the same principle, even if it were more difficult to deal with, is consistent with our findings for conservation training (Beilin, 1965). In an experiment testing the efficacy of various conservation training procedures, verbal rule instruction was the most effective training method used. The difference in cognitive functions studied, however, may account for the superiority of verbal training for conservation performance, that is, water level representation may rely more upon symbolic imagery than does a conservation task. On the other hand, the prior study demonstrated the limitation of verbal processes despite the superiority of verbal to nonverbal training methods. It was shown that the majority of children given the conceptual rule in verbal form were unable, as in the present instance, to use it in relevant tasks.

In regard to the influence of SES and race upon training, there were significant pretest differences between white and Negro *S*s and between middle- and lower-class *S*s. When operational *S*s were removed from the analysis, there were no significant posttest differences attributable to either SES or race—only an SES × race interaction was significant. This interaction resulted from the larger means in the lower-class white group than in the middle-class white group, a difference which is reversed for the Negro group means. This reversal is probably due to the disproportionally great withdrawal of middle-class white *S*s from the sample due to their successful pretest performance. This is reinforced by the indication that when pretest operational *S*s are combined with posttest operational *S*s there are again significant race differences ($p < .02$). The gains from training are least among lower-class Negro *S*s, although on the whole, training is equally effective for both Negroes and whites. Training, however, does not make for enough gains among Negroes to make up for pretest performance differences.

Greater difficulty in conceptualizing water levels in jars in an oblique orientation has been demonstrated. The greater difficulty in the oblique than horizontal and vertical orientations is consistent with findings for children (Rudel and Teuber, 1963) and for a variety of subhuman species (Mackintosh and Sutherland, 1963) in studies of perceptual discrimination. Whether the greater difficulty in dealing with the conceptualization of water levels with obliquely oriented jars is reducible to a perceptual process difficulty should be more fully investigated. The data suggest, however, that the differential representation problem is a conceptual one, albeit more nonverbal than verbal, since the Rudel study shows that by the age of 7–6 (the age of the sample reported on here) most children were able to discriminate between oblique lines oriented to the left and right, whereas 3- to 4-year-olds could not.

REFERENCES

Beilin, H. (1965). Learning and operational convergence in logical thought development. *J. exp. child Psychol.*, 2, 317–339.

Inhelder, B. (1965). Operational thought and symbolic imagery. In P. H. Mussen (Ed.), European research in cognitive development. *Monogr. Soc. Res. Child Develpm.*, 30, 4–18.

Kramer, C. Y. (1956). Extension of multiple range tests to group means with unequal numbers of replications. *Biometrics*, 12, 307–310.

Mackintosh, J., and N. S. Sutherland (1963). Visual discrimination by the goldfish: the orientation of rectangles. *Anim. Behav.*, 11, 135–141.

Piaget, J., and B. Inhelder (1956; orig. French ed., 1948). *The child's conception of space.* London: Routledge.

Rudel, R. G., and H. L. Teuber (1963). Discrimination of direction of line in children. *J. comp. physiol. Psychol.*, 56, 892–898.

Smedslund, J. (1963). The effect of observation on children's representation of the spatial orientation of a water surface. *J. genet. Psychol.*, 102, 195–201.

Vernon, P. E. (1965). Environmental handicaps and intellectual development. *Brit. J. educ. Psychol.*, 35, Pt. I, 1–12; Pt. II, 13–22.

Warner, W. L., M. Meeker, and K. Eells (1949). *Social class in America.* Chicago: Science Research Assoc.

AN EVALUATION OF PART OF PIAGET'S THEORY

G. A. Kohnstamm[1]

THE PURPOSE OF OUR STUDY

We Saw that:

(1) The quantification of inclusion relations—which means the quantitative comparing of two classes A and B in which one (B) contains the other (A)—is considered by Piaget to be the best criterion for diagnosing

---

[1] [The introductory comments include a detailed discussion of the Morf study cited in Kohnstamm's bibliography. Since Morf's findings are briefly reviewed by Kohnstamm and by Smedslund in this chapter, it is omitted here.] I.E.S./F.H.H.

Reprinted with the permission of the author and North-Holland Publishing Company, Amsterdam, from *Acta Psychologica*, 1963, 21, 313–315. This article is a shortened version of a doctoral thesis. The subject is more thoroughly treated in the book *Teaching children to solve a Piagetian problem of class inclusion*, North-Holland Publishing Co., Amsterdam, 1967 (in English). Two coworkers of Piaget have published an answer (in French) in *Acta Psychologica*, 1966, 25 (5). A translation and a discussion of this Genevan answer form part of the above mentioned book. It also contains the results of a Canadian extension and replication study and the results of new experiments done by the present author.

the presence or absence of a certain stage of development in children's thinking: the stage of concrete logical operations.

(2) 75% of children reach this stage by their seventh or eighth year, thanks to spontaneous development.

(3) Various studies have shown that between 10 and 40% of 5-year-olds can deal quantitatively and spontaneously with inclusion relations.

(4) This development is brought about, according to Piaget, by a long period of interaction between the child's own actions (which become thought operations via internalization) and his environment.

(5) One of Piaget's co-workers, Morf, tried to train children who had not already done so to reach the above mentioned stage of being able to quantify inclusion relations.

(6) Of the three techniques he used the last produced enough success to teach 7 of the 30 children (aged 4–7) to discover and then apply the knack.[2]

(7) Piaget and Morf created the impression that because of this the possibilities of *"l'apprentissage"* as far as logical operations is concerned were exhausted.

The Main Purpose of Our Study

With these facts in mind we thought it would be useful to try to teach, in a short time, the majority of a group of 5-year-olds the skill of comparing quantitatively the two classes A and B by using a completely different learning technique from Morf's, thereby demonstrating that:

(1) More can be effected by "learning" than Piaget's school maintains possible.

(2) The quantification of inclusion relations (as shown by correct answers to questions like: Are there more A or more B? and the reverse) is of doubtful value, if a criterion is sought for a certain stage in general thought development, supposed to be independent of chance environment variables. Because a child gaining control over this criterion need not necessarily have reached the complete thought stage characterized by a group of operations.

(3) Piaget's equilibration theory would be confronted with an irreconcilable sort of learning process.

Besides these three main points there are two sub-purposes.

---

[2] [The three techniques Morf used were as follows: (1) collections of objects were presented simultaneously and the child was asked to verify if there was more A than B; (2) inclusion relations were created visibly with strings and chalk (for example, boxers, dogs, domestic animals, animals) and the child was taught to include superordinate classes; (3) children were trained to see objects as belonging to two or more classes simultaneously—a procedure like one of those involved in the Sigel, Roeper, and Hooper (1966) series. It is with this third technique that Morf had some success.] I.E.S./F.H.H.

Sub-purposes of the Study

(4) Piaget and Inhelder maintain that in spontaneous development some inclusion operations develop considerably later for some material (animal pictures) than for other material (flowers and flower pictures). These authors give a hypothetical theory to account for these differences based on the theory of the interiorization of actions: the interiorization of familiar actions occurs sooner than that of those seldom performed. Consequently the interiorized thought actions are dealt with more easily if the child has often been in contact with the material (for it is these very actions which are able to be internalized) than if he has had little contact with the material.

We want to see if we can trace any of these differences in our study. If Piaget is right one can expect 5-year-olds to experience more difficulty in applying inclusion operations to classes little familiar from their own dealings.

(5) Also in accordance with this interpretation Piaget and Inhelder see a still greater difficulty in applying inclusion operations to objects not present in concreto.

A child of 8 years, 6 months can apply the inclusion operations (perfectly correctly) to flowers on a table in front of him, but "We only had to ask him to apply the same to primroses and flowers found in the woods to have to begin all over again."

We want to see if we can trace any of these differences in our own study. One can expect 5-year-olds to have difficulty in applying inclusion operations to purely verbal problems, that is, without material being present to which these thought actions can be applied.

EXPERIMENTAL DESIGN

Broad Survey

The experiment was carried out with 60 5-year-old nursery school children. They were divided into 3 groups of 20 which were as comparable as possible in age (in months), sex, and intelligence (according to Pintner-Cunningham).[3]

Every child was experimented with separately. There was only one Experimenter (E) (writer of this article).

The first group (group I) was trained in dealing with the inclusion relations of solely verbally presented classes. The effects of the instruc-

---

[3] We used this test in order to obtain quickly a comparable performance of all *S*s on a standard test of cognitive development and not because we had so much faith in the value of the thus acquired IQ as an indicator of "intelligence."

tion was studied during the first session using the same sort of verbal problems.

The second group (group II) was trained in dealing with the inclusion relations of classes consisting of flower pictures, animal, people, vehicle pictures, etc. The effect of the instruction was studied during the first session by using both the same sort (pictures) of problems and those of group I (verbal).

The third group (group III) was trained in dealing with the relations of classes consisting of Lego-building blocks of various colors and sizes. The effect of the instruction was studied twice: (1) during the first session using both the same sort of problems (Lego-blocks) and those of group II (pictures); (2) three weeks later, using all sorts of problems (blocks, pictures, and verbal).

A session seldom lasted for more than half an hour. Protocols were made as complete as possible by E. A tape-recording was made of group III, session 2.

The Composition of the Group

SOCIAL BACKGROUND   The children were all pupils at a Municipal Nursery school in Amsterdam. Most of the children in this school come from the socio-economic middle group. Information about father, occupation, etc., was not available.

AGE   The age composition of the three groups was as follows:

Table 1

Survey of the Ages[a] of the Ss

	N	Mean	Range
Group I	20	5;8	5;1–6;0
Group II	20	5;7	5;2–6;0
Group III	20	5;7	5;1–6;1
Total	60	5;7	5;1–6;1

[a] The age given is that on the day of the experiment; if 15 or more days had passed since the child was exactly 5 years and x months, these 15 or more days were reckoned as a full month.

SEX   In every group there were 10 boys and 10 girls.

INTELLIGENCE   The children were tested in groups of five with the Pintner-Cunningham test, a non-verbal test for preschool children. The I.Q. of the three groups was composed as follows:

Table 2

Survey of the Pintner-Cunningham I.Q. of the Ss

	N	Mean	Range	s
Group I	20	105	94–125	10,1
Group II	20	104	76–139	11,2
Group III	20	104	81–131	15,0
Total	60	104	76–139	12,2

The Experimental Situation and the Attitude of E

THE EXPERIMENTAL SITUATION   The children sat a low table. E sat at a table pushed against this. E handed out material and recorded answers in front of him on the table. When coming for the individual study the children already knew E; he had had them in groups of five for the intelligence test. They also saw him frequently taking children from and bringing them back to the class. . . .

THE ATTITUDE OF E   As the purpose of the study was that E had to do his utmost to teach the Ss the thought operation, he could dispense with the usual neutrality of the experimental psychologist.

THE STUDY OF GROUP I

Material

Survey of the leading questions used:
(The questions were all in the form of: "In the whole world are there more .... or more ....?")

(1) More mummies or more women.
(2) More boys or more children.
(3) More people or more men.
(4) More pigeons or more birds.
(5) More animals or more cows.
(6) More dresses or more clothes.
(7) More men or more policemen.
(8) More things to ride or more bicycles.
(9) More bread or more things to eat.
(10) More toys or more dolls.
(11) More fruit or more apples.
(12) More lions or more animals.

(13) More roses or more flowers.
(14) More cars or more Volkswagens.
(15) More daddies or more men.
(16) More girls or more children.
(17) More tulips or more flowers.
(18) More people or more women.
(19) More birds or more sparrows.
(20) More dogs or more animals.
(21) More trousers or more clothes.
(22) More things to ride or more cars.
(23) More water or more things you can drink.
(24) More sweets or more gum drops.
(25) More animals or more birds.

Procedure

EXPLANATION METHOD   E indicated any wrong answers[4] (more A) explaining why they were wrong, in terms that the child could understand.

We gave the following explanation in a talk with the child: "You have to say that there are more B because A are *also* B. A and A′ are *all* B and so there are always more B." Example:

Experimenter:	*Subject:*
(5a) More animals or more cows? No, that's not right. You're supposed to say that there are more animals, because cows are also animals. Cows, horses, sheep, dogs and cats are *all* animals and so there are always more animals.	More cows.
(6a) More dresses or more clothes? No, that's not right, etc.	More dresses.
(7a) More men or more policemen? Yes, that's right, why?	More men. Because there aren't so many policemen, they're only on the street.
No, you're supposed to say that there are more men because policemen are also men. Don't you remember?	Yes.
Now, more men or more policemen?	More men.
Yes, very good, why?	Because men er . . . . . because policemen are also men.
Very good, do you understand? etc.	

E usually continued giving the explanation until he thought he had exhausted the child's possibilities.

---

[4] Morf in his discovery method never tells the child if an answer is wrong and seldom if it is right. Here too is shown that Morf left untouched the most important aid to "learning."

Scoring

An answer was only considered correct if the child answered "more
.... (B)"; answers such as "both" were not counted as correct.

In giving the explanation one rule was always strictly maintained:
the child first had to give an answer to the leading question so that it
could be scored. Only when a scorable answer had been given was the
explanation of that item begun.

If the leading question was repeated during or after the explanation the
answers were not scored again. Only the first answer to the first leading
question of each item was ever scored.

Answers to non-leading questions (why? etc.) were not scored. These
non-leading questions were asked to gain insight into the thought processes
behind the answers to the leading questions.

The percentage of each subject's correct answers to the 25 leading
questions was calculated.

Results of Group I

No child gave from the start correct answers to the leading questions.
After 4 items one child gave correct answers spontaneously. E gave a
varying amount of explanation to the remaining 19 children.

The children were divided into three sub-groups, "success," "partial
success," and "no success," as can be seen in Table 3.

Table 3

*How the Children of Group I Were Divided
in Three Sub-Groups according to Their Learning Results
(Row 2) and What other Characteristics
These Groups Had (Row 1, 3, 4)*

		"success"	"partial success"	"no success"
1	Number of Ss	6	7	7
2	Mean percentage correct answers to all leading questions	89%	62%	33%
	Range	93%–79%	70%–53%	48%–23%
3	Mean age	5;10	5;6	5;6
	Range	5;7–5;12	5;4–5;11	5;1–5;10
4	Mean I.Q.	106	103	106
	Range	96–114	90–119	95–125

Into which sub-group an *S* was placed depended not only on the percentage of correct answers but also on his account of them and of the total impression made during the protocol.

The average percentage of correct answers is, therefore, not very informative because it does not indicate a possible learning process in which faults made at first were later eliminated.

Thus one *S* with a total of 79% correct answers had a total of 95% correct answers *after* the learning period.

While forming the sub-groups we took into consideration the influence of the total percentage to prevent any misinterpretation of the learning process: the six *S*s in the "success" column achieved practically 100% correct answers toward the end of their questionnaires.

The remaining mistakes of this "success" group were mainly caused by concentration collapses or by the relative difficulty of some items. Thus item 11, "more fruit or more apples," appeared to be insurmountably difficult even for children who had answered 20 similar questions faultlessly. The concept "fruit" is too unfamiliar at this age it seems.

Question 23 "more water or more things you can drink" evidently presented difficulty because of its ambiguity: one of the children pointed out that there is more water you "cannot" drink than that you "can" drink.

Thus a child did not need to have a 100% correct result to be placed in the group possessing the skill of being able to compare in size two classes of which one contains the other (but not the reverse) for it is, of course, a self-evident stipulation that the child must be familiar with the classes.

We are not going to discuss the group of seven who had partial success; we cannot say that at the end of the session this group commanded a stable method for solving these problems. In this they are comparable to the group of seven *S*s to whom we were not able to teach even the rudiments of the problem.

Summary of the Most Important Results of Group I

(1) A number of questions in the form of "In the whole world are there more A (or B) or more B (or A)?" were put to 20 five-year-olds.

(2) We were able to teach six of them to answer the purely verbal leading questions correctly.

(3) The great diversity of the classes, as well as the impossibility of a child guessing time and again at random the correct one of the two classes presented[5] by blindly applying a drummed-in principle, enables

---

[5] Here we expose ourselves to possible critics who might say that we merely taught the children to recite mechanically a drummed-in lesson, which would make our results of a lesser quality than the skill observed by Piaget in the 7–8 age group. We shall return to this point.

us to say that these six children had learned to compare in size two given (familiar) classes verbally presented.

The restriction must be made about this size-comparison that it took place only in the form of "more A (or B) or more B (or A)" which happens to be the form used by Piaget and Morf.

(4) The six achieving the desired result were older than the rest (by an average of 4 months) but not more intelligent (according to Pintner-Cunningham).

Comparison of These Results with Morf's

(1) Morf never asked verbal questions only.

(2) In the study of the quantification of inclusion relations as done by Piaget and Morf there was always a percentage of Ss (10–40%) who apparently possessed this skill spontaneously.

In our group I no child gave correct answers from the start; so either our children were less bright or our problems were more difficult than theirs.

(3) The group I results are not much better than the learning results acquired in a completely different way by Morf's discovery method with concrete material (7 out of 30).

(4) We were not able to demonstrate with group I that the development of inclusion relations described by Piaget can be more greatly accelerated by our learning technique than was already known from Morf's results.

THE STUDY OF GROUP II

Material

(1) Some of the pictures of people, animals, food, etc., used by this group are reproduced in black and white in the illustration.

(2) As well as these pictures, purely verbal problems were presented as in group I.

Purely verbal questions used for group II: (The same form as those of group I.)
  (1) More boys or more children.
  (2) More cars or more Volkswagens.
  (3) More sweets or more gum drops.
  (4) More trousers or more clothes.
  (5) More lions or more animals.
  (6) More roses or more flowers.
  (7) More mothers or more women.
  (8) More pigeons or more birds.

(9) More animals or more dogs.
(10) More clothes or more dresses.
(11) More birds or more animals.
(12) More ticket collectors or more men.
(13) More children or more girls.
(14) More schools or more nursery schools.

Procedure

The following were consecutively presented to the children:
(1) Two sample pictures (sample 1 and 2) about which many questions were asked.
(2) Ten pictures (practice phase).
(3) Ten pictures (test phase).
(4) A list of purely verbal problems (14 leading questions).
As intensively as possible, an explanation of points (1) and (2) was given by E in a similar way as to group I's verbal problems.

An example of the pictures protocol will clarify this:
S Jan (5;6) (I.Q. 106) (see illustration, picture of boys and girls).

Are there more girls or more children on this card?	More children.
How many girls?	Three.
How many children?	Two.
The girls then, aren't they children?	Yes.
Point to all the children.	(does so)
Point to all the girls.	(does so)
Now, are there more girls or more children?	More girls.
No, have a good look, are there, etc.	Just as many.
No, that's not right you know. Here are three girls but they are children too, do you see? *They're all children.* The boys are children and the girls are children too. There are two boys and three girls and they are all children.	
Now which are there more of, more girls or more children?	Children.
Yes and why?	Because... er... because...
They are *all* children! The boys *and* the girls, do you remember?	

After the ten pictures of the practice phase, ten pictures were presented for which in principle no more explanation was given (test phase). This was done to see if the child could continue to apply the acquired skill, while getting no support from E. We deviated from this principle with some children and consequently did not place them in the group who had learned the knack (the "success" group).

ARE THERE ON THIS CARD MORE . . . . . . OR MORE . . . . . . ?

PEOPLE OR WOMEN

AUTOMOBILES OR VEHICLES

CAKES OR THINGS TO EAT

ANIMALS OR HORSES

TULIPS OR FLOWERS

"FLY-THINGS" OR BIRDS

THINGS TO EAT WITH OR FORKS

PANTS OR CLOTHES

GIRLS OR CHILDREN

Scoring

This was the same as for group I.

Group II Results

In Table 4 it can be seen that the number of correct answers in the test phase fell easily into three groups, a "success," a "partial success," and a "no success" group.

Table 4

Group II Results in Practice (Row 2),
Test Phase (Row 3) and Verbal Phase (Row 4);
Division in Three Sub-Groups is Based Upon
Results in Test Phase

		"success"	*"partial success"*	*"no success"*
1	Number of *Ss*	8	5	7
2	Mean number of correct answers to the 10 leading questions of the practice phase	5,5	3,6	1,3
	Range	8–2	6–2	2–0
3	The same to the 10 leading questions of the test phase	9,9	5,8	1,0
	Range	10–9	7–5	3–0
4	Mean percentage of correct answers to a purely verbal phase	91%	51%	36%
	Range	100%–80%	87%–30%	50%–20%

Of the seven children who had to be placed in the "no success" group, four answered all the leading questions wrongly in the test phase, two gave two correct answers, and one gave three correct answers.

There is a clear explanation for this perhaps amazing result which we should like to report here (actually one would expect a child grasping absolutely nothing and therefore just guessing to have about as many correct as incorrect answers):

A child with no understanding of inclusion relations always (and only) compares A with A' and never A with B or A' with B. To the question "more people or more women" he answers "more women," "because there are only two people," thinking that the B name refers to A'.

If sub-class A always contains more elements than sub-class A', as was the case in most of our items, the non-grasping child is drawn, as it were, to the wrong answer. The amounts of part A are misleadingly large, and if the child cannot see that the whole B is still larger he always chooses in a comparison of "more...... or more......" the largest part.

This explanation was given by Inhelder and Piaget (1959) and seems to us to be fully justified.

The three groups formed from the learning results have the following characteristics apart from the learning differences.

We see that there is no question of an age difference within the group which was the case in group I (average of 4 months).

But there is in group II a difference in I.Q. between the "success" children and the rest of the group.

This result was not present in group I. There, no difference in I.Q. existed between the "success" children and the others.

Summary of Group II Results

(1) More than 20 pictures were presented to 20 five-year-old children, in which were constantly changing classes A and B (A larger than A' and smaller than B). At every picture the question was asked "Are there more A (or B) or more B (or A)?" The child always had to produce the answer to this question himself. Only after having answered did he get an explanation (if necessary). This was made as intensive as possible.

Table 5

How the Children of Group II Were Divided
in Three Sub-Groups according to Their
Learning Results (Row 2) and What Other Characteristics
These Groups Had (Row 1, 3, 4)

		"success"	"partial success"	"no success"
1	Number of Ss	8	5	7
2	Number of correct answers to the 10 leading questions of the test phase (range)	10–9	7–5	3–0
3	Mean age	5;7	5;7	5;7
	Range	5;2–5;11	5;2–5;10	5;2–5;12
4	Mean I.Q.	112	97	101
	Range	97–139	89–106	86–122

One child answered nearly all the leading questions correctly from the start. We were able to teach 7 other children in the first half of the study (practice phase) to grasp the problem to such an extent that in the second part of the study (test phase) they gave a faultless performance. Moreover they were able to answer almost perfectly a series of leading questions without further practice when the classes referred to were not present in concreto.

(2) Thus we were able to teach 8 of the 20 children to answer the leading questions correctly.

(3) The dissimilarity of classes, the constantly changing number of elements in the classes A and B, and the constantly changing proportions of A and B made it impossible that these children were merely blindly reciting a drummed-in lesson when solving problems which were constantly changing (see footnotes [4] and [5]).

We shall support this with some arguments:

(a) The ability to apply unhesitatingly the picture learning result to the purely verbal phase questions is clearly a *transfer* of the learning result.

(b) The discontinuity in the learning process (how abruptly all mistakes could disappear was shown by the "success" children in the test-phase) indicated an abrupt moment of insight into the problem and not to a gradually increasing rewarded reaction as might be expected from a conditioning process. In fact it is hard for us to see how, with these problems and the way in which they were presented (in continually changing guise)[6] a learning result like this could be obtained by mere conditioning.

(c) Eight of the children were completely successful, five were partially successful, but seven were not successful at all, although the amount of training of the latter was the same if not more. Were it merely a question of learning "parrot-fashion" and not a question of active behavior probably consisting of some restructuring of the perceptual field, then there would not have been such a clear division between the eight with total success and the seven total failures after an equally intensive learning program.

We may say then, that eight of the children learned to compare in size two given (if familiar) classes of which one (B) contained the other one (A), both in situations where the classes were present in concreto and where they were absent.

(4) The eight children achieving the desired result were not older than the others but they were more intelligent (according to Pintner-Cunningham).

Comparison of the Results with Those of Piaget and Morf

(1) The picture material was in many ways similar to the material used by Morf in his learning attempt.

[6] This too is a defense against the possible criticism that our learning result resembles an irreversible S-R connection and is of inferior quality to the skill acquired by spontaneous development.

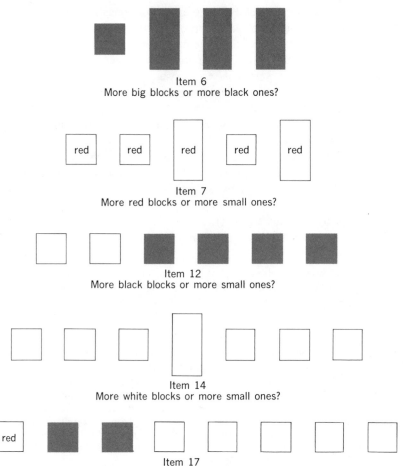

Figure 1 Examples of Lego-block material. The items are shown as from above and are printed at one-half of the actual size (for Items 1 and 2 see below, Figures 2 and 3).

(2) In their study there was always a percentage of children who apparently possessed this skill spontaneously. In our group II only one child gave correct answers from the start.

(3) The learning result of group II is not much better than the learning result acquired in a completely different way by Morf's discovery method using similar material (7 out of 30).

(4) We were not able to demonstrate with group II that the development of logical inclusion operations can be accelerated more by our learning technique than was already known from Morf's study.

(5) One of our learning results with group II, conflicts with one of the opinions of Piaget and Inhelder borne out of their observations: our eight

"success" children were able unhesitatingly (and almost faultlessly) to apply what they had learned with concrete material to purely verbal problems.

THE STUDY OF GROUP III

Material

This group was experimented with twice, with an interval of three weeks between.

We began the first session with the blocks hitherto unused (see Fig. 1), then followed the pictures used in group II.

In the second session purely verbal problems were presented as well as the blocks and the pictures.

Procedure (First Session)

Here is a fragment of protocol to give an impression of the lesson method:

S José (5; 9) (I. Q. 97), (we first explained that there were "large" blocks and "small" ones, and that only three colors were used: red, white, and black).

(1) On this card [Fig. 2] are there more red blocks
   or more small ones?   More small.
   How many small ones are there then?   Two.
   And how many red blocks?   One.
   Aren't they red then? (points to small red
      blocks)   Yes they are.
   How many red blocks are there then?   (counts) Three.
   What is the most, the red or the small?   The small.
   How many small are there?   Two.
   And how many red?   One... er... three.
   What is more, three or two?   Three is more.
   Yes, and what are there more of here, more
      red or more small?   More small.
   What is the most, three red blocks or two
      small blocks?   Two small.

Figure 2

(2) On this card [Fig. 3] . . . etc., more large or
   more white?   More white.
   How many white blocks are there?   Two.
   And how many large blocks are there?   Three.
   Very good! Now which is the most,
      three large, one, two, three (E points) or
      two white?   (Long pause) Two white.
   No, that's not right. Look, there are one,
      two white blocks and one, two, three large
      blocks, and three is more than two, isn't it?
      Three large is more than two (points) white,
      do you see? So there are more large, one,
      two, three, than white because there are
      only two white, but there are three large.
      *They are all large and only two of them
      are white*, do you see?

Figure 3

The material consisted of 18 problems. Usually we began item 10 when the child had shown in the previous items that he had mastered the principle. That is, items 1 to 9 were repeated until the principle had been grasped. We did this because the explanation was easier for items with fewer blocks.

After the blocks came a picture series; first five practice pictures and then a test series which was almost the same as for group II.

Scoring

The same as for group I.

Results of the First Session

Learning by means of Lego blocks proceeded very well. Again, scoring as right or wrong the first answer to the first leading question of each item, we counted the total number of mistakes made by 18 subjects[7] at every item of the block series and presented them in a graph (see Fig. 4).

---

[7] No protocol was recorded for 2 of the 20 children; one could be taught absolutely nothing and with the other the learning process had a normal course.

Referring to the graph it must be remembered that items 1 to 9 were repeated until the principle was grasped and established. The number of wrong answers *at first presentation* of the item is given in the graph. After the first one new presentations of that item followed (i.e. of items 1 to 9) until E thought that the highest possible level had been reached with these easier items (which consisted of at most five blocks).

However, E did continue to explain every wrong answer during the whole series (even after item 9) trying to stabilize the acquired principle.

The few mistakes made on the final items cannot be attributed to two or three *S*s who kept on making mistakes right up to the end; *none* of the 18 *S*s made more than one mistake in the last five items!

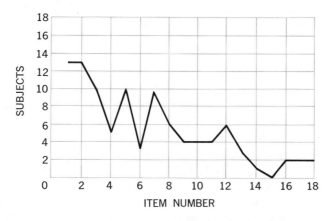

Figure 4 Compiled Lego-blocks learning graph for 18 children. Number of wrong answers of 18 *S*s to first leading question per item. Example: of 18 *S*s 13 gave a wrong answer to Item 1, 13 to Item 2, 10 to Item 3, and so on.

In Table 6 we compare the number of *S*s making 5, 4, 3, 2, 1, and 0 mistakes in the first five items of the block practice and in the last five items.

It is clear that all 18 *S*s could, by the end of the block practice, by and large, answer all the leading questions correctly. Here we might add the child for whom there is no recorded protocol but there is a note saying "went well." One child remains with whom the block method failed.

It must be remembered that the real learning phase (items 1 to 9) took no longer than 15 minutes and frequently only 5.

From the above survey it can also be seen that only one *S* made no mistake from the start, and we must assume that he had mastered the skill on solving these problems before the experiment began.

Table 6

Comparison of the First and the Last Five Items
of the Block Practice

	Number of subjects who gave wrong answers	
	first five items	last five items
5 (Items wrong)	1 (subjects)	0 (subjects)
4	4	0
3	6	0
2	6	0
1	0	7
0	1	11

Example: One *S* answered all leading questions wrongly at his introduction to the first five items.

Summary of the Results Obtained with the Lego Blocks

Every child except one learned to answer the leading questions correctly although this was more difficult for some than for others. This took place in various situations which we think became progressively more difficult although always consisting of the same simple elements.

As these results could not, because of the simplified learning material, supply us with sufficient certainty that these *S*s possessed the general skill studied by Piaget and Morf (the comparing in size of two classes A and B (A being contained in B)), we had to investigate what use the acquired principle was when different material was presented.

The Picture Test

To familiarize them with the material the children were first presented with five practice pictures.

Considering these five items as an interval phase we calculated the number of correct first answers to the leading questions on these items separately (see Table 7).

The effect of the block practice can clearly be seen from the third row of figures in this table.

Of the twenty children sixteen were placed in the "success" group, three in the "partial success" group, and one in the "no success" group. (In groups I and II the numbers were respectively 6;7;7 and 8;5;7.)

Just as in group II, we considered 9 out of 10 correct answers enough reason to place a subject in the "success" group. All the more reason when it was apparent from group II that *S*s with no insight have an average of only one or two correct answers because of the above mentioned "error attraction" (see Table 4).

In Table 8 we compare the results of this test with the group II results.

Table 7

Group III Results in Interval Phase (Row 2) and
Test Phase (Row 3); Division in Three Sub-Groups
Is Based upon Results in Test Phase

		"success"	*"partial success"*	*"no success"*
1	Number of Ss	16	3	1
2	Mean number of correct answers to the 5 leading questions of the interval phase	4,0	2,7	1
	Range	5–2	3–2	—
3	The same to the 10 leading questions of the test phase	9,7	5,0	3
	Range	10–9	5–5	—

Table 8

Comparison of Results of Groups II and III with
a Picture Test of Almost the Same Composition

Number of Ss in the three sub-groups:	*Group II* *(after picture practice)*	*Group III* *(after block practice)*
In sub-group:		
"success"	8 (Subjects)	16 (Subjects)
"partial success"	5	3
"no success"	7	1

Procedure of the Second Session

After a period of 17–23 days a number of children of group III were studied for the second time.

This was mainly to discover:

(1) If the principle learned during the first session had remained intact during a period in which it had not been practiced (clearly, a five-year-old needs this skill neither at home nor at school).

Considering that we were not expecting any of them to have retained this skill our next question was:

(2) How long would it take to reteach the operation? We did not expect this to be long.

(3) We also wanted to study in this group the transition from the pictures to the verbal problems for which there had been no time earlier.

The Results of the Second Session

Ten of the sixteen "success" children were used (chosen at random); the results were then so clear that we left out the remaining six children. We then restudied three of the four subjects in the "partial success" group. The one child in the "no success" group was sick.

Here Are the Results:

(1) The ten "success" children:

The second session began with a short retention test consisting of 5 pictures which had been part of the test series of session I. Of the 10 "success" children 9 answered all the leading questions correctly and without hesitation. One child gave 3 wrong answers.

These unexpectedly good results amazed us. Effortlessly and frequently accompanied by laughter, correct answers flowed from the 5-year-olds. The tape recordings made of both sessions show clearly with how much ease the answers were given. Obviously the children had not lost the skill in the interim and were able to reapply it immediately.

The original repetition of the block practice planned for this session which was supposed to rapidly re-establish the learning result was completely dispensed with; the few items tried with it yielded nothing but correct answers.

Strangely enough the one child who had answered 3 of the 5 leading questions wrongly now answered immediately and effortlessly correctly the 7 block items presented to him.

As a consequence of these findings we usually followed up with a picture test consisting of 5 pictures hitherto unknown to the Ss. Nine of the 10 "success" children answered immediately all the leading questions on this test correctly. One child made one mistake. Again a big success.

(2) Before reporting the results of a further study (purely verbal problems) we shall follow the three "partial success" children in their second learning attempt. These three now gave each 5 correct and 5 wrong answers to the picture test questions. Two of them continued with a follow-up test in which both got 65% correct results. We immediately began a repetition of the block practice with these three children. After this another 5 picture items were presented to them as well as the

pictures already mentioned (2×5), so that in all they were presented with 15 pictures.

Of these children who, a few weeks earlier, had made many mistakes, two now answered *all* leading questions correctly. One child gave four wrong answers.

And with this, the number to whom we had taught, the skill rose from 16 to 18.

(3) The results of a series of purely verbal questions:

Without any further preparation the children from group III, session II, began a series of purely verbal problems carried out in the same way as . . . in group II. All the "success" children (18) got high percentages of correct answers here ($> 80\%$).

Summary of the Results of Group III (Both Sessions)

(1) After practicing with Lego blocks 20 5-year-old children had, as well as a few samples, 10 pictures presented to them on which were continually changing sorts of classes.

(2) The large variety of classes, the continually alternating proportions of A and B, the continually alternating elements in the classes, make it possible for us to say that we were able to teach 16 of the 5-year-olds to compare in size two given (if familiar) classes in which one (B) contains the other (A).

(3) In comparison with group II it was apparent that the block material had a much greater learning effect than the picture material (both verified in the same way).

(4) The learning result was still present in full strength after a 2–3 week period at a test consisting of 5 old and 5 new pictures. Thus *relearning* was not necessary.

(5) Two of the 3 children mentioned in (1) who only answered half of the leading questions correctly at the first session achieved at the second one after a bit more training a 100% good result. Thus the number in the success group increased from 16 to 18.

Comparison of the Group III Results with Those of Piaget and Morf

(1) In their studies there was always a percentage of children (10-40%) who already possessed the skill spontaneously. In group III we found only one child who answered correctly from the start.

(2) Morf eliminated at a pre-selection 30% of his Ss because they were unable to grasp certain elementary points of the test. In our study we used all available children.

(3) The group of 30 Ss with whom Morf finally experimented was, according to him, composed as follows:

4–5 years	5–6 years	6–7 years	total
9	13	8	30

Presumably this group consisted of children of average capacity, the top layer (spontaneous success) and the bottom layer ("échec aux épreuves préalables") both having been eliminated. Considering the intelligence of our group we assume that it was not more talented than Morf's.

(4) Morf achieved the desired learning result with 7 of the 30 children; it is not reported to which age group they belonged. In our third group (Morf's was also his third group) first 16 and then 18 of the 20 children got the desired result.

Even when we deduct the children younger than ours from the total number of children used by Morf in his third study (the nine 4- to 5-year-olds, assuming that 4–5 means < 5;0), while assuming that none of his "success" children were in this group, so that his success proportion increases from 7 to 30 in a 4- to 7-year-old age group to 7–21 in a 5- to 7-year-old age group, then the difference between his success proportion and ours remains still very significant. What is more, a considerable number of his Ss were older than ours.

(5) The quality of our learning results was certainly not inferior to that of Morf's; being able to switch easily from concrete to purely verbal problems and the retaining of the principle for several weeks are quality tests not carried out by Morf.[8]

A HYPOTHESIS TESTED

. . . We wrote this about one of the sub-purposes of our study: "Piaget and Inhelder maintain that in spontaneous development some inclusion operations develop considerably later for some material (animal pictures) than for other material (flowers and flower pictures). These authors give a hypothetical theory to account for these differences, based on the theory of the internalization of actions. The interiorization of familiar actions occurs sooner than that of those seldom performed. Consequently the interiorized thought actions are dealt with more easily if the child has often been in contact with the material (for it is these very actions which are able to be internalized) than if he has had little contact with the material. We want to see if we can trace any of these differences in our study. If Piaget is right one can expect 5-year-olds to experience difficulty in applying inclusion operations to classes little familiar from their own dealings."

We now wonder if our study has shown that some (less familiar) classes present more difficulty than others, i.e. whether a child whom we

---

[8] On top of this we presented very many more sorts of classes than Morf did.

try to teach to compare in size two classes is able to do this with one kind of class but not with another.

At least we think that the hypothesis stated by Piaget to explain the age differences found in the spontaneous development of the operation may be changed in this way in our study where we only had the 5-year-old group at our disposal.

Of course here we must keep two things separate: a child may often deal with some classes and not with others, yet be very familiar with *the names of both sorts* of classes. He can, for instance be very familiar (carrying out actions etc.) with flowers and not with animals and yet be very familiar with the *names of both* classes, knowing what elements belong to which classes. On the other hand, he does not need to know all the classifications and names used by adults and older children for things with which he has to deal every day such as "furniture" or "provisions." *Thus the two sorts, an action- and a name-familiarity, are (up to a point) independent of one another.*

Piaget claims that action familiarity is far more important than name familiarity, and not only in this special case where certain operations have to be applied to various classes, but also in the general development of child thought.

Language is certainly, according to him, an indispensable factor for the completion of thought structure, but has definitely not that dominating influence on the thought development of the 5-year-old child which many other investigators attribute to it.

With which classes, then, are 5-year-olds familiar from personal action and with which not?

Let us first compare those classes in which the differences mentioned have in fact been observed by Piaget and Inhelder. They are the animals and the flowers.[9]

The material most corresponding with Piaget's were our pictures.

A survey of the percentages of correct answers to various leading flower- and animal-questions taken from several sections of the study is found on page 418.

This data shows that there is no reason to suppose that our children had more difficulty with the animal- than with the flower-questions.

Let us now examine the situation where we ourselves find differences in the degree of familiarity 5-year-olds have with certain material from personal experience.

Here again we find no support for the hypothesis proposed by Piaget and Inhelder.

With these samples we let the matter drop for we know that none of our results, with either the pictures or the talks, either the "success" children

---

[9] Though it seems doubtful to us to say that 5-year-olds have more action familiarity with flowers than with animals.

Table 9

Percentages of Correct Answers to Animal- and Flower-Questions (Picture Material)

Group II *Practice phase* (N = 20)[10]		
item 2. More animals or more cats.	25%	*Percentage of correct answers to:*
item 4. More flowers or more roses.	40%	*animal questions 33%*
item 5. More monkeys or more animals.	25%	*flower questions 43%*
item 9. More flowers or more tulips.	45%	
item 10. More sparrows or more birds.	50%	

Group II *Test phase*		
item 16. More animals or more horses.	60%	
item 18. More flowers or more tulips.	55%	*Percentage of correct answers to:*
item 19. More lions or more animals.	65%	*animal questions 62%*
item 23. More crocuses or more flowers.	55%	*flower questions 55%*
item 24. More birds or more ducks.	60%	

Group III *Interval phase* *and Test phase* *(after block practice)*		
item 18. More hyacinths or more flowers.	85%	
item 25. More kittens or more animals.	80%	
item 5. More animals or more monkeys.	85%	*Percentage of correct answers to:*
item 9. More flowers or more tulips.	70%	*animal questions 86%*
item 19. More lions or more animals.	80%	*flower questions 77%*
item 24. More birds or more animals.	100%	
item 4. More roses or more flowers.	75%	

Total percentage of correct answers to:
animal questions 60%
flower questions 58%

Picture Material
Group II Interval Phase and Test Phase

Familiar:	
item 11. More milk or more things you can drink.	55%
item 12. More toys or more dolls.	50%
item 21. More potatoes or more things you can eat.	60%
Total percentage of correct answers	55%

Unfamiliar[11]:	
item 16. More animals or more horses.	60%
item 19. More lions or more animals.	65%
item 20. More things you can ride in or more trains.	55%
Total percentage of correct answers	60%

[10] Only the first answer of every *S* has been scored and calculated. Thus 25% means that 5 of the 20 *S*s gave as first answer a correct one.

[11] Unfamiliar from personal action but not unfamiliar by name and content.

or the failures, either in the beginning or in the end of the learning process, confirm this hypothesis.

It is our belief that in a learning attempt such as ours the crux of the matter is whether the child is familiar with the classes by name and content and not whether he has much or little experience with them.

If a 5-year-old child could learn the principle of comparing two classes, one containing the other, he could apply it to any problem of that type, providing he was familiar with the *name* of the classes referred to and providing he had an idea of their *content*. To the children who grasped the principle, the question "In the whole world are there more cars or more Volkswagens" presented no problem, but "In the whole world are there more fruits or more apples" did. Following Piaget's hypothesis one would have expected the reverse because with which classes are the children more familiar from personal action? With cars or with fruit, with Volkswagens, or with apples?

Of course, Piaget interpreted the differences found in the various age groups and during spontaneous development.[12] But surely some of these developmental differences ought to be found when one tries to teach 5-year-olds to answer these questions.

Inhelder and Piaget (1959) end the paragraph devoted to this subject with these words:

> A reprendre l'explication que nous suggérions au début de ce paragraphe, on peut donc admettre que quand le classement ne prolonge plus directement une action effective possible, telle que cueillir des fleurs pour en faire un bouqet ou de rassembler des images évoquant cette action, mais porte sur des objets impossibles à rassembler, alors l'inclusion ou sa quantification se trouvent beaucoup plus difficiles . . . . Un tel phénomène nous permet de conclure à la nature proprement opératoire, et non pas simplement linguistique, du schèmes de l'inclusion.

which is followed by a criticism of the views held formerly by Welch and Long.

Now that we did not discover this "phénomène" in a situation where we might reasonably expect it we feel a little more justified in doubting the dominating role which Piaget and Inhelder attribute to action and their interiorization and the subordinate role they give to language as carrier of thought.

CONCLUSIONS

Our investigation can be summarized as follows:

(1) We purposely chose a logical operation which has an important function in Piaget's development theory of logical thinking (dealing with inclusion relations).

[12] 67% of a group of 8-year-olds answered the flower questions correctly and 43% the animal questions.

(2) To measure the presence of the operation we used precisely the same method as Piaget in his study of its spontaneous development, and as Morf in his didactic study of it, and which is recommended by Piaget as the method providing *the best criterion* for the presence of the operation (the quantification of inclusion relations by means of a quantitative comparison in size of two classes, A and B, B containing A).

(3) We saw that Morf's learning attempts had little or no success and that Piaget considered this to be in accordance with his development theory. Because, following this theory, only the child's own actions become thought actions (the environment being only a rather passive source of stimulation), and there is no place in that theory for a thought action rapidly forced into being by the environment. Because then the theoretical necessity of first binding these actions into schemas, compensating them into balanced structures while gradually internalizing them would be bypassed.

(4) We then chose children of average level who would certainly not have reached the stage of dealing with the operations had we not thrust this structuring on them.

(5) We made sure that the quality of what the children learned would certainly not be inferior to that attempted by Morf which was comparable to that normally reached by a child at 7 or 8 years. Better still, we designed strict quality tests which were not even demanded by Morf (transfer to purely verbal problems; large variety of class sorts; durability test).

(6) Finally in half an hour we taught 18 of the 20 children to solve the problems designed by Piaget and Morf.

(7) To do this we subjected the children to an intensive learning program in which they were compelled to learn from their faults, while we gave explanation, encouragement, and rejection.

(8) With this strong learning offensive we used methods never used by Piaget c.s. And yet they are not reducible to mere conditioning; because for this the learning process shows too much non-continuity and the learning result is too generally applicable and too durable.

(9) There are several arguments for the insightful quality of the learning result, both in its formation and in its functioning. Presumably we taught the child an active restructuring of the phenomenal field, a restructuring which rapidly became a principle and then a routine for solving certain sorts of problems.

(10) Here we demonstrated that when Piaget c.s. suggest that there is only either the equilibration theory or passive empiricism and that if the latter proves powerless (Morf) then the former automatically takes over, they have not given any consideration to the possibility of other learning methods outside the scope of both passive empiricism and the equilibration theory. Because we wonder how the (rather obvious) learn-

ing method used by us, the process and the result, fit into Piaget's equilibration theory.

(11) We also wonder how this theory can account for the fact that apparently one of the most central operations can, at will, occur two years earlier than "normal." This seems to conflict with Piaget's view that the development of thought operations is fixed in a certain order, independent of chance environment variables, which that half hour lesson must surely be.

(12) We wonder how that complex theoretical construct of direct and invert operation, the mutual coordination and compensation of which is supposed to be essential for the solving of precisely those problems mastered by our 5-year-olds, is reconcilable with our learning result and the way we obtained it. This logical construct of a direct and an invert operation is so closely bound up with the whole theoretical system, since it expresses the *reversibility* which in its turn is *the* characteristic of balanced structures, that it seems to us impossible for Piaget to admit that this whole complex could be established in 90% of the 5-year-olds in half an hour. . . .

SUMMARY OF COUNTER-EXPERIMENT AND RESULTS

Study

We tried to teach children of 5 to learn to answer correctly questions such as: "Are there more horses (A) or more animals (B)?" "Are there more children (B) or more girls (A)?" "Is there more bread (A) or things you can eat (B)?" etc., thus comparing in size two classes, A and B, A being contained by B.

The lesson method was aimed as intensively as possible at the acquisition of insight into this problem. Contrary to the study carried out by Morf, which started from the assumption that the child should discover the solution for himself, we gave a direct instruction, with complete explanation of the problem and examples of correct solutions.

The explanation was always given only after the child had produced a scorable answer, right or wrong.

Three groups of 20 children were used (groups I, II, III). These groups were similarly composed in age (in months), sex, and I.Q.

Group I received instruction by mere verbal problems, group II by showing pictures, and group III by showing blocks. No further material was used with group I. With group II, after the pictures, also purely verbal problems were used. With group III, after the blocks, the pictures were used, and two weeks later again, the blocks and the pictures, plus the purely verbal problems.

Results

(1) Six children from group I, 8 children from group II, and 16 children from group III learned to answer the leading questions correctly. Of the remaining 4 children in group III, 2 more learned to answer the leading questions 2 weeks later ($= 18$).

(2) The 8 "success" children from group II learned to apply their learning result successfully to the purely verbal problems. The 16 (later 18) children from group III were able to apply successfully their acquired learning result (after some practice) to the pictures, and two weeks later from the pictures to the purely verbal problems.

(3) After a 2 to 3 week period the learning result acquired by group III was still completely intact.

REFERENCES

Berlyne, D. E. (1962). Comments on relations between Piaget's theory and S-R theory. In Kessen and Kuhlman (Eds.), Thought in the young child. *Monogr. Soc. Res. Child Develpm.*, **27** (2), Ser. No. 83.

Gréco, P. (1951). L'apprentissage dans une situation à structure opératoire concrète. In Gréco et Piaget, Apprentissage et connaissance. *Etudes d'épistémologie génétique*, Vol. 7. Paris: Presses Universitaires, Pp. 68–182.

Holt, R. R. (1958). Clinical and statistical prediction. *J. abnorm. soc. Psychol.* **56**, 1–12.

Hunt, J. McV. (1961). *Intelligence and experience.* New York: Ronald.

Inhelder, B., and J. Piaget. (1959). *La genèse des structures logiques élémentaires: classifications et sériations.* Neuchâtel: Delachaux et Niestlé. (*The early growth of logic in the child.* London: Routledge, 1964.)

Morf, A. (1959). Apprentissage d'une structure logique concrète (inclusion): effets et limites. In Morf et al., L'apprentissage des structures logiques. *Etudes d'épistémologie génétique*, Vol. 9. Paris: Presses Universitaires. Pp. 15–83.

Piaget, J. (1957). Logique et équilibre dans les comportements du sujet. In Apostel et al., Logique et équilibre. *Etudes d'épistémologie génétique,* Vol. 2. Paris: Presses Universitaires. Pp. 27–117.

Piaget, J. (1959). Apprentissage et connaissance. In Goustard et al., La logique des apprentissages. *Etudes d'épistémologie génétique*, Vol. 10. Paris: Presses Universitaires. Pp. 159–188.

Piaget, J., and A. Szeminska (1941). *La genèse du nombre chez l'enfant.* Neuchâtel: Delachaux et Niestlé. (*The child's conception of number.* London: Routledge, 1952.)

Smedslund, J. (1961). The acquisition of conservation of substance and weight in children: I. Introduction. *Scand. J. Psychol.*, 2, 11–20.

PIAGETIAN RESEARCH AND EDUCATION

Frank H. Hooper

The research reported in this volume testifies to Piaget's substantial impact on current conceptions of cognitive development. Less obvious, perhaps, are the potential contributions of Piaget's theory and related research to educational problems. Piaget's system offers an effective liaison between the developmental status of the child and the curriculum designed to convey society's knowledge, values, and problem-solving strategies.[1]

Piaget's views on the role of educational experiences as a factor in cognitive changes stem from his overall functionalistic orientation. Active individual-environment interactions are the only means by which the child gradually constructs a stable body of information about the physical world, the individual self, and the action sequences themselves. The major focus is upon the central role of an individual's actions and associated outcomes of these actions as mediators of cognitive change. This emphasis upon concrete action colors most of Piaget's educational considerations, especially with regard to the period of middle childhood (ages six to eleven years).

Piaget's ontogenetic model of cognitive development has been viewed as predetermined, invariant, and immutable in the face of diverse social, scholastic, or cultural stimulation (for examples, Kohnstamm 1963, 1966). This may be contrasted with Piaget's (1964, pp. 7–20) recent statements in which active roles are assigned to the four interdependent factors of maturation, experience, social transmission, and equilibration. It is via the latter factor, equilibration or self-regulation, that the individual's actions

---

[1] A number of attempts have been made to relate or apply certain aspects of Piaget's theory to the educational scene. These include general interpretations by Aebli (1951), Beilin (1966), Bruner (1966), Flavell (1963), Peel (1960), Sigel (in press), Skemp (1962), Wallace (1965), and special treatments of mathematics instruction by Dienes (1960, 1963, 1965) and Lovell (1961, 1966). A number of curriculum development conferences focused on the value of Piagetian contributions have been held and these are reported in Bruner (1960), Morrissett (1966), Ripple and Rockcastle (1964), and Sigel (1966a). Finally, a great deal of valuable research directed toward classroom applications of Piaget's theory is being undertaken in the United Kingdom. Many of these research projects are reported in the special publications of the National Foundation for Educational Research, for example, NFER Occasional Publications No. 3, 1959, No. 6, 1961, No. 9, 1965, and No. 12, 1963–1966.

A paper especially prepared for this volume.

operate to alter cognitive structures. The role of learning and educational experiences are not denied by Piaget but they are qualified chiefly through his emphasis on equilibration processes. Thus, he acknowledges the potential effect of the *right kind* of experience at the *right time* for the developing organism. These aspects correspond to curriculum content and timing considerations within the general area of educational application. They provide three points of contact between Piagetian research and the educational field: (1) *when* a certain content or subject area should be taught, (2) *what* content-subject matter is most important, and (3) *how* it may be best presented to the pupil.

PIAGET AND TIMING CONSIDERATIONS

The first question of timing follows directly from a qualitative, stage-dependent theory which stresses accurate assessment of the child's cognitive structure at a given point in time or development. The overriding emphasis rests upon the developmental progression itself, keeping chronological age as a convenient index. The curriculum sequence should be designed in accord with the child's changing cognitive status. Our task becomes one of relating the measures of cognitive function and structure to classroom requirements and schedules. Thus, the Piagetian tasks are viewed as diagnostic tools for educational assessment. Piaget (1962) is quite clear regarding possible differences between the child's cognitive capabilities and the demands of the curriculum in question: "Yet it should be clear that to my mind it is not the child that should be blamed for the eventual conflicts, but the school, unaware as it is of the use it could make of the child's spontaneous development, which it should reinforce by adequate methods instead of inhibiting as it often does" (p. 11).

Although the present status of the Piagetian tasks hardly constitutes a reliable, standardized test series, the research presented in this volume suggests that we are making substantial progress. In each of the areas the core of the replicated findings may form the basis for possible subject matter introduction as additions to the more conventional achievement indices. Piaget's tasks could be valuable adjuncts to those measures designed to determine grade or level placements, subject matter readiness, and corrective or remedial instructional programs. These considerations apply to such topics as quantity-number readiness, scientific concepts, and causality relationships which have a rather direct connection with their respective curriculum areas. For example, utilizing Wohlwill's postulated sequence of number acquisition subtasks or levels (see Wohlwill, 1960, in this volume) the particular child's level of performance tells us when to intervene and what content material to present.

This procedure could be applied to any of the Piagetian concepts or specific content areas which have been shown to develop in an invariant sequence. It is this sequence which provides the basic rationale for determining which skills or abilities are prerequisite to later, more complex functioning. Stated simply, if Stage or Task C achievements are desired in an individual pupil and he has been found to demonstrate adequate Stage A capabilities, then instruction or training should focus on Stage B skills and task settings. Thus, the particular stage specification indicates when to intervene and what to present for the content area in question. In the case of quantity-number concepts (classification skills and spatial concepts), the sequence has been mapped out fairly well. Care should be taken here to distinguish between the *logical* sequences predicted by the formal Piagetian model and the *empirical* task-difficulty orders which result from actual normative research studies. It is the latter pattern, of course, which should be the final arbiter in deciding when to initiate instruction. In this regard, Piaget (1962) has stressed the need for incorporating the logical sequence of spatial concepts (topological-projective-Euclidean) into the school curriculum. Recent research by Dodwell (1963), Fisher (1965), Lovell (1959), and Lunzer (1960), however, has failed to find the predicted primary locus of topological concepts.

PIAGET AND CURRICULUM CONTENT

Closely related to the above discussion are considerations of the curriculum content per se. While many topic areas are directly inferable from the content-specific task areas such as quantity-number, spatial, and time concepts, Piaget's system also includes a more general curriculum directive. This concerns the superordinate role played by the logical operations as they subsume all types of directive thought. The great power of Piaget's model lies in its inherent generality and potential application to a broad range of achievement areas subordinate to logical thought processes or reasoning. This is the essence of the structural components and logical operations, and to the extent that these general factors are found to integrate a wide range of superficially distinct subject disciplines, the impact on educational practice should be far-reaching.

As the name implies, the concrete operations period is characterized by certain first order operations which permit the child to comprehend problem situations in a more effective manner. This period

. . . is attained when the child can dissociate or abstract the part played by himself in ordering his experience rather than on the characteristic of that experience. The ordinary child, by 7 or 8 years of age, can, as it were "turn round on his schemas." Because he can identify the criteria by which he builds his categorizations, he is *aware* of the sequences of his mental actions, and so for any action in his mind he can often see that there are other sequences that give the same results. That is, he can see equivalences for he can coordinate actions in his mind. Thought is now systematized, and the operational structures available correspond to structures which Piaget calls elementary groupings. (Lovell, 1966, p. 215)

These elementary groupings are related to certain functional capacities or achievements including multiplicative classification-relationality skills and the general ability to perceive and utilize reversible transformations. It may be suggested that training in these particular functional skills should generalize to a number of conventional scholastic areas. Instruction in these logical prerequisites has been found to be effective in altering conservation performances (Sigel, Roeper, and Hooper, 1966).

The potential generality of these logical operations and related achievements may be illustrated by pointing out timing and content considerations in a particular subject area, social studies, which is distinct from the usual task situations native to Piaget's investigations. We may do this by indicating correspondences between such cognitive capacities as probalistic reasoning, multiple classification, multiple causation, and conservation of invariants and the teaching of social studies. In this way we shall demonstrate in specific terms how some aspects of Piagetian theory can *directly* apply to curriculum building.[2]

Correspondences between Piagetian Constructs and Social Science Concepts

COGNITIVE PREREQUISITE	SOCIAL SCIENCE CONCEPTS
(1) Probabilistic reasoning	
The idea that combinations of insufficient causes can render an outcome more probable, that is, it is more likely to occur	The fundamental uncertainty of historical predictions of outcomes—the possibility of calculated guesses greater than chance
	The conception of outcomes as the results of stable identifiable determinants plus fortuitous determinants

History and political science seek causative explanations of events, although all the causal information desirable is seldom available. Predictions take the form of educated guesses, or chance modified by what one knows about the situation. The real outcomes are the results of the typical development of stable or inevitable determinants continually acting on situations. In some cases, a fortuitous event may play a catalytic role. It would be a tremendous service to children if, as well as historical narrative, we could teach them the "uncertainty structure" of great amounts of subject matter which will be facing them soon. This uncertainty principle

---

[2] These parallels follow an outline by John Flavell and are adapted from Sigel, 1966a, 1966c.

which permeates all social science is in contrast to the usual physical science model where certainties are taught. Initially, children are extremely absolutistic in the type of information they will search out, accept, and retain, but they lose some of this rigidity in late childhood or adolescence. If we can reach them at this period of relative cognitive mobility, they may accommodate some substantial notions of probability and inference.

COGNITIVE PREREQUISITE	SOCIAL SCIENCE CONCEPTS
(2) Multiple classification	
Multiple relationality Hierarchical groupings	Governmental tables of organization, authority relations, and related classifications of the hierarchical type

Multiple classification and relational understanding probably underlie most abstract thinking or cognition as we normally conceive them. The child of ten to eleven years has mastered the rational manipulation of classes, relations, unit measurements, and numbers insofar as concrete media are concerned. As he makes the transition of analogous operations on the Piagetian formal level, he is capable of meaningful use and comprehension of certain abstract terms and concepts. As an example, the child cannot grasp the essence of an organization table (chain of command, spheres of jurisdiction, interlocking authority) unless he has some mastery of relational structures and superordinate, part-whole classifications as described in systems of logic. Competence in multiple, simultaneous classification and hierarchical relations is the cognitive prerequisite for the acquisition of the concept of multiple causality. In other words, if a student writing about Cardinal Richelieu wishes to be as objective as possible about his life, he must consider the implications of being both a Frenchman and a member of the Catholic church. A "balance" must be made by the student, just as it had to be made by the historical figure in question.

COGNITIVE PREREQUISITE	SOCIAL SCIENCE CONCEPTS
(3) Multiple causation	
The ability to think in terms of natural causes	Causal structure of historical or political outcomes
The ability to regard events as determined by other specific events	The notions of positive, negative, and neutral events in the context of that outcome
The ability to conceive of a variety of types of causes, for example, personal versus impersonal, or individual versus group causes	Concepts of multidetermination of historical and political outcomes Concept of causes continuously operating across extended time periods

A number of causality types can be identified: social, psychological, and multiplicative causality. Whereas children of five or six, for various reasons, could not understand these concepts, there is evidence that children of eight to eleven are beginning, at least with respect to physical events, to have some rational and mature ideas about *the nature of the causes*. They are beginning to look for examples of continuity between physical cause and physical effect. However, there is a difference between spontaneous, self-initiated concept usage and situation-induced usage. In general, children of eleven years have reached only the latter stage. Yet they are able to appreciate cause and effect in their world if the idea is suggested to them.

Does the child who has the intellectual structure to cope with physical, concrete causality also deal adequately with *social causality*? Is there a transfer of competence from one cognitive ability to another? Although there is little experimental evidence bearing on this question, there does seem to be a psychological relationship. The educator can be sensitive to this issue and can observe whether or not this relationship holds.

Rudiments of *psychological causality*, understanding the things that move people to act as they do, appear at approximately this age. Notions of human motivational determinants allow the child to understand how a group of people acting in concert, dressed as Indians, would do things which none of them would do individually on the street in ordinary clothes.

Understanding *multiple causality* is extremely difficult for a child if certain primary conceptual abilities are not present. The younger child is more likely to focus upon a single cause or aspect of an event to the exclusion of other dimensions and causes.

COGNITIVE PREREQUISITE	SOCIAL SCIENCE CONCEPTS
(4) Conservation of invariants	The possibility of across-instance generalizations about historical or political processes, for example, common causal patterns involved in any revolution, or any political process resulting in a new congressional law

It is true that the concept of conservation in various areas (space, length, number, quantity) are not all mastered at the same time or generalized to all forms of presentation. However, the ten- or eleven-year-old child generally has the capacity to understand that, in this world of flux and disorder, certain things stand still or remain constant even in the midst of change.

Most event-generalizations in the social sciences may be viewed as examples of conservation. These may take the form of generalizations or commonalities across time, or instances within a given time period. There may be common causal patterns, for instance, in conflict resolution or political process which result in the passage of legislation. These constancies have to be accepted by the student if historical precedent or political generalities are to have any meaning. The failure to derive any generalities or common threads from traditional narrative history is the most common failing of secondary pupils and college students.

Many of the concepts cited above are arbitrarily chosen from Piagetian theory since they seem particularly relevant for education. There is some evidence that the social science curriculum builders are following a somewhat similar path, although not rooted in developmental psychology. Fenton (1966) has emphasized the need for reflective-analytic questioning in history courses. Gustavson (1955), in stressing the role of multiple causation, states, "No single cause ever adequately explains an historical episode. A 'cause' is a convenient figure of speech for any one of a number of factors which helps to explain why an historical event happened" (p. 55).

PIAGET AND TEACHING STRATEGY

The final question of how to best present the various subject areas to the child is perhaps the most interesting and most controversial of Piaget's contributions. It is here that Piaget's emphasis on the individual's action patterns becomes relevant. As indicated previously, cognitive change is made possible by the active interaction of the child and his surrounding physical and social environment. Experiences in the classroom are no exception to this. Piaget (1964) is quite clear regarding the value of straightforward didactic presentations via lecture or text book:

> Experience is always necessary for intellectual development . . . but I fear that we may fall into the illusion that being submitted to an experience (a demonstration) is sufficient for a subject to disengage the structure involved. But more than this is required. The subject must be active, must transform things, and find the structure of his own actions on the objects. (p. 4)

It is this cognitive reorganization made available by "self discovery" in the classroom which Piaget, along with Dewey and Montessori, stresses as a crucial element.

The student must be actively engaged if the learning process is to be effective. For the concrete-operations-period child, this entails an actual concrete manipulation of the objects or task materials in question. Regardless of content area, the child should perform the actions represented by the concepts. This is especially true insofar as the operational counterparts of the logical groupings are concerned (for example, associativity, reversibility, or the higher order multiplicative relationships and classifications). Thus, in the case of number training, addition-subtraction and multiplication-division experiences should be placed in juxtaposition to accent the inherent reversibility of these activities. Ordination and seriation would best be demonstrated by allowing the child to actually practice on these activities themselves. Similarily, multiplicative classification experiences could be ordered in terms of increasing complexity with the children actually constructing and reconstructing matrices on the basis of single-dimension attributes. This would proceed to multidimensionality experiences with an ever-widening range of concrete media (Sigel, 1966b). In all these instances

> it will be the teacher's task, and one often demanding considerable ingenuity, to analyze the content to be learned in terms of the operations implicit upon it. Having done this, he will arrange the learning materials so that these operations can actually be carried out by the student himself, and then see to it that the student does carry them out. (Flavell, 1963, p. 368)

Once the fundamental action patterns are mastered, the training program could gradually draw the child away from the explicit concrete material settings to higher representational levels in which emphasis would shift to covert, internalized operations at ever-increasing distances from the immediate perceptual context. Here we could utilize pictorial representations, memory-based recall or recognition tasks, and finally, the symbol systems themselves (words or cardinal numbers) to gradually permit the transition to abstract thought levels.

The mechanism invoked by Piaget as a mediator of cognitive restructuring is the equilibration process. This process, centering upon the temporary imbalance between the major functional activities of assimilation and accommodation is usually conceived of as invoking some form of conflict situation. This conflict develops between the child's partially established schemas and new environmental demands which are meaningful to the current level of psychological functioning. Certain task situations are well within the individual's response repertory. The task set for the child has to be just beyond the reach of the child for conflict to occur—neither too easy nor too hard. Theoretically, conflict takes place when just the right amount of discrepancy exists between the established schema and the discordant input, for example, the match-mismatch proposal of Hunt (1961). While the locus of this conflict is within the child's thought pattern, the classroom teacher can create mild conflict within the problem setting. This might involve the introduction of discordant information or illustrative demonstrations designed to carefully challenge the pupil's previous conceptions or partially mastered abilities. In mathematics, for example, alternative methods available for obtaining the same problem solution can be presented (the area of a geometric figure may be determined by different means). As the child is forced to reconcile these distinctive methods to problem solution, he may discover the superordinate rule which subsumes all the methods.

Related to the conflict propositions are Piaget's (1964) views of group dynamics and social interactions. He feels that the child's social setting, in this case the classroom, should be an integral element in the process of cognitive growth.

> When I say "active," I mean it in two senses. One is acting on material things. But the other means doing things in social collaboration, in a group effort. This leads to a critical frame of mind, where children must communicate with each other. This is an essential factor in intellectual development. Cooperation is indeed co-operation. (p. 4)

Thus, peer relationships may be one means of setting natural conflict forces in motion to facilitate the cognitive reorganization of the individual participants. Group problem-solving and discussion situations are one means of accomplishing this. Although the cognitive structure of younger children is generally not influenced by peer-related conflict situations, the concrete-operations child is able to assimilate the differences in viewpoint and alter his conceptions accordingly. The social processes involved here go much deeper than a mere classroom "parliamentary" debate or panel discussion would imply. At issue are such behavioral capacities as role-playing skills, the ability to shift perspectives, and the general use of persuasion and argumentation as instrumental activities in interpersonal situations. Role-playing situations, in particular, offer the possibility of structured emotional involvement in knowledge areas which have traditionally been rather dull and unappealing to the student. Children who actually plan and carry out a rebellion against taxation, organize protest marches against voting infringements or racial discrimination, or exchange role perspectives in the same classroom "drama" are closely approximating the action requirements of Piaget's system. Although the merits of vicarious experiences such as these have been generally recognized by educators, Piagetian theory offers a rationale which justifies their instructional value on theoretical as well as pragmatic grounds.

The group interaction situation may be an ideal means of portraying the essentials of psychological causality to the school pupil. The motivational determinants, goal strivings, power struggles, and so forth, found in the school setting are basically analogous to larger group processes. These considerations could be the basis of introducing content-specific curriculum objectives in social studies (for example, the role of conflicts of interest, biased viewpoints, of "false" positions held in good faith, and diplomatic compromise) as they serve to explain certain political and historical processes.

This discussion has shown the value of Piaget's general orientation to educational issues. Assuming a basic connection between developmental theory and educational application, the research generated by Piaget's ideas should be of great assistance to the teacher and curriculum designer. The major task of implementing these ideas and translating the principles into operational educational procedures remains to be accomplished. In this regard, there are a number of practical considerations of definite interest to the classroom instructor which Piaget has noticeably ignored. Piaget has consistently directed his attention toward very general psychological processes which stress the essential uniformity of cognitive behavior for any particular developmental stage. He has not concerned himself with the problem of individual differences or the role of differential stimulus factors in task settings. Yet, inter-individual and intra-individual variability of behavior across content areas are a familiar difficulty in curriculum planning. Before the complete picture is discovered, additional research may well result in modifications to both educational techniques and the Piagetian conceptual model.

The creation of a general curriculum which incorporates the viable Piagetian ideas should engender renewed interest in the basic goals which have traditionally guided our educational efforts. Piaget's (1964) own views on educational objectives in modern society are probably shared by most educators today:

> The principal goal of education is to create men who are capable of doing new things, not simply of repeating what other generations have done— men who are creative, inventive, and discoverers. The second goal of education is to form minds which can be critical, can verify, and not accept everything they are offered. The great danger today is of slogans, collective opinions, ready-made trends of thought. We have to be able to resist individually, to criticize, to distinguish between what is proven and what is not. So we need pupils who are active, who learn early to find out by themselves, partly by their own spontaneous activity and partly through material we set up for them; who learn early to tell what is verifiable and what is simply the first idea to come to them. (p. 5)

REFERENCES

Aebli, H. (1951). *Didactique psychologique: application à la didactique de la psychologie de Jean Piaget.* Neuchâtel: Delachaux et Niestlé.
Beilin, H. (June, 1966). A cognitive strategy for curriculum development. Paper presented at Fifth Work Conference on Curriculum and Teaching in Depressed Urban Areas, Teachers College, Columbia University.
Bruner, J. S. (1960). *The process of education.* Cambridge, Mass.: Harvard University Press.
Bruner, J. S. (1966). *Toward a theory of instruction.* Cambridge, Mass.: Harvard University Press.
Dienes, Z. P. (1960). *Building up mathematics.* London: Hutchinson.
Dienes, Z. P. (1963). *An experimental study of mathematics.* London: Hutchinson.
Dienes, Z. P. (1965). *Modern mathematics for young children.* Harlow, England: Educational Supply Association.
Dodwell, P. C. (1963). Children's understanding of spatial concepts. *Canad. J. Psychol.,* 17, 141–161.

Fenton, E. (1966). A structure of history. In I. Morrissett (Ed.), *Concepts and structures in the new social science curricula.* West Lafayette, Ind.: Social Science Education Consortium. Pp. 50–56.

Fisher, G. H. (1965). Developmental features of behavior and perception. *Brit. J. educ. Psychol.*, **35**, 69–78.

Flavell, J. H. (1963). *The developmental psychology of Jean Piaget.* Princeton, N.J.: Van Nostrand.

Gustavson, C. (1955). *A preface to history.* New York: McGraw-Hill.

Hunt, J. McV. (1961). *Intelligence and experience.* New York: Ronald.

Kohnstamm, G. A. (1963). An evaluation of part of Piaget's theory. *Acta Psychol.*, **21**, 313–356.

Kohnstamm, G. A. (1966). The gap between the psychology of cognitive development and education as seen from Europe. Paper presented at the Conference on Guided Learning, Educational Research Council of Greater Cleveland.

Lovell, K. (1959). A follow-up study of some aspects of the work of Piaget and Inhelder into the child's conception of space. *Brit. J. educ. Psychol.*, **24**, 104–117.

Lovell, K. (1961). *The growth of basic mathematics and scientific concepts in children.* London: University of London Press.

Lovell, K. (1966). Concepts in mathematics. In H. J. Klausmeier and C. W. Harris (Eds.), *Analyses of concept learning.* New York: Academic Press.

Lunzer, E. A. (1960). Some points of Piagetian theory in the light of experimental criticism. *J. child Psychol. Psychiat.*, **1**, 191–202.

Morrissett, I. (Ed.) (1966). *Concepts and structures in the social science curricula.* West Lafayette, Ind.: Social Science Education Consortium.

Peel, E. A. (1960). *The pupil's thinking.* London: Oldbourne Press.

Piaget, J. (1962). Comments on Vygotsky's critical remarks concerning "The language and thought of the child" and "Judgment and reasoning of the child." In L. S. Vygotsky, *Thought and language.* Cambridge, Mass.: M.I.T. Press.

Piaget, J. (1964). Three lectures. In R. E. Ripple and V. N. Rockcastle (Eds.), *Piaget rediscovered.* Ithaca, N.Y.: Cornell University Press.

Ripple, R. E., and V. N. Rockcastle (Eds.) (1964). *Piaget rediscovered.* Ithaca, N.Y.: Cornell University Press.

Sigel, I. E. (1966a). Child development and social science education: Pt. I. The problem: Pt. II. *Conference report.* West Lafayette, Ind.: Social Science Education Consortium, No. 111.

Sigel, I. E. (1966b). Child development and social science education: Pt. IV. *A teaching strategy derived from some Piagetian concepts.* West Lafayette, Ind.: Social Science Education Consortium, No. 113.

Sigel, I. E. (1966c). Concepts, structure and learning. In I. Morrissett (Ed.), *Concepts and structures in the social science curricula.* West Lafayette, Ind.: Social Science Education Consortium, Pp. 79–85.

Sigel, I. E. (in press). The Piagetian system and the world of education. In D. Elkind and J. H. Flavell (Eds.), *Festschrift for Jean Piaget*. New York: Oxford University Press.

Sigel, I. E., Annemarie Roeper, and F. H. Hooper (1966). A training procedure for acquisition of Piaget's conservation of quantity: a pilot study and its replication. *Brit. J. educ. Psychol.*, **36**, Pt. 3, 301–311.

Skemp, R. R. (1962). The need for a schematic learning theory. *Brit. J. educ. Psychol.*, **32**, 133–142.

Wallace, J. G. (1965). *Concept growth and the education of the child.* The Mere, Upton Park, Slough, Bucks: National Foundation for Educational Research in England and Wales.

Wohlwill, J. F. (1960). A study of the development of the number concept by scalogram analysis. *J. genet. Psychol.*, **97**, 345–377.

CHAPTER

SIX

THEORETICAL

DISCUSSIONS

* * *

THE PREVIOUS CHAPTERS have focused upon the major aspects of Piaget's system which have generated replication and training investigations. The emphasis, throughout, has centered on empirical research issues specific to a given content area or training attempt. The present chapter will deal with theoretical and conceptual issues of a more general nature. These include considerations of Piaget's theory as a general source of research directives, alternative theoretical approaches which may be applied to the Piagetian problem areas, and the relationship of Piaget's major operational constructs to the traditional fields of learning, perception, and intellective assessment. An appreciation of these larger issues and relationships should permit a greater understanding of the empirical research literature.

The first article by Wohlwill minimizes the value of cross-sectional replication research which focuses on the generality of the Piagetian norms, age specifications, and the relationships to conventional achievement or intelligence indices. While information concerning these points is undoubtedly of interest, they are not the most salient issues that Piaget's theory, as an explicit model of cognitive development, must face. For Wohlwill, tests of the adequacy of the Piagetian model should center on the invariant stage sequence and the predicted correspondence of the logical operations constructs and their related behavioral products. The latter issue is the basis for the great power and generality of Piaget's system in organizing superficially distinct forms of logical thinking. Wohlwill's argument is cogent, and he illustrates the dual research possibilities by citing a number of studies found in this volume.

In contrast to the attempted reconciliation of Piagetian and behavioristic conceptions (for example, Apostel et al., 1959; Berlyne, 1960; and Stevenson, 1962), Watson's article represents a straightforward application of learning analysis to the conservation problem format. Utilizing such concepts as discrimination and time-distributed stimuli, he presents an explanation of conservation performance which does not require a logical process rationale. In addition, he applies these stimulus-response considerations to previous training research endeavors including the studies by Beilin (1965), Sigel, Roeper, and Hooper (1966), Wallach, and Sprott (1964).

The need for further conceptual analysis of the conservation paradigm itself is the main theme of Elkind's discussion. Dissatisfied with simplistic views of the processes attributed to conservation performance, Elkind distinguishes between two distinct conservation achievements. These achievements, identity and equivalence conservations, are conceptually distinct but developmentally related. While Piaget stresses the developmental significance of identity conservations in his theoretical explanations, he and later investigators traditionally have used the equivalence format in the actual assessment of conservation performance.

The second theoretical article by Wohlwill considers the relationship of perceptual and inferential processes as they bear on the general area of cognitive development. In many cases, it is extremely difficult to determine exactly when perceptual processes cease to be a factor in cognitive functioning. Similarly, certain theories of perceptual functioning, including Brunswick's probabilistic functionalism and the Bruner-Postman hypothesis approach, stress the role of such ratiomorphic mechanisms as explanatory devices. For Bruner, the perception-cognition dichotomy is merely an arbitrary distinction. Brunswick and Piaget make distinctions between these areas although they stress different criteria in doing so.

Wohlwill discusses these distinctions when pointing out the value of perceptually derived factors as a means of understanding the transition to logical thinking. He suggests three possible dimensions, redundancy, selectivity, and contiguity, which may be applied to perception-conception relationships. An example of research based on manipulations of these dimensions is also presented.

Gruen's article focuses upon differential criteria employed in conservation assessment. Many investigators conducting research in the same general topic area have indicated markedly different age norms and performance patterns for similar task situations and comparable subject populations. The distinctive methodologies have led the respective investigators to emphasize different task requirements and explanatory processes in their theoretical conceptions of the same cognitive behaviors. Certain American investigators, (Bruner *et al.*, 1966; Braine, 1959, 1964; Braine and Shanks, 1965a, 1965b) have not required supporting verbal explanations in the conservation task setting. In contrast, Piaget and his associates emphasize the child's verbal rationales. As Gruen points out, these distinctions not only produce different age norms, but they also reflect basically different conceptions of conservation behavior and what conservation represents in the child's general cognitive development.

These theoretical discussions should contribute to a better understanding of Piaget's overall system and the associated research which it has generated. Some of the major contributions are as follows:

(1) The provision of special criteria for determining the central research issues in the Piagetian approach.

(2) The suggestion of alternative analytic models to employ as explanations of the Piagetian empirical data.

(3) The demonstration of the possible relationship of Piagetian conceptions to the traditional psychological areas of learning, perception, and intellectual functioning.

(4) The indication of certain methodological distinctions in conservation assessment which reflect distinctive theoretical orientations to conservation performance and acquisition processes.

REFERENCES

Apostel, L., A. R. Jonckheere, and B. Matalon (1959). Logique, apprentissage et probabilité. In J. Piaget (Ed.), *Etudes d'épistémologie génétique*, Vol. 8. Paris: Presses Universitaires. Pp. 19–59.

Beilin, H. (1965). Learning and operational convergence in logical thought development. *J. exp. child Psychol.*, **2**, 317–339.

Berlyne, D. E. (1960). Les équivalences psychologiques et les notions quantitatives. In D. E. Berlyne and J. Piaget, Théorie du comportement et opérations. *Etudes d'épistémologie génétique*, Vol. 12. Paris: Presses Universitaires. Pp. 1–76.

Braine, M. D. S. (1959). The ontogeny of certain logical operations: Piaget's formulation examined by nonverbal methods. *Psychol. Monogr.*, **5** (73).

Braine, M. D. S. (1964). Development of a grasp of transitivity of length: a reply to Smedslund. *Child Develpm.*, **35**, 799–810.

Braine, M. D. S., and B. L. Shanks (1965a). The conservation of a shape property and a proposal about the origin of the conservation. *Canad. J. Psychol.*, **19** (3), 197–207.

Braine, M. D. S., and B. L. Shanks (1965b). The development of conservation of size. *J. verb. Learn. verb. Behav.*, **4**, 227–242.

Bruner, J. S., Rose R. Olver, and Patricia Greenfield (1966). *Studies in cognitive growth.* New York: Wiley.

Sigel, I. E., Annemarie Roeper, and F. H. Hooper (1966). A training procedure for acquisition of Piaget's conservation of quantity: a pilot study and its replication. *Brit. J. educ. Psychol.*, **36**, Pt. 3, 301–311.

Stevenson, H. W. (1962). Piaget, behavior theory, and intelligence. In W. Kessen and Clementina Kuhlman (Eds.), Thought in the young child. *Monogr. Soc. Res. Child Develpm.*, **27** (2), Ser. No. 83, 113–126.

Wallach, Lise, and R. L. Sprott (1964). Inducing number conservation in children. *Child Develpm.*, **35**, 1057–1071.

PIAGET'S SYSTEM AS A SOURCE OF EMPIRICAL RESEARCH

Joachim F. Wohlwill

Recently, in discussing Piaget's work in two rather different settings within the space of a week, I came across two remarkably contrasting reactions. The first was marked above all by skepticism and outright disbelief

Reprinted with the permission of the author and the publisher from *The Merrill-Palmer Quarterly*, 1963, 4, 253–262.

in the validity of the phenomena described by Piaget, relating to lack of conservation in young children. The second urged the acceptance of an aspect of Piaget's theory, on the grounds of its elegant internal coherence; it was felt that this feature far outweighed the mere stubborn facts turned up in one investigation, whose results ran counter to the theory.

Most present-day psychologists would be likely to disavow either of these extreme views. The latter would perhaps be more vehemently rejected, if not laughed out of court outright. But the former is also becoming increasingly rare, as research evidence accumulates, attesting to the reality of the phenomena dealt with by Piaget. Indeed, the fast and furious pace of current research directly based on Piaget's work itself bears ample testimony to the viability of the system and its potential for generating research. A rough count of papers published since the mid-fifties reporting Piaget-inspired research shows a steady and impressive increase, from six such papers in 1955/1956 to thirty-three in 1961/1962, and this positively accelerating trend shows no signs of abatement at the present.

The reasons for this fecundity of Piaget's ideas as a source of research are not hard to find. The novelty of so many of the phenomena discovered by Piaget (which are generally intriguing and frequently startling on first acquaintance), combined with the paucity of conclusive evidential support in his own accounts of these phenomena, has inspired a steady stream of studies dedicated mainly to validating the developmental changes he discusses. In addition, the discovery of such new phenomena carries with it the seeds for further research on its parameters and the conditions affecting it. Accordingly we find a fair amount of work relating to Piaget-type phenomena, concernd with such questions as the role of instructions, of changes in the stimulus materials, of vocabulary development, of educational and cultural factors.

There is no denying that research of this kind is of value, if only in providing much-needed data concerning the generality of the phenomena described by Piaget and the kind of influences to which they are subject. It is my belief, nevertheless, that neither of these approaches has materially contributed to the empirical testing of Piaget's *theory*, or has recognized explicitly the essence of Piaget's system and its implications for research. Indeed, without wishing to minimize the very real contributions made by a number of research workers in this area, and the increasing methodological and theoretical sophistication to be noted in much of this research, I cannot avoid at times an admittedly somewhat frivolous, if not unkind, reaction in examining some of these studies. I am reminded here of the hunt for the woozle in Winnie-the-Pooh. Most of you recall, I am sure, the delightful episode in which Winnie-the-Pooh and Piglet set about somewhat apprehensively stalking this animal they have heard about, without any idea of what it looks or acts like. Following with increasing alarm a set of footsteps (which are of course their very own) they wind up merrily going around in circles, until Christopher Robin arrives on the scene to rescue

them from their predicament. I wonder whether some of the currently flour-
ishing work ostensibly aimed at validating Piaget does not show a somewhat
similar lack of appreciation for the nature of the beast which it is trying to
track down. Perhaps the tried-and-true paths along which it proceeds may
likewise fail to lead to any really significant discoveries.

I think, in other words, that we must make more of an effort to come
to grips with the definition of the essential researchable questions which
are implicit in Piaget's theory, and with the most effective ways of approaching them. For instance, data on the changes with age in the percentage of
children who give responses characteristic of the various stages which Piaget
postulates (with respect to the development of a particular concept) may
constitute evidence in agreement, or disagreement, with Piaget's claims.
But such data hardly represent a direct test of his theory. Similarly, studies
dedicated to the proposition that responses in Piaget-type tasks are influenced by variables relating to the stimulus materials used, or to the instructions, or to the socioeconomic background of the respondents, are of
uncertain pertinence to Piaget's theoretical system.

What, then, are the empirical questions which are at the core of this
system? For an answer I believe that we must look at Piaget's (1956) conception of stages, which underlies all of his more recent work. Parenthetically, let me note that we seem at present to be still confronting something
of an impasse in our attempts at handling the problem of developmental
stages—perhaps largely because relatively little attention has been given
to the nature of the research and the appropriate methodological approaches
in the study of this problem. With respect to Piaget's stage-theoretical system in particular, at least two readily testable questions suggest themselves:
(1) Do the steps marking the development of a concept appear according
to a fixed, orderly progression? (2) Do responses to tasks which differ but
which, according to the system, are based on the same mental operations,
develop simultaneously, i.e., in phase with one another?

It seems worthwhile to examine each of these questions in turn, in terms
of their significance for Piaget, their implications for research, and the state
of the evidence regarding them. With respect to the first question, Piaget's
emphasis on invariant, predetermined developmental sequences represents
one of the cornerstones of his developmental psychology, as it does of most
essentially organismic, biologically oriented theories. More specifically, in
Piaget's recent and more formalized work on the development of concrete
and formal operations, the postulation of such developmental sequences is
directly tied to the hierarchical model of levels of operations, which is characterized by a progressive approximation of the processes of reasoning to
the formal system of the logician. A good illustration is provided by Inhelder and Piaget's (1958) formulation of the development of children's
understanding of equilibrium in the balance. The child at Stage I is said
to lack additivity and reversibility, so that he is unable to equalize the
weights on the two arms of the balance, even with distance equated. At

Stage IIa, the formation of additive and reversible schemata allow him to balance the weights by manipulating either weight or distance separately; and at Stage IIb, the principle of the inverse relationship between weight and distance is grasped at an intuitive, qualitative level. Finally, at Stage III, the quantitative, metric proportionality schema is formed, allowing the child to arrive at an immediate, exact solution by direct calculation.

There is a surprising paucity of empirical evidence bearing on this uniform-sequence question. To begin with, a really convincing answer to it would seem to demand longitudinal data. But there are in fact virtually no such data as yet available, at least in published form. This is all the more regrettable, since longitudinal research on Piaget-type problems could be carried out within relatively short time-spans, e.g., of the order of two to three years, and would thus avoid many of the methodological and administrative difficulties which plague long-term longitudinal projects.

In some cases a cross-sectional shortcut exists, however, which may provide answers to essentially the same question, as well as more immediate reinforcement to the investigator. If the developmental sequence can be formulated in terms of a set of hierarchically organized tasks, then an examination of the response patterns made by a group of subjects to these several tasks will yield information of direct relevance to the question of sequential uniformity. Reduced to its barest essentials, this situation might be represented by a two-by-two contingency table, indicating frequency of successes and failures for any pair of tasks. For the postulate of sequential invariance to hold, it would be necessary for the frequency in one of the cells to approach zero, within the limits of reliability of the response measures involved. This would be the cell representing the combination of success on the supposedly higher-level task and failure on the lower-level task. In one study by Keats (1955), the hypothesis that the ability to reason at the level of concrete operations would precede the ability to solve equivalent problems at the level of formal operations was, in fact, tested by the analysis of just these types of contingency tables. Not surprisingly, in view of the nature of the problem, most of these tables did indeed show the expected near-zero frequencies in the appropriate cells.

Similarly, developmental sequences composed of larger number of steps can be tested as a unit, through the analysis of cross-sectional response patterns. This may be accomplished by applying either Loevinger's technique of homogeneous tests, which represents a logical extension of the analysis of two-by-two tables just described, or alternatively its close cousin, Guttman's scalogram analysis (cf. White and Saltz, 1957). The latter has proved somewhat the more popular, although its users have not always recognized some of the statistical problems with which this technique is beset. A particularly ambitious and thoughtful attempt to put this method to use in the uncovering of Piagetian stages is a doctoral research project currently being carried out by Miss Ellin Kofsky at the University of Rochester, under Dr. Flavell's direction. Based on Inhelder and Piaget's (1959) recent book on categorical thinking, Miss Kofsky has constructed a series of eleven tasks, designed to tap the developmental sequence in the domain of the child's concept of classes and classification skills. Her investigation should contribute significantly to our understanding of the developmental process in this area.

It is important to note, however, that Miss Kofsky was only able to base a portion of her sequence directly on Piaget's formulation of the stages in this area of concept development. The typical Piagetian sequence of stages in fact creates a variety of problems for the application of scalogram analysis. To begin with, it rarely comprises a sufficiently large number of definable steps. More important, perhaps, it typically involves a succession of mutually exclusive types of responses to one and the same task, rather than a set of cumulative responses to a series of different tasks. Under certain circumstances it may be possible to construct a series of cumulative tasks so as to tap the various response types suggested by Piaget. More frequently, however, the resulting sequence provides instead a measure of the *generalizability* of a given response along a graded series of problems. This, paradoxically, is not a question which Piaget has handled very systematically. All in all, then, it is not surprising that really conclusive evidence with respect to the sequential invariance of the stage progressions stipulated by Piaget remains somewhat sporadic.

But there is a more fundamental question to be asked in regard to the interpretation of any such cross-sectional data: Does the determination of homogeneity or scalability for a given set of items really provide conclusive evidence as to the essential sequential dependence between one stage and the next on which Piaget insists? For example, reading would be most unlikely to occur in children who had not learned to walk; yet one would hardly wish to argue from this fact that the ability to read was necessarily dependent on walking. Piaget, on the other hand, regards an understanding of the principle of transitivity, for instance, as logically and psychologically prerequisite to the ability to measure the length of an object by dint of successive iteration of a unit of measurement. Evidence on such functionally necessary sequential dependencies would seem to require much more detailed longitudinal analyses of the steps through which children actually pass with respect to a particular concept and of the transitions from one stage to the next. Perhaps a still more rigorous approach to determine whether one step does in fact represent an essential stepping-stone for the next would be to find out whether children at stage X could in any way be taught or given special experience designed to bring them to stage Z, without the intermediary of stage Y. One of the Geneva studies by Morf (1959), on the development of the notion of class-inclusion, contains some evidence of essentially this sort. So far as it goes, it tends to confirm the necessary character of the stage sequence proposed by Piaget with respect to this notion.

It is time now to turn to a consideration of the second general question emerging from Piaget's theoretical formulation, that of the interrelationship between responses to different tasks involving the same operations. As we shall see, this question lies at the core of Piaget's conception of stages of mental development, and the answer to it may well turn out to be something of an Achilles heel in Piaget's system.

Let us look, to begin with, at the origins of this question in Piaget's conception of stages of intellectual development. Essential to his concept of stages is the notion of an underlying generalized mental structure through which all responses characteristic of a given stage are linked. Thus, if a particular stage is characterized by the acquisition of the logical principles of reciprocity, or inversion, or transitivity, the child who has reached that stage should be able to master any and all problems involving this principle. That Piaget really means this quite literally is brought out repeatedly in his writings, notably in his recently translated book, with Inhelder and Szeminska (1960), on the *Child's Conception of Geometry*. This volume abounds in cross-references from one section of the book to another, as well as to other books, all purporting to show the synchronous progression through a sequence of stages exhibited by children in different problem situations having a common operational structure.

For example, Piaget asserts that the stages in the child's approach to the problem of locating a point in two-dimensional space parallel, level for level, those observed in his approach to linear measurement and in his spontaneous conceptualization of spatial coordinates—since these problems are all based on the operation of logical multiplication. Similarly, conservation of area is said to appear at the same time as conservation of distance and length, since all involve the operations of addition and subdivision of parts and coordination of positions. Yet in all of these instances Piaget's evidence is limited to the fairly close agreement between the ages of a few selected subjects exhibiting level-X responses in situation A and the ages of certain *other* subjects showing similar level-X responses in situation B.

This point is clearly amenable to a more rigorous empirical test: one could simply determine the relationship between the performance of a group of subjects on two or more tasks which supposedly involve identical operations in Piaget's terms. It may be noted, in fact, that if we express this question again in the form of a two-by-two contingency table, it turns out to be directly complementary to the one discussed earlier under the heading of sequential invariance of stages. In the present case, the hypothesis would simply stipulate zero-order frequencies in the two cells which represent combinations of success in one task and failure in the other.

The evidence with regard to this question, it seems fair to state, does not bear out Piaget's contentions with any degree of regularity. It suggests, rather, that the situation is far more complex than Piaget's theory allows for. To be sure, the results of a few studies have shown a fairly high degree of consistency in the performance of the same children on two or more related tasks. Thus Braine (1959), who was one of the first to recognize the importance of this question, has shown a very close association between children's ability to respond to the ordinal position of an element in a series, and their success in a measurement task. Lovell (1961), in one of his extended series of studies inspired by Piaget's work, has likewise found substantial intercorrelations between the levels of thinking of children on various groups of related tasks, taken from Inhelder and Piaget's volume on the growth of logical thinking.

The case for the negative is, however, rather more fully documented. To give just a few examples: with respect to the conservation of weight and substance, both Lovell and Ogilvie (1961) and Smedslund (1961) have failed to substantiate the close relationship between the acquisition of conservation and the understanding of transitivity relationships which Piaget's theory postulates. Similarly, Lunzer (1960) has found no consistent pattern in children's responses to tasks involving on the one hand the conservation of volume and the ability to calculate volume by multiplication, and on the other hand the understanding of the notion of infinite subdivision, even though for Piaget the last represents the basis for the first two. Further negative evidence comes from the work of Dodwell (1960), who has been able to show only very moderate degrees of consistency between a variety of tasks in the area of number, which Piaget regards as intrinsically interrelated aspects of the number concept. Most recently, the same author has found an even lower degree of association between formally equivalent problems involving the concept of cardinal number and the logic of classes (Dodwell, 1962).

There is still another investigation by Dodwell (1963) which is relevant in this context. It represents a large-scale attempt to survey the problem areas dealt with in Inhelder and Piaget's book on space. He constructed seven groups of tests, each covering a different area, and each made up of a number of items designed to tap various facets of the same problem. The intercorrelations of performance in the various areas proved to be rather low. There was, moreover, a general lack of consistency among the responses to the items within each of the areas, which merely represented variants of the same task or problems. This is indicated by the large number of subjects who had to be placed into a mixed category, i.e., who failed to show a dominant level in their responses to the various items within any one area. The percentage of subjects in this category varied from a low of 43.5 per cent to a high of 84 per cent.

In the light of such findings, it seems that consistency may well be the hobgoblin of some psychologists, but hardly appears to preoccupy the small minds of children serving as subjects in Piaget-type studies. Nevertheless, in spite of such evidence I would not wish to suggest that we turn in the Piaget model for a new one, just because it may be somewhat out of tune with the real world. Whatever its shortcomings, it still seems a good deal sturdier than any replacements that are likely to be built in the near future.

But what are the specifications for the tune-up which Piaget's system appears to require? With respect to the problem of the lack of inter-task consistency which we have just been discussing, two rather different alternatives should be considered. One possibility is that responses to two situations—supposedly equivalent in terms of Piaget's model—may in fact develop in sequence, rather than simultaneously. This would mean that, instead of all subjects either passing or failing both tasks, some subjects might pass the one and fail the other, though not vice versa. In other words, the situation would be that discussed earlier under the developmental sequence question. Many of the cases violating the parallelity principle appear indeed to fall into this category. For instance, Lovell's data on the relationship between transitivity and weight-conservation show that, of 364 children, 105 (or 29 per cent) mastered transitivity while lacking conservation, while only 27 (or less than 8 per cent) showed the reverse pattern (Lovell and Ogilvie, 1961).

As a matter of fact, Piaget (1956) has to some extent made provision for this possibility through his concept of "horizontal differentials," according to which the same or similar concepts, when applied to different materials or situations, may develop in a staggered sequence rather than simultaneously. A good case in point for Piaget is that of conservation, where we find a progression from substance to weight to volume. Unfortunately such a progression (and in fact the concept of horizontal differentials generally) does not give the impression of having been fully assimilated into his system; it appears rather to have been tacked on almost as an afterthought. In view of the common occurrence of cases of this kind, it would seem important to accord this question more systematic treatment. An attempt should be made to specify the variables and parameters relating to the materials, to the specific content, and to other similar task variables which may affect the developmental timetable with respect to a particular concept or principle. Whether the role of these task variables and the larger problem of the generalizability of a principle or concept can be adequately handled within the framework of Piaget's model of logical operations remains to be seen.

A second alternative to the inter-task consistency postulate must be reckoned with, however. The departure from consistency may in certain cases be such that some subjects attain a given stage for task A but not for task B, while others show the reverse pattern. One possible explanation for such a state of affairs might be simply in terms of the unreliability of the response measures obtained. Indeed, the notion of error, whether based in the subject or in the measuring instrument, is probably one that we shall have to come to grips with more realistically, if we are to make much headway in providing Piaget's system with a solid empirical foundation. This will, however, require a rather less uncompromisingly deterministic and absolutist conception of mental operations, or at least of their overt manifestations, than Piaget has presented us with. Similarly it creates a need for methodological models which include a greater tolerance for error and variability than Guttman's scalogram analysis does, for instance.

It may, indeed, prove necessary to go even further in order to handle some of the stubborn facts indicating lack of any relationship between two supposedly equivalent problems. Even for tasks formally equivalent in their underlying operations, intersubject differences in performance may arise because of factors relating to individual differences in intellectual functioning, such as must be expected at any level of development. For instance, it would hardly be surprising to find reversibility in the area of spatial perspective developing earlier in some children than reversibility in the area of the conservation of displaced volume, while in other subjects the reverse might be true. In other words, the problem of horizontal differentiation of responses must at some point be reconciled with, if not incorporated within Piaget's hierarchical model of levels of mental operations.

The foregoing look at Piaget's system as a source for research may appear to have been a rather narrow, not to say myopic, one. Certainly it has done little more than scratch the surface of this vast area, which remains in large part still terra incognita, with its manifold special problems as well as opportunities. At the same time, this treatment may seem to have been unduly severe in its assessment of the empirical foundation of Piaget's system, particularly in the context of a symposium presumably intended to bring out the positive contribution which Piaget's work represents for developmental psychology. Let me state in closing, therefore, what I would regard as one of the essential benefits which the study of Piaget holds for developmental research.

Piaget's system has impelled us, I believe, to take a fresh look at our field and to ask a host of new questions concerning the nature of developmental stages and of developmental processes generally, as well as of the kind of research approaches which the study of these problems demands. In so doing, it has helped us appreciate the important place of systematic theory in an area of developmental research, essentially comparative in nature, which has not always been noted for its theoretical sophistication. On the other hand, the theoretical significance of research inspired by Piaget's ideas does not prevent it from having direct and important relevance for the resolution of practical questions of pedagogy and educational practice. What is more, research on Piaget-type problems generally turns out to be great fun, not only for the experimenter, but (praise be!) for the subject as well. It would seem uncharitable indeed to ask more of any theorist.

REFERENCES

Braine, M. D. S. (1959). The ontogeny of certain logical operations: Piaget's formulation examined by nonverbal methods. *Psychol. Monogr.*, 73 (5), Whole No. 475.

Dodwell, P. C. (1960). Children's understanding of number and related concepts. *Canad. J. Psychol.*, **14**, 191–205.

Dodwell, P. C. (1962). Relations between the understanding of the logic of classes and of cardinal number in children. *Canad. J. Psychol.*, **16**, 152–160.

Dodwell, P. C. (1963). Children's understanding of spatial concepts. *Canad. J. Psychol.*, **17**, 141–161.

Inhelder, Barbel, and J. Piaget (1958). *The growth of logical thinking from childhood to adolescence.* New York: Basic Books.

Inhelder, Barbel, and J. Piaget (1959). *La genèse des structures logiques élémentaires.* Neuchâtel: Delachaux et Niestlé.

Keats, J. A. (1955). Formal and concrete thought processes. Unpublished doctoral dissertation, Princeton University.

Lovell, K. (1961). A follow-up study of Inhelder and Piaget's "The growth of logical thinking." *Brit. J. Psychol.*, **52**, 143–153.

Lovell, K., and E. Ogilvie (1961). A study of the conservation of weight in the junior school child. *Brit. J. educ. Psychol.*, **31**, 138–144.

Lunzer, E. A. (1960). Some points of Piagetian theory in the light of experimental criticism. *J. child Psychol. Psychiat.*, **1**, 191–202.

Morf, A. (1959). Apprentissage d'une structure logique concrète (inclusion). In A. Morf *et al.*, *L'apprentissage des structures logiques. Etudes d'épistémologie génétique,* Vol. 9. Paris: Presses Universitaires. Pp. 15–83.

Piaget, J. (1956). Les stades du développement intellectuel de l'enfant et de l'adolescent. In P. Osterrieth *et al., Le problème des stades en psychologie de l'enfant.* Paris: Presses Universitaires. Pp. 33–49.

Piaget, J., Barbel Inhelder, and A. Szeminska (1960). *The child's conception of geometry.* New York: Basic Books.

Smedslund, J. (1961). The acquisition of conservation of substance and weight in children: II. External reinforcement of conservation of weight and of the operations of addition and subtraction. *Scand. J. Psychol.*, **2**, 71–84.

White, B. J., and E. Saltz (1957). Measurement of reproducibility. *Psychol. Bull.*, **54**, 81–99.

CONSERVATION: AN S-R ANALYSIS

John S. Watson

Most behavioral events present the tantalizing possibility of multiple interpretation. The behavior which a Piagetian would term an act of "conservation" is no exception. Consider the following example of conser-

A paper especially prepared for this volume.

vation behavior: A child observes one of two equal balls of plasticine being pressed into the form of a pancake and then, in response to inquiry, says the two pieces of plasticine are yet "the same" regarding their substance, weight, or volume. A Piagetian would tend to interpret this behavior as a sign that the child possesses certain logical mental structures which allow him to "conserve" the substance, weight, or volume of the transformed object. An S-R learning[1] proponent would tend to interpret the behavior as a sign that the child has had a history of being rewarded for responding "the same" in stimulus situations similar to this one. The fact that either interpretation can be considered reasonable is a rather obvious point. Less obvious, perhaps, is the fact that research to date does not provide a clear basis for deciding which of these interpretations has the greater relative validity.

While the title of the present paper may have the look of a prelude to argument in support of an S-R interpretation of responses to conservation problems, this will not be the case; nor will there be any attempt to translate relevant Piagetian concepts into mediational S-R terminology after the fashion which Berlyne (1962) initiated. What this paper will undertake is an examination of the stimulus context of the behavior which a Piagetian would accept as evidence that a subject is a "conserver" (hereafter referred to simply as conservation behavior). The analysis will employ the perspective and language of nonmediational S-R learning theory. The principal objective of this analysis is to provide a perspective for designing experiments which would be necessary for estimating the relative validity of Piagetian and S-R interpretations of conservation behavior. A related goal is the identification of causal factors which may play an important role in the growth or acquisition of conservation behavior but which may have remained unemphasized by previous, predominantly Piagetian, analyses. The present analysis is organized around the following three questions: (1) What does conservation behavior look like from an S-R perspective? (2) What are the requirements for an S-R solution to conservation tasks? (3) What are the implications of this S-R analysis for the training of conservation behavior?

WHAT DOES CONSERVATION BEHAVIOR LOOK LIKE FROM AN S-R PERSPECTIVE?

The conservation task employing two plasticine balls, one of which is transformed to a new shape, will serve as the "working example" for much

[1] In this paper, "S-R learning" refers to the theoretical perspective of nonmediational stimulus-response theory as exemplified in the writings of Skinner and the early portions of Hull's writings. This perspective should be distinguished from the S-R theoretical proposals which include a reference to the assumed existence of internal mediating responses as exemplified by the later writings of Hull and Osgood.

of the succeeding discussion. With this in mind, the analysis of conservation behavior can begin by noting that the basic response criterion for conservation is a subject's statement "the same" when asked whether the transformed plasticine is more, the same, or less than the untransformed ball. The verbal statement "the same" is meaningless, of course, without an appreciation of the stimulus context in which the statement occurs. In conservation research, the stimulus context is the conservation assessment task. This being so, let us consider the stimulus dimensions of this task.

Stimulus Dimensions of the Conservation Task

The conservation task lends itself readily to a three-part division for both logical analysis (see Elkind, 1967) and analysis of major stimulus dimensions. For the convenience of later discussion, the initial temporal portion of the stimulus array is here labeled "S1 (sa = sb)" wherein "sa" and "sb" represent the stimulus features of the two objects (for example, the two plasticine balls) and "=" represents the stimulus equivalence of the two objects as they exist within the major stimulus array "S1." Continuing with this form of notation, the second portion of the three-part temporal sequence is labeled "S2(sb→sb′)" wherein "sb→sb′" represents the stimulation produced by the process in which "sb" is transformed to the stimulus object "sb′" (for example, one ball being pressed into the shape of a pancake). The third part of the task is labeled "S3(sa≠sb′)" wherein "sa≠sb′" represents the lack of stimulus equivalence of the two objects due to the transformation of "sb." It is this final stimulus array that confronts the subject as he is queried whether "sb′" is more, the same, or less than "sa." The total stimulus context of the conservation task can now be expressed as "S1(sa = sb) →S2(sb→sb′) →S3(sa ≠ sb′)."

In the following discussion, the three portions of the conservation task will be referred to at times simply as S1, S2, and S3. It should be noted further that one could make additional refinements in this analysis. For instance, one could make many more subdivisions of the S2 portion or perhaps make specific reference to the verbal questioning of the subject in the S3 portion. However, such refinements are not viewed as necessary for the purposes of the present discussion.

S2 (Object Transformation) as a Discriminative Stimulus

From an S-R perspective, the purpose of analyzing the stimulus context in which a particular response is elicited is to uncover the specific stimuli which function in the "control" of the occurrence of that response. It is assumed that a given stimulus controls a response either because it has an "unconditioned" (that is, reflexive) power to elicit that response or because previous occurrences (that is, "emissions") of the response, in the presence of or closely following that stimulus, have been rewarded. Conventional verbal responses are virtually never viewed as unconditioned and thus the S-R proponent seeks to find the stimulus which has marked the occasions in which the verbal response has been rewarded in the past. Now the interesting thing about a subject's conservation response "the same," as it may occur in the S3 portion of the conservation task, is that the immediate stimulus array "sa $\neq$ sb'" would appear to possess eliciting power for nonconservation responses, for example, "more," "less," or "different." From a Piagetian perspective, it is important that this be true. If S3 were to mark an obvious occasion for the response "the same," if sa and sb' indeed "looked the same," then this response would have little bearing on the question of whether the child was "conserving" substance, weight, or volume. If S3 directly controlled the correct response, the child could make the response without conserving anything from S1 to S3 other than his ability to see.

If, on the other hand, one assumes that S3 does not directly control the correct response to conservation tasks (an assumption which at least occasionally should be demonstrated empirically in conservation studies), then an S-R explanation is left with S1 and S2 as potential controlling stimuli. Now a Piagetian would assume that a conserver would not maintain his response "the same" if, during S2, the transformation of sb to sb' were to involve adding or subtracting material. If this is so, then it would appear that the conservation response "the same" would be under the control of S2 since, in both this and the standard situation, the S1 portions would be identical. Thus, it seems that when S2 involves what might be called a "conserving transformation" (hereafter referred to as cS2) in which nothing is added or subtracted regarding the material of sb, the conserver responds "the same." When S2 does involve an addition or subtraction of material (hereafter referred to as ϕS2), this response is not given. From an S-R perspective, then, a conserver's response would be viewed as under the control of S2, with cS2 being the discriminative stimulus for the conservation response "the same."

This designation of cS2 as a discriminative stimulus has an interesting implication. The usual Piagetian definition of conservation involves some statement that the subject conserves a specified aspect of the object (for example, quantity) *despite* his observation of a transformation of other aspects of the object. For example, Flavell (1963, p. 245) defines conservation as "the cognition that certain properties (quantity, number, length, and so forth) remain invariant (or conserved) *in the face of* certain transformations (displacing objects or object parts in space, sectioning an object into pieces, changing shape, etc.)" (my italics). The S-R perspective outlined here, however, would seem to be saying that the subject's conservation behavior occurs not "despite" or "in the face of" the cS2 transformation, but indeed *because of* the cS2 transformation. While this difference in perspective at first may appear to be more semantic than real, the distinction hopefully will become clearer in the course of the following discussion.

WHAT ARE THE REQUIREMENTS FOR AN S-R SOLUTION TO CONSERVATION TASKS?

On the basis of the present S-R analysis, one necessary requirement of the conservation task is that the subject accurately discriminate and remember whether S2 was of the type cS2 or ¢S2. Upon closer examination, it becomes equally clear that the act of discriminating cS2 from ¢S2 is not on the order of a simple discrimination. An S2 stimulus array is what might be called a "time-distributed stimulus." That is to say, S2 does not exist in its entirety at any single moment in time but rather is distributed over a span of time. This can be contrasted to what might be called "static stimuli," of which S1 and S3 can serve as examples. In the case of a static stimulus, the stimulus array can be said to exist in its entirety at any given moment during the span of time it occurs. One rather obvious consequence of this difference is that static stimuli can be accurately assessed even if they are attended to for only a portion of their occurrence. Time-distributed stimuli, on the other hand, can be assured of accurate assessment only when they are attended to for the entirety of the time span they occupy.

Furthermore, the discrimination of time-distributed stimuli requires that the initial portions of the stimulus event be retained in memory while later portions occur. For example, if the time-distributed stimulus red-then-green is discriminated from yellow-then-green and from red-then-yellow, it is necessary that the discriminatory response be withheld until the occurrence of the green light (responding to red would produce errors). Yet, when green does occur, it must be responded to on the basis of whether it was preceded by red or by yellow.

The emphasis this analysis has placed on the requirement that a subject discriminate between cS2 and ¢S2 might be considered as quite compatible with the Piagetian view of the conservation task. Surely a Piagetian would agree that if a subject did not know whether or not some substance was added or removed from the transformed plasticine ball, then, of course, he would not be able to deduce whether the new shape (the pancake) was of equal substance, weight, or volume to the ball which was not transformed. But the interesting point to note is that when a subject fails to produce the conservation response, it is usually assumed that the reason he fails rests in his lack of sufficient logical mental structures for the deductive reasoning, and not because he might possess insufficient information regarding the preceding transformation.

A Piagetian might also propose that a concern for the subject's awareness of the transformational act is quite evident in the usual scoring system for conservation behavior. It is common that a subject who says "the same" be questioned further as to why he has made this statement. Usually the "best" reply a subject can make is a reference to the nature of the transformational act. That is, in the paradigm case, a high conservation rating would be given to a subject who said "the same" and then followed this with "because nothing was added or taken away." However, the absence of this supportive statement normally would not be attributed to the subject's possible inability to see or remember the transformational act, but rather to his lack of clarity about the logical relevance of this information to the statement "the same."

When a subject does make the best reply, the Piagetian interprets it as a reflection of the subject's logical sophistication. Yet, from an S-R perspective, one could contend that when the subject says "because nothing was added or taken away" he is simply reporting his identification of the discriminative stimulus. This would be functionally the same as might occur with a child who had mastered a Skinner box which dispensed candy when a lever was pressed following a red light but not following a blue light. If one asked the child why he had just pressed the lever, he might well be expected to say "because the red light was just on." In this situation, a Piagetian would not be likely to say that the child's response indicates anything regarding his logical sophistication.

Instrumental versus Logical Conservation Behavior

Although the preceding discussion has been centered on highlighting what would appear to be the requirements for conservation behavior from strictly an S-R point of view, the discussion has unavoidably crossed swords with the Piagetian view in order clearly to distinguish the points raised by the S-R analysis. This has raised an issue which is worth pursuing further. The issue concerns the means by which one might possibly distinguish conservation behavior which is theoretically the result of logical thinking and that which is theoretically the result of discriminative instrumental conditioning. If a child's statement "because nothing was added or taken away" is not unambiguous support for claiming that his previous statement "the same" was mediated by logical mental structures, then what behavioral criteria would be sufficient for a claim of logical mediation?

Smedslund (1961b) has introduced one rather objective criterion which appears to have been well received among Piagetians. Smedslund assessed the degree to which the conservation behavior of his subjects resisted extinction across three consecutive conservation tasks which were so contrived that a subject's conservation response "the same" was disconfirmed empirically. This test was given at the end of a conservation training study. Subjects who entered the study as conservers were more resistant than those who apparently learned to conserve during the course of the experiment. Smedslund interprets the greater resistance of the "natural" conservers as reflecting their possession of mediating logical structure. This interpretation would seem quite consistent with Piaget's (1964) contention, "If a structure develops spontaneously, once it has reached a state of equilibrium, it is lasting, it will continue throughout the child's entire life." From this perspective, the extinction of a conservation response stands as a sign that the relevant, logical structures were never really developed. Thus, resistance to extinction takes on the role of a criterion of the logical basis of conservation behavior.

However, it is unlikely that an S-R proponent would be much impressed by this type of data, particularly as regards its relevance to an interpretation of Smedslund's results. Resistance to extinction (even lifetime resistance) can be viewed as the consequence of a variety of variables from an S-R learning perspective (number of past reinforcements, variety of reward, or the schedule of past reinforcement). For example, an S-R proponent would hardly feel compelled to interpret the resistance of Smedslund's subjects as a sign that they possessed mediating, logical structures. The subjects who entered the study as conservers might well be assumed to have had a prior history of reinforcement for conservation behavior. Moreover, if one is to assume that the subjects who entered the study as conservers had an advantage of logic over the trained subjects, because the former developed their conservation behavior "naturally," then it is difficult to reconcile the fact that only six of the thirteen "natural" conservers resisted extinction across a mere three extinction trials.

On the basis of the preceding discussion it would not seem likely that resistance to extinction can serve as an unambiguous criterion for distinguishing between logical and instrumental conservation behavior. As this writer sees it, a more likely possibility would seem to exist in stimulus generalization experiments designed so that when a critical stimulus situation is introduced, a logical response to the situation would be distinct from the predicted generalization of instrumental responding. An example of this type of experiment follows.

The experiment involves three logical variations of the standard conservation task. It will be recalled that the stimulus context of the standard task can be represented symbolically by the expression "$S1(sa = sb) \rightarrow S2(sb \rightarrow sb') \rightarrow S3(sa \neq sb')$." One variation of this task has already been raised by the distinction between $cS2$ and $\not{c}S2$. The standard task is a case of $cS2$ (nothing is added or subtracted in the act of transformation). Thus, the standard task can be varied by substituting $cS2$ with an instance of $\not{c}S2$ (adding of subtracting material while transforming sb). Another means of altering the standard task can be provided by having the initial presentation of the two objects in S1 not equivalent to one another (having one of the two plasticine balls noticeably smaller than the other). This situation would be represented symbolically as "$S1(sa \neq sb)$." We are now in a position to construct three variations of the standard task. They are represented symbolically as follows:

Standard Task	$S1(sa = sb) \rightarrow cS2(sb \rightarrow sb') \rightarrow S3(sa \neq sb')$
Variant 1	$S1(sa = sb) \rightarrow \cancel{c}S2(sb \rightarrow sb') \rightarrow S3(sa \neq sb')$
Variant 2	$S1(sa \neq sb) \rightarrow cS2(sb \rightarrow sb') \rightarrow S3(sa \neq sb')$
Variant 3	$S1(sa \neq sb) \rightarrow \cancel{c}S2(sb \rightarrow sb') \rightarrow S3(sa \neq sb')$

Let us assume that a group of nonconservers are given extended experience with the standard task and specific forms of variants 1 and 2, but no experience is provided with variant 3. Let us also assume that eventually all subjects accomplish complete mastery of the three tasks available to them. That is to say, when queried as to whether the objects are "the same" or "not the same" while facing the S3 portion of each task, the subjects respond in the following way. In the standard task they say, "the objects are the same—because they were the same to begin with and nothing has been added or taken away." In variant 1 they say, "the objects are not the same—because they were the same to begin with and you added some plasticine while making the pancake." And in variant 2 they say, "the objects are not the same—because they were not the same to begin with, the ball made into a pancake was smaller, and nothing has been added or taken away." Now the question is whether these responses represent logical thinking or whether they simply represent instrumental verbal responses and verbal reports of the discriminative stimuli which control these instrumental responses. As yet, one could not be sure of either designation.

The introduction of variant 3 at this time would be quite informative, if it were coordinated with the specific forms of variants 1 and 2 employed in the experiment. Thus, if the smaller of the unequal plasticine balls were transformed to a pancake and while this was being done some plasticine were added, the S1 portion of the task would be the same as the S1 portion of variant 2 and the S2 portion would be the same as the S2 portion of variant 1. Both variant 1 and variant 2 presumably have provided consistent reinforcement of the statement "the objects are not the same." If any generalization occurred then, an S-R proponent should predict that the subjects would respond to variant 3 by saying "the objects are not the same." If they reported the discriminative stimuli, they should be expected to say "because they were not the same to begin with, the ball made into a pancake was smaller, and you added some plasticine while making the pancake." In contrast, a Piagetian should predict that if the responses of the children are mediated by logical structures then they should respond to variant 3 by saying something equivalent to the following statement, "I can't tell, they might be the same because you added some to the smaller one." If this response were to occur, it would be rather difficult to explain in simple S-R terms. On the other hand, if the S-R prediction were to obtain, then it would cast a considerable shadow on the validity of assuming that a child is thinking logically when he makes a correct response, says "because," and follows this with what we view as a logically relevant statement.

WHAT ARE THE IMPLICATIONS OF THIS S-R ANALYSIS FOR THE TRAINING OF CONSERVATION BEHAVIOR?

If one believes that conservation behavior is important, regardless of whether it is best explained in Piagetian or S-R terms, then one might well ask what the present S-R analysis offers in the way of practical suggestions for training of conservation behavior. What kind of training might be fruitful in any attempt to lead a child up the conservation path sooner than he might be expected to traverse that path on his own?

There is a rather clear implication for conservation training within the preceding analysis, and while it is a rather simple proposal, it does not appear to have arisen in previous discussions of conservation training (perhaps because these have been primarily products of the Piagetian perspective). The present analysis has designated the time-distributed stimulus of the transformational act as having central importance in the stimulus context of the standard conservation task. If a subject is to meet the response requirements of the conservation task, his behavior must be under the control of this stimulus. Thus he must be set to attend to this S2 stimulus and be set to discriminate between instances of cS2 and ¢S2. If training is to aid in the acquisition of conservation behavior, then it should be designed to promote a child's capacity for making these necessary discriminations.

How might one train a subject for this type of complex discriminative act? If the act is outside the behavioral repertoire of a subject, there would be little value in simply rewarding "correct" conservation behavior in a set of conservation tasks, that is, reinforcing a child for saying "the same" in a number of standard tasks. The most this procedure could accomplish would be to attach the response "the same" to the static S1 and/or S3 stimulus portions of the standard task. If the act of discriminating S2 is not occurring, then obviously this act could not be reinforced.

When S-R proponents are faced with the problem of training a subject for what is eventually to be a complex behavioral act, and the subject has a small (or even zero) probability of initially producing that response on his own, then some form of "shaping" is usually introduced. Distant approximations of the desired act are rewarded; and as these acts increase in strength, the requirement for reward is slowly shifted in the direction of the desired behavior. This shaping strategy is the heart of much of the modern programed instruction and it would seem likely that this tactic would have fruitful possibilities for training a subject to discriminate complex time-distributed stimuli.

Just what might be the best material or specific shaping procedure to use for accomplishing the present goal is an empirical question. However, the basic idea being proposed here can be illustrated by the following concrete example. The young "nonconserving" child might initially be introduced to a simple discrimination problem in which a specified response (perhaps, though not necessarily, a verbal response) would be rewarded when it followed a "positive" blue light stimulus but not when it followed a "negative" red-then-blue light stimulus. Mastery of this problem would require that, among other things, the subject attend to the antecedent context of the blue stimulus light. To insure that the task was not being solved by the subject simply learning to inhibit the response following the red stimulus, one could later introduce the requirement that the response follow either red-then-red or yellow-then-blue, but not red-then-blue. Later, positive discriminative stimuli might be embedded in varying positions within a longer stimulus series and perhaps later one could introduce longer and more complex stimuli for the required discrimination.

It would even be possible to construct S-R analogues to the standard conservation task and its logical variants. For example, one might start by presenting two blue lights, then vary the color of one light in a sequence which terminates with red. This "transformation" sequence might then be contrasted to an alternative sequence which also terminates with red. If the two situations required different responses for reward to occur, then a symbolic representation of these situations would be virtually the same as that presented in this paper for conservation tasks. Of course, the symbolic similarity in no way guarantees that mastering tasks of this analogue type would aid in the mastery of conservation tasks. But at this point in developmental psychology the question is not one of "guarantees." Rather, one might more realistically ask whether existing studies provide any support for the notion that conservation behavior could be advanced either through training which would be expected to increase a subject's general capacity for discriminating time-distributed stimuli or through training which at least might be expected to increase the salience of these stimuli as they appear within the conservation task. Let us, then, look briefly at the present status of the conservation training literature.

Recent reviews of the training literature (for example, Flavell, 1963; Sigel, Roeper, and Hooper, 1966) make it clear that the large quantity of attempts to facilitate the appearance of conservation behavior have been unable to demonstrate a pretest to posttest change which is significantly greater for children receiving training than for children not receiving the particular training experiences. Of course, a procedure which fails can offer little information as to why it has failed unless it can be precisely related to a procedure which succeeds. An instance of success, on the other hand, at least offers the opportunity of asking whether or not a variable of interest is visibly present. With this in mind, three very recent successful attempts at training conservation behavior are particularly noteworthy.

Wallach and Sprott (1964) report significant training effects in a study of number conservation. Experimental subjects received training in what the authors propose to be a set of "reversibility" situations, while control subjects were engaged in a game session between the pre- and posttests of conservation. Although the authors dismiss the possibility that the training in reversibility may have involved instrumental learning that would have direct transfer value for the posttest in conservation, an S-R proponent would not likely agree. The training and assessment procedures were, in general, very similar. The authors focus their attention on the fact that in the assessment task a subject was asked, "Now are there the same number of dolls as beds?" while in the training tasks the question was, "Do you think we can put a doll in every bed now?" The fact that the word "number" was not used in the training tasks is a crucial point for Wallach and Sprott. From an S-R perspective, on the other hand, it could be argued that the authors have overlooked the fact that while the assessment tasks involved a cS2 (conserving) transformation, the training tasks involved both cS2 and ¢S2 transformations; and the "correct" response to both the assessment tasks and the cS2 training tasks was an affirmative reply (for example, "yes"). Moreover, since the training sessions incorporated a direct contrast between cS2 and ¢S2 transformations, this training procedure would seem to have provided a maximal opportunity for the experimental subjects to learn to attend and discriminate the time-distributed S2 portion of the conservation tasks.

A study by Sigel, Roeper, and Hooper (1966) reports a significant difference between experimental and control subjects in substance and weight conservation following a five-week period during which experimentals received training in classification behavior and reversible transformations. The authors interpret their results as support for the efficacy of training nonconservers in cognitive operations viewed as theoretically prerequisite to conservation. However, it is not untenable that the extensive classification and reversibility training, along with the wide variety of stimulus materials employed, had the simple effect of increasing the attentional and discrimination capacities of the experimental subjects. Moreover, it is interesting to note that the training in reversible transformations, which by their very nature involve time-distributed stimuli, was introduced in the final portion of the training period. This order of training can be viewed as providing a rather good shaping sequence for augmenting skills in the discrimination of time-distributed stimuli. Add to this the extensive opportunity (five weeks) for these children to employ their increasing skills to the conservation problems they encounter in their natural activities of playing, eating, and so forth, and it would seem that the training procedure of this study does contain features which, from an S-R view, might well be expected to have positive transfer to behavior in the posttest conservation tasks. In order to distinguish between the relative validity of this S-R interpretation and the Piagetian interpretation offered by the authors, one would need data from a third group of subjects whose training focused on the discrimination of static and time-distributed stimuli but which was so arranged as to avoid formal classification and reversibility training.

Beilin (1965) also reports a significant training effect in a study of length, number, and area conservation. The effect is rather striking in that it apparently derived from a mere two sessions of training. Most notable, however, is the fact that this study involved a comparison of four different training procedures and only one of these resulted in a significantly greater rise in conservation behavior than that of the control group. One training procedure provided a nonverbal reward for correct conservation behavior. Another procedure involved the nonverbal reward and also provided an "orienting" instruction on every trial. A third procedure incorporated the nonverbal reward, and following incorrect trials, a "verbal rule instruction" was given. The fourth procedure was designed to test Smedslund's (1961a) "cognitive conflict" training hypothesis and it involved no reward. The only procedure to produce significant results was that of the "verbal rule instruction." Beilin interprets this result as the outcome of a "didactic" procedure which would appear to provide the subject "with a model or rule for processing relevant input data." However, that this instruction may have simply provided training in the discrimination of the relevant time-distributed stimuli can be argued by simply quoting that instruction as it was used with the length conservation training: "Whenever we start with a length like this one (pointing) and we don't add any sticks to it or take away any sticks, but only move it, it stays the same length even though it looks different. See, I can put them back the way they were, so they haven't really changed."

Two additional training studies (Frank, as reported by Bruner, 1964; and Smedslund, 1966) involve procedures which also would appear to provide discrimination training which might be expected to increase the salience of the transformation portion of subsequent conservation tasks. However, the apparent success of these two studies cannot be adequately assessed due to the absence of control data. On the other hand, they at least provide a bit of seasoning, if not substance, to the proposal that successful acceleration of conservation behavior may depend largely on the provision of relevant discrimination training.

A CONCLUDING COMMENT

In closing, it should again be stressed that the analysis presented in this paper has not been an attempt to show that what a Piagetian means by conservation can be adequately explained in traditional, nonmediational

S-R terms. The stated objective was to use the S-R perspective as a means of examining the stimulus context of the standard conservation assessment task with the implicit hope that this activity would result in some heuristic products for conceptualization and research in the area of conservation behavior. In retrospect, then, what has this analysis accomplished?

The reframing of the conservation task in S-R terminology would seem to have produced two products of potential value. On the one hand, it has produced a picture of existing conservation research which would seem to designate a prevailing ambiguity in some of the principal criteria of distinguishing the logical nature of conservation behavior. If one assumes that it is important to know when and how various human behaviors attain the stature of logical behavior, then it will be necessary to develop clear criteria of logical conservation behavior. A second product of the present analysis has been the designation of the critical role which a child's ability to discriminate time-distributed stimuli may play in his acquisition of conservation behavior. This is viewed as having a potential value for both the analysis of the natural acquisition of conservation behavior and for the design of procedures to accelerate this acquisition.

REFERENCES

Beilin, H. (1965). Learning and operational convergence in logical thought development. *J. exp. child Psychol.*, **2**, 317–339.

Berlyne, D. E. (1962). Comments on relations between Piaget's theory and S-R theory. In Kessen and Kuhlman (Eds.), Thought in the young child. *Monogr. Soc. Res. Child Develpm.*, **27** (2), Ser. No. 83.

Bruner, J. S. (1964). The course of cognitive growth. *Amer. Psychol.*, **19**, 1–15.

Elkind, D. (1967). Piaget's conservation problems: a logical analysis. *Child Develpm.*, **38**, 15–27.

Flavell, J. H. (1963). *The developmental psychology of Jean Piaget.* Princeton, N.J.: Van Nostrand.

Piaget, J. (1964). Development and learning. In R. E. Ripple and V. N. Rockcastle (Eds.), *Piaget rediscovered: A report of the Conference on Cognitive Studies and Curriculum Development, March 1964.* Ithaca, N.Y.: Cornell University Press.

Sigel, I. E., Annemarie Roeper, and F. H. Hooper (1966). A training procedure for acquisition of Piaget's conservation of quantity: a pilot study and its replication. *Brit. J. educ. Psychol.*, **36**, 301–311.

Smedslund, J. (1961a). The acquisition of conservation of substance and weight in children: II. External reinforcement of conservation of weight and of the operations of addition and subtraction. *Scand. J. Psychol.*, **2**, 71–84.

Smedslund, J. (1961). The acquisition of conservation of substance and weight in children: III. Extinction of conservation of weight acquired "normally" and by means of empirical controls on a balance. *Scand. J. Psychol.*, **2**, 85–87.

Smedslund, J. (1966). Microanalysis of concrete reasoning: I. The difficulty of some combinations of addition and subtraction of one unit. *Scand. J. Psychol.*, **7**, 145–156.

Wallach, Lise, and R. L. Sprott (1964). Inducing number conservation in children. *Child Develpm.*, **35**, 1057–1071.

PIAGET'S CONSERVATION PROBLEMS

David Elkind

The quantity of literature currently growing up around the conservation problems introduced by Piaget and his colleagues (e.g., Piaget, 1952; Piaget and Inhelder, 1962; Piaget, Inhelder, and Szeminska, 1960) testifies to the significance which both Piaget and other investigators attach to these problems. It is not the purpose of this paper to resurvey this research, since much of it has already been summarized by Flavell (1963), Hunt (1961), Sigel (1964), and Wallach (1963). Rather, the aim is to reconsider some fundamental aspects of the conservation problems. More particularly, the aim is to demonstrate that every conservation problem assesses two different forms of conservation and that this distinction helps both to clarify Piaget's discussion of conservation and to resolve some of the misunderstandings about conservation that repeatedly occur in the literature on this subject.

In order to facilitate the discussion, it will be helpful to introduce a symbolic description of the conservation problems in general. Regardless of the content of these problems, they routinely involve presenting the subject with a variable (V) and a standard (S) stimulus that are initially equivalent in both the perceptual and the quantitative sense. The subject is then asked to make a judgment regarding their quantitative equivalence. Once the judgment is made, the variable stimulus is subjected to a transformation, $V \to V'$, which alters the perceptual but not the quantitative equivalence between variable and standard. After completion of the transformation, the subject is asked to judge the quantitative equivalence between the standard and the transformed variable. The entire problem can be symbolized in the following way:

$$S \overset{t_0}{=} V \qquad V \overset{t_1}{\to} V' \qquad S \overset{t_2}{?} V'$$

Reprinted with the permission of the author and The Society for Research in Child Development, Inc., from *Child Development*, 1967, 38, 15–27.

To make this symbolism concrete, consider the problem of weight conservation (Piaget and Inhelder, 1962). The child is presented with two clay balls (V and S) equivalent in size, appearance, and weight, and is asked whether they are the same weight. He is allowed to ascertain this equivalence with the aid of balance if he so desires. One of the balls is then made into a "pancake" or a "sausage" or into a number of "little balls" (V → V'), after which the child is asked to judge whether V' has more, less, or the same weight as S. With this description of the conservation problem in mind, we can turn to the two forms of conservation assessed by the standard conservation task.

ANALYSIS OF THE CONSERVATION TASK

The datum of the conservation problem, the judgment regarding the equality of inequality of S and V', can be viewed as indicative of two different forms of conservation. First of all, the judgment could be viewed as dealing with the conservation of a given weight, length, number, etc., across a reversible transformation and with respect to itself alone. For example, suppose that in the weight conservation problem described earlier one employed only a single ball of clay which was then rolled into a sausage, and the child was asked whether the clay was now the same weight as before (i.e., does V = V'?). This would be a direct assessment of what will hereafter be called the "conservation of identity." In the standard conservation problem, however, the subject never compares V and V' directly, so that identity conservation must always be inferred from the child's judgment regarding S and V, and S and V' in the following way:

Conservation of Identity	Nonconservation of Identity
S judges $S = V$	S judges $S = V$
S judges $S = V'$	S judges $S \neq V'$
E infers $V = V'$	E infers $V \neq V'$

The conservation judgments, however, can also be viewed as assessing the child's knowledge of the invariance of a quantitative relation (of equality, inequality, etc.) across a transformation of one of the elements of that relation. It can readily be seen that the standard conservation problem outlined above provides a direct test of this form of conservation which will hereafter be called the "conservation of equivalence." The assessment of equivalence conservation via the standard conservation problem involves no inference by the experimenter since the child's judgments of S and V and of S and V' are direct indications of the child's belief as to whether a relation changes across a change in the elements of that relation. Either the equality relation between S and V is conserved from the initial judgment to the judgment of S and V', or it is not.

It is probably true, nonetheless, that from the point of view of the subject, the conservation of identity is a necessary condition for the conservation of equivalence. As will be shown later, and as Piaget has often pointed out, there is no perceptual means whereby the child can determine that $V' = S$. He must, therefore, rely on his previous experiences of having judged $S = V$ and of having seen V transformed into V'. The utilization of these past experiences in the form of a deductive argument would seem to be the necessary and sufficient conditions for the attainment of equivalence conservation. The utilization of these past experiences, however, presupposes identity conservation as is demonstrated by the following paradigms:

Conservation of Equivalence		Nonconservation of Equivalence	
	S judges $S = V$		S judges $S = V$
(Covertly)	S judges $V = V'$	(Covertly)	S judges $V \neq V'$
	S judges $S = V'$		S judges $S \neq V'$

To summarize, the conservation problem can be said to assess two types of conservation: equivalence and identity. The conservation of identity, however, must always be inferred from the child's responses, whereas the conservation of equivalence is reflected directly in the child's judgments. Consequently, the conservation of identity would seem to be a necessary but not a sufficient condition for the attainment of equivalence conservation. The latter form of conservation would seem to require, in addition, the utilization of immediate past experience in the form of a deductive argument.

PIAGET'S DISCUSSION OF CONSERVATION

One of the difficulties for the non-Piagetian psychologist in reading Piaget is to determine how much of what is left out of a given presentation is really implicit in that discussion. Piaget appears to write for a highly select audience, namely, his co-workers and students who are immersed in his system and in his terminology. As a result, Piaget may ignore or minimize aspects of a problem which are taken for granted by the group, or which have already been dealt with in detail in some other place, or which are simply regarded as relatively unimportant or self-evident. Unless the reader is a well-read Piagetian, he may well arrive at some erroneous impressions as to what Piaget has said.

A case in point is Piaget's typical discussion of conservation. In such presentations, Piaget generally does not distinguish between identity and equivalence conservation and often devotes the major share of the discussion to the problem of identity conservation. To the unsuspecting reader, this style of presentation may be misleading. Piaget seems to be explaining how the subject arrives at the equality of S and V' when, in fact, he is talking about the equality of V and V'. For instance, when Piaget (1952) talks about how the child recognizes that the amount of liquid in a tall, narrow glass is equal to that in a wide, shallow glass, he is not really trying to explain how the child comes to make an equivalence judgment between the two immediately present quantities, V' and S, but rather how he makes an identity judgment regarding the variable quantity (V') and its previous state (V).

As will be demonstrated in the discussion of equivalence conservation, the mechanism which Piaget postulates to account for the equation of V and V' cannot at the same time explain the equation of V' and S. This seems to be the point on which Piaget is most often misunderstood and is a point which is crucial to a correct understanding of his view of conservation. A brief summary of his discussions of conservation is, therefore, necessary in order to demonstrate that they do in fact deal with identity and not with equivalence conservation.

Regardless of the content of the particular conservation problem, Piaget sees the central difficulty encountered on such tasks as that of how the child comes to deal with an object that is varying in two inverse directions at the same time.

> In all of these examples [of varied types of conservation problems] the subject can hesitate between the responses of "more" or "less" or "equal" as a function of two aspects of the configuration which vary simultaneously and inversely with respect to each other. In the case of the ball of clay made into tiny pieces, or of the large glass full of liquid or pearls whose contents are divided in many small glasses, the two antagonistic factors are the increasing number of elements and their decreasing size. In the case of the ball of clay . . . etc. (Piaget, 1957, p. 49, W.T.)

The basic mechanism which Piaget postulates to account for how the child comes to deal with this problem is what Piaget has called the "equation of differences" (Piaget, 1952) or "compensation" (Piaget and Inhelder, 1962). In brief, Piaget (1957) holds that the child gradually comes to see that for any given object a change in one dimension is exactly compensated by an equal and inverse change in a second dimension. This discovery—that when the dimensions of a given quantity are altered the dimensional differences compensate one another—underlies the child's insight that transformations are reversible and that they leave the object (property or quantity) invariant.

Piaget says, in effect, that the child comes to employ a calculus of discontinuous equations of differences so as to arrive at the notion of a continuous or reversible transformation.

Piaget writes (1957, p. 54, W.T.):

> The processes of retroaction lead [the child] sooner or later to consider as field, not simply the successive changes in A0, A1, A2 (for example,

the increasing length of the ball made into a sausage) nor exclusively the successive changes in B0, B1, B2 (for example, the decreasing diameter of the sausage), but rather their relations:

$$
\begin{array}{ccc}
A0 & \rightarrow & A1 & \rightarrow & A2 \ldots \ldots \ldots \\
\updownarrow & & \updownarrow & & \updownarrow \\
B0 & \rightarrow & B1 & \rightarrow & B2 \ldots \ldots \ldots
\end{array}
$$

To demonstrate that this position has not changed in its essentials over the years, consider the following paragraph segment written more than 15 years before the 1957 article:

> Now the notion of conservation of wholes, which is acquired by children at this stage, presupposes a quantification wide enough to cover the case in which elementary relationships vary in opposite directions, and it there-fore presupposes the discovery of "extensive" quantities. Indeed, if the child is to assume conservation, he must not only be aware that when the width and height of the columns are the same the total quantity remains constant, but also that it remains constant in spite of the fact that the height increases and the width decreases. (Piaget, 1952 [1941], pp. 21–22)

It is thus clear that Piaget's discussion of conservation is primarily aimed at explaining the conservation of identity and not the conservation of equivalence. That is to say, the equation of differences refers to the compensation of changes within one and the same object and not to the relation between standard and variable directly assessed by the conservation problem. Although the notion that conservation always in-volves deduction is implicit and sometimes explicit in Piaget's discussion, the reader may nonetheless sense a discrepancy between what is being as-sessed and what is being explained. This apparent discrepancy may be one reason that Wohlwill (1964) refers to conservation as a mystery and why Bruner (1964a, p. 41) writes that he and Miss Carey continue to "brood on the problem of conservation."

It must be added that this equation-of-difference theory of identity conservation is supported by a host of supplementary experiments, to be found in every book reporting conservation experiments, as well as by care-ful analysis of the behavior of preoperational children on the conservation task. This fact is sometimes obscured by Piaget's apparent use of children's verbal explanations of conservation as if they provided direct evidence as to the processes by which the conservation of identity is attained. In fact, however, the three types of verbal explanations—(*a*) nothing has been added or taken away so it is the same (identity), (*b*) if you made it like it was before it will be the same (reversibility), and (*c*) what it lost in one way it gained in another (equation of differences or compensation)— are really *post hoc* rationalizations rather than veridical reflections of the processes leading to conservation. This is obvious from the fact that each of them is concerned with identity conservation, whereas the problem actually solved was that of equivalence conservation. If the child were really to verbalize the way in which he arrived at the solution to the conservation problem, he would have to say something like this: "This (V) was equal to that (S) before, and the change (V → V') doesn't change anything, so this (V') must still equal this (S)."

The fact that children do not in fact verbalize this deduction is not surprising in the light of Piaget's (1951) early work on childish introspection. Piaget found that when 7–9-year-old children were asked to tell how they had arrived at the solution of an arithmetic problem, they gave logical reasons that had nothing to do with the actual psychological processes involved.

Piaget (1951) wrote:

> When we maintain that children cannot make their reasoning process the object of introspection, all we mean is that it is extremely difficult for them to give an account of the psychological "how" of this process quite independently from the question or whether or not they can give a logical reason for the result obtained. (p. 139)

That Piaget has sometimes been misunderstood on this point is illustrated by the fact that some writers have urged that reversibility (e.g., Wallach and Sprott, 1964) or identity (Wohlwill, 1959) was the prime mechanism of conservation. Such a position seems to miss what seems to be the essence of the Piaget argument with respect to these verbal explanations. In the first place, Piaget often remarks on the fact that the preoperational child knows perfectly well that in the conservation problem nothing was added or taken away and that if it is returned to the starting point it will be the same. The latter judgment is in fact the criterion for the second or transition stage in the attainment of conservation. This knowledge, however, is of little value if the child is not already convinced of conservation. Once conservation is attained, by the equation of differences and the utilization of a deductive argument, the employment of these verbal explanations reflects the attempt to give a logical explanation to the conservation judgment. The significance of these verbal explanations lies not so much in their content as in what they suggest about the child's orientation to the problem. What they reflect is that the child now feels that conservation is a logical necessity and that he must justify it.

In summary, Piaget's discussion of conservation can be misleading both because (*a*) he tends to emphasize identity conservation when the task in question assesses equivalence conservation, and (*b*) he seems to use children's verbal explanations as evidence for the processes by which the child arrives at conservation. As we have tried to point out, however, the notion that conservation involves deduction and that the verbal explanations are of value only insofar as they illustrate the child's new operational or logical orientation is always implicit and sometimes explicit in Piaget's writing.

THE CONSERVATION OF EQUIVALENCE

Perhaps one of the most frequently misunderstood aspects of Piaget's discussion of conservation is the impression that the equation of differences pertains to the comparison of S and V′ and not to the comparison of V and V′. If this were in fact true, the equation of differences could explain both the conservation of identity and the conservation of equivalence, and there would be no point in distinguishing between them. In fact, however, the equation of differences cannot explain how the child comes to judge S equal to V′.

The evidence which demonstrates that the judgment of equivalence between S and V′ cannot be explained by the equation of differences derives from the observation that, if the child were merely presented with S and V′ in isolation without having judged S = V and having seen V transformed into V′, he would never arrive at the conservation of equivalence. This is true because the presentation of V′ and S in isolation confronts the child with an illusion. A sausage and a ball of clay of the same weight appear to be of different weights, just as the same amount of liquid in two differently shaped containers appears to be unequal. If the child (or the adult for that matter) is asked to match a fixed quantity by adjusting (adding or taking away material) a differently formed or contained quantity, he will miss the mark.

That the comparison of S and V′ in isolation presents the child with an illusion has been shown experimentally. Vinh Bang (personal communication), for example, gave both children and adults a ball and a sausage of clay and asked his subjects to equate them in weight by adding or removing clay from the ball. At all age levels, subjects made the sausage much too small to equal the ball in weight. In another study, Beilin (1964) had children compare equal areas presented in different configurations and found that children did not judge the areas as equal. This was true well beyond the age reported by Piaget et al. (1960) for the conservation of area. With respect to weight and area, then, the equation of differences cannot of itself explain the child's judgment that S = V′. This follows because even children who are capable of equating differences cannot arrive at conservation of equivalence when S and V′ are presented in isolation.

A similar conclusion can probably be drawn with respect to the problem of length conservation (Piaget and Inhelder, 1962). In a recent study by the writer (Elkind, in press), 4–7-year-old children were given the classic test for length conservation (two equally long pencils in parallel and then staggered positions). In addition, they were also tested for the conservation of length by means of the Müller Lyer. In the case of the Müller Lyer, *E* first drew two lines of equal length and asked the *S*s to judge if they were the same length and to measure them if they wished. The arrowheads were drawn under the surveillance of the *S*s, who were then asked whether one line was longer, shorter, or the same length as the other. Results showed that children displayed the conservation of length on the Müller Lyer at the same age that they demonstrated it upon the classic length conservation test (75 per cent by the age of 7).

The point of this finding is that the nature of the Müller Lyer is such that it is impossible to equate differences. There is no real displacement of the lines and, in addition, one line looks shorter than the other *at both* ends. Any attempt to equate differences in this situation, between the standard and the variable, would result in failure since both the differences point in the same rather than in different directions as in the pencil test. The fact that children arrived at equivalence conservation in a situation where the equation of differences between the standard and the variable simply would not work adds support to the view that the equation of differences pertains to changes in the variable itself and not to the relation between the variable and the standard. A recent investigation by Murray (1965) with a variety of illusions supports the above finding in the sense that Murray also found conservation at the expected ages across illusory transformations.

The fact that the equation of differences cannot of itself explain the equivalence of S and V' has sometimes been remarked upon by Piaget.

"First of all, it is clear that the child would have no means of gauging the equality of the various quantities in A1 and (B1 + B2) or in P, L, etc., if he were merely asked to compare them" (Piaget, 1952, p. 22). This point is perhaps not sufficiently emphasized, so that it is not difficult to get the impression from Piaget that the equation of differences itself explains the equivalence judgment between S and V'. It is clear from the evidence, however, that the equation of differences cannot explain the equality of S and V' and that the child must employ a form of deduction from immediate past experience to arrive at the conservation of equivalence.

THE CONSERVATION OF IDENTITY

One might well ask, if Piaget is primarily interested in the conservation of identity, why an equivalence problem is used to assess it. The reasons for this would seem to be both practical and theoretical. From the practical point of view, the test of identity conservation runs the risk of memory falsification. If the child is asked to say whether a clay sausage weighs more, less, or the same it did as a ball, it is possible that the child might assume that the ball was actually larger than it was to compensate for the apparent increase in the weight of the sausage. This would be a kind of preoperational conservation, or what Inhelder (1963) has recently called "pseudo conservation." The theoretical reason would seem to lie in Piaget's assumption that identity and equivalence conservation are simultaneous in time, and that the age of equivalence conservation is also the age of identity conservation, so that it is legitimate to infer the age of the latter from the age at which the former is attained. It is on this last assumption that the writer is not in complete agreement with Piaget. But before turning to that issue, we need to show that the problem of memory falsification in the conservation of identity can be overcome.

To avoid memory falsification, all one needs to do—and Piaget himself has suggested this—is to mark the previous state of the quantity in some way. In the case of a quantity of liquid poured from one container to another, one needs to mark the level it attained in the first container; in the case of a clay ball made into a sausage, one might draw a circle on paper to represent its original size, etc. In the interrogation of the child, these previous marks could be referred to if there were a suggestion of "pseudo conservation." While this procedure does not entirely eliminate the equivalence problem, it does focus upon changes within a given quantity, rather than the relation between two quantities. Some pilot work by Robert Ransom supports the view that, at least for length conservation and the conservation of continuous quantities, identity conservation does precede equivalence conservation.

Even in the absence of more definitive data, indirect evidence also suggests that the conservation of identity appears earlier than the conservation of equivalence. As an illustration, Piaget (1952) has reported that, when children were asked to adjust the height of a liquid column in a tall narrow container so that the amount of liquid would be equal to that in a wide shallow one, the children succeeded before they attained the conservation of equivalence. Since a successful solution to this problem presupposes the equation of differences, its appearance prior to equivalence conservation suggests that identity conservation is not simultaneous with the conservation of equivalence. Other evidence of the same kind derives from the recent work on mental imagery. Piaget and Inhelder (1963) report, for example, that for some problems 30 per cent of the children are able to anticipate the results of a transformation before they are able to attain conservation. Once more there is a suggestion that the equation of differences, and hence identity conservation, precedes the conservation of equivalence.

This hypothesized *décalage* between the conservation of identity and the conservation of equivalence would, in fact, help resolve a seeming contradiction in Piaget's conception of conservation. Piaget and Inhelder (1962, p. 15, W.T.) have argued that *true* conservation can only be assessed when there is a "conflict between immediate experience or the givens of perception on the one hand and mental operations on the other." The contradiction arises because as long as identity and equivalence conservation are assumed to be simultaneous in time, operations have to serve both as party to the conflict and the mediator of its resolution.

One possible solution to the problem has been suggested by Wohlwill (1964) who proposes that there is a difference in strength between the perceptual (peripheral) response and the operational (central nervous) response and that the conflict is resolved only when the operational process exceeds the strength of the perceptual tendency. Such a solution, however, is not congenial to the Piaget position which seems to assume a more or less sudden and complete solution to the problem once the child acquires concrete operations. One does indeed observe that, once the child attains conservation, the strength of the illusion seems to make little difference, and children say, "No matter how you change it, it will always be the same."

An alternative solution, and one that would seem to be more in accord with Piaget's mode of theorizing, is that the conflict is between the anticipation of identity conservation mediated by the equation of differences and the perception of inequality presented by the illusion of V' paired with S. Thus when the child thinks of a single quantity and its transformation he is convinced the quantity is conserved because he can equate differences and anticipate the results of the transformation. What he does not anticipate is the illusion presented by S and V'. Since, as we have seen, he can no longer equate them by means of compensation, he must resort to a deductive argument, if such is in his power. This interpretation would make the conservation conflict dependent upon identity conservation and the solution dependent upon the conservation of equivalence. The validity of this point of view must be ascertained by additional research.

While on the subject of conflict, it might be well here to attempt to clarify some of the misunderstandings arising out of "pseudo conservation." In dealing with liquid quantities, for example, the preoperational child has already a pseudo notion of conservation in the sense that he anticipates that, when liquid from a wide shallow container is poured into a tall narrow glass, the level will be the same. When the preoperational child actually witnesses the transformation, however, there is a conflict between his anticipation and the perception of the outcome. Since his concept of liquid quantity is based solely on the level, immediate perception wins out, and he judges the liquid to have changed in amount.

Suppose, however, that the results of the transformation are hidden from the child as in the Feigenbaum and Sulkin (unpublished manuscript, 1961) and Frank (reported by Bruner, 1964b) experiments. In this situation, the child encounters no contradiction to his anticipation of "pseudo conservation" based on level. As both Feigenbaum and Frank report, even 4-year-old children judged that the quantities remained the same when they could not witness the results of the transformation. The 4-year-old children were nonetheless anticipating that the level would stay the same across the transformation to a differently shaped container. The evidence for this came when they were in fact shown the results. Under these conditions, the 4-year-old children changed their judgment. There was an interesting sidelight to these experiments. Some children, in both experiments, seemed to learn conservation on the basis of this screening procedure. Why screening should be more efficacious than the laborious teaching methods employed by Gréco (1959), Smedslund (1959), Wohlwill (1959, 1960), and Wohlwill and Lowe (1962) is not immediately obvious, and the problem calls for further exploration.

It seems, then, that in order to have a full comprehension of Piaget's conservation problems one needs not only to distinguish between the conservation of identity and equivalence but also between true and "pseudo conservation."

SUMMARY AND CONCLUSION

In the present paper we have tried to clarify some of the apparent misunderstandings of Piaget's discussion of conservation. Perhaps the major cause of such misunderstanding is the fact that Piaget is writing for a very select audience, so that much is taken for granted, or is implicit, or is given only passing mention in his discussion. In particular, the distinction between the conservation of identity (the conservation of a given quantity across the reversible transformation and with respect to itself alone) and the conservation of equivalence (the invariance of a quantitative relation across a transformation of one of the elements of that relation) and the mechanisms which mediate them will hopefully enable the non-Piagetian psychologists to obtain a better grasp of the Piaget view of conservation.

Not all of the issues that are raised by Piaget's conservation problems have been taken up here. The relation between conservation and other means of concept assessment remains to be given systematic treatment. Likewise, the place of conservation within Piaget's (1959) little-known two-factor theory of concept formation has yet to be made available to the English-speaking psychologist. It is hoped that the analyses offered here will clear the way for the consideration of some of these broader implications of Piaget's conservation problems.

REFERENCES

Beilin, H. (1964). Perceptual-cognitive conflict in the development of an invariant area concept. *J. exp. child Psychol.*, 1, 208–226.
Bruner, J. S. (1964a). The center for cognitive studies. *Fourth Annual Report*, Cambridge, Mass.
Bruner, J. S. (1964b). The course of cognitive growth. *Amer. Psychologist*, 19, 1–15.
Elkind, D. (in press). Conservation across illusory transformations. *Acta Psychol.*
Feigenbaum, K., and Sulkin (1961). Unpublished manuscript.

Flavell, J. H. (1963). *The developmental psychology of Jean Piaget.* Princeton, N.J.: Van Nostrand.

Gréco, P. (1959). L'apprentissage dans une situation à structure opératoire concrète: les inversions successives de l'ordre lineaire par des rotations de 180°. In J. Piaget (Ed.). *Etudes d'épistémologie génétique,* Vol. 8. Paris: Presses Universitaires. Pp. 68–182.

Hunt, J. McV. (1961). *Intelligence and experience.* New York: Ronald.

Inhelder, B. (1963). Les opérations des images mentales de la pensée et leur symbolisme image. *Cahiers Psychol.,* **6,** 143–171.

Murray, F. B. (1965). Conservation of illusion, distorted lengths, and areas by primary school children. *J. educ. Psychol.,* **56,** 62–66.

Piaget, J. (1951). *Judgment and reasoning in the child.* London: Routledge.

Piaget, J. (1952; first French ed., 1942). *The child's conception of number.* New York: Humanities Press.

Piaget, J. (1957). Logique et équilibre dans les comportements du sujet. In J. Piaget (Ed.), *Etudes d'épistémologie génétique,* Vol. 2. Paris: Presses Universitaires. Pp. 27–118.

Piaget, J. (1959). Apprentissage et connaissance. In J. Piaget (Ed.), *Etudes d'épistémologie génétique,* Vol. 7. Paris: Presses Universitaires. Pp. 21–67.

Piaget, J., and B. Inhelder (1962). *Le développement des quantités physiques chez l'enfant,* second ed. Paris: Delachaux et Niestlé.

Piaget, J., and B. Inhelder (1963). *Traité de psychologie expérimentale. Les images mentales.* In P. Fraisse and J. Piaget (Eds.), Vol. 7. *L'intelligence.* Paris: Presses Universitaires.

Piaget, J., B. Inhelder, and A. Szeminska (1960). *The child's conception of geometry.* New York: Basic Books.

Sigel, I. (1964). The attainment of concepts. In M. L. Hoffman and Lois W. Hoffman (Eds.), *Review of child development research.* New York: Russell Sage. Pp. 209–248.

Smedslund, J. (1959). Apprentissage des notions de la conservation et de la transitivité du poids. In J. Piaget (Ed.), *Etudes d'épistémologie génétique,* Vol. 9. Paris: Presses Universitaires. Pp. 85–124.

Wallach, M. A. (1963). Research on children's thinking. In H. Stevenson (Ed.), Child psychology. *Yearbook Nat. Soc. Study Educ.,* **72** (1), 236–276.

Wallach, L., and R. L. Sprott (1964). Inducing number conservation in children. *Child Develpm.,* **35,** 1057–1071.

Wohlwill, J. F. (1959). Un essaie l'apprentissage dans le domaine de la conservation du nombre. In J. Piaget (Ed.), *Etudes d'épistémologie génétique,* Vol. 9. Paris: Presses Universitaires. Pp. 125–135.

Wohlwill, J. F. (1960). A study of the development of the number concept by scalogram analysis. *J. genet. Psychol.,* **97,** 345–377.

Wohlwill, J. F. (1964). Development and measurement. In R. E. Ripple and

V. N. Rockcastle (Eds.), *Piaget rediscovered*. A report of the conference on cognitive studies and curriculum development, School of Education, Cornell University. Pp. 95–100.

Wohlwill, J. F., and R. Lowe (1962). Experimental analysis of the conservation of number. *Child Develpm.*, 33, 153–167.

FROM PERCEPTION TO INFERENCE:
A DIMENSION OF COGNITIVE DEVELOPMENT

Joachim F. Wohlwill

INTRODUCTION

How shall we conceptualize the changes which the child's mental processes undergo during the course of development? This question has been answered most frequently in terms that emphasize an increase in powers of abstraction or an increased intervention of symbolic processes. More generally, one might say that there is a decreasing dependence of behavior on information in the immediate stimulus field. For instance, in the delayed reaction experiment we find that the maximum delay that may intervene between the presentation of a stimulus and a discriminatory response increases with age (Munn, 1955, pp. 306ff.). Similarly, much of Piaget's work on the development of concepts—particularly that on the conservation of length, weight, volume, number, and so forth—is interpretable in terms of the increasing stability of concepts in the face of (irrelevant) changes in the stimulus field.

We have here, then, the makings of a significant dimension along which to analyze the course of cognitive development. The eventual aim of this paper is to suggest a more systematic approach for such an analysis, based on certain principles relating to the ways in which the organism utilizes sensory information. However, the realization of this aim presupposes an adequate understanding of the interrelation between perception and thinking; it should therefore prove valuable to undertake a prior examination, in some detail, of the various ways in which this relation has been conceptualized, and more particularly of the developmental aspects of this problem.

A prefatory note of caution—given the notoriously elusive and ill-defined nature of such concepts as perception and thinking, no single, uniformly

Reprinted with the permission of the author and The Society for Research in Child Development, Inc., in William Kessen and Clementina Kuhlman (Eds.), Thought in the Young Child, *Monograph of The Society for Research in Child Development*, 1962, **27** (2), 87–112.

acceptable characterization of their relation is to be expected. For the same reason, the analysis of the developmental changes in the relationship between these two functions is beset with obvious difficulties. Nevertheless, we shall find that the alternative formulations that have been proposed to deal with this problem, and especially Piaget's illuminating comparison between perceptual and conceptual development, are not only of great interest in their own right, but contribute materially to the dimensional analysis of mental development.

THREE VIEWS OF THE PERCEPTION-CONCEPTION RELATION

Let us start by reviewing three different ways in which theorists have conceptualized the relationship between perception and conception. These three clearly do not exhaust all the different positions that have been taken on this question, but they probably represent the major trends of thought; of greater importance, they define three sharply differentiated foci from which this problem may be approached, so that their consideration should bring out some major theoretical issues. It should be noted at the outset that all three of these viewpoints are essentially nongenetic, at least insofar as any explicit treatment of development is concerned.

The Gestalt Position

One of the solutions to the problem at hand is to take a model of perception and to attempt to fit it intact to the area of thinking, thus reducing these two functions to a common set of basic processes. This appears to be in large measure the course followed by the Gestalt school in its efforts to interpret phenomena in the field of the thought processes—as seen in Köhler's (1925) classical work on the problem solving behavior of his chimpanzees or Wertheimer's (1959) analysis of "productive thinking" in the solution of mathematical and other conceptual problems. In these works we find a heavy emphasis on such quasiperceptual terms as "insight," "restructuring of the field," "closure," and the like, which seem to represent the sum, if not the substance, of the repertoire of concepts used by the Gestaltists to handle the processes of human reasoning. This point is expressed quite explicitly by Koffka in *The Growth of the Mind*. After paying lip service to the increasing importance in the development of thinking of psychological processes affecting a delay between a stimulus and a consequent reaction of the individual, Koffka (1924), states that:

> . . . the ideational field depends most intimately upon the sensory, and any means that enable us to become independent of immediate perception are rooted in perception, and, in truth, only lead us from one perception to another. (p. 49)

This formulation, quite apart from its rather meager empirical yield, does not seem to have proved overly successful in its theoretical power. Not only has a major portion of problems in the field of thinking been left aside (e.g., concept formation, the nature of symbolic processes, and so forth), but even when applied to the situations with which the Gestaltists have concerned themselves, the explanatory worth of their concepts appears quite limited.[1] Thus, interpretations of problem solving in terms of restructuring of the field have a somewhat hollow ring in the absence of attention to the question of how a Gestalt may be restructured and of what keeps it from being appropriately structured at the outset. In fact, the whole problem of the ways in which conceptual activity may *transform* an immediate percept is ignored. Paraphrasing Guthrie's dictum about Tolman, whom he accused of "leaving the rat buried in thought," one might therefore be justified in criticizing the Gestaltists for leaving the organism too readily short-circuited in closure to permit him to think.

Last, but by no means least, the a prioristic and thus inherently non-genetic bias of the Gestalt school should be noted. In their work, even when it deals with the behavior of children, as in the books by Koffka and Wertheimer cited earlier, there is little interest in matters relating to developmental changes underlying such behavior—a limitation for which Piaget (1946, 1954), among others, has repeatedly taken them to task.

Bruner's Position

Let us examine next a point of view diametrically opposed to the Gestaltists, one which regards perception as basically an inferential process, in which the perceiver plays a maximal—and maximally idiosyncratic—role in interpreting, categorizing, or transforming the stimulus input. This view is represented generally by the latter-day functionalist school of perception, particularly that of the transactionalist variety. Its most explicit statement has, however, come from Bruner (1957), according to whom:

> Perception involves an act of categorization . . . the nature of the inference from cue to identity in perception is . . . in no sense different from other kinds of categorical inferences based on defining attributes . . . there is no reason to assume that the laws governing inferences . . . are discontinuous as one moves from perceptual to more conceptual activities. (pp. 123f)

While Bruner claims neither that all perception processes can be encompassed in such a theory nor that it precludes a distinction between perceptual and conceptual inference, he does argue that the theory covers

---

[1] The work of such investigators as Duncker and Maier might be cited in refutation of this statement. But these psychologists really fall outside the classical Gestalt tradition, utilizing concepts that bear little direct relationship to the principles of this school of thought—cf. Maier's "functional fixedness" and the general attention given to problems of set.

a wide variety of perceptual phenomena which conform in many essential respects to principles akin to those observed in the conceptual sphere.

Bruner's formulation raises a number of difficult questions. What is the implicit definition of perception on which it is based? What is the role assigned to structural aspects of the stimulus in such a model of perception? Most importantly, perhaps, to what extent does the operation of conceptual mechanisms in perception depend on conditions of inadequate or impoverished stimulation? Bruner has not ignored this latter problem, but he is inclined to dismiss its importance; for example, he reduces the difference between ordinary and tachistoscopic perception to a matter of degree— inferential mechanisms are always at work, but categorizations vary in the univocality of their coding of stimulus cues in proportion to the amount of stimulus information provided. Thus, for Bruner (1957), vertical perception is a joint function of redundancy in the stimulus and the accessibility of appropriate categorizing systems, in the following sense:

> Where accessibility of categories reflects environmental probabilities, the organism is in the position of requiring less stimulus input, less redundancy of cues for the appropriate categorization of objects . . . the more inappropriate the readiness, the greater the input or redundancy of cues required for appropriate categorization to occur. (p. 133)

We will find this notion of some interest in connection with one of the dimensions to be proposed later for tracing the development from a perceptual to an inferential level of cognitive functioning. For the present, it may suffice to point out, as Piaget and Morf (1958a) have, that Bruner's model of perception presupposes an adult perceiver; it would be difficult to apply it to the perceptions of a very young child, whose conceptual categories were still in the process of formation. Not surprisingly, under the circumstances, we find that Bruner has thus far failed, as much as the Gestaltists, to consider the developmental aspects of perception and thinking, either in the paper discussed here or in his monograph on thinking (Bruner, Goodnow, and Austin, 1956).

Brunswik's Position

The third viewpoint to be considered is that of Brunswik, who occupies a place somewhere between the two poles just discussed, emphasizing as he does the differences between perception and thinking, rather than attempting to explain one in terms of the other. While his untimely death kept him from pursuing this question beyond the sketchy treatment of it in his last work (Brunswik, 1956), his ideas still may contribute significantly to a workable distinction between perception and thinking—a point which we shall have occasion to acknowledge in the last portion of this paper.

Brunswik starts out by drawing a comparison—based on an actual empirical study—between the achievements of perceptual size judgments in a constancy situation and those of arithmetic reasoning where the equivalent task is presented in symbolic form. The perceptual task yielded the typical clustering of settings within a fairly narrow range of the point of objective equality; in contrast, a majority of the answers given to the arithmetic reasoning task coincided exactly with the correct value, but several subsidiary clusters of answers were found which were quite discretely separated from this mode and which corresponded to false solutions of the problem.

Generalizing from this example—the significance of which is obviously purely demonstrational—Brunswik (1956) contrasts the machinelike precision of the reasoning processes with the more approximate achievements of perception:

> The entire pattern of the reasoning solutions . . . resembles the switching of trains at a multiple junction, with each of the possible courses being well organized and of machinelike precision, yet leading to drastically different destinations . . . the combination of channelled mediation, on the one hand, with precision or else grotesquely scattered error in the results, on the other, may well be symptomatic of what appears to be the pure case of explicit intellectual fact-finding.
>
> On the other hand, . . . perception must simultaneously integrate many different avenues of approach, or cues. . . . The various rivalries and compromises that characterize the dynamics of check and balance in perception must be seen as chiefly responsible for the above noted relative infrequency of precision. On the other hand, the organic multiplicity of factors entering the process constitutes an effective safeguard against drastic error. (pp. 91f)

This conception of the difference between perception and thinking, while hardly exhaustive, is a fairly intriguing as well as plausible one. It has, moreover, definite implications for the analysis of the development of reasoning, although Brunswik has not given these explicit consideration. It is pertinent, however, to note his suggestion in regard to the developmental changes in color and shape constancy which he studied in his early work; he attributed the decline in constancy found in adolescence to the intervention of cognitive mechanisms which lessened the *need* for precise veridical perceptual achievements (cf. Brunswik, 1956, p. 91).

DEVELOPMENTAL APPROACHES TO THE
INTERRELATIONSHIP BETWEEN
PERCEPTION AND CONCEPTION

The three contrasting positions just discussed serve to sketch out the boundaries within which one can trace the course of cognitive development from perception to thinking. As noted above, of the three positions, Brunswik's embodies the sharpest differentiation between these two functions and will be found the most useful for our purposes; in fact, we will presently see a striking similarity between Brunswik's view and Piaget's conception of this problem.

The Views of Piaget

THE TWO PIAGETS   Let us turn, then, to the work of Piaget, who has given us by far the most explicit and formalized comparison between perception and thought and between their respective developmental patterns. We should note at the outset that there appear to be at least two altogether different Piagets. On the one hand, we have Piaget, the psychologist of the development of intelligence, author of a long and impressive series of books covering an array of cognitive functions (language, reasoning, judgment) and of dimensions of experience (time, number, quantity, space, and so forth). On the other hand, there is Piaget, the psychologist of perception, author or sponsor of an equally impressive and even longer series of studies on a variety of perceptual phenomena, published in the *Archives de Psychologie*.

To these two divergent areas of interest correspond two sharply differentiated modes of approach to research. The "clinical" method which Piaget has followed in his study of the development of intelligence, with its deliberate avoidance of standardized procedures and quantitative analysis, stands in marked contrast to the more traditional experimental approach which he has favored in his perception research. Furthermore, while Piaget's aim in his work on thinking is essentially a genetic one, his purpose in tracing developmental changes in perception appears to be rather different. The developmental dimension in the perception research represents primarily an additional variable, coordinate with other situational, experimentally manipulated variables through which basic perceptual processes are exhibited. In this connection it is worth pointing to Piaget's (1956, p. 33) view that developmental stages exist in the realm of intellectual, but not of perceptual, development. We will consider later the possible grounds for such a position.

In view of these various symptoms of a double personality, it is hardly surprising to find Piaget attempting to divorce thinking from perception and to minimize their mutual interrelatedness. Like East and West, "ne'er the twain shall meet"—or hardly ever. One of the very few instances where they do meet, i.e., where Piaget confronts perception and thinking in the context of the same experimental situation, provides an illuminating picture of his basic position. This is a study by Piaget and Taponier (1956), devoted in part to the investigation of a constant error arising in the comparison of the length of two parallel horizontal lines, drawn to form the top and bottom of a parallelogram (without the sides). In this situation the top line tends to be slightly overestimated; this illusion increases, however, from a zero-order effect at the age of 5 years to a maximum at about 8 years; for adults the extent of the error is intermediate. Piaget contrasts this developmental pattern with that obtained when the same judgment is made in the context of a cognitive task: The two equal lines are presented initially in direct visual superposition, so as to be perceived as equal; the top one is then displaced horizontally, the arrangement of the two lines corresponding to that of the previous problem. In this cognitive task, it is the 5-year-old children who show a pronounced bias in their judgment, which leads them to pronounce the two lines as unequal following the displacement. In other words, there is an absence of "conservation of length" in the face of configurational changes. By the age of 8, however, the equality of the lines is maintained fairly uniformly—conservation of length has been acquired. On the strength of these findings Piaget argues against a simple perceptual explanation for the young children's lack of conservation; since their error of perceptual judgment is at a minimum, their failure to maintain the equality of the two lines in the cognitive task must be due to other factors.

This example illustrates well the independence, in Piaget's thinking, between perception and conception or inference—even at the stage of "intuitive thought" where the child's responses appear to be governed by particular aspects of the stimulus field. In fact, as we shall note, Piaget (1946, 1957) has repeatedly stressed that these two functions follow very different paths and arrive at different ends during the course of development. With Brunswik, although on somewhat different grounds, he has been impressed by the statistical, probabilistic nature of perceptual judgments, as opposed to the precise, determinate, and phenomenologically certain results achieved through conceptual inference.

THE CONCEPT OF "PARTIAL ISOMORPHISMS"   Piaget's most recent and most systematic treatment of this question is contained in an article (Piaget and Morf, 1958a) the title of which states his position succinctly: "The partial isomorphisms between logical structures and perceptual structures." In spite of his characteristic reification of such concepts as "structures" and "schemata," Piaget is concerned here with the correspondence between the achievements or end products of perceptual as against conceptual mechanisms, the mechanisms themselves being left largely out of the picture.

In this paper Piaget and Morf discuss a number of phenomena which Werner (1957) has considered as illustrative of "analogous functions," i.e., functions serving similar ends but operating at different levels of cognitive organization. Like Werner, Piaget and Morf draw parallels between perceptual groupings and conceptual classes, between invariance in perception (the constancies) and in conception (the conservations); between the perception of stimulus relationships and the conceptual representation of relationships at the symbolic level. For these authors however, these analogies, or isomorphisms, are only partial; they emphasize, rather, the ways in which perceptual mechanisms differ from the corresponding inferential ones. They point out that perceptual phenomena generally do not meet the requirements of the fundamental operations of logic (reversibility, additivity, transitivity, inversion) except in a limited and approximate sense. For example, with respect to additivity, a line divided into a number of equal segments is actually perceived as slightly longer than its undivided counterpart (the Oppel-Kundt illusion); similarly, in the case of figure-ground reversals the perceptual inversion fails to satisfy the logical criterion of inversion insofar as the boundary line always remains part of the figure. To these examples relating to the logic of classes are added several others involving the logic of relationships. Thus, lack of additivity is illustrated in threshold phenomena, where two subthreshold differences when added together may yield a suprathreshold difference (i.e., $= + = \rightarrow \neq$ is possible in perception). Again, a person's difficulty in judging projective size is considered a case of lack of inversion of the relationship between retinal size, distance and perceived size ($r \times d = p$): given r and d jointly, the subject may "solve" for p, but he cannot obtain r by "dividing through" by d—i.e., by abstracting size from distance.

Finally, Piaget and Morf argue that there are "pre-inferences" in perception which are partially isomorphic to the inferential mechanisms of logical reasoning. Indeed, all perceptual judgment *qua* judgment is thought to involve a decision-process partaking to a greater or lesser extent of the character of an inference from the sensory information given. The extent to which it does so depends on the level of complexity (mediation?) of the judgment, ranging from the simple, direct judgments found in psychophysical thresholds to judgments dependent on "perceptual activity" as in size constancy. Here the difference between these perceptual pre-inferences and conceptual inferences can be found not only in the certainty or univocality of the outcome of the conceptual inference, but also in the subjects' lack of awareness of the separate steps in the inferential chain in the perceptual pre-inferences.[2]

THE PERCEPTION-CONCEPTION RELATIONSHIP IN THE DEVELOPMENT OF THE CHILD   Despite the semblance of a link between perception and inference represented in Piaget's concept of "perceptual pre-inferences," the over-all impression one obtains from his treatment of partial isomorphisms, as well as from other discussions of the differences between these two functions, is of a parallelistic conception—perception and thinking represent two sharply differentiated processes which display certain structural similarities, but even more important differences. Developmentally, too, he considers perception and thinking as following two separate and independent courses, as may be seen in his comparison of the development

[2] This specification of lack of awareness as a characteristic of pre-inferential processes in perception clearly brings to mind Helmholtz's "unconscious inference." Piaget is careful, however, to dissociate himself from those (e.g., Cassirer) who have read into this concept implications of a ratiomorphic process.

of the "conservations" from the conceptual realm with that of the perceptual constancies (Piaget, 1957).

Conservation may be exemplified by the invariance of the volume of a liquid under changes in its container, as when water is poured from a narrow glass into a shallow bowl. Piaget invokes here a gradual process of "equilibration," leading the child from an initial stage at which he focuses only on one biasing aspect of the stimulus (e.g., the height of the container) through an oscillatory stage where he shifts back and forth between this aspect and a competing one (here the width of the container), to a third stage in which the compensatory role of these two aspects begins to be suspected, and then to the final realization, with perfect certitude on the part of the child, of absolute, exact conservation, despite the perceptual changes. In the perceptual constancies, on the other hand, all aspects of the stimulus field, and notably the two stimuli to be compared, are always included in the individual's perceptual exploration of the situation, at least from a very early level of development. The only developmental change is in the extent and efficacy of this exploration or, conversely, in the potency of distorting factors present in this situation. These factors (e.g., a favored attention to the near object) bring about a relative lack of constancy in younger children, which is reduced in later childhood due to more intensive and complete perceptual exploration of the stimuli. But in the domain of perception the exact compensations achieved in the fourth stage of the development of conservation are not realized; instead, the compensations either fall short, as in most illusions, or actually lead to overcompensation, as in size constancy where overconstancy is the rule for adults.

We are now in a position to appreciate the reasons that probably motivated Piaget's denial of the existence of stages in perception, while affirming it for mental development. This distinction would be warranted, not in the sense that ontogenetic change in perception is necessarily more gradual, but rather in the sense that no meaningful structural criteria can be found in the area of quantitative perceptual judgments for distinguishing among different stages. The differences between successive perceptual achievements are necessarily only quantitative, whereas structural differences of a qualitative type, as in the above-mentioned sequence of stages, can be specified for conceptual development.

Some Critical Comments on Piaget's Views

The foregoing presentation is a highly condensed distillation of Piaget's ideas in which many and frequently subtle lines of reasoning—not to mention a number of obscure points—have been omitted. It would therefore be somewhat inappropriate to base an evaluation of the merits of his argument on the picture of it given here. Nevertheless there are several criticisms of Piaget which can safely be anticipated; let us consider three of these points in particular. This will lead us to a somewhat more general question regarding Piaget's approach and will pave the way to a reformulation in the final portion of this paper.

The first objection that is bound to be raised concerns the nonoperational, and at times frankly mentalistic, terms used by Piaget which may seem to leave his analysis devoid of empirical, and perhaps even of theoretical, significance. For example, the criteria which he proposes for a diagnosis of inferential and pre-inferential processes are anything but unambiguous; indeed, his whole conceptual apparatus of schemata, operations, centrations, and so forth appears to lack direct empirical reference. Admittedly, Piaget does little to dispel this impression; concrete illustrations or applications are at best sporadic, and rigorous, systematic efforts at tying the empirical phenomena to his constructs are generally eschewed in favor of ad hoc and post hoc arguments.

It is important to remember, however, that Piaget's ideas on the interrelation between perceptual and conceptual development are not in themselves intended as a theoretical system; they serve rather to explicate, in formal terms, the different models underlying Piaget's theories of perception and intelligence, respectively. Furthermore, a few empirical studies relevant to this discussion can actually be cited (e.g., Piaget and Lambercier, 1946; Piaget and Taponier, 1956; Piaget and Morf, 1958b), and, while the first two of these are mainly demonstrational in character, Piaget and Morf's investigation of "perceptual pre-inferences" represents a step toward a more systematic empirical approach in this area through the manipulation of stimulus cues which change the nature of the task from a perceptual to a more nearly judgmental one. Unfortunately, the experimental design of this study leaves much to be desired, and the rather elaborate interpretations of the results seem unconvincing, if not unwarranted.

A second criticism might well be directed at Piaget's highly idealized conception of adult thought and, at the same time, at his insistence on the distorting and probabilistic character of the processes of immediate perception. In regard to the first point, Piaget has of course been repeatedly taken to task for his inclination to see nothing but perfect logic and rationality in adult intelligence. His reliance on the principles of abstract logic as a model for human thinking has blinded him to the question of the breadth and stability of logic as *used* by the individual. In actual fact, of course, it is little more than a truism that logical principles understood in the abstract may not be applied in particular contexts (as in the atmosphere effects in syllogistic reasoning); likewise, even in the thinking of adults we find frequent instances of failures to apply or generalize a concept or principle when it is presented in unfamiliar ways or extended to novel situations. Differential generalization in the realm of thinking, furthermore, may have all the earmarks of the generalization *gradient* familiar from sensory phenomena.

Conversely, one may argue that Piaget overstates the case for the statistical, approximative, and generally biasing aspects of perceptual achievements. For quantitative judgments, to be sure, Piaget's probabilistic model seems quite appropriate and, indeed, seductively appealing in its simplicity and generality (cf. Piaget, 1955).[3] If we deal, on the other hand, with qualitative judgments and more particularly with judgments of identity or difference among discrete categories of stimuli, we typically find something closely approaching the reliability and specificity of conceptual classifications. Parenthetically, it may be noted that for Bruner it is precisely this type of perceptual judgment which serves as his model of perception, a fact which presumably accounts for some of the ratiomorphic flavor of this model.

If Piaget, then, even more than Brunswik, overestimates the discrepancy between the respective achievements of perception and thinking, he seems also to exaggerate their functional independence. The very fact that the conceptual processes of adults can be characterized along such dimensions as concrete-abstract testifies to the continual interplay between these two functions in much of conceptual activity. Pointing in the same direction are the results from one of Piaget's own experiments (Piaget and Lambercier, 1946) involving size-at-a-distance judgments in which the correct matches could be arrived at inferentially by the intermediary of a reference stimulus. At a certain age level (in middle childhood) there is clear evidence of a "perceptual compromise," showing the mutual interaction, rather than absolute separation, between perception and thinking. We shall attempt to show below how the conceptualization of the development of the symbolic processes in general can be furthered by assigning to perception a differential role in conceptual tasks at different age levels.

PIAGET'S STRUCTURAL APPROACH   If one examines Piaget's thinking further in order to account for his espousal of some of the views just discussed, as well as for the somewhat unsatisfactory explanatory status of the constructs of his system, one finds a ready answer in the structural approach which he has consistently favored in his theory of intelligence. What he seems in fact to have done is to specify the *formal* properties of the products of the thought processes at different stages of development. This has led him inescapably to a picture of successive metamorphoses in the mental development of the child. From this structural point of view, the differences between the reasoning processes of a child lacking "reversibility" and "conservation" and an adult whose thinking does conform to

---

[3] An interesting feature of this model is its ability to account for the instances of nondeforming shape perception represented by the Gestaltists' "good figures" as a special case in which the relationships among the component parts are such as to yield, on the average, zero-order errors due to complete mutual compensation among the various possible distortions arising in such stimuli.

these principles will in fact appear comparable to the differences between a caterpillar and a butterfly—or, to suggest a rather more pertinent analogy, between the pattern of locomotion of the 6-month infant and that of the child who has learned to walk. At the same time, this process of conceptual development will emerge as quite incommensurate with the much less dramatic and seemingly more continuous changes in the area of perception. However, it may be that the structural differences between the *products* of perceptual and conceptual processes obscure the continual interplay between the two in most, if not all, cognitive activity and therefore detract from a true appreciation of the differential involvement of perception in conceptual activity at varying developmental levels.

This interdependence between perception and thinking is the major premise for an alternative conception of intellectual development to be offered presently—a conception built around the person's dependence on various aspects of the information contained in the stimulus field. Such a conception, it is hoped, will contribute to a more truly experimental attack on the phenomena of mental development and their determinants, and thereby serve to supplement the structural analysis which Piaget has given us.

THREE DIMENSIONS OF THE TRANSITION FROM PERCEPTION TO CONCEPTION

If we ask ourselves how one might operationally distinguish between a purely perceptual and a purely inferential task, one criterion for inference would be the opportunity for the subject to supplement or replace the sensory data with information or knowledge not contained in the immediate stimulus field. As a matter of fact, this criterion differentiates the two portions of the study by Piaget and Taponier (1956) referred to earlier in which perception was contrasted to conception within the same stimulus context. The only difference between the two tasks was that in the conservation task the subjects were in effect informed beforehand of the equality of the two lines; this knowledge could take precedence over the lines themselves, and provide a basis for the subsequent judgment under altered stimulus conditions.

It seems possible, however, to formulate this criterion in quantitative, rather than all-or-none terms; that is, the relative amount of information which the subject needs from the stimulus field in order to make the judgment may vary over a wide range. The precise sense in which this quantitative criterion permits us to place perception and conception at opposite ends of a single dimension will be more fully explained below. For the moment, let us simply grant the possibility of doing so and propose this dimension, along with two others that are closely related, as a skeleton for the construction of an experimentally useful conceptual framework within which the cognitive development of the child may be traced.

The three dimensions along which perception and conception can be related may be specified as follows:

(1) *Redundancy:* As one proceeds from perception to conception, the amount of redundant information required decreases.

(2) *Selectivity:* As one proceeds from perception to conception, the amount of irrelevant information that can be tolerated without affecting the response increases.

(3) *Contiguity:* As one proceeds from perception to conception, the spatial and temporal separation over which the total information contained in the stimulus field can be integrated increases.

It should be noted that these dimensions are stated in such a way as to be applicable either to intertask differences or to intersubject differences. Let us examine these three dimensions in some detail from the double standpoint of their relevance to the differentiation of perceptual from conceptual tasks on the one hand and to the analysis of changes during the course of development from a perceptual level of functioning to a conceptual level on the other hand—bearing in mind that these two terms are to be regarded as the poles of a continuum.

The Dimension of Redundancy

The dependence of perceptual functions on a high degree of redundancy in the stimulus input is rather easily demonstrated. Redundancy is basic to the differentiation of figure from ground; similarly it is a requisite for shape perception, the perception of speech, and to some extent for perceptual constancy (as shown in the multiplicity of overlapping cues involved in size constancy). In contrast, at the conceptual end we find redundancy reduced to an absolute minimum—typically zero—in the symbolic representation of mathematical or logical relationships. Whether the average adult is capable of operating consistently at this rarefied level is another question; the difficulty which most people experience in dealing with such nonredundant material, and the fact that a considerable amount of redundancy is built into our language, suggests that there are definite limitations in this respect. This conclusion is supported by work on concept formation, such as that of Bruner, Goodnow, and Austin (1956).

A developmental trend in the direction of decreasing reliance on redundant stimulation can be found in a variety of contexts. First of all, within the area of perception as such, the writer found considerable relevant evidence in a recent survey of the literature on perceptual development (Wohlwill, 1960). The clearest example of this point comes from studies on the identification of geometric or familiar-object stimuli on the basis of partial cues (e.g., Gollin, 1956), where the degree of completion of the figure necessary for its identification gradually decreases during the course of development. It seems justifiable, in fact, to regard such a task as becoming increasingly inferential as the amount of information which the subject has to "fill in" increases.[4] Indeed, this appears to be in part the import of Piaget and Morf's study of "perceptual pre-inference," in which the importance of continuity of lines serving as cues in a perceptual judgment was found to decrease with age.

Looking at redundancy in temporal sequences of events, furthermore, one might conceptualize the formation of Harlow's learning sets in terms of the reduction of redundant information to a minimum; it is of interest, therefore, that the rapidity of formation of such learning sets is strongly correlated with mental age (cf. Stevenson and Swartz, 1958).

This conception is relevant, incidentally, to Bruner's (1957) view of perception as an "act of categorization"; as we noted earlier, he has postulated that the amount of redundant information required for veridical identification is inversely proportional to the availability or accessibility of the particular category in the individual's repertoire of perceptual categories. While the intervention of a specific perceptual category cannot be equated to the operation of general symbolic processes, the fact that the action of both can in some sense compensate for lack of redundancy in the stimulus suggests that Bruner, too, is dealing essentially with a dimension running from immediate perception to conceptually mediated judgment.

The Dimension of Selectivity

The ubiquitous interaction between sensory dimensions in virtually every area of perception (psychophysical judgments and illusions, for example) bears ample testimony to the organism's very limited ability to dissociate relevant from irrelevant information at the perceptual level. At the level of thinking, on the other hand, this discussion represents a *sine qua non* of conceptual functions; the formation of conceptual classes clearly requires the systematic, selective abstraction of relevant (i.e., criterial) from irrelevant information. The same is true in the realm of logical inference, deductive reasoning, mathematical problem solving, and other such manifestations of symbolically mediated behavior.

It is thus noteworthy that one of the major developmental changes that seems to take place in the development of abstract concepts is precisely the differentiation of relevant from irrelevant, but more readily discriminable,

---

[4] The view proposed here offers a resolution to a rather ticklish question which confronted Attneave (1954) in his attempt to analyze form perception in informational terms. Should a task in which the subject has to predict the "state" of a visual field at a point, on the basis of information obtained at preceding points of a contour, be considered a perceptual or a conceptual one?

attributes. This development is shown in various studies of concept formation (e.g., Vurpillot, 1960); it may also lie at the heart of a problem which
Piaget has studied intensively—the development of conservation. Here one
aspect of the stimulus, such as number, weight, volume, or quantity, has to
be conceived as invariant, in the face of highly visible changes in some other
irrelevant attribute with which it is typically correlated. Similar phenomena
are involved in the development of the concepts of time, velocity, and
movement, as studied by Piaget.

The Dimension of Contiguity

The third dimension is perhaps the most obvious one. Indeed, the major
role which spatial and temporal contiguity plays in perception hardly needs
detailed discussion. Spatially, we find it illustrated in the Gestalt law of
proximity, as well as in the variation of illusions, figural aftereffects, and
other perceptual phenomena as a function of the distance between the
central stimulus and contextual portions of a field; similarly, figural after-
effects, among other phenomena, demonstrate the relatively limited temporal
span over which two stimulus events separated in time interact.

It is characteristic of conceptual processes, on the other hand, that they
enable the individual to deal with stimulus information whose components
are widely separated in space or time. To give just one example, conceptual
groupings can be achieved where the objects to be grouped are not in close
spatial relationship and may not even be exposed simultaneously. Here
again absolute independence of contiguity represents an ideal which is
scarcely, if ever, realized even by adults. Thus, Davidon (1952) has shown
that the opportunity for the subject to manipulate the stimulus materials
in an object-classification task so as to provide spatial contiguity for the
groupings made improves performance significantly; yet the results are
perhaps more remarkable for the small size of the effect which manipulation
produced.

Davidon's problem would be an ideal one in which to explore developmental changes; it would be hypothesized that with increasing age this
factor of spatial proximity in conceptual grouping would steadily decrease
in importance. While there is no evidence on this specific point, a variety
of related findings can be mentioned. In the realm of perception, first of all,
the writer's review of the literature on perceptual development (Wohlwill,
1960) uncovered various examples of developmental changes in the direction of an increasing ability or tendency to relate objects in the stimulus
field, independently of their spatial or temporal contiguity. Such a trend
appeared, for instance, in studies of size constancy, which for young children
deteriorates much more rapidly with increasing distance between the stimuli
than for adults, and in the perception of causality, which for children, but
not for adults, requires a perceived contact between the objects in order for
them to appear as causally related. With increasing age, furthermore, rela-

tively remote visual frameworks exert an increasing influence on perception in diverse situations.[5]

With respect to tasks of reasoning or concept formation, we unfortunately have much less direct evidence of developmental changes indicating a decrease in the role of this factor of contiguity, although what we know of the thinking and problem solving behavior of children is consistent with the assumption of such an age trend. One experimental study that might be mentioned in this connection is that by Kendler and Kendler (1956), who found that the ability of 3- to 4-year-old children to respond inferentially in a Maier-type reasoning task was closely dependent on the temporal sequence in which the steps in the inferential chain were presented. Thus, if children were shown that A leads to B, X leads to Y and B leads to G (the main goal object), and if they were then presented with a choice of A or X, the frequency of inferential responses (choice of A) was considerably higher if the B-G experience had immediately followed or preceded the A-B experience, than it was where the X-Y experience intervened between these two. Inferential choices likewise depended on the *direction* of the temporal sequence, being significantly more frequent when B-G followed A-B than when it preceded it—pointing to a rather obvious fact—that the temporal order between two events is of importance quite independently of the interval separating them. It would be of interest to determine whether this ordinal factor also decreases in importance with age.

The Resultant of the Three Dimensions: Specificity

Taken together, these three dimensions yield responses of varying specificity, ranging from those of perceptual judgment, in which accuracy is always relative and error is the rule, to the absolute precision and accuracy of the products of conceptual processes. To this extent they do not represent a departure from Brunswik's and Piaget's conceptions of the problem but rather an extension in the direction of continuity of process from perception to conception.

To illustrate the relevance of our dimensions to this specificity criterion, let us compare the assessment of the relative size of two objects through direct perceptual judgment with that achieved by the conceptual process of measurement, i.e., by the intermediary of a ruler. In the former case, the results will be affected by spatial or temporal separation, by variation in irrelevant aspects, and by lack of redundancy, i.e., one-dimensional stimuli yield larger thresholds than two- or three-dimensional ones (Werner,

---

[5] Certain perceptual phenomena appear, however, to be exceptions to this developmental trend, notably the role played by the factor of proximity in grouping and the role of spatial and temporal separation between stimuli in apparent movement. Thus, there appear to be definite limitations to the applicability of the principles outlined here.

1957, p. 118)—all of these factors interfering with accuracy and precision of judgment. None of these aspects, on the other hand, influences the results obtained through measurement, the precision of which is limited only by the accuracy of the instrument and the observer's visual acuity in reading it. A very similar kind of comparison could have been made between the assessment of quantity by estimation and by counting. It is thus of no little significance that, in the case of length and in the case of number, perceptual discrimination and conceptual measurement appear to develop in close interdependence (Braine, 1959; Long and Welch, 1941).

CONCLUSIONS

Granting for the moment the validity of the dimensions suggested earlier for the representation of important components of developmental change in cognitive functioning,[6] the question of their conceptual fruitfulness arises. Insofar as they do appear to encompass a wide array of phenomena, their status presumably transcends the level of pure description. It is suggested, moreover, that they provide the basis for the construction of a higher-order theoretical framework within which a more systematic and a more generalized approach to problems in this area may be realized.

The major argument in support of this seemingly pious hope is the built-in potential of these dimensions for leading to a set of constructs which can be securely anchored on the stimulus and response sides and which will also facilitate the integration of developmental changes with principles derived from the experimental study of perception and thinking. To give just one example, the conception should prove of heuristic value in the analysis of the perceptual constancies in terms of the role of stimulus variables such as amount of surplus cues, or redundant information, in interaction with organismic variables such as age.

Admittedly, the actual mechanisms mediating the effects of our dimensions of cognitive activity remain quite obscure as yet. Possibly, neurophysiological or cybernetic models of cognitive activity related to the internal activity of the organism in transforming the stimulus input so as to allow for varying degrees of stimulus determination of behavior may provide us with fruitful leads in our quest for such mechanisms. Thus, one might suggest the operation of scanning mechanisms as characteristic of perception, as against digital mechanisms intervening in reasoning. The process of developmental change could then be conceptualized in terms of varying forms of interaction between these two.

It would undoubtedly be sheer pretentiousness to elaborate further upon these highly speculative questions at this point, but one may point to certain

---

[6] For an empirical demonstration of the heuristic value of these dimensions in the study of abstraction see the Appendix to this paper.

empirical hypotheses that appear to be implicit in the postulated dimensions of developmental change themselves. For instance, in the previous discussion of selectivity, it was suggested that the problem of the development of conservation might be handled in terms of the dissociation of a particular concept (e.g., number) from irrelevant, though typically correlated and highly visible, perceptual cues (e.g., length over which a row of elements extends). If this dissociation does in fact represent a factor relevant to the psychological process involved in the development of conservation (as opposed to a mere description of the results of this process), it seems to follow that systematically arranged experiences aimed at untying these two variables for the child should at least facilitate the appearance of conservation.[7]

This brings us, lastly, to the more general question of the bearing of the formulation outlined in this paper on Piaget's work in this area. At first sight, it may seem that the two are at variance in several respects, notably in our postulation of essentially continuous dimensions, as opposed to Piaget's discontinuous stages of development, and in the emphasis here on modes of utilizing stimulus information as against Piaget's system of internal structures, operations, and mental actions. Much of this apparent contradiction disappears, however, if one recognizes that Piaget's concern is with changes in the structural characteristics of the products of intellectual activity, whereas the interest here is in the specification of the dimensions and processes of developmental change.

The distinction between these two essentially complementary approaches may be clarified by reference to their respective handling of the role of external environmental factors. Piaget, as is well known, tends to ignore the effects of antecedent conditions and environmental variables in development, relegating them to a place definitely subsidiary in importance to the unfolding of internal structures. This does not mean that he advocates a strict nativist position, for he has frequently emphasized the continual interaction between external and internal forces. Nevertheless, his biological orientation and interest in structure leads him to take external factors for granted and to regard the form which this interaction takes as largely predetermined from the start. The only problem, then, is that of specifying

---

[7] With respect to the development of number conservation, the writer is currently investigating the role of such experience experimentally, alongside other experimental effects pertinent to the alternative theoretical formulations of Piaget (involving the activation of relevant mental operations, e.g., those of addition and subtraction) and of learning theory (focusing on the role of reinforcement, through direct confrontation with the *fact* of number invariance).

A very similar research project, dealing with experiential effects in the realm of the conservation of weight (under changes in shape) is being conducted in Norway by Smedslund (1959). As regards the effects of dissociating irrelevant perceptual cues, the preliminary report of this author indicates mainly negative results thus far.

the successive stages through which the organism passes; little leeway is left for differential manifestations of external conditions. It is not surprising therefore that his treatment of learning effects in the development of logical processes (Piaget, 1959) is limited almost exclusively to the activation of previously formed structures bearing a logical relationship to the particular structure under investigation. In comparison, the approach advocated here probably is less adequate to the task of analyzing the structural complexities of intellectual activity and its development; in compensation, however, it allows for a more thorough exploration of functional relationships between antecedent condition and developmental change and should contribute thereby to a more explicit understanding of the processes at work in the interaction between environmental and organismic forces.

APPENDIX

An Illustrative Experiment

By way of introducing some substance into the argument developed in this paper, let us consider an experiment specifically designed to show the applicability and usefulness of the first two of the dimensions discussed, namely, redundancy and selectivity. Since the purpose of this study is primarily illustrative, it should not be surprising if the results appear to some extent trivial.

The task was a very simple one—to pick out the odd one from among three stimuli. The stimuli were simple geometric figures, varying along one or more of the following four attributes: shape (square, triangle, pentagon); color (red, green, blue); shading (outline, dotted, solid), and size (large, medium, small). Five different sheets, each containing eight such triplets of figures, were constructed, according to the design outlined in Table 1

Table 1

Schema for Study on the Role
of Irrelevant and Redundant Information

| | Number of Attributes that are: | | |
Sheet	Criterial	Quiet	Noisy
a	3	0	1
b	2	1	1
c	1	2	1
d	1	1	2
e	1	0	3

(the terminology in this table is taken from Bruner *et al.*, 1956). Samples of each type of stimulus set are shown in Figure 1 and the appropriate colors are indicated under each stimulus.

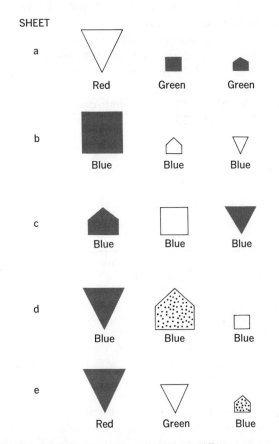

Figure 1 Sample stimulus sets used to represent different amounts of redundant and irrelevant information.

"Critical" attributes in this study were those on which two of the three figures were alike, the third being the odd one. Where more than one attribute was criterial, they were perfectly correlated; thus, sheets *a* to *c* may be said to vary on the dimension of redundancy. Sheets *c* to *e*, on the other hand, vary with respect to the amount of noise or irrelevant information contained, i.e., the number of attributes on which all three figures of a triplet differed. It will be noted that redundancy was varied while keeping irrelevant information constant, and vice versa, this being accomplished by concomitant variation of number of "quiet" attributes—attributes on which all three figures of a triplet were identical. Each attribute was noisy twice on sheets *a* to *c* and criterial twice on sheets *c* to *e*, thus accounting for eight sets of triplets per sheet.

The hypothesis was that, as relevant information decreased or irrelevant information increased, there would be a gradual shift from a perceptual mode to a conceptual mode of functioning, reflected in three different ways. In children errors would increase, and younger subjects would show a larger effect in this respect than older subjects; for adults, time taken to complete each sheet would be directly related to degree of irrelevant or redundant information.

Table 2 presents the means for preliminary results obtained from 15 subjects from a third grade, 15 subjects from a fifth grade, and 15 college students.

Table 2

Mean Number of Errors and Mean Time
(For Adults) per Sheet

Sheet	Mean Number of Errors			Mean Time
	3rd Grade	5th Grade	Adults	(Adults)
a	.6	.5	.1	17.0 sec.
b	.8	.3	.4	19.8
c	1.2	1.2	.4	19.5
d	3.4	3.0	1.2	32.2
e	3.8	3.9	1.9	31.0

Analysis of variance of the error scores discloses highly significant effects of age (third and fifth grades vs. adults), both as a main variable, and in interaction with the stimulus variable. In view of this interaction, which is in accordance with the second hypothesis, no test of the main effect of the stimulus variable was carried out, though the over-all trend is clearly as predicted. For the adults' time scores the effect of stimuli was likewise highly significant, although here, as in the case of the error scores as well, the major difference is between sheets *a, b,* and *c* on the one hand, as against *d* and *e* on the other.

This sharp rise in time and errors between sheets *c* and *d* suggests that the function relating the amount of *irrelevant* information to performance in this type of task differs considerably from that applying to amount of *redundant* information. This difference probably reflects the differences in the processes involved; whereas changes in the amount of redundancy affect primarily the perceptual differentiation of the odd from the even stimuli, changes in the amount of irrelevant information determine the extent to which the subject must try out successive hypotheses with regard to the criterial dimension.

As for the age variable, it is clearly represented in this study in only a very perfunctory fashion. It might be noted, incidentally, that for a small group of younger children (second graders), there was a strong indication that the amount of redundant information played a more important role than for the older subjects.[8]

REFERENCES

Attneave, F. (1954). Some informational aspects of visual perception. *Psychol. Rev.*, **61**, 183–193.

Braine, M. D. S. (1959). The ontogeny of certain logical operations: Piaget's formulation examined by nonverbal methods. *Psychol. Monogr.*, **73** (5), Whole No. 475.

Bruner, J. S. (1957). On perceptual readiness. *Psychol. Rev.*, **64**, 123–152.

Bruner, J. S., J. Goodnow, and G. A. Austin (1956). *A study of thinking.* New York: Wiley.

Brunswik, E. (1956). *Perception and the representative design of psychological experiments*, second ed. Berkeley, Calif.: University of California Press.

Davidon, R. S. (1952). The effects of symbols, shift, and manipulation upon the number of concepts attained. *J. exp. Psychol.*, **44**, 70–79.

Gollin, E. S. (1956). Some research problems for developmental psychology. *Child Develpm.*, **27**, 223–235.

Kendler, H. H., and T. S. Kendler (1956). Inferential behavior in prechool children. *J. exp. Psychol.*, **51**, 311–314.

Koffka, K. (1924). *The growth of the mind.* New York: Harcourt.

Köhler, W. (1925). *The mentality of apes.* London: Routledge.

Lavoie, G. (1961). Contribution à l'étude des relations entre la perception et l'intelligence. Unpublished L. Ps. thesis, Université de Montreal.

Long, L., and L. Welch (1941). The development of the ability to discriminate and match numbers. *J. genet. Psychol.*, **59**, 377–387.

Munn, N. L. (1955). *The evolution and growth of human behavior.* Boston: Houghton Mifflin.

Piaget, J. (1946). *La psychologie de l'intelligence.* Paris: Presses Universitaires. (Trans. from second French ed. as *The psychology of intelligence.* London: Routledge, 1950.)

---

[8] A more extensive investigation of these developmental changes has recently been carried out by Lavoie (1961) with results substantially in agreement with those reported here.

Piaget, J. (1954). Ce qui subsiste de la théorie de la Gestalt dans la psychologie contemporaine de l'intelligence et de la perception. *Schweiz. Z. Psychol. Anwend.*, **13**, 72–83. (Also in J. de Ajuriaguerre *et al.*, *Aktuelle Probleme der Gestalttheorie*. Bern: Hans Huber, 1954. Pp. 72–83.)

Piaget, J. (1955). Essai d'une nouvelle interpretation probabiliste des effets de centration, de la loi de Weber et de celle des centrations relatives. *Arch. Psychol. Genève*, **35**, 1–24.

Piaget, J. (1956). Les stades du développement intellectuel de l'enfant et de l'adolescent. In P. Osterrieth *et al.*, *Le problème des stades en psychologie de l'enfant*. Paris: Presses Universitaires. Pp. 33–49.

Piaget, J. (1957). Logique et équilibre dans les comportements du sujet. In L. Apostel *et al.*, Logique et équilibre. *Etudes d'épistémologie génétique*, Vol. 2. Paris: Presses Universitaires. Pp. 27–117.

Piaget, J. (1959). Apprentissage et connaissance. In M. Goustard *et al.*, La logique des apprentissages. *Etudes d'épistémologie génétique*, Vol. 10. Paris: Presses Universitaires. Pp. 159–188.

Piaget, J., and M. Lambercier (1946). Transpositions perceptives et transitivité opératoire dans les comparaisons en profondeur. *Arch. Psychol., Genève*, **31**, 325–368.

Piaget, J., and A. Morf (1958a). Les isomorphismes partiels entre les structures logiques et les structures perceptives. In J. S. Bruner *et al.*, Logique et perception. *Etudes d'épistémologie génétique*, Vol. 6. Paris: Presses Universitaires. Pp. 49–116.

Piaget, J., and A. Morf (1958b). Les préinférences perceptives et leurs relations avec les schèmes sensorimoteurs et opératoires. In J. S. Bruner *et al.*, Logique et perception. *Etudes d'épistémologie génétique*, Vol. 6. Paris: Presses Universitaires. Pp. 117–155.

Piaget, J., and S. Taponier (1956). L'estimation des longueurs de deux droites horizontales et parallèles extrémités décalées. *Arch. Psychol., Genève*, **35**, 369–400.

Smedslund, J. (1959). Learning and equilibration: a study of the acquisition of concrete logical structures. Pre-publication draft, Oslo.

Stevenson, Harold W., and Jon D. Swartz (1958). Learning set in children as a function of intellectual level. *J. comp. physiol. Psychol.*, **51**, 755–757.

Vurpillot, E. (1960). Etude génétique sur la formation d'un concept: role données perceptives. *Psychol. Franc.*, **5**, 135–152.

Werner, H. (1957). *Comparative psychology of mental development*, revised ed. New York: International Universities.

Wertheimer, M. (1959). *Productive thinking*, enlarged ed. New York: Harper & Row.

Wohlwill, J. F. (1960). Developmental studies of perception. *Psychol. Bull.*, **57**, 249–288.

NOTE ON CONSERVATION: METHODOLOGICAL AND DEFINITIONAL CONSIDERATIONS

Gerald E. Gruen

The recent controversy between Smedslund and Braine (Braine, 1959, 1964; Smedslund, 1963, 1965a, 1965b) has centered primarily on conflicting interpretations of the same data. Braine has argued that his data indicate the presence of transitivity, whereas Smedslund thinks Braine's data reflect fairly simple learning processes. It has become apparent throughout this controversy that Braine and Smedslund are using quite different criteria for diagnosing the presence or absence of transitivity. Smedslund, using his set of criteria, typically has not found the emergence of transitivity in the thinking of children younger than 7 or 8 years of age, whereas Braine, using a different set of criteria, typically finds transitivity present in children 4 and 5 years of age.

Although this controversy has focused on concepts of transitivity, these investigators have equally discrepant findings with respect to the emergence age of concepts of conservation. Braine and Shanks (1965a; 1965b), for example, find that children 4 and 5 years of age are able to conserve, while Smedslund (1961) does not find conservation present in the thinking of children younger than 7 or 8 years of age. While the age norms that Smedslund finds are in agreement with the findings of Piaget (1950, 1952) the age norms that Braine finds are supported by the work of Bruner and his associates at the Harvard Center for Cognitive Study (cf. Frank, in Bruner, 1964). This latter group also finds that 5-year-old children have the ability to conserve.

As Braine (1964) has pointed out, the disagreement involved here is not merely one concerning age norms. If it were, it might be considered trivial. Neither is it entirely a matter of which experimental procedures are the appropriate ones for assessing these cognitive processes. Rather, it is basically a disagreement about the very nature of the processes which underlie the concepts with which Piaget's theory deals.

The disagreement arises over what the necessary and sufficient conditions are for these concepts to be formed. These investigators have been, to a great extent, concerned with the *acquisition* of Piagetian concepts. Because of this, and because they have developed different points of view about the conditions that are necessary and sufficient for children to acquire these concepts, they have come to disagree about the processes that underlie

Reprinted with the permission of the author and The Society for Research in Child Development, Inc., in *Child Development*, 1966, 37, 977–983.

them. This fact is important because the processes that these investigators have assumed underlie conservation have influenced the methods they have employed to study it.

In turn, the different methods they have employed have led them to study qualitatively different phenomena. The discrepancies in the age norms they have obtained suggest that they are not studying the same cognitive processes. It is not enough to say that Braine and Bruner are simply studying the same processes as Smedslund is, only at an earlier, less stable stage of their development. The phenomena that these investigators are studying differ in complexity and quality, and these differences ought to be made clear. The important question, thus, becomes: Exactly what is it that Braine and Bruner find in children 4 and 5 years old that they refer to as conservation and transitivity, and how does it differ, qualitatively, from that which Smedslund finds in children 7 and 8 years of age?

Although this paper will not attempt adequately to answer that question, it is interesting to note that both Braine and Bruner get quite comparable age norms for the earliest appearance of conservation, in spite of the fact that their procedures for assessing the presence or absence of conservation differ considerably. A possible reason why this should occur becomes clear when one looks at the study done by Frank (in Bruner, 1964). Frank found that 70 per cent of the 5-year-old children she studied were able to make conserving responses when distorting perceptual cues were eliminated by a screen. One could interpret her findings in terms of the fact that she forced the children to make a distinction between real and phenomenal properties of an object by screening out perceptual cues. Since Braine and Shanks (1965a) have defined conservation in terms of making a distinction between real and phenomenal properties of an object, it is not surprising that these two investigators get similar results.

In her experiment, Frank (1964) poured one of two standard beakers of water into, alternately, a wider and a thinner beaker of the same height. Before and after the water had been poured, she asked 5-year-old children who had previously been found to be unable to conserve, "Which has more to drink, or do they have the same amount, the standard or the wider beaker?" (Bruner, 1964, p. 6) This question is very similar to the kind of question that Smedslund generally asks. However, following this question, Smedslund always asks the question "Why?" and will not deem anyone a conserver unless he can give an adequate explanation for his answer. Bruner and his group, on the other hand, simply deem the child a conserver if he gives a conserving response to the first question. That is, although the child may be asked to explain his answers, his being labeled as a conserver or a nonconserver is contingent only on his response to the first question.

Smedslund (1963) has referred to this kind of response as a "symptom response" and has presented data intended to show that the explanation criterion has functional significance in at least two ways: (1) in yielding higher correlations than the symptom response alone with certain addition/subtraction operations (Smedslund, 1962), and (2) in being more predictive than the symptom response alone of resistance to extinction (Smedslund, 1962; 1966). Smedslund seems to believe that the simple symptom response criterion is not very meaningful at all.

Recently, Inhelder, Bovet, Sinclair, and Smock (1966) have raised similar objections:

> The operational structure (as defined by Piaget) underlying the conservation concepts appear to us to be a complex, coordinated system that cannot be properly evaluated by rather summary investigation of answers to preselected questions with no exploration of the child's justification of those answers. Nor can such answers be induced by training the child to direct attention uniquely to those aspects of the situation that lead him to a limited (in terms of the criteria for the conservation concept) "correct answer."

Thus it is clear that Bruner uses quite different criteria for assessing the presence or absence of conservation than does Smedslund or representatives of the Genevan cognitive growth projects. These differing criteria, in part, reflect the different theoretical notions these investigators hold concerning the psychological processes that underlie conservation. The remainder of this paper will attempt to illustrate empirically that the discrepancy in the age norms found by Bruner and Smedslund with respect to the emergence of conservation are, to a great extent, attributable to the fact that they have employed different sets of criteria to assess its presence or absence.

CONSEQUENCES OF USING DIFFERENT SETS OF CRITERIA

In an earlier study on conservation of number, I (Gruen, 1965) attempted to control for an ambiguity that exists in the way the conservation question typically is asked. This was done by giving 45 *S*s, who were 5 years of age, verbal pretraining (VPT) designed to insure that they would interpret the conservation question in the way that *E* meant for it to be interpreted. These *S*s were set to interpret "more" and "same" in the question, "Are there more corks in this row, the same number of corks in both rows, or more corks in that row?" to mean more or same in number, and only in number. That is, these *S*s were pretrained to discriminate between the terms "more," which always meant more in number, and "longer," which, of course, always meant more in length. It was suspected that these two possible interpretations of the words "more" and "same" in the number-conservation situation were often confused by 5-year-old children. Forty-five other 5-year-old *S*s were not given this kind of pretraining, but otherwise were subjected to the same kind of experimental conditions as the VPT *S*s. Each *S* was given six conservation problems on the posttest following the training period. The criteria used to assess the presence or absence of number conservation in all Ss were exactly the same as those used by Smedslund. Using these criteria, there were no significant differences between these two groups in terms of the number of conserving responses given by Ss in each group, although there was a trend for more conserving responses to be given by VPT Ss than other Ss. What happens, now, if we reanalyze these same data, only this time using the criteria employed by Bruner and his group?

Table 1 presents the critical information. There were 161 responses that were classified as conserving when the Smedslund criteria were used and 205 when the Bruner criteria were used. The binomial test (Siegel, 1956, pp. 36–42) reveals that this difference is significant ($z = 2.25$; $p = .024$). The Bruner procedure for assessing the presence or absence of conservation thus results in significantly more responses being classified as conserving than the Smedslund procedure.

Table 1

Number and Proportion of Conserving Responses
Made by Ss *on the Posttest of Number Conservation*

Criteria	VPT	No VPT	Total
Smedslund:			
N	100	61	161
Proportion	.37	.23	.30
Bruner:			
N	137	68	205
Proportion	.51	.25	.38

Table 1 also indicates a definite trend for Ss who received VPT to make more conserving responses than Ss who did not, when either the Smedslund or Bruner criteria are employed. The Mann-Whitney U test (Siegel, 1956, pp. 116–127) reveals that the difference between the VPT Ss and the Ss who received no VPT is not quite significant when the Smedslund criteria are used ($z = 1.39$; $p = .16$). When the Bruner criteria are used, however, the Mann-Whitney U test reveals that the difference between these two groups becomes highly significant ($z = 3.44$; $p < .001$). This is because 37 of the 44 responses that were classified as nonconserving responses by the Smedslund criteria, and reclassified as conserving responses by the Bruner criteria, were made by VPT Ss.

It may be that Ss who received VPT in the present experiment are most comparable to the Ss in Frank's (1964) experiment. That is, one effect that the screening out of perceptual cues in Frank's experiment might have had was to eliminate a number of possible interpretations to the ambiguous conservation question, leaving *S* with only one possible interpretation. This is exactly the kind of effect VPT was designed to have. The percentage of *S*s who made conserving responses after receiving VPT in the present experiment was, in fact, quite comparable to the percentage that Frank reports in her experiment, if one looks only at what Smedslund (1963) refers to as "symptom-responses." Seventy-six per cent, or 34 out of 45, of the VPT *S*s made at least one conserving response.

Whether or not Frank's screening procedure can be interpreted as making the conservation question less ambiguous, however, it appears from the VPT effect that at least part of the reason that Smedslund does not find conservation in children younger than 7 or 8 years of age, is as Braine (1964) has suggested, because of the ambiguous way in which he asks the conservation question.

The ambiguity in the conservation question does not completely account for the discrepancies in the age norms found by Bruner and Smedslund, however. Table 1 shows that even within the VPT and no-VPT conditions there is a considerable increase in the number of conservation responses made when the data are classified according to Bruner's criteria, as opposed to Smedslund's criteria. This discrepancy cannot be accounted for by the ambiguity of the conservation question. It seems to be a result, rather, of the fact that Smedslund requires each subject to give a logical, or semilogical, explanation of his "symptom response," whereas Bruner does not.

CONCLUSIONS

The Frank-Bruner procedure for assessing the presence or absence of conservation clearly results in more (and probably younger) children being labeled conservers than does the Smedslund procedure. The difference referred to here is not a function of the screening procedure that Frank employed, but is in addition to it. If Frank had used the Smedslund criteria for assessing the presence or absence of conservation, her age norms would have been older than the ones she obtained; and, vice versa, if Smedslund had used the Frank-Bruner criteria, his age norms would have tended to be younger.

It is an open question as to which set of criteria is the appropriate one for assessing the presence or absence of conservation, but it is not an arbitrary one. The choice depends to a great extent on the psychological processes that one assumes underlie conservation. For example, the criteria that Smedslund has used seem more appropriate for assessing conservation *as Piaget defines it* than do the criteria used by Frank. This is because Smedslund, like Piaget, believes that logical operations such as reversibility, compensation, and logical necessity underlie conservation and must be present in the thinking of a child who has conservation. Smedslund's criteria would not be appropriate for assessing conservation *as Bruner defines it*, however. This is because, in Bruner's theoretical framework, conservation comes into being when the symbolic mode is activated and becomes dominant over the iconic (perceptual) mode and not necessarily through the aforementioned logical operations. Given this framework, the criteria used by Frank seem more appropriate than those used by Smedslund.

Thus, the problem is fundamentally a definitional and theoretical one. Efforts should be expended to reach a general consensus on the definition of conservation. However, if no general consensus can be reached, then investigators should be very careful to specify what they mean by "conservation" and what psychological processes they assume underlie it. Only in the light of such specification does it become possible to evaluate the appropriateness of the criteria that are used to assess the presence or absence of conservation.

REFERENCES

Braine, M. D. S. (1959). The ontogeny of certain logical operations: Piaget's formulation examined by nonverbal methods. *Psychol. Monogr.*, **73** (4), Whole No. 475.

Braine, M. D. S. (1964). Development of a grasp of transitivity of length: a reply to Smedslund. *Child Develpm.*, **35**, 799–810.

Braine, M. D. S., and B. L. Shanks (1965a). The conservation of a shape property and a proposal about the origin of the conservations. *Canad. J. Psychol.*, **19** (3), 197–207.

Braine, M. D. S., and B. L. Shanks (1965b). The development of conservation of size. *J. verb. Learn. verb. Behav.*, **4**, 227–242.

Bruner, J. S. (1964). The course of cognitive growth. *Amer. Psychologist*, **19**, 1–15.

Frank, F. (1964). Cited by J. S. Bruner. The course of cognitive growth. *Amer. Psychologist*, **19**, 1–15.

Gruen, G. E. (1965). Experiences affecting the development of number conservation in children. *Child Develpm.*, **36**, 963–979.

Inhelder, B., M. Bovet, H. Sinclair, and C. D. Smock (1966). On cognitive development. *Amer. Psychologist*, **21**, 160–164.

Piaget, J. (1950). *The psychology of intelligence*. Trans. by M. Piercy and D. E. Berlyne. London: Routledge.

Piaget, J. (1952). *The child's conception of number*. Trans. by C. Gattengo and F. J. Hodgson. London: Routledge.

Siegel, S. (1956). *Nonparametric statistics for the behavioral sciences*. New York: McGraw-Hill.

Smedslund, J. (1961). The acquisition of conservation of substance and weight in children: I. Introduction. *Scand. J. Psychol.*, **2**, 11–20.

Smedslund, J. (1962). The acquisition of conservation of substance and weight in children: VII. Conservation of discontinuous quality and the operations of adding and taking away. *Scand. J. Psychol.*, 3, 69–77.

Smedslund, J. (1963). Development of concrete transitivity of length in children. *Child Develpm.*, 34, 389–405.

Smedslund, J. (1965a). The development of transitivity of length: a comment on Braine's reply. *Child Develpm.*, 36, 577–580.

Smedslund, J. (1956b). Performance on measurement and pseudomeasurement tasks by five- to seven-year-old children. *Scand. J. Psychol.*, 6, 1–12.

Smedslund, J. (1966). Microanalysis of concrete reasoning: I. The difficulty of some combinations of addition and subtraction of one unit. *Scand. J. Psychol.*, 7, 145–146.

CHAPTER

SEVEN

REFLECTIONS

by Irving E. Sigel

*   *   *

THE STUDIES IN this volume are testimonial to the genius of one man, Jean Piaget. They represent but a fraction of the growing literature inspired by Piagetian theory. Whether one accepts or rejects Piagetian concepts and methods, it is impossible to minimize the profound contribution this one man has had on developmental psychology.

To explain Piaget's impact in the last decade would require extensive inquiry into the social and intellectual zeitgeist within which developmental psychology and the study of cognitive processes have assumed tremendous significance. Interest in Piaget's work is but one instance of the growing awareness of the need for intensification of the study of cognitive growth and development. For too long there has been an overemphasis on the affective aspect of development. This growing interest, in conjunction with the contribution of a viable theory of cognitive development, may account for the increased attention to Piagetian contributions. His unique contribution has been described by many writers (Elkind, 1967; Flavell, 1963; Hunt, 1961). From our point of view his significance rests in conceptualizing the development of intelligence within the context of the human condition of adapting to a complex environment. Viewing intelligence in this way removes it from the narrow psychometric view pervasive among American and British psychologists. Piaget's genius is in his ability to use the daily, seemingly commonplace, behaviors of children of all ages as prime data. His interpretations of these behaviors, especially among infants, is remarkable. Coupling these insights with techniques to study cognitive processes, Piaget has produced an incomparable body of knowledge. His monumental theory is independent of modern American behavior theory; his system is self-contained, possessing unity and integrity, as if he is impervious to the achievements of American psychology. This fact, however, does not preclude investigators from different theoretical positions, inspired and stimulated by his contributions, from attempting to examine his work in relation to other theoretical systems. Scholars from around the world have set out to examine his theory from their own theoretical predispositions as points of reference. This volume reflects these efforts.

This is a common occurrence, since scientific knowledge is shared in open societies. To some students of behavior, for example, Piaget's interest in genetic epistemology is not relevant. What is important is that the data Piaget reports provides the developmental psychologist with a body of new information regarding cognitive systems. Thus, knowledge from one discipline can have its impact on diverse and, at times, seemingly unrelated theoretical systems. Einstein's notions on relativity, Cassirer's comments on language, Kant's philosophy, Freud's psychology all have influenced not only the thinkers in the fields from which these scholars emerged, but also many writers and thinkers in more remote disciplines. This is not to say that Piagetian contributions are distant from developmental psychology, for, in fact, they are not. It has been pointed out that Piaget may be criticized because he does not deal with problems as a psychologist (Elkind, 1967; Lunzer, 1960). This argument is specious. Piaget, whatever his discipline, has provided the scientific world with a body of theoretical and empirical information which has relevance to a number of scientific disciplines. We read and study it on its own merit. With whatever approach we take toward it, we are bound to ask questions. The developmental psychologist asks one order of questions, the educator another, the logician may ask a third, and the anthropologist a fourth. Every theory one presents to the public is part of the scientific culture and is open to such examinations. Acceptance or rejection of a theoretical system is a function of its persuasive powers, its logic, its novelty, and above all, its answers to old questions and its posing of new ones.

It is in this frame of mind that we approach Piaget's work. It is open to examination and analysis, to evaluation, and to reinterpretation.

For us, Piaget offers all that we have said and more. He provides an intriguing system. Trained as empiricists with an eye to experimental design and control, to a search for objectified assessments, we come to Piaget with an array of questions. Skeptics all, we then seek to replicate his work with the best techniques at our disposal. We seek to extend his investigations, attempting to enhance our understanding of the conditions accounting for the course of cognitive development so ably described by Piaget and his coworkers—Inhelder, Szeminska, Morf, Gréco, to name but a few. The degree to which these replications have been a success is told in this volume. The degree to which the theory has been extended is also apparent. It must be kept in mind that throughout the forthcoming discussion we are talking about that part of the theory emphasizing concrete operations, and that we are not attempting an evaluation of the entire theory, a task done so ably by the foremost interpreter of Piaget, John Flavell (1963).

REFLECTIONS ON TWO CRUCIAL PIAGETIAN THEMES:
INVARIANCE AND CONVERGENCE

Invariance of Ontogenesis of Thought

The papers presented in this volume offer greater support for the invariant order of stages than they do for the integrative and hierarchical nature of cognitive structures. In those studies involving conservation of particular concepts (quantity, number, space) results are consistent with those reported by Piaget and his coworkers. These studies point to the sequences in which the capabilities of children develop as they deal with these substantive areas. However, the investigations do not offer *definite* proof of *invariance*, since the methodologies employed do not put this question to the crucial test.

Some of the evidence, such as Smedslund's training studies on the acquisition of substance and weight, and Kofsky's study of classification, lead to contradictory inferences regarding the invariance issue. Smedslund's work lends itself to an interpretation of invariance, since a new concept, conservation of weight, could not be assimilated into given cognitive structures. Rather, it was easily extinguished. Kofsky shows that not every identified stage in the acquisition of a classification skill is a necessary and sufficient condition for subsequent stages. Unfortunately, each of these experiments investigated different areas of conservation and thus they do not provide comparable tests of the invariance questions. We are left with inferences from their findings within the broader theoretical framework.

Invariance of stages must be considered from two frames of reference. One framework is based on the interlocking nature of *substantive* material. For many areas of knowledge one has to proceed from the simple to the complex. This would hold true in the study of physical science, languages, and mathematics, where there is an inherent logic to the material. The invariance is substantive, where certain bits of information are necessary preludes to subsequent knowledge. The interlocking is independent of the psychological state of the persons involved.

The second frame of reference by which invariance must be examined is in terms of the psychological-cognitive processes and operations. Although these operations are expressed in the way a child handles particular conceptual material, the psycho-logical operation can be identified. Such mental operations as associativity or reversibility can be inferred, for example, in the context of class inclusion problems or conservation of quantity. Although the evidence to date, inferring at least from the studies reported in this volume, supports this notion, we need more definitive and critical experiments before we may write the laws of invariance.

The major challenge here is to devise appropriate methodologies to undertake such a task. Experimental studies rather than descriptive ones are necessary. Interventions into the hypothesized sequence need be made to determine if cognitive structures can be instituted with permanence and with no deleterious effects on other cognitive functions. The consequences of intervention may upset the balance of cognitve growth, so that overemphasis on particular operations may impede the acquisition of other structures.

One possible solution to this problem may be initial employment of scalogram types of analysis, such as those employed by Wohlwill and Kofsky. These are descriptive studies, allowing nevertheless for delineation of the sequence of the necessary steps. Perhaps by devising a battery of such scales (for example, classification and seriation) a test of the sequence becomes possible. Placing these sequences in the context of longitudinal research would be of inestimable value. Given data from such procedures, rational identification of timing intervention and the identification of the conditions for modifications could be determined. Assessment of intervention consequences could then be done relatively quickly. Such efforts, although appearing as valuable for acceleration, are of import for testing the theory—for us, the major justification. Whether or not acceleration per se is a desideratum has to be assessed on other grounds, for example, the welfare of the child, and the educational needs of the time.

Relationships among Cognitive Structures

In addition to the invariance theme which is evident in this volume, a second one can be identified—*the hierarchical and integrative nature of cognitive growth*. Studies converging on this problem do not present strong support for Piagetian theory. The work of Beilin (1965), Braine (1959), Dodwell (1962), and Shantz (1967) exemplify this effort. Their results are equivocal. It must be kept in mind, however, that each of these studies investigated different combinations of presumed interlocking operations. Thus, definitive statements concerning the hierarchical and integrative nature of Piagetian theory cannot be made.

Herein we come to a conflict in research strategies expressed in the work of empirically-oriented American and British psychologists and the work of the Geneva school. For the former, experimental efforts employ objective tests with the same subjects; the latter employ tests with different children, with integrations of processes and operations inferred.

More fundamental, perhaps, is the theoretical basis upon which such investigations are carried out. Piaget, according to Flavell, argues that no operation can be viewed in isolation because it gains its meaning from the system of which it is a part. This is basic to the equilibration theory. How does one study this type of holistic proposition? Prevalent research strategy among developmental psychologists calls for objective measurement and precise operational definitions of each of the operations. The determination of the feasibility of such an undertaking without doing serious violation to the central theoretical proposition is still to be accomplished.

The issue may be a difference in interpretation, as Lunzer (1960) states it. He undertook a study to determine the interlocking nature of mathematical elements involved in the ability to measure volume. Not finding the predicted linkages, he concludes:

> . . . it is by no means certain that because some relations are fundamental to the *logical* analysis of mathematical properties, these same relations underlie the *psychological* evolution of the recognition of these properties. It may well be that the recognition of such relations is usually delayed far beyond

the understanding of their concrete application. . . . more attention must be paid to what is demanded psychologically in any complex thinking operation: What are the psychological elements and how complete is the integration demanded? (p. 201)

Although the confirmation of the integrative nature of cognitive growth has not been strong, we are not yet in a position to reject this major thesis of Piaget. The research results are equivocal and seem to depend on the nature of the problem, the age of the children, and the methods employed. Braine, for example, finds relationships between transitivity and seriation, while Dodwell finds little to support the relationship between logic of classes and the concept of number.

From a commonsense point of view, one might expect integrating principles to prevail, for how else does man evolve a conceptual structure to handle the multitudinous problems open to him? The oft repeated adage that more research is necessary is obvious, but what kind?

One type of study that may be called for is a retrospective one, in which subjects, already identifiable at a particular state of development, can be examined to determine if they have acquired competence to solve problems from previous periods. The editors (Hooper and Sigel, in preparation) have undertaken such a study with children identified as *conservers*. It was found that they did not represent a homogeneous group when it came to solving logical matrix problems or seriation problems. Are there alternative antecedents to conservation skills? This is unknown. The approaches for study mentioned in the section on stage invariance seem appropriate.

When all is said and done, we are at a point where empirical findings allow for statements concerning the integrative nature of cognitive growth to be made. We have guidelines and evidence to enable us to proceed. This is the challenge we have before us.

Two central Piagetian themes have been identified, the invariance of stages and the integrative nature of cognitive growth. As psychologists, we are interested in those relevant psychological variables that must be considered to provide the proper perspective in which these issues can be examined. It is to this end that we direct our attention in the remainder of this chapter.

REFLECTIONS ON THE ROLE OF EXPERIENTIAL VARIABLES

Perhaps the most poorly defined set of variables influencing the course of cognitive development can be broadly subsumed within the context of experience. The psychologist interested in cause-effect relationships is forced to define relevant environmental variables influencing the child's acquisition of consequent functioning of cognitive operations. Piaget does acknowledge the significance of the environment as a stimulant, and, further, acknowledges the role of linguistic systems as an influence on the quality of emerging logical thought (Inhelder and Piaget, 1964; Piaget, 1950). There is still need to specify the kind and quality of experience that facilitates or inhibits the development of thought from the sensorimotor to the formal reasoning period. Cross-sectional studies do contribute to our general understanding of the role of experience that impinges on the course of cognitive growth. These studies do not, however, provide specific delineation of the factors within the cultures that account for obtained results. The uniqueness as well as the similarities that may be contributory to the outcomes of study need specification.

In this section, emphasis will be placed on a number of experiential variables that contribute to the general developmental trends, as well as individual differences in rate of growth. As the reader reflects on the studies he has read, he will note that children, varying in ability, age, and social class, can solve Piagetian-type problems. What, it should be asked, accounts for intergroup and intragroup variations? A common core of experience holds for organisms coping with the physical world, and even perhaps in certain social conditions. Within these commonalities, individual patterns are found, reflecting the range of idiosyncratic aspects of experience. In effect, we are interested in understanding factors accounting for common trends within a population as well as those factors contributing to individual differences in performance.

The particular life experiences necessary for acquisition of particular concepts (for example, conservation of quantity) have received little attention. To glibly state that "the environment does it" is too gross and nonspecific and of relatively little value. Articulation of the type, quantity, and quality of particular experiences and their direct relationship to the acquisition of logical structures is yet to be done. Piaget's failure to emphasize such psychosocial variables stems from his epistemological, rather than psychological interest, in the development of logical structures (Elkind, 1967). For the investigator, however, approaching Piagetian theory from the stance of psychological growth, the role of experience is a relevant repository of a number of variables which could account for variation in rate and quality of cognitive development.

The focus on experiential factors implies a conviction that sources of variation in performance reside in extra-individual variables. Thus, the particular intensity and magnitude of experiences should account for obtained differences among children.

Closely related to experiential factors is the personality structure of the individual. Personality characteristics play an influential role in determining *how* the child will interact with the environment, how susceptible he is to its variegated influences, and how capable he is in modifying them to his own ends. The outgoing, active child has greater opportunity for greater engagement with objects and people than the child who is withdrawn and prefers the observer role, minimizing action. Thus, the experience a child has with the world about him is in part a function of his effective capability of interaction with it.

Irrespective of his personality, the specifics of the environment as determined by culture and the availability of resources contribute to the quality of the child's contact and the content of his experiences. The rural environment, for example, offers a far different array of experiences than does the urban area; living in an underdeveloped country offers far different opportunities for facing technological conditions than does living in a highly industrialized technological world. Thus, the personality structure interacting with the environmental opportunities contributes considerably to the quality and pattern of children's thought. Greater particularization of environmental and personality variables will be made in the following discussion.

Role of Culture

" 'Culture is the man-made part of the human environment' (Herskovits, 1955, p. 305). This definition subsumes not only the material features of the human environment, but also its 'conceptual features'—the beliefs, science, myths, religions, laws, and so forth, held by a group of people" (Triandis, 1964, p. 2). Culture, according to Triandis (1964), intrudes into the "categories that are organized into schemata, in certain lexical fields, and are associated with each other and with different subjective probabilities. Positive and negative affects and behavioral intentions are attached to such categories" (p. 40).

Such cultural influences affect the thought patterns, creating profound differences in modes of thinking. The Piagetian system is an expression of a logical mathematical system integral to the scientific thought pattern of Western cultures. When applied to non-Western cultures, is not what is studied the commonalities as well as the differences among different cultures?

How children of different cultures fare on Piagetian tasks (quantity, classification) has to some extent been done (Goodnow, 1962; Greenfield, 1966; Hyde, 1959; Price-Williams, 1961, 1962). Many of these are cross-sectional in design, setting out to study the ontogenesis of conservation of quantity. Interestingly enough, there is some consistency in that area, lending credence to the interpretation that some conservation skills may be necessary universally—reflecting just one part of man's coming to terms with his physical world.

Even though some commonalities in developmental trends are found, cultural differences are also reported; for example, different explanations for conservation problems are offered by African Bush children and French-educated ones (Greenfield, 1966).

Similar results with conservation are found by Mermelstein and Shulman (1967) working with lower-class schooled and unschooled rural and urban

Negroes. Where differences are found, Goodnow (1962) attributes them to schooling and social class. Sigel and Mermelstein (1965), working with a group of nonschooled Negro boys and girls in Prince Edward County, Virginia, found similar results; namely, schooling did not seem to make a difference on conservation of quantity, but it did in class-inclusion tasks. Virtually none of the children, the oldest being eleven, were able to solve class-inclusion problems.

The next step, however, is to identify why and how school experiences influence particular cognitive developments, for example, why nonschooling did not affect the acquisition of conservation of quantity but does seem to influence class-inclusion performance.

The selection of cultures to study needs to be done in accordance with specific research requirements, providing environments in which to test the ontogenetic theory. Since we cannot readily manipulate environments, we must select among those already created. The studies of Greenfield, Goodnow, Sigel and Mermelstein reflect this approach. Other examples can be found. To test acquisition of special skills, cultures in which these are evident, with little indication of competence in other logical operations, might be selected. For example, Gladwin (1964) reports the uncanny navigation skills of a group of Polynesians. These individuals, with virtually no instruments, can locate themselves in open sea and orient their course to arrive at their destination in a direct route. Are these skills expressive of their concepts of space? If so, what in their culture enables them to acquire such logico-spatial competence? Is it extended to other similar areas (for example, concepts of land space)? What about their concepts of geometry and measurement?

We have already alluded to schooling as one cultural factor. Another factor is social class, which has been found to influence the rate of developmental change. Almy, Chittenden, and Miller (1966) report that fewer lower-class children show conservation of quantity and number a year later than middle-class children. Explanations of these differences are yet to be fully given.

We have briefly touched on the role of culture in general terms, pointing out that schooling and social class are two culturally relevant variables which contribute to differential patterns of growth. Schooling and social class, however, are still descriptive, static variables, offering little explanatory power. Narrowing our search for greater specificity to define what aspects of class and schooling might be relevant, we wish to focus on two other cultural variables, language and play. For us, these offer important dimensions of experience in relation to cognitive growth.

Role of Language

A considerable body of information is existent on language, embodied in such fields of study as linguistics, psycholinguistics, philology, and so forth. Specifically, our interest is in identifying types of linguistic experience and their role in determining children's ability to deal with Piagetian tasks. It should be made clear that we do not wish to enter the controversy of whether language determines thought in general, a controversy between Piaget and Bruner (Bruner, Olver, and Greenfield, 1966). Piagetian theory holds that cognitive structures are consistently reinforced by the syntactical structure of language (Inhelder and Piaget, 1964). Although this proposition was made in reference to acquisition of classification, there is no reason to expect it not to be true for other types of concepts (quantity, number, space). If syntactical structures may influence thought structure, and if children from different cultural and subcultural backgrounds experience different syntax, then differences in competence for solution of Piagetian-type tasks may in part be explained by such differences in language environments. Bernstein (1961), Hess and Shipman (1965), Sigel, Anderson, and Shapiro (1966), and Sigel and McBane (1967) report social-class differences in language patterns and use of language in classification tasks. For Bernstein, middle- and working-class children experience and express different syntactical structures. Hess and Shipman (1965) found similar type differences among lower- and middle-class Negro children. Sigel, Anderson, and Shapiro (1966) and Sigel and McBane (1967) found differences in the ability of lower- and middle-class Negro children to articulate and label familiar materials. Such data provide support for the hypothesis that linguistic environments influence the quality of thought patterns, their rate of development, and variations in abilities with different types of problems. The social-class differences in rate of development reported by Almy, Chittenden, and Miller (1966), for example, might be interpreted as a consequence of such experiential differences.

The differential reinforcements of particular concepts within these subcultural language environments might account for children having more familiarity with certain classes of concepts than others. Might not there be differences in emphasis on quantity concepts of one class than on classificatory concepts? Might not the level and quality of classificatory labels differ from one class or cultural group to another? It seems eminently reasonable to examine language in such terms, an approach inspired by the work of Basil Bernstein (1961).

One procedure might be to obtain language histories of children through the identification of syntactical structures of adults. Mapping of the children's language environment and testing of the children on tasks reflecting these language structures could be of considerable value in helping resolve issues on the relationship of language to thought.

Developmental histories are needed since quality of language varies as a function of the developmental level of the child. Language does not play a similar role throughout the developmental period (Werner and Kaplan, 1963). Its significance depends on the child's capability of differentiating, interpreting, and integrating language elements. There is some evidence in this volume to support this proposition. Beilin's (1965) training study shows that language is a relevant variable in inducing cognitive changes during the concrete operations period for some tasks. It is during this period that the child apparently possesses the cognitive structure to assimilate these language experiences and to apply them, but with limited generality. The child does not, for example, assimilate these verbal rules when he is faced with perceptual tasks. The partial effect, then, of didactic verbal training may be due to other factors (for example, integration of cognitive operations and complete emancipation of the child from perceptual elements because of the child's age or experiential history). When children are in a particular transitional Piagetian stage, increased exposure to language may well be the stimulus which propels the child forward. The role of language as a determinant of cognitive behaviors must be distinguished from the role of language as facilitating (that is maintaining, modifying positively or negatively) the cognitive skills of the child.

Role of Play

Piaget discusses the significance of play in helping the child acquire appropriate conceptual and representational schemas (Piaget, 1951). Of particular relevance for our discussion are the kinds of play in which the child engages, the kinds of materials available to him, and the mode of utilization he makes of these materials. Play provides the child with a major means of interacting with the physical and social environment, a way of obtaining information feedback.

Children's play behavior varies as a function of age, intelligence, sex, socioeconomic status, to name but a few factors. Let us illustrate difference in play as a function of social class. Underprivileged children's play can be described as highly motoric and hyperactive in contrast to the more ordered, organized play of their middle-class peers. The involvement of children in play activities and their interaction with objects, then, provide different sources of information. The lower-class child who approaches objects in a flitting manner does not attend to details of the objects. His information should be different from that of the middle-class child who approaches objects in a more manipulative and exploratory fashion. Such differential approaches to objects and events should lead to different experiences and learnings about a host of things. These variations in experience with the material and social world provide different kinds of feedback information about the nature of objects and their function (Sigel and McBane, 1967). The information accumulated about the physical world and its actions may well facilitate or inhibit how they might perform in Piagetian experiments. Can it not be that children who acquire conservation or demonstrate conservation relatively early are children who have approached materials in ways which have consistently enabled them to test certain physical principles? Considerable exposure to playing with clay, for example, and manipulation of items of that kind may well account for early acquisition of such ideas (Metcalf, 1965).

The highly energetic child playing with toys and having high exploratory interests, but perhaps limited in the number of materials available to him, may acquire *decentration* earlier than others simply because he wants to avoid boredom and the circumstances force him to use the same objects (Sutton-Smith, 1967).

The kinds of materials available to children offer another source of variation of experiences. The availability of simple versus complex objects, manipulative versus nonmanipulative objects should be explored in terms of the feedback data they provide children about characteristics of materials, structures of objects, reversibility and irreversibility of functions, and so forth. For example, does cooking experience for young girls increase their knowledge of reversible as well as irreversible transformation of some materials (Sigel and Mermelstein, 1965)?

Children's play behavior is also influenced by adults who can influence the child's freedom to maneuver in the environment, who demonstrate various kinds and quality of interference in play, and who voice opinions about the play behavior. Parental sanctions about the goodness and badness or the safety of objects provide additional information for the child. The parents circumscribing the child's play and the kinds of materials provided may yield different bits of information about the world to him. This is particularly true in terms of sex-role typing. Parents type acceptable play behavior of boys and girls. Toys and games are sex-typed from infancy, with boys having greater opportunity to play with mechanical objects, building items, whereas girls play with dolls and more unstructured materials (Sutton-Smith, 1967). In addition, play materials are age-graded; certain kinds of articles are not deemed socially appropriate for children at particular age levels. Finger paints and water play, for example, are frequently thought of as suitable for preschool children. It would not be expected that children, say, in the first or second grade, would be encouraged to deal with these kinds of materials.

During the course of the child's play, whether alone or with peers, he is confronted with the unexpected (Charlesworth, 1964). These confrontations and the degree to which they become possible in the situation may induce cognitive conflict in the child and force a reorganization of cognitive structure. The question has been raised as to the extent of appearance of such opportunities in the natural world in contrast to the laboratory (Wohlwill, in press). There are many opportunities in the natural world of the child for confrontation with the unexpected.

We must not overlook the role of social-play behavior as expressed in formal and informal games. Children are consistently faced with discrepancies between what they expect and what occurs and they must reorganize to meet the demands of the situations. Although games become increasingly structured as the children get older, there are still many opportunities for the unexpected to occur.

The host of experiences the child has in his social world of play and games with animate and inanimate objects deserves serious and systematic study in its own right. The relationship between play and language should not be overlooked. Language is often integrated with play, providing symbolic expression to actions involved in the play (Piaget, 1951). The kinds of play and language expressiveness involved in the child's social experiences interact to provide a set of significant experiences which potentially influence the quality of thought.

Personality as a Variable

Threading through the actions and experiences described to this point is the person himself, a responding, active organism, assimilating and accommodating to the world about him. He is not solely a cognizer; he is also a conator. The picture we have drawn of the child is the one of a cognizing child concerned with the world of reason and logic.

The question before us, however, is to delineate significant variables which impinge on the child's assimilation and accommodation of new information. Some of the variables that immediately come to mind are those trait-dimensions which influence intellectual problem solving: attention versus distractibility, rigidity versus flexibility, impulsivity versus reflectivity, persistence versus giving up, feelings of competence versus incompetence. There is a growing body of evidence indicating the relationship of these types of personality traits to information processing (storage and retrieval), problem solving, categorizing, and so forth (Kagan, Moss, and Sigel, 1963; Kagan, Rosman, Day, Albert, and Phillips, 1964; Sigel, Jarman, and Hanesian, 1967; Witkin, Dyk, Faterson, Goodenough, and Karp, 1962).

A variable that integrates personality and cognition is cognitive style. The term "style" has been used to refer to consistency of behaviors, intellectual or expressive, over a variety of tasks and situations. Three styles of categorization have been identified: descriptive, relational-contextual, and categorical-inferential (Kagan, Moss, Sigel, 1963). Descriptive style refers to classifications based on part or whole cues which are manifest and apparent among an array of material (cat and dog are grouped together because "both have legs"); relational-contextual style refers to groups where items are classed because of their interdependence (cat and dog are grouped because the "dog hates the cat"); categorical-inferential style refers to groupings of items because each represents the class and the cues have to be inferred (cat and dog, because "both are mammals") (Sigel, Jarman, and Hanesian, 1967). One commonly identified type of style is the descriptive part-whole approach, called by some the *analytic* approach (Kagan,

Moss, and Sigel, 1963), where children show preferences for organizing or classifying in terms of manifest details. Although this orientation increases with age, it occurs as early as four or five. This response also reflects the child's ability to disengage relevant from irrelevant cues.

The child, to succeed in a conservation task, has to be able to disengage relevant from irrelevant stimuli and to attend to these appropriately. In effect, he has to use an analytic approach. This is similar to the search-for-hidden-figures task, described by Witkin, Dyk, Faterson, Goodenough, and Karp (1962), Kagan, Moss, and Sigel (1963), Kagan, Rosman, Day, Albert, and Phillips (1964), and Sigel, Jarman, and Hanesian (1967). These studies reveal a range of preferences among children from the ages of four to twelve, expressed in their selection of details by which to organize materials. Modes of classification relate to personality characteristics (Wallach and Kogan, 1965; Kagan *et al.*, 1964). Cognitive style may influence quality of performance since it is a reflection of those cognitive qualities required in the solving of conservation problems (attention to detail).

It seems reasonable to think of performance and acquisition rate of cognitive abilities as related to the kinds of information children process (Smedslund, 1966c). The antecedents of these styles may reside in both constitutional or early developmental experience, for differences in attention span and rate of information processing have been found in children as young as six months of age (Kagan and Lewis, 1965). Thus, one very fruitful line of research that may help uncover variations in rate of growth and level of competence may be in longitudinal studies focusing on the affective features of information processing.

Styles of categorization provide one source of antecedents for study because Piagetian tasks deal with everyday experience. Children are consistently processing the kinds of information that such experimental tasks require. Children deal with quantities, number, classifications. Consequently, by the time the child is six or seven and is faced with these everyday-type tasks in an experimental situation, the habits of processing information that he has established may well impinge on how he behaves in a conservation task.

Another personality characteristic seen as relevant is the impulse-control dimension (Kagan, Pearson, and Welch, 1966). The child must attend carefully to the directions, reflect on the actions of the experimenter, and reason out a conclusion. Attending to a wide array of details and keeping these in mind does require concentration and control of responsiveness. Differences in performance and concept acquisition should occur for the child who is impulsive, who responds quickly without reflection rather than for one who is controlled. Chances are that he has not adequately perceived all the actions of the experimenter and has failed to keep the instructions in mind, resulting in failure on the task. Examination of such types of relationships may be one way to help explain individual differences in performance.

The child's interest in the kinds of tasks involved may also be relevant (Piaget, 1967). Our own experience has indicated that children vary in the degree of interest they have in dealing with physical phenomena. What accounts for this is yet to be identified, but certainly the degree to which the child is interested and sees the experiment as novel and intriguing, or as something boring and to be endured, may also be a significant factor in determining solution.

Our intention in this section was to highlight the relevance of some psychosocial variables. Specific detailing of the interlocking mechanisms in the form of a theory is yet to be spelled out. If we have but pointed toward a significant number of psychological directions, our comments will have served their purpose.

REFLECTIONS ON METHODOLOGICAL PROBLEMS

Piaget's research procedures tend to be less rigorous and standardized than those currently in vogue among American or British psychologists. The discrepancy has given rise to considerable criticism of Piaget's approach, and has stimulated replications under more controlled and standardized conditions, as evidenced by the readings in this volume. The methodological issues, however, still abound, even among the so-called rigorous investigators, and are by no means resolved by the studies reprinted here or others in the literature.

In this section, emphasis will be placed on sampling, the selection and defining of sample characteristics, and on the experimental issues related to tasks, and materials employed.

Issues Related to Subject Samples

Originally, Piaget paid little attention to reporting sample size. Those investigators working from a probability model of behavior hold that control of sample size is essential before any generalizations can be made. Replications using appropriate sample sizes have been reported in this volume. The increase in sample size results in sample variability for given age groups. The "considerable . . . inter-individual variability encountered even in the most well-controlled situations is a great obstacle to making the exact diagnosis" (Smedslund, 1966c, p. 166).

A number of demographic variables, many of them not reported in Piagetian studies, must be taken into account before adequate generalizations can be made, and these same variables offer explanations of individual differences. The studies in this volume reflect concern for such demographic variables as social class of the child, level of schooling, sex, and mental age. Since we discussed the social variables in the preceding section, we shall restrict our discussion here to chronological age, and mental age and IQ. We shall discuss these variables to provide some perspective in our overall task of reviewing Piagetian-based research from the point of view of the developmental psychologist.

Parenthetically, it might be said here that the oft-mentioned criticism of Piaget and his coworkers for failing to take these matters into account may well be due to his scientific goal as a genetic epistemologist. For developmental psychologists, the aim is to uncover generalizations about cognitive behaviors, to understand the psychological bases for them, and to acquire enough information to understand the conditions which influence the course of their growth. Thus, our interest is in group, as well as individual, differences.

CHRONOLOGICAL AGE   Chronological age is a traditional control variable in developmental research. It is the one that Piaget reports exactly in all his studies. Chronological age as a basis for equating subjects is used on the supposition that calendrical time equates subjects for sheer experience and maturity. The studies presented in this volume are all careful to identify their subjects in terms of chronological age, a criterion most accurately and carefully employed. The results of these studies do point to different behaviors attributed to differences in age, attesting to the fact that this is indeed a significant control variable. It must not be overlooked, however, that with all these positive results, there is also overlap between chronological-age groups. Some children at a younger age are able to perform comparably to older children. The lack of perfect correspondence between chronological age and performance leaves open the question, "Why?" The individual differences within age groups must be accounted for. Children vary in rate of growth and in opportunity for experiences which influence the significance of sheer chronological age. Two problems face us: one, to explain what in the chronological-age variable accounts for given behaviors, and second, what accounts for the variations within given age groups. In effect, chronological age is a quantitative, descriptive, control variable, with little explanatory power.

MENTAL AGE AND IQ   Closely related to chronological age is the concept of mental age and IQ. Mental age and IQ, being psychometric concepts of intelligence, are of little use to Piaget in describing his subjects (Tanner and Inhelder, 1960). For Piaget, intelligence is a broader concept than the somewhat restricted notion of the psychometricians. One only knows the intellectual level of his subjects on the basis of their performance on the particular tasks under study. Yet Goodnow and Bethon (1966) report, for example, that for conservation of quantity mental age does play a role, differentiating between dull and normal children. This finding is consistent with that reported by Inhelder (1944).

The results employing mental age and IQ are equivocal. Studying performance on transitivity tasks, Cowan (1964) found that mental age, as well as chronological age, had a very low correlation with the child's ability to solve the problem. Kooistra (1963) also found that mental age accounted for only a small portion of the variance in his study of conservation, transitivity, and relationality with young, high-IQ children. The studies by Hood (1962) and by Woodward (1962) indicate that chronologically older, low mental-age subjects do worse on Piagetian tasks than younger children matched on mental age.

The effect of IQ and MA varies as a function of the task involved. Since some Piagetian tasks have more counterparts in everyday experience than others, CA might be of greater significance in such areas, whereas MA might be more relevant for academic tasks. This may account for the Goodnow and Bethon (1966) finding that CA was more relevant for conservation tasks and MA for combinatorial problems.

Issues Related to Experimental Procedure

Piaget has been criticized on methodological grounds because his experiments are inadequately detailed in terms of testing procedures, unstandardized, and used arbitrary scoring procedures. For example, reliability, in the scoring of children's responses, is not considered. Piaget is indeed aware of the issue, but believes that acquiescence to such procedures would preclude understanding of the children's thought. He, therefore, employs a clinical method (Piaget, 1928). The replication studies, as was indicated earlier in this volume, have attempted to standardize the procedures. Nevertheless, a number of problems still exist and appear even in the studies in this volume. In this section, we should like to focus on issues relating to the testing situation, with particular emphasis on the structuring of the test, response probabilities, materials employed, and the scoring of responses.

Most of Piaget's experiments, as well as those presented in this volume, employ verbal structuring of the tasks, Braine's (1959) study being a notable exception. The task is structured verbally, necessitating comprehension of the terms while attending to the actions of the experimenter, keeping in mind the question to be answered, and responding verbally to the experimenter's interrogation. Smedslund gives three reasons which may account for the child's failure to give appropriate responses to a conservation problem: (1) he does not understand the initial state (in a conservation experiment, he might not perceive initial equality or remember it); (2) he may not be able to clearly articulate his explanation of events, to provide a response indicating similarity or some other characteristic which also is put into a verbal context; and (3) he may not know the answer (Smedslund, 1966a).

Relatively few studies concern themselves with the comprehension of terms in the instructions, especially relational terms. The child's ability to comprehend such terms as "more," "longer," or "same" is prerequisite to solving the problem. Piaget holds that lack of comprehension of these terms indicates that the child has not assimilated this knowledge to the appropriate cognitive structure. Therefore, such lack of comprehension in itself is an indicator of cognitive level.

Gruen's (1965) results suggest that minimal training in the use of such terms tends to help children give conservation responses. That such minimal training as Gruen provides has an effect suggests that the transitory schema may be there, but the verbal experience is limited. One would be hard-pressed to accept that such short-term training alone explains the results.

Griffiths, Shantz, and Sigel (1967) found considerable variation in a group of five-year-olds' ability to respond correctly to such terms as "more," "same," and "less." Understanding such terms did not necessarily relate to conservation skills. Knowledge of the child's level, however, allows one to assign failure in conservation tasks to reasons other than lack of comprehension of instructions.

In addition to the comprehensibility of quantitative terms, perceptual and judgmental terms such as "looks like" and "really is" need to be clarified. These types of instructions, Braine contends, have differential effects on the child's response (Braine and Shanks, 1965).

The Braine-Smedslund (Braine, 1964; Smedslund, 1965) controversy on the role of verbal instructions points to the need to use instruction procedures consistent with the theory. The acceptance of nonverbal responses without detailed inquiry would probably be insufficient for Piaget. He would find discrimination responses, such as those used by Braine, not actually providing an adequate test of the theory (Gruen, 1966).

"INSTRUCTIONAL SET"   The child is often asked to make and agree to comparisons, for example, the equivalence of two items, or, in the transitivity task, to perceive that A is longer than B and B is longer than C. Whether the technique employed is nonverbal (see Braine, 1959) or verbal (see the Gruen or Lovell studies in this volume), there has to be assurance that the child perceives the required comparisons.

The child may agree that things are equal because of the status of the experimenter, or lack of concern and interest, or he may acquiesce, but not actually believe it. In addition, he may forget what is asked of him in the first comparison. Since retention of the experimenter's instructions and subsequent actions are necessary to solve the problem, recall of these data is of particular significance. The memory factor has been found to be related to the child's ability to deal with logical transformations and transitivity tasks (Cowan, 1963).

TASK COMPLEXITY   Performance varies with the complexity of the experimental operations. For example, Feigenbaum (1963) found no difference between using twenty-eight beads and fourteen beads in his experiments assessing the child's ability to conserve quantity. In pretests, he found some children failed the problem when fourteen pairs of beads were used as compared to seven pairs. He says:

> The crucial difference in the Ss' performance might be in their ability to discriminate between one and more than one, two and more than two, and three and more than three, rather than between fourteen and twenty-eight. By using Piaget's definition of conservation, one therefore, in effect, limits the possibility of a more adequate test of the hypothesis, suggesting that reducing the number of beads would increase the success with the conservation task. (p. 431)

Sigel, Saltz, and Roskind (1967) presented two sets of dolls to children, a group of father dolls and a group of doctor dolls, and found that when a father doll was placed among the doctor dolls, the younger child was less likely to attest to the conservation of "fatherness." When the identical problem was presented in a purely verbal context, significant differences were found between the two conditions, although younger and older children still differed. The concretization of the problem, depicted in the doll situation, may well confuse the younger child. What is being assessed in this situation, then, is not precise. Is it the child's ability to emancipate himself from the situation, or his ability to conserve? Can one process not exist without the other?

The issue of the material involved is not new. Critics have argued that the lack of intrinsic interest in the task accounts for young children failing, especially in conservation (Inhelder, 1962). This conclusion has not been verified.

The degree to which the number of transformations affect the child's responses is also equivocal, perhaps due to the type of problem. Sigel, Saltz, and Roskind (1967) find no differences among young elementary school children as a function of number of transformations. The task is the conservation of social role, that is, consistency of role in the face of changing contexts. Smedslund (1966b) does find that number of transformations and order of transformation does make a difference in his study.

We must distinguish between number of transformations and trials (or number of single transformations reiterated throughout) (Saltz and Sigel, 1967). In the former case, number of transformations refers to the number of changes the original item goes through before the child is asked the conservation question; number of trials refers to the number of different examples of a single transformation (for example, the ball is turned into a pancake before the child is asked to respond; two new balls are introduced and another type of transformation occurs, this time a "sausage," and so forth). It is this latter type of alteration that is at issue here.

Intravariability may then be due to differential difficulty of the trials. For example, in a conservation-of-mass problem, transformation into a pancake may be easier for the child than a transformation into a circle or the transformation effected by cutting the piece of clay into bits. Kooistra (1963) found that subjects would give a scorable conservation response on one trial but fail in additional ones. Some children failed on the first trial but succeeded on subsequent ones. The variations in response pattern may be due to the differential difficulty of the trials, and not due to learning within the task or to the fact that the child is in a transitional state. The latter is an oft used interpretation (Smedslund, 1964). Such an interpretation would be convincing if the trials were shown to be truly equivalent.

SCORING   Scoring criteria may determine whether a child is identified as capable of solving a Piagetian-type problem. In the classical Piagetian task, logical justification of the judgment "same" must be given. This is the procedure employed by many of the investigators whose studies are reprinted here. Other studies do not require the explanation (Braine, 1959; Braine and Shanks, 1965b). Gruen has pointed out that these differences are crucial, not because of methodological considerations, but because they reflect a difference in "the very nature of the processes which underlie the concepts with which Piaget's theory deals" (Gruen, 1966). Those investigators asking for reasons test for logical processes, whereas those accepting only acknowledgment of similarity or difference without explanation test for perceptual discrimination. Gruen, for example, reanalyzed his own data and found that altering the scoring criteria for accepting the presence of conservation results in significant differences between the two types of scoring. The nonexplanation condition yields a higher score. Thus, investigators not inquiring for logical explanation would get more conservers—a result that might be used to explain the variance between Braine's and Frank's finding of mean age differences and those findings reported by Piaget and Smedslund. Gruen (1966) concludes:

> It is an open question as to which set of criteria is the appropriate one for assessing the presence or absence of conservation, but is not an arbitrary one. The choice depends to a great extent on the psychological processes that one assumes underlie conservation. For example, the criteria that Smedslund has used seem more appropriate for assessing conservation *as Piaget defines it* than do the criteria used by Frank (1964). This is because Smedslund, like Piaget, believes that logical operations such as reversibility, compensation, and logical necessity underlie conservation and must be present in the thinking of a child who has conservation. (p. 982)

Using logical justification is apparently the only way to truly test Piagetian theory. "The operational structure (as defined by Piaget) underlying the conservation concepts appear to us to be a complex, coordinated system that cannot be properly evaluated by rather summary investigation of answers to preselected questions with no exploration of the child's justification of those answers" (Inhelder, Smock, Bovet, and Sinclair, 1966).

The issue of scoring is more complicated than described by Gruen even if a number of trials are given, each of which is scored on the basis of logical reasons. Children's answers provide an array of responses, reflecting different logical types. The following responses have been found in conservation of quantity experiments: (1) *reversibility* statements, "You can roll it back and it will be the same"; (2) *addition and subtraction statements*, "You did not add or take anything away"; (3) *compensatory statements,* "It is longer and thinner so it is still the same"; (4) *descriptive statements of action*, "You didn't do anything, you just rolled it out"; (5) *reference to previous state.* Usually only one of these types of answer is given. They represent different logical justifications, but are they *equally* acceptable? Are some *better* than others? How does one decide? Cross validation studies examining the relationship between classes of responses and other types of performance may provide the answers. Let it suffice to point out that a careful conceptual analysis of responses, and the defining of the acceptability level from an articulated theoretical definition are necessary (Mermelstein and Shulman, 1967). Procedures for such undertakings are described by Smedslund (1966a, 1966b, 1966c).

LANGUAGE FLUENCY   The failure to explain adequately must not be summarily rejected as evidence of cognitive "lack," but may be due to difficulty in verbalizing. Children may be aware, intuitively, of the invariance of attributes in the face of transformation or of transitive relationships, but cannot "find" the right words to explain them. Some children insist on identity in the face of consistent interrogation, but when asked "Why?" repeat their initial statement. The significance of this type of response must not be overlooked. It is insufficient for a certainty judgment as to the presence of skill, yet it is not totally inadequate.

Conclusion

We have touched on a number of methodological issues which, in their totality, are of import in determining the validity of Piagetian theory. Our intention was to review some of the more cogent problems, thereby offering suggestions for further considerations in this area of research. With the increase in Piaget-based research and with greater concern for methodological rigor, the end product should reveal more substantially-based data on the cognitive development of children. We have not touched on all the issues, but selected those which, in our opinion, are of moment. With increasing work in these complex areas other problems will, no doubt, arise. But is this not the way with scientific undertakings? Our knowledge is definitive until its strengths and limitations are demonstrated. Each step is indeed a closer approximation toward the ephemeral goal each of us seeks—truth.

AN OVERALL REFLECTION

We have presented a number of studies based on Piagetian theory and experimentations. In sum, they reflect an interest and a concern for the body of growing literature explicating Piaget's basic contributions. This volume represents only a temporary assessment of our knowledge since new studies emanating from child development centers throughout the world are currently being undertaken. Above all, new work is still coming from the pen of Piaget, who in this year has celebrated his seventieth birthday. Perhaps some of the issues raised in this volume will be resolved by the originator himself.

Accepting the proposition that a theory is an open system subject to modification, some crucial studies still need to be done. These include testing some of the basic issues dealing with equilibration processes, the interrelationships of various operations, and the validity of the invariant sequences, stemming from the need to construct valid measures of the variables in question and the need to design adequate experimental settings in which to use them.

The basic question, of course, remains. Is all this effort worthwhile? The evidence to date is encouraging. The inherent rationality of Piaget's position and his unique conceptualizations have added a dimension to our view of human development heretofore missing. The acceptance or rejection of any system, in whole or in part, can only come about through adequate evaluation. Piaget's theoretical conceptualizations, methodologies, and empirical data will continue to advance the cause of developmental psychology.

REFERENCES

Almy, Millie, E. Chittenden, and Paula Miller (1966). *Young children's thinking: studies of some aspects of Piaget's theory.* New York: Teachers College Press, Columbia University.

Beilin, H. (1965). Learning and operational convergence in logical thought development. *J. exp. child Psychol.*, **2**, 317–339.

Bernstein, B. (1961). Social class and linguistic development: a theory of social learning. In A. H. Halsey, Jean Floud, and C. A. Anderson (Eds.), *Education, economy, and society.* New York: Free Press. Pp. 284–314.

Braine, M. D. S. (1959). The ontogeny of certain logical operations: Piaget's formulation examined by nonverbal methods. *Psychol. Monogr.*, 5 (73).

Braine, M. D. S. (1964). Development of a grasp of transitivity of length: a reply to Smedslund. *Child Develpm.*, 35, 799–810.

Braine, M. D. S., and B. L. Shanks (1965a). The conservation of a shape property and a proposal about the origin of the conservation. *Canad. J. Psychol.*, 19 (3), 197–207.

Braine, M. D. S., and B. L. Shanks (1965b). The development of conservation of size. *J. verb. Learn. verb. Behav.*, 4, 227–242.

Bruner, J. S., Rose R. Olver, and Patricia Greenfield (1966). *Studies in cognitive growth.* New York: Wiley.

Charlesworth, W. R. (1964). The instigation and maintenance of curiosity behavior as a function of surprise versus novel and familiar stimuli. *Child Develpm.*, 35, 1169–1186.

Cowan, P. A. (1964). A developmental study of logical transformations. University of Toronto, 1963. *Dissertation Abstr.*, 25 (3), 2027–2028.

Dodwell, P. C. (1962). Relations between the understanding of the logic of classes and of cardinal number in children. *Canad. J. Psychol.*, 16, 152–160.

Elkind, D. (1967). Editor's Introduction. In J. Piaget, *Six psychological studies.* New York: Random House. Pp. i–xx.

Feigenbaum, K. (1963). Task complexity and intelligence as variables in Piaget's problems of conservation. *Child Develpm.*, 34, 423–432.

Flavell, J. H. (1963). *The developmental psychology of Jean Piaget.* Princeton, N.J.: Van Nostrand.

Frank, F. (1964). Cited by J. S. Bruner. The course of cognitive growth. *Amer. Psychologist*, 19, 1–15.

Gladwin, T. (1964). Culture and logical process. In W. H. Goodenough (Ed.), *Explorations in cultural anthropology.* New York: McGraw-Hill. Pp. 167–177.

Goodnow, Jacqueline J. (1962). A test of milieu effects with some of Piaget's tasks. *Psychol. Monogr.*, 76 (36), Whole No. 555.

Goodnow, Jacqueline J., and Gloria Bethon (1966). Piaget's tasks: the effects of schooling and intelligence. *Child Develpm.*, 37, 573–581.

Greenfield, Patricia M. (1966). On culture and conservation. In J. S. Bruner, Rose R. Olver, and Patricia M. Greenfield, *Studies in cognitive growth.* New York: Wiley. Pp. 225–256.

Griffiths, Judith A., Carolyn U. Shantz, and I. E. Sigel (1967). A methodological problem in conservation studies: the use of relational terms. *Child Develpm.*, 38, 841–848.

Gruen, G. E. (1966). Note on conservation: methodological and definitional considerations. *Child Develpm.*, 36, 977–983.

Herskovits, M. J. (1955). *Cultural Anthropology.* New York: Knopf.

Hess, R. D., and Virginia C. Shipman (1965). Early experience and the socialization of cognitive modes in children. *Child Develpm.*, **36**, 869–886.

Hood, H. B. (1962). An experimental study of Piaget's theory of the development of number in children. *Brit. J. Psychol.*, **53** (3), 273–286.

Hooper, F. H., and I. E. Sigel (Article in preparation). An initial study of the correspondence between conservation and logical operations.

Hunt, J. McV. (1961). *Intelligence and experience*. New York: Ronald.

Hyde, D. M. (1959). An investigation of Piaget's theories of the development of the concept of number. Unpublished doctoral dissertation, University of London.

Inhelder, Barbel (1944). *Le diagnostic du raisonnement chez les debiles mentaux*. Neuchâtel: Delachaux et Niestlé.

Inhelder, Barbel (1962). Some aspects of Piaget's genetic approach to cognition. In W. Kessen and Clementina Kuhlman (Eds.), Thought in the young child. *Monogr. Soc. Res. Child Develpm.*, **27** (2), 19–34.

Inhelder, Barbel, and J. Piaget (1964). *The early growth of logic in the child*. New York: Harper & Row.

Inhelder, Barbel, C. D. Smock, M. Bovet, and H. Sinclair (1966). Cognitive development: comments on Bruner's Piagetian theory. *Amer. Psychologist*, **21** (2), 160–165.

Kagan, J., and M. Lewis (1965). Studies in attention in the human infant. *Merrill-Palmer Quart.*, **11**, 95–127.

Kagan, J., H. A. Moss, and I. E. Sigel (1963). Psychological significance of styles of conceptualization. In J. C. Wright and J. Kagan (Eds.), Basic cognitive processes in children. *Monogr. Soc. Res. Child Develpm.*, **28** (2), 73–118.

Kagan, J., Leslie Pearson, and Lois Welch (1966). Conceptual impulsivity and inductive reasoning. *Child Develpm.*, **37**, 583–594.

Kagan, J., Bernice I. Rosman, Deborah Day, J. Albert, and W. Phillips (1964). Information processing in the child: significance of analytic and reflective attitudes. *Psychol. Monogr.*, **78** (1), Whole No. 578.

Kooistra, W. (1963). Developmental trends in the attainment of conservation, transitivity, and relativity in thinking of children: a replication and extension of Piaget's ontogenetic formulation. Unpublished doctoral dissertation, Wayne State University.

Lunzer, E. A. (1960). Some points of Piagetian theory in the light of experimental criticism. *J. child Psychol. Psychiat.*, **1**, 191–202.

Mermelstein, E., and L. S. Shulman (1967). Lack of formal schooling and the acquisition of conservation. *Child Develpm.*, **38**, 39–52.

Metcalf, J. W. (1965). Development of quantitative concept in preschool children. Paper presented at American Psychological Association, Chicago.

Piaget, J. (1928). *Judgment and reasoning in the child*. New York: Harcourt.

Piaget, J. (1950). *The psychology of intelligence*. London: Routledge.

Piaget, J. (1951). *Plays, dreams, and imitation.* New York: Norton.

Piaget, J. (1967). *Six psychological studies.* Trans. by Anita Tenzer and D. Elkind. New York: Random House.

Price-Williams, D. R. A. (1961). A study concerning concepts of conservation of quantity among primitive children. *Acta Psychol.*, 18, 297–305.

Price-Williams, D. R. A. (1962). Abstract and concrete modes of classification in a primitive society. *Brit. J. educ. Psychol.*, 32, 50–61.

Saltz, E., and I. E. Sigel (1967). Concept overdiscrimination in children. *J. exp. Psychol.*, 73 (1), 1–8.

Shantz, Carolyn U. (1967). A developmental study of Piaget's theory of logical multiplication. *Merrill-Palmer Quart.*, 13 (2), 121–138.

Sigel, I. E., L. M. Anderson, and H. Shapiro (1966). Categorization behavior of lower- and middle-class Negro preschool children: differences in dealing with representation of familiar objects. *J. Negro Educ.*, Summer, 218–229.

Sigel, I. E., P. Jarman, and Helen Hanesian (1967). Styles of categorization and their intellectual and personality correlates in young children. *Human Develpm.*, 10 (1), 1–17.

Sigel, I. E., and Bonnie McBane (1967). Cognitive competence and level of symbolization among five-year-old children. In J. Hellmuth (Ed.), *The disadvantaged child*, Vol. I. Seattle, Wash.: Special Child Publ.

Sigel, I. E., and E. Mermelstein (1965). The effects of nonschooling on Piaget's conservation tasks. Paper read at American Psychological Association, Chicago.

Sigel, I. E., E. Saltz, and W. Roskind (1967). Variables in determining concept conservation. *J. exp. Psychol.*, 74, 471–475.

Smedslund, J. (1964). Concrete reasoning: a study of intellectual development. *Monogr. Soc. Res. Child Develpm.*, 29, (2), 3–39.

Smedslund, J. (1965). The development of transitivity of length: a comment on Braine's reply. *Child Develpm.*, 36, 577–580.

Smedslund, J. (1966a). Microanalysis of concrete reasoning: I. *Scand. J. Psychol.*, 7, 145–156.

Smedslund, J. (1966b). Microanalysis of concrete reasoning: II. *Scand. J. Psychol.*, 7, 157–164.

Smedslund, J. (1966c). Microanalysis of concrete reasoning: III. *Scand. J. Psychol.*, 7, 164–167.

Sutton-Smith, B. (1967). Novel signifiers in play. Mimeo.

Tanner, J. M., and Barbel Inhelder (Eds.) (1960). *Discussions in child development*: Vol. I, II, III. New York: International Universities.

Triandis, H. C. (1964). Culture and cognition. In L. Berkowitz (Ed.), *Advances in experimental social psychology*: Vol. I. New York: Academic Press. Pp. 2–41.

Wallach, M. A., and N. Kogan (1965). *Modes of thinking in young children.* New York: Holt, Rinehart and Winston.

Werner, H., and B. Kaplan (1963). *Symbol formation*. New York: Wiley.

Witkin, H. A., Ruth B. Dyk, Hanna F. Faterson, D. R. Goodenough, and S. A. Karp (1962). *Psychological differentiation*. New York: Wiley.

Wohlwill, J. F. (1968). Towards a reformulation of the role of experience in cognitive development. In J. B. Grize and Barbel Inhelder (Eds.), Volume of essays in honor of Jean Piaget's 70th birthday.

Woodward, Mary (1962). Concepts of space in the mentally subnormal studied by Piaget's method. *Brit. J. soc. clin. Psychol.*, 1, Pt. I, 25–37.

NAME INDEX

NAME INDEX

SUBJECT INDEX

SUBJECT INDEX